MW01282432

Love and Social Justice

LOVE AND SOCIAL JUSTICE

REFLECTIONS ON SOCIETY

BLESSED CARDINAL
STEFAN WYSZYŃSKI

Translated by Filip Mazurczak

AROUCA
PRESS

Originally published as
*Miłość i sprawiedliwość społeczna. Rozważania społeczne,
fragmenty III Kolekcji—Wyprawa na wyprawy
społeczne* (Pallotinum Publishing House, 1993)

Kind permission granted by the Instytut Prymasowski Stefana
Kardynała Wyszyńskiego (Warsaw) for this English translation.
This publication has been supported by the
©POLAND Translation Program.

Scripture references taken from the Revised Standard Version
Catholic Edition and the Douay-Rheims version.

BOOK INSTITUTE

©POLAND

ISBN: 978-1-989905-90-6 (pbk)
ISBN: 978-1-989905-91-3 (hardcover)

Arouca Press
PO Box 55003
Bridgeport PO
Waterloo, ON N2J 3G0
Canada
www.aroucapress.com
Send inquiries to info@aroucapress.com

Contents

Abbreviations

RN: *Rerum novarum,* an encyclical of Leo XIII (1891)
QA: *Quadragesimo anno,* an encyclical of Pius XI (1931)
DR: *Divini redemptoris,* an encyclical of Pius XI (1937)
MBS: *Mit brennender Sorge,* an encyclical of Pius XI (1937)

Translator's Introduction

I N 2018, JUST BEFORE THE CENTENNIAL OF the restoration of Polish independence, the opinion polling institution CBOS asked Poles to evaluate historical figures in the past century of their nation's history. Unsurprisingly, Pope St. John Paul II enjoyed the greatest support of all, with 97 percent of respondents viewing him in a positive light. He was followed by Józef Piłsudski, the main architect of Polish independence and the country's leader at various times in the interbellum, with 83 percent of Poles having a positive view of him. Blessed Cardinal Stefan Wyszyński came in third place, with a full three-fourths of Poles evaluating him in a positive way.

Throughout Poland, there are streets and schools named after Wyszyński as well as many monuments to him. He is the subject of multiple museums, the most recent of which is the fine Mt 5:14 Museum of John Paul II and Primate Wyszyński in Warsaw, which was opened in 2020. In addition to being beatified in 2021, Wyszyński has also received many secular distinctions in Poland, including the Order of the White Eagle, the highest Polish civilian decoration. Poles regularly refer to him as *Prymas Tysiąclecia*, or "The Primate of the Millennium." It is impossible to understand modern Polish history without knowing about Wyszyński. I hope that this book and my introduction will shed light on one of the twentieth century's greatest Catholic leaders.

Modest Beginnings

Stefan Wyszyński (pronounced "vih-shin-skee") was born on August 3, 1901, in the village of Zuzela in Mazovia in Central Poland; he was baptized the same day. His baptismal certificate is in Cyrillic, for at this time Poland was partitioned between what Herman Melville aptly called the "three pirate powers" of Russia, Prussia (since 1871, Germany), and Austria; Zuzela found itself under Russian rule. Today, the one-room schoolhouse in Zuzela that the young

Wyszyński attended serves as a museum devoted to the future cardinal's early years.

The future blessed had three sisters, one brother, one half-brother, and one half-sister; two of his siblings did not survive until adulthood. Because Wyszyński's father Stanisław was the parish organ player, a position that accorded prestige in rural Poland then, the Wyszyńskis did not suffer from hunger and were better off than most other inhabitants of Zuzela; they even owned a piano, a sign of higher social status in that time and place.

Above all, the Wyszyński family greatly loved Mary. Stanisław Wyszyński had a close devotion to Our Lady of Częstochowa, while his wife, the future prelate's mother, was devoted to the other great Polish Madonna, Our Lady of Ostra Brama in Vilnius (presently in Lithuania). Unsurprisingly given his family's piety, Wyszyński became an altar boy at the age of five.

Apart from a devotion to the Church and Mary, Wyszyński's parents instilled in their children a great love for Poland amidst an ongoing campaign of brutal Russification. Two portraits hung in the family house: those of the great Polish patriots Tadeusz Kościuszko and Józef Poniatowski. The Wyszyński family owned numerous books on Polish history and the classics of Polish Romanticism, while the future cardinal's father took him to a local forest at night to lay crosses on the burial sites of Polish patriots killed in the 1863 January Insurrection, an unsuccessful attempt at gaining independence from Russia. During the First World War, Wyszyński became a scout, which only bolstered his patriotic fervor.

Around this time, the adolescent Stefan Wyszyński decided to become a priest. In 1917, he entered the Pius X Minor Seminary in Włocławek and enrolled in that city's major seminary three years later. Material conditions there were very austere: the seminarians were malnourished, the building lacked proper heating, and poor sanitary conditions led to frequent outbreaks of scabies and typhus. Because of a history of tuberculosis and a recent bout of typhus, of which he was healed thanks to the efforts of a saintly nurse who also happened to be a nun, his seminary's authorities were initially reluctant to ordain him (although he was ultimately ordained a priest on his twenty-third birthday in 1924).

An Activist Priest

After his ordination, Wyszyński served as a priest in Włocławek, which at the time was an industrial city of forty thousand inhabitants where one of the major employers was a cellulose factory; in 1924, he began work at the cathedral. One year later, the young priest began his doctoral studies at the Catholic University of Lublin (today known as the John Paul II Catholic University of Lublin). There, he became acquainted with Catholic social teaching (his impressive familiarity with this topic is on full display in this book). Although he initially wanted to pursue a PhD in Catholic social teaching, he ultimately received a doctorate in canon law. The young Wyszyński's budding interest in Catholic social thought was nurtured by a series of study visits to universities in Western Europe in 1929–1930, where he attended lectures on the topic.

Upon Wyszyński's return to Włocławek, the city, along with all of Poland, Europe, and the world, had been plunged into the Great Depression. Many employees of the cellulose factory were laid off. The resulting mass frustration made Włocławek a fertile breeding ground for Marxist and socialist agitation; the city was then dubbed "Red Włocławek." Many workers there were possessed with a desire for bloody revolution against the capitalists.

At this time, Wyszyński was a professor at the Włocławek Major Seminary, where he also edited its theological journal *Ateneum Kapłańskie* ("The Priests' Atheneum," which is still published today) and worked at a parish in nearby Predecz. He was deeply upset about Włocławek's socio-economic situation.

Between 1930 and 1939, Father Wyszyński published 413 articles, most of which were devoted to improving the plight of the working class and the peasantry (he was a strong supporter of agricultural reform). However, he did not limit himself to ivory tower theorizing.

Pope Francis has famously said that pastors should smell of their sheep. As a seminary professor, Wyszyński made sure that his students, future priests, would as well, and so he took them to factories so they could see the horrible working conditions, not very different from those of Charles Dickens' London in the previous century, in which their future parishioners worked.

Furthermore, Wyszyński organized a "Christian Workers' University" (*Chrześcijański Uniwersytet Robotniczy*), during which he educated factory workers about their rights and about the dangers of both Marxism and laissez-faire capitalism. Wyszyński believed that reading the social teaching of the popes and applying them to socio-economic life would be the best solution to the exploitation of the worker.

Włocławek's working class came to love Wyszyński as their friend and advocate. He often served as an intermediary between factory owners and their employees. He appealed to the owner of one factory on behalf of workers so that soap and towels would be provided for them. In another factory, Wyszyński lobbied to ensure that the workers would have Sundays and holidays off.

A Chaplain to the Polish Underground

Arguably, no country suffered as greatly as Poland during the Second World War. By the war's end, Poland had lost almost six million citizens, including about ninety percent of its Jewish population. Meanwhile, Nazi Germany wanted to turn non-Jewish Poles into a race of slaves for the "master race." In particular, the nation's elites were exterminated: physicians, lawyers, clergymen, university professors, schoolteachers, and political leaders.

Between 1939 and 1945, one in five Polish Roman Catholic priests was killed. The losses to the clergy were the highest in the *Wartheland*, the areas of western Poland to which Germany had (objectively very dubious) historical claims. In the *Wartheland*, more than a third of Catholic priests were killed, while in the Diocese of Włocławek, more than half were.

Although being a priest in Włocławek was itself a death sentence, Wyszyński was also hunted by the Gestapo for his prewar writings criticizing Nazi racism. Włocławek's auxiliary bishop Blessed Michał Kozal, who would later die a martyr's death in the Dachau concentration camp, advised Wyszyński to hide. He did so in various areas across Poland, and ultimately became the chaplain for the community for the blind started by Mother Elżbieta Róża Czacka, who would decades later be beatified along with Wyszyński. Mother Czaczka's community was initially in Laski in the Kampinos Forest just out-side Warsaw but was moved to Żułów in the Lublin region after the destruction of Warsaw.

It was at this time that Wyszyński most likely wrote this book, which was found in his archive. For obvious reasons, it could not have been published under communism, and so its first Polish edition was in 1993 (in 2021, the book was reissued to coincide with Wyszyński's beatification). According to the editors of the 1993 edition, Wyszyński wrote *Love and Social Justice* during the war, probably in 1942. They have arrived at this conclusion because whereas Wyszyński's critiques of Nazism are accompanied by accounts of the German invasion of Poland, his condemnations of Marxism make no reference to the repressive policies of the Polish People's Republic. Furthermore, the most recent Church documents Wyszyński cites in the work come from 1941.

Eventually, the community for the blind returned to Laski, and Wyszyński went along with them. On August 1, 1944, the Home Army, the main branch of the Polish underground, bravely but futilely tried to liberate Warsaw from the Germans. The Warsaw Uprising lasted sixty-three days; the Polish underground had counted on Soviet assis-tance, but the Red Army cynically stood on the right bank of the Vistula and did nothing to help them. Consequently, the Germans completely reduced Warsaw to rubble, while about 200,000 of its inhabitants (mostly civilians) were killed and many Varsovians were deported to concentration camps. On August 5–12, the Germans killed tens of thousands of civilians in the Warsaw neighborhood of Wola; this may have been the single greatest massacre of the Second World War.

At that time, Wyszyński was a chaplain to the Home Army in the Kampinos Forest. In Laski, Mother Róża Czacka established a field hospital for wounded participants of the Warsaw Uprising. Wyszyński consoled them, assisted in operations on the injured, and administered the last rites and heard confessions.

In a remarkable display of Christian forgiveness, the Laski field hospital also provided medical and spiritual assistance to wounded German combatants. One of the nuns in the community, a Jewish convert, spent the entire war praying for Adolf Hitler's soul.

Wyszyński and the Jews

Apart from the late 1970s and 1980s, when it counted on the influence of the Church in its opposition to the communist regime, Poland's liberal intelligentsia has always been anti-clerical, often aggressively so.

As part of its campaign to distort the contributions of the Church to Polish independence, left-liberal media, scholars, and politicians have occasionally tried to paint Stefan Wyszyński as an anti-Semite. This canard has appeared, for instance, in Jan T. Gross's often-tendentious 2006 study *Fear: Anti-Semitism in Poland after Auschwitz*. More recently, anti-clerical social media pages have attributed to Wyszyński quotes from *Ateneum Kapłańskie* that he did not write and that have been taken out of context to make them appear that their author supported Hitler and Mussolini and was hostile to the Jews (in reality, these statements, when read in their entire context, were critiques of Nazism, racism, and fascism).

It is a fact that anti-Judaism (this is a more accurate term than anti-Semitism, as such prejudice was religiously rather than ethnically or racially oriented) was prevalent in the Catholic Church, including in Poland, before the Second Vatican Council. In 1936, for example, Wyszyński's predecessor as primate of Poland, Cardinal August Hlond, issued a schizophrenic pastoral letter in which he, on the one hand, condemned anti-Jewish violence but, on the other, accused the Jews of spreading Bolshevism and pornography and encouraged Christians to boycott Jewish businesses.

With regards to Wyszyński, not only is there no evidence that he was an anti-Semite, but in fact he risked his life to save Jews during the Holocaust. In German occupied Poland, even a minor gesture of sympathy towards Jews was punishable by death (right after the sealing off of the Warsaw Ghetto, for instance, a Pole was shot for throwing a loaf of bread over the ghetto walls).

According to the account of Jadwiga Karwowska, a woman whose parents worked in Żułów, where the Laski community for the blind had been transferred, Wyszyński sheltered a Jewish family, a father and two children with whom Karwowska played, until they were denounced to the Gestapo by a Ukrainian nationalist and consequently killed. Meanwhile, according to a testimony by Esther Grinberg in the archives of Yad Vashem, Israel's memorial to the Holocaust, the Polish woman who sheltered her was inspired by Wyszyński's homily in which he implored his audience to aid those fleeing the burning Warsaw Ghetto.

During the 1967 Six Day War between Israel and its Arab adversaries, Wyszyński, unlike the communist regime, publicly supported the Jewish State. One year later, Poland's communists engaged in an anti-Jewish purge, forcing 13,000 Polish Jews to emigrate. Wyszyński condemned this in his Holy Thursday homily in Warsaw's cathedral in 1968, just weeks after the events: "Maybe I, the bishop of Warsaw, am guilty, because I have not spoken enough about the duty to love all without exception, including those of a different tongue or race, so that the terrible shadow of a renewed racism may never befall us again."

While Wyszyński speaks of "racism" rather than more specifically of anti-Semitism, what he was referring to was quite clear to his audience, as there were not exactly many people of Samoan, Inuit, or West African descent in 1968 communist Poland. In any case, the chief rabbi of Poland at the time, Zew Wawa Morejno, publicly thanked the cardinal for his defense of the Jews twice, in 1968 and 1971.

Interrex

In 1946, Pope Pius XII appointed Stefan Wyszyński as bishop of Lublin. The new bishop chose *Soli Deo* ("Only God") as his episcopal motto. A mere two years later, at the age of only forty-seven, Stefan Wyszyński succeeded Cardinal Hlond as primate of Poland, becoming the archbishop of both Gniezno and Warsaw.

In Polish history, the role of primate is an important one. In pre-partition Poland, the primate was the *interrex*, which meant he exercised the functions of the king before the election of a new one (beginning in 1572, the Polish monarchy was elective).

With Cardinal Hlond, the prestige of the office of primate declined substantially. After the fall of Poland in 1939, Hlond left the country for France (in 1943, he tried to return to Poland but was arrested by the Gestapo). Although Hlond relayed many reports detailing the persecutions of the Polish clergy and Poles more generally to the Vatican, his departure was widely seen as a betrayal. Wyszyński, however, never abandoned his flock.

Already before the war, Wyszyński was harshly critical of Marxism. However, he initially wanted to seek some sort of *modus vivendi* with the communist government to protect the rights of the Church. On April 14, 1950, at Wyszyński's behest, an agreement between the Polish bishops and the communist government was signed. The bishops promised that their priests would not preach anti-communist sermons, support the guerrillas still fighting communist rule, or oppose the collectivization of agriculture, while the government agreed to allow religious education to be held in schools, not censor the Catholic press, permit Catholic charitable organizations to function, and recognized the pope as the highest authority in Church matters.

Non possumus!

Neither the bulk of Polish society nor the Vatican were pleased with this agreement. Indeed, the regime did not keep its promises. The regime continued to sentence priests to death or imprisonment in Stalinist show trials and tried to intervene in the Church's internal matters, such as what was taught in seminaries and Catholic schools.

Wyszyński became increasingly critical of the regime. During an assembly of the Polish bishops in Krakow in 1953, Wyszyński and his colleagues produced a letter to the authorities, famously titled *Non possumus!* ("We cannot!") which ended with the following words: "When Caesar sits on the altar we immediately say: 'We cannot.' We cannot place Godly things on Caesar's altar. *Non possumus!*"

The communist regime was infuriated. Nineteen fifty-three was also a year of increasingly harsh measures against the Church. That year, Bishop Czesław Kaczmarek of Kielce and three priests who closely worked with him were falsely accused of being spies for the Vatican and aiming to "restore the capitalist system, deprive the Polish nation of independence, and reduce Poland and hand it over to the yoke of American and neo-Nazi imperialists." Kaczmarek was sentenced to twelve years in prison (although he ultimately served only four years of his sentence), where he was tortured and mistreated. In 1963, following a series of heart attacks caused by what he had endured, he died.

Meanwhile in Krakow, that same year four priests and three laypeople working for the curia were sentenced to death (later changed to life sentences), life imprisonment, or very long prison sentences. When *Tygodnik Powszechny*, a Krakow-based journal published by lay Catholics, refused to print a panegyric obituary for Comrade Stalin, it was shut down by the authorities.

It was in this atmosphere that Cardinal Wyszyński was arrested by functionaries of the Ministry of Public Security in Warsaw's Archbishops' Palace on the night of September 25–26, 1953. For three years, Wyszyński was kept in several secret remote locations (including former abbeys) across Poland; not even his family was informed of his whereabouts.

As Wyszyński was being arrested, the cardinal's German shepherd Baca bit those who had come for him. Slightly later, the communist regime pressured Poland's bishops to sign a statement supporting the primate's arrest. The only bishop who refused to do so was Wojciech Zink, an ethnic German who was the apostolic administrator of Warmia, one of the regions that had been transferred from Germany to Poland after the Second World War (only under Paul VI were dioceses and archdioceses created in these regions). Wyszyński later bitterly remarked that in 1953, only a dog and a German stood up for their primate.

During his imprisonment, Wyszyński was accompanied by his chaplain, Father Stanisław Skorodecki, and a nun, Maria Leonia Graczyk. It has since been proven that Graczyk snitched on Wyszyński to the communist secret police during those three years. Several historians have accused Skorodecki of the same, but he denied such accusations before his death in 2002.

For many people, the most difficult aspect of Christianity is to love those who persecute us. When Wyszyński was arrested, Poland was ruled by the ruthless Stalinist leader Bolesław Bierut. Wyszyński was so free of hatred that he prayed for Bierut every day of his life.

The Great Novena

Following Khrushchev's famous secret speech denouncing the Stalinist cult of personality in 1956, a thaw followed in Poland. During the speech in Moscow, Bierut died in unexplained circumstances (some have speculated that his death was caused by a major shock to his system when he heard the speech and became afraid that, as a

Stalin-style leader, he would quickly be subjected to imprisonment or worse). He was succeeded by Władysław Gomułka, seen as a reformer. This resulted in a thaw in the harsh persecution of the Church, and Wyszyński was released from imprisonment.

In 966 AD, Mieszko I, Poland's first ruler, was baptized and Christianized the country. While imprisoned, Wyszyński worked hard on a program to remind the Polish nation of its Christian roots, for in his view that was essential to the survival of the nation under a hostile regime imposed from abroad.

The Great Novena was inaugurated at Jasna Góra, Poland's most important Marian shrine, on May 3, 1957. To remind the Poles of their heritage, a copy of the image of Our Lady of Czestochowa peregrinated across Poland, reaching every single parish in the country. In 1957, Wyszyński travelled to Rome to receive his red hat from Pius XII (in 1953, the communist regime did not allow him to travel for the consistory) and had the pope bless the copy of the sacred image.

Celebrations marking the millennium of Christianity in Poland were held in every diocese and were attended by large crowds. The communist authorities were so frightened by this expression of religious devotion, which was supposed to be an opiate for the masses that hinders the proletarian revolution, that they even arrested the copy of the image.

The Great Novena ended with Wyszyński entrusting Poland to Mary at Jasna Góra on May 3, 1966. He had invited St. Paul VI, the first pope to travel outside Italy, for the event, but the communist authorities would not allow for this.

A Critic of *Ostpolitik*

As a young priest, the future Pope Paul VI briefly worked in the papal nunciature in Warsaw. He loved Poland (and even had a basic knowledge of Polish) and enjoyed a good relationship with Cardinals Wyszyński and especially Wojtyła. However, one point of disagreement between Wyszyński and Paul VI was that of *Ostpolitik*.

Ostpolitik was the Vatican's well-intentioned but disastrous policy towards countries behind the Iron Curtain under the pontificates of John XXIII and Paul VI. Both popes have been deservingly canonized as saints; even saints make mistakes, and in this case, *Ostpolitik* was not an error resulting from ill will but rather an incorrect assessment of geopolitics.

The starting point of this diplomatic strategy was the assumption that the post-war division of Europe into two ideological blocs was a permanent fixture (or at least one that would not end anytime soon). Thus, the architects of *Ostpolitik* believed that in order to improve the living conditions of Catholics living under communist rule, the Holy See should not provoke communist regimes but instead seek dialogue with them. As part of *Ostpolitik*, complacent, even quisling bishops were appointed in many Eastern European countries.

The great dry martyr of *Ostpolitik* was Cardinal Jozsef Mindszenty, Primate of Hungary. This courageous man suffered greatly for his defense of the Hungarian nation under the communist yoke, yet was ultimately betrayed by the Vatican, which made him renounce his title as primate and asked him to stop publicly criticizing the communist regime (after receiving asylum in the American embassy in Budapest, Mindszenty was secretly transported to Vienna and toured the world, telling of the plight of his nation).

Ostpolitik ended on October 16, 1978, when a Polish cardinal who actually experienced life under communism ascended the Throne of Peter. Cardinal Wyszyński was a strong critic of this myopic policy, and history has arguably vindicated him.

"We Forgive and Ask for Forgiveness"

Although Polish society overwhelmingly treated Wyszyński as a hero after his imprisonment and during the Great Novena, in 1965 the communist authorities briefly succeeded in arousing resentment towards him.

In 1965, a mere twenty years, less than a generation, had passed since the carnage of the Second World War. Many Poles had survived concentration camps or lost family members; their anger towards Germany was strong and understandable.

Yet Poland's bishops knew that hatred was not the answer. Thus, in 1965 they issued a letter to the German bishops in which they famously forgave and asked for forgiveness. What was most shocking to many Poles was the latter part of that statement. After all that the

Polish nation had endured, what should they apologize for? Yet the Polish bishops argued that even if a single Pole had ever harmed a German, that would be enough to apologize for. While this pales in comparison to the crimes of Nazi Germany, immediately following the Second World War there was nonetheless much popular violence against the German minorities in Poland and Czechoslovakia, even against individual ethnic Germans who were not supporters of Hitler.

While this letter was largely unpopular in Poland, it paved the way for Polish-German reconciliation. Only five years later would West German Chancellor Willy Brandt recognize the post-war Polish-German border, apologize for the war crimes of his countrymen, and travel to Warsaw, where he knelt in front of the memorial to the heroes of the Warsaw Ghetto Uprising and laid a wreath on the Tomb of the Unknown Soldier.

The letter was the initiative of Cardinal Bolesław Kominek of Wrocław, although Cardinals Karol Wojtyła (the future St. John Paul II) and Stefan Wyszyński were among its most vocal supporters. Given that Wyszyński prayed for the Stalinist dictator who caused him great suffering every day of his life, this attitude of forgiveness should not be surprising.

Wyszyński and the Anti-Communist Opposition

One controversial aspect of Wyszyński's life is his attitude towards the pro-democratic opposition in communist Poland. In December 1970, there were riots throughout the Baltic coast in response to increases in the price of food. During his Christmas homily in 1970, Wyszyński did not support the protestors but rather appealed for social calm.

Such an attitude resulted from prudence rather than cowardice or being in cahoots with the communist regime. The December 1970 protests were brutally crushed by the army and militia; forty-four Poles were killed, while a further one thousand were wounded.

Wyszyński simply did not want to provoke a civil war or, worse, Soviet intervention. Given the Soviet invasions of East Germany in 1953, Hungary in 1956, or Czechoslovakia in 1968 following bold reforms or popular uprisings, such fears were not unwarranted.

More complex is Wyszyński's attitude towards Solidarity, the trade union turned peaceful national liberation movement that played a crucial role in the collapse of communism in Poland and across the Eastern Bloc. There is no controversy among historians that St. John Paul II's pilgrimage to Poland in 1979 unleashed a prevalent sense of inner freedom that made that miraculous event possible. There were also numerous priests, including martyrs such as Blessed Jerzy Popiełuszko, and bishops who openly supported Solidarity. Yet Wyszyński's attitude has been somewhat disputed.

According to Ewa Czaczkowska, Wyszyński's biographer, the primate was initially cautious after the strike in the Lenin Shipyard in Gdansk that broke out in August 1980. Shortly afterwards, though, he requested a meeting with Lech Walesa, the charismatic electrician and Solidarity leader who would later be Poland's president. Czaczkowska writes that the meeting with Walesa was very positive, and that from that point Solidarity regarded the primate as their main advisor.

When, on August 31, 1980, an agreement was signed between the regime and Walesa allowing for an independent labor union to function, Wyszyński commented: "You have won, Blessed Mother. May you emerge victorious." He also wrote in his diary: "The workers' government and workers' party have been defeated by the workers."

However, according to Czaczkowska, Wyszyński was nonetheless prudent and had three demands of Solidarity: that they limit themselves to union activities; that they refrain from radicalism and take into consideration Poland's geopolitical conditions; and that the union is Christian in nature and seeks its inspiration from Catholic social teaching. Because Solidarity was ideologically diverse and included leftist secularists, that group was not thrilled with the last of these requests.

Wyszyński and Wojtyła

Unquestionably, the relationship between Cardinal Karol Wojtyła of Krakow, the future Pope St. John Paul II, and Cardinal Wyszyński was close. In their struggles against the communist regime, they supported one another.

When, during the October conclave of 1978, which shocked the world with the election of a pope from behind the Iron Curtain, it became clear that Wojtyła was emerging as a more than plausible candidate, Wyszyński implored him to accept the decision of the cardinal-electors, even though he initially believed Wojtyła was too young and felt that, as Bishop of Rome, the pope should be Italian.

There is a tradition known as the *homagium*. After a conclave, the cardinals pay homage to the newly elected pope. Following John Paul II's election, the pope did not allow two cardinals to kneel before him: Wyszyński and Josyf Slipyj (the latter was a Ukrainian Greek-Catholic cardinal who spent years in the gulag until St. John XXIII appealed to Khrushchev for his release). During the *homagium*, the new pope strongly embraced Cardinal Wyszyński.

During his first visit to Poland, St. John Paul II said the following of Wyszyński: "He is the keystone of the Church in Warsaw. And the keystone of the Church in Poland. This is what his providential mission has been based on for over thirty years. I want to express my admiration for him at the beginning of my pilgrimage here, in the capital of Poland, and once again thank the Holy Trinity for this along with the entire Church and our nation."

A Double Beatification During a Pandemic

Cardinal Stefan Wyszyński died on May 28, 1981. Estimates of the number of people who attended his funeral range from 300,000 to half a million. In 1988, a cause for his beatification was initiated. In 2017, Pope Francis signed a decree recognizing Wyszyński's heroic virtue and two years later approved a miracle through the cardinal's intercession (the healing of a nineteen-year-old girl of cancer).

The beatification, initially scheduled for June 7, 2020, was supposed to be a major ceremony on Warsaw's Piłsudski Square, previously known as Victory Square, where in 1979 St. John Paul II said the famous words: "May Your Spirit descend and renew the face of the earth, of this earth."

In the spring of 2020, many plans — including the beatification ceremony — were cancelled or postponed because of the COVID-19 pandemic. Cardinal Kazimierz Nycz, Archbishop of Warsaw, thus decided to postpone the beatification. When it became clear that the pandemic would be with us longer than most had expected, a date was finally chosen: September 12, 2021.

In the meantime, Pope Francis approved the beatification of Mother Elżbieta Róża Czacka who had ties to Wyszyński. Thus, both were beatified in Warsaw's Temple of Divine Providence. Due to pandemic restrictions, only 7,000 people were allowed to attend, but more than two million Poles watched the ceremony on television while others watched it online.

Róża Czacka (1876–1961) was born to an aristocratic Polish family in present-day Ukraine but moved to Warsaw as a small girl. She was an avid horseback rider. Her brothers noticed that, probably as a result of her nearsightedness, she was poor at judging distances between horses. At the age of twenty-two, she fell of her horse, leading to retinal detachment and blindness.

Upon losing her sight, Czacka became an advocate for the blind. She included Polish phonetics and diacritics in the Braille alphabet and campaigned for a greater inclusion of blind Poles into society; she did not want the blind to merely be the object of pity, but she wanted them to function as independently as possible and be useful to society.

Róża Czacka came from a very religious family; her uncle was a cardinal. In 1918, she founded her own religious congregation, the Franciscan Sisters Servants of the Cross. Upon taking her vows, she chose the religious name of Elżbieta (Elizabeth). She founded a community for the blind in Laski outside Warsaw; as we saw earlier, Wyszyński was the chaplain of the community during the Second World War. More than a century later, the community at Laski is home to about two hundred blind children from across Poland. Laski is also a popular retreat center.

Cardinal Stefan Wyszyński ranks alongside Jozsef Mindszenty of Hungary, Jaime Sin of the Philippines, and St. Oscar Romero of El Salvador as one of the great prelates of the twentieth century who courageously fought for social justice. It is my hope that Wyszyński's recent beatification and this book may make his legacy better known outside his homeland.

Blessed Cardinal Stefan Wyszyński and Blessed Mother Elżbieta Róża Czacka, pray for us!

Filip Mazurczak
October 7, 2021
Kraków

Bibliography

„CBOS. Jan Paweł II najlepiej postrzeganą osobistością społeczną ostatniego stulecia." Dzieje.pl. July 30, 2018. https://dzieje.pl/aktualnosci/cbos-jan-pawel-ii-najlepiej-postrzegana-osobistoscia-spoleczna-ostatniego-stulecia (accessed October 7, 2021).

Czaczkowska, Ewa. *Kardynał Stefan Wyszyński. Biografia*. Kraków: Wydawnictwo Znak, 2013.

Czapla, Tomasz. „Za robotników dałby się pokroić. Młody Stefan Wyszyński." Interia.pl. May 29, 2021. https://tygodnik.interia.pl/news-za-robotnikow-dalby-sie-pokroic-mlody-stefan-wyszynski,nId,5261163 (accessed October 7, 2021).

Huener, Jonathan. *The Polish Catholic Church Under German Occupation: The Reichsgau Wartheland, 1939–1945*. Bloomington: Indiana University Press, 2021.

Jan Paweł II, kard. Stefan Wyszyński. *Listy na czas przełomu*. Kraków: Wydawnictwo WAM, 2021.

„Kardynał Wyszyński a Żydzi. Nieznane karty z życiorysu Prymasa Tysiąclecia." eKai.pl. September 8, 2021. https://www.ekai.pl/kardynal-wyszynski-a-zydzi-sprzeciw-wobec-antysemityzmu-w-czasie-dwoch-totalitaryzmow/ (accessed October 8, 2021).

Kindziuk, Milena. *Kardynał Stefan Wyszyński. Prymas Polski*. Kraków: Wydawnicwto Esprit, 2019.

Lukas, Richard C. *Forgotten Holocaust: The Poles Under German Occupation, 1939–1944*. New York: Hippocrene Books, 1990.

Mazur, Dorota. *Matka Elżbieta Róża Czacka. Życie, duchowość, modlitwy*. Kraków: Wydawnictwo eSPe, 2021.

Weigel, George. *The Final Revolution: The Resistance Church and the Collapse of Communism*. Oxford: Oxford University Press, 1992.

Weigel, George. *Witness to Hope: The Biography of Pope John Paul II*. New York: HarperCollins, 2009.

Wiścicki, Tomasz. „Marzec 1968. Jaka była reakcja prymasa Wyszyńskiego i episkopatu?" Aleteia.pl. March 8, 2018. https://pl.aleteia.org/2018/03/08/marzec-1968-jaka-byla-reakcja-prymasa-wyszynskiego-i-episkopatu/ (accessed October 7, 2021).

VOLUME I

Man and Family in Social Life

PART I

Exsurgat Deus

1

Exsurgat Deus

*"Arise, O Lord, and let Thy enemies be
scattered; and let them that hate thee
flee before Thee" (Numbers 10:35).*

THERE IS A BEAUTIFUL DIALOGUE BETWEEN Christ and His Father in the Easter Sunday liturgy. Amidst expectation and the joyous hope of the moment, we hear Christ's voice: "Why do the nations conspire, and the peoples plot in vain? The kings of the earth set themselves, and the rulers take counsel together, against the Lord and against His, saying, 'Let us burst their bonds asunder, and cast their cords from us'" (Psalm 3:2–3). "How many are my foes, Lord! How many rise against me!" (Psalm 3:2). And here is the Lord "Who sits in the heavens" (Psalm 2:4); the Lord full of power in the joyous work of Alleluia, Who "laughs": "You are my son, today I have begotten you. Ask of me, and I will make the nations your heritage, and the ends of the earth your possession. You shall break them with a rod of iron and dash them in pieces like a potter's vessel" (Psalm 2:7–9).

The stone has been moved! The Lord has been resurrected so that we will never die again! The Lord is king! "Now therefore, O kings, be wise; be warned, O rulers of the earth. Serve the Lord with fear; with trembling kiss His feet. [...] Blessed are all who take refuge in Him" (Psalm 2:12).

"Let them that hate thee flee before thee" (Numbers 10:35).

Hezekiah, King of Judah, was furious about the blasphemies of the Assyrian king who threatened Jerusalem. Hezekiah prayed to the Lord, saying: "O Lord of hosts, God of Israel, Who art enthroned above the cherubim, Thou art the God, Thou alone, of all the kingdoms of the earth; Thou hast made heaven and earth. Incline Thy ear, O Lord, and hear; open Thy eyes, O Lord, and see" (Isaiah 37:16–17).

5

Do we not pray in a similar way when we see how the blasphemers, who amidst their enormous pride have brashly risen up to the throne of the Almighty to blaspheme against Him, have multiplied in the world? Not since the time of Julian the Apostate has there been such powerful, organized hatred of God as today. Indeed, the hatred of the apostates was born in the name of the ancient pagan gods, while today we see hatred of God that directly fights the very concept of God. This is organized hatred, which has been methodically instilled in human hearts, often at a government level, being an inextricable part of political programs and the perceived national interest; this hatred is collective and total. The novel thing is that this hatred is stoked in the name of social, economic, and national well-being, as if God, the Creator of all the earth's resources and the Giver of life to the nations, were humanity's biggest enemy.

Socio-Political Godlessness

Having been influenced by secularist ideas, the governments of various liberal states have at various times struggled against God. However, it was only Socialism and Communism, and especially Bolshevism, that rejected the existence of the spiritual element, considering religion to be the byproduct of economic relations and the "opium for the masses," while considering the struggle against religion to be a political necessity and making it part of their state policy. Since then, there has been a special state department funded by public money that struggles against God and religion in the interest of "the true good of the people." The entire collective economic system is harnessed to this struggle, which swallows people up in such a way that they have neither the will, the energy, nor the time for religion in their lives.

Godlessness is becoming a part of the socioeconomic program. By struggling against the living God, it seeks to close humanity within the limits of temporality, giving it new ultimate aims and offering it new dogmas and moral truths. Communism creates a proletarian religion for its own purposes. Its god is the manufacturing machine, and its symbol is a fist that shakes at the heavens. The highest virtue is breaking production records and the toil of labor, which should completely consume the life of the person. The proletariat leads humanity across the path of these virtues towards the gate of a new redemption, towards a universal revolution.

The racist god, whose creator led an entire nation towards a new paganism, is also a god that has been invented for doctrinal purposes. Likewise, the racist ideology rejects the personal God, instead proclaiming "nature" or "the human spirit" as the new god. The personal God, it has proclaimed, is "a sin against the German nation"! How can one not see this as the rebirth of paganism, which has been correctly called "pantheistic stupor"?

Just like Bolshevism, Nazism has created its own "god," a Nordic, German, national god, for its own purposes. What are these new "gods" if not idols that are useful for the decoration of public speeches?

In a certain Polish home, a German soldier asked a small boy to take the images of saints off the walls. "My god," he explained, "is nature." He was a faithful disciple of neopaganism on an apostolic mission to Poland.

Militant Paganism and Its Fruits

Reborn racist paganism at the service of state policy methodically led its nation to total de-Christianization, to a rupture with Christian culture and morality, which was considered to be the greatest danger to the nation. This aim was achieved through the struggle against moral scruples, in particular through the depravation of young people and the finetuning of an instinct for bloody cruelty within them.

In recent years, we have seen the horrific fruits that this pagan education has borne. The soldier at the front personified not only military efficacy; too often, he was the destroyer of not only the political order, but of religious life as well, destroying all signs of religious devotion with Satanic hatred. We have seen shattered tabernacles, ripped up religious paintings, and broken crosses — not only by roads, but in private homes as well. In many counties, all the roadside crosses and religious figures were "mowed down." Is it not shocking that many churches were bombed during the Sunday High Mass, with their presbyteries targeted in particular?

In one of the churches in the suburbs of Poland's capital, the hands on a church tower clock stopped at the moment of the explosion of a bomb at the time of a war crime, on Sunday at 11:20 in the morning. Was it not Satan's hand that chose this moment on a Sunday morning, when the people gather around the altars to praise God with exaltation? Several hundred churches were destroyed in Poland on that memorable Sunday. It is no coincidence that nearly all the places of worship in Warsaw were destroyed. This was the work of a regular army. Something equally horrific had not happened in previous wars, as the struggle against religion had not before been one of the aims of armed forces at the front. This is the work of this new pagan education.

What a terrible transformation! Christian thinking and morality once had the great power of sanctifying even the knights. Before going into battle, the Christian knight spent the night alone in a church, clad in a white robe, praying, and keeping vigil. The knight was fortified by the Body of Christ in the early morning, used the sword to dispense God's justice, was a defender of women and children, and frequently took pity on the weak and defenseless. The pagan soldier, however, has no ethical code; brutal violence and animalistic timidity, strengthened by his sense of impunity, are his law.

What the occupying army had begun was continued by the occupying pagan administration. This was an enormous change as well. Poland's previous occupiers had fought against the Church as one of the reservoirs of national identity, but today this is supplemented by the struggle against religion more generally and hatred of Christ. The tragedy of the Catholic Church in ravaged Poland attests to this: closed churches; a ban against preaching the word of God and administering the sacraments to the ill and sick, and even of listening to confessions in the Polish languages; the imprisonment and harassment of some priests and bishops and the expulsion of others from their own residences; the confiscation of the Church's property; the closing of seminaries; the disruption of social religious life—none of this should fit the strategy of any general staff.

"He will execute judgment among the nations" (Psalm 110:6).

There is a well-known scene from the Gospels that took place after Christ's sermon in the synagogue in Capernaum: the incited people led Christ out of the city and up a hill in order to throw

Him down from it, "[b]ut passing through the midst of them, He went away" (Luke 4:30). Today, a similar scene happens over and over again. Never before had God's name been so abused as in the military-political propaganda of National Socialism. "God is with us," Hitler's followers claimed; however, this was not Christ, but the "god" of the Nazi Party, of the dictatorship of predatory Germanism, and a god that had been created by man. Christ the Lord walked past this loud gang, just as He had once passed by an agitated crowd of Jews.

What does God have in common with Belial? What does "He Who made us and [Whose] we are" (Psalm 100:3) share with that silver and gold, with that clay that was elevated to the rank of a national deity through a government decree? The Holy Church teaches in *Mit brennender Sorge*, written by Pius XI in 1937: "Our God is the Personal God, supernatural, omnipotent, infinitely perfect, one in the Trinity of Persons, tri-personal in the unity of divine essence, the Creator of all existence. Lord, King, and ultimate Consummator of the history of the world, Who will not, and cannot, tolerate a rival God by His side" (MBS, 9). He is the Creator of the nations, and "all the peoples behold His glory" (Psalm 97:6). "For great is the Lord, and greatly to be praised; He is to be feared above all gods. For the gods of the peoples are idols, but the Lord made the heavens" (Psalm 96:4–5). The Lord will arise in order to demand His rights and the legacy of the nations. "Ascribe to the Lord, O families of the peoples, ascribe to the Lord glory and strength!" (Psalm 96:7).

"The Lord reigns; let the peoples tremble! He sits enthroned upon the cherubim; let the earth quake!" (Psalm 99:1). Meanwhile, the joyous earth, that most faithful daughter of His, "the work of [God's] fingers" (Psalm 8:3), will rejoice and its many islands will be glad (see Psalm 97:1) upon learning that the Lord will honorably protect it against the idols of today's pagans.

"To the King of Ages, immortal, invisible, the only God, be honor and glory forever and ever" (1 Timothy 1:17).

The creators of modern-day gods, the gods of party, blood, and race; national and state gods; the new idols of the atheistic proletariat; all those who instead of giving praise to God, ask for themselves to be praised, should recall the voice from Sinai: "You shall have no other gods before Me... You shall not bow down to them or serve them; for I, the Lord your God, am a jealous God" (Exodus 20:3, 5).

May those who agitate in favor of the idols of the season go and meet the children of the living God in order to stand in defense of the battered honor of the Almighty. Today, we have the unique responsibility to show God our gratitude for His great glory, for His love for us, for the work of Redemption, for sweet Providence, and for elevating humanity. We must praise God on earth, giving witness to Him before all people and all the ministries of the propaganda of foreign gods.

"Hallowed be Thy name" (Matthew 6:9).

We fulfill our first duty of the day with the words of Paul's song: "To the King of the ages, immortal, invisible, the only God, be honor and glory for ever and ever" (1 Timothy 1:17).

"Praise is due to Thee, O God, in Zion" (Psalm 65:1). Taking an example from the holy Church, we thank God for His great glory, which He opened up to us, and which gradually is revealed before our eyes in the works of His hands and in the countless miracles with which He illuminates our souls. "Worthy art Thou, our Lord and God, to receive glory and honor and power, for Thou didst create all things, and by Thy will they existed and were created" (Revelation 4:11). May our mouths proclaim Christ's request: "Hallowed be Thy name" (Matthew 6:9). May it become our imperative to proclaim God's glory throughout the earth!

The hymn of gratitude, "Thy hands fashioned and made me... Remember that Thou hast made me of clay; and wilt Thou turn me to dust again?" (Job 10:8–9), will flow from the depths of my humanity, which has been benevolently shaped by the Father according to His image and likeness. Constantly in God's fatherly hand, in His bosom, in the shadow of His clemency, I am at a loss for words at how wondrous God's creation of my life and soul was. What more could I expect from the idol of race and blood or that of the hammer and sickle? Could I live off scraps for pigs if I have been brought up on the healthy food of the Father's home?

Here is a new title for God's glory! "Hear this, all peoples! Give ear, all inhabitants of the world!" (Psalm 49:2). "Great is the Lord and greatly to be praised in the city of our God! His holy mountain, beautiful in elevation, is the joy of all the earth" (Psalm 48:2). God gave His Son the authority to judge, awakened Him from the dead, and "made Him sit at His right hand in the heavenly places, far above all rule and authority and power and dominion, and above every name that is named, not only in this age but also in that which is to come; and He has put all things under His feet" (Ephesians 1:20–22). "For we know that Christ being raised from the dead will never die again; death no longer has dominion over Him" (Romans 6:9), just as those who trust Him do not die. We give thanks to His power, because He rules over the nations. It is through Him that "we push down our foes; through [God's] name we tread down our assailants" (Psalm 44:6).

Although from the day of Mieszko's[1] triumph of Christ's Cross, "many fight against me proudly" (Psalm 56:2), "He delivered me from my strong enemy, from those who hated me" (2 Samuel 22:18).

Was it not having been strengthened by God's grace and confident in His Providence that King Władysław I the Elbow-High[2] returned with a blessing of the Holy See on a penitential pilgrimage to the tombs of the Apostles in order to build a great Poland and dispense justice during the drama in Płowce?[3]

And what was the force that led Jagiełło at Grunwald?[4] Two armies met. Both were armed with the Cross, but whereas the commander of one yelled: *Gott mit uns*,[5] his opponent humbled himself in front of the Lord, fearing the shedding of Christian blood. The Teutonic Knights, who had God on their lips but not their hearts, were defeated at the feet of a nation supported by God's strength. Poland rescued

---

1 Mieszko I was the first political ruler of Poland, who Christianized the country in 966.

2 The king of Poland from 1320 to 1333.

3 The Battle of Płowce took place in Kujavia in central Poland on September 27, 1331, and resulted in a victory of the Poles over the Teutonic Kings, a German order of warrior-friars which was founded during the Crusades and used violence to convert the pagan tribes of the Baltics to Christianity.

4 At the Battle of Grunwald on July 15, 1410, Polish-Lithuanian knights led by King Władysław Jagiełło (Jogaila in Lithuanian) defeated the Teutonic Knights and ended the order's hegemony in Pomerania.

5 German: "God is with us."

the dignity and glory of the Cross, which in the violent deeds of the Teutonic missionaries had ceased to be Christ's Cross. The servants of the god of thunder and of tribalistic hatred had been the forerunners to those whom the land covered before our eyes.

And what about the famous victory at Khotyn,[6] for which we continue to praise God in our churches even today? It was the only victory for which a joyous *Te Deum* was sung to the heavens even in the days of the Polish nation's greatest slavery!

Could the defense of Jasna Góra[7] be understood in any other way than as a protective sign of Divine Providence in the history of our nation?

And what about our greatest source of pride in the history of Christian civilization — the Siege of Vienna,[8] and the "Miracle on the Vistula"?[9] This is the *gesta Dei per Polonos*[10] known around the world!

Indeed: "Thou with Thy own hand didst drive out the nations . . . for not by their own sword did they win the land, nor did their own arm give them victory; but Thy right hand, and Thy arm, and the light of Thy countenance; for Thou didst delight in them" (Psalm 44:3–4). "Woe to the nations that rise up against my people! The Lord Almighty will take vengeance on them in the day of judgment; fire and worms He will give to their flesh; they shall weep in pain forever" (Judith 16:17).

If God intended on rescuing His nation of Israel and liberating it from the foreign yoke, He did so at the price of the Egyptian plagues, even if all water were to turn into blood and all the firstborn sons of the oppressor were to die. "There is no Holy One like the Lord" (1 Samuel 2:2).

---

6 At the Battle of Khotyn on November 11, 1673 in present-day Ukraine, Polish-Lithuanian troops defeated the Ottoman Empire.

7 In the mid-seventeenth century, Poland experienced a series of devastating invasions by Sweden. In 1655, however, the Poles succeeded in defending Jasna Góra, Poland's most important Marian shrine, from the invaders.

8 On September 12, 1683, an international coalition of Christian troops led by King John III Sobieski of Poland defeated the Turks at Kahlenberg outside Vienna.

9 "The Miracle on the Vistula" refers to the Battle of Warsaw, which took place on August 15, 1920, and resulted in a Polish victory, ultimately leading Poland to defeat the Soviet Union in the Polish-Bolshevik War, which precluded a planned communist overtaking of Western Europe.

10 Latin: "God's deeds through the Poles."

"Put away the foreign gods" (Genesis 35:2).

During the times of Ahab, when the "state" religion was heretical idolatry, the Lord sent the prophet Elijah to the king. Summoning all the pagan prophets from Israel to Mount Carmel, Elijah debated faith with them. He said: "'How long will you go limping with two different opinions? If the Lord is God, follow Him; but if Baal, then follow him.' And the people did not answer him a word" (3 Kings 18:21). This silence of the people is pregnant with meaning. They had to choose to reject God and His one prophet, Elijah, or Baal and the praise of the totalitarian king Ahab and the forty-five prophets of the regime. Was their silence not treason, weakness, and doubt?

We should not condemn this crowd. Let us recall how during our days here and there we "exchanged the glory of the immortal God for images resembling mortal man or birds or animals or reptiles" (Romans 1:23). How many people ran to praise the idols! And, when a bad man strutted, when he built a steel state based on violence and rape, when his armed fist smashed country after country, many fearful hearts were filled with doubt: "Is not the Germanic god stronger than our God?" There was no lack of those who decided it was time to cut ties with the Christian God and go back centuries in our nation's history and reject the Cross, all the while glorifying the Slavic deities.

These are the temptations of the Polish soul! What a great joy it is to be able to say that among us only a few exposed the weak nerves of faithlessness. Instead, the nation as a whole did not succumb to temptation, but during the time of trial, prayed with confident humility: "Fret not yourself because of the wicked, be not envious of wrongdoers! For they will fade soon like the grass, and wither like the green herb. Trust the Lord, and do good... For the wicked shall be cut off; but those who wait for the Lord shall possess the land. Yet a little while, and the wicked will be no more; though you look well at his place, he will not be there" (Psalm 37:1–3, 9–10).

This is over! We see with our very eyes the works of God's power. If the vapors of the past still turn up, let us scatter them with our faith: "Be still, and know that I am God. I am exalted among the nations; I am exalted in the earth!" (Psalm 46:10). Let us respond to the pagan deities with Christ's response: "Begone, Satan! For it is written: 'You shall worship the Lord your God, and Him only shall you serve'" (Matthew 4:10).

"Annihilate the pride of the enemies of thy name"

... and break their resistance with your right hand. "Let them be like chaff before the wind, with the angel of the Lord driving them on!" (Psalm 35:5). "Pour out Thy anger on the nations that do not know Thee and on the kingdoms that do not call on Thy name!" (Psalm 79:6). It is with these words that the Church tells the faithful to pray with the Psalmist for the victory of faith in God. A duty of one's faith is to pray: "Let them know that Thou alone, Whose name is the Lord, art the Most High over all the earth" (Psalm 83:18).

The courage and intimacy with which the Psalmist speaks to God is strange: "Rouse Thyself! Why sleepest Thou, O Lord? Awake! Do not cast us off forever!" (Psalm 44:24). He is so strident that he even arms God against His enemies: "Take hold of shield and buckler and rise for my help!" (Psalm 35:2).

If our strength is flagging in our onerous struggle against evil and infidelity, let us ask for God's succor so that He may protect us in His glory. Even if it were God's will for our faith to be tested and "the cords of death encompassed me, the torrents of perdition assailed me" (Psalm 18:4), then we will say with joy that "all this has come upon us, though we have not forgotten Thee, or been false to Thy covenant" (Psalm 44:17). Our faith and trust in God will grow from our sufferings and persecutions. At such times, God will not release us from His hands, and His intentions are different from those of our enemy. Who does not know that many of our brothers, who have been thrown into prison by the heathens, have attained complete freedom in the Lord? Indeed, "how great are Thy works, O Lord!" (Psalm 92:5). It is unsurprising that "we rejoice in our sufferings, knowing that suffering produces endurance, and that endurance produces character, character produces hope, and hope does not disappoint us, because God's love has been poured into our hearts through the Holy Spirit Who has been given to us" (Romans 5:3–5), "so that the genuineness of your faith, more precious than gold" (1 Peter 1:7) may enrich our hearts with treasures, which to our enemies' shame brings a rich harvest. The enemy who wanted to rob our treasure of faith did a stupid thing and did our nation a favor by awakening our slumbering souls.

"The Lord sits enthroned forever" (Psalm 9:7).

Struggling against God is folly. It is the typical way of the powerful of this earth who in their pride, which piles up to the heavens, have no way of returning other than by falling: "But the wicked perish; the enemies of the Lord are like the glory of the pastures, they vanish — like smoke they vanish away" (Psalm 37:20). "Now is the judgment of this world, now shall the ruler of this world be cast out" (John 12:31). The history of this judgment is so rich that it is surprising that the successors to the fallen heathens have learned so little from the past. Evidently, this is how God cleanses the evil of this world "to repay with affliction those who afflict you, and to grant rest with us to you who are afflicted" (2 Thessalonians 1:6–7).

The idol of the earth, kingdom, state, or nation is built on the tears and oppression of the people, and when God wants to liberate His people from the Egyptian yoke, Pharaoh's heart hardens, and he boastfully ignores God's voice.

Now, all you who walk the path of the heathens in order to fight against the living God will experience your end on this earth, just as Gog, prince of Meshech, and Tubal met his end (see Ezekiel 39:1). "As for you, son of man, thus says the Lord God: 'Speak to the birds of every sort and to all beasts of the field, assemble and come, gather from all sides to the sacrificial feast which I am preparing for you, a great sacrificial feast upon the mountains of Israel, and you shall eat flesh and drink blood. You shall eat the flesh of the mighty and drink the blood of the princes of the earth — of rams, of lambs, and of goats, of bulls, all of them fatlings of Bashan. And you shall eat fat till you are filled, and drink blood till you are drunk, at the sacrificial feast which I am preparing for you. And you shall be filled at my table with horses and riders, with mighty men and all kinds of warriors,' says the Lord God. And I will set My glory among the nations; and all the nations shall see My judgment which

I have executed, and My hand which I have laid on them" (Ezekiel 39:17–21).

A struggle between faith and unbelief, between the buckler of prayer and faith in the Lord, and the military scowl of Gog and Magog, has taken place in our land. Our eyes are filled with terrible visions, apocalyptic battles, and unprecedented amounts of hatred and crime that afflict not only the body, but also the depths of the soul in order to tear it out, separate it from God, and stomp on it on the ground: "If it had not been the Lord Who was on our side, when men rose up against us, then they would have swallowed us up alive" (Psalm 124:2–3).

This is a brief history of the last rebellion against the Almighty. "Of old Thou didst lay the foundation of the earth, and the heavens are the work of Thy hands. They will perish, but Thou dost endure; they will all wear out like a garment. Thou changest them like raiment, and they pass away; but Thou art the same, and Thy years have no end" (Psalm 102:25–27).

"'I am the Alpha and the Omega,' says the Lord God, Who is and Who was and Who is to come, the Almighty" (Revelation 1:8). God is the beginning for those who trust in Him and the end for all who fight against Him!

As it was at the beginning of our nation's history, when the holy baptismal waters cleansed our eyes so that they may see God's true luminosity; likewise, today, "The Lord our God be with us, as He was with our fathers; may He not leave us or forsake us; that He may incline our hearts to Him, to walk in all His ways, and to keep His commandments, His statutes, and His ordinances, which He commanded our fathers" (1 Kings 8:57–58).

2

"I Will Sing of Thy Steadfast Love, O Lord, Forever"[1]

*"For Thou art just in all that Thou hast done to us
[...]. For we have sinfully and lawlessly departed
from Thee and have sinned in all things and
have not obeyed Thy commandments [...]. For
Thy name's sake do not give us up utterly, and
do not break Thy covenant" (see Daniel 3:23,
The Prayer of Azariah in the Furnace).*

IT IS UNLIKELY THAT ANYONE WHO HAS READ
the Book of Genesis has not focused his attention for an extended
time on the strange conversation between Abraham and God on
the road to Sodom and Gomorrah. This road was marked by God's
justice and His justified wrath for the countless sins of the inhabitants
of those wicked cities. This is what Abraham said on the way there:
"Suppose there are fifty righteous within the city; wilt Thou then
destroy the place and not spare it for the fifty righteous who are in it?"
(Genesis 18:24). "And the Lord said: 'If I find at Sodom fifty righteous
in the city, I will spare the whole place for their sake'" (Genesis 18:26).
A bartering about the limits of God's love began: encouraged by God's
compliance, Abraham, who was "but dust and ashes," insisted once
again. And the Lord promised that He would not destroy the city
for forty-five, forty, thirty, twenty, or even ten righteous (see Genesis
18:32). However, not even ten righteous could be found. Up until the
present, the Dead Sea is witness to the Lord's wrath and punishment.
One cannot forget that it was precisely in this way that God's great
mercy saved Lot from the destruction of those iniquitous cities so
that the righteous are not slain as the wicked (Genesis 18:25).

As on the road to Sodom, on the way to numerous nations and cities today, many souls try to barter with God, who at all costs wants to
be merciful. Today, when we are experiencing a great global catastrophe, if we were to ask people who have emerged out of the rubble of

---

1   (Psalm 89:2; see Isaiah 63:7).

crumbling cities, from the burning fires and the terror of bombings, how many would speak of the miracles accomplished thanks to God's mercy? "A thousand may fall at your side, ten thousand at your right hand; but [death, pestilence, and terror] will not come near you" (Psalm 91:7), because "He will give His angels charge of you to guard you in all your ways" (Psalm 91:11).

As in the life of every person; likewise, in the life of our nation, the Lord has become our salvation. Thus: "I will recount the steadfast love of the Lord, the praises of the Lord, according to all that the Lord has granted us, and the great goodness to the house of Israel, which He has granted them according to His mercy, according to the abundance of His steadfast love" (Isaiah 63:7).

I. In Memory of God's Great Mercy

It is God's will for the holy books to record the history of His mercy in the life of the Chosen People so that it may be remembered forever. The "stiff-necked people, uncircumcised in heart and ears" protested against the spear of the Merciful One; having forgotten God's great kindness and love, they constantly betrayed Him. Every time they bowed their proud necks before God's reproachful hand, the Lord, jealous of love, always saw the people's heart like wax that has melted in hot contrition; thus, He returned to His people and saved them.

"Our fathers, when they were in Egypt, did not consider Thy wonderful works; they did not remember the abundance of Thy steadfast love, but rebelled against the Most High at the Red Sea" (Psalm 106:7). Their faith was small, as they frequently doubted God's power, although they lived in the light of a fiery cloud, surrounded by miracles that had become their daily bread. They murmured against Moses for having led them out of the land of Egypt: "What have you done to us, in bringing us out of Egypt? [...] For it would have been better for us to serve the Egyptians than to die in the wilderness" (Exodus 14:11–12). They placed slavery and even debasement above trust in the Lord. They scorned the food of freedom of the sons of God. Nevertheless, He liberated them in His name, to show them His power. "He rebuked the Red Sea, and it became dry" (Psalm 106:9); "Then they cried to the Lord in their trouble, and He delivered them from their distress" (Psalm 106:13). Although they had believed His words and praised God's glory, "they soon forgot His works [...] But they had a wanton craving in the wilderness and put God to the test in the desert" (Psalm 106:13–14). They called: "Would that we had died by the hand of the Lord in the land of Egypt, when we sat by the fleshpots and ate bread to the full" (Exodus 16:3). The idol of the belly that they had hitherto faithfully served paralyzed their spirit: incapable of making sacrifices, they valued fleshpots over freedom. "He gave them what they asked but sent a wasting disease among them" (Psalm 106:15), as they were envious of Moses in the camp and of Aaron, who was holy in the Lord.

The rebellion of Korah, Dathan, and Abiram expressed the pride that several generations experienced: "Why then do you exalt yourselves above the assembly of the Lord?" (Numbers 16:3). This same pride is expressed in the evident rebellion against God Himself: "They made a calf in Horeb and worshiped a molten image. [...] They forgot God, their Savior, Who had done great things in Egypt" (Psalm 106:19, 21). Moved by wrath at the unfaithful people, God wanted to destroy them: "Therefore, He said He would destroy them — had not Moses, His chosen one, stood in the breach before Him, to turn away His wrath from destroying them" (Psalm 106:23; see Exodus 32:11). However, their infidelity did not end: "Then they attached themselves to the Ba'al of Pe'or and ate sacrifices offered to the dead" (Psalm 106:28). "They sacrificed their sons and their daughters to the demons; they poured out innocent blood, the blood of their sons and daughters" (Psalm 106:37–38). One betrayal led to another; they irritated God with their affairs, incensing His spirit (see Psalm 106:7). Thus, the Lord struck them: "Then they cried to the Lord in their trouble, and He delivered them from their distress" (Psalm 107:13).

"Then they despised the pleasant land, having no faith in His promise. They murmured in their tents and did not obey the voice of the Lord" (Psalm 106:24–25). They scorned the land of milk and honey, raising their quarrelsome and cantankerous voices against God's gifts. This once more provoked the Lord's rage: "How long shall this wicked congregation murmur against me?" (Numbers 14:27). Only Moses, the Lord's servant, stopped God's right hand from not sending pestilence upon them.

19

"[T]he land was polluted with blood. Thus, they became unclean by their acts and played the harlot in their doings" (Psalm 106:38–39). They rejected God's ways and Godly matters, instead walking the winding roads of their countless iniquities. Thus, "the anger of the Lord was kindled against His people, and He abhorred His heritage; He gave them into the hand of the nations, so that those who hated them ruled over them" (Psalm 106:40–41).

Here are but a few fragments of the Chosen People's constant struggle against their Lord, a struggle that renewed God's love. "Many times, He delivered them, but they were "rebellious in their purposes, and were brought low through their iniquity. Nevertheless, He regarded their distress, when He heard their cry. He remembered for their sake His covenant, and relented according to the abundance of His steadfast love. He caused them to be pitied by all those who held them captive" (Psalm 106:43–46).

II. Our Great Sins

We began the history of our nation with the experience of God's mercy. What else was being cleansed by the waters of holy Baptism, if not the initiation of the nation onto the paths of great graces and great forgiveness? The Lord has been no less generous to us than to His Chosen People, since thanks to holy Baptism, we have become a holy chosen nation that is loved up to the heights of the Holy Cross. As a nation, we have always been faithful to the Cross; never in our history have we had national betrayals. However, we have not been free of sins that have disarmed our spirit and pushed us away from the paths of God's great vocations and destinies. God punished our grandfathers for the sins of our great-grandfathers, so that He could bring freedom back to their sons.

How often in our reborn fatherland have we forgotten about the greatest commandment of love for God and the second greatest commandment, similar to the first, that of love for one's neighbor and of social love. On the first day of the Resurrection, the Lord gave us a warning right at the gates of the capital. When we "cried to the Lord in our distress" (Psalm 120:1), when the churches of the capital had become filled with a crowd of people praying and its streets became filled with processions of suppliants, He liberated us from our oppression and brought us joy on the very day of the Intercessor of all graces, the Lady of all mercy, Mary, the Queen of Poland, who has ascended into heaven.[2]

However, the more time passed from the "Miracle on the Vistula" and its significant lesson began to fade in the Polish memory, "you waxed fat, you grew thick, you became sleek; then [...] forsook God Who made [you] and scoffed at the Rock of His salvation" (Deuteronomy 32:15). This began to give rise to apostasy: "For my people have committed two evils: they have forsaken me, the fountain of living waters, and hewed out cisterns for themselves, broken cisterns, that can hold no water" (Jeremiah 2:13).

"They sacrificed to demons which were no gods, to gods they had never known, to new gods that had come in of late, whom your fathers had never dreaded" (Deuteronomy 32:17).

Dumbfounded by freedom, some conceived of freedom above all as liberation from God's laws, from the commandments of the Holy Church, up to the point of breaking with the highest truth and rejecting Christianity. In fact, there were even calls for Poland to return to the feet of the Slavic deities, to not serve Christ but Światowid...[3]

How little time did the Holy Church have in Poland in order to heal the wounds from the persecutions of her invaders; she walked the Stations of the Cross in the Poland whose life she had saved during the time of slavery. The Church's servants, who in an earlier age had been deported to Siberia, often were considered to be "occupiers" and often became second-class citizens.[4] We must recall the difficult

---

2   Wyszyński is referring to "the Miracle on the Vistula," the Polish victory over the Bolsheviks during the Polish-Bolshevik War of 1920. Many Poles then fled to churches and chapels to pray to God and Mary to deliver their nation from Soviet captivity. The turning point in the battle coincided with August 15, the Feast of the Assumption.

3   Światowid: A pagan deity from pre-Christian Poland.

4   Wyszyński is referring to the well-known 1939 anti-clerical essay *Nasi okupanci* ("Our Occupiers"), written by Tadeusz Boy-Żeleński, a famous translator of French literature into Polish and physician who criticized the Catholic Church's role in Polish society and campaigned for the legalization of abortion and promotion of contraception in interwar Poland. Boy-Żeleński met a tragic end: in July 1941, he was one of forty-five Polish professors and their family members killed by the Germans in Lwów (present-day Lviv, Ukraine) as part of their campaign against the Polish intelligentsia.

battles that the Polish Church had to fight for the Christian nature of our state, for schools and education, for Catholic marriages: how alone she was in her struggle against the weak, but influential cults that broke down religious unity; what painful things she had listened to in the parliaments or during discussions on the concordat. This powerful "conspiracy of silence" when various social and political organizations were being formed, whose names evoking sad memories need not be recalled here and that tried to be completely silent about the Good News, and in their educational work, financed by public funds, acted as if Christ had not come to the earth, and Poland had not been Catholic for a thousand years!

Three months before the war broke out, I attended a meeting of a semi-public education organization. During three days of sessions, the word "Christ" was not said a single time, although there was talk of "internal life," of shaping the character, etc. We recall not only the destructive spread of Communism, which has made not only our eastern borderlands, but also our salons, numerous organizations and magazines, and even the doors of our schools. "You were unmindful of the Rock that begot you, and you forgot the God who gave you birth" (Deuteronomy 32:18).

"Our fathers, when they were in Egypt, did not consider Thy wonderful works; they did not remember the abundance of Thy steadfast love" (Psalm 106:7).

Is it not telling that the nation that "with the smoke of fires, with the dust of blood consanguine with Yours, O Lord," which once yelled with all its heart: "God save Poland," forgot "its Creator" so easily? By reviving our fatherland right now, at a time that is so momentous for the world, God has led us through a land of wonders. Was it not a miracle that three powers[5] have been crushed so that the tied-up Lazarus, who had been in the tomb for four days, could arise? Was it not a miracle that Poland, which was still pale from death, weak, and exposed, unarmed and lacking allies, alone defeated one giant from the east who moved westwards not only to conquer our lands, but also to foment global revolution? However,

5   In 1772, 1773 and 1795, an internally weakened Polish-Lithuanian Commonwealth was partitioned by Russia, Prussia, and Austria, ceasing to formally exist until the restoration of Polish and Lithuanian independence in 1918.

God, Who has miraculously resurrected us, also gave us power; He wanted us to be confident in our strength. He wanted to elevate our importance in the eyes of the world, and thus strengthened our right hand so that we could understand that we are still to be the bulwark of Christianity. He liberated us not so that we would drown in our old sins, but so that we could be a model for Christian states and move forward. We are to serve God, not the Egyptians.

Do we not perceive God's finger in the history of our resurrection? Did we humble ourselves before the Majesty of the Lord in recognizing that "Thy right hand, O Lord, shatters the enemy" (see Exodus 15:6)? How much pride, arrogance, disregarding one another's accomplishments, and extorting reasons for praise! Amidst this petty market hubbub, we did not understand God's miracles or remember His great mercy. Have we already forgotten that the Lord Who had "saved a people out of the land of Egypt, afterward destroyed those who did not believe" (Jude 1:5)? We remember this well!

"But they soon forgot His works; [...] they had a wanton craving in the wilderness and put God to the test in the desert" (Psalm 106:13–15).

Although this is painful, let us recall how much complaining and murmuring there was against our fatherland in our poor Poland. They murmured when hungry, recalling how during the time of slavery they "sat by the fleshpots" (Exodus 16:3); they murmured when satiated, and "they despised the pleasant land" (Psalm 106:24). Instead of working to rebuild the fatherland, they praised what is foreign. So many have cursed the free fatherland, saying: "This is not the Poland we had waited for!" Disputes and class conflicts, the pride of the rulers, selfishness and economic exploitation, and the egotism of possession were all our sins. And we believed Mary was to blame for them!

Could not poor Poland, worn out by slavery and a century of plundering, have immediately judged her sons before fleshpots and feed them with bread until they were satiated? And those who first sat at the Father's table, who arrived first, did they not push away the weaker ones who would only later arrive? Does the good son admonish his mother for being weak and poor because she moves forward slowly in pain?

"Men in the camp were jealous of Moses and Aaron, the holy one of the Lord" (see Psalm 106:16) and called: "Why then do you exalt yourselves above the assembly of the Lord?" (Numbers 16:3).

23

The long period of slavery did not free us of rebellion. In partisan battles, it was forgotten where the good of the party ends and where the Blessed Mother's common good begins. Were not the partisan battles that Poland experienced not too often subversion at the cost of the fatherland? We have seen this system in practice right up to the last moment. Even the most outstanding representatives of society, whose lips proclaimed love of the fatherland, sabotaged the state on the eve of the war, stubbornly denying it tax revenues. What villainy was done in order to avoid fulfilling one's duties! Many created legal fictions and endowed themselves with the right to property; many among them later eagerly paid taxes to the invader, whereas they had nothing besides curses for their own state, claiming it had left them homeless.

"They sacrificed their sons and their daughters to the demons; they poured out innocent blood, the blood of their sons and daughters" (Psalm 106:37–38).

We also witnessed an orgy of lawlessness in the morality of family life. It seemed that Poland was returning to the Saxon period.[6] It was with difficulty that the Church succeeded in protecting the state from the danger of Bolshevik matrimonial law, as the worst example came from the top, from Polish literature, which praised free love, collegial marriage, trial marriages, and so forth. The sins of marital infidelity, sexualism, and hedonism promoting infanticide on a huge scale spread across our land. The breakdown of marriage, changing religion to be able to change spouses, abandoned children, broken homes, the tragedies of abandoned mothers, who included the wives of people with high positions in the state apparatus, and cheated not only the mothers of their own children, but often the fatherland, the mother of mothers, as well; all this was common in recent years. Can such people set a good example? Because of their attitude, they promoted widespread licentiousness! Could such people, who lacked the strength to curb their own lust, have had the strength to defend the nation in times of terror? They lacked the strength that they had not practiced in their family homes. It can be said of them: "But Jeshurun

---

6 Under the reign of Augustus III, the Elector of Saxony (1733–1763), Poland-Lithuania was in a political union with the German state of Saxony. In the Polish popular imagination, this period is synonymous with license and decadence.

waxed fat, and kicked; you waxed fat, you grew thick, you became sleek; then he forsook God Who made him" (Deuteronomy 32:15). These average, ordinary people, fattened by the prosperity the state had ensured them, quickly forgot where they had come from, from what lowly social positions they had been pulled out by the fatherland; they grew fat and indulged their unconquered desires, putting themselves and their entire nation in jeopardy.

"The Lord saw it, and spurned them, because of the provocation of His sons and His daughters. And He said, 'I will hide my face from them, so I will stir them to jealousy with those who are no people; I will provoke them with a foolish nation. [...] And I will heap evils upon them; I will spend my arrows upon them; they shall be wasted with hunger and devoured with burning heat and poisonous pestilence. [...] In the open, the sword shall bereave, and in the chambers shall be terror, destroying both young man and virgin, the sucking child with the man of gray hairs'" (Deuteronomy 32:19–25).

"Know and see that it is evil and bitter for you to forsake the Lord your God; the fear of Me is not in you" (Jeremiah 2:19).

III. God's Great Compassion

When David demanded that Joab conduct a census among the people of Israel, God punished his pride. He brought upon him the prophet Gad, giving him three punishments to choose from. "Then David said to Gad, 'I am in great distress; let us fall into the hand of the Lord, for His mercy is great; but let me not fall into the hand of man'" (2 Samuel 24:14). David acted properly, entrusting himself to God's hands and supplicating himself to God's mercy, not man's. The enemy strikes to kill, while even when God strikes, He does so in order to revive someone, to bring him back to life. When He uses an invader as a whip, He does so in order to admonish a lost nation. However, He allowed them to act only within limits that are consistent with God's plan. If the hostile person forgets that he is only an ax in the hands of a lumberjack, God crushes and rejects him as a useless tool "lest their adversaries should judge amiss, lest they should say, 'Our hand is triumphant, the Lord has not wrought all this'" (Deuteronomy 32:27).

When God sent Assyria in order to make the Israelites come to their senses, He threatened: "Ah, Assyria, the rod of my anger, the staff of my fury!" (Isaiah 10:5). Assyria quickly forgot that he was an ax in the hands of the lumberjack and decided "in his mind to destroy and to cut off nations not a few" (Isaiah 10:7). As soon as God's whip begins to implement its plans and not those of God and when pride and impetuosity grow, then God's voice speaks to the conquered people: "O My people, who dwell in Zion, be not afraid of the Assyrians [. . .]. For in a very little while, My indignation will come to an end, and My anger will be directed to their destruction" (Isaiah 10:24–25). Great is the mercy of God, Who does not lose sight of the hostile hand "for Thou, O Lord, hast not forsaken those who seek Thee" (see Psalm 9:11).

The cries of the oppressed, who have themselves experienced the seven deadly sins of hostile enemies, have called out to the heavens from the Polish lands: "Yet, O Lord, Thou art our Father; we are the clay, and Thou art our potter; we are all the work of Thy hand. Be not exceedingly angry, O Lord, and remember not iniquity forever. Behold, consider, we are all Thy people. Thy holy cities have become a wilderness, Zion has become a wilderness, Jerusalem a desolation. Our holy and beautiful house, where our fathers praised thee, has been burned by fire, and all our pleasant places have become ruins. Wilt Thou restrain Thyself at these things, O Lord? Wilt Thou keep silent and afflict us sorely?" (Isaiah 64:8–12). "Vindicate me, O God, and defend my cause against an ungodly people; from deceitful and unjust men deliver me!" (Psalm 43:1).

Only the heavenly Father and the Mother of His Son, the Consoler of the oppressed, know the enormity of pain and the sea of tears that have been poured out in the nation's pleading prayer in the time of the greatest calamities that we have ever experienced.

"Then they cried to the Lord in their trouble, and He delivered them from their distress" (Psalm 107:13).

"The Lord brings the counsel of the nations to nought; He frustrates the plans of the peoples" (Psalm 33:10). "The Lord has broken the staff of the wicked, the scepter of rulers, that smote the peoples in wrath with unceasing blows, that ruled the nations in anger with unrelenting persecution" (Isaiah 14:5–6). He came to our aid more quickly than we had expected; He wanted to see lively smiles in our sorrowful eyes and joyous gratitude in our hearts. "For a brief moment I forsook you, but with great compassion I will gather you. In overflowing wrath for a moment, I hid My face from you, but with everlasting love I will have compassion on you. [...] For the mountains may depart and the hills be removed, but My steadfast love shall not depart from you" (Isaiah 54:7–10).

* * *

Today, when the Lord drew us out of many waters (see Psalm 18:16), our lips will sing the song of gratitude and praise for the greatness of His compassion, as did Moses' lips after crossing the Red Sea: "I will sing to the Lord, for He has triumphed gloriously; the horse and his rider He has thrown into the sea. [...] The floods cover them; they went down into the depths like a stone. Thy right hand, O Lord, glorious in power, Thy right hand, O Lord, shatters the enemy" (Exodus 15:1, 5–6).

"Therefore, strong peoples will glorify Thee; cities of ruthless nations will fear Thee. For Thou hast been a stronghold to the poor, a stronghold to the needy in his distress, a shelter from the storm, and a shade from the heat" (Isaiah 25:3–5).

"I will give thanks to the Lord with my whole heart; I will tell of all Thy wonderful deeds. I will be glad and exult in Thee, I will sing praise to Thy name, O Most High" (Psalm 9:1–2).

27

3

The Heart of God Is
the Heart of the Nation

"You have seen what I did to the Egyptians
and how I bore you on eagles' wings and
brought you to Myself" (Exodus 19:4).

REBORN POLAND EXPRESSED ITS GRATITUDE
by unveiling a monument in Poznan with a loving heart: *Sacratissimo Cordi Jesu—Polonia Restituta*.[1] As it grew out of the heart of the nation, it became for all of us a symbol, not only of the unification of the Polish state, but also of its marriage with the Sacred Heart of Our Lord Jesus Christ.

It is here, where the soul of the reborn Poland was expressed most beautifully, that a crime of sacrilege took place, while we unfortunately lacked the fortitude to prevent it. The hand of the "hostile man" was not stopped, but it dealt the "pain of pains" to our martyred soul. The "monument of gratitude" fell to the rubble, while the gold heart, a votive offering of grateful Poles, was ripped out of the bronze figure of Christ. The significance of this crime is terrible. And how instructive it is! The enemy knew from where the nation draws its strength. He knew that the nation cannot live without a heart. He knew that the heart of the nation is in the Heart of God. Here lies the essential meaning of this crime: in order to kill Poland, one must kill within her God's spirit and tear her heart away from God's Heart. How much did we learn in that rubble! The invader's crime is the *felix culpa*[2] as a sign of reborn Poland.

---

1 Latin: "To the Sacred Heart of Jesus, Reborn Poland." This monument was unveiled in Poznan in 1932, as an expression of gratitude for the rebirth of the Polish state. In 1939, it was torn down by the German occupiers, which was personally overseen by Eckhart Greiser, son of Arthur Greiser, the sadistic ruler of the *Warthegau*, the areas of Lesser Poland incorporated into Germany from which Poles and Jews were expelled; the people of Poznan dubbed Greiser "The Monster." In 1946, Greiser was publicly executed in Poznan; tens of thousands of Poles watched in satisfaction.
2 Latin: "blessed downfall"; in Christian theology, a term that often refers to Adam and Eve's fall.

I. The Heart of God in the Life of the Nation

At Mount Sinai, at the feet of which the Lord entered into a covenant with the people of Israel, His thundering voice resounded across the land: "You shall have no other gods before Me" (Exodus 20:3). God's breath, which shattered "foreign gods," gods of stone, silver, and gold, and made by human hands, the gods of Egypt, Moab, and Edom, liberated the people from the yoke of polytheism. The living God rescued man from the tyranny of countless idols. The same power that caused Baal to fall also annihilated Światowid, Tryglaw, Swarog, and Perun,[3] liberating our nation from the truly Egyptian yoke of the spirits that populated the fields, mountains, waters, and homes; it liberated our nation from unknown powers. "For I the Lord your God am a jealous God" (Exodus 20:5).

United in faith in the one God, we went towards national unity with our heads raised high. This was the first common love of the Polish nation, the love of God Who shows "steadfast love to thousands of those who love me and keep [His] commandments" (Exodus 20:6).

1. God Chooses His People and Is Jealous

Today, there are no chosen peoples in the supernatural order that are loved by God more than others, like the Israelites, who had been called to preserve and transmit to the world the commandments of faith in the One God, as well as to prepare the way for the Redeemer. Christ called His followers to be "disciples of all nations" (Matthew 28:19). However, the moment the nation becomes obedient to God's call and lowers its head before the Holy Cross, and the water of rebirth cleanses the souls of its sons from sin, it becomes "a chosen race, a royal priesthood, a holy nation, God's own people" (1 Peter 2:9), and God's wonderful love, which thrills us as we read the Old Testament, reappears in its history. In fact, it becomes a hundred times greater, because it is enriched by the merits of our Lord Jesus Christ.

Led out of the darkness of unbelief through an uncanny sentence of God's love, fortified by the words of life at the dawn of its history, and beginning its history at the Cross, the Polish nation must meekly confess: "For the Lord's portion is His people, Jacob His allotted

---

3 Pagan deities from pre-Christian Poland.

29

heritage. He found him in a desert land, and in the howling waste of the wilderness; He encircled him, He cared for him, He kept him as the apple of his eye. Like an eagle that stirs up its nest, that flutters over its young, spreading out its wings, catching them, bearing them on its pinions, the Lord alone did lead him" (Deuteronomy 32:9–12). Cannot the history of God's love in the life of our nation be expressed in the following words of the Lord's Psalmist, which have been passed on to later generations?

"We have heard with our ears, O God, our fathers have told us, what deeds Thou didst perform in their days [...] for not by their own sword did they win the land, nor did their own arm give them victory, but Thy right hand, and Thy arm, and the light of Thy countenance; for Thou didst delight in them" (Psalm 44:1–3).

We see, then, who we are in the face of God: "For you are a people holy to the Lord your God; the Lord your God has chosen you to be a people for His own possession, out of all the peoples that are on the face of the earth" (Deuteronomy 7:6). He elevated us out of love for us: "It was not because you were more in number than any other people that the Lord set His love upon you and chose you [...] but it is because the Lord loves you" (Deuteronomy:7–8).

2.God Is Inculcated in the Nation

God surrounds His people, just as the mountains surround Jerusalem (see Psalm 125:2). The nation reborn in Christ becomes the vineyard planted by God, surrounded by His Providence and flourishing, thanks to Him. This is how Isaiah speaks of this vineyard: "I, the Lord, am its keeper; every moment I water it; lest anyone harm it, I guard it night and day" (Isaiah 27:3). The vine that feeds the branches with its grace, which causes us to bear many fruits (see John 15:5), is Christ the Lord. It is this miracle of inculcation that gives birth to astonishing joy: "For what great nation is there that has a god so near to it as the Lord our God is to us, whenever we call upon Him?" (Deuteronomy 4:7).

3. God Is the Heart of the Nation

"Know therefore that the Lord your God is God, the faithful God Who keeps covenant and steadfast love with those who love Him and keep His commandments, to a thousand generations" (Deuteronomy 7:9).

The nation's unity with God is its strongest covenant; there is no earthly power that would be capable of annihilating a nation that fears God: "For the eyes of the Lord run to and fro throughout the whole earth, to show His might on behalf of those whose heart is blameless toward Him" (2 Chronicles 16:9). A tree that bears fruit for its Lord cannot be cut down and thrown into the fire; the heart that drinks the life-giving nectar of the Vineyard, whose rhythm is coordinated with the rhythm of the Heart of the Almighty, cannot wither or grow weak. "When He is quiet, who can condemn?" (Job 34:29). Even if there were moments of quandary among the people, as once in the desert, at "the waters of Meribah"; even if God's impetuosity were to cause the infidel to revolt against the Chosen People, God will recall His ancient covenant and rebuild the ruined wall of the vineyard, because His mercy is great.

A struggle for the hearts of the people can be waged between God and the nation; however, God's generous Heart is always the victor in this struggle. Does not the history of Israel attest to this? Let us look at a few examples:

"And the people of Israel did what was evil in the sight of the Lord and served the Baals. [...] So the anger of the Lord was kindled against Israel, and He gave them over to plunderers" (Judges 2:11, 14).

"And the people of Israel again did what was evil in the sight of the Lord. [...] And the Lord sold them into the hand of Jabin king of Canaan" (Judges 4:1–2). "The people of Israel did what was evil in the sight of the Lord; and the Lord gave them into the hand of Midian" (Judges 6:1).

"And the people of Israel again did what was evil in the sight of the Lord; and the Lord gave them into the hand of the Philistines for forty years" (Judges 13:1).

However, every time they were oppressed by an enemy, "the people of Israel cried to the Lord" (see Judges 3:9), while God's fieriness left Him, and He felt regret, so He awakened a man filled with His strength in order to liberate His people. For this God's heart is strong, although it easily grows soft upon hearing human cries and is contemptuous of no one (see Job 36; Hebrews 5). Admittedly, He says: "I will hide my face from them," and even if God "will provoke them with a foolish nation," it will only be to arouse jealousy in His prodigal sons (see Deuteronomy 32:20–21). For "He wounds, but He binds up; He smites, but His hands heal" (Job 5:18). He desires the nation's health and cannot tolerate its infidelity. Even when He submits the unfaithful nation to the hand of the enemy, He watches over the latter so that it would not cross the limits intended by God in its hatred: "If it had not been the Lord Who was on our side, when men rose up against us, then they would have swallowed us up alive" (Psalm 124:2–3).

"Blessed is the nation whose God is the Lord, the people whom He has chosen as His heritage!" (Psalm 33:12). When the heart of the nation goes to meet the Heart of God, the Lord Who commands you will be with you and will not leave you; have no fear!

II. The Heart of the Nation Towards God's Heart

"The steadfast love of the Lord never ceases; His mercies never come to an end" (Lamentations 3:22). In the last "morning" of our national life, the mercy of God, Who freed us from the yoke of the oppressor with His strong hand, became renewed within us so "that you should not be their slaves," and God has "broken the bars of your yoke and made you walk erect" (Leviticus 26:13). The cuffs fell from our hands, and we raised our martyred body: "Let us lift up our hearts and hands to God in heaven" (Lamentations 3:41), from where our redemption comes.

1. The Nation Unites in the Heart of God

Bound together by a common Grapevine, Jesus Christ, we, the grapevine branches, become wondrously united in the Lord through the life-giving juice of His grace. Happy is the nation that can say this about itself! This is God's ready, gratuitous participation in the life of the nation. We can confidently build our homeland on this Rock. This structure can grow in no way other than by fulfilling God's laws: "If you walk in My statutes and observe My commandments and do them [...] And I will have regard for you and make you fruitful and multiply you and will confirm My covenant with you [...] And I will make My abode among you, and My soul shall not abhor you.

32

And I will walk among you, and will be your God, and you shall be My people" (Leviticus 26:3–13).

This is the most succinctly conceived program of national unification and at the same time the path towards power and strength. In our nation's soul and thanks to God's commandments, we will develop hearts of gold, in which the Lord will open the door to His house and not bother our nation. We will walk towards the source from which all our strength flows; we will drink from it with full hands and full hearts, and we will live from generation to generation!

2. The Nation Becomes Ennobled and Fortified in the Heart of God

The nation that awaits the Lord and is faithful to Him strengthens its existence in order to avoid the fate of those who followed Belphegor and whom the Lord destroyed. We can understand so many tragic disappearances of nations, states, and powers once we study their attitude towards God. "They who wait for the Lord shall renew their strength"(Isaiah 40:31); the names of fools are erased from the land of the living, as they have erased God's name from their legislation and their national life and customs. We are at times witnesses to a pathetic contest in which a bifurcated nation pulls in two directions; how often the forces that ruin the strength of the nation begin to battle. It is sometimes the case that the nation is overtaken by the servants of Baal and remains at the surface of life only by the offering, sacrifice, and strength of "bigots, religious fanatics, and clericalists" who give the state new generations of citizens, maintain the legal order and the gravity of state power, save the honor of the soldier, stay after hours at work to complete the backlog of their "liberated" colleagues, and fill the state budget with conscientiously paid taxes, protecting it from plunder and squandering.

It has often happened in human history that having been led to ruin by the servants of Baal, the nation and the state have entrusted themselves to "second-class citizens," those who have the courage to believe in something, in their last instinct of self-preservation; it is then that "the miracle of will and courage," be it bravery on the battlefield, devoted work at the head of the government, or quiet service to society, lifts them up from agony. The nation united in the

33

Heart of God and looking for him with all its heart gains wondrous trust and deep faith that God will not abandon it even in the most difficult moments: "They who wait for the Lord shall renew their strength, they shall mount up with wings like eagles, they shall run and not be weary, they shall walk and not faint" (Isaiah 40:31).

In our eagle's nest, we need many eagle's hearts and eagle's flights, because our way leads across mountainous paths.

As an example, let us compare two distant, yet strikingly similar, historical events.

During the times of the prophet Isaiah, the Assyrian king Sennacherib encircled Jerusalem. He said to the king of Judah, Hezekiah, through his messengers: "Do not let your God on Whom you rely deceive you by promising that Jerusalem will not be given into the hand of the king of Assyria. Behold, you have heard what the kings of Assyria have done to all lands, destroying them utterly" (2 Kings 19:10–11).

In more recent times, our faith was similarly reviled: "No god of any nation or kingdom has been able to deliver his people from my hand" (2 Chronicles 32:15). Our prayers to the Immaculate Virgin Mary as well as our trust and the calm with which we awaited our liberation were mocked. And the nation prayed as Hezekiah: "O Lord the God of Israel, Who art enthroned above the cherubim, Thou art the God, Thou alone, of all the kingdoms of the earth; Thou hast made heaven and earth. Incline Thy ear, O Lord, and hear; [. . .] hear the words of Sennacherib, which he has sent to mock the living God" (2 Kings 19:15–16). Like He did once through the prophet Isaiah, the good Lord today also gave an answer to our invader: "Because you have raged against Me and your arrogance has come into My ears, I will put My hook in your nose and My bit in your mouth, and I will turn you back on the way by which you came" (2 Kings 19:28).

The trust that comes from deep faith in the Heart of God steers the nation, gives it fortitude during the greatest persecutions, and is the source of power and hope, despite all difficulties.

3. The Nation's Wisdom Comes from God

When its life is tied to the Heart of God, the nation gains new strength from respecting the laws of God, Who is the wisdom of all nations. These laws, which save the man who is subjected to them, also save the nation. The life of the national community gains its strength from God's will; thus, if the nation bases all its legal order on His laws, if they are very close to the nation, in its mouth and in its heart (see Deuteronomy 30:14), then they will become a blessing to both social life and the citizens themselves.

"Keep them and do them; for that will be your wisdom and your understanding in the sight of the peoples, who, when they hear all these statutes, will say, 'Surely this great nation is a wise and understanding people'" (Deuteronomy 4:6). It is in vain that nations look for wonderful, life-giving, and eternal wisdom outside of God's laws. How fleeting are the efforts of secular states that fear even the weakest link between their laws and those of God! It is a kind of historical irony that the more nations have abandoned God's commandments, the thicker are their legal codes, and the more numerous and unreliable are their laws: "The Lord brings the counsel of the nations to naught; He frustrates the plans of the peoples. The counsel of the Lord stands for ever, the thoughts of His heart to all generations" (Psalm 32:10–11).

When a survey on the causes of the economic crises was conducted among writers and scholars, the most concise response was: "We must return to God's Ten Commandments." This fruit is sweet to our taste (see Song of Songs 2:3) at all times; it is a compass and a rudder for all human laws.

Our nation's covenant with the Heart of God, having experienced a difficult test of love, will not allow for the severing of the eternal bond: "I held him, and would not let him go until I had brought him into my mother's house, and into the chamber of her that conceived me" (Song of Songs 3:4). Let us humbly plead to the Lord: "Set me as a seal upon your heart, as a seal upon your arm" (Song of Songs 8:6). The Lord will command you to proclaim to the corners of the earth: "'Say to the daughter of Zion, 'Behold, your salvation comes; behold, His reward is with Him, and His recompense before Him.' And they shall be called the holy people, the redeemed of the Lord; and you shall be called sought out, a city not forsaken" (Isaiah 62:11–12).

* * *

Countrymen who are bound to the Heart of God!

"You stand this day all of you before the Lord your God; the heads of your tribes, your elders, and your officers, all the men of Israel, your little ones, your wives, and the sojourner [. . .] that you may enter into the sworn covenant of the Lord your God, which the Lord your God makes with you this day; that He may establish you this day as His people, and that He may be your God" (Deuteronomy 29:10–13).

We have returned here after walking a thorny and bloody path. We have walked across fire and water, but we have not ceased to call Thy Name. The "hostile man" who struck at the bond between the Heart of God with the heart of the nation has destroyed our nation, but he has not destroyed the faith in the Heart of God in the heart of our nation. It is easier to rip the heart out of bronze than it is to do so from the soul of the nation. Let us know where our power and strength lie. The enemy knows this best! He instructed us by striking at the monument of the Heart of God. He struck at bronze but aimed for the heart. Although he shattered the bronze, the heart has remained intact. This is the heart of the nation, which we will join with the Heart of God; our national program is to become rooted in His Heart. Let us kneel before the Lord of hosts in zealous submission and humble prayer:

"O Lord, Thou wilt ordain peace for us, Thou hast wrought for us all our works. O Lord our God, other lords besides Thee have ruled over us, but Thy name alone we acknowledge" (Isaiah 26:12–13).

The ever-merciful Lord will send His blessings to the fatherland in its new path of life:

"Whereas you have been forsaken and hated, with no one passing through, I will make you majestic forever, a joy from age to age. [. . .] Violence shall no more be heard in your land, devastation or destruction within your borders; you shall call your walls Salvation, and your gates Praise" (Isaiah 60:15, 18).

4

In Homage to the Queen of Poland

"Blessed be the Lord Who made heaven and earth [...] Because He hath so magnified thy name this day, that thy praise shall not depart out of the mouth of men" (Judith 13:24, 25).

"Virgin, Mother of God, God-famed Mary!"

DAZZLED BY THE MIRACLE OF LOVE, THE immensity of mercy, the depths of God's wisdom; with eyes glistening with tears of joy and with hearts filled with gratitude, let us go to the tabernacle of glory where Mary lives amongst her people. Let us open the heart of the history of the nation and learn the wisdom of life from past centuries, grow stronger, proceed courageously, and fortify the soul, for a long road is still ahead of us.

Following the example of Christ, Who proceeded from the tomb of His resurrection "to His most beloved Mother", today all of resurrected Poland directs its steps to the Throne of the Queen of Poland, for a solemn *Te Deum*. Here, we will first place our tears of joy and gratitude; it is here that we will entrust our hearts.

Pursuant to the Polish bishops' decision, September 8 is the day of our nation's solemn vows to the Heart of Mary. We have prepared for this day by entrusting our parishes and dioceses to the Heart of Mary. Today, the entire nation is summoned to the hill of Jasna Góra to dedicate itself to the Heart of Mary, to ask for blessings for the free fatherland. On this day, it is worth looking to the past. It is good to see how the ceremony of entrusting the heart of our nation to the Heart of Mary flows from our history.

Here are several thoughts.

1. The history of the Polish nation opens with a Marian song. Regiments of Polish knights emerge from the darkness of the ages; they cut new paths for Christian civilization and the following hymn emerges

from their hearts: "Virgin, Mother of God, God-famed Mary!"[1]

Embraced by the arms of Christ's Cross, we have heard Him say: "Behold, your mother!" (John 19:27). Like the Master's beloved disciple, we took Mary into our home at that moment without hesitation. A new light has flowed to us, and astonished eyes ask: "Who is this that looks forth like the dawn, fair as the moon, bright as the sun, terrible as an army with banners?" (Song of Songs 6:9).

We have understood that a new, exceptional force, "full of grace," thanks to which we have found grace in the Lord, enters the history of the nation. Is it possible to take in the enormity of joy resulting from our nation's vows to Mary? "And why is this granted me, that the mother of my Lord should come to me?" (Luke 1:43). All Polish hearts have opened up to the sound of Mary's name in humble gratitude; and since then, we have been the chosen nation of the Mother of God. "Like a terebinth I spread out My branches, and My branches are glorious and graceful" (Sirach 24:16). Our hearts have resounded with love for the Mother of God and the exceptional veneration that fills our life to the brim.

Like a garland around defensive watchtowers at our borders, Mary has made our Polish land a capital of miracles and grace, where she has sustained hearts, wiped away tears, healed, and consoled. Beginning with the north, where the "Queen of the Polish Sea" keeps vigil in Swarzewo in Kashubia and including Tuchola, Chełmno, Gostyń, Jasna Góra, Gidle, and Piekary, to where the Silesian people swam through oceans of blood to get to the free Poland, defending talk of the fatherland in Marian song; and next, by moving south from Kalwaria Zebrzydowska through the capital of Our Lady of Podhale, Our Lady of Ludźmierz, through Tuchów and through Jazłowiec, where commands are given by the "Hetmanness of the Polish Cavalry," crowned by Polish knights who each year reported on horseback to their Lady, grateful for the succor she had presented them in need; to the feet of Our Lady of Latyczów, a Holy Exile who found refuge in the Łuck Cathedral, up through the capital of the Grand Duchy of Lithuania at Ostra Brama.[2] And, Jasna Góra was the heart of it

---

1 This is a quote from *Bogurodzica* ("Mother of God"), a medieval Polish hymn that Polish knights said in battle.
2 Marian shrines in Poland.

all! That was the source of the strength that accompanied kings and hetmans in fields of battle. This is where national unity is forged at times of adversity. Here, the nation humbled itself with the pilgrim's song, "Kind Mother." Here, the different estates and professions fraternized, proclaiming their solemn vows. This is where the strength to work was drawn and the saber of the spirit was sharpened. It is here that light was imparted. This is because this is the capital of the Queen of the Crown of Poland!

It is characteristic that Poland's great trails of civilization are at the same time paths across which the inextricably linked veneration and glory of Mary flowed; the number of miraculous places on those paths equals the capitals made famous by Mary's generosity!

Through Mary, the Lord has shamed our enemies on so many occasions. The history of the nation contains a series of decisive victories that were possible thanks to her intercession. Grunwald, Orsha, Kircholm, Kłuszyn, Khotyn, Beresteczko, Jasna Góra, and Trembowla, as well as Vienna and Parkany call in unison:[3] "The Lord hath blessed thee by His power, because by thee He hath brought our enemies to naught" (Judith 13:22). It is not through their own strength that our kings and hetmans emerged victorious, but through God's power, which kindled in their hearts living respect for Mary. The soldiers' hearts of Chodkiewicz and Koniecpolski; Batory and Sobieski; Żółkiewski, Czarniecki, and Kordecki[4] were all hearts that beat with veneration for Mary: "Return, return, O Shulammite, return, return, that we may look upon you. Why should you look upon the Shulammite, as upon a dance before two armies?" (Song of Songs 6:13); "Your neck is like the tower of David, built for an arsenal, whereon hang a thousand bucklers, all of them shields of warriors" (Song of Songs 4:4).

The "shields of warriors," with which Poland stopped the hordes of Gengis Khan as well as the Turkish and Swedish deluges, is the weapon of "the tower of David."

---

3 Military victories of Poland and Lithuania over the Teutonic Knights, Muscovy, Sweden, and the Ottoman Empire.
4 These are the names of various hetmans, or military commanders, and kings of the Polish-Lithuanian Commonwealth known for their bravery and victories over the Turks, Swedes, Cossacks, and Russians.

2. The Commonwealth emerged from the dangerous waves of the Swedish deluge[5] at the feet of Jasna Góra. The victory of the defenders of Jasna Góra became a general mobilization of the spirit and will to defend the country. Called by its Queen, the nation threw off itself the yoke of the invader. Led by gratitude and conscious of its faults, it decided to reject all misdeeds and clad itself in the "armor of brilliance," of social love and justice. It is telling that in Poland, veneration of Mary has always been tied to a desire to change one's life and correct social relations and institutions. That has been the case from King John Casimir's vows up through the academic vows at Jasna Góra.[6]

All the estates — kings and senators, the nobility, the people — humble themselves before the image of Our Lady of Grace in Lvov. Mary was proclaimed Queen of the Polish Crown: "Mother of God and Virgin, whose humanity is great! I, John Casimir, make the following vow at your holy feet, in front of your Son, King of Kings and my Lord. Today, I elect you to be my Patroness and my Queen."

3. Once again, tempests and storms struck at the home of the fatherland, which wavered under their weight. Not supported in time, it fell, burying its children in the rubble of slavery. And when the powerlessness of torpor and pain ended, a painful complaint flowed up to the heavens from the soul of the torn nation: "O Lord, how many are my foes! Many are rising against me; many are saying of me: there is no help for him in God" (Psalm 3:1–2). Will the sown corncockle seed bear fruit? No! Insurgent banners with Our Lady of Jasna Góra, Our Lady of Ostra Brama, and Our Lady of Koden will be raised, and they will lead grandfathers, fathers, and sons, one generation after another, in the struggle for freedom! The knights of Bar will lie next to one another and the land will flow with the blood of the insurgents,[7] but no force will tear the voice and the heart apart from the heavenly gates.

---

5   The Swedish Deluge was a series of Swedish invasions that devastated Poland between 1655 and 1660.

6   On April 1, 1656, King John III Casimir made vows to Mary in the Lvov cathedral, making the Virgin Queen of Poland and promising to improve the plight of Poland's peasants.

7   This refers to the Bar Confederation, an association of nobles formed to defend Poland's independence from Russia that also opposed King Stanislaus II Augustus.

"Why dost Thou stand afar off, O Lord? Why dost Thou hide Thyself in times of trouble?" (Psalm 10:1). "My soul also is sorely troubled. But Thou, O Lord — how long?" (Psalm 6:3).

The clanging of handcuffs rings from the sorrowful funeral procession of the living but buried nation. However, in its soul, it carries images of the one that "defends Czestochowa and shines at Ostra Brama." Tenacious love and hope and a medallion with the Mother of God on one's breast are the only decorations the nation continues to bear; this is their *Virtuti Militari* and *Polonia Restituta*[8] all at once! In the dungeons of mines, chained to wheelbarrows, beaten, and worn out; their eyes feeding on a pre-mortem fever, they see the Queen of the Heavens and of Poland rushing to them with their last rites. A penitential complaint emerges: in his pride, the vengeful persecutes the poor at every time... He says in his heart: "I shall not be moved; throughout all generations I shall not meet adversity" (Psalm 9:6; Hebrews).

"Turn, O Lord, save my life; deliver me for the sake of Thy steadfast love" (Psalm 6:4). Penitential contrition gives rise to hope: "O Lord my God, in Thee do I take refuge; save me from all my pursuers and deliver me" (Psalm 7:2).

> Ask Thy Son, our Lord,
> God-named Mary,
> To have mercy upon us and hand it over to us!
> *Kyrie eleison!*[9]

Sorrows and insipid moans be gone; the nation is atoning for great sins, but it also enjoys God's boundless graces. The nation is strong in its faith and in Christian confidence, a heroic and victorious nation that has overthrown its enemies through the strength of its faith and the hymn "Mother of God." Today, that trust is our bread!

"I am not afraid of ten thousands of people who have set themselves against me round about. Arise, O Lord! Deliver me, O my God! For Thou dost smite all my enemies on the cheek; Thou dost break the teeth of the wicked. Deliverance belongs to the Lord" (Psalm 3:6–8).

Go to the Queen of the Polish Crown, O pilgrim nation! Go on your knees to the gates of Resurrection! Through prayer, all of Poland

---

8   Polish military decorations.

9   These are words from *Bogurodzica*.

is standing in offensive formation!

Victorious Mother of God, thanks to whom Władysław the Elbow-High emerged victorious; the Help of our forefathers at Grunwald; mighty Lady at Khotyn; Savior of our nation during the miraculous defense of Jasna Góra; you supported winged regiments during the Siege of Vienna... Pray for us.

"The Lord has heard my supplication; the Lord accepts my prayer. All my enemies shall be ashamed and sorely troubled; they shall turn back and be put to shame in a moment" (Psalm 6:9–10).

4. "This is the day of blood and glory"! "The one that has perished" is rising from the dead; "Poland does not want to die!"[10] The Lord's right hand was strong; God looked at the infliction of His servant and struck down her oppressors with His strong arm! We were born despite all hopes, despite the designs of world politics!

Poland embraced its children with its wings like a hen embraces its chicks. However, she did not yet get to keep it warm with the motherly emotion of its suffering body, as new trials have struck at the nation. Valiant defenders of the fatherland fell at nearly every border like springtime flowers withering from the midnight chill.

The Hereditary Ruler of this land, Our Lady of the Herbs walks across our land with the Child of God in her arms. Flowers fall on the vestments of the heroic priest whose love for his country is expressed by a red stream of blood on his white stole; on the gray uniform of the fallen lieutenant whose dead hand seems to still point towards the line of defense; on the female breast which, it seems, blocks access to the gates of the heart of the nation by sacrifices of life; they gild the bloodstained uniform of the soldier with a harvest wreath from the fields of the fatherland.

The mournful moan of the evening song flows from the distant fields to great the Queen of Poland:

> At the ringing of the Angelus bells,
> May Mary forever be praised,
> Let Christ forever be praised...[11]

---

10 From Pius XII's address to Polish immigrants in September 1939.
11 From the poem *Na Anioł Pański* ("For the Angelus") by Kazimierz Przerwa-Tetmajer.

In it, the echo of Warneńczyk's[12] battlefield and the prayers of Poles who are grateful for victory resounds: "Eternal rest grant upon them, O Lord."

Your children and your defenders, faithful servants of the Lord who do not know song without complaint, have fallen in these fields. They have shed their last blood. They had little blood to begin with because these are the first days of their resurrection.

"Raise your arm, Child of God; bless the sweet land!"

"Give them strength against Your enemies . . . "

"The Father's right hand gives strength!" The Father's right hand has struck the enemies. . .

Great powers tremble. . .

"May Mary forever be praised,

Let Christ forever be praised . . . "

5. "Listening to the powerful voices of our great past and admiring the luminous image of national glory, we firmly believe that our beloved fatherland will be strong and happy only when it persists by you and your son like a daughter for ages!"[13]

Jasna Góra is experiencing a new siege! This is not by your enemy, although the fortifications of your monastery are continuously being stormed! This is a siege of hearts, a mobilization of the spirit of the nation! All of Poland, inspired by the example of brave academic youths, has arrived here to thank Mary, praise her, and beg for her intercession.

"Behold, you are beautiful, my love, behold, you are beautiful! Your eyes are doves behind your veil [. . .]. Your lips are like a scarlet thread, and your mouth is lovely [. . .]. You are all fair, my love; there is no flaw in you. You have ravished my heart, my sister, my bride, you have ravished my heart" (Song of Songs 4:1–9).

Winds of freedom have swept Poland, as has the call: "Everyone who is alive, go to Jasna Góra!" On the eve of a great trial, which the nation instinctively sensed was coming, our hearts were fortified at

---

12 At the Battle of Varna in Bulgaria in 1444, the Christian armies of Poland, Hungary, and Wallachia commanded by King Władysław III Warneńczyk of Poland were defeated by the Turks, while Warneńczyk perished in battle. This was the final battle of the Crusade of Varna, an unsuccessful attempt at preventing Turkish Muslim spread to the Balkans.

13 The Academic Oath at Jasna Góra, 1936.

the feet of Mary, the nation's Holiest Queen! Is not how our Mother has bolstered our hearts, how the works that have occurred in the recent thanks to new graces and visitations past worthy of admiration? Although she was poor as a widow, all of Poland erected a forest of monuments to her Queen and decorated her temple with crowns from Swarzewo to Piekary and Jazłowice as signs of fidelity and gratitude; Poland professed her vows not only in the spirit of praise and pleading, but also that of sacrifice and offering, the gift of obligations, promises, and vows willingly made out of love. The power unifying the nation in its veneration of the Blessed Virgin Mary; its decisive will to profess, protect, and spread the Catholic faith, applying Christ's laws in professional, social, national, and state life resonates from these vows of nearly all the estates.

We were witnesses to a great coming together of the nation; Mary strengthened Poland, binding together the hearts of all with her love. As during John Casimir's vows, new forces of peaceful reform, an augury of harmony and collaboration in the mutual recognition of our laws and duties in the spirit of justice and Christian love have flowed from these pronouncements at Jasna Góra. Mary has become the glory of our Jerusalem, the joy of Israel, and the pride of her people.

* * *

New tempests have passed. Fortified by the vows of freedom, we were sustained by their words in times of slavery. Strengthened by the "Tower of David," our nation has resisted the assaults of Nazism and paganism. We have shed much blood, given many sacrifices, and suffered through much adversity, humiliation, and many insults. And yet, we did not break down. We have risen up, and we are alive! Where are those who looked down on us? They are gone! Not a single one is left!

Today, we carry our hearts, repeating the words *Sursum corda*. We carry them in offering to Jasna Góra. Today, Polish hearts have gone around Mary›s capital and won her Heart. It is truly righteous, just, proper, and redemptive to stand here and implore that the heart of the nation be offered to the Heart of Mary.

May our thoughts, wills, and hearts run towards Jasna Góra, where cardinals, bishops, priests, and the faithful from across Poland bring them to God's throne through Mary's hands. It is through Mary that God awoke us from the dead; through Mary, we pay grateful homage to the Lord of Hosts, the King of the nations and the ages, Whom no one can oppose, because He wants to save Israel!

Through tears of gratitude, let us say the following prayer:

> Son of God, for Thy Baptist's sake,
> Hear the voices, fulfill the pleas we make!
> Listen to the prayer we say,
> For what we ask, give us today:
> Life on earth free of vice;
> After life: paradise!
> *Kyrie eleison!*

PART II

Man and the Family

1
"Man: An Unknown Being?"

THE BOOK OF THE PROPHET DANIEL RECORDS the following historical event: "King Nebuchadnezzar made an image of gold, whose height was sixty cubits and its breadth six cubits. He set it up on the plain of Dura, in the province of Babylon. Then, King Nebuchadnezzar sent to assemble the satraps, the prefects, and the governors, the counselors, the treasurers, the justices, the magistrates, and all the officials of the provinces to come to the dedication of the image which King Nebuchadnezzar had set up" (Daniel 3:1–2). Pursuant to the king's instruction, all those at the front came and stood in front of the golden image, while the king's herald proclaimed: "'You are commanded, O peoples, nations, and languages, that when you hear the sound of the horn, pipe, lyre, trigon, harp, bagpipe, and every kind of music, you are to fall down and worship the golden image that King Nebuchadnezzar has set up; and whoever does not fall down and worship shall immediately be cast into a burning fiery furnace.' Therefore, [. . .] all the peoples, nations, and languages fell down and worshiped the golden image which King Nebuchadnezzar had set up" (Daniel 3:4–7).

We know this image from the recent past and from our own experiences! This image is not only historical, but it is prophetic as well! Every age has its Nebuchadnezzar, and every age has its golden idol. The unfortunate man turned to dust by a golden idol, a tyrannical ruler, under the threat of being sent to the fiery crematoria is a familiar image to us. It does not matter if he has been conscripted to serve the golden idol of accumulating wealth or if he has become enslaved by the materialistic communist state; man's woe remains the same. He lies with his face down, stripped of his own dignity and respect, faith and freedom to think what he likes. Is this still man?

I. Who Is Contemporary Man?

You will say that this is a superfluous question, but we have a ready answer: "Man is an unknown being." This is true: people today do not quite know who man really is. In this regard, previous centuries were more fortunate. Today, only religion knows who man truly is, but the world, which has liberated itself of religion, prefers to wander in the darkness than to return to the Christian response. For how else can we call these contradictory views that are expressed in the aims that are imposed on man today than wandering in the darkness?

Some proclaim man as his own god.

They multiply man's rights at the cost of God Himself and their weaker brethren, and at the cost of society and the state. Everything must bow down to man. There are no limits here. They subject everything to the highest and irrevocable judgment of the person; they profess his moral liberty and freedom from all social obligations. They acknowledge only private morality for their own use. Man can do whatever he pleases, and morality is his private business. They do the same with God. Religion is also each person's private matter. Perfection and striving for God have absolutely no social meaning. Man's highest aspiration is happiness in this world. All means can be used to achieve this aim because here there are no binding moral principles. Economics and ethics are fields that are foreign to one another. There are no higher laws or divine commandments to which man's social and economic life should be subjected. The freedom to grow wealthy is the highest economic principle. Everything should serve man's aspirations to personal wealth; even religion and the state should not take precedence over his temporal interests. Man is *homo oeconomicus* and nothing more. Everything else is merely an accessory to life and should serve but one aim. Man's neighbors are "human material," that is, of the same value as raw material on the balance sheet of the costs of production; the value of one's neighbor's is reduced to the amount of labor or physical strength, a weekly wage, and one's position in the labor hierarchy and nothing more. Besides that, nothing binds them together.

In this way, man has been turned into a paralytic who usually acts against others, walking his own, unforeseen paths.

Others, on the contrary, consider man to be nothing.

In their eyes, man possesses no personal value. Not only is he no longer at the center of the world, but he simply is reduced to nothing. His entire value comes from social relations designated by the state. Thus, man is denied his basic human rights: the freedom to think and to act. Man is subjected to absolute obedience to supreme power; he must listen to people rather than to God. The human person is subjected to complete disdain, a merciless harshness in the system of governance, the inhumanity of limitless official lawlessness, despotism, and terror. In practice, this leads to the enslavement of the citizen in favor of the collective.

Second, man is denied the right to believe in God and give Him praise. Man's transcendent element is not recognized, nor are any purposes apart from temporal ones. This is the source of the organized, official struggle against religion as a new aim of the modern state. This is organized hatred!

Communism aims to create a world without God. It seeks to bring up man without God's commandments and religious morality, only with the morality of the masses. Thus, all religion must be destroyed. Technology has become man's new god, while proletarian equality is the greatest source of joy. In this way, man, who has been created in God's image and likeness, is separated from his Creator and thrown into the hopelessness of godlessness and temporality.

Third, man's own purpose and aims are rejected. Man no longer has a soul or his own purpose. In no way is man permitted to seek happiness in God. Man is obliged to strive for the aims assigned to him by the state. He must be completely socialized in both spirit and body. He is obliged to make sacrifices and listen to all the commands of the collective.

Finally, a new aim indicated by collective life is imposed upon man. Because spiritual values have ceased to have a purpose, the highest aim of man's life is the good of the state, nation, class, party, or economic well-being, the production of an organized, typically atheistic temporal and material happiness, a paradise on earth or a capitalistic heaven that is achieved to one's own profit or that of the communist system. In other words, this is a deification of the material, profit, production, and technology.

Others still worship the achievements of the modern age.

They say that the greatest disgrace is for man to have any relationship to God, especially any such relationship in a Christian conception. Man is God's creation? This expression itself suffices to make him subjected to the entirety of hatred that is felt towards God. It professes complete disdain for the image of God in man, which is easy to consolidate, as people do all they can in order to not resemble God in the least.

Completely stripped of what remains of his bond with God, man is directly considered to be the manure, thanks to which future generations will grow. He leads a purely animalistic life; he eats in order to live and work, works for the masses, and depletes his strength. Once he becomes less productive, he must be sent away so that there is food for the young. His highest value is his race and pure blood that should be transmitted to later generations. Membership in a given race determines man's value. If he lacks a specific blood type, he is not human and has no right to life. He is a parasite! Removing a parasite becomes a contribution to allowing so-called "complete people" to live and grow without constraint.

This is the cross of our times to which man has been nailed.

In order to find out who today's man is, let us reflect upon this cross. He is nailed to it like Christ Himself! His hands, which are used to serve every form of oppression, become incapacitated, while his legs are nailed to hard wood. He no longer has his own will! Subservient science explained to the world that man is devoid of free will for so long that people finally started to zealously believe this. The chains of a crown of thorns were placed on the head, while the thorns scatter away free thinking. They attack the heart with the sharp blade of a soldier's spear. Man is stripped of his clothes like Christ and has neither property nor possessions. He is fed vinegar on the spear at the expense of the state. That is all they can give in response to the human cry: "I am thirsty!"

The story of Christ has been faithfully reproduced. When man loses his ties to God and ceases to be a child of God, he ceases to be human. This is the great finale of the struggle for man. In the past, it was repeated that the proletarian is not human. In response, it was shouted that the bourgeoisie and the kulaks are not human.

This is the death of man in the twentieth century!

II. The Christian Exaltation of Man

The zeal of modern attempts at degrading man today have the benefit of underlining the huge difference between the pagan degradation of man and his Christian dignity. We turn away from such wretched images with relief. We have not lost what remains of our hope, because the Cross is not hopeless! Each man's cross leads him to glory. We have not ceased to be children of God! None of these forceful doctrines will succeed in stripping us of this honor. Man's yearning for humanity and to be a child of God are stronger than all doctrines.

Man was created in God's image and likeness.

Michelangelo beautifully expresses this notion in *The Creation of Adam*. God touches Adam, whom He brings to life, with the tip of His finger. There is solitude all around; there are no witnesses in God's workshop, only God and man. This solitude speaks volumes: it means that in his primal state, man is dependent solely on God. He came into the world without a passport, without the permission of the nation, without the resolutions of economic institutions, and without the permission of the commission on provisions and lodging. . . . Everything he possesses comes solely from God and is the work of His fingers. Man recognizes this in himself: "Thy hands have made and fashioned me" (Psalm 117:73). We have received from God the most important, basic gifts that attest to our human nature: our immortal soul, reason, and will. Nothing more can be added by the nation, state, or society. They can develop these divine gifts and make use of them, but their absence cannot be replaced with anything. Thanks to these divine gifts, man is a person; that is, a free being endowed with reason, created in God's image and likeness.

Thus, the rights that attest to the essence of our humanity come solely from God, not from our blood and race or the decisions of legislative bodies, statesmen, or constitutions. This is a counterrevolutionary statement against the contemporary state, which does not want to have such dignified citizens so that they do not overthrow it. Yet, God's words are not wrong: "Let us make man in Our image, after Our likeness" (Genesis 1:26). God did what He had announced: "Lift up the light of Thy countenance upon us, O Lord" (Psalm 4:6). From that point, only man is a person, a being with reason and will in the rich array of earthly creatures. God will speak only to such a being, and only a being endowed with reason and free will is capable of understanding and loving God. Only God can embrace man, His creation, with the fullness of fatherly feeling, because only God is his Father. All others are impostors. The world has mistreated man because it is not his father.

Man is called to be a child of God.

God's grace, which served Christ the Lord on the Cross, has elevated us to the supernatural dignity of being God's children.

"It is the Spirit Himself bearing witness with our spirit that we are children of God" (Romans 8:16). "For you did not receive the spirit of slavery to fall back into fear, but you have received the spirit of sonship. [...] [W]e cry: 'Abba! Father!'" (Romans 8:15).

In this way, we have inherited God's will: we are "heirs of God and fellow heirs with Christ" (Romans 8:17); Christ is our Brother. We have entered the oldest family, God's family. Every Christian has the right to call God his Father: "For in Christ Jesus you are all sons of God, through faith. [...] There is neither Jew nor Greek, there is neither slave nor free, there is neither male nor female; for you are all one in Christ Jesus" (Galatians 3:26, 28). This leads to wonderful conclusions of which we must remind the world:

• man's right to life as a person and his inviolable dignity are sacred and cannot be usurped, because man is immortal and redeemed by the Blood of Jesus Christ;

• the right to life is sacred, for we have received this right not from our nation, state, or society, but from God;

• man's right to make use of all resources that are necessary on the path to heaven is sacred and inviolable.

In light of these basic truths, there are no differences between people; "the same Lord is Lord of all and bestows His riches upon all who call upon Him. For, 'everyone who calls upon the name of the Lord will be saved'" (Romans 10:12–13).

How far removed this truth is from modern doctrines! It is evident that man is not the fertilizer that must improve the soil for future generations, nor is he a mere slave and employee of the state. He is something incomparably greater and has a different, higher aim. Man was created in God's image and likeness. Just as eternity is a trait of

God, immortality is a characteristic of man. Of all the creatures that live on this earth, only man is immortal! Apart from man, no other entities are immortal: not families, not nations, and not states. Only man is redeemed by Christ's Blood; thus, he is a member of not only his earthly family, but of God's family as well. There is a time when each man will sever his ties to this earth and leave his family, nation, and state, but he will not cease to be a child of God and a citizen of Christ's kingdom.

Man has a purpose in his life, one that is higher than a temporal aim.

The temporal aim is transitional with regards to our ultimate aim. Man's highest earthly aim is perfection in worldly life. It encompasses all the temporal duties that make up our personal, family, professional, social, national, economic, cultural, political, and religious life. Striving for this aim is man's moral duty, which entails a sense of responsibility with respect to society and God. In order to achieve this aim, we need the full harmony of the natural gifts we have received from nature and God, the Creator of nature, as well as society.

The responsibility of the Christian's conscience is to perfectly fulfill all the temporal tasks of his life at every level of his vocation and profession. Experience shows that even if we fully achieve the perfection of earthly life, temporal aims are not capable of satisfying all the desires of the human soul, which is much richer in its aspirations. Created in God's image and likeness, man can find respite only in God. Thus, man's ultimate aim is to become united with God in eternal life. We strive for this by fulfilling God's commandments and sanctifying ourselves: "For this is the will of God, your sanctification" (1 Thessalonians 4:3). Our task is to become united in God's love: "God is love, and he who abides in love abides in God, and God abides in him" (1 John 4:16). Through love of God, we also become closer to our neighbors. Thus, there is a further growing together of human society.

Another duty is to become like God: "You shall be holy; for I the Lord your God am holy" (Leviticus 19:2). God's efforts in the human soul and our cooperation with God's grace so that we become worthy of entering Christ's kingdom are related to this.

The next duty is to praise God. Our life's hymn is: *Gloria in excelsis Deo* (Luke 2:14): "Glory to God in the highest" — *Te Deum*, *laudamus—Jubilate—Cantate—Exsultate...* How much joy flows from this here on earth! Praising God turns into joy and peace: *et in terra pax hominibus bonae voluntatis.* When praising God, we find our dignity and glory, because God Himself is the subject of our praise.

Finally, we are called to friendship with God: "No longer do I call you servants [...] but I have called you friends" (John 15:15). "You are my friends if you do what I command you" (John 15:14). God did not create us to be slaves, vassals, or proletarians, but He revealed His wondrousness in the fact that He repays our readiness to serve Him with friendship. Man and Satan act differently; they transform service into tyranny and slavery. God tells us through the first pope: "But you are a chosen race, a royal priesthood, a holy nation, God's own people, that you may declare the wonderful deeds of Him Who called you out of darkness into His marvelous light" (1 Peter 2:9).

God repeats the same through the most recent pope!

III. The Fruits of the Previous Pains of Man's Cross

A struggle over who man is and who he should be in human history is being waged before our eyes. The basis of this struggle is new, but simultaneously old, truths. They are new because the world has recalled them only recently, but they are old because they have been professed by the Church for twenty centuries.

1. The truth that only man, not society, the nation, or the state, is immortal is inviolable. Only man is loved by God and redeemed by Jesus Christ.

2. Irrespective of his nationality, state, class, or wealth, each man has the great dignity of a human being.

3. Apart from his temporal aims, which are achieved within one's family, profession, state, or nation, every man has eternal and ultimate aims that are to be achieved during life on earth. No authority on earth can deprive man of the freedom to strive for those aims. Separating man from them would be the greatest offense and would imprison his noblest desires and aspirations.

4. Inviolable human rights, which are older than anyone else's rights, including those of the family, nation, and state, protect man's

ultimate aim; they are also independent of any social, economic, or political system. Every political system that threatens these aims will be unjust and lead to slavery, even if it offers the liberty to commit all the possible sins. Nothing can replace these laws in the human soul: neither the most fertile area of life, nor a collectively glorious and monstrous state that breaks production records.

5. However, man can achieve none of his temporal or ultimate aims without cooperation with other people; according to God's will, this elevated man, who is lesser than the angels (see Psalm 8:6), must make use of other people's help. Man strives for heaven in a human community as well: in the Church.

6. Entering a family, national, professional, political, or religious community, man must subordinate his aims in accordance with the nature and purpose of each of these communities.

7. Living within them, man gives witness to his personality, which he perfects thanks to them.

8. Thus, they must recognize man's highest and ultimate aim and negotiate their own aims with him.

* * *

Doctrines and political systems that tried to strip man of God's likeness are dying before our very eyes. The racist elite of blood has fallen into oblivion, proving to history that "it is the spirit that gives life; the flesh is of no avail" (John 6:63). Others will come . . . *qui non ex sanguinibus* — who are not of blood (see John 1:13).

The materialistic, money-obsessed elites have fallen. You have seen from their deeds that "man shall not live on bread alone" (Luke 4:4), and that economic life is not the entirety of life, while the economic states are not the entirety of the nation or even its primary layer. "What will help man?" Others will come . . . *neque ex voluntate viri* — nor of the will of man (see John 1:13).

The godless proletarian elite has fallen. It has warned us that man cannot be subjected to the soulless law of the herd, crowd, and mass. Others will come . . . *neque ex voluntate carnis* — nor of the will of the flesh (see John 1:13).

A new age is coming! That of those "who were born [. . .] of God!" — *Ex Deo nati* (John 1:13) — God's elite! It will bind its life to

57

kinship with God and justify the value of its life through the work of the entirety of man: his soul and body, in nature and in grace. It will bind together heaven and earth. It will bring God back to earth and return the earth to God but making the earth conducive to life for all and to the search for God!

We will see the joy of the Lord's glory here on this earth. The spectacle of Nebuchadnezzar in the plain of Dura will never be repeated. Meanwhile, one day all the nations, peoples, and tongues will stand in glory before the Lamb; all those "who have come out of the great tribulation [...]. They shall hunger no more, neither thirst anymore; the sun shall not strike them, nor any scorching heat. For the Lamb in the midst of the throne will be their shepherd, and He will guide them to springs of living water; and God will wipe away every tear from their eyes" (Revelation 7:14–17).

2

"Woe to Him Who Is Alone"

(Ecclesiastes 4:10)

G OD, THE FATHER OF ALL CREATION, CRE-
ated His world in such a way that everything that flows from
His thought has a natural tendency towards social coexistence. Although as human beings people transcend all other creatures
in their dignity, they are not free of universal laws. God does not
want man to be alone, but to be together with his brothers. There
cannot be division and natural hostility in the world, because everything has come from the hand of the one Father. Even though all
people have their own life goals, thanks to God's will, they achieve
them through living in a community. In order to attain God, they
need the help of other people, such as those they are united within
the Church.

"There is one body and one Spirit, just as you were called to the
one hope that belongs to your call, one Lord, one faith, one baptism,
one God and Father of us all, Who is above all and through all and
in all" (Ephesians 4:4–6).

I. Man: A Social Being

Having judged man in paradise, God pondered His most perfect
creation in light of the entire created world. He saw all the birds
in the air and all the creatures that walk and crawl the earth. "For
the man there was not found a helper fit for him" (Genesis 2:20).
There must have been something incomplete in Adam's life if God
Himself stated: "It is not good that the man should be alone" (Genesis 2:18). Another person must stand at man's side, a helper and
companion in his life and work. Thus, God concluded: "I will make
him a helper fit for him" (Genesis 2:18); this expresses the needs of
human nature. These words contain an introduction to social life
in every form.

Man is not a self-sufficient being.

No man — not even a child that calls for help by crying for the first time — can live and flourish without the support of others. People need the assistance of others from the cradle to the grave. Let us consider how much human work makes up our lives, even the most self-sufficient work, and how much good will our neighbors exhibit in the lives of every person. Everything we have — our food, our clothing, the roof above our heads — we owe to some sort of human effort. Only benefactors surround us! If we reject everything that comes from our neighbors, we will experience poverty and helplessness. There is some great service of social love in the entirety of this collaboration with our neighbors. The organization of the world is so permeated with love for service and owes so much to it that the world cannot defend itself against it. At every corner, we experience aid and service. How many people bring us good things without which we could not survive on our own! There is some love in every good, even the smallest one.

Man feels the need to coexist with other people.

Human nature, which was created by a loving God, is such that man cannot be alone, but must love something. The qualities of our body and spirit attest to this. Man not only is the recipient of the good will of others, but himself also serves his neighbor.

Our body is intended not only to serve ourselves, but also for coexistence with others. The human hand seeks contact with that of another person. Not a clenched fist, but an open hand signifies readiness for cooperation and coexistence. Only a sincere, open hand free of deceit is capable of engaging in a brotherly embrace with another person. Our eyes seek contact with those of our brothers. Our eyes are expressive, as we can use them to express our feelings without even knowing the same language as someone else. How easy it is to guess what is going on in another's soul by looking into his or her eyes! The human face is like an identification card that identifies us throughout our lives. Speech is exceptionally social. We can spend time with God through our thoughts and feelings, but we connect with our fellow man through speech.

We could proceed to reflect on all of man's natural gifts in this way and demonstrate his natural inclination towards his neighbor.

Although it is covered by a body, our spirit tries to break out to be among others. We have the need to spend time with others, to share our feelings, knowledge, and thoughts. We constantly preach our *eureka* to the world! Our talents and faculties — those of knowing, wanting, and loving — constantly push us out of the boundaries of our "personality." Let us encounter some joy: how eagerly we search for listeners who would accept and share it with others. That is the case with man, who has his own small or great truths and joys. Thus, it is no surprise that God is full of joy and happiness. Could He not have been capable of creating man in order to tell him about his unending happiness in Revelation? A good, wise, and happy man wants to instruct, improve, and console.

"Behold, Lord, the half of my goods I give to the poor" (Luke 19:8). These are actions that come from God!

At every corner, we experience assistance and feel the need to serve others.

Man is bound to God and other people through the service of a powerful love, much more so than he is aware. We feel a duty to work, kindness, bringing help to others, friendliness, and love. Even the hermit must have his raven that brings him half a piece of bread each day or his lion that digs his grave. That is how God has created us! He wants us to have a complete sense of our social bonds through the social nature of our personality. It is unsurprising that we consider helping our neighbors to be an obligation of social justice.

II. Human Life in Different Societies

The Triune God says: "Let us make man in Our image, after Our likeness" (Genesis 1:26). This is not vain talk. In his personality, man is similar to God, Who wants him to be His reflection and image. There are indications for human activity that flow from this.

God acts in collaboration. The act of creation took place thanks to the perfect cooperation of the Persons of God. Everything that God does unites the intimacy of the Divine Persons through love and acts of charity.

"God is love" (1 John 4:16), and from this flows the fundament upon which we should build our relations with other people. Just as there is triunity in unity, and unity in triunity in God; similarly, personal unity and social community must be reflected in man, who was shaped in God's image and likeness. We have nowhere to look for the source of humanity's social nature apart from God Himself. That is man's inclination to live with others and with God the Father: to live alongside God the Son and the Holy Spirit. God wanted human nature to be shaped in such a way that it would be itself unity, a unity that strives for coexistence with others.

God, the creator of human nature, places man within a community. He wants man to be part of a community to enable the full flourishing of his personhood.

Through God's will, man is tied to his family.

God created man only once; He left the rest to the family. If the family community ceased to exist, the world would become depopulated.

Man is to follow a two-fold vocation: he can either follow God's voice and start a family or follow God's love and remain alone in it. In both the former and latter cases, man lives in community, either with other people or with God. Both communities are ruled by love.

God Himself prepared the family community for man. He based it on the sacrament of marriage, which He made a temple of God. God gave something like a reflection of His own fatherly authority in the authority of the family. Parents' dignity comes from this divine authority. God situates man in a family that is designed in this way. In His fatherly goodness, He protects the infant-like inability to exist with the greatest love: parental love.

Every person must come into being through some family: when he lacks the most natural love for oneself, Christian love becomes a substitute family for him. In the family, man experiences the most wondrous feelings of love. God sets the hearts of parents aflame with such love for their children. Only this love makes one capable of fully forgetting about oneself and becoming completely devoted to one's child. Children who are raised in an atmosphere of love and their parents' sacrifices leave their homes with the most important gift to social life: social love.

The mere fact that God wanted all people to come into the world through the family and prepare them for the world thanks to the family suggests that He wanted to accustom us with the first form of social life. We receive almost everything from our families: not only our first names, but our surnames as well. Sometimes, we cannot liberate ourselves of the legacy we have received from our parents throughout our entire lives. This right to a legacy is either a blessing or the source of our tears. Thus, the Christian family is so important to us. That is also why other social groups are built in a way that is modeled after the family community. However, the family itself cannot satisfy all of man's needs. It must rely on the help of other communities that we become entrusted to and that determine our fate on earth.

Man is also connected to the social life of his nation.

A nation is one great family. This is the first community which we encounter in the family. Our families bring us into the nation; it is in the family that we receive the gift of our native tongue, which our mothers teach us. The dearest word, "God," is so kind to our ears when we hear it in our native tongue that it seems most beautiful and dearest to us. We become part of a nation, and even grow closer to God through national language, culture, history, and song. The first words with which we address God are in our native tongue.

God wants us to develop our personhood by coexisting with the nation; this divine will is also reflected in love for one's fatherland. Even if our fatherland's life consisted only of the tears and blood of its martyred children, if it were not only the "Christ among nations" but also "a nation of Christs," it will always be closer to us and loved more by us than the richest foreign land. We will always yearn for it. This is the voice of nature; therefore, that is what God wanted. God also wanted man to be bound to his fatherland through moral obligations towards it.

Man is also connected to the social life of his state.

The life of each nation flourishes best in our own state community.

As Pope Leo XIII teaches, the entirety of worldly matters is contained in two communities: the spiritual and the secular. Each community has its own aim: the state community strives for temporal well-being, while the Church community wants to achieve eternal life. Each is, in its own sense, the highest good, and each is necessary for the person. However, only when both act together do they allow man to achieve the right goal, the perfection of life.

Man cannot be indifferent to the state. He cannot live without the state's aid. This community comes from the will of God, the creator of human nature, and it is necessary in the temporal order for the development of the human person, just as the Church is necessary in the supernatural order. The state can cooperate with the Church and help it in fulfilling its role, which is protecting the divine law. When the state respects God's law, when it gives God the highest praise, and when it and all its laws come from God, then it helps itself and its citizens. We then understand well what our duties to the state invested with God's authority mean. We understand how far they reach, since we are expected to even sacrifice our own lives in defense of the state. This is evidence that we are bound up with the good of the state, which in turn is our good.

Man is bound to the Church community.

We cannot be alone even when we strive for God. To enable our soul's access to His grace, Christ the Lord deposited everything needful in the Church. All works of salvation happen from God's will through the Church. On the way to heaven, each person is guided by the Church. All the graces of the Crucifixion flow onto humanity through Christ living in the Church. Jesus Himself had His Simon of Cyrene and His Veronica on the way to Calvary. And what about man in his path to God?

Our absolution in the sacrament of penance as well as the Eucharist on the altar are dependent on other people. This is strange, yet Christ the Lord made His presence at the altar dependent on man's presence. All sacramental graces come through human hands. "Woe to him who is alone" (Ecclesiastes 4:10). Woe to him! We know this pride that rejects the priestly ministry because one "wants to talk to God alone." God certainly knows the paths to the human soul, although He has yet to send angels from heaven in order to celebrate Mass and sit in confessionals in churches that lack priests. Thus, we must cooperate in the Church community, which leads us to heaven.

* * *

Christ the Lord preaches a sacred community, calling Himself a vineyard and us a grapevine. Every other community in which people love themselves socially is modeled after the supernatural community.

Although human dignity is elevated, through God's will, we achieve all our aims through people. This attests to the fact that man is a social being of the highest order. Man's own destiny is bound to social fruits. Man is to proclaim all his life: *Gloria in excelsis Deo*,[1] and this is to result in "peace to all people of good will" on earth. Our entire aspiration for God and for humanity is expressed here. Love for God is inextricably linked to love for man. Love for one's neighbor feeds off God's love and finds its full expression in good deeds done for others. The human community is the collective family of God's children, of brothers in Christ: "All are yours; and you are Christ's; and Christ is God's" (1 Corinthians 3:22–23). "Woe to him who is alone." God's assistance shown us in our neighbors becomes social love.

---

1 Translation from Latin: "Glory to God in the highest."

3

Human Rights[1]

T HE RECENT WAR HAS DEALT A MAJOR BLOW
to man, stripping him of what had remained of his rights, honor,
and dignity. Almost everywhere, people were deprived of personal freedom, property, a roof over their heads, a corner to call their
own, and the warmth of a home; instead, they were deported to
forced labor and concentration camps. People were taken away from
countries, cities, and villages like potatoes in crammed wagons from
one end of Europe to another. Meanwhile, people were hunted in the
streets of cities like wild animals. They were imprisoned in dungeons,
casemates, and bunkers, packed together like herds of sheep. Finally,
human life was assaulted.

There no longer exists a legend about bloody thugs; what we have
gone through exceeds even the most imaginative legends. In the Majdanek concentration camp, we saw film footage of a huge mound,
more than a dozen meters high and made of the ashes of cremated
human bodies. In the camps, several hundred ovens called crematoria
in which supposedly twenty million people were killed operated for
the sake of the destruction of humanity.[2]

All this fills us with anxiety about the future of man on earth.
We ask if man still has any rights. What more can we do if today

1   This is an article that was initially published in *Ład Boży* ("The Divine
Order") on September 16, 1945, nr. 3.
2   Officially known as *Konzentrationslager Lublin* ("The Lublin Concentration
Camp"), the Majdanek camp operated on the outskirts of Lublin from 1941 to
1944. Its fatal victims included 50,000–60,000 Jews as well as 19,000 Slavs, mostly
Poles and some Belarusians, Ukrainians, Russians, and others. In November
1943, Majdanek, along with the Poniatowa and Trawniki camps, were the site
of "Operation Harvest Festival," when the Germans and their Ukrainian collaborators shot about 40,000 Jews over just two days. This is the largest single
massacre of Jews during World War II. The mound composed of human ashes
Wyszyński refers to can be seen today at Majdanek; it is enclosed in a mausoleum
designed by Polish architect and sculptor Wiktor Tołkin, himself a member of
the Polish wartime resistance and a survivor of Auschwitz. The mausoleum
contains the inscription: "Let our fate be a warning to you."

millions of people have been turned to ash? A great shout of horror and outrage does not suffice. We have to demand that human rights are respected. How wise and necessary was God's old law: "Thou shalt not kill."

I. From Previous Centuries

Once, God proclaimed on Mount Sinai: "You shall not kill; You shall not commit adultery; You shall not steal; You shall not bear false witness against your neighbor; You shall not covet" (Exodus 20:13–17). This was the first written law in defense of man. Under its protection, man could be safe. Today, it is said that God's laws are unnecessary and that human ones suffice.

Christ once taught on the Mount of Beatitudes: "You have heard that it was said to the men of old, 'You shall not kill; and whoever kills shall be liable to judgment.' But I say to you that everyone who is angry with his brother shall be liable to judgment; whoever insults his brother shall be liable to the council, and whoever says, 'You fool!' shall be liable to the hell of fire" (Matthew 5:21–22). That was God's constitution of human rights. In its name, slavery was abolished, and man became liberated of savagery and cruelty.

Once, having listened to the Sermon on the Mount, Europe overcame its bloodthirsty tendencies. The rulers of nations put their swords away in their sheathes; they were not allowed to kill without an important reason. The Polish kings proclaimed: we will not deprive anyone of freedom, only those who have been convicted by the law. This made life on earth possible.

Once constitutions whose spirit was Christian proclaimed declarations of the rights of man and citizen, considering the defense of human liberty, life, and property to be their most basic duty.

Over the past quarter-century, all this has fallen into oblivion. God's law and human wisdom were violated. We are anxious about the future of humanity on earth. If the most recent war was so hostile to man, what will the next one bring? And who can swear that there will be no more wars on earth?

II. The Struggle for Human Rights

In order to protect man against the violation of his dignity, we must fight for the reinstatement of basic human rights today. Pope Pius XII courageously dealt with this matter in his December 1942 speech. Looking at the blind steamroller that was the war that had annihilated so much human life, the Pope called for respect for humanity.

These are the most basic human rights that must be respected if we do not want humanity to perish.

The most basic human right is the right to life.

It is certain that man did not receive life from himself or from the state, but from God. Thus, only God and no one else has authority over the life of a person. Thus, neither man himself nor anyone else can assault human life.

Man has the right to develop his physical life in accordance with his own aims and the purpose of that life. This right to life is inextricably linked to the right to the development of freedom and will, especially the right to an education and religious upbringing, as well as the right to resources, which are necessary and sufficient to the preservation and flourishing of human life. Thus, a human being cannot be imprisoned, persecuted, or deprived of his life because of his faith. Only when it is harmful to society in such a way that this harm is inevitable can the authorities limit this human right.

Man has the right to praise God.

Man's strongest aspiration is God, even if it is restricted by persecution. Therefore, man has the right to both private and public prayer. Thus, if serving God does not violate the healthy and proper social order, it should be permitted. Consequently, the state cannot close places of worship, destroy religious symbols and signs, prohibit access to the holy sacraments, have police patrol confessionals, or control human consciences. The German lawlessness that prohibited confession in Polish was savage.

Regardless of his tongue and race, every person has the right to freely aspire towards God.

Man has the right to a family.

Inviolable human rights include the freedom to enter into marriage and aim for the natural purpose of family life, as well as the right to start a family and own a home. Thus, no authorities have the right to destroy the family, to deprive families of their own children, and to deport them to perform forced labor. No one can unlawfully deprive the family of a roof over its head, expel it from its home, or seize what is left of its property.

The right of the family to exist—in other words, the rights to transmit life, one's surname, and property to one's children—should also be respected. Thus, we cannot demand that families make such sacrifices in a way that would obliterate memories of the family. We have read so many times in the German obituaries about the death of the fourth, fifth, and last son of the family.

Man has the right to work.

For many people, work is the only means of supporting their own lives and those of their families. Man cannot be denied work merely because he does not belong to the ruling political party or because he has different beliefs. Social, economic, and political life is not the domain of one social class or another, but it is the common good of all citizens who make up society. Thus, everyone has the natural right to make reasonable use of its goods.

Man has the right to freely choose his state in life.

No one can be forced to perform a specific kind of work. Every person is somewhat different; everyone has his unique preferences, vocation, and talents. This must be respected. A person can be encouraged to choose a certain kind of work that at a given moment corresponds to the needs of society. However, the use of coercion and violence leads to the creation of a society of slaves. We have seen the Germans use this violence with respect to our youth, who were deprived of the right to an education; professors, who were sent to work in the quarries; and artisans, whose profession was changed each hour. Today, we see how great the losses of our nation are, and how our talent and strength has been destroyed.

Man has the right to make use of his temporal goods.

Everything we possess is intended to satisfy the needs of the person and the family. What we dispose of, however, can serve others. There is such a thing as social obligations, and the good of one's neighbors requires certain limitations of freedom. Correct limitations of property, however, do not amount to its abolition. We were appalled when we were expelled from our homes and not even allowed to take a piece of bread for the journey. All of Poland, especially Warsaw, experienced this painfully.[3] This is a painful lesson on how great a national good respecting the property of citizens is.

These human rights are strong as steel, and no one can violate them. Every violation of them is a kind of lawlessness that destroys social life as well as the natural order established by God and confirmed by human wisdom. The bedrock on which social life rests must not be destroyed. The world order must once again respect human rights.

---

3 During the Second World War, Warsaw was badly damaged and experienced massive civilian losses. During the September 1939 campaign, 10 percent of Warsaw's buildings were completely ruined, and a further 40 percent were heavily damaged, while at least 18,000 civilians perished. Following the Warsaw Uprising of 1944, 85 percent of Warsaw's buildings were razed to the ground, while up to 200,000 Varsovians, mostly civilians, were killed. In both instances, tens of thousands of Poles had to flee the battered Polish capital. At the end of the war, most of Warsaw's population had either perished or fled, and the city was populated by a mere couple thousand "Warsaw Robinson Crusoes," the most famous of which was Władysław Szpilman, whose wartime fate is documented in the well-known book and film *The Pianist*.

4

Mother: To the Mother
of the Fatherland

*"A woman who fears the Lord is to
be praised. Give her of the fruit of
her hands" (Proverbs 31:30–31).*

ON THE VAULT OF THE SISTINE CHAPEL,
Michelangelo presents the creation of Eve, mother of all who
have ever lived. This work awakens many sublime thoughts
and is expressive of the deep truths it communicates about life. Coming from the rib of a sleeping Adam, Eve approaches her Creator with
folded hands, in a humble and grateful pose. Directed by the deep
sense that all her power and glory come from God, Who is the only
aim, the entire purpose, and the most lasting joy of her life, she thanks
Him for the gift of life.

How close Eve, our mother, is to us! How willingly we find the con-
tours of our mothers in her, thanking God for the gift and miracle of
life. All the creative power of the Christian woman is enclosed in that
image of Eve who directs her first steps and feelings towards the Father
of all things. From that point, the hands of every woman who gives birth
will be pointed towards the Creator. The Lord opens our hands and fills
them with blessings (see Psalm 144:16–23). He will begin and end her life.

I. The Christian Mother Before the Face of God

It is because of the heavenly Father's will that there is a close
connection between the Christian mother and God's designs. This
connection gives birth to unique gifts and duties. Let us ask: what
does the mother owe to God? What are her obligations to Him?

1. What Does the Mother Owe to God?
These are wondrous and numerous gifts: some are shared by
the entire human species, which has been elevated by God to be

worthy of being called sons of God, while others involve only women and mothers.

The mother owes her entire religious dimension to God.

God, Who Himself generously gifted the female soul, counts on the woman's further cooperation so that she would become clad not in expensive clothes "but by good deeds, as befits women who profess religion" (1 Timothy 2:10). It is not so much the external decoration that determines the woman's glory, as the beautification of her soul through prudence, chastity, and kindness (Titus 2:5). "Charm is deceitful, and beauty is vain, but a woman who fears the Lord is to be praised" (Proverbs 31:30).

St. Peter emphasizes the duty of women in the words: "Let not yours be the outward adorning with braiding of hair, decoration of gold, and wearing of robes, but let it be the hidden person of the heart with the imperishable jewel of a gentle and quiet spirit, which in God's sight is very precious" (1 Peter 3:3–4).

Christianity's greatest contribution to the woman is that, unlike the entirety of paganism and pagan-influenced Christianity, it demands of her internal and spiritual values as the basis for all her veneration and happiness: "A holy and shamefaced woman is grace upon grace" (Ecclesiasticus 26:19). Similarly, the Church has based coexistence within the family not on material fundaments, wealth, or physical beauty, but on spiritual unity and the sacramental bonds that tie together God's love and grace on the example of Christ, Who is bound to the Church through the sacrifice of His death. Thus, it is unsurprising that the Apostle requests that husbands love their wives just as Christ loved the Church for which He sacrificed His soul.

Mothers owe the gift of fertility to God.

Eve, the first mother, expressed the truth that every mother feels and witnesses: "I have gotten a man with the help of the Lord" (Genesis 4:1). The mother of the heroic Maccabean brothers was also aware of this truth: "I do not know how you came into being in my womb. It was not I who gave you life and breath, nor I who set in order the elements within each of you. Therefore, the Creator of the world, Who shaped the beginning of man and devised the origin of all things, will in His mercy give life and breath back to you again" (2 Maccabees 7:22–23).

Every child senses this truth: "Upon Thee I have leaned from my birth; Thou art He Who took me from my mother's womb" (Psalm 71:6–23). "My frame was not hidden from Thee, when I was being made in secret, intricately wrought in the depths of the earth" (Psalm 139:15).

This trust in the mother, in whose hands God entrusted the fate of mankind, is His great gift. God helped man only once by creating the first parents, and left the rest to mothers, who from that point on cooperate with God the Father. Mothers naturally derive all their creative power from God, but their role is no less wondrous and mysterious.

Mothers receive the soul of their children from God.

The Maccabean mother told her sons: "It was not I who gave you life and breath, nor I who set in order the elements within each of you" (2 Maccabees 7:22). The good Lord responds to the will of parents and uses them to determine the creation of a child's soul.

The great privilege of the mother is that she bears responsibility for two souls: her own and that of her child. This is a unique phenomenon in which the soul of one person is dependent on that of another; no two other persons are so closely linked as the soul of a child and the life of its mother. The impact that a mother has on her child in the first months of its life attests to how tremendous this influence is.

Mothers also receive the gift of sacrificing themselves for their children from God.

The enormity of the sacrifice that mothers make for their children cannot be relieved by anyone apart from God. Only He shares with mothers the difficulties in transcending the challenges of life with mothers. "Upon Thee was I cast from my birth, and since my mother bore me, Thou hast been my God. Be not far from me, for trouble is near and there is none to help" (Psalm 22:9–10).

The woman whose soul grows cold and whose faith in God weakens is not capable of making sacrifices; where religiousness disappears, cradles grow silent, and the nation dies out. Not even the most powerful state can teach such sacrifice to children, the family, and the fatherland. Only God, through the natural law which He deposited in the mother's heart, can make sacrifice of one's one comfort, blood, and life possible. Since God gave man five talents, He demands another five. The requirements with respect to His mother, whom He so generously gifted, are no smaller.

2. What Should the Mother Do for God?

Above all, she should return her child's soul, which she has received from God, back to the Creator.

Divine and Christian in nature, the soul seeks out the God that has created it. The duty of those who have received gifts is to ensure that they be properly evaluated and respected. Thus, the mother who is grateful to God must put all her effort into making sure that God receives His glory in the life of a child whose first steps on earth are directed towards His commandments.

She is to save her own soul by giving birth to children.

Thus, God wanted her, a "transgressor" (1 Timothy 2:14) through Satan, to repay the debt she owes to God. From that point, she will experience pain during childbirth (see Genesis 3:16), and her pain and suffering can be healed only through the radiance of Christ's Cross.

St. Paul the Apostle teaches: "Woman will be saved through bearing children, if she continues in faith and love and holiness, with modesty" (1 Timothy 2:15).

Life clearly demonstrates how much of God's grace and how much exceptional strength is received by women who are obedient to the Father of all who live and His laws. The pains of childbirth turn into joy; thus, "she no longer remembers the anguish, for joy that a child is born into the world" (John 16:21–23). When this person is alive, when he fills the world with glory, then his mother receives all that glory: "Blessed is the womb that bore you, and the breasts that you sucked!" (Luke 11:27).

II. Mothers Before Their Fatherland

The Maccabean mother, who received seven sons from God and brought them up in a spirit fidelity to the laws of God and the fatherland, is worthy of admiration. Both the youngest among them and the six eldest ones gave witness to their exceptional courage and love for God and their fatherland: "I, like my brothers, give up body and life for the laws of our fathers, appealing to God to show mercy soon to our nation" (2 Maccabees 7:37). At the same time, he gave the best testimony to his mother, who full of wisdom "encouraged each of them in the language of their fathers" (2 Maccabees 21), to be faithful to the laws of God, and their own nation. From that point, the model of the mother preserved in the holy books is an example of fulfilling one's duties: giving her child to God and her fatherland.

Just as she does with respect to God, the Christian mother also has a twofold relationship with her nation, which gives her gifts and to which she has responsibilities.

1. What Does the Polish Mother Owe to Her Fatherland?
Above all, she owes her natural gifts to it.

Although it has been destroyed by ravenous invaders and is poor, our fatherland is a good mother that generously provides us with all the gifts of the earth. It gives us our daily bread, which is as harsh as the Polish fate but nutritious; it is bread that transforms its sacrificial life into food for all its children. This is mother earth's gift to the human mother, which provides the soil with its defenders.

Your fatherland gives you the gift of your mother tongue with which you can not only express your maternal acts of love, but thanks to which, your children also praise you for your sacrifices and efforts. The Polish language provides your children with the dearest words which they will scatter upon you as if it were the flower of glory.

Your fatherland's soil provides you with the sonorous melodies of fields and forests with which you sing childhood fairytales, and beautiful, tender accounts of sleeping knights and national heroes at Warna, Grunwald, and the Vistula who populate human hearts and with which you will sow love for the fatherland that is as powerful as death as if it were the best grain.

Next, you owe your safety and the defense of your family home to your fatherland.

The fatherland looks after not only all the borders of your land, but also after the safety of your homes and the calm sleep of your infants. Every soldier at the border is your ally, and every guardian of public safety looks after you; every educator, priest, and thinker is your collaborator, while harmony and internal order are your friends.

You owe the respect and dignity you receive to your fatherland.

Notice how joyous it is that your fatherland has decorated its eagle's heart with Christ's Cross and is always faithful to the Church. From its gates, your praise and glory flow, and Christ's Church has taught the Poles respect for its mother. You owe two types of gratitude: gratitude to God for summoning Poland to the light of the faith and to the fatherland for having been faithful to its vocation.

This is a great fruit that fell from this tree upon you: there is no other nation where mothers are treated with such veneration and respect as Poland. Look at the harm that the racist pagan state has caused women by turning them into a tool for reproduction; look at what the Bolshevik state has caused the woman to experience by separating her from her family and home, instead making her work in mines and factories. Only a Catholic nation knows how to surround your heads with halos, because that nation is a child of the Church which, like God, turns Eve into Mary, elevates Magdalene to the altars, and preaches the veneration of being God's Mother. This gives you twofold obligations: to the Church and to the nation.

2. What Are the Polish Mother's Obligations to Her Fatherland?

The first obligation is to give life to your children.

God expanded the commandment He gave to the first parents to the entirety of the human race: "Be fruitful and multiply and fill the earth and subdue it" (Genesis 1:28). Parental fulfillment of this commandment is strengthened in the hierarchy of love. The greater the degree of love that binds you to God, family, and fatherland, the more persistently you should seek to fulfill that duty.

Love for God requires you to seek God's greater glory, which is revealed in the number of His worshipers and witnesses and those who participate in His joy.

Love for the family necessitates looking after its growth, praise, and good name, which are transmitted from generation to generation. Hence, Sacred Scripture gives us evidence of God's blessing in many children: "Your wife will be like a fruitful vine within your house; your children will be like olive shoots around your table" (Psalm 128:3).

Love for the fatherland requires us to populate the Polish soil and subdue it. Just as God gives the entire human race duties towards the whole earth, He also demands that the Polish nation be populated by citizens and subjected to them. If there will be a deficiency of Polish citizens, then our land will instead be subdued by foreign nations that will fulfill God's natural law towards life. This natural love is more powerful than any historical laws. Thus, we witness how the names of the "unwise nations" that rebelled against the duty to give birth to children are erased from the earth; the homes of their great-grandparents are seized by foreign invaders in the name of the right to living space.

The Lord says to Israel: "None shall cast her young or be barren in your land; I will fulfill the number of your days" (Exodus 23:26). This is both a blessing and a reminder of God's requirement. This is a blessing because selfless mothers provide their nations with numerous healthy children; those that will build up the strength of the nation, live and work for their fatherland, and defend its borders. It is also a reminder because where mothers are selfish and incapable of making sacrifices, the nation dies in the cradle or, worse, in the womb of the "mother-coffin." There is no room for great talents or great people; this is an anemic, frail, and truly less valuable nation.

Before the war, the Nazi press reported, not without satisfaction, that for every three "dog moms" in Berlin, there was just one woman with a child. And what about Poland? Let us not forget that, over the course of just ten years, our birth rate fell from 15 to 12 births per thousand inhabitants. Over just four years (1928–1932), the number of children fell by 40,000, or the population of a sizable city.

Poland is moving backwards. There are more decorated dolls, but fewer mothers on our streets.

How different were the Hebrew mothers who experienced the harshest persecutions in the cradle of the nation during the time of the Exodus! The laws of the pharaohs that demanded the killing of young Israelites did not change this. Instead, the mothers of the oppressed nation gave the following venerable testimony: "The Hebrew women are not like the Egyptian women; for they are vigorous and are delivered before the midwife comes to them" (Exodus 1:19).

What gave them that strength? Love for God and their fatherland! How imperative it is that Polish mothers conquer selfishness and place the laws of God and the fatherland before love of themselves. Then, the Polish soil will be populated and subdued to the Polish nation.

The second duty is to turn their children's heart towards God and the fatherland.

It is turned first towards God, because what is God's should be rendered unto Him (see Matthew 22:21). Children's souls are God's, and they are entrusted to their nation only for their time on earth, after which they are completely returned to God. Thus, mothers whose faith is strong must make their children's faith strong as well, for both God and the good of the fatherland, because love of the fatherland and fidelity to it are taught in the shadow of the wings of God's law.

Children's hearts should be directed towards the fatherland! This will occur through bringing them up in a Christian, rational, and strict way. The hearts of youths should become imbued with a proper hierarchy of duties: towards God, from which the strength to fulfill all obligations flows; towards the family, so that there is enough strength to perform difficult duties and so that no one escapes from making self-sacrifices; and towards the fatherland, so that they can be faithful to it, ready to sacrifice their lives for it.

The education of young people must be rigorous and heroic. This is demanded by the circumstances of our state's existence and the enormity of work in which we must engage and do. The experiences of the previous war demonstrate that the upbringing of some of our youth was too soft, which made them incapable of sacrifice and deprived them of national pride. Experience shows that bringing up children in a tough and strict way is easier in a larger family, as having only children leads to the upbringing of selfish youths who recline in their family nest, which has been prepared by Providence for their non-existing brothers and sisters. How can such spoiled young people be brave defenders of the fatherland? Will their weak, infirm hand suffice where three or four others are needed? Will they be capable of replacing those who have fallen in making sacrifices for the nation and in the trenches?

Our fatherland requires numerous families and for people to be brought up heroically. This is the responsibility of Polish mothers!

* * *

When describing the death of the brave defender of the nation, the Book of Judith concludes this description with the following beautiful words: "And all the people mourned for seven days. And all the time of her life, there was none that troubled Israel, nor many years after her death" (Judith 16:29–30).

If Polish women diligently fulfill all their obligations towards God and their fatherland in light of God's laws, they will gain not only glory in the nation, but the borders of the nation will see peace for many years.

"A woman who fears the Lord is to be praised. Give her of the fruit of her hands" (Proverbs 31:30–31).

5

"Blessed is the Fruit of Thy Womb"

(Luke 1:42)

---

*"God of your fathers Who will help you, by
God Almighty Who will bless you with
blessings of heaven above, blessings of the
deep that couches beneath, blessings of the
breasts and of the womb" (Genesis 49:25).*

THIS BEAUTIFUL BLESSING WAS GIVEN BY THE
patriarch Jacob, the dying father of the Chosen People, who
stretched his weak hands over the head of Joseph, who had
revived Egypt. Before his eyes were the vast lands of his descendants,
Ephraim and Manasseh, which were filled with numerous people
who were busy reaping the fruits of the blessings of heaven and earth.
The hardworking and brave people who worked their paternal land
are like a testimony to their submission to the will of their Father
of fathers: "Be fruitful and multiply, and fill the earth and subdue
it" (Genesis 1:28).

The children of the earth are an evident blessing of the breast
and life as well as the joy of their fathers' eyes. They make a blessed
change, giving the earth a new face, whose fruits they possess. They
praise Divine Providence, which has deposited so many inexhaustible
treasures in the womb of mother earth, with their work. What great
things those hardworking hands do! The world will become more
noble and submissive to man, whose mind will inspire creation to
sing a hymn of praise for God. From that point, the birth of every
person will be a joy for the world, not only that of the woman who
"when she is delivered of the child [...] no longer remembers the
anguish, for joy that a child is born into the world" (John 16:21),
but also that of all of nonrational creation which has sensed with
its natural instinct that it has received a king, the only rational being
capable of grasping the meaning of creation and directing it towards
aims indicated by God.

Man is God's greatest gift to the earth! Every new human life is an increase in hope for the entire world, because thousands of possibilities are hidden in this life. The world experienced the greatest joy of "creation", thanks to Mary's words: "Behold, I am the handmaid of the Lord. May it be done to me according to your word" (Luke 1:3), and thanks to the words of the angel: "Be not afraid; for behold, I bring you good news of a great joy, which will come to all the people; for to you is born this day in the city of David a Savior" (Luke 2:10–11).

We know very well how much this world owes to the birth of God. "But to all who received Him, who believed in His name, He gave power to become children of God" as they "were born, not of blood nor of the will of the flesh nor of the will of man, but of God" (John 1:12, 13). Why, then, is the contemporary world so afraid of new births? Why is it sad upon learning that "a child is born into the world" (John 16:21)? Why does it perceive fertility as a curse? Read the pronouncements of learned economists and philosophers who complain about the improperly constructed world, which is supposedly threatened by an invasion of children, and huge segments of humanity, entire nations and peoples, dying of starvation. The world, they say, has been improperly constructed, because the soil cannot provide all its children with bread. Thus, they say, we need a crusade against the "unjust invaders." Solemn, gray heads looking up from volumes containing population statistics have given the verdict: "Death to children!"

Where does this pettiness come from? What is the source of this selfish fear, this anxiety and retreat from new life? Could this be because man has placed more trust in economics, statistics, and himself than in the eternal law and God? Today, so-called "economic considerations" are used to justify war. Millions of young beings are deprived of the right to life, the greatest good, in the name of the good of the economy. We know that man's ultimate purpose has no relation to economic aims, as it infinitely surpasses it, by all of eternity. Economic life is but a modest fragment of man's temporal life; furthermore, it completely pales in comparison with the infinite joy of being in God's presence.

Therefore, does not this economic pronouncement contradict common sense and God's rational creation of the world?

81

I. God Wills That the Earth Be Populated

When reflecting upon His creation and "everything that He had made," the Creator of the world saw that "it was very good" (Genesis 1:31). However, it was God's will for man to complement His work so that earth itself and the goods that come from it would become usable in order to prepare it for the direct fulfillment of human needs. Thus, God obliged man, a rational being, to work in paradise, so that he would "till it and keep it" (Genesis 2:15). God gave us the commandment to create new life so that His will would never be forgotten: "Be fruitful and multiply, and fill the earth and subdue it; and have dominion over the fish of the sea and over the birds of the air and over every living thing that moves upon the earth" (Genesis 1:28).

Although the aims of human life are not limited to work, they are achieved by fulfilling God's will, for which He needs the cooperation of every person within the limits of his vocation and in accordance with God's plan to bring nourishment to all in the appropriate time (see Psalm 145:15).

Making complete use of the goods of the earth is possible only with a higher level of population.

From the time of Abraham's memorable agreement with Lot, the world is filled with God's people. "Let there be no strife between you and me, and between your herdsmen and my herdsmen; for we are kinsmen. Is not the whole land before you? [. . .] If you take the left hand, then I will go to the right; or if you take the right hand, then I will go to the left" (Genesis 13:8–9). Lot chose the land of Jordan and subjected it to his rule. God's plan to populate the earth moved one step forward. From that point, the subjugation of the earth will follow those paths.

Economic history teaches us that as people increase in number, they gain access to new territories, the first of which are the most fertile, after which they conquer uninhabited territories and, finally, colonies. Today, we are witnesses to how the slightest wasteland is carefully tilled and used. It can be said that the direct cause of this subjugation of every corner of the earth is man's obedience to God's will: "Be fruitful [. . .] and fill the earth" (Genesis 1:28).

As the earth becomes more populated with peoples and nations, man puts more work into its every fragment; the intensification of economic life increases, which makes the earth more productive. Meanwhile, as agriculture achieves its peak, peoples and nations look for new territories, trying to make them hospitable to human life. Thanks to this and through their benevolent work, they fulfill God's commandment, subjugating the earth to themselves. God wanted not only Europe and America, but the entire world, to have a foretaste of earthly paradise thanks to the earth's cultivation by man. Thus, obedience to God is the main cause of progress and the growing home to civilization. After so many thousand years of the world's existence, the earth is not completely populated and remains in a wild state, not capable of presenting its resources and riches.

How much is a mother without children worth? What is the earth without people? The desire to present its nourishing, maternal feelings and concern for man slumbers within the earth. Its sons must rest in the earth's womb. Earth wants to open her heart and give nourishment.

Divine Providence blesses man's obedience.

"Therefore, the Creator of the world, Who shaped the beginning of man and devised the origin of all things [. . .] not [. . .] out of things that existed. Thus, also mankind comes into being" (2 Maccabees 7:23, 28). He did not leave humanity in an empty, dry, and untrodden land, but instead He surrounds it with providential, probing concern. God the Father cannot be worse than a woman who does not forget about her infant. "Even these may forget, yet I will not forget you" (Isaiah 49:15).

The astonished world, which a century before had been told of death from overpopulation, now opens its wonder-filled eyes and sees new riches, which have been uncovered from the oblivion of previous centuries, in the earth. God responds to the worried: "Fear not [. . .]. For I will pour water on the thirsty land, and streams on the dry ground; I will pour My Spirit upon your descendants, and My blessing on your offspring. They shall spring up like grass amid waters, like willows by flowing streams" (Isaiah 44:2–4).

As the human population grows, the earth's fruits likewise multiply. Mother earth's generosity is truly moving. She provides more necessary fruits than the earth's inhabitants are capable of consuming. Why should this be surprising? After all, the earth is our mother. Meanwhile, she learned her maternal feelings in the school of the Father of all creation. We see, therefore, how infinite the possibilities of nature are in our history. Today we make use of goods that were unknown to our fathers, while our children possess new economic goods and will tame the forces of the earth more than we. Earth's hospitable womb has greatly expanded since the time of Abraham and Lot.

II. A Growing Human Population Is Conducive to Economic Progress

Historical experience teaches us that progress and prosperity are always correlated with an increase in population; it is not overpopulation but rather an unjust division of the goods of the earth and an unjust socio-economic system that are the cause of humanity's misery. Thus, in a new universal system we should strive for all nations' equal participation in the natural goods of the earth, as Pope Pius XII teaches.

Thanks to an increase in population, economic life has a greater possible number of human talents at its disposal.

We are witnesses to healthy competition in which there is no longer room for mediocrity; instead, honest work, skills, and talents can be developed and nurtured. They force us to arise from sloth and sleepy lethargy, instead working dutifully and making use of the talents God has given us not only for our own use but also for the good of our neighbors. Thanks to this, there is a work environment in which we have to be vigilant and have in mind both our temporal and eternal purposes. From a moral perspective, such an environment is always healthier than one of indolence, idleness, and sloth.

If God wants us to conscientiously make use of our talent in our supernatural lives and wants another five talents in addition to the five we have been given, then this law has its power in earthly life as well. Just as God's demands lead us to sanctity in supernatural life, we likewise achieve it in temporal life thanks to the perfection of earthly life. The fruit of such arduous work is not only the development of technology and civilization as well as the progress of culture, but also bountiful economic goods in the place of previous scarcity.

Thanks to this, it is possible to achieve the Christian economic goal that satisfies the needs of all of society.

The increase in the human population also makes the division of human labor easier.

The modern organization of labor, which does not need to be stopped but instead needs to be Christianized, requires industrious hands that are ready to undertake it. An increase in the supply of the labor force is not only fear of unemployment, but it is also the will to work. "We want work!" the crowds cry out to us. However, such a phenomenon is always healthier than a deficiency of labor, for it contains the will to act and the will to overcome difficulties, not a fearful retreat from those who want to live. Helping these people and entrusting to them a fragment of the labor market that is adapted to their skills and education fulfills a unique kind of providence that God has entrusted to human prudence and anticipation.

Economic development creates new opportunities for prosperous life for a growing number of people.

After all, we see how the gradual population of the earth and our efforts create new possibilities for labor and new living conditions. If our work is determined by love for our neighbor and our nation, if we are directed by the principles of Christian justice, then we create greater and better living conditions for people. Then, one's own flimsy profit will cease to be the driving force behind economic efforts, and it will instead be replaced with concern for the prosperity of one's neighbors. People come closer to one another and find their brethren in God's face: "Did not He Who made me in the womb make him? And did not One fashion us in the womb? If I have withheld anything that the poor desired or have caused the eyes of the widow to fail [. . .] If I have seen anyone perish for lack of clothing, or a poor man without covering; if his loins have not blessed me, and if he was not warmed with the fleece of my sheep" (Job 31:15–21).

All people who through their lives help those who are willing to find work and new opportunities for existence are deserving of praise: "Blessed is the womb that bore you, and the breasts that you sucked!" (Luke 11:27). However, this will happen only at the price of the second blessing: "Blessed rather are those who hear the word of God and keep it!" (Luke 11:28).

III. Depopulated Lands Will Grow Poor and Fall into Ruin Amidst Poverty

The days of the Final Judgment have not yet come, but the glorification of the infertile already resounds. Many people today believe that lethargy is the greatest accomplishment; all deficiencies and crises should be resolved through the sloth they so praise. When there is a surplus of grain, it should not be sown; instead, a bonus should be given for idleness! When there is a surplus of products, manufacturing facilities should be stopped! Fearing the overpopulation of their own earth, people call: "Blessed are the barren, and the wombs that never bore, and the breasts that never gave suck!" (Luke 23:29).

One of the signs of the decadent thinking of our times is the retreat from difficulty. A certain Catholic writer has characterized our age as follows: in the Christian age, when there were seven children's heads in one household but only six hats, people wondered how to get the seventh hat. Today, however, they ponder how to get rid of the seventh head!

It is unsurprising that idleness, which is praised in economic life even though there are millions of starving and needy people, is also a crime, just like the propaganda of infertility. A systematically depopulated land will turn into a desert, which has happened wherever there lived once rich and large nations, but that today have left behind them nothing more than ruins that are worthy of admiration. "How could nations that have built such wonders died out?" we ask. The decline in prosperity always goes hand in hand with a decline in the birth rate. Unemployment has never been eliminated through the artificial limitation of births; unemployment has remained among the nations that noted the largest decrease in the birth rate.

When the labor force will run out, the natural goods that have been prepared by Providence will decay, and all the riches of the villages and cities will fall into ruin. You ask why ruined cities and villages have not been rebuilt. They have not because these goods belong to no one, and those lands have no heirs; they are populated by people with "a miscarrying womb and dry breasts" (Hosea 9:14). They are too prudent and excessively cautious: "Their root is dried up; they shall bear no fruit" (Hosea 9:16).

The names of fools are erased from the books of the living (see Psalm 69:29).

IV. We Stand Before the Face of Our Mother Earth

What will we bring her as a gift? We expect so much of her! It is to her that God's commandment "Be fruitful and multiply, and fill the earth and subdue it" (Genesis 1:28) refers. The earth which Providence has given us hungers after our love; this is not only the love of words and songs, but above all the love of action and work. Is it not completely subjugated to us? Although its cloak is shabby, because it has been destroyed and covered by rubble, it is nonetheless graceful and pleasing to the eye. Its womb contains God's gifts, which have not yet been used up; so far, we have not yet known our mother, the earth. Let us wipe all wastelands and sandy deserts off its face, instead looking into its heart in order to extract from it the treasures that are hidden to its own children and have been protected against the lustful eye of passersby with trembling. Let us give our mother earth children, our faithful sons; let us provide it with thrifty plowmen, miners, and workers who love her and are devoted and faithful to her, pouring out their blood, sweat, and tears over her. Let generation after generation walk across it in faithful service so that the efforts of the entire nation could renew the face of the earth. "Shall a land be born in one day? Shall a nation be brought forth in one moment?" (Isaiah 66:8). For this, work across the centuries is needed!

Earth, which is grateful for its hardworking sons, will bear its fruit!

* * *

God gave the commandment to populate the earth with human sons. He wants man to subjugate the earth to itself. He has calculated the opportunities and riches of the earth correctly; God's earth is capable of nourishing all its children.

Trust in Divine Providence! "Hearken to me, O house of Jacob, all the remnant of the house of Israel, who have been borne by me from your birth, carried from the womb; even to your old age I am He, and to gray hairs I will carry you. I have made, and I will bear; I will carry and will save" (Isaiah 46:3–4).

Have we possessed the entirety of the earth's mysteries? Have we completely studied its parental powers? Have we put all our zeal and talents into it? Do we want to set barriers to God's creation and power? Are we of little faith? Why do we doubt? "'Shall I bring to the birth and not cause to bring forth?' says the Lord; 'Shall I, who cause to bring forth, shut the womb?'" (Isaiah 66:9).

Faithful to God's laws and message, we will fulfill the Lord's Covenant, and the whole world will be filled with the joy of the earth's goods.

"Rejoice with Jerusalem, and be glad for her, all you who love her; rejoice with her in joy, all you who mourn over her; that you may suck and be satisfied with her consoling breasts. [...] For thus says the Lord: 'Behold, I will extend prosperity to her like a river, and the wealth of the nations like an overflowing stream; and you shall suck, you shall be carried upon her hip, and dandled upon her knees. As one whom his mother comforts, so I will comfort you; you shall be comforted in Jerusalem. You shall see, and your heart shall rejoice; your bones shall flourish like the grass; and it shall be known that the hand of the Lord is with his servants" (Isaiah 66:10–14).

6

The Family in Society and the State

"Whatever house you enter, first say,
'Peace be to this house!'" (Luke 10:5).

THESE WORDS FROM THE GOSPELS CONTAIN Christ the Lord's instruction to His disciples who spread the Good News. God's Word is to bring His peace to every home, every family, and the personal life of all its members. Respecting and preserving the family home, as well as surrounding it with care and love, are the works of the Christian spirit. The superiority and magnificence of Catholic culture consists of the fact that it has surrounded the family with the spirit of sanctity and inviolability, making everyone treat its laws with respect and veneration. Here, new life is born for God, the nation, and the state. If God Himself demonstrates so much subtle concern and reveals so much love for the family, He instructs all through His attitude: parents, priests, politicians, and rulers. All mouths must proclaim the good news to the family: "Peace be to this house!'" This is the Christian spirit!

Why, then, is the contemporary family attacked with such fury? Many ideologues seek to unravel it and hurl some strange and passionate words in the calm of the home: "The family is not of God; it belongs to the state!" "Your marriage must be a civil one!" "You cannot give yourselves up to God!" "Your wedding vows can be dissolved." "Throw away your love; keep looking for new and different loves." "Hand your children over to the state or the municipality; it does not matter to whom!" "These children are not yours! You gave them life? You are only functionaries of the state!" "We don't want families; we want a herd!" "We don't want family love!"

Such cries have driven peace out of the family home, separated hearts, separated parents from their children, tipped over cradles, killed the mutual trust of spouses, and pushed the family away from a safe wharf and onto the rough waves of the passion of people who are typically the worst and lack families. This is the work of the pagan spirit!

However, tempests pass, and screams die down. People who publicly experience their own suffering and seek vengeance against the family for the disappointment they have experienced within it quiet down and grow silent. Yet the family persists. Everything will survive because it is of God!

Let us therefore return to the family; let us remove the noisy rabble from it, close its door, and remain amidst anxious parents and fearful children. "Peace be to this house!"

I. What Does the Family Give to Society and the State?

The family provides society with the most wondrous gifts, without which it would be incapable of functioning.

It distributes God's gift: man.

No one can give society a greater gift. This gift is taken directly from God, as all of life comes from God's hand. The world has come to possess man through God. He is the cause for the birth of all people. God gives the world man and outlines his history. This is beautifully expressed by the Psalmist: "My frame was not hidden from Thee, when I was being made in secret, intricately wrought in the depths of the earth. Thy eyes beheld my unformed substance; in Thy book were written, every one of them, the days that were formed for me, when as yet there was none of them" (Psalm 139:15–16).

Only God sees man's conception "in the depths of the earth," in the mother's womb. Only He is the Lord of the life-giving force. Only He knows the number of the nations. In His books, man's entire life is outlined from the start, even before man has arrived on earth. However, God directly created the human body only once. Thus, He has summoned parents to continue His work of creation. He entrusted to them the fate of the earth as well as that of human life on it. From that point, God collaborates with parents, but He fully respects their free will: "Let it be to me according to your word" (Luke 1:38).

Thus, according to God's will, parents give life to their children, thus becoming His direct collaborators. God will give them the most wondrous gift — that of children — as a reward for their faithfulness. It is a child that comes from God's hand that is to be "the image and likeness of God"; it has a rational and free nature and is capable of full development. It has the full dignity of an immortal being that is capable of being God's child, of friendship, and of happiness in God. The family is to prepare the man received from God with His grace in the soul for living in society.

The family provides the state with citizens.

The family brings up man and thus prepares him for co-existence with other people. The family makes man capable of not only physical life, but of social co-existence as well. It is in the family that man first learns social and moral concepts, thus developing the human personality. Man receives the sense of social bond that is the important basic element of all social co-existence and that gives birth to a sense of civic duty from the family as well. This bond is forged through common religious beliefs as well as identical ideals and loves. Such a bond is inoculated all the more powerfully that it nestles in not only the child's mind and will, but in his heart as well. Thus, the family often binds its child to God, the nation, and the state. Parents also instill a civic sense of law and order in their children's souls, not through power and violence, but through love. This is its major contribution. No society, not even a total and collective one, can exist without this sense of duty. It results not only from a sense of justice, but also of love, veneration, and gratitude at the same time.

This is much more than even the best organized state that uses external force can provide.

The family takes upon itself the greatest difficulties and sacrifices.

Often having only modest means at its disposal, the family achieves the best fruits of bringing up its children, which are all the more certain if they are not ruined by social customs and the political system, in the most frugal possible way. Without the concern of society and without state budgets, the family carries the entire burden of bringing up children, covering their expenses, and preparing them for independent lives. Every person with a sensitive heart and a grateful memory has the most tender recollections of their parents' sacrifices and love, thanks to which they become useful members of their state and nation. If the family does not fulfill its duties, typically nobody else is capable of fully executing them.

Thus, the family is the "mother" of society.

Society is born in the family. The family is not only the basic unit of society. It is the womb of society! The family nurses its fate in its hands. The end of the family means the downfall of society. Empty cradles and sad households are a harbinger of the emptying streets of cities and villages. Because the state emerges out of society, everything that society has received from the family becomes a blessing for the state itself. That which citizens receive from the family is their contribution to national and state life.

The aim of family life is not restricted to the aims of public society. The state is not man's highest purpose; it is not capable of encompassing and satisfying all the needs of the human soul. The state makes use of the gifts of family life and can develop them in accordance with its natural purposes. However, the state is not the only successor to the family. Above all, God and His Church and the entire nation have the right to it. Nonetheless, public society is greatly indebted to the family, and it should repay that debt.

II. What Should Society and the State Give to the Family?

At the beginning, let us establish the basic principles. They are of basic significance with respect to more detailed solutions. If they are not accepted as the cornerstone of the entire edifice, not even the best and most detailed intentions will bear fruit. According to Pope Leo XIII, every healthy system should organically create public and private prosperity. The basic elements of a healthy political system must include pure mores, order, and honesty in family relationships, respect for religion and justice, a proper separation of burdens and taxes, and the flourishing of the national economy. In particular, grounding the family in a healthy political system in accordance with its earthly and ultimate aims ensures the permanence of the state's existence.

Thus, it should be accepted that:

• Man (human life) is the most important resource at the disposal of the state and society.

• The family, which creates human life, should be surrounded with the state's and society's most benevolent care.

• The sanctity of the family and its relationship to the Church through the sacrament of marriage as the strongest bond of family life must be recognized. Civil law should protect the indissolubility of marriage.

• It should be remembered that the family needs favorable economic conditions; the entire state structure must be conducive to this aim.

• Healthy demographic policy should above all be pro-family policy.

• The collaboration of the Church, society, and state in favor of the family must be considered essential.

These general rules should lead to detailed efforts with positive results.

1. The Moral and Legal Protection of the Family

The family must be a priority of the national budget, while the state must stand in defense of the family community. It must oppose attitudes in opposition to the family, child, and mother; such attitudes are often so hostile that people think that bearing life is the greatest crime against which the state should defend itself using all possible means.

The tasks of society and the state include:

The ratification and faithful respecting of laws protecting marital fidelity and the mutual assistance of spouses.

History teaches us that the good of the state and the temporal happiness of citizens cannot be safe and intact where the fundaments on which they are based, the family and the legal protection of morality, are not upheld. The resulting divorces and "temporary marriages," broken family homes, and abandoned children violate not only God's law, but also the natural law applied to the nation and state.

Anti-natalist tendencies must be opposed.

The right to fertility can be supported by both the needs of the fatherland and state as well as the Church. This is particularly evident amidst the growth of selfishness in "families on strike", whose attitude threatens the existence of the nation and the state. Voluntary infertility achieved through immoral contraceptive practices attests to a failure of society.

Experience shows that all systems of rewards and profits and favorable tax measures are meaningless where immorality has devoured consciences. The family requires too great sacrifices for it to be repaid with mere pennies. Where there is a need for sacrifice and love, money does not suffice, although it can support healthy, large Christian families. All that is left is to appeal to cooperation with the Church, who is capable of reaching human souls. However, the state can fruitfully support the Church by fighting against pornography, immoral art, and the disintegration of public customs. In particular, public authorities have the right and duty to struggle against neo-Malthusian doctrines and the propaganda of contraceptives; they should end their active participation in neo-Malthusian policies and ban the production and sale of all immoral articles that prevent conception.

The state and society must stand in defense of the life of the unborn.

Neither the individual nor society may assault the life of a child. The state must not tolerate the practice of abortion. The duty of legislative bodies is to stand in defense of life with the aid of the appropriate laws and punishments. Such a duty is all the greater, as those who are threatened with death have fewer means of self-defense. In the mother's womb, children have no possibility to defend their lives! They are defended only by God, through the voice of conscience and the Church. When the conscience is blurred, all that remains is the kind of punishment that in human society only the state can levy. Through its laws, the state cannot entrust the lives of children to dishonest physicians and selfish parents. God the Judge Who avenges spilt blood calls all who have contributed to the death of the innocent, either through the ratification of laws or through supporting or implementing them calls: "What have you done? The voice of your brother's blood is crying to me from the ground. And now you are cursed from the ground" (Genesis 4:10–11). This curse falls on dying families and nations.

2. The Economic Protection of the Family

Economic assistance to families can be applied especially in the spheres of family property, the work of fathers, and general social welfare.

The well-being of the family must be based on private property.

According to Leo XIII, nature itself has bound private property to the existence of human society, especially with the existence and development of the family. On the fiftieth anniversary of *Rerum novarum*, Pius XII said that if the concept of living space had to be justified in any field, it should be with respect to the family: we must think of living space for families.

Thus, the aims of the state are:

• To protect private property as the basis for the organization and upkeep of the well-being of the family. A man who starts or already has a family has a somewhat dual right to possessing private property: his personal right and that of those he looks after.

• To aim for such a system in which the largest possible part of humanity can fulfill its desire to attain and maintain property.

• In particular, families have the right to property, because property supports their desirable permanence and security. According to the Catholic *Social Code*, "It is important that legislation facilitates the acquisition of property, especially for the tilling of parcels of the native land, for families" (29).

The fathers of families should be given the conditions in which they can work.

In his encyclical *Rerum novarum*, Leo XIII instructed that social and economic relations be established in such a way that, depending on their state and where they live, all the fathers of families could ensure themselves, their wives, and their children a decent living. The *Social Code* affirms: "When the head of the family is a sober and honest person, and conscientiously performs the duties of his profession, should, thanks to social organization itself, find sufficient resources to support and raise his family in his work." "The laborer deserves his wages" (Luke 10:7).

Justice itself seems to demand that those who give society citizens and bring them up have preference under equal conditions of general arrangements and preparations in receiving employment over those who do not have families.

Appropriate legal protection should be accorded to salaries for work, as a salary is the basic resource for the livelihood of not only the individual, but of the family as well. All attempts at denying due wages must be decisively rejected. The law of the Old Testament demanded: "You shall give him his hire on the day he earns it, before the sun goes down (for he is poor and sets his heart upon it)" (Deuteronomy 24:15). Such abuses cause great damage, not only to families that suffer because of this, but also to the entirety of social life. It is also unacceptable that remuneration for work is so modest that it would be insufficient to feed a frugal and resourceful family.

Finally, the family must be given social protection.

In this case, the interested parties, society which assists them, and, finally, the state, which complements the efforts of both, have an enormous role to play.

According to Catholic social activists, healthy demographic policy should above all be pro-family policy. This means that "in the womb of civilian society, the family deserves the right to distributive justice. Taxes, burdens, social benefits, welfare payments, dearness allowances, and disability pensions should be determined in relation to the family, not to the individual."

So far, policies have been different. Those employees in both the public and private sectors who typically raise the largest number of children are given the lowest salaries. High salaries for officials usually encompass small families. Families that endow society with the largest number of citizens receive beggars' wages. There is a strange tendency to further limit benefits to the working fathers of families; furthermore, state legislation introduces new restrictions that above all affect families. Private employers sometimes follow this example.

This attitude and such ignoble practices must be stopped. Conditions in which families can more easily realize their needs and fulfill their duties must be created. When private assistance fails, the duty of public authorities is to supplement it. The contemporary housing system, which already is hostile to large families because of the small size of apartments, is not conducive to children. This practice must be ended through the construction of apartments for the middle class and the poor. Starting a family, which already is expensive today, and the even more costly education of children in typically expensive schools, should be facilitated through tax breaks for large families, family allowances, and the ensuring of a balance between family incomes and duties. The mounting difficulties facing the fathers of large families in looking for work must be overcome; crimes against fathers who lose their jobs only because they have many children must end. Meanwhile, the system of family salaries must be developed so that all job contracts include family benefits.

* * *

"Whatever house you enter, first say, 'Peace be to this house!'" (Luke 10:5). Let us bring peace to weary fathers, exhausted mothers, and impoverished children. They will bless us in their prayers to the Father of all families. "Peace to all people of good will" will descend on the earth.

7

Compensation for the Family for Labor

"Masters, treat your slaves justly and fairly, knowing that you also have a Master in heaven" (Colossians 4:1).

S T. PAUL'S WORDS INTRODUCE US TO THE very essence of the topic I would like to touch upon. In them, the Apostle has combined God, masters, and slaves into one whole. As is usually the case in the Pauline teaching, everything moves towards unity, collaboration, and co-existence; everything constantly complements itself. The Apostle to the Gentiles is the apostle of the community as the basis for Christian social co-existence. Out of this sense of community, he will arrive at conclusions obliging people at every moment of their lives.

Masters also have a Master Who is superior to them! Every entrepreneur, factory owner, or workshop organizer is bound by the demands and laws of He Who is above him: the Lord in Heaven. He will also treat them "justly and fairly." One day, He will also summon them to His currency exchange. At the Final Judgment, God will repay everyone according to his deeds. This will be a just remuneration for the work of one's life.

You cannot forget about this final payment when your servants — employees and workers who have the same Lord in Heaven as the capitalists — stand before you. God's justice should be a model for every dimension of justice, which Providence has placed in your hands. We must look at the numerous hardworking people through the prism of the kinship we share with them through the Lord Almighty. Only then will we succeed in liberating ourselves of the countless errors and sins that dehumanize human labor, which turn it into a commodity and make a person completely subjected to the proletarian ideology and have broken up the family and caused pauperization and unemployment to spread, thus subjecting human labor to the cruelest and most erroneous laws of supply and demand.

In this reflection, I plan on taking into consideration the needs and demands of the working-class family in order to arrive at an opinion on what just and righteous remuneration for human labor should be.

I. A Just Wage Must Be Measured by the Value of Human Labor

This value is comprehensive: it is not only personal, but also economic and social. With regards to legitimate labor, one cannot forget the various properties of human labor.

1. The Personal Value of Human Labor

The personal value of human labor is two-fold. First, labor, which is a human activity, directly strives for the perfection of our personality; second, the fruits of labor provide us with the resources, without which life is impossible.

The personal value of labor has hitherto been appreciated the least. In the fierce dispute over the value of wages, people almost completely forget about the fact that all kinds of labor, even those that are contractual, are related to the human person, and thus are inextricably linked with it. Labor as such above all has personal significance and value for the working person. Hence, it shapes and expands the mind, strengthens the will, orders feelings, and develops spiritual and physical functions. As such, it is necessary for man; it becomes his most personal need and duty. It is not only a demand of the stomach, but also a need of rational human nature.

Can personal value conceived as such be subjected to some material evaluation or payment? If labor is judiciously organized, then man is generously compensated in his humanity. We can at best speak of one full and righteous payment, of God's payment for the deeds of one's life.

Here, however, the second personal value of human labor is added. Labor is not only a need of our rational nature; it is also a necessary, and often-times the only, means of obtaining bread. It is the livelihood for people who do not possess property or their own enterprise. Its personal value consists of satisfying the necessities of life for themselves as well as their families.

99

Having this in mind, from the very beginning, God has fine-tuned a strong sense of responsibility for the fruit of the worker's efforts within people. Not only Christ the Lord has forcefully recalled that: "The laborer deserves his wages" (Luke 10:7). A wage for labor is an equitable and just means of meeting the costs of life. Deuteronomy instills within employers the practice of repaying employees with the fruits of their labor: "You shall not oppress a hired servant who is poor and needy, whether he is one of your brethren or one of the sojourners who are in your land within your towns; you shall give him his hire on the day he earns it, before the sun goes down (for he is poor, and sets his heart upon it)" (Deuteronomy 24:14–15). Here, the importance of this wage to one's life does not arouse any doubts. This is the main reason why God is so lovingly concerned for the repayment of labor. God is the creator of the oldest labor law that defends laborers. God inspired these words: "From the fruit of his words a man is satisfied with good, and the work of a man's hand comes back to him" (Proverbs 12:14). God considers depriving workers of the wage they have earned to be a shameful sin: "Behold, the wages of the laborers who mowed your fields, which you kept back by fraud, cry out; and the cries of the harvesters have reached the ears of the Lord of hosts" (James 5:4).

According to God's design, binding the fruits of the work of human hands with the needs of life and the protection of a wage that suffices for life reveals to us the real spirit of this Divine legislation: in every just wage for labor, the value of work as a human activity in which man engages in order to support himself and his family must be taken into consideration.

2. The Economic Value of Labor

This is another value that must be taken into consideration when establishing a just wage. Every rational and intentional form of human labor has economic value, as it makes use of physical and spiritual efforts as well as human skills and talents. It also attains other values. This economic fruit of labor always has its value independent of the demands and sacrifices that labor entails. It also cannot solely be subjected to its evaluation in the labor market. "The work of a man's hand comes back to him" not according to the job market or the blind laws of supply and demand (Proverbs 12:14). This economic value of labor, which typically significantly exceeds the received payment and accumulates so richly amidst constantly growing prosperity must at the very least correspond to a payment that would suffice for the renewal of the strength depleted when working. The most basic and just exchange of services demands this.

3. The Social Value of Labor

Man is not isolated from the rest of society when doing any work. Social life consists of the fact that man constantly receives something from society and constantly gives something back to it. Human labor is at the same time collaboration with people. It is possible only in cooperation with others and their work, which has already been completed or at least intended. Man cooperates with others both through the tools of labor and through the very aim of labor, whose attainment is tantamount to performing some service for one's neighbor. Likewise, every kind of human labor, even that of the most selfish entrepreneur or limited worker, makes use of social protection and the existing legal order, as well as the working conditions that have been created by the employer. It also directly or indirectly consolidates the social order and multiplies the common good.

Likewise, the mere consumption of the fruits of human labor is not purely personal. Man uses the resources he has received to support his family, bringing back to society a large portion of his possessions in the form of citizens who are ready for life and skilled for further labor. The fruits of man's labor are usually shared with the needy; labor provides the resources for social, professional, public, national, and religious co-existence, thanks to which it is applied to collective society in a new form.

Everything that makes up this rich social life man makes possible through the fruits of his labor, thanks to the wage for his labor; this is also where the further value of human labor rests. Thus, the essential value of human labor can be evaluated only when we take into consideration all these factors.

4. A Just Wage Should Encompass the Entire Value of Labor

A just wage must correspond to the fruits and importance of labor. Indeed, not all labor can be evaluated in the same way. Labor is not only exchange value that is measured by what it brings to the employer in an economic sense. Labor is above all a social value that impacts the entirety of social life. Thus, not only the employer, but the entirety of organized society that labor serves must participate in compensating a just wage. Here, we have ample room for social initiatives, both private and state-sponsored, that should aid the employee's family if his needs cannot be met by a wage for his labor itself. Just compensation for labor is compensation for the family. It is to cover the needs of not only the employee, but also of his family. After all, the needs of the family are in reality the needs of the employee.

God has given every person the right to start a family: he "shall leave his father and mother and be joined to his wife, and the two shall become one flesh" (Ephesians 5:31). Thus, there are no dual needs here; there is but one need of the head of the family, who through God's will makes up one whole along with his wife and children. However, the family is not only the right of the individual; it is above all a social need and a condition necessary for its existence. Compensation that can support the family is only just in terms of human rights and the needs of society. The great majority of humanity receives these resources from labor; thus, they must be at such a level that they can satisfy the needs of the family. In this spirit, Pope Pius XI teaches: "In the first place, the worker must be paid a wage sufficient to support him and his family" (QA, 71).

Naturally, not every place of employment will be capable of meeting all those needs that should be encompassed by a just wage. The existence of a family, which is the fundament of national and state life, cannot be dependent solely on economic factors. The entire social system should be directed towards the family. Through its special services, which it provides to society, especially when it is large, the family should receive assistance from both the national economy and the organized society and state for the difficulties in bringing up children that entail making great sacrifices amidst modest means. It will receive this assistance through the creation of funds assisting families through social insurance, institutions supported by the state budget, etc.

II. For What Should Family-Sustaining Compensation Strive?

Psalm 128 presents to us an image of a happy family, predicting an arising social order: "You shall eat the fruit of the labor of your hands; you shall be happy, and it shall be well with you. Your wife will be like a fruitful vine within your house; your children will be like olive shoots around your table. Lo, thus shall the man be blessed who fears the Lord" (Psalm 128:2–5).

This image will become reality in nearly every family if human labor and social conditions protect its existence. The instructions of Catholic social teaching strive precisely for that. According to them, labor should facilitate the starting of a family and supplement its living costs. Only such a wage corresponds to the moral value of labor as a moral activity of the human person. Thus, above all *compensation for labor should be sufficient for supporting a family.*

Pius XI believes that a wage should be such that "[e]very effort must therefore be made that fathers of families receive a wage large enough to meet ordinary family needs adequately" (QA, 71). This thought is underscored in *Rerum novarum*: the natural laws of justice require that a wage suffices so that the frugal and moral worker can support himself and his family.

Developing this matter in detail, Catholic social activists believe that supporting a family encompasses: food, clothing, lodging, light, and fuel; the bringing up and education of children, as well as the worker's own education; the fulfillment of religious, national, social, professional, and state responsibilities; rest on holidays, vacation days, and reasonable forms of recreation; insurance against accidents, old age, and common illness; and savings necessary for acquiring modest property that ensures the permanence of the family home.

Family compensation should make the bringing up of children possible.

The labor system should not preclude the meeting of one of the most important life duties for the worker: the transmission of life and the bringing up of offspring. In *Rerum novarum* (14), Pope Leo XIII writes that: "'The child belongs to the father,' and is, as it were, the continuation of the father's personality." Bound to their parents through the natural law, children can expect to be brought up in preparation for independent life. And increasingly better life! That is the essence of social progress, which is dictated by the need for growth, so that man wants an increasingly better life.

The family brings children into society, bringing up new citizens for the fatherland, Church, and state. The better it fulfills its duties, the more evident its usefulness to all will be. Bad education — resulting in an impoverished, sickly generation demoralized by poverty and coming out of families that have been deprived of the most basic needs without which man can not only not exist, but that make salvation difficult — causes damage and even failure to the family. It is clear that the entire social system should aid the family in the exercise of its duties.

A wage must facilitate the acquisition of modest property.

Property is the basis for the existence of the family. If it is a demand of the common good and a natural right of the individual, it is all the more a demand of the family, which consists of multiple individuals. Through the aid of property, it secures not only the well-being of the family, but it furthermore facilitates the upbringing of the family and the improvement of living conditions. The right of parents to secure a future for their children defends the natural right to inheritance, which is as strong as the right to possession.

In order to bolster the family, the property on which it supports itself must be secured. All legislation should support this aim. According to Leo XIII: "The law, therefore, should favor ownership, and its policy should be to induce as many as possible of the people to become owners" (RN, 46). A healthy spirit of the desire for property and savings, which completely disappears in the workers' milieu, depriving people of the faith in the possibility of liberation from any permanent, professional poverty, must be rebuilt. Ceasing to see workers as proletarians through the aid of property will of course be possible only when a wage for labor will ensure people healthy savings. Thanks to it, the family will attain the family living space recommended by Pius XII.

Finally, family compensation must facilitate the social progress of the working masses.

This will be the result of all the above-mentioned achievements, thanks to which the moral growth of workers will be possible.

Liberating man from the milieu of proletarian existence and making him a living and useful member of society is one of the most important aims of social life. This aspiration cannot be foreign to the aims of human labor, which strives for social progress. The Church, whose main purpose is to support all kinds of progress up to the highest limits of sanctity in God, desires this with all her heart.

Pius XI clearly writes that economic "goods ought indeed to be enough both to meet the demands of necessity and decent comfort and to advance people to that happier and fuller condition of life which, when it is wisely cared for, is not only no hindrance to virtue but helps it greatly" (QA, 75).

Thus, we see here that the potential for growth has no boundaries. They will constantly increase alongside the increase in general prosperity. The Catholic concept of a just wage is not closed, but widely open for further progress. Compensation for the family is the chief principle of Catholic social teaching. Pius instructs that "if this cannot always be done under existing circumstances, social justice demands that changes be introduced as soon as possible whereby such a wage will be assured to every adult workingman" (QA, 71). Thanks to such reforms, we will attain what the Psalmist proclaims: "You shall eat the fruit of the labor of your hands; you shall be happy, and it shall be well with you" (Psalm 128:2–3).

III. The Good of the Family and the Common Good

Complete good will be achieved only when the state of an enterprise and the good of its owner, as well as the good of society, and the righteous aspirations of workers will be taken into consideration.

The good of workers and their families requires that labor provides them with the means that are necessary for the achievement of the full development of the person, so that workers receive such wages that they can fulfill their duties and support large families, without breaching Christian morality.

The good of their families necessitates that workers do not renounce a righteous wage, as labor is not only personal in nature, but is also necessary for supporting the life of the family and satisfying its needs. There is a natural law of justice, a higher and older one, that requires that wages suffice for the frugal and moral worker to support his family. This same good requires that excessive demands of work will not completely deprive them of the ability to make a living; for example, the closing of places of employment caused by them generates unemployment, which is a danger to family life.

The good of the enterprise must also be kept in mind. Pius XI rightly cautions against leading places of work to decline through the demand for excessive wages. Under certain justified conditions, it is better to concede to a lower wage than to lead to the downfall of a place of employment. However, lower wages do not justify the bad state of an enterprise resulting from sloth, a lack of initiative, or technical and economic backwardness in the organization of the workplace.

Finally, we must remember the common good. This is broadly understood: it teaches us a social sense, thanks to which we can subordinate our own requirements to matters of a higher order. It also teaches us concern for the good of citizens, requires us to overcome idleness and imprudence, the narcissism of both employers and workers, and the spirit of interest and class. This common good requires that the largest possible number of people in society can have their well-being secured: "Workers and other employees, by setting aside some part of their income which remains after necessary expenditures, [can] attain gradually to the possession of a moderate amount of wealth" (QA, 74). The common good also demands "that the opportunity to work be provided to those who are able and willing to work", and receive the resources that are necessary to live at a decent level (QA, 74). Thus, a proper balance of wages must be found; they cannot be too low, but neither should we allow excessively high wages to be the cause of unemployment. The level of wages must therefore be determined not by personal gain, but by a concern for the common good.

* * *

Even if we created the most perfect social system and accepted the best will of employers and employees bolstered by the cooperation of all the layers of society, justice achieved in this way would only be human justice. Likewise, the greatest harm will be the work of man.

The good Lord did not leave these things only to the human will. And although He does not defend employers here on earth, the ultimate truth is that God Himself is the fullest and most righteous wage. God experiences the value of every kind of labor. "Each man's work will become manifest; for the Day of the Lord will disclose it, because it shall be revealed in fire; and the fire shall try every man's work, of what sort it is" (1 Corinthians 3:13). God also "judges each one impartially according to his deeds" (1 Peter 1:17). Then it will turn out if the wage we have received was justly received; it will become known what was just or unjust. God will even everything out: "For the Son of Man is to come with His angels in the glory of His Father, and then He will repay every man for what he has done" (Matthew 16:27). This will be a general payment, God's reckoning which we will receive with an interest rate on all the injustices we have caused and ourselves suffered through. "For God is not so unjust as to overlook your work" (Hebrews 6:10); "Watch over them, lest thou fall, and bring dishonor upon thy soul" (Ecclesiasticus 1:38). "Whoever gives you a cup of water to drink because you bear the name of Christ, will by no means lose his reward" (Mark 9:41).

8

The Salt of the Polish Earth

"You are the salt of the earth" (Matthew 5:13).

ONE EVENT FROM ISRAEL'S FORTY-YEAR wandering in the desert on the way to the Promised Land must be recalled. The weary people raised their voice against Moses for leading them out of the land of Egypt. "O that we had meat to eat!" they called (Numbers 11:4). This was not the first time that Moses listened to his people's grievances. Throughout all the years that he led them to the land of milk and honey, Moses bolstered their flagging spirits, yet he experienced such a lack of faithfulness. There were constant complaints of: Why did you lead us out of Egypt? Were there not enough tombs there so that we could die there rather than in the wilderness? Moses was a titan of faith and witness to God's greatest miracles; he engaged in a lonely conversation with the Lord for months at a time. Yet, Moses broke down under the weight of responsibility that had been placed on his powerful but nonetheless merely human shoulders. He went up a hill to the Lord. This telling complaint flowed from the depths of the weary soul of that leader of the Jewish people: "Why hast Thou dealt ill with Thy servant? And why have I not found favor in Thy sight, that Thou dost lay the burden of all this people upon me? Did I conceive all this people? Did I bring them forth, that Thou shouldst say to me, 'Carry them in your bosom, as a nurse carries the sucking child,' to the land which Thou didst swear to give their fathers? [...] I am not able to carry all this people alone, the burden is too heavy for me" (Numbers 11:11–14). The Lord had mercy on Moses and instructed him to select seventy elders from the people and place them before the tent of meeting: "I will take some of the spirit which is upon you and put it upon them; and they shall bear the burden of the people with you, that you may not bear it yourself alone" (Numbers 11:17).

That was the first time that the summons: "You are the salt of the earth" (Matthew 5:13) was given.

I. The Salt of the Earth of the Fatherland

The incident in the wilderness teaches us that those whom God has destined to carry the weight of their people exist in society thanks to His will.

Man, who by his nature is a social creature, follows the voice of the natural law, developing his life amidst different groups of people who are bound together by one aim, that of the social good, which causes them to create a social organism. Thanks to the natural inclinations that have been given to him by God, the Almighty Creator of Nature, man coexists in family, national, professional, public, and religious communities. Each of these communities may seem like a merely human work, yet our social nature, received from God, ultimately binds them together, as it helps man to attain human personality within a social organism.

The life of society is similar to that of the human body: "For the body does not consist of one member but of many" (1 Corinthians 12:14). This multiplicity of members is at the same time a sign of their diversity, which is so essential that, without those differences, social life would be unthinkable. "If all were a single organ, where would the body be? As it is, there are many parts, yet one body" (1 Corinthians 12:19–20).

Just as is the case with the human body, God's activity likewise takes place in the social organism, which for the good of the whole gives a distinct role and purpose to each part: "But as it is, God arranged the organs in the body, each one of them, as He chose" (1 Corinthians 12:18). God directs man's life in such a way that He puts everyone in place, giving him distinct tasks in temporal life, which are intended to facilitate striving towards man's ultimate aim. The so-called social position is a vocation, the voice of God who created every person "as He wanted."

It is instructive that everyday experience shows that individual parts of the human body are always ready to sacrifice themselves in order to preserve the whole; when the head is threatened, the arm instinctively strives to assist it, because the individual's life depends on that arm. A good citizen endangers his life in order to protect a threatened common good. The reason for this is simple. What is an arm without a head and a citizen without the society of which he is a part? "The eye cannot say to the hand, 'I have no need of you,' nor again the head to the feet, 'I have no need of you'" (1 Corinthians 12:21). God wanted "that the members may have the same care for one another" (1 Corinthians 12:25).

Although all have the same God and Lord, there are different kinds of service and different affairs (1 Corinthians 12:5–6). God distributes both the speech of wisdom and various gifts; God gives one person five talents, and another only one. God gives every person however many talents He wants! Everything in His activity is purposeful; everything entails duties and growing responsibility so that we can give back five different talents from the five we were given, and that good grain gives a hundred-fold harvest.

Through His Son, God has said to the world: "You are the salt of the earth" (Matthew 5:13) and demanded that the salt not lose its taste. He also said: "You are the light of the world" (Matthew 5:14) and demanded: "Let your light so shine before men, that they may see your good works and give glory to your Father who is in heaven" (Matthew 5:16). Thus, it must be seen that the salt not lose its taste, but instead adds flavor to the world, while the "light" must follow the admonition: "Therefore, be careful lest the light in you be darkness" (Luke 11:35–36).

Just as the human body consists of not only just legs and arms, as it needs a head in order to live; likewise, in the social organism, the head is of leading importance that is so crucial that it is easier for a body to fulfill its duties without arms or legs than without its head. This is that light of the social world, that salt that is sometimes sprinkled on the social organism. Just as God has venerated various body parts by determining their usefulness depending on their purpose; likewise, in the social organism, veneration and grandeur follow social usefulness. Christ the Lord has clearly emphasized: "A city set on a hill cannot be hid" (Matthew 5:14). Since lightness illuminates, it is not for it to be hid under a bushel; since it is placed on a candelabrum, it is obvious that it is intended to bring "light to all in the house" (Matthew 5:15).

This admonition is bound to the summons to honor God: "that they may see your good works and give glory to your Father who is in heaven" (Matthew 5:16). The good Father ordered the world in such a way that a glimmer always touches those who perform their works well from the glory God deserves. Thus, a grateful society shows respect to its elite when it sees its good deeds; it rejoices upon its good works, respecting and elevating them above all those who are in the house.

Therefore, God's command to be the salt of the earth and the light of the world corresponds to social hierarchies. It is imperative to not lose sight of these duties that follow this exhortation; unfortunately, we often forget that bearing the proud name of the intelligentsia entails personal and social obligations. Interchangeable justice demands that those who have received more from God and society, those who have been elevated and placed upon the candelabrum, should give more to God and society. This justice requires that we be healthy salt in order to shed pure light and build using good works.

"Like living stones, be yourselves built into a spiritual house, to be a holy priesthood, to offer spiritual sacrifices acceptable to God through Jesus Christ" (1 Peter 2:5) was given. Here, it is fitting to cite words that are frequently applied to the Catholic elites, who are called to cooperate with the Church hierarchy: "But you are a chosen race, a royal priesthood, a holy nation, God's own people, that you may declare the wonderful deeds of Him who called you out of darkness into His marvelous light" (1 Peter 2:9–10).

The most important duty is to praise God, Who has elevated us towards Him regardless of our personal merits, only because He wanted it that way and chose us so that we would be a vessel for glory (2 Timothy 2:20). We were mere clay in the hands of God the potter; how can we be boastful and proud before Him? Furthermore, knowing our insufficiency and the magnitude of our expectations we should accept the demand to acquire all virtues in order to become elevated to perfection "so that no fault may be found with our ministry" (2 Corinthians 6:3) as our righteous duty. It is only "from the fullness of the heart" that the mouth can speak and tell of God's justice; only then will it fulfill the demand: "As each has received a gift, employ it for one another, as good stewards of God's varied grace" (1 Peter 4:10).

The higher one's social position, the greater the duty to become living stones in the spiritual home of one's soul (1 Peter 2:5). Christ's

Parable of the Talents is an instructive example. Those who have received five talents are expected not only to give them back to their Host, but also to bring back another five, while those who have received two are expected to bring back another two. The useless servant who has hidden his talent from the Lord in the ground will be thrown into external darkness. God sows where He did not reap and harvests where grain has not been scattered (see Matthew 25:14–30). The same applies to social life: those who have received more and have been elevated more and those who have been called to leadership must give more, elevate themselves higher, and control themselves. These talents are indefinite: "For this very reason, make every effort to supplement your faith with virtue, and virtue with knowledge, and knowledge with self-control, and self-control with steadfastness, and steadfastness with godliness, and godliness with brotherly affection, and brotherly affection with love" (2 Peter 1:5–7). This will follow infinitely up to sanctity! God has the right to receive His hundred-fold harvest.

A hierarchy of service follows from the hierarchy of exaltation. Just as salt is to serve the earth and light is to serve those who are at home; likewise, "whoever would be great among you must be your servant, and whoever would be first among you must be your slave" (Matthew 20:26–27). Social exaltation entails being destined to serve society. By washing the feet of His disciples, Christ, our Lord and Teacher, gave the example "that you also should do as I have done to you" (John 13:15–16). Through this gesture, Jesus revolutionized the hitherto binding views, so that, "You know that those who are supposed to rule over the Gentiles lord it over them, and their great men exercise authority over them" (Mark 10:42). From that point, everything will be different: "Even as the Son of Man came not to be served but to serve, and to give His life as a ransom for many" (Matthew 20:28). This is how the socially exalted are called to serve their neighbor.

What is the value of light that does not illuminate the darkness? What is the worth of the life of an elite that lives only for itself? The new social order is enclosed in the following words: "Bear one another's burdens, and so fulfill the law of Christ" (Galatians 6:2).

II. When the Salt Loses Its Taste

"You are the salt of the earth; but if salt has lost its taste, how shall its saltness be restored? It is no longer good for anything except to be thrown out and trodden underfoot by men" (Matthew 5:13). Nobody has described the salt of society that has lost its taste more bluntly. In these words, Christ the Lord has described the history of numerous social revolutions and revolts in which the salt has lost its taste and is trampled upon by people.

Social life must have its own salt; if a soulless and withered intelligentsia does not play this role, then it must abdicate. The laws of sociology demand that their place is taken by someone else, because society must continue living.

We are witnesses to the struggle for a new face of the intelligentsia, for a new elite. The great social revolutions of recent history, white and red alike, have rejected old models in order to impose upon us a new kind of social elite. Until recently, the aristocratic, wealthy elites, those "messengers of materialistic racism," were dominant. Such people were of noble birth, but they typically lived shabby lives, entering life through the open gates of their money and family crest, without any personal effort, not knowing the importance and value of labor and incapable of overcoming themselves and the world. The curse of gold, the mysterious power of wealth, and the pleasures of this earth have had such a tragic impact on this group. They depleted their strength and overpowered them so much that they were incapable of making heroic sacrifices amidst social changes, wasting away in animal-like fear.

"For this people's heart has grown dull, and their ears are heavy of hearing, and their eyes they have closed, lest they should perceive with their eyes, and hear with their ears, and understand with their heart, and turn for me to heal them" (Matthew 13:15). Their glory comes entirely from their wealth: "But he that is glorified in poverty, how much more in wealth? And he that is glorified in wealth, let him fear poverty" (Sirach 10:34), because he will lose his social status upon losing his wealth.

Scientific progress has pushed a different kind of elite to the forefront: illustrious scientists who have much knowledge, but often do not know how to live; people whose adulation of reason has led them to completely destroy their will. Outstanding experts who are focused on the narrow fragment of life they study, but do not perceive the deeper meaning of the world and its ultimate meaning have come from this milieu. This is also salt that has lost its taste. We can tell them what the angel of the Laodicean Church heard: "I know your works [...]. For you say, I am rich, I have prospered, and I need nothing, not knowing that you are wretched, pitiable, poor, blind, and naked" (Revelation 3:15, 17).

The communist myth has introduced the working elites into its world, the heroes of effort and production pioneers, proclaiming them to be the giants of the future and the creators of a new culture, morality, and religion. This is the most narrow-minded kind of elite: they bravely control their hammers, tractors, and machinery, but they are incapable of gaining control over their own souls. The young Bolshevik generation has revealed itself to the world as "the ugliness of devastation."

Here and there, there is a political elite, the salt of the ruling party, and the crib elite that "for a piece of bread [...] will do wrong" (Proverbs 28:21), and pretend to be either scoundrels or angels of light depending on what winds blow. These people have numerous talents, but in essence, they are dilettantes who flaunt the venal price of their worth. Those who graze alone are "waterless clouds, carried along by winds; fruitless trees in late autumn, twice dead, uprooted [...] wandering stars for whom the nether gloom of darkness has been reserved forever" (Jude 1:12–13).

There is one more kind: the pagan elites, well-bred people of "pure blood" who have been brought up in the national kennel of state breeding facilities. They elevate the pride of the body to the altar of service to society, while they proclaim purebred animals in the human body that are well-fed, athletic, and endowed with the full laws of the state, thanks to the virtues of their body and blood as a deity. They do not want to know that Christ the Lord has redeemed everyone, regardless of the virtues of their blood or race, through His Blood, and that God's likeness is reflected in the soul of every person, hence their great value. Man's majesty wholly results from his spirituality, not from the test tubes of laboratory experiments; the ideal of the pure body being a temple of a filthy soul is the reborn Phariseeism of uncleansed hearts.

The struggle for a new face of the intelligentsia is taking place in our homeland. The Church considers such new models to be worthless to social life; it has a ready evaluation of them in the following words from the Gospel: "Every plant which My heavenly Father has not planted will be rooted up" (Matthew 15:13); "You will know them by their fruits. Are grapes gathered from thorns, or figs from thistles?" (Matthew 7:16). Thorns and thistles are useful only to be thrown into the fire; they are the new man of Bolshevism and racism, just like the new man that was born in the previous century. "Every sound tree bears good fruit, but the bad tree bears evil fruit" (Matthew 7:17); meanwhile, "the good man out of his good treasure brings forth good, and the evil man out of his evil treasure brings forth evil" (Matthew 12:35). The material and political-partisan elite, as well as that of blood and race or that which sets records of physical labor and is deprived of all religious and moral values "are blind guides" (Matthew 15:14). "Can a blind man lead a blind man? Will they not both fall into a pit?" (Luke 6:39).

It is a great misfortune for the nation if its leaders, who are called to carry their people's burden, themselves are led by their selfish interests. Are they not capable of adding salt to their maternal soil? "They have healed the wound of My people lightly, saying, 'Peace, peace,' when there is no peace" (Jeremiah 8:11). That is the moment when catastrophe comes. The people follow the desires of their wandering stars until they all fall into a pit together.

There have been cases in the history of Israel when God punished entire nations for the faults of their leaders. God punished not only the house of Jeroboam for his crimes, but the entire people: "And He will give Israel up because of the sins of Jeroboam, which he sinned and which he made Israel to sin. [...] The Lord will smite Israel, as a reed is shaken in the water, and root up Israel out of this good land which He gave to their fathers and scatter them beyond the Euphrates" (1 Kings 14:16, 15). "The Lord sent against [Manasseh] bands of the Chaldeans, and bands of the Syrians, and bands of the Moabites" (2 Kings 24:2), although Josiah, Manasseh's successor, renewed his covenant with the Lord (2 Kings 23:3). Nebuchadnezzar, the king of Babylon, took away "all Jerusalem, and all the princes, and all the mighty men of valor" into slavery; thus, no one was left in Jerusalem "except the poorest people of the land" (2 Kings 24:14), so that they could be vinedressers and plowmen (2 Kings 25:12).

God stands up for His people, whom He wants to protect and liberate from those who cause scandal: "'Woe to the shepherds who destroy and scatter the sheep of my pasture!' says the Lord. [...] 'I will attend to you for your evil doings,' says the Lord. 'I will set shepherds over them who will care for them, and they shall fear no more, nor be dismayed, neither shall any be missing'" (Jeremiah 23:1, 2, 4).

Just as the Lord "will utterly consume the house of Jeroboam, as a man burns up dung until it is all gone" (1 Kings 14:10), He will throw out the salt that has lost its taste so that people trample on it. Justice arrives, through which God "slew the strongest of them, and laid low the picked men of Israel" (Psalm 78:31). "But if you will not hearken to me and will not do all these commandments [...] I will send faintness into their hearts [...] the sound of a driven leaf shall put them to flight [...]. I will break the pride of your power. I will make your heavens like iron and your earth like brass; and your strength shall be spent in vain [...]. And I will bring a sword upon you, that shall execute vengeance for the covenant [...] Ten women shall bake your bread in one oven and shall deliver your bread again by weight; and you shall eat and not be satisfied. [...] And I will devastate the land, so that your enemies who settle in it shall be astonished at it. [...] And you shall perish among the nations, and the land of your enemies shall eat you up" (Leviticus 26:14–38).

The salt has been trampled upon so many times in history. Great wars and revolutions take place, and entire segments of society die from the sword of hatred. A people who wants not so much your gold as a good example from you, not alms but the lifting up of their spirits arises; if you die, it will not be so much because of your wealth as because of your moral indignities and violating God's command: "You are the salt of the earth."

III. Adding Salt to the Maternal Soil

In order for the salted soil to not lose its taste, the holy Church makes harsh but necessary demands of every person. Above all, she instills within us the conviction that working to improve ourselves is of great social importance. We should reject the superstition that the private life of every person is of solely personal significance. There is no such thing as the private life of a person; he forms a whole with the rest of the world, influencing his surroundings, even unwillingly, and this influence can be either good or bad. The enormous impact of the individual on the history of societies and nations in the spheres of thoughts, words, and actions is undeniable. The force of good, which is granted to others, scatters all around itself. The good Lord must share His happiness with others, while the Good News, threatened by St. Paul's "woe to you", must be preached.

St. John Chrysostom explains that mild, modest, merciful, and just persons cannot keep these virtues to themselves, as their impact brings benefits to their entire surroundings. Thus, those that are pure of heart and lovers of peace, those that endure persecutions for the truth lead their lives in a way that brings benefits to the good of society (Homily 15 on Matthew). "The good man out of his good treasure brings forth good, and the evil man out of his evil treasure brings forth evil" (Matthew 12:35), "for out of the abundance of the heart his mouth speaks" (Luke 6:45).

The richer a citizen's soul, the richer the society in which he lives. A nation composed of courageous people is brave, while a nation of cowards is craven. Adam Mickiewicz encompassed this truth in his famous axiom: "However much you expand and improve your souls, the more you will improve your rights and expand your frontiers."

No less known is the terrible power and solidarity of evil, even if it were to come from one person, from one of his thoughts or one of his books. The most private, secret license violates the social value of the unit and has social consequences. "So have no fear of them; for nothing is covered that will not be revealed, or hidden that will not be known" (Matthew 10:26).

People are bound to society through thousands of ties by a kind of solidarity, both in good and in evil; they do not have the power to limit the impact of their actions to their own use. In their cohabitation with their family and neighbors, in their professional, social, and political lives, their righteousness will rise up to the olive tree-covered peak. The mystery of a man's glance, his hidden thoughts, and his facial expression will be revealing, for "the heart of a man changeth his countenance, either for good, or for evil" (Sirach 13:31). "You brood of vipers! How can you speak good when you are evil? For out of the abundance of the heart the mouth speaks" (Matthew 12:34).

This gives birth not only to a personal admonition that binds our souls to God, but also a social admonition to work on ourselves internally. Only a decadent society can respond with passivity to souls that give birth to thorns and thistles. A society that has the will to live must for its own good make sure that every patch in the fatherland is well-tended and yield a hundred-fold harvest. A young talent that is led astray is such a painful loss for the nation. Such a talent was to be great, the salt of the earth, its joy and pride; it was supposed to blossom into a tree from which bluebirds would be nourished from generation to generation, but it turned out to be so small. This is a pain among pains! This responsibility grows in the souls of those who lead their nation. The fatherland, a good mother, has surrounded us with splendor and gravity. So many have risen up from the lower ranks of society and can say that, like David, they are summoned from the sheep, yet today they are so magnificent and powerful! The majesty of the Republic cannot shroud an internal void. Even if our breasts are decorated with the ribbons of all orders and golden braids, this will not save you! You must not make it possible for others to say of you: "So you also outwardly appear righteous to men, but within you are full of hypocrisy and iniquity" (Matthew 23:28). So that those of you who are first today will not be the last, you must elevate yourselves in order to bring good fruits and illuminate others that live alongside you in Poland, our common home.

The second command is to gain victory within ourselves; only then will victory in the nation be possible. We cannot strive for the elevation of the nation when there is a void in our souls. We should above all ask ourselves: are we capable of carrying the burden of the nation? How do I bring the light to those that are in our maternal home? The Apostle to the Nations has given us a command regarding the salt of the earth: "That the man of God may be complete, equipped for every good work" (2 Timothy 3:17). And there is a second one: "Finally, brethren, whatever is true, whatever is honorable, whatever is just, whatever is pure, whatever is lovely, whatever is gracious, if there is any excellence, if there is anything worthy of praise, think about these things" (Philippians 4:8). "Finally, be strong in the Lord and in the strength of His might" (Ephesians 6:10), "for not by might shall a man prevail" (1 Kings 2:9).

Social exaltation cannot be tantamount to the slogan: now my soul can eat and drink (see Luke 12:19), but it must be an initiative for greater self-denial and struggle against oneself not only for one's own good, but for that of society as well. The Book of Proverbs admonishes those who are leaders of the people: "It is not for kings to drink wine [...]. Give strong drink to him who is perishing and wine to those in bitter distress" (Proverbs 31:4–6). Thus, we have to arouse within ourselves the will to conquer ourselves, the will to create within ourselves the power of the spirit and of courage, through God's grace, in order to struggle with ourselves so that we can give our fatherland strong people, "the new people of a tribe that has not yet been seen... a tribe strong in faith and armed with love" (Eugeniusz Małaczewski)[1].

Only when the grain of wheat falls into the soil and dies will it bear great fruit (see John 12:24). Let it be our internal commandment, a commandment of righteousness towards those who we are to illuminate, so that we would "not be left to ourselves" and our desires, but that we would die for our good land, our beloved fatherland and society and yield a hundred-fold harvest (Matthew 13:8).

The strength that is drawn from faith will increase our social usefulness, and one day history will remember us in the chronicles of our nation, just as they have written down Gideon, Jephthah, David, Samuel, and the prophets "who through faith conquered kingdoms, enforced justice, received promises, stopped the mouths of lions, quenched raging fire, escaped the edge of the sword, won strength out of weakness, became mighty in war, put foreign armies to flight" (Hebrews 11:33–34). The power of your spirit will allow you to be above many without violence or the sword. You will lead the people of this earth towards a powerful Poland along completely new paths; you will build a powerful Poland, not merely write and speak about it!

---

1 Eugeniusz Małaczewski (1897–1922) was a colonel in the Polish Army who participated in the Polish Bolshevik War of 1919–1921 and was the author of novels and poetry.

I will ask myself: what benefits come from my life? What will I leave behind me? That depends on me! I will build up great powers within me and place a great desire "in Him who strengthens me" (Philippians 4:13). I am a Christian; and therefore, nothing is foreign to me! Everything comes from the hands of the heavenly Father, and everything is given to me. Everything is mine, because I belong to Christ, just as the whole world is His. My life's program is: "Test everything; hold fast what is good" (I Thessalonians 5:21). Everything that comes from God's hands must lead towards God! I will convert my faith into good works. "If a brother or sister is ill-clad and in lack of daily food, and one of you says to them, 'Go in peace, be warmed and filled,' without giving them the things needed for the body, what does it profit? So faith by itself, if it has no works, is dead" (James 2:15–16). Who better understands God's thought in the world than those who believe Him? "For it is God's will that by doing right you should put to silence the ignorance of foolish men" (1 Peter 2:15). Go, therefore, everywhere, doing good for all!

"Be fruitful and multiply, and fill the earth and subdue it" (Genesis 1:28). This includes our Polish land! You cannot leave the place that Providence has designated for us. Let us arouse within our souls the will to tenaciously struggle for God's kingdom on earth, for our fatherland's fidelity to our God.

"Therefore, encourage one another and build one another up, just as you are doing" (1 Thessalonians 5:11). Let us arouse within ourselves the will to elevate our brethren. Let us struggle against spiritual mediocrity and its children: selfish fear, compliance, pettiness, duplicity, and averageness. Let us be sowers of the good seed and the light and salt of the earth. Let us share our spirit: "Wisdom that is hid, and treasure that is not seen: what profit is there in them both? Better is he that hideth his folly than the man that hideth his wisdom" (Sirach 20:32–33). Let us have the will to help others, following the example of St. Paul, who wanted to remain in the body only because it "is more necessary on your account" (Philippians 1:24).

"Do not quench the Spirit" (1 Thessalonians 5:19). Let us create a chosen race, "God's own people" (1 Peter 2:9) for our fatherland; let us bring up those that love God's truth and are ready for all sorts of toil, sacrifice, and struggle, and who are faithful and devoted.

Let us want to populate Poland with powerful spiritual leaders and saints, as sanctity certainly is masculine, powerful, and brave, and it knows neither obstacles nor concessions. Is this pride? Perhaps it is in the eyes of Satan, whose kingdom we want to fight off. But it is not so in the eyes of God, Who has commanded: "Be holy" (Leviticus 11:44). Blessed is the land where each of its rulers will draw inspiration from the spirit of Jadwiga; every knight, from the power of Czarniecki, Kordecki, and Żółkiewski; every priest, from the spirit of St. Stanislaus, Bishop and Martyr; and Andrew Bobola; every citizen, from the homilies of Skarga; every scholar, from the wisdom of St. John Cantius; and every youth, from Casimir. Let us kindle the great fire of holy greed; let us gather the fruits of the spirit in order to overcome the power of darkness. Blessed are the eyes that will see this!

* * *

When fleeing from Jezebel's vengeance for having beaten Baal's prophets, Elijah went to Beersheba. On his second day there, he sat underneath a broom tree and demanded of his soul that it dies: "Enough! Now, Lord, take my life, for I am no better than my fathers" (1 Kings 19:4). We take part in such a state of the spirit when we stand before the enormous social duties and responsibilities in our sense of powerlessness. And when Elijah sleeps, God acts! As for a prophet in the wilderness, God will likewise send us nourishment and a jug of water. Then, there is the commandment: "Arise and eat, else the journey will be too great for you" (1 Kings 19:7).

In our journey on the road of destinies and duties up to God's hill, the Lord, who is our strength and the torch that illuminates our way, supports us. "Finally, be strong in the Lord and in the strength of His might. Put on the whole armor of God, that you may be able to stand against the wiles of the devil. [...] And therefore, having girded your loins with truth, and having put on the breastplate of righteousness, and having shod your feet with the equipment of the gospel of peace" (Ephesians 6:10–15).

9

The Real Liberation of the Working Class

*"Let the mountains bear prosperity for the people,
and the hills, in righteousness!" (Psalm 72:3).*

THE WORLD OF THE "WISE OF THIS EARTH" became filled with astonishment, anxiety, and distrust when Pope Pius XI called for the fulfillment of the most important socio-economic task: the liberation of the working class. How could this be? Is the Church of one mind with those who set the world aflame by calling: "Workers of the world, unite"? Has the Church been deluded by the illusion of the proletarian state and its dubious achievements? Who now will be the anchor of social harmony and order?

Why are you who are fearful and whose faith is small and think evil thoughts in your hearts surprised? The first liberation of the proletariat took place through Christ the Lord; indeed, the Church has been doing this for twenty centuries by preaching the Gospels to the poor. Does it not have the right to ask for "its legacy," as neither the international proletarian movement nor the proletarian state have the strength that is necessary to liberate the working class? Furthermore, they do not want to liberate it, as they consider the existence of the working class to be something indispensable and useful to themselves.

As a constant phenomenon that is inextricably tied to contemporary socio-economic life, it has been appearing in recent decades to an increasingly serious degree alongside pauperism, the impoverishment of entire layers of the working class, or so-called proletarism. Its essential trait is the uncertainty of living conditions that has been caused by the lack of property for all; the only value they have is a capacity to work, which a worker cannot make use of if there is no employer who would be willing to give him the opportunity to earn a wage. Having the will but not the opportunity to work, or having work that does not allow one to maintain an existence that is deserving of a creature of God, man is prone to the destructive influences of destitution, which lead not only to material poverty, but also to moral proletarism.

It is telling that apart from an insignificant improvement of its lot, the working class has also increased in size in today's world. Pius XI discusses this in his encyclical *Quadragesimo anno:* "But since manufacturing and industry have so rapidly pervaded and occupied countless regions, not only in the countries called new, but also in the realms of the Far East that have been civilized from antiquity, the number of the non-owning working poor has increased enormously and their groans cry to God from the earth" (QA, 59). Their ranks continue to swell: "Added to them is the huge army of rural wage workers, pushed to the lowest level of existence and deprived of all hope of ever acquiring 'some property in land,' and, therefore, permanently bound to the status of non-owning worker unless suitable and effective remedies are applied" (*ibid*).

The Church considers the existence of increasingly numerous regiments of people at a proletarian level of existence as well as the proletarization of ever-growing segments of society to be a harmful phenomenon in every respect: public, social, national, economic, moral, and religious.

I. The Catholic Sursum Corda

Those err who quote the Gospel passage: "For you always have the poor with you" (Matthew 26:11) to justify idleness and passivity in the struggle against proletarism. Indeed, the poor will exist in this world until it ends, and they have a necessary social role. However, this does not mean that there must exist countless people who are insecure about their existence and are dependent on the whims of speculation and exploitation resulting from badly organized socio-economic life. Also wrong are those who organize the working class, telling it that it is condemned to an eternal proletarian existence and that it must gain power and create its own proletarian state through a bloody revolution. They are the sowers of proletarian revolution who annihilate within people the will for social progress and leave them without hope for a better tomorrow.

The Church has never accepted proletarism; she has never claimed that there must exist a layer of people who are condemned to a proletarian existence. On the contrary, the Church has considered lifting man up from proletarian existence to be her most urgent task. The entire work of

Christ the Lord and His Church consists of lifting up and exalting man. Although the Church's mission is not primarily economic, through her teaching, she demands efforts to accomplish the de-proletarization of the person, just as she accomplishes the de-proletarization of his soul.

Many years ago, the division between slaves and free men was so stark that no one could bridge this chasm. This was considered to be completely natural that an entire class of people lived at the same level as animals. Meanwhile, Christ came to our world in a stable, which He changed into a temple, while an animal knelt before His humanity in order to elevate man above animal. Man discovers that he is redeemed through "the precious blood of Christ, like that of a lamb without blemish or spot" (1 Peter 1:19), Who cleansed our souls "by your obedience to the truth for a sincere love of the brethren" (1 Peter 1:22). Having become brothers in Christ's blood, we become "heirs of God and fellow heirs with Christ" (Romans 8:17), almost "gods"; we are no longer slaves, but free.

The understanding that had once been given to Peter is born in the human heart: "God has shown me that I should not call any man common or unclean" (Acts 10:28). When Cornelius falls to his feet before him, Peter lifts him up and says: "Stand up; I too am a man" (Acts 10:26). Both, however, humble themselves before God. This is a redemptive example that initiates a new era in relations between people. No man will kneel before his brother, nor will any servant kneel before his master; there will no longer be any violence, oppression, rape, or the humiliation of some and elevation of others; we are the children of the Father who "executes justice for the fatherless and the widow, and loves the sojourner, giving him food and clothing" (Deuteronomy 10:18).

For Peter, it is a joyous illumination and nearly a revelation that "God shows no partiality, but in every nation anyone who fears Him and does what is right is acceptable to Him" (Acts 10:34–35). This discovery will revoke the archaic division between the rich and poor in order to establish a new divine measure of the gift of faith. James' speech is significant: "My brethren, show no partiality as you hold the faith of our Lord Jesus Christ, the Lord of glory. For if a man with gold rings and in fine clothing comes into your assembly, and a poor man in shabby clothing also comes in, and you pay attention to the one who wears the fine clothing and say, 'Have a seat here, please,' while you say to the poor man, 'Stand there,' or, 'Sit at my feet,' have you not made distinctions among yourselves, and become judges with evil thoughts? Listen, my beloved brethren. Has not God chosen those who are poor in the world to be rich in faith and heirs of the kingdom which He has promised to those who love Him?" (James 2:1–6).

Thus, there are no differences between those who believe in our Lord; there is no exaltation because of one's purse, ring, or shawl. There is no potential proletariat here, because what St. Paul said to Peter is binding: "Love one another earnestly from the heart" (1 Peter 1:22). Man cannot lead a life unworthy of a rational being, as Christ has "called you out of darkness into His marvelous light" (1 Peter 2:9). A person can choose voluntary poverty, but it is unacceptable that socio-economic conditions condemn millions of people to an existence that makes it impossible to strive for Christian perfection, for sanctity. Both man's noble vocation and his ultimate aim, as well as the great dignity of the human person, who is destined for the freedom of God's sons, cannot be reconciled with the atmosphere the proletarian movement has created. In order to be capable of fully exploiting all the riches of his soul, man should make use of those resources that God's benevolent Providence has prepared for us as assistance in our temporal existence.

If the socio-political system deprives man of these most basic resources, it is unjust and incompatible with God's plan. An economic system that forces man to constantly violate God's law in order to obtain the most basic resources that are necessary for life, one that pushes man farther from God rather than bringing him closer to Him and changes the whole world into the arena of a hateful struggle for a piece of daily bread cannot be consistent with God's intentions.

Thus, every Catholic is obliged to love his neighbor and make contributions to liberate the working class from its difficult socio-economic situation; this is the greatest responsibility. Leo XIII writes that those that neglect it through their recklessness with respect to themselves and the state are sinners, "[f]or no one lives only for his personal advantage in a community; he lives for the common good as well, so that, when others cannot contribute their share for the general good, those who can do so are obliged to make up the deficiency" (*Graves de communi re*, 19).

Every person has the responsibility to collaborate with others for the common good. Man cannot be limited to his personal goods, profits, and interests. By living and thriving in the human community, man gains goods and benefits from it; thus, he must feel obliged to give back to society. Hence, there is a duty to cultivate within oneself the virtue of social justice, or a disposition to make one's personal good compatible with the common good. If good requires this, man should even eagerly give up part of his personal goods in order to liberate his brethren from proletarian existence. By sacrificing his property, he acts not only for the common good and that of the exploited, but in that way, he preserves his personal good.

The same applies to moral life. The proletarian morality is a social failure whose corrosive impact extends to all areas of social life. Even the most morally exalted people suffer because of this. It is impossible to protect oneself and society; no one can stop this wave of proletarian sins in a way other than by effectively struggling against proletarism in its socio-economic origins. There is no other way to protect "public order, peace, and the tranquility of human society" (QA, 62).

The following admonition of St. Peter must rest at the basis of the liberation of the working class: "As each has received a gift, employ it for one another, as good stewards of God's varied grace" (1 Peter 4:10). The spirit of justice and Christian love as well as the awareness that we are the children of one Father and of our common mother, Poland; understanding their interconnectedness and social usefulness as well as the role of various goods and services that must contribute to our common good are the necessary conditions by which a real liberation of the working class can take place.

II. The Social Liberation of the Working Class

Today's striving for the social liberation of the working class is healthy in its general intentions, although much chaff has become mixed up with this good grain.

Significantly, religious-moral matters, or, rather, the struggle against the Christian religious world view, play a major role in the struggle of the working class for liberation. Both in cities and in the country, some have claimed that the liberation of the working class must begin with the liberation of man from the demands of religion; in other words, from an evident or hidden struggle against it. Intellectuals like the Journalist in Stanisław Wyspiański's *The Wedding* came to factories or to the country, and said in one breath:

> [L]et everything be swept away:
> those Polish fast-days to exalt
> the names of poets sanctified —
> rainbows of sentiment to vault
> the desert wastes of crucified;
> those folklore virgins wearing crowns —
> and all Beliefs along with them![1]

Socialist and communist programs have openly presented the struggle against the clergy as a prerequisite for the liberation of the working class. Although they spoke of "the clergy," in reality, they had the struggle against religion itself in mind. They undertook a major educational campaign that systematically saturated the soul with distrust and doubt that led the people to disbelief. They were more cautious in rural areas, where under the guise of liberating the people from hierarchical influences and the magnates, they corroded the basic truths of the holy faith and presented the entire history of the Church in false hues. We owe it to the deep faith of our common people that all these attempts were not met with major successes. Their efforts faced healthy instincts:

> But do not desecrate those shrines!
> They had to play their sacred part.
> No, do not desecrate those shrines:
> that's vile![2]

The struggle against religion is the "vilest" part of the liberation of the working class, because this cannot be accomplished without the assistance of religion and the principles of the Gospels. Who can say with any authority that human life cannot be subject to speculation, like cotton, grain, or oil; that man's rights and good are more important than the economic good, which must always serve people;

---

1   Translation from: Stanisław Wyspiański, *The Wedding*, trans. Noel Clark, London: Oberon Books, 1998, p. 84.
2   Ibid., p. 85

that the right to property cannot violate the laws of the soul but must instead serve it in its path to God? Did not the popes have this in mind when they bravely and boldly struggled for social justice and taught that the liberation of man cannot take place without invoking God's laws and the teaching of the Church?

The most important issue in the program of the liberation of the working class is its liberation from godlessness and the useless wasting of one's talents to struggle against God. Let the people know that "God's Mother, crowned, in royal attire, [sits] on Wawel Castle's throne."[3]

Social liberation also is greatly significant. The working people in cities and villages strive for civic exaltation and to gain respect for their human dignity. In particular, the country often speaks of the need to overcome the "spirit of serfdom" within itself and an independent kind of education that is conscious of its social duties, role, and class pride. Why is this odd? After all, it is the Church that has aroused within man the aspiration for constant elevation. The Church's entire dogmatic, moral, and social thought aims for the elevation of man's dignity to a sense of full freedom as sons of God. Furthermore, the Church considers depriving people of the right to dignity to be harmful, while Pius XI complains that large multitudes have turned away from the Church, as the Church denied them the respect they deserved.

Cultivating within people a spirit of independence is an aspiration that is worthy of support as long as man is aware that there is but one dependence from which we cannot liberate ourselves: a sense of dependence on God and His holy laws. If this sense will accompany human aspirations, independence will not only not be harmful, but it will also be desirable for personal, social, and national reasons. We cannot constantly nurture the fears that were castigated by the Headman in *The Wedding*: "Afraid we might kick up a fuss? / Behind our backs, you laugh at us."[4] For great forces could assuredly revive Poland's life if refined layers of the common folk entered into it:

"As I see things, you gentlefolk might not have been so taken in, if you'd not lost your will to win!"[5]

---

3 Ibid., p. 163
4 Ibid., p. 24
5 Ibid., p. 24

Cultivating a sense of professional and class pride, that of both the working class and the farmers, as well as healthy ambition and a sense of one's social role and the value of the services that are rendered also would be of great significance. The majesty and value of the people's humble work for the entire nation, the persistence of those silent plowmen and workers, as well as their modest demands and minor use of social prosperity, are fact. Making proper use of it is completely consistent with the assumption of the future class and trade-based system: binding those masses to the nation in the spirit of cooperation in solidarity with other layers of society; permeating them with the spirit of high professional morality would grant Poland the strongest basis for development.

Liberating the Polish working class from the hydra of Marxism is an urgent task; instead of illusory doctrines that are foreign to the Polish spirit, Poland needs a healthy education system. A Catholic nation that is internally bound together in one faith can easily attain agreement without the search for other sources of aid. We can accomplish the liberation of the working class of the city and the country through our own efforts inspired by Catholic social teaching, which is so full of light and the potential for rebirth.

With brave hands, armed with Christian love, and wise in justice, let us contribute our efforts to the plow of social liberation; in this way, we will also attain economic liberation!

III. The Economic Liberation of the Working Class

The Book of Proverbs contains the following request of God: "Give me neither poverty nor riches; feed me with the food that is needful for me, lest I be full, and deny Thee, and say, 'Who is the Lord?' or lest I be poor, and steal, and profane the name of my God" (Proverbs 30:8–9). Here, the concern for an honest relation to God is striking; serving God is foremost, irrespective of both poverty and wealth. Concerned about fidelity to God, the inspired author fears both wealth, which emboldens man, and extreme poverty, which typically leads to moral decline and rebellion. The satisfaction of needs corresponding to the demands of one's state and environment "according to my needs" is something of an ideal of economic balance in the life of the person.

The same thought is found in the Church's social teaching. The Church condemns neither wealth nor poverty; she considers full access to economic goods and a certain standard of living corresponding to moderate prosperity to be necessary for man's moral development. Such a state of economic development in which a maximally large number of people would be capable of leading "lives worthy of people" would be greatly desirable from the perspective of moral development. This thought is frequently emphasized in papal social encyclicals.

Catholic social teaching evaluates the order of socio-economic relations through its moral usefulness; and therefore, favors making private property accessible to all strata of society, which it sees as an effective and desirable means for ensuring a sense of full freedom in one's own trade, which has a major impact on the elevation of man's personal dignity and the overall moral level of society. Yet, absent other solutions, Catholic social teaching allows for a limited right of the state to redistribute wealth when excessively large concentrations lead to the growth of the rural proletariat, which becomes prone to poverty and is forced to move to the city, emigrate, or some other alternative that is harmful to the common good.

In order to counter uncertainty of the working-class man's life and in order to facilitate the exercise of his duties, the Church believes it is necessary to encourage ownership. "The law, therefore, should favor ownership, and its policy should be to induce as many as possible of the people to become owners. Many excellent results will follow from this; and, first of all, property will certainly become more equitably divided" (RN, 46–47).

Ownership among the working classes can be expanded by ensuring them a just wage, which, according to Leo XIII, would cover not only the frugal and morally upright worker's living costs, but would furthermore help him to acquire a modest estate. The mere possibility of obtaining savings and other modest property has a very positive impact on the worker's life, level-headedness, diligence, and family virtues through which man is freed from a sense of homelessness, loneliness, social alienation, existential uncertainty, etc. In this way, society should "aim for the dissemination of family benefits as well as increasing wages and limiting the time one spends working accordingly to the needs of the profitability of companies and the creative capacities of the worker" (*Declaration of the Social Council of the Primate of Poland*, 1937). Likewise, in order to eliminate uncertain living conditions, especially pertaining to the security of one's family home, it is necessary to: "endow the workers of huge production facilities with a parcel of land or at least allotted gardens", and end the system of barrack-like housing for workers instead of one or two-family homes with gardens when lodging facilities are provided by the employer (*Declaration of the Social Council of the Primate of Poland*).

Mere concern for ensuring the freedom and dignity of the working person is emphasized in the Catholic postulates concerning manorial service. "Independent workshops for agricultural workers currently consist of livestock premiums as well as annually allotted plots of land. There should be an effort to expand the above scope of one's own farm's servants within a certain structure and accordingly to the demands of the profitability of one's production facilities, while limiting the possibility of exchanging the right to one's own livestock premium for a different benefit" (*Declaration of the Social Council of the Primate of Poland*).

When implementing these guidelines, which due to the religious nature of the Church's teaching is contingent in details, we should bear in mind the truth that socio-economic life is not an ultimate goal in itself, but instead it is an intermediate means in man's striving for God. The Catholic employer will fully acknowledge the humanity of his employee, and in the spirit of Christian love, offer his hand to his brother in order to support him in his path towards God. United by a common faith, we will perform the deeds that result from it so that we are not met with the following reprimand: "If a brother or sister is ill-clad and in lack of daily food, and one of you says to them, 'Go in peace, be warmed and filled,' without giving them the things needed for the body, what does it profit?" (James 2:15–16). Let us strive not only for unity in faith, but also for the integration of our deeds. How often we shield our property from God's laws!

The unfailing performance of good deeds demands the sacrifice of part of one's personal property. The people of the Gadarenes were incapable of it, as Christ the Lord exorcised a legion of demons from the possessed and allowed them to occupy a herd of swine. When the herd threw itself into the sea and drowned, "all the city came out to meet Jesus; and when they saw him, they begged him to leave their neighborhood" (Matthew 8:34). And Jesus trod a different path.

Today, we want liberation, but we do not want to lose our "swine." Thus, Christ the Lord is dismissed from the factories, the gates of barns, and the limits of manors. Liberation from our times cannot take place without making sacrifices! Thus, it is better to lose swine than one's entire property, man, and . . . Christ.

* * *

Christ the Lord, Who knows the human soul and all its anxieties and unlimited desires, including the most secret ones, has seen man's struggle for his daily bread and his unflagging efforts to multiply the abundance of this earth. He gives us the following admonition, which we cannot forget in our struggle for the real liberation of the working class: "For what will it profit a man, if he gains the whole world and forfeits his life? Or what shall a man give in return for his life?" (Matthew 16:26). Indeed! What will it help man even if he had kept his entire estate for himself and multiplied it greatly; if he did not give a glass of cold water to his neighbor or even a spikelet, even though he had built up his homestead and built new factory chimneys? What will it help a worker even if he succeeded in taking over all the factories and all of industry, if he elevated his own political party above the interest of the state and his professional organizations above the good of other social classes? What good is it if he created a proletarian state and ruled the world through one more international, one more powerful than the others; if he walked to all the ends of the earth with a red flag and placed it on the tallest factory chimneys, cathedral towers, and even the proud peaks of the Tatra Mountains? What good is all this if it brought harm to his soul?

The real liberation of the working class took place on the Cross, and without this no liberation can take place in either social or economic life. Liberated with respect to class, society, or the economy, the member of the political party or union does not cease to be a person, husband, father, brother, or son; he is still burdened by the tasks and difficulties of human life and conscience. He still has to service not only his machine, but also his soul; he must learn how to direct not only his workplace and skillfully navigate the treacherous tangles of conveyor belts and the greedy mechanisms of factory wheels; he must deal with himself, order his own life, and struggle against his own passions, which he sees in others. The social injustice that outrages and depresses us is not only outside ourselves, but also within us; thus, we have to begin this struggle with ourselves. If this struggle does not end in victory, then we will waste the most wondrous fruits of socio-economic liberation.

There is a Life and Truth that infinitely transcends all of earthly life and social and economic truths; it infinitely transcends the entire world of the working class's aspirations and struggles. Christ, the one who justifies Himself before no one: before neither the factory owner nor the worker; the heir nor his servant; Who judges the living and the dead; whose passion redeemed the suffering of the whole world, walks across the earth. All must justify themselves before Him. Only then will a genuine and complete liberation of the working class take place.

Having liberated our hearts from godless hatred, let us arm them with the power of brotherly love and unite before our common Father in our humble prayer: "Give the king Thy justice, O God, and Thy righteousness to the royal son! May He judge Thy people with righteousness, and Thy poor with justice! Let the mountains bear prosperity for the people, and the hills, in righteousness!" (Psalm 72:1–4).

Liberated through Christ from the proletarian yoke, let us become participants in the great joy: "May all kings fall down before Him, all nations serve Him! For He delivers the needy when He calls, the poor and him who has no helper. He has pity on the weak and the needy and saves the lives of the needy. From oppression and violence, He redeems their life; and precious is their blood in His sight" (Psalm 72:11–15).

10
Catholic Education[1]

A NEW AGE WHEN MAN WILL LIVE IN THE fullness of his being is dawning. So far, he has led something like half a life: either a biological, materialistic existence, subjected to the yoke of money and profit, or stripped of his own aspirations and subjected to a different yoke, that of service to the state. Both lifestyles were erroneous. Only great saints were capable of successfully attaining the fullness of human life. In order to avoid repeating old mistakes, contemporary man must obtain a comprehensive education for benefit to himself, the nation, and society. Education must concern the entire human person; that is, it must encompass his personal and social nature.

1. Educating the Human Person

A good understanding of oneself must be the basis for every healthy upbringing of the person and making him capable of fulfilling the basic demands of life. Thus, we must be aware of who we are, our nature, and what we strive for.

As a being composed of both body and soul, I aim for closeness with God through the perfection of temporal life. Thus, I am destined for life both on earth and in heaven. I am destined for life on earth within the boundaries of earthly goals and for heaven within those of eternal unification with God. This means that I must be prepared for both heaven and earth. Thus, I must make my body capable of exercising its earthly duties through physical education, in order to avoid feebleness and decrepitude. I also have to perfect my spiritual faculties — my reason, will, and heart in order to perform those duties — through intellectual, spiritual, and religious education.

The belief that in the new system man must take second place only to God must play a leading role in educating the human person. Only

[1] This is an article that was initially published in *Ład Boży* ("The Divine Order") on October 28, 1945.

then will the person remember his great dignity and both worldly and ultimate destiny. A person educated in such a way will be saved from self-neglect and will be obliged to respect his neighbors and be prevented from abusing others.

2. Educating a Social Nature

The truth about man's social nature is the basis for this education. By God's will, man is a social being; his nature inclines him towards co-existence with other people. People feel a need for others and have a duty to co-exist alongside them. People must be prepared for such co-existence by fine-tuning a social nature inside them. This task can be accomplished in two ways: by rejecting egotism, which is contrary to social life, and by gaining social virtues.

The man who violates the rights of his neighbor when his real or imagined privileges come to the fore is egotistical. Every sinner is the most common kind of egotistical man, because nearly every sin violates the rights of other people. In social life, the selfish man is the one who evades social duties and responsibilities. In economic life, meanwhile, the selfish man is the one who is motivated by the capitalist spirit of profit. Every man is obliged to struggle against those bad tendencies and habits that make his surroundings hostile to him; he must cultivate the virtues that facilitate co-existence with others and make him or her useful to them.

Egotism that is not tempered can quickly become collective egotism. National education that does not recognize the right of other nations to freely develop their national qualities is egotistical. Equally egotistical is state-focused education that considers one's state in society to be privileged and superior to all others, denying other means of participation in social goods. Also egotistical is class education that professes the superiority of one's class over that of others to which only the language of class struggle can speak.

Social virtues must be acquired. We begin to refine them within ourselves by implementing Christ's principles: "A new commandment I give to you, that you love one another" (John 13:34). This is the guiding principle of socialization. Apart from Christ, nobody has given a more important principle for social co-existence. St. Paul the Apostle expressed this in words: "Let no one seek his own good, but the good of his neighbor" (see 1 Corinthians 10:24). We must reject constantly thinking only about ourselves, our benefits, personal comfort, profit, and security. Furthermore, every person has the duty to solidary work that multiplies good. Not good, but evil, must become our source of pride. We are obliged to work on ourselves in order to multiply good deeds and make them known. Thus, we must awaken within ourselves the will for personal moral progress in order to become more useful for society through our virtues, talents, and skills. Even our religious life must be aimed at not only personal happiness and peace of one's conscience, but also towards praise of God and benefit to society. Religiousness cannot be egotism. It is insufficient to protect oneself from evil; one must protect his neighbors from it as well.

In Poland, the will to do good to one's neighbor must be revived. We have to awaken within every citizen the need for a living relationship with his nation, state, and Church. We must develop a sense of social and professional community as well as responsibility for our personal actions throughout our entire lives.

These are the guiding thoughts in the new education of the person.

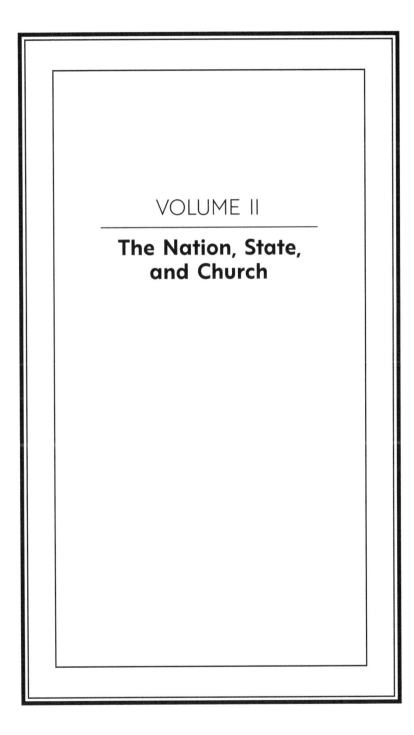

VOLUME II

The Nation, State, and Church

PART I

The Nation and the State

1

God and the Nations

"Let the peoples praise Thee, O God; let all
the peoples praise Thee!" (Psalm 67:5).

THE GOD AND LORD OF ALL CREATION IS THE Father of the nations. Why would the Creator of man and his soul not be the Father of the body and soul of the nations? After all, the nation is not a god! The nations are God's children; through their common Father, they are brothers! The family of the nations is called to a higher purpose, to praise its common God: "Praise the Lord, all nations! Extol Him, all peoples! For great is His steadfast love toward us; and the faithfulness of the Lord endures forever. Praise the Lord!" (Psalm 116:1–2). This is the constitution of the coexistence of the nations. The principles of Catholic nationalism flow from it.

Throughout the history of the Jewish nation, the model of God's providential care over the life of one nation was maintained. God gave such tender care to this nation because He had called it to fulfill particular tasks in the salvation history of humanity. Does salvation history, then, not repeat itself in the history of every nation that has been called to the light of faith in God? Thus, "Thy faithfulness endures to all generations; Thou hast established the earth, and it stands fast" (Psalm 119:90). That is why we can see a reflection of God's exceptional benevolence in the history of the Chosen People; it is infinitely repeated throughout human history and the history of every Christian nation.

I. God Protects His Nation

Let us refer to examples from the history of Israel. Beginning with Abraham, Isaac, and Jacob, we can follow the history of God's care for the Chosen People, whom He has endowed with wondrous gifts: "The Lord said to Abram [. . .] For all the land which you see I will give to you and to your descendants forever" (Genesis 13:14–15). God's care is truly moving. God sends Joseph to Egypt in order to save the entire nation during a time of famine. Once the voice of the oppressed calls from the land of the pharaohs several centuries later, God sends Moses and brings His people "out of the land of Egypt, out of the house of bondage" with a strong hand (Exodus 20:2). He leads His nation in the light of the fiery cloud and guides it unmolested across the Red Sea; He makes bitter waters sweet for them, feeds them manna in the wilderness, quenches its thirst with water from a rock, and breaks down the defensive walls of cities in order to lead them to the Promised Land. And yet, God instead hears the complaints of His people; despite His numerous miracles, He sees much distrust, a lack of faith, and rebelliousness: "Would that we had died in the land of Egypt!" (Numbers 14:2).

However, "The Lord is slow to anger, and abounding in steadfast love, forgiving iniquity and transgression" (Numbers 14:18), and did not neglect the Chosen People. Furthermore, God Himself has delineated the boundaries of the earth and became its defender, a foe of all His people's enemies and their succor whenever they are in need. The Lord's fiery right hand, which is fearful to all of Israel's enemies, stood at the borders of the earth. Woe to the nation that rises up against God's people! "Ah, the roar of nations, they roar like the roaring of mighty waters! The nations roar like the roaring of many waters, but He will rebuke them, and they will flee far away, chased like chaff on the mountains before the wind and whirling dust before the storm" (Isaiah 17:12–13).

Is it a mere coincidence that the history of God's struggle with His people for the right to love and good has gone on until today? Did Divine Providence care merely about historical accuracy? No! This is a testimony for future centuries and peoples in order for them to awaken faith and trust in the power of the King of the ages, the immortal Lord of the nations.

II. God Grants His People the Gift of the Earth

As in the history of the Chosen People, our fathers' journey to the Promised Land has been repeated. We can say the following about our nation: The Lord "made him ride on the high places of the earth, and he ate the produce of the field; and He made him suck honey out of the rock, and oil out of the flinty rock" (Deuteronomy 32:13).

Our fatherland is God's gift to our nation! In His work of creation, God anticipated this place to which the history of the Polish nation was to be bound. Will we not accept this gift with joyous hearts? How many times have we heard laments about our fatherland, which Providence has given to us! Just like the people of Israel once complained in the wilderness before seeing the land of Canaan; likewise, there are those in our fatherland today who claim that it is a land that devours its own inhabitants (Numbers 13:33). Let us respond with Joshua's words: "The land, which we passed through to spy it out, is an exceedingly good land. [. . .] Only, do not rebel against the Lord" (Numbers 14:7, 9).

God married our nation to its paternal land, setting aflame a zealous love for it in our hearts, a love in life and in death! What is the source of this nearly tragic love for the Polish soil? Why are those who leave it tormented by a yearning for it? Where does this intoxicating power that led them out of their houses across the sea for land come from? What is the source of this irrevocable marital bond between the nation and the soil of the fatherland? This has happened through the Lord! This love, which closely binds the human soul to our land, comes from God's will. Love for one's maternal land contains something of that powerful love of God, who created the world.

Consequently, there is the right to one's own land and fatherland. It was God's will that we live as a separate nation. It was not we who gave life to our nation; God wanted us to be a distinct nation and imbued us with the will and capacity of evolving into a nation. Thus, if we exist and live, we are of God's will. Since we have survived for so many centuries, God apparently wants us to be a distinct nation. Since we have created our own language and national culture, we have responded to God's designs. This gives us the greatest right to our existence, life, and freedom!

The history of our nation is bound together with the land that Providence has given to our forefathers. We have become bound to it through a feeling of love and God's gratitude for such a wonderful gift. This land is so closely tied to our souls that there is no force that would be capable of annihilating this bond. We have worked hard on this soil, which is made fertile thanks to the blood of many genera-tions; it has become our property through our enormous national work that is demonstrated by our historical monuments, which have taken root in its heart. We have expressed the entire nature of our national character on the face of this earth, so the Polish soil *res clamat ad Dominum.*[1] It calls to its lord, the Polish nation. However, it also calls the Lord Almighty, the King of Kings and Father of the nations every time it is pillaged by invaders. God's care over our land can never expire, which is why the Lord Almighty returned our land to our nation after a century and a half of slavery.

III. The Nation Prolongs Its Life in God

God not only gives land to the nations; He also populates it and brings up the nation in the spirit of God's service and conscientious-ness. God instructed the following: "Be fruitful and multiply, and fill the earth and subdue it" (Genesis 1:28). No nation that follows this instruction needs to fear about its future.

Following the voice of God, the Holy Church blesses Polish cra-dles and gives the nascent nation the right to refuge from the deadly current of human suicide. The Church blesses young hearts, binding together hands and souls so tightly through the power of the Holy Spirit that these bonds must last until death. "What therefore God has joined together, let not man put asunder" (Matthew 19:6).

Through this work of God, the Church provides a constant service to the nation, as she protects it from suicide. The Church resists selfishness and sloth; although God's laws, which it preaches, seem harsh to many, they are the only salvation of the nation. Every nation can say of itself: "If Thy law had not been my delight, I should have perished in my affliction" (Psalm 119:92).

IV. The Nations in God's Designs

The Lord Almighty and the Father of humanity "made from one every nation of men to live on all the face of the earth, having determined allotted periods and the boundaries of their habitation" (Acts 17:26).

---

1 Latin: "A thing calls for its owner."

God's history is present in every land. God's activity on the rich soil of the nation's natural properties is turned into new, usually completely different and rich, forms. Religious life and praise of God in our fatherland, which eagerly prays Vespers and *Gorzkie żale*[2] and seeks strength from Resurrection Masses and the child-like joy of the May devotions to the Blessed Virgin Mary, greatly differs from that in the history of the nation of St. Joan of Arc and St. Vincent de Paul or in the fatherland of St. John of the Cross, St. Teresa of Ávila, and St. Ignatius Loyola; and finally, in the history of the nation of St. Catherine of Siena, St. Gemma Galgani, and St. John Bosco.

All this happens in the body of one universal Church. No one will say that this does not multiply God's glory and usefulness to souls! What a wondrous international exchange of goods has grown on the fields of nations, on God's great field! How much poorer the religious life of every human soul would be if it did not have the ability to make use of these diverse gifts and resources that have been laboriously gathered by God's children from various nations. Indeed, "there are varieties of gifts, but the same Spirit; and there are varieties of service, but the same Lord; and there are varieties of working, but it is the same God who inspires them all in everyone" (1 Corinthians 12:4–6). And although there are various languages, all "are inspired by one and the same Spirit, who apportions to each one individually as He wills" (1 Corinthians 12:11). This is a kind of "communion of saints," the nations of the world.

We witness how various nations rise up and fall; how some grow ill while other persist in their strength. We witness how some spread disease around themselves while others effectively fight them off. When some persecute God's Church, which preaches the revealed Truth, others praise and take care of it. In this way, the Master's instruction is realized: "When they persecute you in one town, flee to the next" (Matthew 10:28). Meanwhile, God's messengers preserve and bring God's light to all the nations so that it is not extinguished until the end of the world.

---

2   Literally "bitter lamentations," *Gorzkie żale* are traditional Polish hymns on Christ's Passion that are sung after Sunday Masses during Lent. This devotion remains popular: according to a 2020 CBOS poll, 53 percent of Poles take part in *Gorzkie żale* devotions.

The Church of God is like the father who supports his numerous sons and daughters on his old shoulders; when one of them grows weak, another replaces it, thus enjoying the privilege of Simon of Cyrene, who helped the Redeemer of the world to carry His cross. In this way, the Church, who is supported by the nations and blesses their life, walks across history, bringing life-giving words to all the nations and peoples, tongues, and lands.

Let us take a look! Great failures in the form of false doctrines and the possession of one nation by the demon of pride and the lust of the eyes are making their way across the world. Cain revolted against Abel, just as the prodigal son did so against his good father! In that case, is not the only defense the plurality and diversity of nations? When one nation prepares the disease of Communism for the use of others, the borders of the nations are the "trenches of the Holy Trinity" that protect other nations "until iniquity passes." When one nation raises its pride against the thrones and altars of the entire world, the "remainder of the nations" gathers in order to end its license. It also sometimes happens that an arm or an eye is cut off from this human body in order for the entire body to survive.

V. Forces That Unite the Nations

Christianity has an uncanny capacity for bringing the nations closer together. Today, as the nations become increasingly pagan, the influences of nationalism, which is a centrifugal force, increase, thus breaking up the remains of the ancient Christian family of nations. Pagan nationalism has elevated the nation above the person. This leads to the overestimating of one's nation and self-adulation, the idolatrous worship of oneself, and, finally, the dictatorship of national egotism. With respect to other nations, this leads to a lack of objectivity, blindness, and the disappearance of all semblance of reality and a lack of respect for other nations, which leads to often-painful mistakes.

Everyone knows of the great misfortunes that nationalism brought upon not only the nations that were poisoned by their own arrogance, but upon the entire world. We can and must fight against this great evil of today's world! This can happen only in the face of the truth that all the nations come from God's hand and that the highest meaning of their existence brings them to God's feet. There is no other way to create a family community of the nations than by calling: "Sing to God, O kingdoms of the earth; sing praises to the Lord, to Him who rides in the heavens, the ancient heavens; lo, He sends forth His voice, His mighty voice. Ascribe power to God, whose majesty is over Israel, and His power is in the skies" (Psalm 68:32–34).

It is only in the face of God that we can understand that no nation or its history can be elevated above other nations with impunity; in the designs of ever-wise Divine Providence, each nation has its proper place and tasks that have been given to it that can in no way disturb the paths of others. Just as in every human community, there are mutual dependencies in the community of the nations as well. The source of the life of nations is outside of them. A nation owes its life not only to itself, but it lives thanks to the One Father of all nations, thanks to God's natural law, which is deposited in the human person; it lives thanks to morality and religion. Can it be the highest value in life? Can nationality be the gauge of one's morality?

Just as no nation exists through itself and by itself, no nation is capable of survival on its own, whether culturally, morally-religiously, or politically. Claiming that a nation can be completely independent, innate, and autonomous is utopian thinking! Today, this is most evident in the field of the international exchange of economic goods, where self-sufficiency has completely failed. Every nation is destined to be dependent on some other, as they complement each other and must follow the path of co-existence and serving one another. We especially see this in the sphere of culture. If you try to cleanse the Polish nation of the cultural influences of ancient Greece and Rome and erase the Italian Renaissance from its history, and deprive it of the background of Catholic thought, you will see that not only the Collegiate Church of Sts. Peter and Paul in Kruszwica, but also Wawel Cathedral's Chapel of Sts. Felix and Adaukt, Gniezno Cathedral, the Poznan City Hall, Sigismund's Column, and the Józef Poniatowski Monument will disappear; we will lose not only religious art and Polish hagiography, but with it Christian virtue, morality, and the very soul of the nation! There is no other way. "The stone which the builders rejected has become the head of the corner. This is the Lord's doing; it is marvelous in our eyes" (Psalm 118:22–23).

Today, in an age of such vibrant intellectual relations, the exchange of thoughts, and international conferences, if you protect the nation from the rest of the world, as happens in the Bolshevik and totalitarian states, you will cut it off from the living body of humanity, and thus from the source of life-giving blood. Just as everything leads to God in supernatural life, because "you are Christ's; and Christ is God's" (1 Corinthians 3:22); likewise, in cultural life, we arrive at the conclusion that we are the children of one Father.

Just as a nation cannot and should not separate itself from the contributions of others, it must keep its soul on guard in order to protect it from those destructive currents that flow from the heart of sick nations. This is completely understandable. Chesterton wrote that superhumans who are not good are monsters. The nation should care for its self-preservation, as its duty is to seek good. We have to seek the salvation of our citizens.

However, a nation cannot be concerned solely about its own existence and expansion, regardless if this be the path of self-development or that of rape and violence. According to Friedrich Wilhelm Foerster, "A nation that considers the preservation of its existence to be its highest goal is bound to die." If a nation does not want to die of internal weakness and moral decomposition, it must also care for the salvation of other nations, especially neighboring ones, for the kingdom of truth and morality, and follow all of God's laws. Contemporary nationalism, which rejects all these duties, must be considered the greatest evil for every nation.

When these truths stand before our eyes, we must refer to God's unifying force, to the heavenly Father who has brought us together in His bosom. How wonderful it is that "Thy kingdom is an everlasting kingdom, and Thy dominion endures throughout all generations" (Psalm 145:13).

* * *

The God Who chastens the nations (see Psalm 94:10), Who brings light to living beings, gives them a place and time in history and uses them to implement His wondrous, providential rule over the world. Today's pagan nationalism has failed to understand this wonderful plan of the Father of the nations. National selfishness preached that the nation is man's greatest good. It is in its name that a destructive struggle has been waged between the nations. Meanwhile, the Father of the nations transcends all nations; He directs them. Only God is the highest good. Only God presents to the nations their paths and tasks. How God looks after and cares for individual nations in the development of the history of the world has been evident from the most ancient times; in the history of Abraham of Ur of the Chaldeans through Egypt, Babylon, and Assyria, through Greece and Rome, up through the journey of the peoples who all realize God's plans and His fullness throughout the ages.

What is the future of these ways of the nations? None of the people of "this world" will comprehend God's ways! Only one faith gives us the strength "that Thy way may be known upon earth, Thy saving power among all nations" (Psalm 67:2). Nations that have been led into slavery by others do not fully know God's ways; Israel lamented over the rivers of Babylon, while the Pompeian prisoners of war wept while being led to Rome; the temples of pagan Rome fell apart as the Goths and Vandals arrived, not knowing that they would bring the beam of faith in Christ to Europe on the way back. Similarly, the Christian Crusaders did not predict that they would bring the new goods of civilization as a gift to Europe.

What seed does God today sow before the future history of the world when we ourselves are witnesses to contemporary migrations of the nations? No one knows this, only He, the Father of the nations! Faith, however, which trusts that God chastens the nations, alone gives us certainty that God can always bring good out of humanity's greatest misfortunes. The last word about the future of the world belongs to faith. Our greatest hopes and our confidence in the wise and wondrous economy of God's rule over the world all cumulate in the almighty hand of God's Providence. Such faith requires that we calmly sing the eternal hymn of humanity: "Let the peoples praise Thee, O God; let all the peoples praise Thee! Let the nations be glad and sing for joy, for Thou dost judge the peoples with equity and guide the nations upon earth. [. . .] God has blessed us; let all the ends of the earth fear Him!" (Psalm 67:3–7).

2
Service of the Fatherland

*"If I forget you, O Jerusalem, let my
right hand wither!" (Psalm 137:5).*

THE SONS OF ISRAEL PRAYED WITH SUCH
zealous promises over the waters of the rivers of Babylon where
they had been spending long days engulfed in sadness and mourn-
ing their yoke. They had hung their harps on willows; no one heard
their song. Although their mouths were silent, their hearts were filled
with yearning for Zion to which they ran for the glory and joy of their
nation and to which they were bound by the power of the promise:
"Let my tongue cleave to the roof of my mouth, if I do not remember
you, I do not set Jerusalem above my highest joy!" (Psalm 137:6–7).

Such promises are not alien to us, as we know the depths of the
source from which they spring: love for the poor maternal fatherland,
the joyful will of faithful service, and fixing past negligence that has
caused so many misfortunes: these are the feelings that brought life
to our hearts during the time of slavery. At that time, we learned of
everything we had done wrong; our eyes opened to see our great errors.
Now is the time to fulfill those promises; today is the best time to begin
our faithful service to our mother by fulfilling the zealous obligations
in our hearts that have been performed amidst tears.

When we are to begin our sacred service of our fatherland, we are
overwhelmed with fear that our hearts might grow cold too soon and
that our will might grow weak. Let us strengthen our hearts and will
through ardent prayers to our heavenly Father:

We implore you with our foreheads planted in the ground,
With our temples steeped in the warmth of Your spring-time breeze. . .
We implore you: create within us pure hearts,
Renew our senses and root out the corncockle from our souls as
    well as the blasphemous illusions — and give us eternal
good in addition to Your numerous other gifts — Give us good will!
       (Zygmunt Krasiński, "Psalm of Good Will")

I. Serving the Fatherland in Love

There is no great service without great love. Should we speak of love for our fatherland? It is true that we love our mother, but do we not love her more in word than in deed? Our love for our fatherland is too often expressed through tender hearts and tears in our eyes, but it is not expressed often enough through actions in everyday fidelity to our obligations and in our small but constant devotions and labors from which the common good of the nation arises.

1. The First Love: For One's Maternal Land

The first fruits of our love belong to our fatherland, which we have received from God in order to expand our life in it. Once again, does this even require mentioning? After all, everyone knows that the Poles ardently love their land. Who has not heard about our proverbial patriotism and our heroic sacrifices of our lives in defense of our nation? All this is true! Who among us will ever be capable of extinguishing within ourselves the memories of our fatherland, even if we spend all our lives outside it? If you ask our exiles who are abundantly blessed with bread, you will learn that their greatest ailment is their yearning for their fatherland and the unforgettable charm of their familiar landscapes, the quiet and beauty of the fields, and their maternal fertility.

Yet, we often complain about this gift from God, accusing God Himself: "Thou dost make us the scorn of our neighbors; and our enemies laugh among themselves. [...] Why then hast Thou broken down [the vineyard's] walls, so that all who pass along the way pluck its fruit?" (Psalm 80:6, 12). Do not too many among us fruitlessly complain about the indefensibility of our borders? Do not too many yearn for the Italian sky, the Swiss air, and French bread? Do we not too often envy others yet look down upon everything that is from our fatherland? In other words, do we not constantly think that the grass is greener on the other side? It seems to us that if God had granted us a different land, then we would have been happier, wealthier, better, and given more from ourselves to other nations.

Our first obligation is to temper our ingratitude and pettiness. God gave us porous borders, but He gave our fatherland brave hearts and courageous breasts that will be defenses as effective as mountain ranges. We have become so accustomed to open fields that the greatest national victories are tied to their infinite plains. God trusted us and thus did not hide our nation in an inaccessible corner of the earth, but in an open and visible place so that we would serve the nations through our example of courage and sacrifice so that everyone "may see your good works and give glory to your Father who is in heaven" (Matthew 5:16).

Our location demands of us arduous efforts on behalf of our fatherland; it demands blessed work that destroys within us sloth and complacency, which is so typical of other nations but is foreign to us. In our harsh climate, we have shaped our tough natures, perseverance, patience, and intransigence; when properly tamed, all these traits will multiply the new glory of our national virtues.

Do you complain of the poverty of our land? It is not the poorest land; after only a few years of patient work, it will provide enough bread to everyone in the house of their father. Let us look at the sad fate that has befallen many powerful nations in this world; in the prosperity of their fatherland, their souls have grown fat. In their comfort, they have lost not only their courage, but also love for their fatherland, falling behind their enemies. May no one say that prosperity is the greatest blessing of a nation and the aim of ruling it, because a nation is like man in that it does not live on bread alone; it does not live on its wealth and everyday satiation and the fullness of the safes in its banks alone, because the enemy empties those. A nation does not live on shares and dividends from businesses, speculation, and games in the stock market, or the increased productions of its factories working according to the purest "gospel" of economic liberalism alone. A nation living on a harsh rock can have a tougher spirit and be worthier and more powerful than a nation completely submerged in the goods of the earth.

Love for the fatherland requires us to populate our land and subdue it to ourselves. Above all, we must not lament that our mother is poor and clad in a shabby cloak, but instead persistently work so that God's resources and gifts, which have been placed in our hands through Providence, may bear fruit a hundred times over. Furthermore, we have a duty to willingly help our poor land by sacrificing part of our own property and our own abundance. Maybe it would be worth sacrificing our property for the good of the fatherland. Even if this great task were not demanded of us, let us at least perform the everyday tasks of voluntarily paying taxes to the state, protecting the common good, and respecting the property of the state. This is also a means of elevating the poorest land. When we add fidelity and dutifulness in our everyday labors in every position we are given, then our strength will grow three-fold in our strenuous work for our fatherland. How many wondrous virtues have their source here! Our poor land will repay us by enriching our souls.

Can a poor mother of wealthy sons that love her perish?

2. "Love One Another Socially"

Love for one's compatriots is the second commandment of serving one's fatherland. We can discern not only Christ's disciples, but also the sons of one mother through love for one's neighbor. Love for the fatherland is expanded love of one's neighbor. Love of one's neighbor is above all properly understood love of oneself. The greater my joy, the more happy people whose happiness I witness will surround me. Not the struggle against everyone and hatred resulting from fear of one's own existence but respecting the rights of others and giving everyone what they are entitled to is the best guarantee of one's own rights.

When we look at the nation as a social body of which we are members, then this truth becomes even more obvious. We become one body with the nation in which we live; we receive the entire substance of our national life through the nation, and we receive it from its other members. Can we hate those who are members of the same national body as we?

Thus, faithful service to the fatherland demands that we transcend our own egos, putting effort into expanding our own hearts in order to embrace the entire nation with them. For us Catholics, this is not a new demand; it flows from the Christian commandment to love one's neighbor. Such love demands that we overcome our petty prejudices; it requires that we end our disgraceful and petty discussions in the press as well as the Pharisee-like pointing out of other people's errors. On the contrary, the more one of our compatriots has suffered from the enemies of the nation and the more the image of Polishness has become faded and deformed in him, the more he requires care and endearing love so that those injuries are repaired. Love for our compatriots requires that we meticulously improve our national flaws and traces of slavery within ourselves and our neighbors. Healing the wounds of our brothers and improving our fatherland in our own homes is the Christian elevation of the nation of which we are a part. The overcoming of differences between states through love and the struggle against state, class, or professional egotism so that they do not make us blind to the truth that we are the children of one nation will serve these same aims.

3. Providing the Nation with Life

The more effectively one overcomes one's own selfishness, the more capable one is of living in life for the fatherland. We all know how difficult it is for egotists to be good sons and daughters of their nation; they would prefer to see the death of their own nation than to make even the smallest sacrifice for it.

Everywhere Christian family morality is attacked through sexualism, the easy life, neo-Malthusianism, and pornographic literature, the more nations are condemned to the cemetery. Nations that have violated Christian morality and rejected Catholic teaching on marriage are on the way to suicide: the names of fools are erased from the land of the living!

This horror also threatens our fatherland and our nation. Distinguished, honored, and decorated Polish sexualists have created a legend about catastrophic overpopulation. Their iniquitous work has borne fruit very quickly: in our country, the rate of population increase has fallen three times as rapidly as in Western Europe. Whereas the rate of natural increase in Poland was 534,000 people (17 per 1,000) in 1930, by 1934 it was just 402,000 (12 per 1,000). Instead of the legend of overpopulation, Poland faces the threat of depopulation. This has been accomplished by the moral murderers of our nation. It is telling that there are those who blame the Church for this state of affairs. This happens just as others have accused the Church of making people in Poland "multiply like rabbits" and impoverishing the country through its harsh teaching on marital morality. It is known that the Church in Poland has survived the attack on the Christian nature of marriage and has not opened the gates to divorce, through which death typically comes to the soul of the nation. And yet, natural population increase is a good not only for the Church, but for the nation as well. Taking upon herself the struggle against marital immorality, the Church defends the life of the Polish nation.

One must remember that the rapid decline in the birthrate in recent years (not only in big cities, but also in rural Poland) is caused by not one but many factors. It does not matter that the Church proclaims her teaching in defense of budding life if the state attacks it, or it is not accepted by society. We know what the effects of this were in Saxon and Stanisław's Poland,[1] when comfortable lifestyles, divorces, and salon immorality became fashionable in our country. Even if these factors ceased, what would this help if the entirety of socio-economic relations became such that human poverty ended young life along with the first cry of a baby?

Serving the fatherland demands that we openly confess that the Polish nation is in decline. We are squandering the accomplishments of previous generations. We are forced to be ashamed of our national history and reject the idea of being a great power, which begins not with a poster but with the cradle.

The numerical increase of the nation is guaranteed only by the Catholic teaching on marriage and Catholic family morality. They oppose the spirit of egotism and complacency, instead nurturing a spirit of sacrifice and diligence. Thus, it is imperative to create social, legal, moral, and socio-economic conditions in which budding life may find its most solicitous defenders and custodians. Meanwhile, all those who have followed the natural law and formed families must also see their marital duties as service to the nation. Only then will the righteous inherit the earth.

---

1 In 1697–1763, the Polish-Lithuanian Commonwealth formed a personal union with the German Electorate of Saxony; Stanisław's Poland refers to the rule of Stanisław August (Stanislaus Augustus) Poniatowski (1764–1795), the last king of Poland. Both periods were marked by decadence.

II. Social Service of One's Countrymen

1. Preparation for Social Service

Service to society is impossible without the prior socialization of the individual and his subordination to the good of society. Man cannot be subordinated to society in any way unless he is first subordinated to God and His greatest good.

Today, so much has been said about socialization and social work, yet the great contradiction between external socialization and the internal depravity of man has not yet been resolved. Hence, we have so many anti-social social activists who try to build within others what they destroy in themselves and who are glad to socialize others and subject them to the laws of communal life, but leave complete freedom to themselves. As F. W. Foerster has beautifully written, the socialization of man can take place only through Jesus Christ: "The human community was created in Gethsemane and Golgotha. If the natural man is not crucified, then all efforts at human socialization fall apart, resulting in wild mutual hatred. The natural man cannot really become a brother; those who do not see this know neither what man is nor what it means to be one's brother."

The real social approach to the person begins with the washing of feet, as our Teacher and Lord has done: "If I then, your Lord and Teacher, have washed your feet, you also ought to wash one another's feet" (John 13:14). Only then does man sever ties with his own "I" and notice his neighbors around him: "Let no one seek his own good, but the good of his neighbor" (1 Corinthians 10:24). That is when the destruction of the animal and the creation of man begins. A man who wants to have a social spirit within himself and who makes an effort to carry out his social duties should take the Apostle's advice to heart: "Finally, all of you, have unity of spirit, sympathy, love of the brethren, a tender heart, and a humble mind. Do not return evil for evil or reviling for reviling; but on the contrary, bless, for to this you have been called, that you may obtain a blessing. For 'he that would love life and see good days, let him keep his tongue from evil and his lips from speaking guile; let him turn away from evil and do right; let him seek peace and pursue it'" (1 Peter 3:8–11). Having

156

conquered evil within himself, man will "be ready for any honest work" (Titus 3:1). He will also come to possess the attributes that are necessary for all kinds of social work: "Rejoice always, pray constantly, give thanks in all circumstances [. . .]. Do not quench the Spirit [. . .]. [T]est everything; hold fast what is good" (1 Thessalonians 5:16–21).

Prepared in this way, man will be capable of co-existence in the national community.

2. The Socialized Life of a Member of the Nation

God has placed man in all sorts of communities: the family, profession, nation, and political and religious communities. The Church teaches that co-existence with them is absolutely necessary for man. Even hermits, who are unique in their lifestyle, are advised by the Church to live in monastic communities. When asked how to enter the kingdom of heaven, Christ instructed following the commandments that deal with the necessity of co-existing with people (Matthew 19:17–19). It was only in exceptional cases that Christ the Lord advised: "Go, sell what you possess and give to the poor, and you will have treasure in heaven; and come, follow me" (Matthew 19:21). When the young man did not follow this advice, however, Christ did not condemn him.

It is in family life that man has the most opportunities to develop and present his social soul. In family life, there can be no love other than the union of two people in God; the deepest meaning of this love is expressed in the transmission of life, which entails so many sacrifices and self-denial for the good of one's family.

And what about social and economic life? In this case, God's thought also tempers man's egotism, making him conceive of labor as service to God, as an activity that is sanctified by the nature of its cooperation with Divine Providence. In God's plan, the aim of economic activity is the meeting of the needs of the whole, and man must consciously collaborate with God's plan. Although the spirit of business has spurred economic growth and the increase of wealth, this has benefited individuals rather than the nation. It is the source of ruthless, egotistical capitalism, which has turned the "social economy" into the economy of anonymous finances and, consequently, half a century of social struggle and revolutionary anxieties, socialism and

Bolshevism, and proletarism in the broad masses, all phenomena that often eat away at the wealth of businessmen.

Wanting to serve one's fatherland, one must temper within oneself the harmful spirit of profit and become sensitive to the common good, which is more difficult to achieve but is correct and socially beneficial. When man ceases to be blinded by egotism, his eyes are opened to the broad paths of God's thinking, which the Church seeks to implement in the life of the nations. We must stop thinking about whether we are comfortable, and instead ask: are my brothers comfortable? Are their lives worthy of a human being? What can be improved in their lives? This is the starting point for constant social and economic revisionism in which social love is the source of justice that leads across the path of social progress to the gates of *Civitas Dei*.[2]

In professional life, social service provides us with many opportunities for efficient labor. For a Catholic, there exists no concept of a "minimum standard of living" as a principle of balance, order, and justice. As in every other expression of the Catholic life, in this case there is also flexibility inspired by love for one's neighbor and described as social justice: if you have a lot, give more, and if you have little, give less. Having established the concept of a just wage, which encompasses the physical, social, cultural-educational, and moral-religious needs of an individual and his family, the Church has overcome the legend of "the necessity of the existence of proletarism as a constant phenomenon that opens the doors of social progress to the masses." Here, there is great potential for social service to the nation that is provided by neither proletarian society nor the capitalist state.

III. Service of the Fatherland in the Lord

Our nation's ties to God and His Church have been of great consequence. It was the Church that shaped within us a Christian conscience, protecting us against historical lawlessness, which we never applied to any other nation in our history. We were called the "bulwark of Christianity"; apart from pride, this title has also benefited us in the fact that the entire Catholic world prayed for Poland

2 Latin: "City of God."

and provided it with sacrificial aid during times of hardship. This awakens within us the need to not only preserve our nation's external relationship with God but being witnesses to God's truth.

The first duty is to seek strength from our religion for service of the fatherland in order to be like the great leaders of Israel "who through faith conquered kingdoms, enforced justice, received promises, stopped the mouths of lions, quenched raging fire, escaped the edge of the sword, won strength out of weakness, became mighty in war, put foreign armies to flight" (Hebrews 11:33–34). We live in God and in faith not because it is more comfortable and pleasant and safer, and not to please ourselves, but in order to be more valuable and useful to society and our nation: that is true service of the fatherland in the Lord!

When we are faced with our tremendous national duties, we can defeat the spirit of fear and pettiness by the certainty that "I can do all things in Him who strengthens me" (Philippians 4:13). "God is at work in you, both to will and to work for His good pleasure" (Philippians 2:13). No educational system, social situation, or political program can guarantee us this strength "in every good deed"; only a man of strong faith who lives out the faith and gains strength from it can make the greatest and most effective effort in the service of the nation. We have seen many examples of this wondrous strength coming from faith in the lives of many of our compatriots. Before every endeavor, Romuald Traugutt[3] sought wisdom, advice, and strength in prayer. Such heroic figures that have brought light to our fatherland's history as Chodkiewicz, Żółkiewski, Czarniecki, Batory, Sobieski, and Kościuszko[4] arose from the religious spirit of

---

3 Romuald Traugutt (1826–1864) commanded the Polish January Uprising of 1863–1864 against Russian rule, which ended in defeat; the insurgents, including Traugutt himself, were executed or deported to Siberia. Due to his piety and intense devotion to his country and faith, there have been efforts to open a cause for beatification for him.

4 Tadeusz Kościuszko (1746–1817) was a Polish patriot who led a series of insurrections against Russia in the late nineteenth century. Benjamin Franklin met him in Paris and used his support as a military engineer in the American Revolutionary War, during which Kościuszko designed many fortifications, including that at West Point. Thomas Jefferson called Kościuszko "as pure a son of liberty as I have ever known."

our nation. The spirit of faith inspired our national poets. Not only did they not see religion as an obstacle to serving the fatherland well, but they sharpened their souls like swords in it.

In serving our nation, let us bear in mind St. Paul the Apostle's advice "to lead a life worthy of the Lord, fully pleasing to Him, bearing fruit in every good work and increasing in the knowledge of God. May you be strengthened with all power, according to His glorious might, for all endurance and patience with joy" (Colossians 1:10–11).

An equivalent duty is to remember the great worth of our life with regards to both our ultimate aim and our temporal aims. Christ the Lord once wept over Jerusalem: "Would that even today you knew the things that make for peace! But, now they are hid from your eyes" (Luke 19:42).

Just as Jerusalem, every nation and every man living in every nation have their days of visitation. We were given only one life, and we are to spend that life in the bosom of our nation.

What they will write about our nation and if it will be good or, rather, passed over with shame, depends on us. Regardless, we will go down in history with good or ill repute or not at all. Maybe they will say of us: we were unrealized potential, wasted talent, a lost drachma! Perhaps they will think: "This man began to build and was not able to finish" (Luke 14:30). Or, perhaps our entire generation will be evaluated by the historians of our nation just as we write about our ancestors today, harshly judging them: "For men will be lovers of self, lovers of money, proud, arrogant, abusive, disobedient to their parents, ungrateful, unholy, inhuman, implacable, slanderers, profligates, fierce, haters of good, treacherous, reckless, swollen with conceit, lovers of pleasure rather than lovers of God" (2 Timothy 3:2–4).

God willing, may our generation not leave such a testimony. It depends on us if our lives will create the most beautiful chapter in the history of our nation. This will happen when we follow the advice of the Apostle to the Gentiles in our lives: "Finally, brethren, whatever is true, whatever is honorable, whatever is just, whatever is pure, whatever is lovely, whatever is gracious, if there is any excellence, if there is anything worthy of praise, think about these things" (Philippians 4:8).

* * *

When bidding His disciples farewell in the Cenacle, Christ the Lord prayed to His Father before His passion as follows: "I do not pray that Thou shouldst take them out of the world, but that Thou shouldst keep them from the evil one" (John 17:15). Our prayers cannot be any different: wanting to fulfill God's will, we must lead energetic lives and overcome all its difficulties here on the Polish soil! During our time on this earth, one concern must sustain us: that we are delivered from evil and that we do not let evil conquer us, but that we defeat evil through good (see Romans 12:21). The victorious struggle against evil is the most faithful service of the fatherland! In our brave procession towards the greatest Good, our nation will become united in accordance with Christ's request: "That they may all be one; even as Thou, Father, art in Me, and I in Thee" (John 17:21). We can achieve unity only when following God, because in Him we will all become one in Christ our Lord. Just as no force is capable of breaking up unity in God, no force can defeat or scatter a nation so unified in God. Serving our brothers in love and our fatherland in the Lord, "we may lead a quiet and peaceable life, godly and respectful in every way" (1 Timothy 2:2).

3

A Just Poland Is More Pleasing to God

"I am the Lord your God, Who brought you forth out of the land of Egypt, that you should not be their slaves; and I have broken the bars of your yoke and made you walk erect" (Leviticus 26:13).

DURING THE GREAT VISITATION OF OUR nation during the days of suffering, pain, and tears, we humbled ourselves before God's Majesty in the sense of our guilt; martyred by our cruel enemies, we called: "Turn, O Lord, save my life; deliver me for the sake of Thy steadfast love. For in death there is no remembrance of Thee; in Sheol who can give Thee praise?" (Psalm 6:4–5). The Lord who takes "no pleasure in the death of the wicked, but that the wicked turn from his way and live" (Ezekiel 11:33) has led us out of the grave. We give thanks to the Lord's will so that we may praise Him. "He will afflict us for our iniquities; and again He will show mercy" (Tobit 13:5).

Afflicted for our iniquities and liberated by the Lord's great mercy, we are beginning a new course by severing our ties to the path of death: "Depart from me, all you workers of evil; for the Lord has heard the sound of my weeping" (Psalm 6:8). The works of the reborn Poland are the works of great benevolence and justice. Let us undertake them by heeding to the exhortation: "seek justice, correct oppression; defend the fatherless, plead for the widow" (Isaiah 1:17). Our mother Poland will be reborn and free of the violence of the rulers and the misery of the ruled, while exploitation and oppression will not take place among us.

"For Zion's sake I will not keep silent, and for Jerusalem's sake I will not rest, until her vindication goes forth as brightness, and her salvation as a burning torch. The nations shall see your vindication, and all the kings your glory; and you shall be called by a new name which the mouth of the Lord will give. You shall be a crown of beauty in the hand of the Lord, and a royal diadem in the hand of your God. You shall no more be termed Forsaken, and your land shall no more be termed Desolate" (Isaiah 62:1–4).

I. Wise Government

1. Social Justice in Governing the State

Having experienced God's justice, let us become imitators and "slaves of righteousness" (Romans 6:18). "For I will proclaim the name of the Lord. [. . .] 'The Rock, His work is perfect; for all His ways are justice. A God of faithfulness and without iniquity, just and right is He'" (Deuteronomy 32:3–4). A summons to all who rule flows from the mouth of the righteous God: "Love righteousness, you rulers of the earth" (Wisdom 1:1). Works of justice are a blessing that is given to all who walk its paths: "For the Lord is righteous, He loves righteous deeds; the upright shall behold His face" (Psalm 11:7).

2. The Common Good Before the Eyes of the State

The primary task of the state is concern for the common good and the public common good of the entire community and all the segments of society that make it up. State authorities are summoned above all to work for the common good; all citizens are obliged to cooperate with all the efforts of state authority. In order to implement this task, public authorities must act with a sense of social justice. This is beautifully expressed by the inspired author: "When the righteous are in authority, the people rejoice; but when the wicked rule, the people groan [. . .]. A righteous man knows the rights of the poor; a wicked man does not understand such knowledge" (Proverbs 29:2, 7).

This spirit extends to all state and social institutions, which also must be permeated with concern for the common good and a sense of social justice. Pius XI underlines this in his encyclical *Quadragesimo anno:* "Hence, the institutions themselves of peoples and, particularly those of all social life, ought to be penetrated with this justice, and it is most necessary that it be truly effective, that is, establish a juridical and social order which will, as it were, give form and shape to all economic life" (QA, 88).

What good will social legislation bring if the state authorities show citizens a scandalizing example of bypassing them, if they create an entire system of legalized abuses in state enterprises, as well as public offices and institutions? For the good of society, public authorities should be marked by not only social justice, but they must also implement the tasks of social justice so that every person could live well in the broadest meaning of the term, and thus in its moral, religious, social, professional, and economic aspects. There can be no social justice when there are entire classes deprived of the protection of the state and prone to exploitation and poverty in the social organism. "If one member suffers, all suffer together; if one member is honored, all rejoice together" (1 Corinthians 12:26). As a result of the natural internal bonds of the social organism, the suffering of the abandoned masses painfully affects all other groups, even if their own prosperity is well-established, and it can result in revolutions and social unrest that impact both the satiated and the hungry.

It suffices to reference a couple examples from socio-economic life that, according to Pius XI, attest to the need for the public authorities to be concerned and care for the common good. This common good demands that "the riches that economic-social developments constantly increase ought to be so distributed among individual persons and classes to the common advantage of all" (QA, 57). Thus, the aim of the state should be to facilitate the distribution of all the resources that are necessary to live depending on the demands of one's environment through proper social legislation.

Approaching the ideal of social equality is possible thanks to the appropriate value of wages, which should also "be adjusted to the public economic good" (QA, 74). The proletarian state of existence, which maintains that poverty is an irrevocable part of life, is also harmful to the common good. Thus, Catholic social teaching demands that for the common good, both bureaucrats and laborers could receive such a wage that would allow them to satisfy their indispensable needs and have something left over in order to accumulate a modest estate.

Making the entirety of economic life dependent on capital solely intended for private use and completely ignoring the dignity of the working class and the social nature of the economy are also opposed to the common good.

3. The State in Defense of the Economically Exploited Segments of Society

Although every person, individual, and social class must to an equal degree be the subject of the concern of the just state, it is imperative that "in protecting private individuals in their rights, chief consideration ought to be given to the weak and the poor" (QA, 25). Why? Leo XIII explains this in his encyclical *Rerum novarum:* "The richer class have many ways of shielding themselves, and stand less in need of help from the State; whereas the mass of the poor have no resources of their own to fall back upon, and must chiefly depend upon the assistance of the State" (RN, 37).

Sacred Scripture likewise contains incentives in this regard. For example, the Psalmist calls: "Give justice to the weak and the fatherless; maintain the right of the afflicted and the destitute. Rescue the weak and the needy; deliver them from the hand of the wicked" (Psalm 82:3–4). Meanwhile, the Book of Proverbs admonishes: "Open your mouth, judge righteously, maintain the rights of the poor and needy" (Proverbs 31:8). The entirety of social welfare legislation, which the state has the duty to bring to life through its concern for the working masses, finds its rationale here.

Socio-economic life is an area of constant change; hence, it is difficult to permanently state when the state has such a duty.

Leo XIII concisely presented a series of examples of righteous intervention motivated by the common good. "If by a strike of workers or concerted interruption of work there should be imminent danger of disturbance to the public peace; or, if circumstances were such as that among the working class the ties of family life were relaxed; if religion were found to suffer through the workers not having time and opportunity afforded them to practice its duties; if in workshops and factories there were danger to morals through the mixing of the sexes or from other harmful occasions of evil; or if employers laid burdens upon their workmen which were unjust, or degraded them with conditions repugnant to their dignity as human beings; finally, if health were endangered by excessive labor, or by work unsuited to sex or age — in such cases, there can be no question but that, within certain limits, it would be right to invoke the aid and authority of the law" (RN, 36).

Burdening public authorities with the responsibility for particular concern for the working masses deprived of wealth, Catholic teaching has in mind above all the working class, bureaucrats, and "those who are able and willing to work" (QA, 74). Public authorities should "offer to the greatest possible number the opportunity of getting work and obtaining suitable means of livelihood" (ibid.). Society should make haste to assist the state, using its surplus revenues to create places of employment and sources of income.

II. A Wise Nation

1. Bringing the Working Masses to the Life of the Nation

We can use Isaiah's words to summon those who are at the forefront of the nation: "Open the gates, that the righteous nation which keeps faith may enter in" (Isaiah 26:2). Whom do we want to summon? Let us look around us and ask: who do we lack? Who remains outside our joys and sorrow, our family community? Once again, let us reply with Isaiah's words: "Go through, go through the gates, prepare the way for the peoples" (Isaiah 62:10).

Oddly enough, we have never succeeded in building strong ties of national unity between the workers and the peasants. One nation has two paths that run concurrent to one another, but do not merge into one; as it were, its arms, only one of which fully maintains its ties to the national body, tremble. Piotr Skarga[1] said: "Bad are the arms of which one is ill; both must be healthy." Both hands must come together in a kind, brotherly embrace, in solidarity work for the common good and active service of the fatherland; both hands must grasp the hilt of the sword in its defense. This is our most urgent national task: to return the worker, who has so far been wandering in the wilderness of internationalist yearning, back to the nation. Although the worker has on numerous occasions expressed his love for his mother in bursts of heroic struggle against invaders, in times of peace he is attracted to ideals that are alien to the soul of the

---

1 Piotr Skarga (1536–1612) was a Polish Jesuit, champion of the Counter-Reformation, pundit, and critic of many policies of the Polish-Lithuanian Commonwealth. A cause for his beatification was launched in 2013.

nation; he is prone to illusory inspirations and expects liberation from hostile forces.

So far, the people's strength, whose sacrificial work increases the nation's wealth but does not enrich the soul of the nation, has been slumbering in a half-sleep. We can still hear the calling of the village Headman in Wyspiański's *Wedding*: "It's light!" Now is high time for illumination so that "the righteous nation which keeps faith" (Isaiah 26:2) may enter the life of Poland and give its heart, soul and hands in service to the country.

According to God's design, social life should encompass all the segments of society; it should above all serve and be supported by all. Only then is attaining the common good possible. "For the body does not consist of one member but of many [...]. The eye cannot say to the hand, 'I have no need of you,' nor again the head to the feet, 'I have no need of you'" (1 Corinthians 12:14, 21). The ruling elites cannot carry the burden of the entire life of the nation by themselves, if they are not bolstered by the brawny arms of the working and peasant masses.

God's wisdom should be the source of models for social co-existence. God unites all the states in His glory: "Let the desert and its cities lift up their voice, the villages that Kedar inhabits; let the inhabitants of Sela sing for joy, let them shout from the top of the mountains. Let them give glory to the Lord and declare His praise in the coastlands" (Isaiah 42:11–12). Brought together by a common song praising God's glory, the burghers and the villagers and the highlanders and the islanders will more easily find a common language in the service of the fatherland.

2. Social Emancipation

"See that you do not despise one of these little ones; for I tell you that in heaven their angels always behold the face of My Father who is in heaven" (Matthew 18:10).

It seems imperative to recall these words in this age of constitutions and the legal emancipation of citizens. Unfortunately, today we are very far from this beautiful image: "Every valley shall be filled, and every mountain and hill shall be brought low, and the crooked shall be made straight, and the rough ways shall be made smooth; and all flesh shall see the salvation of God" (Luke 3:5–6).

Christ the Lord did not attempt to bring equality to the world in the Marxist sense, but instead He strove for social emancipation that is much deeper at a collective level, and equality in the face of the power of grace which has come from Him and healed all; this is why the people sought Him (see Luke 6:19). Unfortunately, many pagan customs that cast a shadow on the co-existence of the different segments of society have remained among Christians.

In Poland, there is a great distance between the city and the country, the villager and the official, the laborer and the intellectual; this is caused not only by the standard of living, but furthermore and primarily by the anti-social attitude of the guardians of state authority and those that execute it with regards to the working class in the city and country. Rural Poland has experienced the overwhelming dominance of others, which is the source of much suffering and humiliation; its inferiority and civic subordination in its contact with the administration of the same state.

An imperative of the common good is to overcome the spirit of pride and humiliation, which is described in Ecclesiastes: "If you see in a province the poor oppressed and justice and right violently taken away, do not be amazed at the matter; for the high official is watched by a higher, and there are yet higher ones over them" (Ecclesiastes 5:7).

It should not be this way in our fatherland; our hearts must become filled with a zealous desire for justice. The fruits of bolstered social bonds will grow out of this strong will supported by the feeling of Christian love for one's neighbor; above all, they will be the spirit of brotherly love and friendly benevolence as well as helpful assistance to one another. Before our eyes, Poland will become a powerful construction that unites all the social classes in solidarity and service. The spirit of arrogance and domination will disappear, while the belief in mutual necessity, dependency in rendering services to one another in the name of social justice in exchange for receiving services from one's neighbor, will blossom. The spirit of assistance and recognition for mutual usefulness will be awakened within us. The burgher will respect the humble work of the farmer, while the farmer, when standing before the window of an official, will have no need to say: "I have no need of you" (1 Corinthians 12:21). The Christian social order, influenced by Pauline instructions, will take the place of mutual humiliation and debasement. It will unite Poland through spiritual ties; it will bring the peasant and working-class masses to their fatherland. Then, the nation will manifest all the strength given to it by God. Poland will be the ideal of social balance in the spirit of St. Paul's words: "[T]he whole body, joined and knit together by every joint with which it is supplied, when each part is working properly, makes bodily growth and upbuilds itself in love" (Ephesians 4:16).

This leveling of social inequalities in the spirit of Christian social love paves the way for economic reforms, which would defeat proletarism and ensure a standard of living corresponding to man's great dignity to every citizen of the state.

3. The Social Role of Love

Christian love must be the soul of the new social order; it prepares the way for greater justice. This is the love for one's neighbor prescribed by Christ the Lord: "A new commandment I give to you, that you love one another; even as I have loved you, that you also love one another" (John 13:34).

Social love is not exhausted by works of mercy, in giving alms to the poor and succor to the needy. Love in social life is something greater still. Love knows no limits. Love does not limit itself to healing wounds; it wants to prevent them. If it had limited itself to kind deeds, it would not be a fulfillment of the Covenant; it would also not be Christian love. In its preventive role, love will lead to the growth and progress of social justice. Love shapes the national conscience, inspiring the creation of new laws in defense of the injured. Thanks to this, it is the source of social progress. A certain Catholic writer wrote that today's justice is yesterday's love, while today's love is the justice of tomorrow.

Happy is the nation whose social co-existence is at its gilded heart. In this kind of society, every citizen can quote Job: "When the ear heard, it called me blessed, and when the eye saw, it approved; because I delivered the poor who cried, and the fatherless who had none to help him. The blessing of him who was about to perish came upon me, and I caused the widow's heart to sing for joy. I put on righteousness, and it clothed me; my justice was like a robe and a turban. I was eyes to the blind, and feet to the lame. I was a father to the poor, and I searched out the cause of him whom I did not know. I broke the fangs of the unrighteous and made him drop his prey from his teeth" (Job 29:11–17).

In a land filled with the spirit of love and justice, "[s]teadfast love and faithfulness will meet; righteousness and peace will kiss each other. Faithfulness will spring up from the ground, and righteousness will look down from the sky. Yea, the Lord will give what is good, and our land will yield its increase" (Psalm 85:10–12).

* * *

In the life of the state, justice is its blessing. It is blessed by its citizens, wealthy and poor, worker and craftsmen alike, by its orphan, widow, and vagabond. It solidifies in God's power and blessing.

"Blessed shall you be in the city, and blessed shall you be in the field. Blessed shall be the fruit of your body, and the fruit of your ground [...]. The Lord will cause your enemies who rise against you to be defeated before you; they shall come out against you one way, and flee before you seven ways. [...] The Lord will establish you as a people holy to Himself [...]. The Lord will open to you His good treasury the heavens, to give the rain of your land in its season and to bless all the work of your hands; and you shall lend to many nations, but you shall not borrow" (Deuteronomy 28:3–12).

"And the effect of righteousness will be peace, and the result of righteousness, quietness, and trust forever" (Isaiah 32:17).

4

The God-Fearing State

*"Unless the Lord builds the house, those
who build it labor in vain. Unless the
Lord watches over the city, the watchman
stays awake in vain" (Psalm 127:1–2).*

WHEN ISRAEL FOUGHT THE AMALEKITES
in the wilderness, Moses ascended the summit of the hill
and prayed to the Lord of Hosts for the victory of His
people. "Whenever Moses held up his hand, Israel prevailed; and
whenever he lowered his hand, Amalek prevailed. But Moses' hands
grew weary [. . .]. Aaron and Hur held up his hands, one on one
side, and the other on the other side; so his hands were steady until
the going down of the sun. And Joshua mowed down Amalek and
his people with the edge of the sword" (Exodus 17:11–13).

There is a true division of labor in this event. In the valley, the war-
rior people are fighting under Joshua's leadership, while Moses' hands,
stretched out towards the Lord and asking for the Lord's succor, are
above them. Weak is the hand amidst the enormous tasks, although it
is wielded by the strong man; that is why Aaron and Hur, the envoys
of the people, stand at the side of the spiritual leader of the nation in
order to keep the hand facing the Lord through their common effort
and prayer. They fight through prayer, and they emerge victorious
in prayer! In order to defeat the enemy, it is not enough to raise up
the sword; pleading hands are also necessary. They then fight using
two swords: the temporal and the spiritual. They will win thanks
to this holy alliance!

Human strength flags not only in military struggle, but especially
in mundane, tedious concern for the existence of the state. As a form
of social cohabitation that is necessary for society, the state has taken
up some of God's works and thus needs God's aid to implement
them. Its existence coming from God's will, the will of the Creator
of nature, whenever the state is deprived of the spiritual sword and is

not supported in its prayerful being by the priest's hand, the nation will inevitably decline. God's ancient words to Job are relevant to every state in today's world: "Have you an arm like God, and can you thunder with a voice like His? Deck yourself with majesty and dignity; clothe yourself with glory and splendor. Hide them all in the dust together; bind their faces in the world below. [. . .] Then will I also acknowledge to you, that your own right hand can give you victory" (Job 40:9–14). However, God sees that there is not a single nation under the sun that could trust even His right hand. Thus, international law has been created for mutual assistance; hence, the entire elaborate network of global politics: numerous alliances, pacts, agreements, and treaties among those who look for the human right hand and human assistance. History, however, teaches how disappointing all these human efforts are. The right hand of the state, nation, and man must always rest against God's right hand. Every man and every nation must support the right hand that is raised towards the heavens.

1. "What therefore God has joined together, let not man put asunder" (see Matthew 19:6).

In the Epistle to the Romans, St. Paul teaches: "Let every person be subject to the governing authorities. For there is no authority except from God, and those that exist have been instituted by God. Therefore, he who resists the authorities resists what God has appointed, and those who resist will incur judgment" (Romans 13:1–2).

From these words, a strange radiance falls on the authority of those who are "God's servants", both for the glory of those who do good and to execute God's wrath on evildoers (see Romans 13:3–4). God wanted to adorn the temples of governing bodies with a halo of glory, in order to facilitate the implementation of its great tasks. Pope Leo XIII writes: "Government authority will be radiant and protected when it is considered from God, Who is the most majestic and holiest source. If it is something akin to the administration of God's authority, the authority of those who govern the state immediately takes on supernatural majesty. [. . .] Not wanting to recognize that God gives the right to decree debases political authority of its most beautiful radiance and weakens it in its fundament."

By elevating the dignity of authority so high, God has created two kinds of authority, the sacred and the secular, which He has given two separate aims, something like two different directions, but has strongly embedded them in a single source: God's power. Leo XIII continues: "God has divided authority over mankind into two kinds: the spiritual and the secular, of which the former has been entrusted with directed divine matters and the latter with human affairs. Each is the highest in the sphere of its scope; the limits of each are precisely described in its nature and destiny; each has its own sphere in which it executes its activity." Through God's will, two sovereign communities that are formally distinct, Church and state, govern over people. Although each community has its own aims, one is endowed with supernatural goods and brings people closer to eternal salvation, while the other brings people to earthly good through peace, progress, and temporal prosperity. Both communities rule over the same people, who are God's children and who will ultimately be given over to our common Father. It is here that they come together: in their common source, the Father; in His work, man; and in their ultimate aim, God. In His greatest wisdom, God has married both communities together, expecting divine offspring from this permanent bond. Only a permanent bond between Church and state can give birth to a full man and a full citizen. Both these communities need one another; none is sufficient for man on its own. Although it brings man closer to heaven, through God's will, the Church does so on this earth. The state, meanwhile, is supposed to provide man with worldly goods, but it cannot effectively do so without summoning the help of the Church. The state, however, cannot fully educate its citizens; a man brought up by the state will always be incomplete.

Thus, this bond between Church and state comes from God's will. "What, therefore, God has joined together, let not man put asunder" (see Matthew 19:6). As in Christian marriage, there must be a bond of love between the Church and state. What would a marital contract be without the love of the spouses? A similar legal bond, which is strengthened by the concordat, will never replace necessary respect, sincere friendship, and internal cooperation. The concordat, which only separates the limits of each institution's powers, but does not create a friendly atmosphere of cooperation and trust in a sense of mutual usefulness and cannot replace values, is a dead letter.

The Church is too firm in her aims in order to be a serious rival to the state in the struggle for the souls of citizens. The Pharisee anxiety over the influences of the Church in the state and the power of its teaching, as well as the pusillanimous question: "What are we to do? For this Man performs many signs" (John 11:47), and the fear for the people: "The world has gone after Him" (John 12:19), should be calmed with Isaiah's words: "Fear not, daughter of Zion; behold, your King is coming, sitting on an ass's colt!" (John 12:15); "'Behold, your salvation comes; behold, His reward is with Him, and His recompense before Him.' And they shall be called the holy people, the redeemed of the Lord; and you shall be called Sought Out, a city not forsaken" (Isaiah 62:11–12). He who brings the kingdom of heaven does not take away worldly existence. The Church will return Poland's children to Christ, and Christ will give them back to the nation.

2. State Education in the Church

Both Church and state call for "the strong man" today. However, the contemporary state frequently understands the concept of the strong man as one with a strong and healthy body, even if the person is in reality weak. The Church, however, believes that the strong man is not a brutal one, but one who is capable of overcoming himself and can temper the lust of his eyes, lust of his body, and pride within himself.

When the Church calls for the reform of the spirit, what it means is the need to make life compatible with the rules of faith, because that is the only way that any reforms — moral, social, political, and economic — are possible. A so-called strong person is forged only through the path of sanctity; that is, the only path through which he can learn to love God and neighbor. All other paths give rise to troublemakers and phonies who pass like smoke, because the "power of the spirit" of an old man allows him only a few years. Only the Church gives rise to figures whose fame has persisted throughout the centuries. "It is the greatest fortune of every kingdom," Piotr Skarga preached, "when it is home to people who kindly love one another, are sober and have a sense of shame and love modesty; when they are submissive, punitive, brave, and love one another."

F. W. Foerster, a contemporary Christian thinker, believes the same: "The greatness of a state does not consist in its territorial vastness, wealth, military strength, population, trade, and industry, or even its scientific and technical progress, but rather in the moral and religious strength of its citizens, their fidelity to the laws of their conscience, and, finally, their religiousness."

A state must consciously play the role of the educator of society. It is not enough for the state to preserve its existence, maintain internal order, and ensure the security of its citizens; it is insufficient for its citizens to be able to live; they must live well. Apart from the state's will and assistance, the citizens must put in their own will. Here, we encounter two wills: the will of the state, which will influence the entirety of the conditions of the existence of citizens through its public offices, thanks to which the state will want to make citizens good; and the will of the citizens, who themselves must want to encounter those efforts of the state and become subject to its educational influences.

The educational ideal of the state cannot be merely the citizen and his civic virtues, but the entire person. In order to be rightly constituted, the state needs all human virtues, not just civic ones. The state cannot perform this task on its own, without the aid of the family, Church, nation, society, and professions.

The Church is especially capable of comprehensive education; it educates people for their personal lives, family, nation, state, and God. The Church shapes these virtues, which the state in no way can shape on its own, in the citizen.

Above all, the Church teaches citizens the truth. Citizens' respect for one another as well as the state must be based on the truth: "Therefore, putting away falsehood, let everyone speak the truth with his neighbor, for we are members one of another" (Ephesians 4:25). This is of great significance to public life and protects against all illusions and disappointments, making life easier and more efficient! Let us teach citizens the truth, and we will build a mighty state: we will fill the state coffers with the money of conscientious taxpayers, protect ourselves against illusions, and extricate dishonesty, deceitfulness, and humbug from public life. This spirit of truth is possible only in Jesus Christ, because only through Him can we possess "the Spirit of truth, Whom the world cannot receive, because it neither sees Him nor knows Him; you know Him, for He dwells with you, and will be in you" (John 14:17).

Meanwhile, when the state bases its attitude towards its citizens on the truth rather than pernicious propaganda, which masks lies, and will not estrange others from itself through distrust, a strong state will arise.

And humility! Is this not one of the strongest fundaments of state power? Teach citizens humility, you will move them to perform solid work and cultivate thorough knowledge, which in today's competitive labor market is the nucleus of victory. Today's "strong man" shudders at the thought of humility. He says that the Church supports people "of a worse kind," and talk of humility fosters within them a sense of inferiority. It is true that the Church defends the weak. However, in her view, those whose bodies are weak are not the inferior ones. The Church has the power to carry and raise up the weakest, and her history attests to how many people rejected by the world have become the pride of the Church, states, nations, culture, science, art, etc. Through humility, we will open the gates of social equilibrium and mutual respect, while we will put everyone in their proper relationship to state authority, one that is worthy of a Christian.

Moderation, a life of restraint, a rigorous personal life, in which man learns to struggle against himself, courageous attitudes towards sloth and complacency in life, sacrifice, renunciation, being content with one's lot, frugality, and all the "economic virtues" lead not only to spiritual power and physical health, but also to national prosperity! Is it not here that citizens capable of the greatest sacrifices for the state, of the greatest troubles and personal limitations are educated? Like Uriah, who when asked by David why they do not enter their homes, they reply gallantly: "The ark and Israel and Judah dwell in booths; and my lord Joab and the servants of my lord are camping in the open field; shall I then go to my house, to eat and to drink, and to lie with my wife?" (2 Samuel 11:11). Oh, how much we, a generation brought up softly, need Uriah's virtues in order to respond to the duties of the chivalrous nation, to which Providence has called us.

And the virtue of valor! Who can shape it better than the Church? The Church requires that we act courageously when she demands the most difficult of all struggles: the struggle against oneself. When man is ready for this struggle, who can resist him? Supposedly, death requires the most courage, although it is a universal and inevitable necessity, especially such a death that can be easily avoided by making easy concessions. The Church teaches us to die valiantly. Let us look at the martyrs! Who does not know the history of Christian virgins who have thanked Christ for the strength to be victorious in death? Did this Church, who has taught people to bravely die for God, not teach them to bravely die for the fatherland?

You say: Christians only know how to die bravely, but they have not learned to courageously live for the fatherland. Know that if not for the courage of Christians, their patience, tenacity, and sacrifice, no state would be capable of surviving. Those who can perform the most difficult task — that of dying well — are capable of an easier art, living for the fatherland. Great courage flows only from the hardship of everyday life subjected to God's laws. Otherwise, the citizens of the state are like Ephraim's armed sons who knew how to shoot a bow but retreated on the second day of battle because they did not respect God's covenant and refused to follow His law (see Psalm 78:9–10).

However, love is the greatest virtue; it is a wonderful virtue that is very patient and kind and is not envious; it is not boastful or prone to anger; it does not rejoice at injustice but rejoices at the truth (see 1 Corinthians 13:4–5). Love never ceases, and regardless of how well man fulfills all his social duties, it constantly moves him to constant, increasingly greater efforts for the common good. It is a beautiful sign of the most righteous sovereign, how wonderfully it complements the best-governed state, and how strongly does it bond the most compact society together!

These are only examples that have been fortuitously taken out of this encyclopedia of the Christian treasury. However, they are an image of the great force that enters into the body of the state when its citizens live out those virtues.

The Church is the most reliable reformer of public life and a doctor who knows well two eventualities: life and death. No political program has succeeded in changing humanity. Only man's return to Christ and the conversion of man leads to miracles that are worthy of the attention of every state: "No longer proud, one becomes humble; no longer stingy, one becomes generous; a libertine becomes pure and chaste; each wound finds its medicine" (G. Savonarola).

177

Equally meaningless is the change of the social, economic, or political system when the old, sinful man lives in it. One can rearrange the furniture in a home, but if its inhabitant is not subject to major reform, he will not find happiness or bring it to others. It is a great danger to reform the system without reforming man; the disappointment this leads to can bring about catastrophe. The state is incapable of reforming man without the Church and her supernatural power. The Church teaches us to give the Word of God to all to whom it is due: "Pay all of them their dues, taxes to whom taxes are due, revenue to whom revenue is due, respect to whom respect is due, honor to whom honor is due" (Romans 13:7).

3. The God-Fearing State

The state lives thanks to the conscience of its citizens.

Deeply shaken by John's words, "the multitudes asked Him, 'What then shall we do?' And He answered them, 'He who has two coats, let him share with him who has none; and he who has food, let him do likewise'" (Luke 3:10–11). Having received this general response which obliges every person, they asked for guidelines concerning their duties in their everyday life. Thus, the tax collectors came and received the following response: "Collect no more than is appointed you" (Luke 3:13). Soldiers also asked and heard the reply: "Rob no one by violence or by false accusation, and be content with your wages" (Luke 3:14). This is how God ordered the people's consciences through the words of a prophet, elevating the value of their life and teaching them to dutifully live out their vocation, state, and profession.

For the Church, the behavior of Christ the Lord was an example of how to comprehend one's tasks in society. Like our divine Master in the past, today the Church, when she is asked and when she is not, reminds all people of their duties, constantly shaping the consciences of citizens. The state can live thanks to this moral-religious effort of the Church, because her existence is contingent on fidelity to one's conscience, love of one's duties, a spirit of righteousness, and the obedience of citizens.

The Church recalls St. Paul's words: "Therefore one must be subject, not only to avoid God's wrath but also for the sake of conscience"

(Romans 13:5). The Church does not limit herself to teaching, but in her educating activity implants love for the internal order and order in the soul, in the most personal and social life. "The Catholic citizen, farmer, official, officer, soldier, member of parliament, senator, or member of the government," Cardinal Hlond[1] writes, "cannot have two consciences: a Catholic one for private life and a non-Catholic one for public matters. Christ's law is obliging in all areas."[2]

The deeper man's life is shaped, the more accurately the following commandment is implemented in public life: "Be subject for the Lord's sake to every human institution, whether it be to the emperor as supreme, or to governors as sent by him to punish those who do wrong and to praise those who do right" (1 Peter 2:13–14). Full submission to "all human government" and the entire external organization of the state is possible only thanks to education and the internal organization of the soul. Telling man of God, salvation, his duties towards God, souls, and one's neighbor, the Church inculcates him with a civic sense, while the state places the entirety of social organization on a strong and unwavering stance, on Christ, "for in Him all things were created, in heaven and on earth, visible and invisible, whether thrones or dominions or principalities or authorities — all things were created through Him and for Him. He is before all things, and in Him all things hold together" (Colossians 1:16–17).

Surrounding state authority with the majesty of God's will, the Church teaches not only obedience towards the state like obedience towards God Himself, but she binds together the community living in the state with the strongest bond: that of mutual love in Christ. The Church does the state a great service in that she binds her citizens with Christ through love, simultaneously binding together their coexistence through the spirit of love, bringing social peace to an estranged milieu.

Sin is the greatest enemy of the state.

Sin ruins and leads to the disaster of not only individual people; sin also has social consequences, which leads to the ruin and disaster of the state. Not only the human soul, but also the "soul" of the state

---

[1] Cardinal August Hlond (1881–1948) preceded Wyszyński as Primate of Poland, an office he exercised from 1926 until his death.

[2] The pastoral letter *O chrześcijańskie zasady życia państwowego* ("On the Christian Principles of Public Life").

is the site of the hopeless struggle against sin and the struggle... for the right to sin. This is a struggle in which people commit the greatest acts of heroism and sacrifice.

Sin is the greatest enemy of the state because it destroys it from within in an imperceptible, insidious, and cunning way. Sin deforms God's thought, which God realizes within the state. The state was supposed to be "the City of God" married to God and the Church; it was supposed to be its faithful collaborator in man's path through the "wooded forest" of temporality towards heaven; it was supposed to surround man with comprehensive concern so that he would not only not become worse, but in fact, perfect himself. Meanwhile, the state itself often becomes the antechamber of hell, where the image of God is torn out of the soul, with Satan taking His place. Sin not only distorts God's image of the state, but it strikes at its very fundaments, efforts, and aspirations; it strikes at all the efforts of the state and its entire organization, sowing destruction everywhere. Sin spares nothing; it undermines the authority of the state, paralyzing its guardians with the leprosy of a bad example that leads to decomposition; thus, they are no longer the light of the world, but instead the source of shame. Sin gives rise to resistance among subordinates, boycotting the most salvific laws and the wisest actions; it breeds resistance and sabotage, which undermines the very existence of the state, unscrupulously destroying personal values. The sin of sloth and unconscientiousness fills all offices, scattering sand in the cogs of the state machinery. Through venality, bribery, theft of the state's money, and squandering of the public estate, sin empties the state's budget and reduces the nation's assets. Sin is unafraid of revealing secrets of national defense, thus digging the grave for one's own fatherland. As a result of the sins of pride, ignorance, and negligence, the state can no longer count on anyone, while the people it values and pays the most disappoint in times of trial, exposing all their vile neglect, amateurishness, emptiness, and arrogant, pretentious foolishness. How can the state be meaningful in public life and in fulfilling the social duties of people who have not learned to heroically struggle against sin in their own souls? Only those who bravely struggle against themselves and defeat themselves thanks to God's grace will disappoint neither the state, the nation, nor society.

In the struggle against this invasion and deluge, this rocky wave of sin, the state is powerless and helpless. How can it counter sin? With the criminal code? With the threat of imprisonment? With the police, who itself is not without sin? All this is too little. We know that even the most arrogant, atheistic, and secular state recognizes its powerlessness in its struggle against sinful citizens. Only the Church is unafraid of sin, and only the Church will emerge victorious from the struggle against sin. Only the Church can bravely look sin in its eyes, and only the Church knows the repulsive truth about it. Only the Church has the right to pardon and stop sin. Only the Church can say to the sovereign and his ministers, taxpayers and tax collectors, soldiers, and policemen: "Go in peace and sin no more" (see John 8:11). These who hear these words will feel inside them the renewed power of God's grace, which regenerates man for a new life.

Without the aid of the Church, the state will be unsuccessful in the struggle against sin, crime, and delinquency. A concordat is necessary here, one that is stronger than a mere exchange of documents; it must be a concordat of active and benevolent mutual assistance. The state can help the Church in the struggle against sin by creating an atmosphere that is hostile to sin and decisively struggling against all forms of scandal with all its available and appropriate means: legislation, the judiciary, and administration. The Church will do the rest.

God's laws stand in defense of the state.

Just as sin destroys the state, respecting God's laws elevates, bolsters, and preserves it. "If you walk in My statutes and observe My commandments and do them [. . .] you shall [. . .] dwell in your land securely. I will give peace in the land, and you shall lie down, and none shall make you afraid [. . .] and the sword shall not go through your land" (Leviticus 26:3–6).

What is the source of this power? Is it not the fact that in the life of the nation, God's law always encounters the state? It had existed before the state and ordered the lives of people, acting as the glue that bound together the citizens of the state community even before political bonds had been created. By educating the person, God's law prepares him for co-existence in society and inclines him to create a state community. The state owes all its existence to God's law, from which it also receives all its legislative power. Even when the state begins to exist independently of God, it cannot liberate itself from God's law, as it is the only soil where righteous legislation can sprout.

How wondrous God's care for the state community is! Can it not say of itself: "My help comes from the Lord, Who made heaven and earth [...]. Behold, he who keeps Israel will neither slumber nor sleep" (Psalm 121:2–5)? The stronger a state's relationship to God, the more confident it can be of its existence: "And I will have regard for you and make you fruitful and multiply you and will confirm My covenant with you. [...] And I will make My abode among you, and My soul shall not abhor you. And I will walk among you, and will be your God, and you shall be My people" (Leviticus 26:9–12). The God-fearing state can confidently count on His care and aid, as one can always trust citizens who are ready for faithful service of God.

4. A Prayer for the State

In the First Epistle to Timothy, St. Paul instructs "that supplications, prayers, intercessions, and thanksgivings be made for all men, for kings and all who are in high positions, that we may lead a quiet and peaceable life, Godly and respectful in every way" (1 Timothy 2:1–2).

The liturgy of the Church is filled with prayers for the state and those that govern it. The Church also summons the people, like Aaron and Hur in the past (see Exodus 17:12), to raise their hands to God, the King of Kings, and the Lord of all rulers so that they may receive wisdom. God places an enormous burden and responsibility on those who govern states; thus, they cannot be left to their own fate, but instead they must be surrounded with zealous prayer for all they do. Their efforts must be met with blessings.

The state, however, has its sins that provoke God's wrath. Then, the Lord calls: "How long will this people despise Me? And how long will they not believe in Me, in spite of all the signs which I have wrought among them? I will strike them with the pestilence and disinherit them" (Numbers 14:11–12). Like the voice of Moses in the past, in such moments, the voice of the Church is needed to beseech the Lord's wrath: "Now if Thou dost kill this people as one man, then the nations who have heard Thy fame will say, 'Because the Lord was not able to bring this people into the land which He swore to give to them, therefore He has slain them in the wilderness'" (Numbers 14:16). "Pardon the iniquity of this people, I pray Thee, according to the greatness of Thy steadfast love, and according as Thou hast forgiven this people, from Egypt even until now" (Numbers 14:19).

Just as the princes of Israel once summoned Samuel, today the rulers of states should beseech God's aid and blessing for all their efforts at every time of need. "Do not cease to cry to the Lord our God for us, that He may save us from the hand of the Philistines" (1 Kings 7:8), to the Lord who ends wars to the ends of the earth, "breaks the bow, and shatters the spear [and] burns the chariots with fire!" (Psalm 46:10).

"A false witness will perish, but the word of a man who hears will endure" (Proverbs 21:28). To achieve full glory, the leader of the nation and sovereign of the state need to be anointed by God. "This God is my strong refuge and has made my way safe [...] so that my arms can bend a bow of bronze" (2 Samuel 22:33, 35). May he not be ashamed that it is not he, but God who is the Victor! King John's *Veni, vidi, Deus vicit*[3] is the most wonderful expression of a ruler's glory. "For Thou didst gird me with strength for the battle; Thou didst make my assailants sink under me" (2 Samuel 22:40). Only then will the nation understand that God is with it and that God does not abandon leaders during the most difficult moments of their struggle. On the contrary, do not allow yourself to fear; do not let your spirits sag, but trust in God, who is your ally! Grab your weapon and shield and come to help me! As you strike with your sword, you will call to Him with the voice of faith: "Draw the spear and javelin against my pursuers! Say to my soul, 'I am your deliverance!'" (Psalm 34:1–3).

The nation, the state, and the sovereigns who know the path of prayer to heaven fear not Isaiah's words in days of joy and sadness, glory and terror: "Woe to those who go down to Egypt for help and rely on horses, trust in chariots because they are many and in horsemen because they are very strong, but do not look to the Holy One of Israel or consult the Lord!" (Isaiah 31:1). The state's covenant

---

3   Latin: "I came, I saw, God conquered." After defeating the Turks at Vienna on September 12, 1683, King John III Sobieski of Poland wrote this in a letter to Pope Innocent XI (although in reality, Sobieski wrote *Venimus, vidimus, Deus vincit* — "We came, we saw, God conquered").

with God bolsters any other covenant because then God becomes our allies' ally.

May our nation learn to publicly and collectively pray for its own state. When days of misfortune come, let us cry like the prophet Joel: "Blow the trumpet in Zion; sanctify a fast; call a solemn assembly; gather the people. Sanctify the congregation; assemble the elders; gather the children, even nursing infants. [. . .] Between the vestibule and the altar let the priests, the ministers of the Lord, weep and say, 'Spare Thy people, O Lord, and make not Thy heritage a reproach, a byword among the nations'" (Joel 2:15–17). When our nation is no longer castigated, and we experience peaceful days, let us not cease to call to the heavens: "Save, O Lord, our Republic, which places its trust in Thee."

* * *

When Nehemiah rebuilt the ruined walls of Jerusalem upon returning from the Babylonian captivity, the enemies of the Chosen People gathered together in order to ride and "fight against Jerusalem and to cause confusion in it" (Nehemiah 4:8). The brave leader of the nation did not fear; in fact, he demanded that all pray to our God and "set a guard as a protection against them day and night" (Nehemiah 4:9). "From that day on, half of my servants worked on construction, and half held the spears, shields, bows, and coats of mail; and the leaders stood behind all the house of Judah, who were building on the wall. Those who carried burdens were laden in such a way that each with one hand labored on the work and with the other held his weapon. And each of the builders had his sword girded at his side while he built" (see Nehemiah 4:16–18).

Is this not a touching example? May it be a model for us who rebuild the walls of our state yet are surrounded by enemies. Let us persist in prayerful reflection, our spirits vigilant and keeping a sword at our hips, unvanquished in our struggle. The walls of our household, which we will support with our arms, protect with our own breast, and surround with God's victorious power, will appear. If the Lord is with us, no one can be against us. The Lord is my savior, refuge, and helper for the ages!

5
Caesar in the Life of the Nation

I N HENRYK SIENKIEWICZ'S NOVEL *QUO VADIS*, a certain dialogue that takes place between Paul of Tarsus and Petronius in Antium attracts our attention. We are surprised by the encounter of two worlds: that of nascent Christianity, the religion of the slaves of Suburra, with the exquisite world of Rome's patricians, the elite among the elites. St. Paul says: "You call us enemies of life [. . .]. But wouldn't your life be safer and surer, Petronius, if Caesar were a Christian?"[1]

This distant echo from the period of transition from paganism to nascent Christendom leads to a persistent reflection in the depths of our soul! How is it possible that contemporary social currents as well as major revolutions and upheavals in the name of the liberation of man cause the life of the free person to be increasingly difficult, threatened in its elementary existence, and, in fact, nearly impossible? The state of the "liberated working class" has become a tyranny to not only the so-called bourgeoisie, but to the victorious proletariat as well. The totalitarian state has led not only to catastrophe, but also to total anxiety, fear, and terror, organizing a model prison that is the last stop before execution. The citizen at the mercy of the regime is frightened by the distant echo of the totalitarian ruler from the time of the pyramids: "I am Pharaoh, and without your consent no man shall lift up hand or foot in all the land of Egypt" (Genesis 41:44).

If only today's Caesar was a Christian! If only he acted according to our teachings!

I. Contemporary Caesar

It is telling that today everyone expects great spiritual virtues of all who exercise authority. Wearied by democratic irresponsibility and excessively tried by "secular" morality devoid of any moral principles

---

1   Henryk Sienkiewicz, *Quo Vadis*, trans. W. S. Kuniczak, New York: Hippocrene Books, 2017, pp. 415–416.

as well as the politics of sordid business and filthy hands, we demand Christian ethics and morality in political life. Leaders sense the desires of the masses; indeed, recent dictators have put on the gowns of often-harsh asceticism and self-abnegation in their personal lives. There were those who led the lives of monks and those who practiced comprehensive asceticism at times in their lives; finally, there were those who even provided "an inspiring model of family life." At the same time, they so often have themselves engaged in striking acts of lawlessness, cruelty, and ruthlessness; how inconsistent they were! They often acted like demons, even as they appeared as angels of light before the crowds. What is the source of this extreme discrepancy, this facility with which they transitioned from lofty actions to the most repulsive crimes? If only today's Caesar was a Christian!

Today's Caesar has all the anxieties of the pagan soul.

He enters the life of his nation with unparalleled pride, as if everything that the nation had done before him was worthless and meaningless and the positive construction of something began only with him. Hence, "they named lands their own" (Psalm 49:11).

The pomp of rulers was never expressed in such a grotesque, theatrical, and calculated way as in recent times. The ruler appears before the crowds like the Roman emperors used to appear before the plebians, amidst often phony, sleazy, and pompous decorations that seem to be symbols of the internal emptiness of the leader these people are supposed to adore. They have modeled their methods after those of cunning peddlers who try to cover up the fact that their wares are actually rubbish through loud shouts intended to attract passersby. What a painful idea — an advertisement for authority, which comes from God; an advertisement for a ruler who participates in God's power! By selling a substitute to the masses instead of the essential value of the soul, which they lack, "they conceive mischief and bring forth evil, and their heart prepares deceit" (Job 15:35). Iniquity resides in the lies to which they have given birth; such lies are all the more harmful as they have deceived millions who blindly trust them and lead them towards painful disappointment.

"For there is no truth in their mouth; their heart is destruction, their throat is an open sepulcher" (Psalm 5:9). How could it be any different? Hiding behind empty slogans and self-promotion, they fill their nation with the anxiety that fills their own souls: "But the wicked are like the tossing sea; for it cannot rest, and its waters toss up mire and dirt" (Isaiah 57:20).

"For they sow the wind, and they shall reap the whirlwind" (Hosea 8:7). Is it not telling that a society ruled by modern Caesars is like a volcano roaring internally and like the eternally wrathful sea that throws foam all around itself? The masses, who do not know the path of peace, come to share the ruler's anxiety (see Psalm 14:3).

The Christian ruler receives the command to "learn to fear the Lord [his] God" (Deuteronomy 17:19).

The ruler's fear of God guarantees the happiness of the people. Called to be the leader of the people, Joshua hears the following command from God: "Only be strong and very courageous, being careful to do according to all the law which Moses my servant commanded you; turn not from it to the right hand or to the left, that you may have good success wherever you go. This book of the law shall not depart out of your mouth" (Joshua 1:7–8).

In the mind of the ruler, God's law is the way to His wisdom, and "wisdom is better than strength, and a wise man is better than a strong man" (Wisdom 6:1), for only a wise ruler can appropriately make use of the power bestowed upon him for the common good. The Christian ruler should never forget Ben Sira's advice: "If they make you master of the feast, do not exalt yourself; be among them as one of them" (Sirach 32:1). "That his heart may not be lifted up above his brethren, and that he may not turn aside from the commandment, either to the right hand or to the left" (Deuteronomy 17:20). The road to greatness in the nation leads only through the path of service to the nation.

National leaders need numerous virtues; above all, purity of the heart, altruism, and total self-sacrifice in the service of their nations. "Those who do not give themselves wholly," Savonarola writes, "and who look for themselves apart from the affairs of the state will soon not want it without themselves. Thus, they will soon want only themselves... and sacrifice the entire nation! Meanwhile, the opposite is true! The fatherland is not for you, but you are for the fatherland, and you and the fatherland are for God."

A Christian leader with such a preparation will find the way to the heart of his subjects. He demands much of himself in the vein of the wise principle of all authority: "Like the magistrate of the people, so are his officials; and like the ruler of the city, so are all its inhabitants" (Sirach 10:2). Thus, if he wants to elevate his nation and improve it, he should above all strive for God. He will bless his own nation with the generosity of God's blessings that will gather in his own soul. The words of Ben Sira are confirmed very often.

II. Caesar and His Housemates

"When the wicked rise, men hide themselves, but when they perish, the righteous increase" (Proverbs 28:28). "When the righteous are in authority, the people rejoice: but when the wicked rule, the people groan" (Proverbs 29:2).

That from which "men hide themselves" and why "the people" ruled by an unjust ruler "groan" comes from his wicked soul. Threatened by his enemies and his surroundings, he tries to cling to authority through violence, terror, fear, and tyranny. Despots expand the limits of crimes, seeing almost all citizens as potential criminals. Nowhere are human life, property and the basic right to life valued so little as in the state marked by terror, which slowly becomes one big prison. Let us look at the examples of lawlessness that communist and totalitarian states have given us. They became filled with concentration camps, where the flower of the nation was ruined and where the victims of the regime were treated like ordinary criminals, except that ordinary criminals are protected by the criminal code. All human accomplishments that are flaunted using the slogans of "freedom, equality and brotherhood" bow before the will of the despot. There no longer is civic freedom; there is only the freedom of the ruling party and the lawlessness of tyranny towards ordinary citizens.

In one of his sermons, Father Piotr Skarga advised rulers: "Look after your health, not causing harm to anyone. Those who harm no one are suspicious of no one." The time a ruler is in power is extended by love and social justice. However, the godless ruler does not tread this path, while his lawlessness is filled with sorrow and the groans of his unfortunate land. The lawlessness in his heart gradually spreads to the nation, which is infected by its leader's evil actions, multiplying them infinitely. A wicked ruler will use his negative influence on his nation in order to climb an even higher level of iniquity. Bolstered in strength by defaming the nation, he agrees to commit mad deeds that lead to perdition.

Only a Christian ruler can introduce the Christian spirit to the life of his nation in place of Caesar's spirit. When this happens, his soul, which had hitherto been oppressed and trampled on, will regain his social and civic significance, as will the sanctity of human life. Only a Christian ruler will be able to understand man's great value and how his soul and person are higher than any social goods. Only then will he appreciate the momentous contribution that the Christian citizen makes to public life.

Then, respect for human rights, human dignity, and active Christian love for one's fellow citizens becomes a requirement of state policy. Respecting human dignity, freedom, and personhood is the simplest path to permanently binding man to society and to gaining people who cooperate toward beneficial social goals. This aim cannot be achieved through terror and violence, which can bind the body, but cannot subdue the soul.

The folly of all dictators is that they build up an elaborate system of terrorizing the citizen, deluding themselves that this is the means to unifying society. May the tyrant who oppresses not think that he rules humanity; he merely drives the flock. There is no soul in the totalitarian state, the collective state, or the dictatorship of the proletariat; there is only the mechanization of robots who have hidden their souls before the bloody hand of tyrants. No tyrant can kill the soul, for the soul is God's work. The human soul is so independent and free that God has respected its freedom up to the limits of sin. Nor can tyranny subdue the soul, for it is receptive only to love and freedom. God, the most perfect model of all rulers, walks with us in love, as He does not want to be the lord of slaves. Those who get rid of love cannot ensure anyone freedom. Thus, Christian rulers cannot reject love as a means of social influence.

The aim of the Christian sovereign cannot be to make people blindly submissive and obedient in a way that is not worthy of man; instead, he must strive to make them good. When he approaches the Christian ideal of a righteous man, he will possess the most valuable treasure in building a permanent and close-knit society.

III. Caesar and the Nations

The ruler who has violated God's law in his soul and who has allowed himself to be directed by pride leads his nation to mad "tourism," from one abyss to another. The de-Christianized soul serves selfishness in all its perversity. Dishonesty and hypocrisy become the moral code in international politics: They "speak peace with their neighbors, while mischief is in their hearts" (Psalm 28:3), while this wrath leads them to bloodshed. Woe to weak nations that have had the misfortune of entrusting themselves to others and have allowed themselves to be deceived. There would be no succor for them if rule of the world remained only in the hands of a tyrant. However, God does not allow rulers to escape His hands. He stands in defense of the poor and lowly; He protects nations against being devoured by cruel despots. This is their fate: "In a moment they die; at midnight the people are shaken and pass away, and the mighty are taken away by no human hand" (Job 34:20).

And this is the fate of the tyrant and all the works of his hands: "Woe to him who heaps up what is not his own — for how long? [...] Because you have plundered many nations, all the remnant of the peoples shall plunder you, for the blood of men and violence to the earth, to cities and all who dwell therein. [...] Woe to him who builds a town with blood and founds a city on iniquity!" (Habakkuk 2:6–12).

The Christian ruler will not follow the bloody path of tyrants. He knows that God has intended for there to be an international community and that He gave birth to numerous nations, which He has entrusted with distinct tasks, and that only the labor of these nations, based on their own cultural values developed in light of God's law, will influence the richness of the soul of the world. Understanding the value of his own nation best, he will not disdain the property of others and their contribution to the common treasury of humanity, which lives in the house of the common Father. Thus, the Christian ruler will follow the high standard of Catholic universalism to whose laws he will subject love for one's own nation out of concern that it could descend into national selfishness or self-love. The good of one's own nation will be evaluated in the light of the good of humanity, and he will strive for that good, directed by the principles of Christian ethics, believing that only such good is the permanent prize of the nation, which is consistent with the highest good and God's law. It is insufficient to accept only the most convenient Christian principles; the life of the entire nation and all its aspirations and politics should be permeated by the spirit of God.

The Christian ruler will be governed by this spirit when entering into contact with other nations. He will not forget that a bad tree cannot bear good fruits and thus he cannot have anything in common with Belial; he cannot support blatant godlessness and the crimes of other nations, even if they were to bring the greatest benefits to his nation. A ruler who enters into an evident alliance with a nation that violates God's laws and whose actions are condemned by the Holy See summons God's wrath, using the words of the Psalmist: "Scatter the peoples who delight in war" (Psalm 68:30).

IV. God in Caesar's State

In recent years, we have witnessed attempts at building a modern state without God. No totalitarian states, which violate the freedom of the citizen, could completely enslave him before enslaving Christianity, which has always stood in defense of human freedom. Thus, the Catholic Church must fight against the totalitarianism of modern states, in defense of the citizen.

The Idol of the State Against God

When we recall the event of the terrible struggle against God's Church by the modern state, we have before our eyes the Apocalyptic kings who "receive authority as kings for one hour, together with the beast. [. . .] They will make war on the Lamb, and the Lamb will conquer them, for He is Lord of lords and King of kings, and those with Him are called and chosen and faithful" (Revelation 17:12, 14).

We were witnesses to the liberation of pride. Those who say the following to God have risen up: "'Depart from us! We do not desire the knowledge of Thy ways. What is the Almighty, that we should serve Him? And what profit do we get if we pray to Him?'" (Job 21:14–15). The contemporary dictator has swallowed the hook of Satanic temptation, which had long been hanging over the world from the hill of

191

temptation. He was shown "all the kingdoms of the world" and "all this authority and their glory" (Luke 4:5, 6), which could be attained by just one bow to Satan. This temptation is too strong for the weak person. Tempted by Satan, he tempts his subjects: "If you, then, will worship me, it shall all be yours" (Luke 4:7). You will maintain all your property and that which you will steal from others for the good of the national interest as well as a strong position, broad influence, profits from the state budget, privileges, orders, distinctions, and respect. Everything will be yours if only you bow before me!

In the twentieth century, man was called a god; we witnessed the deification of the leader of the nation and his being called the god of the nation. It was preached that God was revealed not in the person of Jesus Christ, but in Adolf Hitler. Hitler was called a holy spirit and a light that illuminates. In servile blindness, the abysmal difference between the Creator and His creation was forgotten. The hymns of praise of *Sieg Heil* and *Sacro Duce* and the nation falling to its knees before tyrannical propaganda were possible thanks to the acceptance and approval of the sinful man, "who opposes and exalts himself against every so-called god or object of worship, so that he takes his seat in the temple of God, proclaiming himself to be God" (2 Thessalonians 2:4). Struggling against God's name in order to inscribe one's own on the names of all the roads and monuments, overthrowing God's law in order to impose state-sanctioned lawlessness, replacing God Himself to become the god of the terrorized masses: such are the political aims of the modern ruler!

"For although they knew God, they did not honor Him as God or give thanks to Him, but they became futile in their thinking and their senseless minds were darkened. Claiming to be wise, they became fools, and exchanged the glory of the immortal God for images resembling mortal man or birds or animals or reptiles" (Romans 1:21–23).

If today's Caesar occasionally refers to God, it is only in order to summon Him to be an accomplice in his crimes and to hide his tyranny behind His majesty. In the name of the slogan "God is with us,"[2] the freedom of nations was violated, country after country was ravished,

---

2 *Gott mit Uns* ("God is with us") has been a slogan of the German military since the Middle Ages. Here, however, Wyszyński is referring to the fact that it was present on the uniforms of the Wehrmacht, Nazi Germany's army.

churches filled with praying people were bombed, the property of widows and orphans was plundered for public aims, and families, villages, cities, and even entire regions of helpless people were disinherited.

Is it not telling that the modern, supposedly sophisticated leader is on the level of Nero, Diocletian and Julian the Apostate whenever he struggles against God, displaying brutality, savagery, refined cruelty, and inhumanity? The coarse gladiator tormented his innocent victim with the cold blood of a professional executioner. Today, the orders of rulers make civilized people resemble animals: the elegant, fragrant, educated, enlightened, and progressive police functionary who preaches slogans of comprehensive tolerance calmly shoots his Browning pistol at the equally elegant, educated, and enlightened twentieth-century martyr for his faith in Christ.

Let us recall the images of the persecution of the Church in Bolshevik Russia, Mexico, Red Spain, and racist Germany: how are they any different from the persecutions of the first centuries of Christianity? At best, they differ only in that they have perfected their techniques of murder! How little has changed in the hatred for God and His saints. The struggle against God always turns even the most civilized man into a beast.

> For those who deify themselves in the world
> On the contrary slowly de-humanize themselves.
> (Zygmunt Krasiński, "Psalm of Sorrow")

Meanwhile, "He who sits in the heavens laughs" (Psalm 2:4). The Lord hates "haughty eyes, a lying tongue, and hands that shed innocent blood" (Proverbs 6:17). Soon, "all worshipers of images are put to shame, who make their boast in worthless idols" (Psalm 96:7).

2. The End of State Idols

Christ's sword has been hanging over the godless ruler and his life from the very beginning of his rule: "Woe to the world for temptations to sin!" (Matthew 18:7). The higher the corrupter of God's children is elevated, the mightier the power of Christ's sword. God goes to make His judgment: "Now shall the ruler of this world be cast out" (John 12:31). God "cuts off the spirit of princes [and] is terrible to the kings of the earth" (Psalm 76:12). The elevated idol will hear above himself the Almighty's shocking, powerful question: "Will you condemn Me that you may be justified? Have you an arm like God?" (Job 40:8–9).

"Why do you boast, O mighty man, of mischief done against the Godly? [...] You love evil more than good and lying more than speaking the truth" (Psalm 52:1, 3). "Woe to those who decree iniquitous decrees" (Isaiah 10:1). Remember, that I am the Lord of the ages! "I have seen a wicked man overbearing and towering like a cedar of Lebanon. Again, I passed by, and lo, he was no more; though I sought him, he could not be found" (Psalm 37:35–36).

How ephemeral is the memory of tyrants in God's eyes! How quickly their days pass! "The enemies of the Lord are like the glory of the pastures, they vanish — like smoke they vanish away" (Psalm 37:20). The faster they are elevated, the more terrible their downfall.

"Before his days be full, he shall perish and his hands shall wither away" (Job 15:32), for "men of blood and treachery shall not live out half their days" (Psalm 55:23). Will not all their false glory, with which they have reviled God Himself and belittled people, turning God's free sons into degraded slaves, end along with their entire arrogant lives? "When his breath departs, he returns to his earth; on that very day his plans perish" (Psalm 146:4). Lackeys are the first to sprint away from a decaying house of infamy. How often has Job's prophesy been fulfilled before our very eyes: "His memory perishes from the earth, and he has no name in the street" (Job 18:17).

The corpse of the tyrant has not yet cooled, but portraits and plaques proclaiming his pride have already been torn out of walls. He has fallen into oblivion like a mere rock! You have released Your wrath, which has consumed it like straw; they have sunk in turbulent waters like lead; You have stretched out Your right hand, and the earth has devoured them; the greatness of Your arm will make them motionless like a stone (see Exodus 15:5–16). Indeed, "your remembrance shall be compared to ashes, and your necks shall be brought to clay" (Job 13:12).

This is God's historic response: Get behind me, Satan, for "you shall worship the Lord your God, and Him only shall you serve" (Luke 4:8; see Matthew 4:10). Instead, they have worshiped their own glory, the power of horses and panzers, the rattle of tanks and bombers! Yet, "the war horse is a vain hope for victory, and by its great might it cannot save" (Psalm 33:17). "His delight is not in the strength of the horse, nor His pleasure in the legs of a man; but the Lord takes pleasure in those who fear Him, in those who hope in His steadfast love" (Psalm 147:10–11).

Are we not witnesses to this truth that has shone before our eyes? All those who know the Lord's paths look to the future with confidence and the calm of faith: "I have seen the fool taking root, but suddenly I cursed his dwelling. His sons are far from safety, they are crushed in the gate, and there is no one to deliver them. His harvest the hungry eat, and he takes it even out of thorns" (Job 5:3–5).

That has also happened! Such is the eternal path of leaders and nations that rebel against the Lord in their pride: "For the nation and kingdom that will not serve You shall perish; those nations shall be utterly laid waste" (Isaiah 60:12).

* * *

Isaiah called against the Babylonian king: "The Lord has broken the staff of the wicked, the scepter of rulers, that smote the peoples in wrath with unceasing blows, that ruled the nations in anger with unrelenting persecution. The whole earth is at rest and quiet; they break forth into singing. The cypresses rejoice at you, the cedars of Lebanon, saying, 'Since you were laid low, no hewer comes up against us.' [...] 'How you are fallen from heaven, O Day Star, son of Dawn! How you are cut down to the ground, you who laid the nations low!' [...] Those who see you will stare at you, and ponder over you: 'Is this the man who made the earth tremble, who shook kingdoms, who made the world like a desert and overthrew its cities, who did not let his prisoners go home?'" (Isaiah 14:5–17).

Such are the age-old paths of the blind rulers of blind nations. May the nation learn to distinguish between good and evil forces; may it remember that God overthrows state idols today, just as He once overthrew Belial. God "leads counselors away stripped, and judges He makes fools. He looses the bonds of kings and binds a waistcloth on their loins. [...] He pours contempt on princes and looses the belt of the strong. [...] He enlarges nations and leads them away" (Job 12:17–23).

We learn of the Lord's paths and His power! Today, God is no weaker than at the beginning, when He established the fundaments of the earth and its kingdom.

"Who shall not fear and glorify thy name, O Lord? For Thou alone art holy. All nations shall come and worship Thee, for Thy judgments have been revealed" (Revelation 15:4).

6

Poland in the Family of Nations

"We love Poland, our Fatherland, not only because it feeds us, but because it is of God's design." (Piotr Skarga)

"THE RIGHT HAND OF THE LORD DOES VALiantly, the right hand of the Lord is exalted [...]. I shall not die, but I shall live, and recount the deeds of the Lord" (Psalm 118:16–17). Gratitude to God is the program that the Psalmist proscribed for his nation.

When we enter the ranks of free nations, we should have no other program before our eyes: "I will sing of Thy steadfast love, O Lord, forever; with my mouth I will proclaim Thy faithfulness to all generations" (Psalm 89:1). Indeed, we have reached the gates of freedom calling: "Open to me the gates of righteousness, that I may enter through them and give thanks to the Lord" (Psalm 118:19). Today, when our cries have reached the Lord's ears and we are once again in the family of free nations, let us reflect on what we, a young and gifted Catholic nation, are to do in this proud assembly!

We have called for justice to the Lord of Hosts, and when our right hand is filled with His gifts (see Psalm 25:11), let our righteousness be revealed and enter the life of our nation and our coexistence with other nations as we tread the Lord's paths together.

I. Our National Values

We know our national flaws, which we talk about with the relish and passion of those who flagellate themselves. There is nothing wrong with this as long as this does not violate the truth and does not shape within us a sense of worthlessness and powerlessness.

However, there is nothing wrong with making ourselves aware that our national character has not only flaws.

Polish Catholicity

We draw our nation's greatest value from deep faith and zealous piety. Poland is famous for being a Catholic country (*Polonia semper fidelis*) and as the land of crosses and sites of miracles where God reminds the world of the importance of faith. We astound the nations with our deep reverence for the Holy Mother. These are priceless values that make us apostles of a good example despite our sins. Just as St. Paul in Romans, we can also thank God that our faith "is proclaimed in all the world" (Romans 1:8). This has won us widespread trust among the nations, even during the most challenging trials and experiences. Yet we never understood our Catholicity in a selfish way, only for the sake of our convenience; we have never had any material gains from the Church. Instead, we have righteously understood our dignity as a daughter of the Church: we took this as God's truth and lived a life of grace, in return being, as Pope Innocent XI said in 1678, *praevalidum ac illustre christianae rei publicae propugnaculum* ("a mighty bulwark of Christianity").

Poland has always defended the Church and Christian civilization. Our struggles were never aggressive in nature; our struggle against the East was a struggle over the limits of the influence of Latin Christian culture and a struggle for Rome in the East. This has been the case from time immemorial! The paths of Poland's eternal struggle in defense of Christian civilization lead through the fields of Legnica, where we defended Christian Europe against the Mongols; and through our numerous struggles against the Tatars and Turks that stretched throughout the centuries, from the campaign against the Turks by the Danube during the Jagiellonian dynasty (1426) to Varna, where our king, a Christian knight, fell; at Cecora, where Żółkiewski perished; and Vienna and Párkány, from which King John III Sobieski emerged victorious. We defended Christian civilization in our wars against the Teutonic Order, schismatic Muscovy, and heretical Sweden. We defended Christian civilization not only at Grunwald, but also at Orsha, Kłuszyn, Chudnov, Kircholm, and the slopes of Jasna Góra; finally, we defended it at the Vistula in 1920 and in the rubble of Warsaw.

It is important to note that no one ever aided us in our struggles; in fact, the entirety of Christian Europe often stood against us. If it did not take up arms against us, then it at least opposed us in spirit, as if God wanted us to be isolated in order to implement *Gesta Dei por Polonos*.[1] As Poland fought in defense of Christian culture, Europe, protected by the breast of our forefathers, destroyed this culture in wars of religion.

Latin Rome went to the East, to the Dnieper and the Daugava, when Poland was independent. When Poland was gone, Rome retreated to the Bug and the Narew Rivers. We can correctly say that the partitions of Poland were the greatest crime against Western culture. Today, Poland's strong connection to Latin culture likewise means the Roman Church's safe and secure movement eastwards; undermining Polishness in the East means the retreat of Latin culture from the Vistula. The Latin Church has always moved eastward when Poland was strong and retreated when Poland was weakened. Poland always guaranteed the Church freedom in its own lands as well as in neighboring lands in its sphere of influence. In our fatherland, the Church was always persecuted by invaders and never by the Polish nation.

2. The Nobility of the Polish Character

Our national character is exceptionally noble thanks to the Catholic religion; thanks to this, Poland has protected itself from causing harm to others throughout its history. We ourselves have suffered greatly at the hands of other nations, but we have never consciously harmed any of them. One of our thinkers, Feliks Koneczny, has noted that "the Poles are ready to harm Poland in order to not harm others at any moment." Hence the proverbial religious and political tolerance of our nation.[2]

Vindictiveness and a spirit of revenge are foreign to us, even with respect to the sworn enemies of Polishness. Have we ever harmed the children of hostile nations? Have we not given ourselves many excuses, saying that the fattest piece of Polish bread typically is meant

---

1   Latin: "Acts of God for Poland."
2   Pre-partition Poland was arguably the most religiously tolerant and ethnically diverse state. With some exceptions, such as the expulsion of the Polish Brethren, a Protestant sect that rejected the Trinity, in 1658, the Polish state afforded protection to religious minorities and was free of wars of religion. King Sigismund II Augustus (1548–1572) famously said: "I am not the king of your consciences."

for others? There were moments when this aversion to revenge was good for us. St. Paul's words have been verified among us: "If your enemy is hungry, feed him; [. . .] for by so doing you will heap burning coals upon his head" (Romans 12:20). How many times have we seen tears of gratitude in the eyes of our generously endowed enemies! It is significant that hatred directed towards Poland had to be officially organized, because neighboring nations, tempted by their rulers, did not share it.

The spirit of bloody revolution was completely alien to us; we were defeated by neither red nor brown communism, even though we were surrounded by both like an island in the sea for many years.

> A childish slaughter is not a good act,
> Nor is destruction.
> Only God's love is active.
> Through love, it leads to transformation.
>   (Zygmunt Krasiński, "Psalm of Love")

The spirit of guile, betrayal, and assassination, which other nations consider to be the apex of political wisdom, was also alien to us. We were too noble and upright to build our state with the dagger and poison.

> My brothers are not my murderers.
> I love the saber, but the knife is shameful.
>   (Zygmunt Krasiński, "Psalm of Sorrow")

3. Love for Freedom, Equality, and Justice

Our Fatherland has always been faithful to the teaching of the Church, from whose treasury it has taken beloved freedom and brought it to the coexistence of both estates and nations.

We have preached the principle of the equality of all before the law for many years. Social justice is not a new concept for us. When the rest of Europe fought to increase royal authority, in our country such thinkers as Andrzej Frycz Modrzewski and Piotr Skarga spoke out in favor of improving the lot of the peasants and plebians.

The concept of subordination to the state was alien to us; we instead preferred the concept of citizenship. We understood the Gospel principle of "whoever would be first among you must be slave of all" (Mark 10:44), in such a way that society was supposed to serve not the king but the common good. Even our notorious landowners were a hundred times milder than in Western countries. Honesty with respect to the spirit of our own nation requires that we acknowledge this fact!

We even knew how to mitigate the co-existence of various religions and denominations in the heart of one nation. In our struggle against the Teutonic Knights and the rest of Europe, at the Council of Constance Poland defended, through the words of Paweł Włodkowic,[3] the principles of natural law, emphasizing that pagans are subjected to the same laws as Christians and that the Christian faith cannot be imposed using violence, fire, and the sword. As far back as the fifteenth century, Poland defended a thesis that has yet to be adopted in the policies of colonial powers, which continue to treat people as merchandise to be traded, primarily for economic reasons.

Although it was deeply Catholic, Poland was never hostile to anyone who professed a different faith. With regards to our attitude towards neighboring nations, we have always maintained that the weak should be respected and should be afforded the same rights as the strong. Poland rejected the Teutonic Knights' principle of "apostolic spoils," instead defending the thesis that another's land cannot be invaded even in the name of spreading the Gospels. We proclaimed that every nation has the right to self-determination and to its own politics of war and peace, while the right to self-determination belongs to all organized nations because of natural law itself.

When we recall these Polish theses at the Council of Constance from half a millennium ago and listen to Pope Pius XII's 1941 Christmas Eve address on the moral law that binds together the coexistence of nations as well as the linguistic distinctiveness and the right of the nations to free economic activity, we sense our nation's close kinship

---

3 The Council of Constance (1414–1418) convened to end the Western Schism, which resulted in three men claiming to be the pope, condemn the heresies of reformers Jan Hus (who was sentenced to burning at the stake at the council) and John Wycliffe, and resolve the conflict between Poland and the Teutonic Knights. The Polish delegation was led by Paweł Włodkowic, a priest and the rector of the Krakow Academy, and defended the pagan peoples of the Baltics whom the Teutonic Knights sought to convert to Christianity using violence. Włodkowic also defended Hus. Włodkowic's arguments were some of the earliest public defenses of the notions of international human rights.

with the Holy See. Poland has always been magnanimous towards the weak. Not violence and the sword but love and unity have been our political tools. Thus, it is correctly said of Poland that if the fate of the world depended on it, the world would be filled with free and happy nations. It is unsurprising that the ideal of the struggle for freedom has always been popular in Poland and that Poland takes part in all struggles for liberation under the slogan: "For your freedom and for ours!" Meanwhile, "Poland Has Not Yet Perished" has become something like a hymn of freedom for all the oppressed Slavic nations.

A universalistic mindset has always dominated in our public life. We never limited ourselves to what is useful only to ourselves, instead asking ourselves what we can do for others.

4. The Morality of Collective Life

Poland always struggled to implement moral principles in public, political, and international life. Our political thought has always dealt with the question of how to introduce Christian ethics into the coexistence of nations. Our national philosophy, poetry and literature attest to this. We have always linked progress to morality, always convinced that there can be no progress without morality. From the Council of Constance to the present day, we have always fought for these principles at the international level. Although the whole world believed that morality in politics is a lost ideal, and all acted in political life as if they had been liberated from all notions of morality, we have always dreamed of "the City of God in the world."

The once-despised Polish ideal triumphs in today's world. Contemporary experiences have proven that one cannot violate moral principles in public, state, and international life. We have finally arrived at the conclusion that truly healthy policies can be implemented only by moral people. We will remain the defenders of one kind of ethics, of Christian ethics, in the life of the states and nations.

This is the invaluable contribution of the Polish soul to the life of the nations! Half a century ago, it was not appreciated. Such harsh experiences as the catastrophe of the recent war were needed in order to recognize what was so obvious and what was Catholic in our soul. Today, the stone rejected by the builders has become the cornerstone for the new generation.

II. Poland in God's Plans for the World

Our fatherland is a clear sign of God's power over the nations. "When the Lord restored the fortunes of Zion, we were like those who dream. Then our mouth was filled with laughter, and our tongue with shouts of joy; then they said among the nations, 'The Lord has done great things for them'" (Psalm 126:1–2). May the nations continue to admire the miracles of God's power in our history and may they learn respect for His will.

Pope Pius XI, a friend of our nation, once said to us: "I am convinced that God, who so miraculously returned freedom to your nation, wants to implement His plans through it and will do so despite everything." We lack the courage to guess God's plans, for they stand before every God-fearing nation "in due time." Today, we can say that the most important manifestations of God's will are not alien to us.

Above all, let us bear witness to God in the face of the nations.

Our national bard Zygmunt Krasiński, who welcomed Poland's aspirations for freedom with his prophetic spirit, spoke to the nation as follows:

> Poland! Poland! Your tomb was only
> The cradle of a new dawn.
> Against eternity, it was one brief moment
> In which the day of God was conceived!
> ("Psalm of Hope")

Today, when "the day of God was conceived" within us, let us say to one another: "Awake, awake, put on your strength, O Zion; put on your beautiful garments, O Jerusalem, the holy city [...]. Shake yourself from the dust, arise, O captive Jerusalem; loose the bonds from your neck, O captive daughter of Zion" (Isaiah 52:1–2).

With our heads raised high to the Lord, let us listen to Him, who says: "'You are my servant, I have chosen you and not cast you off;' fear not, for I am with you, be not dismayed, for I am your God; I will strengthen you, I will help you, I will uphold you with my victorious right hand. I will strengthen you, I will help you, I will uphold you with my victorious right hand" (Isaiah 41:9–11).

Having learned of God's great love for us, let us profess with joy: "Who delivered me from my enemies; [...] Thou didst deliver me from men of violence. For this I will extol thee, O Lord, among the nations, and sing praises to thy name" (Psalm 18:48–49).

This universal will flow from the grateful heart to the nation: "O give thanks to the Lord, call on His name, make known His deeds among the peoples!" (Psalm 105:1). It is our national duty, the duty of a grateful and noble heart and the obligation of international justice to bear witness to God's power and glory! When a brave and noble nation becomes a herald of God's glory among the nations and a living testimony to God's omnipotence, it revives numerous hopes, liberates many forces, and strengthens countless hearts that are weakened by the power of evil and faithlessness. This will be an eloquent testimony to the truth that there is such a thing as God's justice and that not brutal violence, but God rules the world, while the fate of the nations rests in His hands.

From this point, God's justice and law must become international law, for "the Lord's hand has exalted us," and this hand will continue to protect us.

Just as our distant ancestors defended God's natural law in the coexistence of nations before the entire world, let us likewise undertake this task that we have abandoned and that has not yet been undertaken by anyone.

Let us continue to be a bulwark of Christendom.

The world needs an example of political idealism. When all the principles of international law were violated; when hypocrisy, guile, and political lies were elevated to the level of the state's national interest; when the greatest political wisdom became the art of cunningly deceiving one's opponent and striking him from behind when he stumbles; when Machiavellianism can be considered to be a virtue compared with pagan brutality and contemporary savagery, the world must hear the vibrant protests of the state that has the courage to be humane, moral, and religious in its international politics. Let us be attracted to the ideals of justice and truth, the ideal of high morality on which the coexistence of nations rests.

> Raise the sword against hell
> And fight Satan's black minions!
> Cut through the bloody knout of the Barbarian hordes with
> your saber!
>
> (Zygmunt Krasiński, "Psalm of Love")

We were a religious state, and we must remain one if we do not want to slip away from our historical role as defenders of Christendom. Catholicism is the source of our nation's strength; this has been clearly expressed by our enemies, who have tried to defeat the nation above all by striking at the Church. The most recent blow was the strongest, but at the same time it was instructive, as it provided testimony to the truth that the Church in Poland has served the nation well and raised it in the spirit of love for the Fatherland. Was it not our enemy who confirmed that the Roman Church is our national Church? By striking at the Church, the "hostile man" struck at the bulwark of Christendom; in his hatred for religion, he fought against not only Poland but also the religious state. We know how comforting the sense that the enemy was the enemy of not only our nation but also of God Himself was, and how it was a deposit of Divine justice. Who that fights against God with impunity can ward off the prod (Acts 9:6)?

There was no way that God could have more effectively defended veneration of Him than through elevating those who trusted Him from our downfall.

The always-unique idealism that has marked the history of our nation has always been the source of our pride. Although we had created a powerful state, our weapon was that of culture, which brought nations together, rather than the methods of partition and bloody conquest.

Whenever we were a nation state, we never forgot about the ideal of the common good. How willingly we faced trials whenever matters of the utmost importance were threatened. We protected Christian Europe from the Islamic invasions.

It suffices to recall the stubborn conflict between the Christian and Muslim worlds. The East did not succeed in defending itself, for it lacked pure, selfless hands. In the West, only the Holy See represented universal Christian thought, which was expressed by the former apostolic nuncio to Poland, the famous Enea Silvio Piccolomini, who would become Pope Pius II. He did not succeed in uniting the bickering Italian and German states or overcoming the egotism of French leaders and Hungarian self-interest. In the struggle against Islam, only Poland, which was always moved by the pure thought of defending

Christendom, never disappointed. When summoned, Poland marched to Varna, hurried to Vienna, and emerged victorious from Khotyn.

Just as regiments of Tatars and Turks once broke down when they were met with the brave breast of Polish kings and hetmans, likewise Polish breasts stopped the march of Red Asia to conquer the West at the dawn of our nation's rebirth. Poland's defensive will inaugurate the failure of the totalitarian state in the West; only Poland, which trusted God's historical justice, repulsed this violence. Although she was defeated, Poland awoke the slumbering conscience of the world and initiated the worst failure of Godless pride. Then, we looked the "ugliness of devastation" of a state without God right in the eyes. Who knew the godless state better than Poland, who was first to be confronted with the furiously unrestrained hatred that stormed eastwards? This was a warning to us in order to fend off this monstrosity, which we saw with our own eyes and personally experienced, as the most terrifying and harmful plague to the state.

How many times we have stood in defense of Christian civilization! This is our pride and contribution to history, which is greater than the industrialization of Europe and all its civilization. When Poland bled in defense of Europe, the West, which was protected by our breast, worked calmly and grew richer. May it remember this today!

In light of these achievements, can we not be proud of the witness of the Father of Christianity, Pope Benedict XV, who so accurately evaluated the greatness of Poland's contributions to the clash of two civilizations on the fields of Radzymin and Ossów?[4] "It is this benevolence of the Lord God Our Benefactor," he wrote to the Polish bishops on December 4, 1920, "who has strangely been good to not only your nation but to other peoples as well. Everyone knows that the enemy's mad onslaught intended to destroy Poland, that bulwark of Europe, and later undermine all of Christianity and the culture that flows from it, all the while planning on spreading a mad and pathological doctrine."

Today, all political profiteers and hucksters should recall this knot that binds together the nations in one Christian culture and the holy faith; today, all these sorrowful Marthas that aim for much should learn that they need nothing more than God. Without God, the most

---

4 Radzymin and Ossow were the sites of two major battles of the Polish-Bolshevik War of 1918–1921, which resulted in a Polish victory.

powerful rulers, the richest empires, the oldest and proudest nations, and in fact all of Europe will perish!

Let us inscribe in bronze Pope Pius XI's words addressed to the Polish nation: "You are knights of the faith; in this role, you will be the best knights of Poland."

This is our national task, which is not new to us and which nobody has done for us since Poland's downfall! As in the past, may it once again be our pride and a call to struggle for a righteous soul in the coexistence of nations.

Finally, let us give the world a model of a righteous Christian state.

If God led us "through fire and through water" (Psalm 66:12) in order to take us to a place of refreshment, it was to make us champions of God's order in the nation and world by allowing us to know the power of suffering and wretchedness. Our soul is completely Christian, and we have seen the entire repulsiveness of the pagan world with the eyes of our soul.

May this historical spectacle in which we took part be an incentive for arduous work: "I will come into Thy house with burnt offerings; I will pay Thee my vows, that which my lips uttered, and my mouth promised when I was in trouble" (Psalm 66:13–14).

We were to be Christ's Simon of Cyrene in His procession across the ages. Let us bear witness to God's truth and show that the Christian world order is not a utopia and the fantasy of good but weak people, but that a political system based on the Gospels and a social order based around the principles of justice and Christian love is *unum necessarium,*[5] the only and ultimate means to rescue humanity from its ultimate catastrophe.

May the augury of the bard be fulfilled within us:

> Poland was the only fatherland in the past
> From whose breast love and not banditry flows.
> (Zygmunt Krasiński, "Psalm of Good Will")

* * *

The Lord's Psalmist enclosed the entire wisdom of the coexistence of the nations in a well-known couplet: "Praise the Lord, all nations!

---

5   Latin: "The only thing that is necessary."

Extol him, all peoples! For great is his steadfast love toward us; and the faithfulness of the Lord endures forever. Praise the Lord!" (Psalm 117:1–2).

Indeed, God's mercy for us is so great that the Lord summoned all His nations. For the laws of freedom and brotherhood, love and the mutual respect of all the nations are enclosed "in the Lord's truth, which lasts for ages." When all the nations will become united in praising God, then the Psalmist's vision will be implemented: "Let the nations be glad and sing for joy, for thou dost judge the peoples with equity and guide the nations upon earth" (Psalm 67:4).

PART II

Church and State

1

The Church in the Life of the Nation

"You are knights of the faith; in this role, you will be the best knights of Poland." (Pius XI)

"GIVE EAR, O MY PEOPLE, TO MY TEACHING; incline your ears to the words of My mouth! [...] And that they should not be like their fathers, a stubborn and rebellious generation, a generation whose heart was not steadfast, whose spirit was not faithful to God" (Psalm 78:1, 8). Concerned about his nation's sacred bond with God, the Psalmist prays with these words. We send the same words of prayer to the heavens today, when "led through water and fire" we are to begin the new chapter of our nation's co-existence with our Lord.

We know how often doubts arise in our souls about whether our nation is treading the right path by following the voice of the holy Church, especially during times of great trial. Are not the nations that do not know the Lord and do not invoke His name better off? We have already received an answer to these questions when we look at the dying sons of iniquity: "Fret not yourself because of the wicked, be not envious of wrongdoers! For they will soon fade like the grass, and wither like the green herb. [...] For the wicked shall be cut off; but those who wait for the Lord shall possess the land" (Psalm 37:1–2, 9).

Today, after we have inherited our land anew, let us look at the history of our nation's marriage to God's Church in order to invigorate an old relationship with new love. In our reflections, let us never lose sight of the following truth:

God is the Creator of the entire world and not just of one nation; He is the King and Lawgiver of all.

There is one Church for all times, just as there is one God.

The frontiers of the Church are so vast that all the nations can find a place in them. The Church can understand and help every nation, rejoicing at the progress of each one, as long as the principles of the holy faith are not violated.

The Church leads man to God and to eternal bliss and thus cannot be subordinated to the volatile slogans of nationalism.

Religion is not a subject that serves only one nation, but it instead is a light that gives the Christian nation a new direction for life.

Even the mightiest nation is as tiny as a drop of water in a pail when compared to God.

Called to preach God's truth to the world, the holy Church sees traces of God's hands in everything. The attitude of the Church to the nation can only be Divine.

I. The Nation in the Hands of the Church

Christianity has indicated our aim: eternal happiness in God. Through this, it has led man out of his cramped cell and bound him to the Creator. Everything that happens in the world should help man in his aspiration towards God.

All societies can fulfill this auxiliary task. The Church has created the Christian society of peoples; hence, different nationalities can flourish on this earth. Christianity has developed national life. The national community is brought into life not so that some nations could separate themselves from others, but in order to show them a higher purpose and to support man, the individual unit that makes up the whole, in his aspirations for God.

The statement that the nation is the greatest good and aim is false. The nation does not exist for itself; it can serve either God or Satan. The struggle between good and evil takes place in every nation, just as it occurs in every person; every nation carries Cain's stigma and can be the source of either death and destruction or of love. The holy Church explains and orders this struggle; the Church's teaching ennobles not only man, but also the nation, helping it to invigorate and elevate everything that is good within it. Thanks to this, the Church lifts up and preserves the nation.

One great thinker, F. W. Foerster, who was impressed by this grand mission of the Church towards the nation, has said that "from the moment of the advent of Christianity there is no death for the nations as long as the nations will renounce the spirit of conquest, arrogance, pride, egotism, and self-worship and will agree to fulfill their moral duties; that is, they will serve the truth, justice, love, man's eternal destiny, and praise of the Creator." This contains not only the secret of the persistence of the nation, but also that of its cohesion and power, the secret of ordered love for the fatherland.

There exists a hierarchy of values in life: lesser goods must be subordinated to higher ones, while temporal goods must be subjugated to eternal ones. There is a hierarchy in love as well. Love in which the fatherland is the greatest value is useless for the fatherland itself. "Only a man who recognizes God above the nations," F. W. Foerster instructs us, "will also find a true bond between himself and his fatherland."

The spirit of true patriotism is created in a moral and religious atmosphere, the same one in which the individual and the family are obliged to life. Thus, a spirit of justice, truth, morality and love for one's neighbor must be the basis of love for one's fatherland; if it does not want to be useless to the fatherland itself, it must depend on something that is higher than man and his fatherland. "Patriotism," Chesterton wrote, "becomes an offense the moment it is considered the greatest virtue."

Man must always remember that he is something more than a patriot and a citizen: he is above all a child of God and a brother in Christ.

The Church grants the nation the great favor of being internally bound together through unshakable ties. The Church does not encourage individuals who act alone; she is free of isolated people, for all are bound together through the Mystical Body of Christ. The Church teaches that man must co-exist within a society in order to achieve all his goals, fulfill all his duties, and fully develop his personality. In the Catholic conception, the nation is a bond of the highest order, as it is not only external but spiritual as well. "The fatherland," Cardinal Mercier said, "is not an assembly of individuals or families living in the same land who are bound together solely because they live near together or have a kinship of transaction, living only off memories of happiness or suffering. No; the fatherland is a relationship of souls in service of one social organization that should

213

be protected and defended even at the cost of shedding one's blood, under the leadership of those who direct its fate."

The bonds of souls in the fatherland must be supported through religious, family, professional, and political ties. Hence the commandment that all these communities be bound together, so that national life will not be based on powerful, uniform attitudes. The religious bond of the nation is forged through the "one holy, Catholic, and apostolic Church" that encompasses not only the groups making up the nation, but also educates and shapes the mystic and the butcher, the soldier and the virgin, the factory owner and the worker, the heir and the agricultural laborer, the king and his courtier, the priest and the child; she speaks to all of these groups using their own language, although everything leads to one Father.

The Church has succeeded in maintaining national unity even when the "hostile man" tried to destroy that unity. Even during the times of social warfare and class antagonism, the Church did not change her behavior; she always had only one table of the Lord for both the magnates and the people, one bloodless Sacrifice in the temple and one court of penitence, one Word of God and one uniform priestly blessing. In this way, the Church is responsible for not only a major social reform, but she also internally unites the nation, protecting it from its greatest misfortune: a spiritual national schism.

Jealously protecting the strength of family ties, the Church built the nation on a foundation of stone. Through an indissoluble marital bond and close-knit family, she has led her members to the national family: the fatherland. It is worth noting that this supranational Church does not accept people without a fatherland and without a nation; the slogan "The worker has no fatherland, no family, and no home" from the *Communist Manifesto* is completely foreign to her.

In order to bolster national bonds, the Church is glad to see society organized into professional estates, through which professional bonds can ensure everyone's place in the social organism so that people may be ready to serve the nation through, in, and for their profession. The Church wants to see the national community encapsulated in legal, political, and state forms. In that case, the nation's sovereignty and fullness increase; it becomes not only a spiritual community, but also a consensual legal community, a bond based not only on love and freedom, but also on civic loyalty and unity; it is not only the bosom of maternal tenderness, but also the right hand of the Father's authority. The nation achieves the fullness of its development only in its own state.

II. The Church in the Soul of the Nation

Entering the life of the nation and its temple, which has been prepared by the Creator's hand, God's Church treats it like a good mother treats the soul of a child God has given her. She cannot destroy it, but instead must carry out God's works within it.

The Polish nation has gained many virtues from the Slavic family: benevolence, peace, cordial feelings, and hospitality. Even the early religious concepts of the Slavs were marked by peace: unlike in the Germanic mythology, there was no place for bloody, vengeful, or cruel gods in the Slavic mythology.

After the Church had embraced our nation, she did not kill our Slavic traits; on the contrary, she respected our national properties and facilitated the development of Polish culture as an extension of the development of Slavic culture. Christian in its nature, the Slavic soul has been enriched by the Church with all its power and ability to overcome itself. Catholicism has taught us the rigorous asceticism of self-control, the restraint of one's lower desires.

Protestantism, meanwhile, encouraged its followers to: "Believe strongly, sin strongly." Hence the great crimes that were perpetrated against other nations by a nation that was Protestant to the marrow of its bones. Although Catholicism teaches: "Be strong, and let your heart take courage" (Psalm 26:14), it simultaneously calls us to overcome ourselves. Thus, the Church has taught the nations greatness. Teaching her followers to suffer and overcome themselves, she has shaped the Christian virtues of courage, rectitude and magnanimity. The savagery, brutality, and cruelty that grew out of man's stubborn nature and were liberated by the Lutheran constitution of the freedom to sin have fought against this path.

The Slavic soul of the Christian Polish nation continued to express itself in its folk rituals; in the numerous blessings and sanctifications of fire, water, the fields, domesticated animals, and herbs; the blessings which preserved their continuity with the nation's historical traditions and customs even though they became imbued with a new Christian substance. The Church gave new impulses to folk culture, which has been expressed so uniquely in human art; in Marian hymns and Christmas carols; in Nativity plays and the holiday traditions that are woven into the canvas of the liturgical calendar. Does not our ardent veneration of the Mother of God contain within itself the entirety of the Slavic soul, which is simultaneously very Christian? What is more Slavic than the nation's powerful song of: *O, holy God?* When we look at Catholic churches in our fatherland, we see that they are so indigenously Polish that they feel very comfortable in our soul. It is true that the Church brought art to Poland, just as our—and not only ours!—civilization comes from the Church. We see how subtly sacred art has expressed itself with respect to the Polish nation, how greatly it has respected the distinct traits of our soul. What can be more Polish than Wawel Cathedral or St. Mary's Church in Krakow, than the cathedral in Gniezno or Plock?

Should it surprise anyone that during the time of slavery we felt most Polish in churches, which were like our native home for us? The spirit of Polish folk song was so powerful that the enemy could not defeat it for centuries. The fact that the Church has skillfully educated the Polish nation in the national soul is attested by the moving example of a Polish immigrant in France who once complained that everything there was in French and "only one Mass was in Polish." The Latin Mass!

The universal Church has become for us a national Church to the extent that when we think of Poland we think not only of the chessboard of fields, meadows and forests, extensive willows, and fragrant lupines; not only a flock of birds flying below the heavens, blossoming lindens, and country huts surrounded by hollyhocks, but above all: "The country church with a pipe organ filled with people immersed in prayer and singing an ancient hymn. This is the melody of a Christmas carol or of May devotions to the Blessed Virgin Mary; this is a soaring plea to the 'Star of the Sea,' a Corpus Christi procession, rural weddings, and funerals that walk across soft paths with black banners towards a cemetery that is guarded by birches and spruces" (Z. Dębicki).

Thus, we must state that this universal, Roman Church is at the same time a Polish Church, for she does not destroy the soul of the nation, but instead allows it to speak in its own way to preserve unity for its own sake. Furthermore, the Church even demands respect for the properties of the nation's soul. The Church preaches love for one's surroundings because of the principles of hierarchy in love; she preaches love for the language of one's fatherland, customs, and unique national atmosphere. This was the case not only in the time of St. Augustine, when she required teaching the faith in one's own language, but in the early Middle Ages, when the Church built up the system of education, as well. This remains true today, when Pius XII speaks of the protection of the cultural and linguistic uniqueness of nations. Thus, the Church can be universal, which means that she is Polish in our Fatherland and French in the land of St. Louis, while the leader of the Italian nation can say that he cannot envision the history of his own nation without the Church. Similarly, no Frenchman can imagine the history of his fatherland without St. Joan of Arc; even an author of textbooks for secular schools would violate the principle of neutrality by keeping her out of his work. In Poland, not only a peasant will call the Catholic faith Polish and nonetheless find it difficult to conceive that a German can be a Catholic as well. Indeed, only a true Church can succeed in being so universal!

Although the same Church educates everyone, we know well that a Catholic in Poland, Spain, Italy, France, or Germany is different because the Church does not shut itself off in one national organism, nor does it consider providing one pattern for all to be wise. The Church is not afraid of a richness and diversity of forms, unlike the suffocating collectivist and totalitarian ideologies that want to close off every brain and every human will in the party uniform. On the contrary, the Church strives to maintain the rights with which people are endowed so that they may remain who they are, speak the language that they received from their mothers, wear their fathers' clothing (indeed, priests have always been the most zealous defenders of folk costume), and sing folk songs that have resounded for centuries (after all, Polish songs have always been present in our churches).

At the same time, the Church does not want to be alone in her work of educating the nation, which would be neither desirable nor possible.

The statement that the contemporary Pole is a work of the Church is erroneous. The character of the nation depends not only on the religion that the nation professes but also on a series of other factors, such as the family, profession, environment, state, socio-political institutions, forms of economic activity, territory, soil, climate, race, geo-physical environment, and many other factors, which the sociology of education has analyzed in detail. Naturally, religion is of primary significance here, but it is not the only factor. The Church realizes this and thus does not want to replace anyone in the process of educating the nation, not the family, the professions, nor the state. The Church only demands that the religious influence on the nation's education be guaranteed and that other factors that also are qualified to educate it do not eliminate these efforts. The Catholic ideal of education will be achieved when all involved in education will fulfill the tasks that God has granted them.

We understand that people frequently disappoint, hence the fact that although our nation's character is fundamentally Catholic, it not infrequently strays from the Catholic ideal. Would not the Polish nation be happier if our compatriots were more consistently Catholic, displayed more of God's power, and lived in the spirit of grace?

III. Hetmen[1] of the National Spirit

Not long ago, there was a struggle against the Catholic clergy in our country. The accusation that the Roman clergy are "our occupiers" was thrown at our faces. God corrected this insult not long after: the author of this slander collaborated with our eastern enemy, while "our occupiers" in black and violet cassocks filled both the invaders' prisons and concentration camps, generously shedding their blood for love of their martyred Fatherland and Church! How could it be any different? Love for God is the most effective way of teaching us love for the Fatherland. The Church plays a leading role in this![2]

The bond between the nation and the Church is most strongly expressed in the patriotism of the Roman clergy. Thus, priests have

---

1   The Hetman was the chief of the armed forces of the Polish-Lithuanian Commonwealth and the second highest-ranking military officer of the nation after the king.
2   See earlier note on Tadeusz Boy-Żeleński.

always been leaders in national movements and have been leading patriots. Priests have fought for the people's rights and their right to their national languages in Flanders, Ireland, South Tyrol, Slovenia, Croatia, and Slovakia; they fought in Lithuania, Latvia, and the Basque Country.

It could be no different in Poland! The same natural law that comes from God functions here, that of love for the Fatherland, a love that is our moral obligation. This was recognized by our enemies, who always struck at Catholic bishops and priests and who saw black cassocks as a provocation and sabotage whenever they wanted to oppress our nation.

Polish priests shaped their love for their Mother before the altars, where the nation pleaded through their hands, offering God the chalice of their suffering. How many sufferings and torments did they endure! Countless souls have opened the secrets of their heroic struggles to them. If only you were privileged to hear the final confession of those awaiting to be executed, who were forcibly deported to Siberia, or Polish soldiers who offered their sacrificial blood when going into battle! The sanctuary of the most intimate and deepest feelings and the full power of love for the Fatherland can be found there. Polish priests are the ministers to the nation, which "knows no song without complaint." It is they who were burdened with the weight of the wrath of the righteous God. They protected the nation from ever-new calamities before God's face. It was Polish priests who learned of the greatness of God's love among even the harshest suffering in the mysterious power of grace. During the time of slavery, all our national yearnings were expressed through the mouth of religion. In order to maintain its existence, the nation, torn apart from statehood, seemingly instinctively cleansed its soul, strengthened itself, gathered its strength from dark cemeteries and exploded with the power of resurrection between ancient church walls. That was also the case in our recent days, when churches became the only asylum for our nation, while the fraternal melody "Kind Mother" became our national anthem.

Why should it be surprising that heroes with crosses in their hands and stoles on their shoulders, which the savage enemy would later often carve on their breasts with his bayonet, have come out of this school? Why should it be surprising that "your occupiers" came from the bosom of the Church and who stood at the forefront of the nation's stations of the cross up until Siberia, as did those who fell in the trenches of the bulwark of Christianity in order to protect Polish and Christian civilization, and those valiant men of martyred Podlachia and Chełmo as well as the ambassadors of Poland in the sea of red Bolshevism who voluntarily renounced the historical path of the nation's movement to the East? Read the long histories of priests who struggled for national liberation, and you will learn of the martyred ranks of the sons of the Church and our nation!

Is not the testimony of the enemy frequently closest to the truth? In recent days, we have learned that we are not lesser sons of our nation than our glorious ancestors. The enemy closed Catholic churches and surrounded them with guards as if he feared that the soul of the nation hidden there could be prematurely resurrected. He became afraid of the power that came from these churches; he was afraid of the *Sursum Corda* breaking out of the heart of the Polish priest like a mysterious summons; he feared the power of the confessional, prohibiting the people from declaring their sins to the Almighty God. The hand of the invader, who in something unprecedented in the history of religion attacked the Lord's table justified only by a gendarme's pass, closed off the "holy of holies."

> You have given us everything you could, O Lord!
> Our oppressors provide a model of vile violence,
> Of scarlet massacres and iniquitous slavery,
> Which curses the sobbing of infants.
> (Zygmunt Krasiński, "Psalm of Good Will")

Thanks be to God for the witness of truth to the universal Church who, as we know in our fatherland, is the most wondrous model of a national Church. The Roman Catholic Church is our true national Church, while Jesus Christ and not Dažbog[3] is our Lord.

IV. Days of Glory and Suffering

Throughout our nation's history, we have been inseparable from the universal Church, who participated in both its joys and sorrows and strengthened our history even when it was called "history

---

3 Dažbog: one of the major Slavic pagan deities.

without history." Would not the Church have never left the stagnation of the local wars of the Piasts if she had not enclosed the young nation within her uniform hierarchical forms, thus preserving national unity? The Church moved the borders of the nation towards the East; Poland was wherever the Latin Rite existed, and when the Latin Rite retreated, Poland also retreated whenever the nation fell away from the Catholic faith. Polish Wilno is Catholic, Polish Lvov is Catholic, and Polish Silesia is Catholic. However, the nation lost the distant borderlands of Masuria, just as the Church once lost it, although she has maintained Catholic Pomerania. What protected Silesia, Greater Poland, Pomerania, and Kashubia from de-nationalization if not their bond with the Catholic Church through the Latin liturgy? What has protected Poland's Eastern borderlands if not the Latin Rite? Compare the boundaries of rites and national boundaries. Certainly, one can point towards Polish Protestant villages, but these are islands![4]

History creates a rule: Latin Catholicism supports Poland, while Poland supports Catholicism in the East. This is the only natural concordat of two communities married together through God. Its fruits must be sweet for both the Church and for Poland. The golden era of the nation's history coincides with the golden era of the history of the Church in Poland. Catholic baptism gave Poland Jagiełło and along with him the entire East; all this was thanks to the fact that Jadwiga's soul belonged to God.[5] We cannot forget this! Similarly, the religious decline of the periods of the Saxon dynasty and King Stanisław August Poniatowski are tied to the downfall of the nation. Would this downfall have taken place if the nation had listened to the prophetic voice of Piotr Skarga and if it had understood the Church's teaching on love for the Fatherland?

No one whose senses are intact and possesses at least a bit of intellectual honesty could ever demonstrate that the Church led to the downfall or death of any nation. Nations have perished through their own fault, because of their own sins! "Every nation that will continue

---

4   Here, Wyszyński is referring to such small towns in Cieszyn Silesia like Szczyrk and Wisła that have large Lutheran populations. As of 2021, there are about 70,000 Lutherans living in Poland, mostly in the region of Cieszyn Silesia.

5   See earlier note on St. Jadwiga, Jogaila, and the Christianization of Lithuania.

to speak of God will live!" Only the names of foolish nations that rebel against God's law are eradicated from the land of the living.

Despite the nation's close relationship with the Church, never in its history was Poland an ideal Catholic nation. First of all, state-building is not the Church's mission; second, she cannot achieve this effort alone, as she needs the cooperation of all creative factors. We know well that all who are resistant to the truth harm God's work in the nation's soul in their own way: "Behold, this child is set for the fall and rising of many in Israel, and for a sign that is spoken against" (Luke 2:34). The Gospels' permeating the soul of the nation is always tied to a struggle that requires the most difficult victory in history; namely, victory over oneself. The Church's great merit is that she will show the path to that victory; however, the will to emerge victorious over oneself depends on the person who is responsible for warping the Christian ideal in the life of the nation.

Despite this, we have deserved the commendable title: *Polonia semper fidelis.* And rightly so! Throughout our history, we have lost our statehood, but we have never lost our own Church whose organization was in those times practically the only external form of binding the nation together. Only once in her history did Poland tolerate infidelity to God, when during the Prussian Homage an arrogant former Teutonic Knight whose knees no longer wanted to kneel before God knelt before the Polish king.[6] We know the enormous price of this infidelity, for we painfully atone for this foreign betrayal that has led to nearly all our national calamities. We also know our historical fidelity to God and know that we are generously repaid for it today. How many times have we referred to it, basing our right to life on our fidelity in our prayers of contrition! And how grateful we were to those who recalled our fidelity before God.

In our most recent trial, Pope Pius XII's words addressed to the representatives of our life were a "veil of Veronica": "One thing that never existed in your history was an unfaithful Poland separated from Jesus Christ and His Church. Throughout the centuries, the nation of St. Casimir and St. Jadwiga, the nation of two St. Stanislauses,

---

6 The Prussian Homage took place on April 10, 1525, when Albrecht Hohenzollern bowed before Polish King Sigismund I the Old, thus becoming the ruler of the Duchy of Prussia, which would become a fiefdom of Poland.

St. John Cantius, and St. Andrew Bobola has lost its territories, its riches and its independence, but never its faith. It also never lost its sincere devotion to the Blessed Virgin, to that mighty and sweet Queen of Poland from Czestochowa." Indeed, as a nation we have never betrayed God, although individuals and families have at times done so. We have never persecuted the Church, although our invaders have tried to pit our nation against it or even to sever our ties with it. In our country, only the enemies of Poland have fought against the Church. We can accept the pope's message, which summoned the civilized world to the defense of "the most Catholic nation, which is dear to us" with joy. We were historically entitled to this!

* * *

The Book of Esther contains the words of the following prayer: "O Lord, Lord, almighty king, for all things are in Thy power, and there is none that can resist Thy will, if Thou determine to save Israel" (Esther 13:9). Let us pray in this way with the zealous spirit of faith and love under the starry ceiling of our sky so that it may reach the Lord, who was always our Leader.

"Thou didst bring a vine out of Egypt; thou didst drive out the nations and plant it. Thou didst clear the ground for it; it took deep root and filled the land. [. . .] It sent out its branches to the sea, and its shoots to the River. [. . .] Turn again, O God of hosts! Look down from heaven, and see; have regard for this vine, the stock which thy right hand planted. [. . .] Let Thy face shine, that we may be saved!" (Psalm 80:8–20). "Then we Thy people, the flock of Thy pasture, will give thanks to Thee forever; from generation to generation, we will recount Thy praise" (Psalm 79:13).

2
Church and State

*"Render therefore to Caesar the things
that are Caesar's, and to God the things
that are God's." (Matthew 22:21).*

"**I**S IT LAWFUL TO PAY TAXES TO CAESAR, OR not?" (Matthew 22:17). This is a timeless dilemma! Why, then, should it be surprising that it was presented before Christ the Lord? The insidious malice of Jesus' enemies has become the cause of His greatest glory. At the same time, it is an immortal service to humanity, for those words contain Christ's most important reform.

I. Christ's Reform

Our Lord's concise and firm words have resolved a historic problem. Christ the Lord has divided power: "Render therefore to Caesar the things that are Caesar's, and to God the things that are God's." This fact is of tremendous importance to man, freedom of thought, and the human spirit.

The pagan world knew no division between secular and religious authority.

Nor did it know the problem of the relationship between spiritual and temporal matters, the spirit and matter, Church and state. The pagan state was always marked by the bond of spiritual and secular authority, which was contained in the same hand. The state was the absolute ruler of the body and the soul. In the pagan state, religion was only one branch of public administration. Pagan priests were usually ordinary state officials. That was the most essential characteristic of paganism! At the same time, it is the most momentous warning sign when the world begins to return to paganism. Whenever secular authority enters into the realm of ecclesiastical affairs and violates the freedom of religion and conscience, it is evidence that a new wave of paganization is approaching.

Christ's reform distinguishes between spiritual and secular authority.

From this point, there exist two separate kinds of authority. Christ the Lord teaches: "My kingship is not of this world" (John 18:36). Religion is not something of this earth, and so its strength is not drawn from temporal things. It also does not usually meddle in temporal matters, and when it does so, it limits itself to a very narrow and necessary range of topics. In Christ's verdict: "Render therefore to Caesar the things that are Caesar's, and to God the things that are God's," God and the state are distinguished so clearly for the first time. Christ the Lord proclaims that religion is no longer subjected to state authority and that listening to Caesar is not the same as listening to God. Caesar ceases to be the highest priest. The pagan state clearly felt this degradation and so as a sign of protest it has so generously shed the blood of the Christian martyrs.

The Lord Jesus has established His Church and entrusted her with the execution of spiritual authority. The Church is "God's kingdom" on earth; she is a tangible kingdom with her own constitution, hierarchy, teachings, laws, and worship. All people in all places and times are summoned to this kingdom. They already know that they frequently must tell the state: "We must obey God rather than men" (Acts 5:29).

This reform becomes the cornerstone of Christian civilization.

Thanks to the power of one sentence by Christ, man becomes free, has a conscience, and is liberated from the omnipotence of all temporal authority. Christ has placed man in the face of something that exceeds temporal authority. He has poured comfort and the confidence that he will never be completely oppressed into man's heart. Man has received the right to appeal to a higher court than the state. The entirety of Christian civilization and West European culture has been born from this sense of higher human rights. It has abolished the despotic principle that proclaims that Caesar possesses all authority, including religious authority.

By distinguishing between spiritual and temporal authority, the Lord Jesus has definitively deprived the state of a great part of its old powers. Thanks to this, Christianity has liberated the human conscience from the yoke of state authority. From that point, the human conscience depends solely on God. Caesar must renounce the violation of conscience. Whenever state authority wants to assault the conscience of citizens, it must begin with the struggle against the Church, which stands at its guard. Thus, every form of persecution of the Church is a warning sign for the citizens: your good is at stake here!

Despite numerous persecutions of the Church, Christ's reform has never been completely destroyed. Christians died in the arenas of ancient Rome not only to give witness to evangelical truths, but also to protest against the state's violation of freedom of conscience.

Christ's reform has changed state authority and made it more noble.

The duty to take care of one's citizens and ensure that their rights are respected replaces unrestrained authority over one's subjects and absolute rule. The Christian ruler becomes the defender of peace and justice. The state itself ceases to be a form of tyranny and instead becomes an institution of concern and care for the common good of citizens. Furthermore, the concept of the common good expands, increases its scope, and grows. If not for Christ's reform, which has created a division of authority, there would be no "declaration of the rights of man and citizen."

The sovereign has not only rights but also duties with respect to his subjects, for he who has authority "is God's servant for your good" (Romans 13:4).

II. Church and State: Separate Communities

By determining social relations in the state of Israel, God gave Moses authority over his nation and made him His deputy, while God bestowed the office of high priest to Aaron. However, Moses and Aaron were biological brothers who constantly supported each other in the task of guiding God's people.

The Church constantly has this example before her eyes. Looking at it, the Church teaches that the state is a community that is separate from the Church, with a different aim. Like the Church, the state has its own sovereignty; it has the right to select such a form of government that best corresponds to its tasks.

Both Church and state are two separate communities; they are perfect and independent with respect to their own aims. The aim of the Church is to bring people to happiness in God, spiritual and supernatural good, and God's glory through the aid of supernatural resources. The Church is to take care for the spiritual social order that is the order of God's grace and glory. The task of the state, meanwhile, is to foster peace and temporal as well as supernatural well-being; the state must look over the temporal order and its factors.

Thus, it is clear that both Church and state have their own spheres of activity. The domain of the Church's activity encompasses solely spiritual matters: the internal life, the holy sacraments, the organization of public and private devotion to God, religious orders, the Church hierarchy, etc. These belong solely to the Church's authority. The state, meanwhile, deals solely with temporal matters: public safety, the organization of administration, economics, finance, technology, etc. These matters solely belong to the state's authority.

However, separation does not mean division! There are matters that concern both Church and state because they above all concern man, who is both a citizen of the state and a member of the Church. The most important matters pertain to marriage and the family, education in the family and school, public morality, public freedom, the veneration of God, etc. Once again, Moses and Aaron converge at this point! Just as a man cannot be divided, areas of common life that are so closely related likewise cannot be separated. There exists a need for Church and state to cooperate.

The experience of the past few decades shows that contemporary states tend to all too frequently infringe on the sphere of religious matters and their independent regulation. Such states maintain that they want to protect themselves against the Church who, in their opinion, has a tendency to expand her authority. However, the Church's activity was never harmful to the state, while the state's exceeding its authority has often led to the Church's enslavement. History demonstrates this. The state possesses physical strength that it can and has abused with respect to the Church. In this respect, the Church is not a threat. Her impact is spiritual and thus has long-term consequences.

Considering this tendency of the contemporary state, we must recall the warning that was given to king Uzziah when he entered the Jerusalem Temple in order to burn incense on the altar: "It is not for you, Uzziah, to burn incense to the Lord, but for the priests the sons of Aaron, who are consecrated to burn incense" (2 Chronicles 26:18). After the king had failed to heed this warning, he was stricken with leprosy.

The Church exercises her teaching, legislative, and juridical authority within the scope assigned to her and with her own solemnity. Thanks to this authority, she is the Church in the full meaning of this word. This three-fold authority must be executed independently of the state; that is, through a hierarchy that receives its authority from God, not people. Only the Catholic Church has a priesthood whose authority absolutely does not come from the state. Only the Church has a hierarchy that has been established by God and that is allowed to speak to the people in the name of God: "He who hears you hears Me" (Luke 10:16). If the Church did not have her own hierarchy and if her authority were dependent on the state, she would cease to be a Church and would instead become an administrative body of the state, while her activities would be reduced to purely state functions. Spiritual authority would drown in secular authority; Caesar would swallow what belongs to God. At the same time, the Christian, West European culture that renders unto Caesar what is Caesar's and unto God what is God's would perish. Wherever the state deprives the Church of her three-fold authority, the greatest harm is done to the Church, human souls, and culture. When the state deprives the Church of her independence and makes her a mere tool of her authority, the Church's authority over souls perishes.

The history of so-called state and national Churches demonstrates how crucial it is to maintain the distinction between Church and state authority. So-called national churches have always turned into bodies of state administration. The Anglican and Lutheran Churches, as well as all so-called official state churches, have lost their independence from the state. The shepherds of those churches have become state officials not only because they lacked the sacrament of holy orders. Although they preserved their priesthood, even schismatic churches have lost their independence from the state, become subjugated to it, and lived off its power as a result of the mixing up of authority. After all, the head of those churches was not a priest, but a secular official: a tsar, king, or president. This kind of church loses its authority over souls, which the state usurps. Will it succeed? Can the state exercise spiritual authority? From whom did it receive spiritual authority? When the state usurps this authority over souls, it hands it over to the police. A priest in a stole is replaced with a policeman with a rubber truncheon. Freedom of conscience dies. Caesar removes God from the temple. Man loses the ability to appeal to God's laws when he faces abuse from state authority. Left alone, man painfully feels the weight of his abandonment and helplessness. Thus, we have to persistently repeat the words of Christ the Lord: "Render therefore to Caesar the things that are Caesar's, and to God the things that are God's."

III. Harmonious Cooperation Between Church and State

In its essence, religion is universal and eternal; the Church will outlive all states. Only the Church has received the promise that she will persist until the end of the world. Thus, various states will perish, while the Church will live on.

Only the Church is not enclosed in a demarcated territory, but instead transcends all boundaries. Meanwhile, states are subject to the constant volatility of temporal life both within their boundaries and in their subjects. Thus, both state and Church are distinct in their existence and their qualities. However, they converge at one point: man. Here, we see the image of agreement between God and Caesar. The soul is an element of God, while the body is a human element. However, one preserves the other. We are called to save the soul through the body and the body through the soul; we are called to save both. Indeed, Christ has redeemed not only the soul but also the body. When they work together, they survive; when they are in conflict, both perish. Woe to both the body and soul when the body overrides man's soul. Woe to us when temporal life becomes our Caesar. We cannot render both what is Caesar's and what is God's to Caesar. Nor can we forget about the laws of the body, as God wanted not only the soul but also the body, which serves the soul, to be praised in the glory of the heavens.

This is a revealing comparison! It clearly shows that despite distinctions in existence and qualities, Church and state must act concordantly. Separation and distinction cannot be division.

"Every kingdom divided against itself is laid waste" (Matthew 12:25). We see the truth of these words in the history of Israel. When Israel served its only God under King David, it was politically united. When Israel's descendants began to "commit adultery with foreign gods" and practice polytheism upon rejecting their God, they were broken up. Some stayed at God's side, while others followed Baal; some followed Rehoboam, while others followed Jeroboam. During Christ's time, the Israelites were divided between four rulers.

The division of the state typically begins not with the territory, but with the soul of the nation, the human soul. Man's rejection of God is the first division. This is followed by the nation's rejection of God, the division between Church and state, and the division between spiritual and physical power.

It is unsurprising that the Israelites rejected Christ when they were ruled by Pilate, Herod, Philip, and Lysanias: "We have no king but Caesar" (John 19:15). Although Christ was crucified by the Roman state, this happened because of the demands of the crowd, which had rejected God's authority over that of the state. The result of this rejection was terrible. Caesar listened to the pleas of those who had rejected their God. The blood flowed onto the nation and its sons.

That always happens whenever a nation rejects God and trusts only in Caesar, for every division between Church and state contains a division between the body and soul of society. A state without a soul is as tragic as a man in whom a spiritual division has taken place. The state must gain its spirit from somewhere. If it rejects the spirit of the Church, it must create "national gods" to which it will sacrifice its citizens. We know how terrifying these state gods can be. In the communist state, the Bolshevik party has become a god; it is supposed to be a spirit that invigorates the state and creates its own religion. The case with other totalitarian states is similar.

In his encyclical *Immortale Dei*, Pope Leo XIII teaches: "There must, accordingly, exist between these two powers a certain orderly connection, which may be compared to the union of the soul and body in man." These two forms of authority must be distinct, as each is independent in its own sphere. However, this independence does not preclude relations, especially since these two forms of authority have the same subjects. When both remain in their sphere of activity, there will be few opportunities for dispute. Naturally, disputes cannot be completely avoided, as there exist matters of convergence in which it is difficult to distinguish with precision the scope of each community's authority; at times, human passions, ambitions, and pride come into play, which incline each community to make use of its perceived superiority. However, just as the human good requires respect for the rights of both body and soul, similarly it requires that the difference between the Church and state is recognized in their co-existence.

In contemporary Church-state relations, when countries are not uniform with respect to denomination, it is difficult to lead to a desirable degree of cooperation between Church and state. However, the state should seek to co-exist with the Church as well as it can. It should protect the Catholic faith, recalling that the state is still "God's servant" (Romans 13:4). Other kinds of worship should sometimes be tolerated to avoid greater evils and to enjoy freedom within the limits of natural morality.

In a religiously homogeneous state, co-existence with the Church should have the marks of a marriage. There must be mutual assistance in every marriage. In the co-existence of two communities, there must be a spiritual collaboration in the sense of mutual usefulness and the mutual necessity of accepting the services of each.

Both Church and state are great organizers of social life: one imbues social life with spiritual and supernatural forces, while the other contributes temporal and natural forces. They neither destroy nor preclude one another; instead, they need and complement each other. The state must recognize the Church and co-exist alongside it, recognizing the necessary bond between its life and that of the Church in the souls of its citizens. The Church, meanwhile, must preserve all the traits of her apostolic fidelity. She will never abandon the state, even if it is sinful, rebellious, or stricken with the greatest misfortune. The Church never abandons her position; she is always ready to console and elevate. The Church can be thrown out by the state, but she cannot back out on her own. She will never renounce the concordat. She will never recall her nuncios, even if they lived in the middle of Sodom and Gomorrah, just like Christ who ate with sinners and tax collectors and even died alongside common criminals.

The diplomatic arrangements into which the Church enters have in mind the salvation of souls that never die. This is the fidelity of the universal Church to the Catholic state!

* * *

The history of the Israelites gives us instructive examples of the co-existence of spiritual and secular authority.

Upon his return from the Babylonian exile, Zerubbabel began the reconstruction of the state; the first walls he lay towards the heavens made up God's temple.

Likewise, Hezekiah renews God's glory, which had been violated during the rule of the godless Asher: "In the first year of his reign, in the first month, he opened the doors of the house of the Lord and repaired them" (2 Chronicles 29:3). He presents a manifesto to the nation: "For our fathers have been unfaithful and have done what was evil in the sight of the Lord our God; they have forsaken him and have turned away their faces from the habitation of the Lord and turned their backs. They also shut the doors of the vestibule and put out the lamps [...]. Therefore, the wrath of the Lord came on Judah and Jerusalem [...]. For lo, our fathers have fallen by the sword, and our sons and our daughters and our wives are in captivity for this. Now it is in my heart to make a covenant with the Lord" (2 Chronicles 29:6–10).

These are examples of how to rebuild the state in accordance with God. "Render therefore to Caesar the things that are Caesar's, and to God the things that are God's" (Matthew 22:21).

3

The Divine Right of Nations

THE BOOK OF JUDITH DESCRIBES A TELLING and momentous event. Holofernes, a general of the Assyrian army who has been sent by his king to conquer the world, stands at the border of Judah. The victorious leader, whom nobody had previously succeeded in conquering, has learned that "the people of Israel had prepared for war and had closed the passes in the hills." Thus, he decides to investigate and posed the following question to the princes of Moab and the commanders of Ammon: "What people is this that lives in the hill country?"

Achior, "the leader of all the Ammonites," stood up and summarized the history of the Israelites in one long speech. That was a strange history! It was inextricably tied to Israel's relationship to God. No one was capable of defeating that nation whenever its sons were faithful to God Himself. Whenever they betrayed their God, however, "they were given to spoil, and to the sword, and to reproach. And as often as they were penitent for having revolted from the worship of their God, the God of heaven gave them power to resist." What Achior describes almost became a law that determined their political success: "And as long as they sinned not in the sight of their God, it was well with them: for their God hateth iniquity." What advice did the leader receive? "Now therefore, my Lord, search if there be any iniquity of theirs in the sight of their God: let us go up to them, because their God will surely deliver them to thee, and they shall be brought under the yoke of thy power: But if there be no offense of this people in the sight of their God, we cannot resist them, because their God will defend them: and we shall be a reproach to the whole earth" (see Judith 5:1–25).

Holofernes was scornful of that advice. His punishment is described later in the Book of Judith. Are we to imitate his example? No; instead, we should open the pages of Sacred Scripture in order to learn the wisdom that leads to the auspiciousness of nations in order to evaluate God's unwritten law of the nations.

233

I. Infidelity to God as a Cause of the Downfall of Nations and States

Not only every man but also every society, nation, and state are required to respect God's commandments in public life. If the sin of a single individual is a misfortune for the world, sins committed by the powerful apparatus of public authority are infinitely more devastating! If a murder committed by a person shakes the heavens, organized murder committed by a state is all the more outrageous! If the infidelity of the individual poisons the souls of one's neighbors, think of how great a calamity godlessness sanctioned and performed by the state is! Thus, God's justice, sanctioned by the natural law, comes into play, requiring the state to defend His created order and to punish evildoers.

In the history of Israel, which is an image of God's rule over every nation, we clearly see how its political power grows proportionately to the growth of moral power and fidelity to the one God. Israel's political power reached its apex during the rule of King David, who was the most faithful executioner of God's plans. However, his successor, Solomon, became influenced by the pagan religions, thus beginning a period of apostasy and paving the way for Israel's downfall in the time of the greatest flourishing of its state. Infidelity to God became Israel's daily bread. Sirach gives a sad testimony on his nation: "Except David, Hezekiah, and Josiah, they all sinned greatly, for they forsook the law of the Most High; the kings of Judah came to an end; for they gave their power to others, and their glory to a foreign nation" (Sirach 49:5–7).

The concise history of God's benevolence to the nation and that nation's ingratitude is presented by Jeremiah, the national prophet of Israel. In exchange for God's dear concern and providence, the nation "commits adultery with foreign gods." The abandoned God asks Israel: "What wrong did your fathers find in Me that they went far from Me, and went after worthlessness, and became worthless?" Israel is incapable of providing an answer. God, however, does not give in; on the contrary, He levels accusations: "And I brought you into a plentiful land to enjoy its fruits and its good things. But when you came in you defiled My land and made My heritage an abomination

[...] for My people have committed two evils: they have forsaken Me, the fountain of living waters, and hewed out cisterns for themselves, broken cisterns, that can hold no water." This betrayal will not go unpunished; a punishment will flow from its inside: "Your wickedness will chasten you, and your apostasy will reprove you" (see Jeremiah 2:5–19).

The nation is tied to God "as the waistcloth clings to the loins of a man" (Jeremiah 13:11). According to Jeremiah's beautiful words, the aim of this unification is "that they might be for Me a people, a name, a praise and a glory" (Jeremiah 13:11). Whenever the nation betrays its Lord, however, God tells the prophet to take off the loincloth and lay it before the Euphrates so that it may spoil. This is a prophesy of the Babylonian exile, the effect of a lack of faith in God.

Every yoke follows unfaithfulness towards God and His eternal laws. There is nothing surprising in this! The nation knows the price of infidelity: "Son of man, when a land sins against me by acting faithlessly, I stretch out my hand against it and break its staff of bread and send famine upon it and cut off from it man and beast" (Ezekiel 14:13). God's punishment occurs in light of this admonishment: "Behold, the Lord will lay waste the earth and make it desolate, and He will twist its surface and scatter its inhabitants. And it shall be, as with the people, so with the priest [...]. The earth shall be utterly laid waste and utterly despoiled; for the Lord has spoken this word. [...] The earth lies polluted under its inhabitants; for they have transgressed the laws, violated the statutes, broken the everlasting covenant. Therefore, a curse devours the earth, and its inhabitants suffer for their guilt; therefore, the inhabitants of the earth are scorched, and few men are left" (Isaiah 24:1–6).

Just so that there are no doubts as to the fact that the Lord is the ruler of the nations and the avenger of the infidels, we receive a clear response from the Prophet: "Who gave up Jacob to the spoiler, and Israel to the robbers? Was it not the Lord, against Whom we have sinned, in Whose ways they would not walk, and Whose law they would not obey? So, He poured upon him the heat of His anger and the might of battle; it set him on fire round about, but he did not understand" (Isaiah 42:24–25). He will give one more explanation to people with "stiff necks" and "uncircumcised ears" who do not want to understand God's paths: "And when your people say, 'Why has the Lord our God done all these things to us?' you shall say to them, 'As you have forsaken Me and served foreign gods in your land, so you shall serve strangers in a land that is not yours'" (Jeremiah 5:19). Now, there is no room for any misunderstanding: "So will I break this people and this city, as one breaks a potter's vessel, so that it can never be mended" (Jeremiah 19:11).

Sacred books have recorded the history of the Chosen People to give us a warning so that we may not repeat the same sins and betrayals, for God's punishments contain a note of trust in human reason, certain hope that man can in fact learn something from the history of other peoples and nations.

"Thus says the Lord, your Redeemer, the Holy One of Israel: 'I am the Lord your God, Who teaches you to profit, Who leads you in the way you should go. O that you had hearkened to My commandments! Then your peace would have been like a river, and your righteousness like the waves of the sea; your offspring would have been like the sand, and your descendants like its grains; their name would never be cut off or destroyed from before Me" (Isaiah 48:17–19).

We know that God is faithful to His words.

II. God Revives Nations and States Through His Punishments

This is God's didactic thought. God has "plans for welfare and not for evil" (Jeremiah 29:11). Whenever we summon Him, He listens to us and leads us out of all forms of slavery, just as He led Israel out of the Assyrian and Babylonian yoke. "And He will come to Zion as Redeemer, to those in Jacob who turn from transgression" (Isaiah 59:−20).

God settles accounts with His people in advance, just as He did with Israel through Isaiah. He is repulsed by idle external worship and praise of Him with only one's lips, even if it was tied to a multitude of generous sacrifices. God does not trust in lies, even if they are repeated on end: "This is the temple of the Lord, the temple of the Lord, the temple of the Lord" (Jeremiah 7:4). God's temple will be preserved among the people "if you truly amend your ways and your doings, if you truly execute justice one with another, if you do not oppress the alien, the fatherless or the widow, or shed innocent blood in this place" (Jeremiah 7:4–5). Otherwise, the temple will become filled with people whose actions are heathen and thus it becomes "a den of robbers" (Jeremiah 7:11). Even the house of God will not survive before the Lord's eyes: "Therefore I will do to the house, which is called by My name, and in which you trust, and to the place which I gave to you and to your fathers, as I did to Shiloh. And I will cast you out of My sight" (Jeremiah 7:14–15). "Even though you make many prayers, I will not listen; your hands are full of blood" (Isaiah 1:15).

God recalls the nation's past fidelity and good works. "How the faithful city has become a harlot [...]. Your princes are rebels and companions of thieves. [...] They do not defend the fatherless, and the widow's cause does not come to them" (Isaiah 1:21, 23). God most wants the old works of justice. Therefore, He admonishes: "Turn now, every one of you, from his evil way and wrong doings, and dwell upon the land which the Lord has given to you and your fathers from of old and forever; do not go after other gods to serve and worship them or provoke me to anger with the work of your hands" (Jeremiah 25:4–5). When admonishments do not help, God sends forth punishments that are intended to make those who resist Him come to their senses to perform the "first deeds" of love: "I will turn My hand against you and will smelt away your dross as with lye and remove all your alloy. And I will restore your judges as at the first, and your counselors as at the beginning. Afterward you shall be called the city of righteousness, the faithful city" (Isaiah 1:25–27).

We cannot forget the only factor that induces God's punishment, however. God constantly wants a transformation of our mind and heart; He does not seek revenge and retaliation.

God gave an instructive lesson to Babylon, which was sent to punish Israel and all the other nations of the earth, thus becoming the "hammer of the whole earth" (Jeremiah 50:23). Israel, however, forgot that it was only God's tool; it exceeded what it was entitled to and abused its power. Thus, it was crushed and broken by God, because it offended the Lord (see Jeremiah 50:25). Now, Babylon will hear words of punishment: "Requite her according to her deeds, do to her according to all that she has done" (Jeremiah 50:29). We cannot abuse God's mandate, for only He rules over the nations.

237

This gives birth to trust in love of the Lord: "Take courage, My people, O memorial of Israel! It was not for destruction that you were sold to the nations, but you were handed over to your enemies because you angered God. [. . .] You forgot the everlasting God, Who brought you up, and you grieved Jerusalem, who reared you. [. . .] For He who brought these calamities upon you will bring you everlasting joy with your salvation" (Baruch 4:5, 8, 29).

A prayer is raised to the King of Nations following the ray of trust: "May God be gracious to us and bless us and make His face to shine upon us, that Thy way may be known upon earth, Thy saving power among all nations. Let the nations be glad and sing for joy, for Thou dost judge the peoples with equity and guide the nations upon earth. [. . .] Let the peoples praise thee, O God; let all the peoples praise Thee!" (Psalm 67:1, 3, 4).

This is a hymn of gratitude for "God's law of the nations"!

* * *

"For thus says the Lord: 'Behold, I will extend prosperity to her like a river, and the wealth of the nations like an overflowing stream; and you shall suck, you shall be carried upon her hip, and dandled upon her knees. As one whom his mother comforts, so I will comfort you; you shall be comforted in Jerusalem. You shall see, and your heart shall rejoice; your bones shall flourish like the grass" (Isaiah 66:12–14).

4

The Church as the True Defender of Human Freedom

EBUCHADNEZZAR, THE RULER OF BABYlon, ordered that a humongous gold image be placed on the field of Dura and called upon all his subjects to venerate the idol: "You are commanded, O peoples, nations, and languages: that when you hear the sound of the horn [...], you are to fall down and worship the golden image that King Nebuchadnezzar has set up; and whoever does not fall down and worship shall immediately be cast into a burning fiery furnace" (Daniel 3:4–6).

"Then the satraps, the prefects, and the governors, the counselors, the treasurers, the justices, the magistrates, and all the officials of the provinces were assembled for the dedication of the image that King Nebuchadnezzar had set up; and they stood before the image that Nebuchadnezzar had set up" (Daniel 3:3), wanting to keep the grace of the totalitarian tyrant of long-gone times, the tyrant who even reached for human souls in order to chain together his will with the handcuffs of worship of the state, at the price of idolatry. When he made the people fell before the idol; when he trampled on their neck with his heavy foot; when he struggled against the dignity of man, an intelligent and free being, he understood that he ruled over not people, but an enslaved herd. He defeated humanity in the subordinated nation and tore down the last bastion of dignity — religion — to build a state of tyranny, violence, and rape on the ashes of humanity.

Only three Judean youths who in their hearts carried faith in the God Almighty, Who transcends all the transient gods of the state, did not follow this command, although they ended up amidst the flames of the fiery oven, as if they were the only mouths praising the God of Hosts. They are the defenders of the dignity of man, who, being God's own property, cannot submit to anyone, even the most ruthless leader.

239

I. The Totalitarian Assault on Human Freedom

This image from the history of Babylon has been repeated many times throughout the history of the world. Humanity has survived not only the pagan world's stubborn struggle against nascent Christianity, but also the somber history of the inhuman Protestant principle of *cuius regio, eius religio*; the sea of lawlessness of the new deity, the secular state; as well as the cruelty of the state god of collective production and the deification of race. Whenever a new idol was forged, the nation was violently forced to bow before the golden god, while the powerful state ignited the fiery oven of persecutions in which all who dared to defend the freedom of their hearts against the totalitarian assault of the state perished.

Man Falls Prey to Communist Production

In recent years, we have witnessed a great struggle against human freedom within the humongous body of the communist state. Communism has proclaimed unlimited and universal freedom, considering freedom to be the privilege of every person. However, this was nothing more than a slogan in a propaganda campaign. In reality, communism has led man to the most burdensome and complete slavery: socio-economic slavery. Communism proclaimed the myth of production as a god, thus completely subjugating man to its laws.

The citizen of a communist state is theoretically the owner of everything, but in practice he owns nothing, while all citizens are hirelings of the state. All the means and tools of production as well as all places of work are in the hands of the state's economic administration. Without the will of the state, no citizen will ever find employment. The state wields total control over its citizens' lives and deaths from starvation. The state becomes man's only providence. Thus, if it deprives someone of work, it sentences him to death; the communist state can deprive man of a roof over his head, a cup of hot water, a slice of bread, and even the most modest clothing.

What is man to communism? Man is by no means an important concept; in fact, this concept is suspect and even indecent! It smacks of great exaggeration. Why should we speak so much? Man is only a means of production. One of his aims is the development

240

of production. The entirety of man's worth is measured by his productive potential, which becomes the measure of all human rights. The entire system of production has sought to devalue the concept of "man," deprive man of freedom, and intentionally destroy human dignity through the system of labor competition.

In the communist system, man has sacrificed his humanity in favor of the state. A system of slave labor was created. First, the humanity of those who had the courage to think in a different way than the official party line was sacrificed. The state controlled all the means of cultural development; normal academic and cultural life were no longer possible. Their absence can be replaced only by intellectual and cultural slavery. Only the "law-abiding" citizens had any right to speak; others had to remain silent.

Nor did the reforms bypass the proletariat, which was liberated from the yoke of capitalism only to become the slave of the collective. In the communist state, the laborer subjected to the laws of a mad pace of production becomes the victim of no smaller oppression. He was deprived of his personal will; the state struggled against individuality and the freedom to act; and slaves handcuffed to factories were compelled to perform involuntary labor. All were subjected to a collective template, thus becoming deprived of freedom and the liberty of a quiet home and the choice of one's food, clothing, and place of employment. A free social life was replaced with violence, while people were violently forced to join unions, attend party rallies, and engage in politics whose only aim was to preserve the propagated system rather than improve the lot of the worker.

No better is the fate of the peasantry, which has ceased to own its land and crops, homesteads, and houses, as the state has subjected it to the harsh laws of a truly feudal system of slave labor.

And what are we to make of the freedom of conviction, belief, and faith? Do we not have before our eyes that golden idol of Nebuchadnezzar when we read how a complex system of godlessness was created to struggle against "the old God of Christianity" and "a hunt for God" took place within the human soul, thus leaving only the freedom... to disbelief? This example is infectious, as the communist regimes learned about the struggle against religion from the Soviets and other opponents of human freedom.

If there is no freedom to believe in God, how can we speak of civil liberties? It is telling how briefly humanity could make use of this accomplishment of civilization! Civil liberties were misused to struggle against religion, and when religion's influence was curbed, civil liberties fell along with the branches that were sawed off. Thus, it is unsurprising that today human freedoms are expressed by overflowing prisons, mass shootings, the imaginative tortures of the Cheka; the zenith of these "accomplishments" are the Butryka, the Solovetsky Islands, and the State Police Directorate.[1]

Communism has created a whole chain of slavery that has been wrapped around man, causing him to break in the face of the system; subordinating the individual to the masses; leaving the citizen to the whims of the official; replacing the individual conscience with the collective conscience; and violating human dignity through violence. Man has been turned into a soulless machine, a blind tool in the hands of the Moloch-like state.

There exists only one freedom: that of the communist elites, which would be more accurately defined as license and the usurpation of the means that are necessary to live from the hands of the poor.

In this way, a new order has been created, one in which the following words of the Psalmist describe well: "For I see violence and strife in the city. Day and night they go around it on its walls; and mischief and trouble are within it, ruin is in its midst; oppression and fraud do not depart from its marketplace" (Psalm 55:9–11).

2. The Brutality of Enslaving Totalitarianism

Totalitarianism also wages war against human freedom. It seeks to usurp the entire life of the nation in all its aspects: social and cultural, religious, political and economic. The totalitarian state is not so much a caretaker as it is a director and commander in all areas of life. Its worldview is National Socialism, and every citizen must

---

1 The Cheka was the first Soviet secret police, founded in 1917 by the Polish aristocrat Felix Dzerzhinsky (Feliks Dzierżyński), that would be succeeded by the NKVD and KGB, among others. Butryka is a prison in Moscow that was founded in Tsarist Russia but would be used by the Soviets to hold political prisoners. The Solovetsky Islands are an archipelago that was home to the first prison in the Gulag system. The State Police Directorate was the immediate successor to the Cheka.

accept it. Only the "truths" preached by it are of civic value and only they deserve to be called the truth. Truths that do not spread the military spirit, the spirit of struggle, are meaningless and cannot be the worldview of the human citizen.

In the totalitarian state, the individual has no rights. The state is everything; it is the new god, and the individual takes on meaning only in the state. In the sphere of social relations, brute force determines everything. The weaker must become subordinated to the stronger. Man has only those rights that he can gain through his own strength. The state sees man as nothing more than a representative of certain forces.

Like in the communist state, in the totalitarian state the individual is merely the means, the tool which the state freely uses in order to achieve its collective goals. In it, man's spiritual values are not taken into consideration. The entirety of education boils down to expanding physical strength. Distrust in reason, the expansion of strength and energy, and honing obedience are the principles of education that are instilled in the name of faith in "blood and race."

In the totalitarian state, religion is not absolute truth and worth; it is merely a tool in the hands of the state. "It is not the nation that should follow the principles of religion, but religion should be first created according to the aims and aspirations of the people" is the leading principle which the Church had to accept. When this failed, there were attempts at separating the nation from Christianity to unite it at the feet of the Germanic god, who supposedly better fit the spirit of the nation. Aiming for the unity of the nation, the propaganda rejecting Christianity has broken the nation up into thousands of cults that fight one another amidst the deluge of the accounts, fairy tales, and mythical illusions of Germanism.

The struggle against man and his connection to God leads to the frightening terror that the nation has not yet experienced or witnessed. The strength that was worshiped turned into a terrible tool that ravaged many nations, but above all brought misfortune upon the German nation itself, which turned its homeland into a concentration camp where the highest authority is the omniscient secret police.

Once again, it has turned out that it is not "flesh and blood" that reveal man's greatest strength, but the "Father who is in heaven" (Matthew: 16:17). Man cannot be reduced to race and cannot be explained away through race and blood; he has a higher life, a spiritual life which is the source of his entire worth, dignity, and rights.

All this pride, whose power rests in dishonest verbal propaganda, should be confronted with Christ's words: "You brood of vipers! How can you speak good when you are evil? For out of the abundance of the heart the mouth speaks. The good man out of his good treasure brings forth good, and the evil man out of his evil treasure brings forth evil. I tell you, on the day of judgment men will render account for every careless word they utter" (Matthew 12:34–36).

II. The Church as the Defender of True Human Freedom

In his revelation, St. John describes the work of the beast of the Apocalypse: "Also it causes all, both small and great, both rich and poor, both free and slave, to be marked on the right hand or the forehead, so that no one can buy or sell unless he has the mark, that is, the name of the beast or the number of its name" (Revelation 13:16–17). We see what a step forward the heirs to the apocalyptic beast have taken: today, one not only cannot "buy or sell," but he is not even allowed to breathe without the mark of the beast.

In this sad situation, man has found his defender in Him whose strength flowed from the Cross of the Highest Consoler of humanity, in the Church. The Church engaged in a decisive battle in defense of man, protecting him from the crushing roller of totalitarianism. Through the words of Pius XI, the Church has fought against integral nationalism, Nazism, pagan totalitarianism, fascist errors, and the excesses of capitalism, collectivism and communism, thus serving the dignity of the human person everywhere. This is a testament to the Church's contributions to civilization!

1. Man and His Personal Destiny

In the struggle for human dignity, the Church reminds the state of the great dignity of the human person and his personal fate. The Catholic *Social Code* states that: "Not society, but only man, and each man, who was created in the image and likeness of God, is immortal. The Lord God has loved, and Jesus Christ has redeemed only man, each man without exception."

Before encountering society, every man met God, as during the act of creation he received from Him an immortal soul; along with it, he heard God's voice, which designated the path of his earthly vocation and ultimate destiny. From that point, man follows his paths towards God; God has personally created these paths so that they lead to salvation.

In this way, God's hand has forged the greatest work before which creation stands astounded, asking the Almighty Creator: "What is man that Thou art mindful of him, or the son of man, that Thou carest for him? Thou didst make him for a little while lower than the angels, Thou hast crowned him with glory and honor, putting everything in subjection under his feet" (Hebrews 2:6–7; see Psalm 8:5–7). The state receives such a citizen from God's hand. Thus, it is unsurprising that God has endowed man with rights that not even the most totalitarian state can destroy. The right to life comes from God's hands. It is so precious that the Church defends it from the womb until the moment of death. Through her example, the Church instructs the state to not violate that law without apparent necessity for the common good. Today's totalitarian currents have provided an example of a great violation of this law when terror liquidated not only individual persons but also entire segments of society, groups of people, and social classes that were inconvenient or had the courage to think independently. Furthermore, the totalitarian state has embarked on the mad plan of exterminating entire nations in order to expand their "living space."

Another law is bound to God's law of the protection of life: the integrity of the human body. Those possessed by racist theories violate this law in unprecedented ways in their own nation, influenced by national egotism.

The right to life is tied to the right to the possession of means that are necessary to live. State authority can neither create nor support an economic system that would deprive entire social classes of the means necessary to life, for man has received the right to them from nature and not the state. We know that the totalitarian state has all too often used the specter of death from starvation in the struggle against its own citizens.

It is also from God that man has received the right to strive for his ultimate purpose on the path He has designated. The state must ensure that citizens have the freedom to pursue their vocation, as doing so ensures the flourishing of their personhood. In the pursuit of his purpose, man can and should make use of social assistance, which is ensured by the state that respects the right to property and its individual use.

The above-mentioned rights create a framework in which freedom, God's greatest gift to man, can function and flourish. Freedom as conceived by the Church is not a god, but it is the first gift that God gives to man, elevating him above all other creation.

Because freedom is not a god, everything cannot be sacrificed for it, but we can strive for it through grace, of which the Church is a steward. The Church, who ties freedom to responsibility for human actions, guarantees that freedom is used in the best way: "Live as free men, yet without using your freedom as a pretext for evil; but live as servants of God" (1 Peter 2:16–15). "For you were called to freedom, brethren; only do not use your freedom as an opportunity for the flesh, but through love be servants of one another" (Galatians 5:13–15). "Only take care lest this liberty of yours somehow become a stumbling block to the weak" (1 Corinthians 8:9).

Personal freedom, based on the concept of responsibility, will be the best contribution to the social good. Thus, the Church, who has shaped within the person a sense of responsibility, is the best guarantor of freedom of not only the individual, but of society as well. Social freedom must be subordinated to the common good; for freedom to not be a delusion that turns into license and the tyranny of the strong over the weak, it must be rightly grounded.

In collective society, the freedom of the individual is the guarantor of the common good. If everyone will work in the spirit of Christian love for one's neighbor in order to expand God's kingdom on earth, then freedom and civil liberties will not be divergent, but will instead lead towards a common goal, for "where the Spirit of the Lord is, there is freedom" (2 Corinthians 3:17).

2. The State and Civil Liberties

Although man is a person, he nonetheless lives in society and is a social being; thus, he cannot achieve all his aims without society. It is not true that man is self-sufficient; he is incapable of surviving and achieving the perfection of mind and heart without assistance from society. Thus, according to the Catholic *Social Code*, society is for man "a necessary means that facilitates the achieving of his own purpose. Human rights result from his very nature. From the perspective of society, they are subject to certain limitations that are required by social co-existence."

Thus, man must co-exist with people and create different communities: familial, professional, and political. When an individual becomes a part of such communities, he does not lose the personal rights he deserves or the aims proper to him. No community can have such authority over man that it can erase his rights that are proper to the human person or to deprive him of the freedom to think and to act, thus making him a dead cog in the social machine.

In his activity, man has the duty to look after the common good and even sacrifice his well-being and personal rights for the sake of society. He can never lose sight of the truth that the state society, like every other society, is not man's ultimate purpose. The contemporary totalitarian state forgets this all too often and proclaims itself as man's ultimate purpose, thus subjugating him to itself. At the cost of the person, the state is deified and becomes the master of life and death.

The contemporary state that violates human rights should remember that it is not a good or even a person. The state is a legal, economic and political community whose aim is the temporal good of the people; with respect to the person and to humanity it maintains its laws, strength, freedom to act, and authority, but, according to Cardinal Pacelli, "the individual participates in collective life not in order to lose his personhood, but instead to develop it." Human personhood will always be the greatest value in the world. Efforts must be undertaken to harmonize the life of the individual with social life. Those who deny the rights of the person turn society into a great herd. This has been successfully accomplished in the collective state.

In particular, the state lacks the right to interfere with its citizens' spiritual lives and especially their human conscience, for reason and conscience are of greater worth than the state; they are the cornerstone of the existence of the state itself.

Excessive emphasis on the laws of society, the nation, and state, organization and unity will always be erroneous. This causes the state to become a tyrant that violates human rights, not respecting its duties towards its own citizens and other nations. Such a state digs its own grave.

Equally erroneous is excessive emphasis on the freedom and security of the individual. In this way, cooperative national life, which is a life-giving source for man and fully flourishes through the exercise of social obligations, is violated.

The wisest political solution is a synthesis of, on the one hand, the instinct of personal dignity, independence and freedom, and, on the other, the social instinct, extrapersonal unity, obedience, discipline, and social organization. This work is accomplished thanks to the religious perspective on man, who is the citizen of the state community. The ancient state did not understand the human soul and thus it oppressed man. Christianity began to speak of the great dignity of the person as a child of God, of the infinite value of his soul, and of his long-term destiny, thus liberating man from the tyranny of the state. The first major charter of human and civil rights was written by the Church: "For whatever is born of God overcomes the world; and this is the victory that overcomes the world, our faith" (1 John 5:4).

Thanks to our faith, a new, major victory is taking place before our very eyes.

* * *

In recent decades, humanity has faced great, historic challenges. Nations that have rejected God have killed their children. God's right hand has liberated man from the tyranny of godless rulers. We are on the path towards the new rebirth of man. Let us go to the House of the Lord. From there, justice, peace and the happiness of peoples will flow.

"Many nations shall come, and say: 'Come, let us go up to the mountain of the Lord, to the house of the God of Jacob; that He may teach us His ways and we may walk in His paths.' For out of Zion shall go forth the law, and the word of the Lord from Jerusalem. He shall judge between many peoples, and shall decide for strong nations afar off; and they shall beat their swords into plowshares, and their spears into pruning hooks; nation shall not lift up sword against nation, neither shall they learn war any more [...]. For all the peoples walk each in the name of its god, but we will walk in the name of the Lord our God for ever and ever" (Micah 4:2–5).

PART III

The Kingdom of God on Earth

1
"So, You Are a King?"
(John 18:37)

I N THE LITURGY OF THE MASS ON THE FEAST
of Christ the King, the Church reminds us of a scene that took
place before Pilate's court. "So, you are a king?" Pilate asks with
mistrust. Christ the Lord affirms this: "You say that I am a king.
For this I was born, and for this I have come into the world, to bear
witness to the truth. Everyone who is of the truth hears my voice"
(John 18:37).

When the Church recalls these words at such an appropriate time
and they are heard from parish pulpits, today's people are overcome
with the same skepticism as Pilate: "So you are a king?" "But we
have not heard anything of this before! The Good News has been
preached around the world for centuries, but it has not entered our
own minds!" Today, in the twentieth century of Christianity, this
news, which is recalled by Pope Pius XI, arouses greater anxiety, for
the world has become so unaccustomed to Christ's dominion.

As she praises the glory of Christ's kingdom in the Preface during
Mass, the Church professes the kingdom of truth and life; the king-
dom of sanctity and grace; the kingdom of justice, love, and peace.
The Preface describes the most essential traits of Christ's kingdom.
However, the Pilate-like world does not understand these words. What
the Church says is harsh! Why is it supposedly so irrelevant?!

I. The Church Has Proclaimed Christ's Kingdom of Truth and Life

The world doubts: The kingdom of truth? The kingdom of life?
But what is the truth? And what is life? Today's world has so little
faith in the truth and the possibility of its existence that it has such
great expectations of the truth; all its own "truths" have disappointed
it. It is unsurprising that this world is so mistrustful of every mani-
festation of the truth.

The Church reminds the world of Christ's words: "I am the way, and the truth, and the life" (John 14:6).

"For this I was born, and for this I have come into the world, to bear witness to the truth. Everyone who is of the truth hears my voice" (John 18:37).

In the prologue to his Gospel, John adds: "The true light that enlightens every man was coming into the world" (John 1:9).

"In Him was life, and the life was the light of men" (John 1:4).

There is a close bond between the light of the truth and life. Life is possible only thanks to the presence of truth. And God is the truth! Just as there is but one God, there is also only one truth: God's truth! Every truth flows only from God's truth. Every fragment of human truth rests in God. Only the truth that is discovered in God gives the world life. Even if an untruth is accepted and professed by the whole world, it cannot ever become truth despite its prevalence. Today, we know of many untrue "truths" that the whole world defends. The opposite is also true: even if truth coming from God were ridiculed by the world, just as Pilate ridiculed Christ, it will never cease to be the truth.

The world's misfortune rests in the fact that it seeks truth that is contrary to God.

There is a struggle between God's truth and man, who seeks it out: "The true light that enlightens every man was coming into the world" (John 1:9). Today's world knows this, and this infuriates it! It also knows that God "was in the world" and that "the world was made through Him" (John 1:10). This truth is the source of the world's rebellion! "He came to His own home, and His own people received Him not" (John 1:11). On the contrary, people today openly strive so that certainly untruths will become universally accepted, in the vain hope that they will become new "truths" and a new anti-Christian revelation. They believe that this world can contain such "truths" that are against God and that will help to overthrow God's kingdom.

Such hopes can be discerned even among certain representatives of the social sciences: they are ready to accept anything as long as it has nothing to do with God's name and His truth. The greatest absurdities will find their educated defenders who will create elaborate systems of scientific lies and delusions only because they have nothing to do with God.

The error of today's science consists in the fact that it seeks to create a contradiction between God's truth and the so-called scientific truth. Many believe that only such an approach is scientific, even if it contradicts God's revelation. They seek out what divides and not what brings people together. Creating contradictions is the greatest triumph. People do not so much seek out the truth as they try to detect lies. A rich imagination seeks out, suspects, and pursues lies everywhere. God Himself has been subject to such morbid mistrust: "He was in the world, and the world was made by Him, yet the world knew Him not. He came to His own home, and His own people received Him not" (John 1:10–11).

Errors and pride come at a cost. The misfortune of such science is that it has divided everything and subjected everything to doubt. Today, it does not even trust itself!

Separation from God's truth is the death of science and morality.

There was a time when many preached that God would be replaced with reason, science and knowledge. It was commonly believed that widespread education would be a miraculous cure-all. Heaps of books and journals were written in this hope, and schools and academies were built everywhere, while man died powerless and surrounded by darkness beneath that Tower of Babel. The world has produced scholars, but these scholars profess truths they themselves do not believe in, just as they do not believe in any value of human knowledge. Throngs of youths descend upon universities, yet several years later they leave them wielding diplomas and asking with anxious minds: "What is truth?" Are they capable of grasping the meaning of life without knowing the truth?

Pupils take after their masters! Lifelessness flows from books and writings today. Indeed, how weak in life those scholars are! "These are waterless springs and mists driven by a storm; for them the nether gloom of darkness has been reserved. For, uttering loud boasts of folly, they entice with licentious passions of the flesh men who have barely escaped from those who live in error. They promise them freedom, but they themselves are slaves of corruption; for whatever overcomes a man, to that he is enslaved" (2 Peter 2:17–19).

"And the Word became flesh and dwelt among us, full of grace and truth" (John 1:14).

When the world dies, it must summon its heavenly Doctor, for it is incapable of healing itself. It must reject the mistrustful question: "What is truth?" It is time to accept the only acceptable method of seeking the truth: "Everyone who is of the truth hears My voice" (John 18:37).

When we seek the truth in the sign of the Eternal Word, we will regain life, which was born "not of blood nor of the will of the flesh nor of the will of man, but of God" (John 1:13).

"For he who finds me finds life and obtains favor from the Lord; but he who misses me injures himself; all who hate me love death" (Proverbs 8:35–36).

II. The Church Has Proclaimed Christ's Kingdom of Sanctity and Grace

Christ's Kingdom is not of this world: "My kingship is not of this world; if my kingship were of this world, my servants would fight" (John 18:36). Christ's Kingdom is the kingdom of the spirit, whose rule is exercised in the human soul, mind, will, and feelings; it is a kingdom of sanctity and grace.

If the kingdom of truth and life infuriates the contemporary world, then the kingdom of sanctity and grace causes it scandal: What is it? What is it worth? What does it give to the world?

Today's world yearns for sanctity.

We can say the following about entire societies, peoples, and nations in today's world: "For my people have committed two evils: they have forsaken Me, the fountain of living waters, and hewed out cisterns for themselves, broken cisterns, that can hold no water" (Jeremiah 2:13).

Although it has rejected Christianity, today's world's yearning for sanctity has not been quenched. We know its desire and hunger well. Although it rejects the Christian saints, the world creates its own "saints;" it is still infatuated with the ascetic and the abnegate. The world does not want to see states ruled by well-fed, satiated people concerned about their own self-interest. It mistrusts them. The only kind of statesman who conquers human hearts and can gain power is the one who has forgotten about himself and his rights, well-being, estate, and prosperity. In recent decades, we have seen numerous statesmen who were ascetics in their own way. There were both pagan and Christian ascetics. The world desires rulers who have successfully ruled over themselves. The world demands such virtues of all those who have the desire to be in dominant positions; it does not reject the worshipers of the "old God," having ever-greater expectations of priests, monks, and the apostles of God's affairs in the world. How easily it is scandalized when it sees their flaws and deficiencies.

It seems to us that a new age is dawning, one in which social hierarchies will be determined not by one's estate or title, but by an exemplary moral life.

The world forgets that such yearnings are exceptionally Catholic.

Today's world searches for a new religion: strength.

In the search for new ideals, the world rejects the Church; it trusts that it will receive strong people Christianity is incapable of producing thanks to a new, natural religion devoid of sacraments, grace, rituals, and ceremonies.

Wherever we go, we hear calls for a "new morality" and a "new man." In the Soviet Union, a new collective religion was forged, one in which the hero of labor, the Udarnik,[1] the "saint" of production who was ready to sacrifice everything that is personal and belongs to him was worshiped. Many contemporary states consider the man who is raised in a martial spirit, in the spirit of military heroism, to be the ideal; he is a strong, resolute, relentless man deprived of all Christian ideals and liberated of any sentiments: love, compassion, kindness, and tenderness. A harsh and even, if the good of society demands it, cruel man is the new ideal. In order to achieve such an ideal, they profess a new religion that requires struggle, victory and death.

Furthermore, the call for a new perfection has become the national interest. The old man; that drunken, filthy sensuality; that suffocating immorality that was praised and that was omnipresent in books, in the theater, in movies, and in art; that touted freedom to debase oneself and all who surround him has grown old and is now considered distasteful. We have had enough of all this! Look at how we burn heaps of pornography, which has been created in the name of freedom of

[1] A highly productive manual laborer in the USSR and other communist regimes who was awarded by the state for his hard work.

255

expression; we want to pull people away from pubs and brothels, all those vile places where the soul is pillaged. You want to accomplish this? So do we, and we have wanted to do so for a long time! In fact, we have wanted to do this from time immemorial... There was a time when you did not want this. Thanks to God, you do want this today! But how do you plan on achieving this? Do you want to struggle against Beelzebub, the diabolical prince? Renounce the devil!

The Church offers old truths in response to new yearnings.

The good Lord responds to these human yearnings through the holy Church by recalling old truths. You say that there are no brave, strong, or heroic people in today's Church. In that case, think of all those martyrs who have given their lives for their religious convictions in the twentieth century, that age of sloth and softness. They died no less heroically than their comrades and friends who were paratroopers and bombardiers, and they did so voluntarily, not because they were following commands. The Church has new martyrs of the twentieth century, its new Cecilia, Anastasia, Agnes, and Lucy. They did not sacrifice their lives for orders and crosses of merit, nor did they do so for fame and publicity or the favor of the powerful of the world, but for the most disdained Cross, for the distant Leader who will reward His soldiers in the next life.

What is the greatest heroism? All power coming from Christ! He also contains the goodness without which there can exist no sage power. The martyrs of the Church are the true strongmen! They know not only how to live the truth, but to die for it as well.

III. The Church Has Proclaimed Christ's Kingdom of Justice, Love and Peace

Upon hearing these words, the world once again experiences Pilate's doubts: "A kingdom of justice? Love? Peace?" These are empty words! Neither justice nor peace can exist in this world! And we do not want love!

Various forms of freedom have been proclaimed as new ideals.

The separation between politics and moral demands has been proclaimed. The statement that "politics can never be moral" has been elevated to the status of a dogma. Why should politics be subjected to God's old commandments? It must be as far away from Christ as possible! The Church should never try to make politics more moral; such efforts are clericalism.

And what about economic life? What can Christ say about factories, banks and trade? Economics and ethics are polar opposites! It is impossible to make a profit with the aid of God's commandments. The commandments of merchants are contrary to those of God! You say that man will become a human wolf; why, then, should he be a brother? We need power, and not neighbors, for labor! Love is such a soft word! And a costly one!

"Freedom from Christ" has given birth to a new slavery.

"For the nation and kingdom that will not serve you shall perish; those nations shall be utterly laid waste" (Isaiah 60:12).

When God's law disappeared from political and economic life, these were overwhelmed with lawlessness. Wherever there is a lack of truth, lies become the most important means of rule and victory. Hatred triumphs wherever there is no love. Freedom from God's laws is the liberation of deceit, lies, fraud, violence, and the law of the fist. Selfish exploitation, filthy greed, and the struggle over a piece of daily bread flourish wherever love dies. That is the path to the destruction and ruin of the entire world.

* * *

Guided by the inspiration of the Holy Spirit, God's Church reminds the world of Christ's right to His kingdom. Christ struggles for His legacy when the world is overcome with the tumult of anarchy and rebellious shouts of "I will not serve" everywhere. He brings life to the world, which prefers to die in its foolish protest than accept the sweet bonds of His rule.

"Why do the nations conspire, and the peoples plot in vain? The kings of the earth set themselves, and the rulers take counsel together, against the Lord and his anointed, saying, 'Let us burst their bonds asunder, and cast their cords from us'" (Psalm 2:1–3).

Indeed, we must ask: why did they rebel against their Ruler? They perish in a flood of lies and death, in waves of iniquity and tyranny, shackled by injustice, hatred and struggle. Yet they do not want to recognize the authority of the King of peace and life, sanctity and grace, justice and love above themselves. Why? This is the riddle of the twentieth century.

"He who sits in the heavens laughs" (Psalm 2:4). "And now, O ye kings, understand: receive instruction, you that judge the earth. Serve ye the Lord with fear: and rejoice unto Him with trembling. Embrace discipline, lest at any time the Lord be angry, and you perish from the just way. [. . .] Blessed are all they that trust in Him" (Psalm 2:10–13).

2
Building Christ's Kingdom

"Thy kingdom come" (Luke 11:2):

*"For behold, the kingdom of God is
in the midst of you" (Luke 17:21).*

*"For the nation and kingdom that
will not serve you shall perish;
those nations shall be utterly
laid waste" (Isaiah 60:12).*

I N THE ENCYCLICAL *UBI ARCANO DEI*, PIUS XI,
the servant among God's servants, concisely explains what
Christ's kingdom is on earth: "Jesus Christ reigns over the minds
of individuals by His teachings, in their hearts by His love, in each
one's life by living according to His law and imitating His example.
Jesus reigns over the family when it, modeled after the holy ideals of
the sacrament of matrimony instituted by Christ, maintains unspot-
ted its true character of sanctuary. [...] Finally, Jesus Christ reigns
over society when men recognize and reverence the sovereignty of
Christ, when they accept the divine origin and control over all social
forces, a recognition which is the basis of the right to command
for those in authority and of the duty to obey for those who are
subjects, a duty which cannot but ennoble all who live up to its
demands" (48).

These concise words contain the entirety of the authority which
"the first-born of all creation" (Colossians 1:15) has received from the
heavenly Father, "for in Him all things were created, in heaven and
on earth, visible and invisible, whether thrones or dominions or principalities or authorities — all things were created through Him and
for Him. He is before all things, and in Him all things hold together"
(Colossians 1:16–17).

Through the will of the heavenly Father, "in Him all the fullness
of God was pleased to dwell, and through Him to reconcile to himself all things, whether on earth or in heaven" (Colossians 1:19–20).

I. What Is Christ's Kingdom?

We ascribe royal authority to Christ the Lord because of His humanity. Being Divine, Christ the Lord possesses everything with His Father, and so the highest authority over all the world's creation. This authority flows from the strange union in which Christ's Divinity and humanity are unified: thanks to this unity, Christ has received full authority over all of creation from His Father. Christ the Lord binds together within Himself not only Divinity and humanity, but through the Blood of the holy Cross He has also bound together everything on earth with everything in heaven.

As the King and Highest Authority, Christ the Lord has concentrated within Himself triune authority: lawgiving, judicial, and penal authority. These forms of authority are the essence of Christ's Kingdom.

As the Lawgiver, Christ the Lord has not come to dissolve the ancient Covenant, but to fulfill it. He taught the people "as One who had authority, and not as their scribes" (Matthew 7:29). Christ the Lord creates a law which firmly defends against the abuses of those who ruled at the time: "You have heard that it was said to the men of old, 'You shall not kill; and whoever kills shall be liable to judgment.' But I say to you that everyone who is angry with his brother shall be liable to judgment; whoever insults his brother shall be liable to the council [. . .]. You have heard that it was said, 'You shall not commit adultery.' But I say to you that everyone who looks at a woman lustfully has already committed adultery with her in his heart. [. . .] It was also said, 'Whoever divorces his wife, let him give her a certificate of divorce.' But I say to you that everyone who divorces his wife [. . .] makes her an adulteress; and whoever marries a divorced woman commits adultery. Again you have heard that it was said to the men of old, 'You shall not swear falsely [. . .].' But I say to you, do not swear at all [. . .]. But I say to you, love your enemies and pray for those who persecute you" (Matthew 5:21–44).

How different are the conditions that accompany Christ's legislation, which is proclaimed from the Mount of Beatitudes, compared to those under which Moses heard God tell him His laws on Mount Sinai. There, God spoke in the glory and terror of thunderbolts, while the people did not dare approach the foot of the mountain. Here, however, Christ pronounces His words powerfully, albeit in an atmosphere of peace and calm, to a crowd that has thronged at His feet.

Christ's law is related to the concept of punishment and menace, but this results from love and is based around love: "If you keep My commandments, you will abide in My love" (John 15:10). There is no other ruler who would be willing to rule over people without police and prisons, only with love.

As the Judge, Christ the Lord has inherited the entirety of judicial authority. Peoples and nations who have opposed His signs will stand before Him, for "the Father judges no one, but has given all judgment to the Son" (John 5:22). "Behold my servant, whom I uphold, my chosen, in Whom my soul delights; I have put my Spirit upon Him" (Isaiah 42:1).

Finally, Christ the Lord possesses the right to punish, and the resistant will hear Him say: "Depart from Me, you cursed, into the eternal fire" (Matthew 25:41). Indeed, Christ the Lord has redeemed the world with His most precious blood and therefore is completely entitled to it! Everything rests in Christ's hand: "I have manifested Thy name to the men whom Thou gavest Me out of the world; Thine they were, and Thou gavest them to Me" (John 17:6). Everything is beneath Christ's feet.

II. Christ's Kingdom Is Exceptionally Spiritual

Christ's Kingdom deals with spiritual matters and spiritual life. The Lord Jesus has decisively rejected all the temptations of the crowd, which was fascinated with His miracles. Neither those satiated by the miraculously multiplied Bread, nor the Palm Sunday crowds succeeded in changing Christ's true attitude: "My kingship is not of this world" (John 18:36). Whenever Christ saw crowds coming to kidnap Him and make Him the king of Zion, He always hid from them. He frequently told parables that made it clear that His would be a kingdom of a completely new order.

We enter Christ's kingdom through penitence, faith, and baptism, and therefore through an internal path of transformation and rebirth. Christ said to Nicodemus: "Truly, truly, I say to you, unless one is born of water and the Spirit, he cannot enter the kingdom of God" (John 3:5).

Internal transformation is the essence of Christ's kingdom. The rulers of this earth have a different criterion: they dress their members in uniforms and inquire about blood and race. By contrast, Christ looks into the soul! He has emphatically communicated this through His first miracle at Cana, where He turned water into wine, that from that point the transformation of everything would become even deeper: bread would turn into Christ's Body, the earth would turn into heaven, and man would turn into God: "You are gods, sons of the Most High, all of you" (Psalm 81:6). Only this kind of preparation bears witness to belonging to Christ's kingdom. This kingdom opposes only Satan's kingdom and the rulers of darkness.

Satan's highest ideal is also transformation, but the transformation of stones into bread. This digestive ideal ends his worldly success. Satan even seeks out Christ's assistance to embody this ideal but receives the following brief response: "Man shall not live by bread alone" (Matthew 4:4; Deuteronomy 8:3). The struggle of Satan's kingdom against God's kingdom begins on earth at that moment on the Mount of Temptation. Satan will attempt to transform the King of Heaven into the king of Jerusalem, the king of the satiated, with the aid of the satiated crowds that dream of sitting in high positions on His left and right (see Matthew 20:21). Rulers like Nero, Diocletian, and Stalin arise and undertake Satan's struggle under the slogan of *panem et circenses*,[1] which continues to be professed until today in all the languages of the world.

Christ's struggle against Satan's kingdom will be a protest against the adoration of the satiated: "Truly, truly, I say to you, you seek me, not because you saw signs, but because you ate your fill of the loaves" (John 6:26). Christ wants to transform this bread into His Body: "Do not labor for the food which perishes, but for the food which endures to eternal life, which the Son of Man will give to you" (John 6:27).

This is where the enthusiasm of the masses fizzles out. "This is a hard saying" (John 6:60), and so the crowds leave Christ's kingdom, going to adore their own riches and experience the yoke of cattle.

---

1 Latin: "Bread and circuses."

III. "The Kingdom of God Is in the Midst of You" (Luke 17:20–21)

When the Pharisees ask Christ when the Kingdom of God will dawn, He replies: "The kingdom of God is not coming with signs to be observed; nor will they say, 'Lo, here it is!' or 'There!' for behold, the kingdom of God is in the midst of you" (Luke 17:20–21). Indeed, Christ, "the way, and the truth, and the life" (John 14:6), founds His kingdom in souls; He becomes the King of minds through the truth, the King of the will through the commandments and sanctity, and the King of hearts through love.

Christ is the king of our minds. In Him "are hid all the treasures of wisdom and knowledge" (Colossians 2:3). He is not an encyclopedia of human wisdom, but He is the Truth itself. Through Christ the Lord, the world has become filled with the Spirit of Truth and its love. The pagan world had to doubt in the Truth, while the Christian world learned how to seek it out. "For this I was born, and for this I have come into the world, to bear witness to the truth. Everyone who is of the truth hears my voice" (John 18:37). Thus, Christ's kingdom is built on truth as well as the search and love for truth. All mortals must receive the truth from Christ and obediently accept it.

They must recognize God's truth, which is revealed in the created world. This world is God's work, and therefore it is the truth. It is not the whole truth, but it leads us to the Highest Truth, which is God. This entire world gives witness to God; we experience His face in the work of His hands. His truth is revealed in the entirety of creation. The world overflows with questions, and every being is the truth to the degree to which it is a particle of God's truth.

"The earth is the Lord's and the fullness thereof, the world and those who dwell therein" (Psalm 24:1). This basic truth makes us accept the entirety of God's truth, which is revealed in the world: the world is the Fatherly home for those of His children who believe in His name, while the earth belongs to His children. God blesses the earth so that it would bear abundant harvests for those who glorify Him. The goods of the earth above all are intended for His children. The world is not for the unbelievers, but only for those who accept His truth.

We are to accept God's truth not only in the world itself, but in every creation. The Creator Himself praised the work of His hands:

263

"His work is perfect" (Deuteronomy 32:4). We must recognize with gratitude that God has created the entire world in truth. In the process of creation, truth and good are one.

We must also accept the revealed truth that God initiated through Moses and the Prophets and gave to the world, which Christ the Lord ultimately placed in the holy Church. Those who accept this truth will receive salvation from the Lord, while those who reject it will themselves die.

History has confirmed God's truth all too often. Every heresy is an assault against some revealed truth. We know that we cannot do this with impunity. The history of heresy demonstrates how every error hurts the people. Humanity was torn apart by the proud Eastern Schism, which did not want to acknowledge the authority of the Roman pope and became a slave to the tsar, while the rebellion against God's grace in the Western heresy starved the souls of entire nations living without the holy sacraments, without God's Bread, and without the priesthood, leaving them to lifelessness and the powerlessness of death.

"For the nation and kingdom that will not serve you shall perish; those nations shall be utterly laid waste" (Isaiah 60:12).

Christ the Lord is king in the human will. Christ extends His authority over our will through the power of His example. He united within Himself God's holy will with the perfect human will, subjected to God's will. Through this submission, He constantly prompts our will to become subordinated to God's highest will. He who fully controls His human will "was oppressed, and He was afflicted, yet he opened not His mouth" (Isaiah 53:7). Christ is conscious of His will and therefore voluntarily submits to His Father's will: "Not as I will, but as Thou wilt" (Matthew 26:39). "Not my will, but Thine, be done" (Luke 22:42).

Binding conclusions flow from this model. Inspired by the example of Christ the Lord, let us eagerly take on the most beautiful acts, sacrifices and commitments. Just as the most wondrous works, the blessing of the Cross and Redemption, took place in Christ the Lord thanks to this harmony of His human will with the will of God, the same should happen in every human soul. We ardently desire to possess the whole world for God and Christ the Lord.

Christ takes over our will not through orders, but through love. This is a completely different approach than that of contemporary powers, which have elaborated systems of violence to incline the human will to submission. By having violence as their fundament, they themselves experience violence!

Christ the King reigns in our hearts. The fullness of mildness, clemency, and love are in Christ the King, Who after all is love. Thus Christ, Who is the beginning of all love, becomes the unity of all hearts so that He is one heart and one soul for many believers. Christ takes our small hearts and transforms them into one big heart. So great is this heart that although so many who thirst have come to it and drank, none has ever left it still thirsting (see John 7:37). Never in history has anyone been loved as much as Christ the Lord. This has oftentimes aroused the admiration and jealousy of the powerful of this world, who so desired to gain the love of their subjects.

Napoleon, who often contemplated the mystery of Christ the Lord's influence, arrived at the conclusion that Christ was not merely human. Even Stalin sought out the love of Russian children and demanded he be present in the company of youths. Propaganda posters pretentiously read: "Allow children to come to me." What good can posters do without the spirit of love and the sacrifice of the Cross? Neither Napoleon nor Stalin, but Christ died for the people on the Cross! It was through the wood of the Cross that He gained to right to love, which does not end with death or a state funeral, heap of flowers, and flood of eulogies, as happens in this world. Only when they touch the heart of God can human hearts permanently rule over human hearts. Look at the saints: they are loved because they love in God.

IV. Christ's Kingdom Gives Birth to God's Peace on Earth

Christ the Lord said that His kingdom is not of this world. How strange is the power of this spiritual authority when thanks to it our hearts will be dominated by "the peace of Christ" (Colossians 3:15), which will flow from our hearts onto all of humanity.

Souls that have become entrusted to God's truth, that have submitted to God's will, and that have loved all in God can no longer be happy alone. They desire to share their joy with others; hence the instructions: "Go therefore and make disciples of all nations" (Matthew 28:19) and "Unite all things in him" (Ephesians 1:10). From there flows the powerful wave of Christian mercy, charity and social work as well as Catholic and missionary action, to lead the entire world to happiness in God.

Christ's Kingdom is born in the soul, but it does not remain enclosed within it. Christ is the Lord of all creation and has authority over the entire created world. Through the Blood of the Cross, he has the right to the world.

Christ's dominion moves from the human soul to the life of the family, nation, state and all human life. His kingdom is inscribed in souls not only in the lives of the saints, but in all human history: not through the history of wars, but through the communion of saints. God inscribes this history not on stone tablets, but on the tablets of our hearts (see 2 Corinthians 3:3). The Kingdom of God comes not with publicity and fanfare, nor does it come through propaganda and external effects; instead, "the kingdom of God is in the midst of you" (Luke 17:21). Arising amidst peace and humility, it dies like a grain of wheat to bring hundred-fold fruits through its death, which are love and social justice. Christ the Lord establishes His social kingdom on the cornerstone of the reborn soul. Isaiah says of Christ: "Behold, My servant whom I have chosen, My beloved with whom my soul is well pleased. I will put my Spirit upon Him, and He shall proclaim justice to the Gentiles. He will not wrangle or cry aloud, nor will anyone hear His voice in the streets [...] and in His name will the Gentiles hope" (Matthew 12:18–21; see Isaiah 42:1–4).

It depends on us if Christ's kingdom will pass judgment on the nations. It will pass through the human soul. Let us make room for Christ in our souls, and He will be present in our family, nation and state. There is no other way!

"Worthy is the Lamb Who was slain, to receive power and wealth and wisdom and might and honor and glory and blessing [...]. To Him be glory and dominion for ever and ever. Amen" (Revelation 5:12;1:6).

VOLUME III

The Social Crusade

1

The Causes for the Existence
of the Social Question

*"For the love of money is the root
of all evils." (1 Timothy 6:10).*

WHAT ARE THE SOURCES OF THE MISFOR-
tune of contemporary societies? How can we understand
that the fact that the world, which is filled with God's
gifts and is becoming increasingly prosperous, is at the same time so
full of poverty and people who lack the means to live? What is the
origin, the cause of the so-called social question?

This is not a new question, and the matter itself remains conten-
tious. We see how differently it is resolved in both the social sciences
and in practice. Some see its origins as moral in nature, others consider
their causes to be social, and yet others blame economic factors. The
proposed solutions depend on the assumptions one has regarding the
root of the problem. Capitalism fails to recognize any impairment of
the working class that would result from the flaws of the economic
system. Socialists and communists, meanwhile, reduce the system
to purely economic matters. They say that it is enough to create a
commonwealth of goods, and then all evil will disappear.

What are we to think of this? The answer to this question is even
more significant as this problem is becoming increasingly prevalent.
Whereas Leo spoke of the question of the workers in his encyclical
Rerum novarum, Pius XI was forced to speak of the reworking of the
entire social system, for the social matter encompassed not only the
working class, but almost all of society. Looking at the contemporary
struggles of nations and contemplating their causes, Pius XII sees an
even greater scope to this topic. This applies not only to a single social
class, nation or state, but to nearly all states so that we must now campaign for the equal participation of all nations in the goods of the earth.

Otherwise, if this evil is not eradicated in its germinal stage, it
will expand and extend to the entire world with its tentacles. This

is no longer solely the problem of laborers, that of the relationship between the employer and the industrial worker. This concerns urban workers, agricultural laborers, and people who own no property; it encompasses nearly all who are in a dependent labor position, and not even the world of officials is exempted from this problem. Furthermore, it even encompasses small-scale industry, which is dependent on big, anonymous finance. "If one member suffers, all suffer together" (1 Corinthians 12:26).

Because the riches of the nations are nonetheless growing and the goods of the earth are increasing, this is evidence that this phenomenon is much deeper and more complicated than it would seem at a superficial level. There are four causes for this contemporary socio-economic calamity: they are spiritual, economic, legal-social, and moral-religious in nature. Knowing the causes is essential to uprooting these evils. The selection of the medicine depends on the diagnosis of the causes.

I. The Spiritual Causes of Social Evil

Leo XIII begins his encyclical *Rerum novarum* by speaking of "the spirit of revolutionary change," claiming that it inclines people to look for new paths of social life. In this way, he demonstrates that the cause of the social question is much deeper than economic in nature; it rests in the human soul, in its constant torment and anxiety. People, even those whose economic status is secure, are prone to that same spirit of revolutionary change. The drawing-room communism of well-fed and rich people can serve as an example. It is telling that the wealthy intelligentsia is often a hub of revolution.

This is an eternal secret of the human soul: "I will not serve" (Jeremiah 2:20). It will never be overcome. The desire for revolutionary change will always accompany human life. When it is expressed within reasonable limits, it can overcome idleness, insensitivity to human suffering, and dystrophy of the heart and mind. When this desire is not tamed, it can be the source of constant unrest and disorder. We should not delude ourselves that people who are satiated with bread will satisfy all their desires. Even well-off laborers are prone to revolutionary demands and create centers of social unrest, rebellion and revolution. These are the depths of the phenomenon that reminds us that "man does not live by bread alone" (Deuteronomy 8:3).

II. The Economic Causes for Social Unrest

The economic causes for social unrest are the most tangible; they simply cannot be denied. Indeed, the social question is not only a moral affair, as some erroneously maintain, but it has a great impact on economic and political life.

The indisputable cause of social unrest is "the vast expansion of industrial pursuits and the marvelous discoveries of science" (RN 1), or machine production, which harms the working man, even though it increases his efficacy. Machinery makes labor easier, but at the same time it makes it exceptionally difficult; it increases wealth, but it creates a proletariat as well.

Another economic cause of the disruption of the economic balance is "the enormous fortunes of some few individuals, and the utter poverty of the masses" (RN, 1). Thus, the contemporary system can be considered unjust, which Pius XI has mentioned: "The immense multitude of the non-owning workers on the one hand and the enormous riches of certain very wealthy men on the other establish an unanswerable argument that the riches which are so abundantly produced in our age of 'industrialism,' as it is called, are not rightly distributed and equitably made available to the various classes of the people" (QA, 60).

The economic causes of social unrest also include the fact that production and trade have nearly become the monopoly of a few; thus, a handful of wealthy people has imposed a nearly slave-like yoke to the working class (see RN, 2).

In the encyclical *Quadragesimo anno*, the Holy Father discusses in detail the roles that free and unfettered competition plays in the shaping of social disorder. It has changed the nature of economic life and the co-existence of people; thus, "it is obvious that not only is wealth concentrated in our times but an immense power and despotic economic dictatorship is consolidated in the hands of a few, who often are not owners but only the trustees and managing directors of invested funds which they administer according to their own arbitrary will and pleasure" (QA, 105). In the economic sphere, this leads to a three-fold struggle: for the enslaving of economic life itself, the domination of the state and its resources, and, finally, economic dominance in the world facilitated by struggle between states.

It is evident here how much the expanding causes of social unrest are harming one's neighbors. Small businessmen usually suffer alone under the yoke of the great financial organization of the universe, whose burdens make it more difficult to undertake social reforms.

Contemporary economic life has been criticized by the Holy See; its main misfortune is the volatility that rests at its organizational fundaments, which usually leads to ruthless conflict. A man who wants to live at a decent level and not become swallowed up must forget about everything, including God's laws and the duties of his conscience. Oftentimes, this is the price he must pay to survive. This leads to an insensitivity of the conscience and the desire to increase one's profits at all costs. Nobody in such a situation can be sure of his property and existence, while this prevalent uncertainty only increases the chase after profits.

Another danger is the anarchy of the trade market, which creates opportunities for easy profits; hence all the wild speculation, which is driven by inordinate greed. The ease with which one can make money attracts above all those who want to gain a profit through the smallest labor input, with the assistance of speculation. The more conscientious, honest, and moral individuals retreat from economic life, while only people free of any conscience remain there. Under such conditions, the most moral entrepreneur is in a hopeless situation. Trade becomes immoral when it is difficult to maintain it within the limits of morality under the conditions of honest competition.

Another danger to economic life results from anonymous companies, under whose guise the worst sorts of injuries and swindles take place: constant fake bankruptcies and the squandering of savings entrusted to petty money-grabbers. The stock market ceases to be a kind of economic service, instead becoming an area of easy speculation.

Finally, industry that deals with the production of means serving indecent aims is immoral; it not only demoralizes, but it also foments lust, desires, envy, and the willingness to make use of all forbidden fruits, which are presented as attractive through advertisements.

III. The Social-Legal Causes

The social-legal causes of this crisis are no less important. They have adversely affected both legal relations and social customs. Leo XIII directly speaks of "the changed relations between masters and workmen" (RN, 1). In the past, these relations were familial; today, the old bonds of the labor community have disappeared, having been replaced with contracts. The employer directly tells his employee: I do not care about your life apart from your labor and your salary; I do not want to have any personal relationship with you.

The familial and social relationship has become supplanted by the worst form of economic relationship: class struggle. Furthermore, this relationship has become worsened because artisans' guilds were shut down in the previous century, but not replaced with anything new (see RN, 2). The guild system was destroyed because it resisted improperly understood freedom. People became deprived of social bonds, scattered, broken, and prone to plunder by the strong without an opportunity for self-defense.

The spirit of struggle against the right to association has survived until the present day. The natural law and the necessities of life force laborers to join associations. Confidence in laborers' own strength and closer bonds between them are awakened among those who are affiliated (see RN, 1). Attempts at association are constantly met with hostility, which is one more cause of the embitterment of the working class.

IV. The Moral-Religious Causes

The moral and religious causes of this crisis are almost completely ignored; both socialists and capitalists are silent about them. However, they are very closely tied to socio-economic life.

Sins and moral negligence are the most frequent causes of injustice.

Leo XIII has generally said that this increasing moral decline devastates both social and economic life. Original sin is dangerous to not only laborers, but to capitalists as well; its terrible effects have placed them on the same level. Moral evil increased even more when its development was assisted by an immoral system. Thus, it is unsurprising that as legislation and the public sphere became increasingly deprived of the Christian spirit, craftsmen were left to the mercy of the capitalists and their rivals, whose greed knew no limits (see RN, 2).

Pius XI has expressed this even more explicitly by pointing out the moral cause of the erosion of economic life. The main responsibility rests in the liberal economy, which argues that ethics and economics are distinct disciplines and thus must be separated. An economic philosophy that is alien to true morality has appeared under the influence of individualist thinking. This is a major topic, although it has been entirely overlooked.

Contemporary experience demonstrates that the resolution of social problems through only legal or economic means will not bear the expected fruit. Providing immoral people with new resources that will be utilized for sin will greatly worsen their situation. Hence, efforts to improve the lot of people should encompass both the economic and moral areas.

* * *

This is the totality of the causes of today's social unrest, which causes many people anxiety by depriving them of peace and social harmony. One must discern how they affect and complement one another, how they create a knot that can become untied only when all who are capable and ready to untie it in their own way contribute to it.

Only the common efforts of the Church and state as well as of employers and employees will conquer evil. All must become moral and learn of God's commandments; all must be imbued with love of one's neighbor and a sense of social justice and the will to work for the common good. Only then can we expect social harmony.

"For the love of money is the root of all evils" (1 Timothy 6:10), while social peace is the work of social justice and justice towards one's own soul, neighbors, and God.

2
God's Law and the Working Class

*"I have seen the affliction of My people who are
in Egypt and have heard their cry because of
their taskmasters; I know their sufferings, and I
have come down to deliver them" (Exodus 3:7–8).*

OD UNDERTOOK THE EFFORT TO LIBERATE
the Israelites "out of the land of Egypt, out of the house of
bondage" (Exodus 20:2) under exceptional circumstances.
A new ruler "who did not know Joseph" (Exodus 1:8) or his great
contributions to saving his nation from death from starvation came
to power; thus, seeing the proliferation of God's Chosen People, he
began to fear for the future of his own nation. To save it from becoming dangerously outnumbered, a devilish plan was devised: Pharaoh
then "set taskmasters over them to afflict them with heavy burdens;
and they built for Pharaoh store-cities, Pithom and Ramses" (Exodus 1:11). Harsh was the plight of the poor people who "made their
lives bitter with hard service, in mortar and brick, and in all kinds
of work in the field" (Exodus 1:14). Although a cruel ruler had died,
the lot of the oppressed and exploited people did not improve: "And
the people of Israel groaned under their bondage, and cried out for
help, and their cry under bondage came up to God" (Exodus 2:23). It
was then that God summoned Moses, His servant, and said to him:
"I have seen the affliction of My people who are in Egypt and have
heard their cry because of their taskmasters; I know their sufferings,
and I have come down to deliver them" (Exodus 3:7–8). The Lord
sent Moses before Pharaoh to lead His people out of slavery through
the power of signs and miracles.

The struggle of the Egyptian ruler against Israel's leader is telling:
"Moses and Aaron, why do you take the people away from their work?
Get to your burdens" (Exodus 5:4). Do we not recognize this language? "Behold, the people of the land are now many, and you make
them rest from their burdens!" (Exodus 5:5). Do we not recognize
this means of struggle whose aim is to strike down all desires for the

275

improvement of one's lot? Pharaoh decreed: "You shall no longer give the people straw to make bricks, as heretofore; let them go and gather straw for themselves. But the number of bricks which they made heretofore you shall lay upon them, you shall by no means lessen it; for they are idle; therefore, they cry, 'Let us go and offer sacrifice to our God.' Let heavier work be laid upon the men that they may labor at it and pay no regard to lying words" (Exodus 5:7–9). That is the beginning of the terrible exploitation of labor, whose echoes have come to our ears thanks to works of history. The dejected people lost their confidence in Moses' vocation such that "they did not listen to Moses, because of their broken spirit and their cruel bondage" (Exodus 6:9). But who can fight against God if He has decided to save Israel? The Lord hardened the heart of the unjust ruler through the Egyptian plagues, while He proudly led His people across the Red Sea and out of the house of slavery. God immortalized His miracles in this historic work; He became the defender of the oppressed and exploited, and such He has remained through all revealed history.

Let us read the holy books and become acquainted with the Mosaic law, which was dictated by God; let us reflect on the Psalms and closely study the writings of the prophets: everywhere, we will find God's same will, which aids and defends the poor, widows, strangers, servants, and mercenaries. Let us pick up the Gospels, and we will easily see that they continue to realize God's work. Jesus Christ, who came to fulfill the Covenant, Himself said that the heavenly Father demanded that He be concerned for the small and weak: "The Spirit of the Lord is upon Me, because He has anointed Me to preach good news to the poor. He has sent Me to proclaim release to the captives and recovering of sight to the blind, to set at liberty those who are oppressed, to proclaim the acceptable year of the Lord" (Luke 4:18–19).

I. God's Law in Defense of Laborers

Israel went through a great trial under the yoke of the Pharaohs. What it experienced, however, was intended to awaken in the nation repulsion to all forms of exploitation and injustice; it was supposed to be a necessary but painful memory that would encourage Israel

276

to respect the rights of its neighbors, servants, and laborers, and it was intended to hone social sensitivity and a spirit of justice. "You shall remember that you were a slave in Egypt and the Lord your God redeemed you from there; therefore, I command you to do this" (Deuteronomy 24:18). Thanks to the memory of this, God has paved the way to human hearts to prepare them for an even more perfect Covenant: Christian love and justice.

God has closely bound together religious-moral and socio-economic life.

God has subjected humanity to religious and moral evaluation throughout nearly all its existence. All creation, with which God has so generously endowed man, has been placed before His feet: "All sheep and oxen, and also the beasts of the field, the birds of the air, and the fish of the sea, whatever passes along the paths of the sea" (Psalm 8:7–8). God wanted all of creation to serve our earthly journey to fulfill its vocation, which has been eternally established by God and sacrificially given to man, serving him with its life and forces. Through this service, creation's purpose is to facilitate the performance of the duties of both the mundane and eternal dimensions of life. By making use of creation in a way that is in accordance with God's plan, man is to not only achieve his earthly goal—the perfection of life—but also perfect union with God. In its service to man, creation is to attest to its submission to God, so that the people of God many know and understand the Lord as "the ox knows its owner, and the ass its master's crib" (Isaiah 1:3).

Thus, everything that encompasses the fullness of creation is tied to God through a common aim: praise of God; everything is brought together in this unifying hierarchy of mutual services. Can there exist an intentional division between religious and economic life if the entirety of economic life and all economic goods are to facilitate and make possible man's praising of God? Man is not to serve creation, but creation is to serve man; man is not to be subjugated to land, money, or riches, but land, money and riches are to be subjugated to man. Man is not to be subjected to the laws of economic life, but economic life must be directed by man, who is devoted to service and love of God. Ultimately, therefore, economic, and religious life cannot be separated from one another; on the contrary, they are to be closely interrelated in human life in order to reflect God's nature and anointment upon all human activity.

As long as this order of primacy is maintained, creation is a servant of man, while man is God's friend; when this order is disrupted, man becomes God's foe, the enemy of his neighbor, and the servant of matter, money, cattle and the ass, as well as all the deadly sins.

Upon God's commandment, Moses closely bound together all economic and religious matters and subjected them to religious evaluation so that this misfortune would not befall humanity. In this way, an economic life based on equitable distribution of goods was developed; it especially protected laborers and their wages, widows, orphans, and debtors. It protected the property of the poor and ensured that working conditions were adequate, ensuring all laborers the right to holy day rest and limited working hours; it earnestly fought against all kinds of usury and abuses of its economic domination.

"The Lord is a stronghold for the oppressed, a stronghold in times of trouble" (Psalm 9:9).

God defends the poor and the working class.

The books of the Old Testament contain many testimonies indicating that our heavenly Father does not let anyone out from under His protection, but "is our refuge and strength, a very present help in trouble" (Psalm 46:1). Today, we are so proud of social legislation, which, although it is imperfect, contains Christian influence because it aims for the solidification of social justice, a virtue whose assumptions are Christian. Is it not in the holy books that we must look for the beginnings of all those laws that secure that the work of laborers is protected?

Indeed, the protection of human labor began at the moment when God spoke to Moses from the burning bush: "Come, I will send you to Pharaoh that you may bring forth My people, the sons of Israel, out of Egypt" (Exodus 3:10). Do not Moses' discussions with Pharaoh remind us of the conversations that take place today in labor inspectorates? Is it not there that we often hear, on the one hand, the harsh accusation: "for they are idle; therefore, they cry, 'Let us go and offer sacrifice to our God.' Let heavier work be laid upon the men that they may labor at it and pay no regard to lying words" (Exodus 5:8–9), and, on the other, should we not recall God's words and laws as well as our duties towards Him, which are forgotten in today's economic life: "Let my people go, that they may serve me" (Exodus 8:2)? Today, the heathen representatives of economic interests reject God's intervention with the question: "Who is the Lord, that I should heed His voice and let Israel go? I do not know the Lord, and moreover I will not let Israel go" (Exodus 5:2). Indeed, they do not know the Lord, but God has not forgotten about His rights to the people who are still His, even though they are lost in the machine halls of factories, in the depths of mines, and alongside blast furnaces. Thus, God has extended His protection over the toiling people, from the days of Pharaoh up through the age of businesses and cartels, Soviet collective farms, Udarniks, and forced labor camps; from the days of Moses and Aaron to those of Leo XIII, Pius XI, and Pius XII.

The law defending the rights of the laborer once decided: "And if your brother becomes poor beside you, and sells himself to you, you shall not make him serve as a slave: he shall be with you as a hired servant and as a sojourner. [. . .] You shall not rule over him with harshness but shall fear your God. [. . .] For they are my servants, whom I brought forth out of the land of Egypt" (Leviticus 25:39–42). How often God reminds the employer of the human duty to treat his laborers well; He defends their physical strength and their great human dignity, making evident the truth that God is the defender of man: "For to Me the people of Israel are servants, they are My servants whom I brought forth out of the land of Egypt" (Leviticus 25:55).

God's law defends a wage paid to a laborer for his work. He prohibits coveting another's property, thus protecting the property of the weak against its plundering by the strong. He extends His protection over all payments in the name of this universal law, while all abuses will be judged before His tribunal. "You shall not oppress a hired servant who is poor and needy, whether he is one of your brethren or one of the sojourners who are in your land within your towns; you shall give him his hire on the day he earns it, before the sun goes down (for he is poor and sets his heart upon it)" (Deuteronomy 24:14–15). The Mosaic law frequently recalls this: "The wages of a hired servant shall not remain with you all night until the morning" (Leviticus 19:13).

Jeremiah's admonition to those who violate God's will sounds even more powerful than any contemporary labor laws: "Woe to him who [...] makes his neighbor serve him for nothing and does not give him his wages" (Jeremiah 22:13). Contemporary legal codes, labor courts, and even strikes and the efforts of unions are often powerless when faced with the viciousness of the human will. However, God, "who shows no partiality to princes, nor regards the rich more than the poor" (Job 34:19), will repay all according to their deeds.

Indeed, who else has imbued the human heart with the obligation to rest from work, having closely bound it to the holy day? God's law has always spoken of the inseparable connection between paying homage to God and respecting the needs of the burdened body. Every article of the Mosaic Law that established a new holy day simultaneously recalled: "And you shall make proclamation on the same day; you shall hold a holy convocation; you shall do no laborious work: it is a statute forever in all your dwellings throughout your generations" (Leviticus 23:21). That which religion has instilled in the human conscience has succeeded in resisting human greed, which wanted to empty churches to fill the factories with people who have broken with God. We know the works of capitalism, which has violated all of God's laws and human laws, destroying veneration of God in souls and the remnants of human strength in bodies for the good of production. Are the works of communism any different? People working in factories have been downtrodden for the good of the proletarian class, the Bolshevik state, and the international revolution, while working without rest has become the ideal for the new farm. God's law, which demanded that all labor cease and outstanding payments be given before the setting of the sun in order to give not only man, but also creation the opportunity to rest, is a stark counterpoint to such evils.

The struggle against the exploitation of human labor certainly took place in the holy books. The book of Job condemns all who "thrust the poor off the road" (Job 24:4) and those who have stripped the clothing of those who "lie all night naked, without clothing, and have no covering in the cold" (Job 24:7); it also condemns employers whose laborers "go about naked, without clothing, hungry; [and] carry the sheaves; among the olive rows of the wicked [i.e., their masters — author's note] they make oil; they tread the wine presses but suffer thirst" (Job 24:10–11).

God's law even protects the means of human labor, which are the only source of man's subsistence: "No man shall take a mill or an upper millstone in pledge; for he would be taking a life in pledge" (Deuteronomy 24:6).

Is not God's following demand a beautiful augury of today's social insurance? "And if your brother becomes poor, and cannot maintain himself with you, you shall maintain him; as a stranger and a sojourner he shall live with you. Take no interest from him or increase but fear your God; that your brother may live beside you" (Leviticus 25:35–36). How many diverse social laws there are in the holy books which, it would seem, foreshadow the contemporary ideals of social welfare!

God's law expresses particular concern for poor widows, orphans, and refugees, for whom the gates of all households are to be opened so "that they may eat within your towns and be filled" (Deuteronomy 26:12). Furthermore, tables are to be set for the poor across the land, while the head of the household is implored to leave for them ears of grain in the field, grapes in the vineyards, and forgotten sheaves "so that the Lord your God may bless you in all the work of your hands" (Deuteronomy 24:19). There is so much love in the following demand: "When you reap the harvest of your land, you shall not reap your field to its very border, neither shall you gather the gleanings after your harvest. [. . .] You shall leave them for the poor and for the sojourner" (Leviticus 19:9–10). Today's economical, frugal, and calculating views will call this profligacy, although it is through the stinginess and prudence of those who profess them that the number of paupers, beggars, and, yes, thieves has multiplied.

The statutes of God's laws led to social balance.

The law with which God has encompassed the entire religious life of His people has had such a major social and economic impact that it created a perfect balance in which no one was poor, exploited, or oppressed. As long as the people were faithful to the Ten Commandments, as long as they respected all of God's demands and judgments, there was complete agreement and religious-economic unity in the state of the national economy at the time. However, there were times when the nation abandoned God's paths and betrayed the Lord's Covenant. The less there was of God in Israel's heart, the more sins, injuries, and human misery there was. When religious life faded, the socio-economic institutions of the Mosaic law died out, which led to the exploitation of labor, usury, and speculation, while landholdings grew, and trade-based capitalism flourished.

God admonishes the unfaithful people; He sends prophets who castigate all offenses and sins, warning of God's wrath: "For three transgressions of Israel, and for four, I will not revoke the punishment; because they sell the righteous for silver, and the needy for a pair of shoes—they that trample the head of the poor into the dust of the earth, and turn aside the way of the afflicted" (Amos 2:6, 7). Improperly acquired wealth hardens hearts, making them deaf to God's voice and to human tears.

These prophetic visions contain an increasingly clear figure of the Redeemer, who "set at liberty those who are oppressed, to proclaim the acceptable year of the Lord" (Luke 4:18–19).

II. Jesus Christ: The King of Justice and Peace

Christ built the kingdom of justice and peace that was prophesied in Psalm 71 to "judge [His] people with righteousness, and [the] poor with justice. [...] For He delivers the needy when He calls, the poor and him who has no helper. He has pity on the weak and the needy and saves the lives of the needy. From oppression and violence He redeems their life; and precious is their blood in His sight" (Psalm 71:2, 12–14).

Christ the Lord came to the earth not to organize economic life or build factories and businesses, nor did He do so in order to devise five-year plans; He did not spur a revolution to create paradise on earth. It was through His teaching and the work of the Cross that Christ achieved the greatest transformation in the world: the redemption of human souls and their liberation from the slavery to possessions. Meanwhile, through His royal judgment Christ has summoned all in order to "judge His people with righteousness, and the poor with justice."

Coming to earth and descending to the Egypt of the New Covenant, Christ the Lord could have repeated His Father's words, which had once been said to Moses: "I have seen the affliction of My people who are in Egypt and have heard their cry because of their taskmasters; I know their sufferings, and I have come down to deliver them" (Exodus 3:7–8).

Christ the Lord brought liberation above all to the human soul.

Christ often looked at man through the prism of the body as if He did not notice it, even though He was sensitive to the suffering of the human body. Christ did not care if He had before Himself a cripple—a beggar in filthy rags by the portico of Solomon's temple or the Pool of Siloam—or an arrogant Pharisee or wondrously-clad rich man approaching Him. Even when the Lord Jesus healed bodies, He reached deeper, to the human soul, where he looked for man's fates, vocations, and dignities in the human person.

It was thanks to this that Christ opposed the entire world of His day, in whose eyes man had no worth (as in the case of many eyes today). Christ the Lord taught that every man without exception is exceptionally valuable, for He bears likeness to the heavenly Father. Every person is called to union with the Father.

Man's destiny is to come into closer union with God than with any other human being. Professional, national, social, or political bonds; the unity of the proletariat; or even the corporal unity of marriage are nothing compared to the union with God to which man is called.

During the years of democratic rule, much has been said about man's civic rights; apart from the pagan age, however, never has man been as downtrodden as today. The cornerstone of all human dignity and worth was rejected: the vocation to eternal unity and friendship with God. Only Christ the Lord perfectly knew this dignity, for He paid for it very dearly, with the last drop of His blood. He who is incapable of realizing this does not know who man is.

Having loved us above all human measures, Christ wanted everyone to value and love man as God did. For only then "God abides in us, and his love is perfected in us" (1 John 4:12). Just as there is no perfect unity between people and God without love, there is no love of God without simultaneous love of one's brother: "If anyone says, 'I love God,' and hates his brother, he is a liar; for he who does not love his brother whom he has seen, cannot love God whom he has not seen" (1 John 4:20).

It is only in love that the Covenant will be fulfilled; this "fulfill-ment of the Covenant" is an indispensable condition of all social well-being. Thus, Christ the Lord, who liberated the soul from sin and human life from selfishness, gave the greatest favor to the world in not only the religious-moral, but also the socio-economic dimension. From that point, there can be no reconstruction of the socio-economic system without first reforming the soul; the "liber-ation of the proletariat" despite God or even against God is a truly Sisyphean task! Look at the bitter fruits of the social revolutions of recent years, those that have fought more against God than for your daily bread. The proletariat was persuaded that in order to satiate the human body, they must kill God in their souls; although God had been ousted, the bodies were neither satiated nor clothed.

The Lord Jesus refers to His mission.

The event in the Nazareth synagogue, when Christ went to "His fatherland" and sat to preach Sacred Scripture, was greatly emphatic. When He was given the book of Isaiah, He read the following words from it: "The Spirit of the Lord is upon Me, because He has anointed Me to preach good news to the poor. He has sent Me to proclaim release to the captives and recovering of sight to the blind, to set at liberty those who are oppressed, to proclaim the acceptable year of the Lord" (Luke 4:18–19; see Isaiah 6:11). Isaiah's words foretold of a great jubilee, "proclaim[ing] liberty throughout the land to all its inhabitants" (Leviticus 25:10), a year when every slave would become free, while those who were freed would in no vain way be allowed to part, but the Lord "shall furnish him liberally out of your flock, out of your threshing floor, and out of your wine press; as the Lord your God has blessed you" (Deuteronomy 15:14).

As He gave the book to the servant, Christ said: "Today this scrip-ture has been fulfilled in your hearing" (Luke 4:21). Indeed, Christ has come to fulfill the Covenant rather than to overturn it; thus, He took upon Himself the effort that was initiated by the Covenant. He would later pursue this effort and summon all to Himself: "Come to me, all who labor and are heavy laden, and I will give you rest" (Matthew 11:28). Could not that Son of the Tiller of the Heavens and of an earthly craftsman, Jesus of Nazareth, who had been brought up among the poor and the lowly, knowing their plight, suffering, and their brows sweaty from the struggle for bread; that witness to human anxieties about food, drink and clothing, who knew hunger, destitution, and homelessness, could He not have understood His people? Could He not have felt compassion for them? Having resting on His breast and thus knowing the pulsating desire of that heart better than anyone else, Christ's beloved disciple wrote: "But if anyone has the world's goods and sees his brother in need, yet closes his heart against him, how does God's love abide in him? Little children, let us not love in word or speech but in deed and in truth" (1 John 3:17–18). That is what the disciple says, but "a disciple is not above his teacher" (Matthew 10:24).

Christ is the people's friend.

Our Lord's evangelical efforts are distinctly social in nature: He usually speaks amidst great crowds of people. Christ is only born in the solitude of silence, "increas[ing] in wisdom and in stature" (Luke 2:52), far from hubbub; however, when He begins to act and teach, He stands amidst the crowds. He will not enjoy solitude or silence until the benevolent darkness of the last moments of His death on the Cross, where "it is finished" (see John 19:30).

We see Christ amidst the masses of sick, poor, and shoddily clad people, but Christ the Lord was not a demagogue, people's tribune, or agitator; He was far removed from the self-interested arrogance of party representatives, leaders, and candidates who sow anxiety around them with which we are so familiar. Christ the Lord went into the crowds as a good teacher, as the teacher of their sufferings and souls; He was a friend Who did not look for His own benefits. Christ avoided the applause and adoration of the crowds; He was always ready to hide when they wanted to crown Him king. However, since He only saw great crowds, He had mercy on them and healed the powerless.

A huge crowd usually followed Jesus and often clung to Him for many days. Thus, it is unsurprising that He felt compassion for them when He saw that "they were like sheep without a shepherd" (Mark 6:34). The miraculous multiplication of the loaves resulted from this compassion for the hungry people who followed Him: "I have compassion on the crowd, because they have been with Me now three days, and have nothing to eat; and I am unwilling to send them away hungry" (Matthew 15:32).

How thought-provoking is Christ's response to the proposal of the apostles to scatter the crowd so that they could go to the towns and purchase food: "They need not go away; you give them something to eat" (Matthew 14:16). Did He not know that those who have abandoned everything to follow their Master lack money in their traveling bags? He knew this very well, but He wanted His disciples to emphatically see that He was not indifferent to human misery, that if it is accepted, His teaching can likewise today multiply the loaves of the daily bread so that all may eat and be satisfied (see Matthew 15:37).

We see a great fraternization among the crowds that followed Christ: "And all the crowd sought to touch Him, for power came forth from Him and healed them all" (Luke 6:19). They were overcome with a common desire.

They felt with their hungry souls and afflicted bodies that the One who could lead to their entire liberation and social fraternization was approaching. It was as if they sensed St. Paul's prophetic words: "For in Christ Jesus you are all sons of God, through faith. For as many of you as were baptized into Christ have put on Christ. There is neither Jew nor Greek, there is neither slave nor free, there is neither male nor female; for you are all one in Christ Jesus" (Galatians 3:26–28).

As in the past, likewise today the Lord Jesus' greatest friends and advocates were among those people. Whenever the elders and leading Pharisees wanted to seize Jesus, "they feared the multitudes, because they held Him to be a prophet" (Matthew 21:46). It was the multitudes that sensed in Him "the Father of the poor, widows and orphans." They knew the loving glance with which Christ embraced the faces of those who listened to Him, sincerely admiring His comforting words, and accepting them with all their hearts: "And whoever gives to one of these little ones even a cup of cold water because he is a disciple, truly, I say to you, he shall not lose his reward" (Matthew 10:42). Only this poor, undernourished and overworked crowd could be completely concerned with the sentence of the Final Judgment, which had been prophesied in such exceptionally understandable words: "Come, O blessed of my Father, inherit the kingdom prepared for you from the foundation of the world; for I was hungry and you gave me food, I was thirsty and you gave me drink, I was a stranger and you welcomed me, I was naked and you clothed me, I was sick and you visited me, I was in prison and you came to me" (Matthew 25:34–36). In other words, this is nothing of the publicized acts, great victories and conquests, or even recollections of the great and famous of the world they admired. Only such meek words and actions?! Without a doubt, they understand this and know how aggravating hunger is; how hollowing the fever of thirst is; how sweltering being covered only in rags is; how painful it is to be abandoned when suffering... Great are these "small works," especially since Christ brings all of them onto Himself: "And the King will answer them, 'Truly, I say to you, as you did it to one of the least of these My brethren, you did it to Me'" (Matthew 25:40). This is such a privilege! You, the small of the world, are one with Christ; you are the living Christ who walks the earth.

If the world would have loved Him, all the hungry of the earth would have been fed and all the naked would have been clothed; the proletariat would disappear, as would social hatred and envy, class struggle, and the exploitation of labor. Meanwhile, all the unemployed, who stand all day at the market, would go to the vineyard, while every laborer would be righteously paid. Would this not be the most wonderful fulfillment of the Covenant?

The Mosaic Law was written on stone tablets, but Christ's law is "written not with ink but with the Spirit of the living God, not on tablets of stone but on tablets of human hearts" (2 Corinthians 3:3). If the Old Covenant liberated the poor of the earth from usury and injustice, how many more gifts have Christ's law of love and justice borne?

Death, sin, hatred, struggle, exploitation, injury, and social injustice enter the gates of the world when we leave God's threshold. When God enters the soul, He can even live in the factory; when you oust Him from the soul, how can you maintain His justice in your places of work? There is no justice in this world without His law, and there is no social love without His love.

* * *

"I am the Lord your God, who brought you forth out of the land of Egypt, that you should not be their slaves; and I have broken the bars of your yoke and made you walk erect" (Leviticus 26:13). You have believed this for centuries. In recent times, however, your faith has wavered. Some have stood up and told you: "We will turn

287

all these stones into bread." The laborers worked hard; the cogs of machines grated; the world became filled with the whistle of conveyor belts and the peal of steam hammers. Prosperity for all! May strength-giving loaves of bread be given to all! They zealously called out: Let us become wealthy! Warehouses have become filled with all sorts of goods. The world grew wealthier, but you have remained poor. Why? Because goods have been improperly divided! In order to divide them righteously, you must have Christian minds and hearts. Not all believed this.

Others, meanwhile, stood up and said: "Workers of the world, unite!" Our god is class struggle! Heaven is for the sparrows, but paradise on earth is for the proletariat! You have believed in a new god. You have faithfully prostrated before him, killing the bourgeoisie and allowing your blood to flow on the streets on every holiday of the proletariat. Your efforts were great, yet you were so sorely disappointed.

Others stood up and said: "Religion is the opium for the masses." Long live the God-less state! The revolution will liberate us! A God-less state was established; it struggled for decades, murdering the bourgeoisie, tearing down churches, and oppressing the proletariat. Everything was destroyed! Poverty was all that was liberated.

And you let out a sigh. So many times your faith was in vain. Has hell opened before us? Must we abandon all hope? There is no hope outside of God! Hope comes from faith in God. For centuries, He has seen your anguish, O unfortunate sons of Eve. He comes to you not to explain Himself before you, because God excuses Himself before no one, but to summon you to the freedom of being sons of God. The one God has "broken the bars of your yoke and made you walk erect" (Leviticus 26:13). Trust in God! People have disappointed you. Who if not God?! Through faith, you will enter the kingdom of hope and love, and through love you will enter the kingdom of justice and peace.

3
The Church and Economic Matters

A RATHER STRANGE EVENT OCCURRED IN Christ the Lord's apostolic life. Someone from the crowd said to Him: "Teacher, bid my brother divide the inheritance with me" (Luke 12:13). One would think that because this request resulted from the sincerest faith and complete trust, it would be a field where Christ could emphasize His influence. Yet Christ's response was unusual: "Man, who made Me a judge or divider over you?" (Luke 12:14). This response is unusual in that the man who asks could have correctly believed Christ to be the Lord and Ruler of everything in heaven and on earth. Christ did not deny this. However, He wanted to underscore His appropriate role on earth, which was much more important than the function of dividing inheritance. Christ instructs: "Take heed and beware of all covetousness; for a man's life does not consist in the abundance of his possessions" (Luke 12:15). The parable of the rich man whose soil has borne a plentiful harvest resolves His audience's doubts. To everyone whose life's priorities are: "eat, drink, and be merry," Christ will say: "Fool! This night your soul is required of you" (Luke 12:19–20).

This is Christ the Lord's essential task. It is also the role of the Church. Christ the Lord instructed not only the people of Israel, but also His Church.

So often today we hear voices summoning the Church to decisively enter the field of socio-economic affairs and make her impact visible there. How much hope is enclosed in this challenge! When numerous doctrines and aspirations failed and when both the capitalist and state economies disappointed, who can say something more if not the Church? Those who do not know the Church's social teaching await more detailed instructions and guidelines. Do they have the right to await them? We must answer this important question.

What is the Church's authority in economic matters?

In her teaching, the Church clearly distinguishes between her own authority and the rights and duties of Catholics. The Church clearly speaks of her right to enter economic life.

The Church knows very well that Christ the Lord unified His Divinity with His humanity and spirit with matter, also so that the whole world would take this unification as a model and so that all unification would occur in God from that point, so that the world would want to pour God's spirit into matter. Christ the Lord did not come to live in stone church buildings; He came to souls and because He wants to sanctify earthly life, He will go with them wherever they will lead Him: to the stock market and to trade; to the school and to the kitchen.

This is the important role of the Church, who wants to permeate everything with God's spirit and give everything to God. Here, there is no distinction such as: "All are yours; and you are Christ's; and Christ is God's" (1 Corinthians 3:22).

Thus, it is unsurprising that Leo XIII, Pius XI, and Pius XII have all clearly stated that the Church has not only the right but even the duty to enter the socio-economic sphere and subject everything that happens there to her judgment.

What is the nature of the Church's social interests?

That the Church feels entitled to deal with economic affairs does not mean that she considers herself to be an omnipotent lord of all areas of human life. Instead, she remembers Christ's words: "Man, who made me a judge or divider over you?" (Luke 12:14). Hence, the Church does not write or proclaim any economic programs; the Church's teaching deals with religion, not economics. The Church does not proclaim economic dogmas, nor does she deal with the elaboration of economic life; she does not create institutions whose sole purpose is to "serve tables" and multiply the mundane goods of this world. However, she has been keenly interested in economic life from the beginning of her existence. She never cursed material gains; she remembers and reminds the people of God's commandment to subdue the earth (see Genesis 1:28).

The Church's interest in earthly life is demonstrated by her entire history as well as the most valuable monuments that have inspired her. The bond between religious-moral and socio-economic life is evident everywhere: in Sacred Scripture and the entirety of Church writing; the Gospels and the teachings of the Church Fathers; medieval theology and contemporary theology; synodal and conciliar legislation;

and the Church's penal law. The Church evaluates forms of economic life through the prism of their moral usefulness. Moral usefulness is the gauge of the value and honesty of individual economic institutions. This path is evident in both the oldest and the contemporary teaching of the Church.

The Church designates her authority in economic affairs

The attitude of Christ the Lord is an example for her. The Church supports the division of obligations; she teaches that the entirety of human affairs is entrusted to two sovereign communities: the Church and the state. Only religious-moral affairs and matters related to supernatural life are subject to the Church's direct authority. In this sphere, the Church implements her own tasks, which no one else can exercise. Meanwhile, all earthly affairs and everything related to them are under the direct jurisdiction of the state's authority.

Naturally, there is an extensive list of topics that equally concern the Church and the state. Agreement between the two forms of authority must appear in this area.

The Church directly addresses the human soul, which it transforms and prepares for co-existence with other people through supernatural means. She impacts man through the entirety of her Gospel teaching; through education and the life of grace; and through her practice, especially in Christian works of mercy. The Church impacts earthly, and therefore economic, life through people brought up in such a way. The influence of the Church will be indirect, while her efficacy depends on the submission of Catholics and how they have accepted the Church's educative influence.

We know from history that this influence was enormous and that in her first centuries the Church changed the social and economic mores without revolution but through the path of development; that she shaped the spirit of the Christian community in the economic life of the Middle Ages; that she effectively resisted degenerate capitalism; and that she was nearly the sole opponent of socialism and was most persistent in the struggle against communism.

For the Church, the boundary in economic matters will be the moral evaluation of life

The Church is above all the teacher and guardian of moral-religious truths whose significance is not only religious, but social as well. The

Church evaluates economic phenomena and man's economic deeds at the moral level. The Church is not indifferent to the nature of human deeds; she is not indifferent to the social service of industrialists, merchants, bankers, engineers, farmers, manual laborers, and stable workers, for every human deed, even that which seems the most material, is essentially good or evil and depends on the intention that accompanies it.

There is no distinction between the religious man and the social, political, or economic man. The social activist, politician, and economist must all be honest and moral in their work. In this area, they and all their work and activity are subjected to the Church.

The same goes for the evaluation of socio-economic currents and systems. Let us read *Rerum novarum:* The Church evaluates socialism through not economic, but moral values. Meanwhile, in *Quadragesimo anno* the evaluation of capitalism, production techniques, and the organization of labor are not economic, but moral and religious. Because moral and religious goods are man's greatest goods, the Church has a ready evaluation for the systems and doctrines themselves. The world will hear from the Church: "Take heed and beware of all covetousness; for a man's life does not consist in the abundance of his possessions" (Luke 12:15).

These are the boundaries of the Church's socio-economic authority. One cannot say that this role is small and without significance to man's earthly life. The Church deals with the value of economic deeds from the pulpit and in the confessional; she forces man to constantly revise his behavior, teaching conscientiousness and fidelity, but above all justice and love. In this way, she gives the greatest service to economic life, without which the world would be incapable of exercising its mundane duties.

The economic rights and duties of Catholics go further

Although she designates the boundaries of her economic activity, the Church does not create analogous limits for Catholics. She only demands that they completely exercise the duties they have undertaken. The Church demands of their faithful that they be Christians not only in church buildings, but also in professional, economic, and political life. Catholics must implement the principles of the Gospels in worldly life. The aim of their activity is the sanctification of earthly life and the incarnation of the spirit in matter. They are to work in favor of the primacy of the spirit over matter and man's primacy over that of objects. They are to liberate themselves from the primacy of objects. They must sanctify their entire professional lives, make economic life moral, and perfect themselves through labor and the exercising of their everyday duties.

We see here that one cannot escape from this earth. Only people with a unique vocation are obliged to sell everything they possess and follow Christ (see Matthew 19:21). The masses of Catholics are to bind their supernatural lives with their earthly lives, which they must focus on serving God and their neighbors. This is the essence of Christianity: to service Christ in our brothers, the hungry, thirsting, naked, and homeless Christ.

The Church will remind all who serve the table of Christ's words: "Take heed and beware of all covetousness; for a man's life does not consist in the abundance of his possessions" (Luke 12:15).

* * *

This is the division of roles between the Church and the faithful in the sphere of economic life. May the Church then continue to preach the Word of God, while you will go to serve the tables. We will fulfill the Lord's commandment and inherit the earth through this sacred cooperation.

4

The Church and
the Working Class

"No longer do I call you servants [...]
but I have called you friends" (John 15:15).

"You were bought with a price; do not
become slaves of men" (1 Corinthians 7:23).

O N THE DAY OF CHRIST'S BIRTH, THE
Church reads to us the words of the Apostle Paul: "Thou,
Lord, didst found the earth in the beginning, and the heavens
are the work of Thy hands; they will perish, but Thou remainest; they
will all grow old like a garment, like a mantle Thou wilt roll them up,
and they will be changed" (Hebrews 1:10–12; see Psalm 101:26–28).

These words of granite and steel strike at the turbulent and volatile
world. How fragile are these soaring comparisons! Yet they say nothing
about the Master, the Father of the future age who will look at the
death of the centuries. Some limitless Power rules over the world;
"all kings fall down before Him, all nations serve Him!" (Psalm 72:11).

We find this boundless force in all of God's works; it is the root
of the world. If man accepts it, he will become a child of God, and
when it enters the Church "the powers of death shall not prevail
against it" (see Matthew 16:18). Such is God! He is truly strange in all
His works. However, man loses sight of this truth. The matters and
affairs of this earth so hide God from him that he would be glad to
bend God's thought to suit his own thoughts and aspirations. "The
Lord looks down from heaven upon the children of men, to see if
there are any that act wisely, that seek after God" (Psalm 13:2–3).

Is it not strange that man desires to adapt God Himself and His
great works to his petty thoughts and purposes? He feels that God
will only then succeed in saving his existence on earth, while the
Church will fulfill her mission only when she will be at his service.

The Church is always accused of having to serve someone. One
century ago, there were efforts to convert the Church to liberalism;

today, we see that the Church was right when she responded to her tempters with: "The freedom of the wealthy is the slavery of the poor." Half a century ago, the Church was encouraged to convert to socialism so that Catholicism would become red; today, when socialism is dying because of its own powerlessness, we see that it is true that "no one can be at the same time a good Catholic and a true socialist" (QA, 120). There were also proposals from the red communist front: "Catholics, we are extending our hands out to you." This unsupported hand fell. All these human aspirations will grow limp; they will be changed, but "Thou remainest"! Nothing in this world is permanent or eternal. All social, economic, and political systems pass like a shadow; none of them has received the promise of eternal existence. Thus, the Church is bound to no system and serves none.

Nothing has survived on the battlefield, although the Church's only weapon was "the sword of the soul." But God's truths have shone with new strength! Hopefully, people will understand that salvation is only in Jesus Christ, our Lord.

Glory to God and the salvation of our souls is the only service of the Church throughout all the centuries. Only God and the human soul last forever. There will come a time when you will cease to be factory owners, workers, capitalists or communists, professionals, day laborers, unskilled workers, etc. However, you will never cease to be children of God; you might be prodigal sons, but you will be His sons nonetheless! Therefore, the Church stands at your side and supports you with your great dignity as the children of God, remaining by your immortal soul.

Every wolf that will open his mouth to devour your soul will perish, stricken by the sword of God's Spirit. You will then see who is devoted to you in life and in death. God is not the God of a specific class, but He is the God of the universe, while the Church is a mother, not a stepmother, for all the Father's children.

I. The Church Uses the Pulpit to Defend the Workers

From the days of Christ the Lord's sermon in the Nazareth synagogue until the days of Pius XI, nothing in the Church has changed. Christ preached: "The Spirit of the Lord is upon me, because he has anointed me to preach good news to the poor" (Luke 4:18). Nineteen centuries later, His successor, the visible head of the Church, will writes the same in one of his encyclicals: "Go to the workingman, especially where he is poor; and in general, go to the poor" (DR, 61).

Go to Catholic churches and listen closely to the words of the priest that come from the pulpit, and you will easily recognize the same Spirit of the Lord that was above Christ and that today speaks using the mouths of people sent to all the corners of the world.

For centuries, the Church has preached God's law, the oldest of all laws, which stands in defense of man and his life and dignity, in defense of his property.

There can exist no sound social or economic system that could exist without God's Ten Commandments; there can be no sound economy and effective social policy or labor legislation without the Church's moral principles. Thus, every priest who preaches the Word of God most effectively works to ground social justice among the people and to secure and improve the lot of the workers.

There is no separate social or economic morality that is good for today but will be opposed tomorrow depending on the political system or the dominant economic philosophy; there is natural law and God's law, which has always been unchanging and has been preached by the Church in every century, era, and system. The most basic duties towards one's neighbors result from God's law. The Church strictly binds the necessity to realize these tasks to the entirety of religious life, so one cannot be a good Catholic if one neglects them.

Hence the entirety of Catholic social teaching, which speaks of the exercise of these duties, is not an occasional supplement to theology, but it is internally bound to the most basic theological truths.

One cannot listen to God's law and protect one's conscience from pangs of guilt if one violates his duties with respect to his neighbors. Perhaps this is why a certain group of people avoids the doors of churches, so that they will not awaken their slumbering consciences; maybe that is why they avoid sermons in which they hear an appraisal of their own lives, and criticism of the injury you do to people, which results from a stubborn rejection of the basic duties of love of one's neighbor.

The Church awakens and forms the social conscience.

This is one more great contribution of the Church to the workers.

The entirety of social and economic life, both the world of the employers and that of the workers, must heed to moral principles and must hone within themselves a spirit of self-control; meanwhile, the workers must deepen their religious life, for it is the source of true love and conscientiousness. "Put on then, as God's chosen ones, holy and beloved, compassion, kindness, lowliness, meekness, and patience, forbearing one another and, if one has a complaint against another, forgiving each other; as the Lord has forgiven you, so you also must forgive. And above all these put on love, which binds everything together in perfect harmony" (Colossians 3:12–14).

The Church preaches the moral responsibility of all without exception — industrialists, factory owners, directors, employers, and foremen and workers — before God. In addition to this moral responsibility, she adds economic responsibility for goods that are intended for the use of all. The obligation to conscientiously conduct the affairs of a business and in the fulfillment of all bilateral obligations resulting from labor contracts results from this.

Without this difficulty, it is impossible to create social order and ensure the workers participation in the goods of the earth. Without religion and the conscientiousness resulting from religious life, one cannot speak of the improvement of the lot of the workers.

Most social of the reforms that the workers demand cannot be justified if we limit ourselves to the economic sphere; to demonstrate their necessity, one must reference Christian truths, man's great dignity and destiny, familial obligations, and the moral value of labor. This cannot be achieved by social policy, economics, or sociology. Only religion can speak of these matters boldly and powerfully.

We clearly see that the notion that religion is a merely private affair is erroneous. In the factory or the office of the management board, the worker clearly sees that it is not without meaning if the factory owner, director, or engineer is religious and moral or if he is not. You have experienced the burden of the seven deadly sins of your heathen factory owners, for whom God means less than the social labor inspector. You thought that people who have scoffed at God would respect you? That those who have violated God's law would respect your rights? Oh, no; religion is not a private affair!

The Church can forcefully speak to the consciences of directors and factory owners. She speaks to your consciences with the same forcefulness! Whoever disturbs the Church in these efforts and whoever opposes them harms the workers. If the Church cannot exercise many of her tasks, if she has not helped you as you would have liked, this was often the fault of the employers and even the workers themselves. Both have undermined the importance of religion, rejected the Church's laws, and opposed her social activity, labeling it as politics. Meanwhile, the workers, who have been enticed by communist slogans, have together with them struggled against their ally and collaborator.

It is from the pulpit that we hear the most forceful defense of the dignity of the working man.

Contemporary social, political, and economic life have greatly depreciated human dignity. Wherever you will go, they will see you as merely half-human; they will see you as physical, qualified, or professional means of production or an unskilled laborer; their respect and appreciation for you will be solely according to your purely external value.

Only when you will enter the church and stand before the shadow of the altar and at the feet of the pulpit will you be reminded that you are someone greater: "You were bought with a price; do not become slaves of men" 7:23). "No longer do I call you servants [. . .] but I have called you friends" (John 15:15).

You will see how the problem of your economic liberation is presented. It recalls an image from the distant past. When Moses led Israel out of the Egyptian yoke and into the wilderness, the people complained about him: "Would that we had died by the hand of the Lord in the land of Egypt, when we sat by the fleshpots and ate bread to the full" (Exodus 16:3). Today, similar yearnings are accepted as the loftiest ideals of the working classes, as their only aspiration and their only right: to seat the workers in front of fleshpots and change them into working beasts that are well-fed by the state or their employer. Let them work, eat, digest, and remain silent until the moment when rational animals with healthier muscles will replace them and throw them onto the street.

From the pulpit, the Church present the worker a much greater, more majestic purpose.

Man cannot be tempted by just meat and bread. Paradise on earth understood as just a mountain of meat cannot be organized. Man cannot be at the center of the world and serve all his whims. He cannot be seen as merely a producer and consumer of goods, rational tool of factory production, proletarian, or party member. Worldly happiness cannot be arranged for people in a way that would violate their ultimate destiny.

The Church illuminates the darkness of these contemporary errors, which are so enticing yet so illusory and dangerous to people, by stubbornly insisting that man is a rational being that has been created not according to the statute of a party or a factory, but in God's image and likeness, while man has his own destiny, obligations, and rights that are above production and the organization of social and economic life; his mouth's destiny is the praise of God, joy, and bliss in God: "For this is the will of God, your sanctification" (1 Thessalonians 4:3); man's entire activity is enclosed within the limits of his vocation and purpose. All this means that man should be given the dignity of a free being, the entire freedom of humanity: "For you did not receive the spirit of slavery to fall back into fear, but you have received the spirit of sonship" (Romans 8:15).

Any other solution — including the communist paradise on earth — is an illusion, the greatest temptation that infinitely delays the true liberation of the proletariat.

And what about your liberation as the working class?

Judge the value of these eternal solutions yourselves. It has been said that the workers are injured in economic life, in their family and civic rights, etc. One great voice shouted in response: The worker has no religion, family, fatherland, society, or state! The worker is merely a proletarian! Do away with religion and fatherland, and instead unite! Many listened. They left the Church and national life in great numbers, separating themselves from society. However, the Church thinks and acts differently. Here is one example: In the Epistle to Philemon, St. Paul implores his addressee to receive an escaped servant as "no longer as a slave but more than a slave, as a beloved brother, especially to me but how much more to you, both in the flesh and in the Lord" (Philemon 1:16).

This is the Church's social aim: to transform workers and their supervisors into "beloved brothers in the Lord." For this reason, the Church reprimands all supervisors: "Masters, do the same to them, and forbear threatening, knowing that he who is both their Master and yours is in heaven, and that there is no partiality with Him" (Ephesians 6:9). In this way, the Church attempts to bring workers into the community from which they have been excluded by economic relations and erroneous social doctrines.

The Church summons the workers to religious life and co-existence with their own nation and society, bringing them to collective life and demanding that their rights are recognized.

This is where the wandering and homelessness to which capitalism, socialism, and communism have condemned you will end.

II. The Church Supports the Workers' Just Aspirations

Jesus Christ's redemption has flowed onto the entire world and onto all of man, both his soul and body, introducing a new, universal order in all relations in human life. From that point, your aspirations are not limited, "for you did not receive the spirit of slavery to fall back into fear," but you have received the spirit of sonship. [. . .] We cry: 'Abba! Father!'" (Romans 8:15).

In Christian social life, there is a dynamic drive to go higher, one that breaks up all ossified forms of slavery and constantly leads humanity across degrees of perfection; just as perfection is unspoken and limitless in God, the entirety of creation aims for participation in ever-greater perfection: "We know that the whole creation has been groaning in travail together until now; and not only the creation, but we ourselves, who have the first fruits of the Spirit, groan inwardly as we wait for adoption as sons, the redemption of our bodies" (Romans 8:22–23). For this reason, the Church has her Christian *rerum novarum cupiditas*, or a desire for novelty: a new and increasingly better life; she strives for change, reform, and renewal. The Church is not afraid of being accused of novelty or revolutionary fervor, for her aim is perfection.

We see the same at the social level, which the Church has boldly entered and become the source of constant initiative and progress. The Church was not afraid of speaking out in matters related to the workers even when the state did not understand her; in fact, she often spoke out against the state, against hackneyed and hallowed views, powerful currents, and even against the aspirations of her members.

The Church reminded the state of its obligations with respect to the workers.

When capitalism opposed the state's intervention in economic life, it depriving it, in the name of freedom and of inquiry into the relationship between capital and labor, the Church spoke not only of the state's rights, but also of its duties; she recalled that the state that is "conformable in its institutions to right reason and natural law, and to those dictates of the divine wisdom" (RN, 32) is also obliged to be concerned about not only general prosperity, but should especially embrace the workers with care.

The Church teaches that the entirety of socio-economic life cannot be left solely to man's good will, because then primarily people liberated from all morality and conscientiousness would profit, while "the richer class have many ways of shielding themselves, and stand less in need of help from the State; whereas the mass of the poor have no resources of their own to fall back upon, and must chiefly depend upon the assistance of the State" (RN, 29).

Despite the numerous accusations that were then leveled against Leo XIII, who was even called a socialist, the pope did not back down, for he did not proclaim the false teachings of socialism but authentic Christianity, which could appear as red radicalism only to ignoramuses. Whenever we are dealing with the fulfillment of God's commandments, we cannot speak of radicalism, but only of duty, which is justice and love.

The Church was right in demanding that the living conditions and labor of the worker be guaranteed legal protection; Leo XIII has sketched out a detailed program pointing out to the state when and under what circumstances it should use the law, which is a tool God has endowed it with for the protection of human labor.

Thanks to the full support of the Church of the legal protection of the workers, a new law has appeared: social legislation, whose spirit and aims, most generally conceived, correspond to these great currents of social care whose traces we see in the holy books.

Thus, it is unsurprising that Pius XI, who upon observing social legislation in the modern state, expressed his joy in the encyclical *Quadragesimo anno* that "a new branch of law, wholly unknown to the earlier time, has arisen from this continuous and unwearied labor

301

to protect vigorously the sacred rights of the workers that flow from their dignity as men and as Christians. These laws undertake the protection of life, health, strength, family, homes, workshops, wages and labor hazards, in fine, everything which pertains to the condition of wage workers, with special concern for women and children" (QA, 28).

Here, we have the victory of the Christian spirit, which deepens social morality, the spirit that teaches us to love our neighbors "not love [...] word or speech but in deed and in truth" (1 John 3:18).

The Church demands the lifting up of the workers from proletarian poverty.

The Church has never accepted the proletarian lifestyle of the workers. Although they were constantly told that they are proletarians and although a proletarian state in which the living conditions of the proletarian were elevated to a special dignity and although the workers were brought up in the spirit of proletarian pride, the Church has always spoken of the liberation from the chains of the proletariat, of de-proletarizing all.

In the world of the worker, there is a pervasive yearning for existence that is worthy of a human, for the possibility for an honest family life, prosperity, and the ability to attain a decent living. These aspirations are correct, as they are the result of the understanding of one's own rights and dignity; they are human rights, and as such they must be recognized and respected through Christian love.

The Church reaches out to these proper yearnings, as she wants the working classes to lift themselves up from poverty and for their material conditions to improve (see RN, 23). The Church desires that within them would be awakened the aspiration towards honest possession: "The law, therefore, should favor ownership, and its policy should be to induce as many as possible of the people to become owners" (RN, 46). For this aim, the Church is adamant in demanding a just wage as a means that makes the meeting of one's needs possible. Furthermore, it supports the right to property, so that through it the workers may "emerg[e] from the insecure lot in life" (QA, 61).

The Church supports the right of the workers to association.

From time immemorial, the Church has preached social wisdom, which brings people together in a fraternal handshake: "Two are better than one, because they have a good reward for their toil. For if they fall, one will lift up his fellow; but woe to him who is alone when he falls and has not another to lift him up" (Ecclesiastes 4:9–10). The Church considers this demand of natural law, which leads to co-existence in social groups, to be the correct and legitimate aspiration of the workers in any era, especially in the present economic system.

Leo XIII elaborates in detail on the need for and importance of well-organized workers' associations and labor unions; he writes that "it were greatly to be desired that they should become more numerous and more efficient" (RN, 49).

When there was a conflict between labor unions and patrons in northern France in recent years, this dispute was brought to the Holy See; Rome confirmed the right of the workers to association. The encyclical *Quadragesimo anno* goes further, for it demands the recognition of "the natural right to form associations to those who needed it most to defend themselves from ill treatment at the hands of the powerful" (QA, 30).

There was a time when states opposed all efforts towards organized labor, considering them to be the enemy of freedom, while there were others when the state of the proletariat deprived the workers of all protection, turning their labor unions into police centers. This has occurred in our times. The Church opposed these aspirations, wanting the permeate the life of the workers through the spirit of fraternal cooperation. In the corporatist system, which is recommended today, this thought will be further elaborated.

The Church fully recognizes the aspirations of the workers to social emancipation.

Among the workers, there is a clear aspiration towards social progress, towards the attaining of respect in collective life and emancipation in social life. Such activity is fully supported the Church, which has since antiquity taught to: "Love one another with brotherly affection; outdo one another in showing honor" (Romans 12:10).

The Church also struggles for the respect of these healthy aspirations because they are the demands of social justice. The contributions of the world of labor to society are so great and the fruits of its efforts are expressed in such countless riches that it would be only proper that those who have contributed to those goods be surrounded by society's respect proportional to their achievements.

However, the Church goes further in her aspiration for social respect: she demands that the workers constantly improve not only their social position, but also their moral and religious values. Only then, when the workers will attain a high level of moral life, will they be capable of skillfully making use of their material achievements; the profligate worker, constantly drunk and immoral, will lose even the greatest earnings and will not be respected, even if society would bring him to the forefront of society.

Demanding participation in social life, in cultural goods, and in social progress, the Church simultaneously calls the workers to constant progress in their virtues. "For freedom Christ has set us free; stand fast therefore, and do not submit again to a yoke of slavery" (Galatians 5:1), for the slavery of the soul and the yoke of sin lead to the bottom of social and economic penury.

* * *

In these reflections, we see that the Church has been engaged in a lonely struggle for the rights of the poor for centuries; the Church frequently had to overcome the opposition of the state and powerful economic forces in defense of man and his right to honest and decent existence.

The Church exercises her duty: yesterday, today, tomorrow, and until the end of the world! Protected by God's truth; free from the bonds of political groupings and social and economic doctrines; higher than the volatility of earthly life; greater than the greatest of the earth; taken from the people and established for the people—the Church freely, straightforwardly, and truthfully preaches the words of life to all people, states, nations, and even ages. The more freedom the Church possesses, the better for the small of this earth and the better for the entire earth.

This is your bedrock. Let us enter the gates of God's Church. Christ is in Peter's Barque amidst this "Sea of Galilee"! His tired disciples were by Him, trying to catch fish. They toiled greatly, like yourselves, casting their nets all night in vain. Yet they caught nothing, much like yourselves! At the gates of the Church, you will hear Christ's summons: "Put out into the deep and let down your nets for a catch" (Luke 5:4). Listen to Christ, just as your hardworking companions.

You have worked in the darkness of the night, without God's illumination. Cast your net in Christ's light. You will reap a reward like they: "And when they had done this, they enclosed a great shoal of fish; and [...] their nets were breaking" (Luke 5:6). The power Christ exudes and that once healed all is not smaller today. Today, it is also capable of renewing the face of the earth. Only one thing is needed: faith! For nothing is impossible for those who believe.

5

The Church and the
Spirit of Capitalism

*"All these evil things come from within,
and they defile a man" (Mark 7:23).*

*"For the love of money is the root of all evils;
it is through this craving that some have
wandered away from the faith and pierced
their hearts with many pangs" (1 Timothy 6:10).*

THE IMPACT OF ORIGINAL SIN IS ALL-ENCOM-passing. Every area of human life, including socio-economic life, has its original sin. The sad shadow of Eve's greedy eyes fell onto the world like the seed of the "new world order," from which the desire for all stones to become bread has sprouted.

The admonition that Christ would later express in the words: "For what will it profit a man, if he gains the whole world and forfeits his life?" (Matthew 16:26) died in the human heart. Why not try gaining the whole world? Why search for God's Kingdom and its justice? Why not accumulate earthly treasures? Can rust, moths and thieves still scare us away? Indeed, we are more prudent as "the sons of light" (Luke 16:8), as Christ Himself has confessed. Let us agree with him at least once!

In this way, human eyes disdain of eternal economics; instead, a worldly economy has been born. A *magna charta libertatum* of man and citizen was proclaimed in socio-economic life. The natural law and God's law have fallen, instead being replaced by the "holy and inviolable laws of economics"; the morality of Christian love has disappeared in order to give way to love of the pocket and one's own profit. What does morality have to do with economics? Is morality not the greatest enemy of the economy? Man, before whom all creation bowed at the time of the Bethlehem Star, has once again paid divine homage to the Mammon of injustice.

A new religion has appeared, that of money and wealth. Its dogmas are unlimited economic freedom, free competition, the separation of capital from labor and economic life from ethics, the law of supply and demand, and the mechanism of prices. Its morality, meanwhile, is marked by a lack of all morality, the supremacy of capital over man and his labor, the good of production, and profit as a good deed. Its altars are all factories, machines, tools, cartels, syndicates and banks, where human life is sacrificed for the price of greed.

The ultimate aim is to become the blessed rich man. Let us be wealthy at all costs, all who can and however they can!

Behold, the god of this world: pagan capitalism. Everything that the world has since experienced is closely bound to this system, for abyss calls upon abyss (see Psalm 41:8).

Pagan capitalism is the birth father of all revolutionary currents: socialism, communism and Bolshevism, all those aspirations that supposedly fight against reactionary laws and defend human rights which are violated.

Can a wicked tree bear good fruit? Sin gives birth to sin. The sins of socialism, communism and Bolshevism have opposed the sin of capitalism. The Marxist heresies have demonstrated that capitalist technology gives rise to a collectivist system. "For the love of money is the root of all evils; it is through this craving that some have wandered away from the faith and pierced their hearts with many pangs" (1 Timothy 6:10). You say that this sounds radical? Every sin is radical, be it the individualistic sin of capitalism or the collectivist sin of Bolshevism. All sins belong to one family, however, and so both the gold and red internationales flow from one source: greed.

In our reflections, we will above all deal with the spirit of capitalism, for it is most contrary to the Christian spirit; it bears fruits that poison the entirety of economic, social and political life, while their destructive influence impacts the moral and religious life of entire states, nations and societies.

Can the Church remain indifferent in the face of this poisoned well from which her children so frequently drink?

The Church evaluates all human life with her ultimate measure, which she applies to economic life: everything that facilitates man's achieving of this aim is useful and good, while everything that makes this way more difficult is evil or useless, and even if it brings economic benefits its must be rejected, for "man does not live by bread alone" (Deuteronomy 8:3).

The Church evaluates all economic currents and directions with this measure, which she also applies to the capitalist economy. Let us see what part of it we can reject, and what is worth keeping.

I. The Church and the Mechanisms of the Capitalist Economy

How many times have embittered workers shouted: "The Church is on the side of the capitalists!" "The Church has sold us out to the wealthy!" Communist propaganda and socialist tactics, which carefully hide true Catholic teaching from the people, have only bolstered this view. The capitalists themselves have at times used the Church to justify their practices, thus sowing mistrust of this greatest guardian of truth and morality, which reminds the capitalists of their duties as well.

It is not true that the Church supports Godless capitalism.

It is very unfair to proclaim that all that the Church had to say to the workers was that they must be obedient and patiently bear the capitalist yoke, while she supported industrialists and defended plutocracy. Did you not hear that until very recently the Church had the courage to tenaciously oppose the widespread practice of interest on capital, even though the economic system at the time frequently scoffed at her, seeing her as the preacher of obscurantism and backwardness? If the Church had been listened to, the development of capitalism in its present form would have been stopped among the Catholic nations. Do you not know that it is the non-Catholic nations that are the strongest bastions of capitalism? Did you not hear that the Church's teaching and morality are being accused of having delayed the development of industry and trade in Catholic countries?

Yet the Church has not ceased to preach: "Lend, expecting nothing in return; and your reward will be great, and you will be sons of the Most High" (Luke 6:35). Wherever the word of the Church is accepted, this teaching has had a benevolent impact on alleviating the razor of human greed.

The Church never praised nor supported capitalism, but from the oldest times up to the present she has vigorously campaigned against all sorts of usury. During the time of the greatest expansion of usury, Leo XIII condemned "rapacious usury," which up through the present day "is nevertheless, under a different guise, but with like injustice, still practiced by covetous and grasping men" (RN, 2). Meanwhile, the Code of Canon Law which Benedict XV proclaimed condemns all forms of usury, and therefore the abuse of labor contracts as well; meanwhile, Church sanctions apply to usurers (Canon 1543).

Likewise, today we can hear the following words of the Book of Proverbs in Catholic churches: "The people curse him who holds back grain, but a blessing is on the head of him who sells it" (Proverbs 11:26). And also: "Diverse weights are an abomination to the Lord, and false scales are not good" (Proverbs 20:23).

Exploitative and Godless capitalism has always been condemned by the entire teaching of the holy Church.

The Church rejects the licentiousness of selfish capitalism that is not limited by any legislation.

The Church defends freedom, as freedom is an indispensable condition for human activity and best corresponds to man's rational nature. However, the Church strongly condemns such a form of freedom that liberates the individual from natural law and God's law as well as all moral commandments. Such a freedom becomes a poisonous well; the slavery of the poor flows from such freedom of the rich.

Economic liberalism has been condemned by the Church because it preaches freedom from all of God's laws. Modern capitalism has rejected all of His assistance in economic life; it did not want to lower its boastful head before the warning of the Psalmist: "Unless the Lord builds the house, those who build it labor in vain. Unless the Lord watches over the city, the watchman stays awake in vain" (Psalm 127:1–2).

The fact that Godless capitalism has rejected God in the factory is not in itself tragic; the Christian God watches human hearts and hands all too closely. The capitalists have begun to serve the idol of Mammon, which has filled their pockets. They received their payment of Judas' pieces of silver for their betrayal of God. What did the laborers gain from a betrayal of God? Why did they oust Him from their factories and workshops, from the platforms of their political parties and unions? Was it to hasten the victory of Godless and selfish capitalism? This betrayal of God's laws by the capitalist world and the world of the workers was a shared fault! It facilitated the breakdown of the economic body of healthy professional life, leading to disorder and, consequently, the exploitation of the economic supremacy of capital. Would it be possible to maintain the morality of economic life without God's laws? And old piece of revealed wisdom states: "As a stake is driven firmly into a fissure between stones, so sin is wedged in between selling and buying" (Sirach 27:2). Thus, it is unsurprising that economic life separated from God's law by both factory owners and workers became a land of sin, a new Sodom and Gomorrah that in places has turned into the Dead Sea.

The Church recognizes respectable economic institutions.

God's world is a big house where human life should function according to His models. After all, God is the creator of the great "machine" about which we read in the Book of Proverbs: "Wisdom has built her house, she has set up her seven pillars. She has slaughtered her beasts, she has mixed her wine, she has also set her table" (Proverbs 9:1–2). Now, messengers are faced with the challenge: "Whoever is simple, let him turn in here! [. . .] Come, eat of my bread and drink of the wine I have mixed" (Proverbs 9:4–5). This is a model for men who live in the world in accordance with God's law. Many are called by Providence to cooperate with it in the feeding of the world; it is their duty to participate in the "building of the house" and call people to cooperate and co-exist, to their participation in the fruits of this work.

God encourages man to conquer the earth: "Be fruitful and multiply and fill the earth and subdue it" (Genesis 1:28). Man is called to the great effort of gradually rebuilding the world. The development of world economies is the result of the laws of progress. Thus, today's big industry cannot itself be something evil and deserving of condemnation if it cooperates with God's law, for "the wage of the righteous leads to life" (Proverbs 10:16). If it is devoted to the creation of truly useful goods, every honest human labor is man's cooperation with God in His plan of feeding the world.

The Church likewise does not condemn the credit-based economy that big industry uses, as long as it functions in a just way. Through His attitude, the Lord Jesus has proven that there can be both flaws and merits in every area of human life; the flaws can be fixed through man's good will. Thus, He accepted the invitation to the feast of Levi where "there was a large company of tax collectors and others sitting at table with them" (Luke 5:29). When the Puritans of the day were scandalized by this, He ensured them that those people can also enter the Kingdom of Heaven if they will honestly exercise their duties (see Luke 5:27–32). Thus, Christ the Lord went under Zacchaeus' roof so that his house would also be saved; for the same reason, He called Matthew to be an apostle and evangelist who would teach the world how human labor could and should be sanctified through God's grace.

The Church likewise does not condemn the fact that contemporary workers are in a mercenary relationship with their employers; she only encourages the search for a new form of this relationship that better corresponds to human dignity. Today, however, the Church demands that contractual workers be secured with a just wage, elaborate social legislation and charity funds, while encouraging the improvement of the living conditions of the laborer.

II. What Aspects of Contemporary Capitalism Does the Church Oppose?

The holy Gospel contains a description of a feast prepared by a king, one in which he summoned a select few through his servants, but those who were invited refused to participate in the feast, "but they made light of it and went off, one to his farm, another to his business" (Matthew 22:5). This is an image of contemporary economic life, whose organizers and directors are completely absent from the feast of the Heavenly King and are totally subordinated to their cattle, villages and commerce. This is the source of all the sins of contemporary capitalism.

The Church rejects the worldliness of the capitalist economy.

Having rejected God's law, capitalism feeds on the illusory happiness of earthly life, and, like communism, wants to create paradise on earth. For this purpose, it demands unlimited freedom of private property and rejects all social obligations. It prescribes to its believers a principle that has been condemned by the Church: Grow wealthy first, and then everything else will be given to you. Pursuant to this principle of accumulating wealth, all the savage forms of economic anarchy that lead a handful of people to conquer the world through money and credit are promoted: excessive speculation and other maximizations of profits; depriving workers and laborers of their livelihood; ubiquitous dishonest advertising; dubious bankruptcies; cheating; manipulating the stock market; brutal warfare between trusts, cartels and department stores; the perverse rivalry of joint-stock companies. Thus, should it be surprising that in *Quadragesimo anno* the Holy See strongly condemns these modern sins of which no one is accused and whose injuries are never corrected?

The truth is that the rights of the owner are not exclusive, and goods are not intended primarily for the satisfaction of his desires. These laws are not unlimited, for man is not the absolute master of his goods, but only their steward; he must account of his stewardship before God.

For the system of the capitalist economy to fulfill its duties, it demands many moral virtues of its directors. No society, let alone the entire sphere of economic life, can exist without moral virtues.

The Church earnestly condemns the spirit of profit, the creation of wealth only for oneself.

In its essence, capitalism does not desire the satisfaction of the needs of all of society, but the greatest possible enrichment of the individual. This is capitalism's greatest flaw: its main aim is profit.

Capitalism has brought up man in such a spirit. A man who is governed by the capitalist spirit wants to turn all stones into bread; he sees attaining profit as the ultimate aim of his entire life and work. All the natural relationships between people fall before his eyes: the familial, professional, national and religious communities. All the works of God's hands mean little to him: nature is no longer beautiful; it is perceived as merely the source of raw materials and income from the land and cattle. Such men see others not as neighbors, but only as hired hands, or the owners of stocks.

The spirit of profit breeds a feverish pursuit of money. The capitalist seeks to gain time in order to make as many profits as possible in as brief a time as possible. A mad rush to save on time, interest, labor and the laborer's wage begins in order to make a new investment possible. This is the secret of the feverish tempo of modern production, in which capitalists compete with Udarnik Bolsheviks in tempting the laborer with the vision of a wage in order to force him to increase his production at the cost of his own body and soul.

What are the fruits of this? Do we not have before our eyes now the landowner who is described in the Gospel, who has gathered an unexpected harvest and spoke within his soul: "Eat, drink, and be merry?" Yet their fate is the same: "This night your soul is required of you" (Luke 12:19–20).

Death stands before the gate of greed. "There is not a more wicked thing than to love money: for such a one setteth even his own soul to sale: because while he liveth he hath cast away his bowels" (Sirach 10:10). Man becomes overcome with the desire to overwork himself in anxious haste, in the constant pursuit of income. This leads to anxiety; hence all the madmen, degenerates, perverts and semi-humans who lack the time and effort for anything that is not money or profit.

This is the new *homo oeconomicus*.

The Church struggles against capitalist exploitation and the humiliation of those whose work.

The Church has assertively cautioned the entire world against the pernicious consequences of capitalism, which have struck at the individual dignity of the exploited worker.

Capitalism first equated man with machinery and reduced people to merely soulless tools; it later ennobled machinery, on which it bestowed the status of a divinity man should serve. As a sad consequence of this slavery, man's efforts only increase, prematurely depleting the strength of the labor force by hastening the tempo of production. "Among the olive rows of the wicked they make oil; they tread the wine presses but suffer thirst; from out of the city the dying groan" (Job 24:11–12).

Through the far-reaching division, mechanization and rationalization of labor, capitalism has struck at man's greatest gift, his rational nature, destroying all his interests in reference to the object of labor. How accurate is Pius XI's statement that inanimate objects leave the workplace sanctified, while man becomes worse and more commonplace. Furthermore, by situating man below a machine, capitalism has lost all its sensitivity to the basic needs and conditions of human life. It has thought that man, like a machine, is not prone to exhaustion but only the laws of shock absorption. Thus, it has placed upon him burdens it cannot carry itself. How similar today's capitalists are to the ignoble farmers about whom Job laments: "They go about naked, without clothing; hungry, they carry the sheaves" (Job 24:10).

Capitalism is also indifferent to man's moral and religious needs, making it difficult for him to exercise the basic responsibilities towards his own soul and salvation. When we add to this the constant lowering of wages for labor, or the sabotage of workers through the specter of reductions and unemployment, the Church's reasons for protest become even more apparent.

Isaiah once threatened those who exploit: "Woe to those who join house to house, who add field to field, until there is no more room, and you are made to dwell alone in the midst of the land" (Isaiah 5:8). Greed makes the eyes blind to the economic truth that the destitution of the masses will have a terrible effect on their purchasing power and therefore production and the state of businesses.

The fruits of the capitalist spirit are truly terrible. The laborer has become spiritually impoverished, abandoning God's and man's laws, trying to save himself from violence and economic tyranny at all costs. The soul of the laborer, which was disappointed in its worldly lot, has become filled with anxiety, greed, ruthlessness, envy and the lust for inaccessible earthly goods. Subjected to material poverty, he persisted in moral poverty, while in his impoverished soul and body he became reduced to the proletarian life that is not worthy of a man; he became prone to all the temptations of revolution, communism and Bolshevism. These are the bitter fruits that cry out to the heavens.

The Church uncompromisingly condemns plutocracy, or the domination of money over the entirety of economic life.

The individualist spirit that dominates economic life has led to capitalism, whose extreme form has led to the dictatorship of money. Pius XI has noted a sad phenomenon of our times: dangerously potent and despotic economic power is concentrated in the hands of only a few. Such power "is being most forcibly exercised by those who, since they hold the money and completely control it, control credit also and rule the lending of money. Hence, they regulate the flow, so to speak, of the lifeblood whereby the entire economic system lives, and have so firmly in their grasp the soul, as it were, of economic life that no one can breathe against their will" (QA, 106). Through the complicated system of monopolies, trusts and businesses, it has led to the domination of all means of life, violating the principle of justice. All sorts of industrial and trade associations as well as useless banking and credit institutions have been used for egotistical self-enrichment so that they no longer serve the ordinary citizens for whom they were established: instead, they serve the exploitation of not only individuals, but entire classes, segments of society, nations and states.

As Austria's Catholic bishops write in their pastoral letter, plutocracy systematically leads to robbing nations of their savings and the intentional impoverishment of the masses in order to make not only laborers, but also artisans, the middle class, and even the entrepreneurs and factory owners who are dependent on it. We read in this letter that in certain countries bankers have become the new dominant power, wielding power over state authority, which then is no longer sovereign. Having exchanged money for merchandise, which they sell at usurious prices in their gilded bankers' stalls, the Godless world of finance, which wants to become wealthy without bounds, is prone to "temptation, into a snare, into many senseless and hurtful desires that plunge men into ruin and destruction," as St. Paul says (1 Timothy 6:9).

"This accumulation of might and of power generates in turn three kinds of conflict. First, there is the struggle for economic supremacy itself; then there is the bitter fight to gain supremacy over the State in order to use in economic struggles its resources and authority; finally, there is conflict between States themselves" (QA, 108). Having achieved these two forms of power, the financiers attempt to prevent social legislation and all reforms, instead multiplying sin. Here is a brief list of such transgressions:

They burden the services of bank and credit institutions with excessive, usurious interest; they exploit both laborers and small-scale artisans and suppliers through bad working conditions and unjust wages and prices; unjust interest or the direct usurpation of savings, especially small ones, through fake bankruptcies, inflation, artificial increases and decreases in prices, stocks, etc.; they have changed the guiding force of economic life, rejecting the remedying of human needs, making financial profit the aim of all economic activity.

Thus, it is unsurprising that great power has led to the universal struggle of all against all: capital against labor, great capital against small capital, the bourgeoisie against the proletariat, etc. Finally, it has ruined the dignity of those who rule, reducing their rule to that of slaves who have sold themselves to all human passions and selfish interests. "Gold has ruined many and has perverted the minds of kings" (Sirach 8:2). But that is not all! It leads to "conflict between States themselves, not only because countries employ their power and shape their policies to promote every economic advantage of their citizens, but also because they seek to decide political controversies that arise among nations through the use of their economic supremacy and strength" (QA, 108). This is where the most terrible chapter in human history begins: cruel, bloody, ruthless wars whose filthy, mercenary aims are at times cloaked under the guise of the noblest ideals; these are wars that trample on everything that should be holy and sublime.

* * *

All abuses of God's laws will be avenged; He will not allow for His laws to be mocked.

"For the love of money is the root of all evils; it is through this craving that some have wandered away from the faith and pierced their hearts with many pangs" (1 Timothy 6:10).

It is sobering how dangerous is the unjust reaping at the cost of one's soul and how great riches pit human pride against God, while they immerse the world in the materialism of consumption and in unbelief. What is more atheistic today: communism or capitalism? Whom do you prefer on your threshing floors: an apparent arsonist who sets fire to your own house, or a devious one who sets your patrimony to fire quietly and at midnight? Judge for yourselves!

Indeed, their hearts will be pierced with many pangs. God will be the first to abandon them. "For thus says the Lord: For three transgressions of Israel, and for four, I will not revoke the punishment; because they sell the righteous for silver, and the needy for a pair of shoes — they that trample the head of the poor into the dust of the earth and turn aside the way of the afflicted" (Amos 2:6–7). God will reject them and end their stewardship because the most prudent were not unlike the sons of lightness: "Hear this, you who trample upon the needy, and bring the poor of the land to an end, saying, 'When will the new moon be over, that we may sell grain? And the sabbath, that we may offer wheat for sale, that we may make the ephah small and the shekel great, and deal deceitfully with false balances, that we may buy the poor for silver and the needy for a pair of sandals, and sell the refuse of the wheat?'" (Amos 8:4–6).

Such hopes are in vain! A month or a Saturday will not pass for you; on the contrary, your improperly acquired property will be taken away from you:

"Therefore because you trample upon the poor and take from him exactions of wheat, you have built houses of hewn stone, but you shall not dwell in them; you have planted pleasant vineyards, but you shall not drink their wine" (Amos 5:11).

"Therefore, thus says the Lord God: 'An adversary shall surround the land, and bring down your defenses from you, and your strongholds shall be plundered'" (Amos 3:11).

"Whoever accumulates by depriving himself, accumulates for others; and others will live in luxury on his goods" (Sirach 14:4).

"But woe to you that are rich, for you have received your consolation" (Luke 6:24).

If only they would bring this punishment only onto themselves. Unfortunately, however, every individual sin gives rise to universal sin, just as original sin does. Thus, this egotistical betrayal of social duties leads to terrible shocks in which all goods — not only worldly, but spiritual ones as well — fall victim to revolutionary catastrophe.

Behold the old, yet surprisingly relevant, image of catastrophe that we have ourselves experienced all too often:

> Then a mighty angel took up a stone like a great millstone and threw it into the sea, saying, So shall Babylon the great city be thrown down with violence, and shall be found no more; and the sound of harpers and minstrels, of flute players and trumpeters, shall be heard in thee no more; and a craftsman of any craft shall be found in thee no more; and the sound of the millstone shall be heard in thee no more; and the light of a lamp shall shine in thee no more; and the voice of bridegroom and bride shall be heard in thee no more, for thy merchants were the great men of the earth, and all nations were deceived by thy sorcery. And in her was found the blood of prophets and of saints, and of all who have been slain on earth (Revelation 18:21–24).

Does this not remind us of the not-too-distant past? Are not the princes of the earth today merchants and financial potentates? Have not all the nations yielded to their charms? Do not this mad dance of gold and the dizzying melody of the flute of greed fill the ears of the entire world with their din?

Let us recall "the blood of prophets and of saints, and of all who have been slain on earth" (Revelation 18:24). May we not be blind leaders. May we not heal the regret of the daughter of Zion too superficially. We must remember that "treasures gained by wickedness do not profit, but righteousness delivers from death" (Proverbs 10:2).

Let us ask the God of hosts: "Give the king Thy justice, O God, and Thy righteousness to the royal son! May He judge Thy people with righteousness, and thy poor with justice! Let the mountains bear prosperity for the people, and the hills, in righteousness! [...] May He defend the cause of the poor [...] and crush the oppressor! [...] From oppression and violence He redeems their life; and precious is their blood in His sight. Long may He live, may gold of Sheba be given to Him! May prayer be made for Him continually, and blessings invoked for Him all the day! [...] Amen and Amen!" (Psalm 72:2–19).

6

Catholics and Communists

T HE QUESTION OF THE CHURCH'S ATTITUDE
towards socialism and communism is often presented in an
erroneous way. It should not be interpreted through a parti-
san-political lens, as is usually the case; the most important matter
is not if someone belongs to one party or another or if one supports
or rejects class struggle. While socialism today is changing its attitude
towards both property and class struggle, communism still aims for
the harshest form of class struggle and the complete renunciation
of private property; and the weight of the matter rests elsewhere;
it can be reduced to essential differences in views. Even if socialism
renounced universal ownership and ended class struggle, one cannot
speak of concurrence with Church teaching.

I will now devote several separate reflections to the attitude of the
Church first to socialism and later to communism.

I. The Church and Socialism

In his encyclical *Quadragesimo anno*, Pius XI notes the changes
that have been occurring in contemporary socialism. Although socialism has kept its name, it has changed its attitude towards previously
praised social reforms: "The other section, which has kept the name
Socialism, is surely more moderate. It not only professes the rejection
of violence but modifies and tempers to some degree, if it does not
reject entirely, the class struggle and the abolition of private ownership. One might say that, terrified by its own principles and by the
conclusions drawn therefrom by Communism, Socialism inclines
toward and in a certain measure approaches the truths which Christian tradition has always held sacred; for it cannot be denied that its
demands at times come very near those that Christian reformers of
society justly insist upon" (QA, 113).

These words of the Holy Father are very important. One must
remember that the pope does not have in mind Marxist doctrine itself,

which is the most extreme form of socialism, because this doctrine is impervious to change. However, its explanation and application in life, or its political practice, changes.

According to Marx's conception, class struggle is closely tied to the entire process of political change: from capitalism through the concentration of the masses, their complete impoverishment, and the final period, that of revolution, which will someday liberate the world of capitalism. In this process, class struggle plays an essential role, without which Marxism does not exist. In political life, some variants of socialism have deviated from this means of the reconstruction of the world, which is so essential to it. This is what the Holy Father had in mind when he noted the changes in the heart of the socialist movement and new intellectual currents. Life itself has inclined it towards ending the boycott of existing forms of the political system and making use of those achievements that the new state had given them long ago, through labor legislation, which initially was so fiercely opposed in socialist milieus. Although it renounced class struggle in practice, it did not break with it in theory. Revolution on a global scale has not ceased to be the subject of socialist yearnings.

The same goes with respect to socialism's attitude towards private property. Along with the improvement of the well-being of the laborers, who have ceased to be a proletariat clad in rags and have begun to achieve what might even be called a kind of prosperity, this doctrine's hostility towards all forms of private property became very difficult. The enfranchisement of the proletariat, the growing savings of laborers, and the housing cooperative movement provided such visible benefits that one could not struggle against it. Thus, socialists had to discourage the struggle against property, for this struggle threatened the accomplishments of the working class; it was thanks to ownership that their previously sad state has improved.

The essential difficulty that precludes the reconciliation of socialist and Catholic doctrine rests in its view of society. Under the influence of the changes I have mentioned above, there began to appear hopes that there could be agreement between the two. Within the Church, there were even attempts at meeting people affiliated with socialism. Attempts at "baptizing" socialism began to appear among the socialists themselves. They typically ended with the confusion of concepts, for everything was reduced to fundamental conceptions: the view of the world. Pius XI noted this when he wrote: "Whether considered as a doctrine, or an historical fact, or a movement, Socialism, if it remains truly Socialism, even after it has yielded to truth and justice on the points which we have mentioned, cannot be reconciled with the teachings of the Catholic Church because its concept of society itself is utterly foreign to Christian truth" (QA, 117).

We are very familiar with the Christian view of man and society. Pius XI continues: "For, according to Christian teaching, man, endowed with a social nature, is placed on this earth so that by leading a life in society and under an authority ordained of God he may fully cultivate and develop all his faculties unto the praise and glory of his Creator; and that by faithfully fulfilling the duties of his craft or other calling he may obtain for himself temporal and at the same time eternal happiness. Socialism, on the other hand, wholly ignoring and indifferent to this sublime end of both man and society, affirms that human association has been instituted for the sake of material advantage alone" (QA, 118).

The errors that result from this are common to both socialism and communism, with the difference that the socialists merely profess these errors, while the communists implement them. There is an intellectual, ideological kinship between socialism and communism. Both systems have accepted the materialistic conception of world history; both have the same fathers and children. Studying the history of socialism, we see that it constantly loses its supporters to communism; it is simply a nursery, a preparatory school for communism. Polish socialism has brought up large masses of people who have organized the Soviet state.

Both socialism and communism have an equally hostile approach to God. Although socialism's attitude towards private property and class struggle has been mitigated, its approach to religion was not subject to significant changes. In the Polish socialist literature, there are books that, despite their authors' intentions, indicate that socialist education typically leads to atheism, even if it is not the direct intention of socialist leaders. Pius XI has made note of this, noting "a certain new kind of socialist activity, hitherto little known but now carried on among many socialist groups. It devotes itself above all to the training of the mind and character" (QA, 121).

The simple conclusion is that Catholicism and socialism are two contradictory concepts, while attempts at reconciliation will not bring the desired fruits as long as socialism remains socialism.

II. The Church and Communism

Over time, socialism, a movement that was initially homogeneous, divided into two camps "often opposing each other and even bitterly hostile, without either one however abandoning a position fundamentally contrary to Christian truth that was characteristic of Socialism" (QA, 111).

Communism is the continuation of socialism; it is the introduction of the correct conclusions from materialist principles, which do not impose themselves but that conciliatory socialists fear and therefore do not fully implement. Thus, others appeared who were irritated by socialist compliance; they had two main aims: "Unrelenting class warfare and absolute extermination of private ownership" (QA, 112). They achieve these aims "by employing every and all means, even the most violent. [. . .] To achieve these objectives, there is nothing which it does not dare, nothing for which it has respect or reverence; and when it has come to power, it is incredible and portentlike in its cruelty and inhumanity. How much an enemy and how openly hostile it is to Holy Church and to God Himself is, alas, too well proved by facts and fully known to all" (*ibid.*).

Catholics see in communism errors that strike at the very mind and heart of man. In the eyes of the communist, matter is god and the main source of all progress and perfection; it is matter that will transform and redeem the world. Communism seeks redemption not from Jesus Christ, but from matter. The personal God does not exist; He is ruthlessly thrown off the face of the earth.

Catholics cannot fail to notice that communism wants to create a world without God and that its designs are filled with radical hatred for religion and a rejection of the Church as a timeless community that exists alongside the state.

Catholics likewise could not fail to notice that anti-religious propaganda holds a central place in the program of the communist state. They will not be deceived by insidious voices whispering: "Catholics, we are extending our arms to you," for Catholics cannot forget that this same outstretched arm murdered priests and dynamited the Lord's churches.

Catholics likewise cannot forget the mundane, silly struggle against God and religion that employed caricatures and satire. In this struggle, communism could not find any serious arguments. It has limited itself to mockery, ridicule, jokes, commonplace lies and cruelty. This is the "modern" weapon in the struggle against God.

Catholics cannot fail to notice communism's aspirations towards the rejection of the soul and its destiny, its aversion to recognizing any spiritual forces in love or the will to introduce personal, familial or social ethics devoid of God.

Catholics cannot forget that communism throws masses of people, who have been created in God's image, into the abyss of materialism and atheism; it subjects people to a sort of obedience that only God can demand of man, although He never forces anyone into obedience, for He does not want to mistreat His creation.

Catholics cannot not notice communism's aspirations towards the adoration of the social value of hatred. They see communism as the cause for stripping man of his personal and social worth. One likewise cannot be blind to the abysmal difference between the Catholic and communist views of man.

Communism has impoverished the concept of the human person; it has created an artificial man who is no longer a person, but merely an individual without his own purpose. Only the state community gives man a purpose. However, the aim that the communist state has outlined demands a higher aim. This is where the horizon of communist thought ends. It can say nothing more to man.

Communism destroys man's social life, which is developed for his own aims. There is no intermediary between the citizen and the state, neither the family, the nation, nor one's profession. Thus, we can see that communism looks at the individual in an individualistic way. Is this not a contradiction? Unfortunately, it is not. Through communism, all of man falls prey to the state. Although it speaks of the socialization of man, it completely rejects his social nature and the possibility of existing in so many rich forms of social life. The state destroys the family, guilds, labor unions, the nation and the religious community. Is this not individualism? We see here that socialist thought has not succeeded in completely liberating itself from the legacy of liberal thinking, which has done the same.

The Church acts in a different way. She teaches that the state is a community consisting not of individuals, but of smaller social cells in which man develops his personal and social worth, thanks to which he becomes capable of living in increasingly higher forms of social life: the state, the supernatural community, and, finally, the Church. Man is capable of preserving his personal liberty in the family, in his profession, and in his national and religious community. Having stripped man of his personal and social worth, communism demands of him further sacrifices for the sake of collective life, which becomes inhuman. It is scornful of the human person, subjecting it to inexorable rule, despotic bureaucratism, terror and inhumanity to the highest degree. Communism wants to socialize both the human body and soul.

Bureaucratic despotism and terror reduce man to being a means of production; capitalism does the same. From that point, the aim of human life is economic output. To attain this goal, one must sacrifice man and his personal good; he must become harnessed to the chariot of production, which leads him to the abyss of practical slavery. In communism, the natural community is replaced with an artificial, monstrous social and political machine. It exists in collective farms, factories and housing.

Man, who is deprived of the protection of the family and society, has been handed over to a giant, a Leviathan who has crushed him with his enormity. Man perishes. His land is seized and forcibly added onto huge farmlands that stretch beyond what the eye sees and are tilled by tractors. His property is seized and subjected to the crushing dominance of gigantic plans and monstrous factories where he completely loses himself in enormous production halls. Those who are not fit to be tools, cogs in the great machine must perish. Those who reject being tamed are liquidated. Leviathan does not know clemency or human dignity; it only knows the human mass. The mass sucks up, absorbs and transforms individuals within its body. The mass dominates everywhere! What does one man mean? Even the field of battle is conquered through the dominance of the masses.

This is how communism has "complemented" man.

Catholics cannot accept such a system, because they see that the communist man is stripped of his own personal aims, reason, will and feelings; there is only the reason and will of the collective. All supernatural aspirations that transcend temporality are sabotage.

The Church preaches the need for social co-existence in the Christian milieu, while communism demands an atheistic environment stripped of personal social elements. Thus, "religious socialism, Christian socialism, are contradictory terms; no one can be at the same time a good Catholic and a true socialist" (QA, 120). It is therefore even more true that one cannot be a good Catholic and a true communist.

III. The Communist "Tombs of Craving"

Today, the world's entire rebellion against God and its insatiable greed has concentrated around communism. Just as the people once rebelled against God in the desert because He fed them manna, today the world is satiated with quail meat yet dies in its greed.

Communists accuse the Church of condemning the opponents of matter: the Manicheans, Puritans and Protestants. They forget, however, that matter comes from God's hands and that man is called to process it according to God's plan. They also forget that the Church condemns those who worship and praise matter, for matter is not the only aim of human life. Those who are angry at the Church for supposedly fighting against matter themselves violate human bodies, which the Church venerates after death, elevating them to the altars, raising them up, and piously placing them in sanctified places until the day of resurrection. The communists, those worshipers of matter, have turned the human body to ash in thousands of execution sites, while the Church, the supposed enemy of matter, professes the resurrection of the body.

They accuse the Church of opposing democracy, while they themselves have created a tyrannical dictatorship on the rubble of democracy. When the Church created democracy at the Lord's Table, in religious orders, and in conclaves, the communists turned what they called democracy into plutocracy. They have overthrown altars and thrones, and a dictatorship appeared, much to the surprise of communist sympathizers. They fought against the medieval state, while they themselves created a state in which man cannot even freely breathe and has been turned into a working animal at the service of the state. They do not want to see that the Church has created a Christian community without the aid of the State Political Directorate, Cheka and Solovetsky Islands. We see here the entire tragedy of the rebellion against God; in every aspect of their evil, they sin even more than those who have been the cause of their hatred.

These are true tombs where "they buried the people who had the craving" (Numbers 11:34).

Communists mock the "prudishness" of the Church, whose nuns have taken vows of chastity and are sent to hospitals and operating rooms to serve the human person and have devoted their entire lives to countless children, orphans and families that have been abandoned by their fathers.

Communists accuse the Church of blessing cannons and tanks, saying that it blesses wars. However, they are silent about the fact that they not only have not ended war, but in fact they prepared for the worst armed attack against all of Europe. The communist laborer will attack the Church for blessing arms that he himself has created. He is, however, silent about the fact that as far back as seven hundred years ago the Church implemented God's peace, at a time when knights were the dominant state; that she constantly begs the Lord for peace during the Mass; and that she could ennoble the knights, giving them swords not for aggression, but for the protection of the oppressed and the poor.

In all countries, communists struggle against the death penalty, demanding amnesty for prisoners, while they themselves have created the most monstrous penal system, contrary to all the principles of criminal law; they praise euthanasia, abortion and so forth.

This is the communist "paradise" which is armed to the teeth and rattles from the constant marches of armies.

* * *

In the struggle against communism, we should bear in mind that, above all, principles should be distinguished from people. The principles themselves are unacceptable; their errors must be highlighted. However, when it comes to people and the parties and organizations they create, they are typically inclined towards compromise, both with respect to their principles and their environment. The ranks of social-ists and communists are not free of evil and devious people focused on their self-interest, as is the case in nearly every social movement. However, there are also those who desire justice and seek out God, Whom they at the moment do not need for a happy earthly life and Who has no place in their vision of the future state. We must discern the best approaches to ideologues and to the well-meaning.

We should have a similar approach to various social efforts as we reach out to those who encourage them. We must remember that we live in a Christian culture that shapes and develops in us a social instinct and desire for the practical love of one's neighbor. Morality that has for so many centuries been honed by the Church's teaching continues to develop and grow stronger. It even has an impact on those who have fallen away from the Church and boast that they are good without the aid of religion. It is true that man is endowed with a basic aspiration towards what is good. However, it is also true that this aspiration is enhanced by the Church. Christian morality will become an increasingly strong need and desire of the human soul. This desire will even attract socialists, communists and atheists. If a social initiative's aspirations and aims are healthy, one should not reject it simply because it has come from the opposing camp. If it is good, it is also Christian, just as everything that the Church has done either directly or through her faithful. Even if it came from "the other side," it can Christianize the world and serve the cause of God, despite the intention of its authors.

One should also avoid purely negative struggle; one must indicate a positive, new, better program, a system that lives not only off the crumbs of morality, but off all of God's truth.

One should also notice that even if all the economic aims were achieved in the communist state and if everyone were supplied with bread and liberated from the burden of work, man cannot be com-pletely liberated from evil and suffering. In the state of the future, people will suffer, agonize and experience a hunger that is perhaps even sharper than the hunger of the body: the hunger of the soul. We will always experience an unsatisfied desire for happiness, for man is created for heaven and eternal joy in God. As St. Augustine said: "My heart is restless until it rests in Thee."

When faced with death, the fate of the communist differs not from that which awaits every person. Neither the gigantic city nor the red banner will protect him against God. A man who favored the collective during life will yet die alone. How will the communist identify himself when he stands before the Christian God's tribunal? Not Lenin, but Jesus Christ will come to judge the living and the dead. Not the red star, but the sign of the Son of Man, the Cross, will appear in the heavens.

Only the Church can prophesy God's mercy. The Church offers eternal mercy and "generous redemption." Although it cautions of hell, it sends no one to it; the communists, meanwhile, create hell on earth. They do not know what mercy is. Have you ever heard this term in the State Political Directorate or the Cheka?

Thus, after all the sufferings of human life, the greatest hope is in the gates of the Church.

7

The Social Renunciation
of Catholics

WHEN THE PROPHET ELIJAH STOOD before Ahab, he heard the following reproach from the king's mouth: "'Is it you, you troubler of Israel?' And he answered, 'I have not troubled Israel; but you have, and your father's house, because you have forsaken the commandments of the Lord and followed the Baals'" (1 Kings 18:17–18).

A similar reproach is leveled against the Church today. They say that the Church has become prone to radicalism, that the prelates are red, and the popes and bishops speak in the spirit of communism.

Is the Church radical, or rather are her faithful ignorant? Can the Church be radical?

The Church is the purveyor of truth. The truth is often found between extremes. Radicalism by its name goes to one extreme or another; thus, there can be both right and left-wing radicalism. Every radicalism consists of the upsetting of a balance, the distortion of the truth for ideological ends. However, there is no such thing as the radicalism of the Church. The world constantly receives truths from the Church that can be improperly understood, destroyed or squandered; even prodigal sons take "half of their goods" from the Church that they waste, living opulently but eventually suffering hunger and eating what is intended for pigs, yearning for the past abundance of their father's house. In this way, the communists have borrowed from the Church the idea of community, the communion of saints, which they have deformed with the class interpretation; today's leftist movements have borrowed from the Church the spirit of sacrificing oneself for one's neighbors, veneration of man and his labor, aspirations for liberation, etc. These are the evangelical crumbs from the table at which they do not want to sit.

If many Catholics today think that the Church preaches radical principles, this is because they themselves have strayed so far from the truth that the mere truth seems something unusual to them. The reality is such that Catholics have renounced the Church's social teaching to an enormous degree. There sometimes appear religious heresies, and there can also be social ones, when the truth that the Church professes is rejected.

I. What Does the Social Renunciation of Catholics Consist Of?

The Church has professed her principles of social, economic and political morality from time immemorial. The Holy See has been publishing social encyclicals for a long time. Indeed, an enormous body of Catholic social literature has appeared. Meanwhile, the great majority of the Catholic world has been deaf to the Church's social teaching. In fact, it has even become hostile to it.

The renunciation of Catholics consists of the fact that they did not want to take responsibility for implementing the Gospel in everyday socio-economic and political life. They have become scattered in political systems that are hostile to the Church: they have filled the ranks of communists and socialists; are completely smitten with the capitalist spirit; and in most cases isolate economic life from the influence of Catholic morality. They are very irritated when the clergy mentions the problems of service, a just wage and the decent living conditions of contractual laborers. The mere phrase "social justice" irks them.

Catholics have impoverished Catholic life, which they have limited to the churches and reduced to the sphere of worship and religious rituals. They fearfully make sure that the Church's teaching does not influence earthly life, which they consider to be solely theirs. Thus, they have left earthly life to the mercy of their own frequently selfish and mundane aspirations. The fruit of this attitude is such that today's Catholic world has become divided into two camps: those who accept the Church's teachings and those for whom it is an obstacle; the latter often oppose socially inclined Catholics even more zealously than they do the communists.

As a result of such a headstrong attitude, at times it is the enemies of Christianity who implement the principles preached by the Church (which they understand in their own way), but often using them to oppose God Himself.

From the time of the very first community in Jerusalem, the Church has preached the communion of saints. But have Catholics implemented it? Ineptly imitating the Gospels, communists and Bolsheviks have tried to do this. They have lost, for they conceived of their community in terms of class and reduced the Christian concept of one's neighbor to the proletariat, while they have filled all of social life with hatred. They do not want to accept that the Church leads to a community of thoughts and actions through love, encompassing the community in Christ, our Brother, and all classes and estates.

The Church has long preached the dignity of man and struggled for the liberation of the proletariat. However, she was abandoned by her children in this struggle. Meanwhile, the socialists have sought to implement these principles. They also have lost, for they believed that the proletariat would by itself achieve dignity and liberation, rejecting the assistance of others and denying the rights of any community apart from that of the proletariat.

The Church has fought for the recognition of the dignity of human labor for a long time. Once again, Catholics have failed to appreciate this teaching which the Christians in the catacombs understood better than the holders of degrees in sociology in the twentieth century. They wanted to implement their aims in a radical way; however, their weakness lay in the fact that they only saw the production input, which processes matter and creates economic values; their greatest dignity matured in these efforts. They never thought of the perfection of man through labor.

These symptoms of distrust with which the great majority of Catholics approach the social teachings of the Church are very painful for her.

II. The Basic Flaws of Renunciation

The intellectual renunciation of Catholics in the social sphere was the "original sin" that gave birth to many other basic errors. They include the fact that Catholics reject God's primacy in economic life in both thinking and practice. They worship the independence of the principles of economic life from those of Christian morality; they believe that God's commandments cannot be preserved in industry and trade; they value economic laws over God's laws; they do not want to recognize

331

that there cannot be two primacies and that one must choose either God's sovereignty or that of the power of matter, money and gold.

Catholics reject the Church's authority with respect to the moral aspect of economic life. They believe that economic morality does not befit the dignity and majesty of religious truths. They forget that Christ was born in a stable and does not fear the factory or the mine, just as he did not fear the sinners or tax collectors. Strange is the obstinacy with which they constantly speak as the accusers of the Church, which they do not attempt to understand and whose categories of reasoning they do not try to test. This is why the aspirations of Catholics in their everyday economic life are so secular and mundane.

Catholics practice class renunciation in both theory and social practice. They reject the Church's view on society as a moral organism. They preach and apply the principles of social separation and are especially inclined towards estate and class separatism. They also do not avoid participation in harsh class struggle in the sphere of capital and labor. They are marked by disbelief in the power and necessity of a harmonious cooperation between all segments of society. Meanwhile, there is no social separatism for the Church; on the contrary, the Church has always imbued integral thinking in people, teaching them the synthesis of life. In the act of faith — *Credo in unum Deum* — the Church has emphasized not only her faith, but also faith in the one God who wants everything to be one, just as the Father and Son are one (see John 17:22).

Catholics have the duty to become aware of their social nature, which has been so lacking in the Catholic world, despite the doctrine of the Mystical Body of Christ. They have become more prone to the strong class basis for the errors of capitalism and communism than to the one, holy and Catholic Church.

III. The Holy See's Accusations Against Catholics in the Area of Economic Life

There are at times very painful moments of the examination of one's conscience. Pius XI was very aware of this sad necessity when he saw how all the Church's pleas did not bring any fruit, while social errors, even the most ludicrous ones, enjoy great success, pushing the world into an increasingly terrible abyss of confusion. That was not a time for silence. The Church's encounter with her wayward children must have come for the good of all in order to avoid even greater misfortunes.

Both in *Quadragesimo anno* and in *Divini redemptoris*, Pius XI levels numerous accusations against the Catholic world, above all because it has failed in its fidelity to the Church. The Holy See's accusations are justified by the fact that the Church has never ceased to stubbornly admonish and instruct her faithful. Above all, the Holy Father accuses Catholics of unfamiliarity with Catholic social teaching: "If the manner of acting of some Catholics in the social-economic field has left much to be desired, this has often come about because they have not known and pondered sufficiently the teachings of the Sovereign Pontiffs on these questions" (DR, 55). Certainly, the errors that the pope condemns result from this ignorance: "What is to be thought of the action of those Catholic employers who in one place succeeded in preventing the reading of Our Encyclical *Quadragesimo anno* in their local churches? Or of those Catholic industrialists who even to this day have shown themselves hostile to a labor movement that We Ourselves recommended?" (DR, 50).

These are the real sufferings of a mother, the Church, who was betrayed by her own children.

Later, the pope accuses Catholics of a contradiction between religious and social life that has resulted from religious ignorance: "For there are some who, while exteriorly faithful to the practice of their religion, yet in the field of labor and industry, in the professions, trade and business, permit a deplorable cleavage in their conscience, and live a life too little in conformity with the clear principles of justice and Christian charity. Such lives are a scandal to the weak, and to the malicious a pretext to discredit the Church" (DR, 55).

The Holy Father accuses Catholics of violating the obligations of charity; they have loved in word but not in deed: "These groups have refused to understand that Christian charity demands the recognition of certain rights due to the workingman, which the Church has explicitly acknowledged" (DR, 50). True charity must be bound to justice: "From this it follows that a 'charity' which deprives the workingman of the salary to which he has a strict title in justice, is not charity at all, but only its empty name and hollow semblance. The wage-earner is not to receive as alms what is his due in justice. And let no one attempt with trifling charitable donations to exempt himself from the great duties imposed by justice. Both justice and charity often dictate obligations touching on the same subject-matter, but under different aspects; and the very dignity of the workingman makes him justly and acutely sensitive to the duties of others in his regard" (DR, 49).

The pope accuses Catholics of abusing the right to property and of living in opulence amidst poverty; he calls them to renounce themselves: "Is it not deplorable that the right of private property defended by the Church should so often have been used as a weapon to defraud the workingman of his just salary and his social rights?" (DR, 50). "But when on the one hand We see thousands of the needy, victims of real misery for various reasons beyond their control, and on the other so many round about them who spend huge sums of money on useless things and frivolous amusement, We cannot fail to remark with sorrow not only that justice is poorly observed, but that the precept of charity also is not sufficiently appreciated, is not a vital thing in daily life" (DR, 47).

In order to correct evil, "it is imperative to return to a more moderate way of life, to renounce the joys, often sinful, which the world today holds out in such abundance; to forget self for love of the neighbor" (DR, 48).

The pope also accuses Catholics of reducing the confidence of the working classes in Jesus Christ's religion because of their attitudes in economic affairs. Such Catholics have bolstered the suspicion that the Church was on the side of those who exploit; in other words, they have caused embittered laborers to turn away from God.

The Church accuses Catholics today of not wanting to struggle for the restoration of the dignity of the human person along with her, increasing the dignity of labor, restoring the bonds of cooperation in solidarity rather than atheistic class struggle, the morality of trade and industry, professional ethics, the liberation of the proletariat and the enfranchisement of the masses.

The voice of the popes has become a voice calling out in the desert; the broad masses have not shared the concerns of Leo XIII, Pius XI and Pius XII.

* * *

Many people believe that external, political changes suffice to resolve all difficulties. Something more is needed: we need a return to God's commandments and Christian deeds. The post-war world is burdened with the legacy of terrible social errors, the remains of fallen political directions and doctrines. However, these remains are by no means harmless. Whatever happens in the world always has some sort of impact. In order to struggle against the bad fruits of days past, the animated efforts of all people of good will are needed. Pius XII encouraged such efforts in his beautiful speech on the occasion of the fiftieth anniversary of *Rerum novarum*: "Do not let die in your midst and fade away the insistent call of the social encyclical, that voice which indicates to the faithful in the super-natural regeneration of mankind the moral obligation to cooperate in the arrangement of society and especially of economic life, exhorting those who share in this life to action no less than the state itself. Is not this a sacred duty for every Christian?"

Indeed, the first effect of grace is the strengthening of our sincere efforts in exercising God's commandments every day, both as individuals and as members of society. For two thousand years, there has been preserved "in the soul of the Church the sense of the collective responsibility of all for all; so that souls were moved and are moved even to heroic charity, the souls of the monks who cultivated the land, those who freed slaves, those who healed the sick, those who spread the faith, civilization and science to all ages and all peoples, to create social conditions which alone are capable of making possible and feasible for all a life worthy of a man and of a Christian."

"Keep burning the noble flame of a brotherly social spirit which fifty years ago was rekindled in the hearts of your fathers by the luminous torch of the words of Leo XIII; do not permit it to lack for nourishment [. . .]. Nourish it; keep it alive; increase it; make this flame burn more brightly; carry it wherever a groan of suffering, a lament of misery, a cry of pain, reaches you; feed it evermore with the heat of a love drawn from the heart of your Redeemer [. . .]."[1]

---

1   This English translation comes from: Pius XII, *Pius XII: La solennità della Pentecoste*, trans. P. J. Smith, https://thejosias.com/2017/06/02/pius-xii-la-solennita-della-pentecoste/ (accessed August 14, 2021).

8
The Most Pressing
Economic Task of Catholics

*"Unless your righteousness exceeds that of the
scribes and Pharisees..." (Matthew 5:20).*

I WILL END THESE WORDS IN MID-SENTENCE.
Christ the Lord had the right to end them; He had the right to
admonish. He gave this authority to the Church! She also has the
right to admonish and castigate; however, she rarely makes use of
this power. Instead, she tends to instruct.

The "social crusade" that Pius XI has proclaimed indicates how
the Church makes use of this authority. Once again, the Church calls
upon Catholics to fight for justice on earth alongside the Church.

The tasks and obligations of Catholics in their earthly life are also
becoming increasingly clear. Who can say that he never heard the
Church's voice? May her summons for generous works of justice
resound once again.

We will now point out the most important and basic challenges
that face the Catholic world in the economic sphere.

I. The Most Important Task: To Believe the Church's Teaching

One must believe not only in a church, before a pulpit, or
in a confessional, but also in the factory, workshop, office and
warehouse.

For half a century, the Church has been constantly reminding us
of the most pressing needs of economic life, and for half a century
she has been met with disbelief and the opposition of the Catholic
intelligentsia and elites. Only a small part of the Catholic world —
mostly in the milieu of laborers — has believed the Church. The
rest is indifferent, liberal or communist!

Meanwhile, as we wallow in disbelief, events that should con-
vince us that the Church's admonitions and instructions from half

336

a century before were correct and that her predictions were even prophetic are unfolding before our very eyes.

That the world is wallowing in lawlessness and injury that breeds upheavals and revolutions has, unfortunately, taught us nothing. We still argue with the Church, although we sense that there is no salvation elsewhere. We accuse her of radicalism, a social orientation, and taking on a red hue. When the Church speaks of justice, our hearts close off. We must stop this deadlock.

We must quickly free ourselves of social prejudices, ignorance and un-Christian social errors. We must struggle against the heresy that has thrown God from economic life and reduced His influence on earthly matters. This absurd blasphemy that forgets that "the earth is the Lord's and the fullness thereof" (Psalm 24:1) must be opposed. After all, this is madness and suicide.

We must become acquainted with the Church's social truth and implement it in everyday life along with God's commandments, for they are a consistent part of the Church's teaching. Fidelity to the social encyclicals is among the Catholic's duties.

A Catholic social philosophy and economy must be elaborated. In this area, the Church presents only the most general assumptions in her social encyclicals. They are, however, a reference point for further efforts, which belong to lay Catholics.

Since general principles, one must begin to illuminate the mind with faith. In academic work, researchers should not overlook these most basic truths. The more vigorously they will stand before our eyes, the more safely will we be able to avoid differences and discrepancies. Catholic social philosophy, economics, sociology and social policy must be developed. Thanks to them, we must look for the implementation of "eternal economics" in the life of God's children on God's earth.

How much there is to be done here! Take and read the books of Polish economists and social activists. So far, these works have been silent on Catholic social teaching. The most esteemed economists do not know how to quote the most basic documents of Catholic social teaching. Listen to their lectures in university classrooms. Usually, the good news about Christian social justice has not been proclaimed there. Those elderly people are not familiar with the enormous intellectual efforts of the Catholic world in the sphere of economics.

It is up to lay Catholics to implement this task to bear witness to the Truth.

II. The Second Task of Catholics: The Implementation of the Gospel in Economic Life

This is a necessity that results from the fulfillment of the first task. We must above all remember that economic reconstruction is possible only on the fundaments of moral reconstruction.

The transformation of social legislation and systems is ineffective without the transformation of the human soul, which must implement this legislation in live in these systems. Thus, we must first transform our internal and moral life. The spirit of sanctity must be bound to earthly life, while the internal life should be one with supernatural life. So far, this topic has not been completely resolved. Indeed, many believe that a factory owner, merchant or politician cannot be a saintly person. They are absolved before they even commit any sins. This is at the same time an incitement to further sin that frees them of the effort to transform themselves.

Economic and moral life must be brought together. Catholics have forgotten about this task in economic life all too easily, although the Holy See has called upon them to implement it. Although they have created elaborate works of charity, in the sphere of the economy they have usually loved only with their tongues, not with deeds and the truth.

We must also remember that although the Gospels lead to heaven, they also profess principles for earthly life, thanks to which entry to heaven will be facilitated. Due to the neglect of the sanctification of the earth, one must walk across the pagan earth to get to Catholic heaven. This is a betrayal of the small and the weak. If many of them are condemned because of a bad arrangement of economic relations, will this not be because life on earth has become excessively difficult and so dangerous to souls that only the saints can deal with it?

There are numerous examples today.

There is the proletariat state with its culture of Godlessness, which has appeared as the fruit of social injustice.

There is the struggle against God, which today typically occurs in the sphere of economic life.

Finally, there is contemporary industry, which is the most vigorous area of the struggle against God. The seeds of this struggle are scattered from the factory to the village.

How urgent it is to return economic life to God so that the Father's right hand is not bitten where the heavenly Father breaks the daily bread with His sons.

Finally, a Catholic working environment must be created.

Previously, Catholic laborers lived pagan lives and, rarely, human ones; they only sometimes died in a Catholic fashion. The labor milieu endangers many people with the condemnation of the soul, turning them away from God. It has not yet been baptized. A "life worthy of a human and Christian" must become accessible to people.

III. One Last Point: The Healing of the Contemporary System of the World

Catholics must increasingly engage in contemporary life to heal the mundane system of the world. Above all, they must make the spirit incarnate in matter; they must embed moral principles in the economic body. The Incarnation of the Son of God, who ennobles the body and desires the universal sanctification of human life, is a model for Christians. Just as the spirit is incarnate in the person, a unity of matter and the spirit that guides it must likewise occur in economic life. There is no possibility for two separate paths: that of religion and morality on the one hand and the mundane path of the world, economy and factories on the other. God's spirit, which governs all of human activity, must become evident in all human endeavors.

Catholics must direct all of creation towards God's glory. God's glory is the purpose of the world; creation is at the service of man, while man is at God's service. Every man must attract creation towards himself, elevating and bringing it closer to God by his life's deeds. In particular, Catholics, who are the Father's most faithful children, must reveal the power of the spirit that must rule over the created world.

Today, when we have become subjected to the violence of possessions, when we have bowed before matter and serve the idols of prosperity, wealth and money, it is especially our duty to liberate the world of the practical materialism that permeates all human deeds, thoughts, aspirations and desires.

The sanctification of worldly life must be the aim of Catholic labor. This effort can be attained above all through the spreading of sanctity and the implementation of God's commandment: "You shall be holy" (Leviticus 19:2). This can be attained through the sanctification of the milieu in which we live. A man devoted to earthly matters is also obliged to fulfill God's will, save his soul and attain sanctity. He must also attract all who live beside him towards this path; he has the duty to help his neighbors in their path towards God. "Our justice" must be even more bountiful; it must reach all people and descend to the soil of the earth.

To achieve this aim, we must sanctify our professional life, ground it in the principles of Catholic social morality, and organize Catholic professional life. We must aim for the reconciliation of professional cooperation, protecting it from the spirit of class struggle, the selfishness of profit and the elaboration of artificial contradictions. We must strive for the edification of one's profession through Catholic professional ethics, for spiritual and religious renewal in the socio-economic field.

In order to ground these fruits, we must work on the reconstruction of economic life in the spirit of Catholic professional ethics. It is only at this price that Catholics will be absolved of the accusation that they have not fulfilled their social duties. "Our justice" must be more bountiful than that of the pagan exploiters of slaves, the masters of the old civilization, capitalists and communists; it must be more bountiful than even that of the honest employers, entrepreneurs, merchants and plowmen. This will be the measure of the new social system and new justice; it will be the measure of love and social peace. It is only in this way that you will "lay up for yourselves treasures in heaven" (Matthew 5:20).

9

The Natural Social Order

FROM THE TIME OF GOD'S DECLARATION IN paradise: "It is not good that the man should be alone; I will make him a helper fit for him" (Genesis 2:18), we face the question of co-existence with our neighbors. Is it true, as the advocates of class struggle proclaim, that man is a wolf to another man? Or, on the contrary, is it that "a brother helped is like a strong city" (Proverbs 18:19)?

The world has gone through numerous experiences. The Church and God's grace have brought people together, while the world and selfish sin have torn them apart. Throughout history, there have been periods when people were completely scattered; there were times of fierce conflict between entire estates and classes. The fruits of these conflicts were too bitter for us to return to those paths.

What better serves the world and people, and what is stronger? War or peace, hate or love, division or unification? Is it necessary to refer to extreme forms of relationships between people? Can we not find guidelines in human and social life for the basis of human co-existence, for what should be intact when it best secures internal order and the social good?

There are some unfailing laws whose preservation brings evident benefit and whose violation causes worldly injury. They stem from man's natural nature as well as rational and free being, which is destined for social life and capable of co-existence and cooperation with his surroundings.

All of man's properties must have room for further growth; this can occur only in a social system that will be built on man's image and likeness, just as man is created in the image and likeness of God (see Genesis 1:26).

Every system serves man; every system must aid man and service his person. Therefore, it must bear some similarity to the immutability of human nature; it must create its own framework in which man will feel free.

I. Man and His Aims

Man is the starting point of the construction of every system.
Man is a social being. We emphasize both those words with equal emphasis. This is not a theoretical dispute on whether man stands before society or if the opposite is true. Instead, man's nature is two-fold: it is simultaneously personal and social.

Man is not God; thus, not everything can be thrown before his feet: religion, morality, created goods; he cannot be elevated above the nation and state, although as the only concrete rational reality man is something greater than the state. Yet man strives for exaltation, for he strives for God, who has the capacity of elevating him before all other creation.

Man is not social manure, matter or clay on which the feet of future generations trample; however, man can be humiliated by the social system, which occurs today.

"Man is man": this means he is a rational and free being with his own social, temporal and eternal aims, tasks and destinies.

Man's own human aims — earthly and eternal alike — are strictly tied to his personhood. They are independent of society, although man achieves them in co-existence in various societies. The earthly aim encompasses the perfection of earthly life, which is achieved through the aid of natural talents and aims. Man is obliged to lead the perfection to heights that can be attained on earth, making use of natural and supernatural gifts. Man's earthly aim should not be downplayed, for it must assist in the path towards the eternal aim.

The eternal, supernatural aim of becoming united with God through love and friendship is also among man's aims. Even if his earthly life were most perfect, "man shall not live by bread alone" (Matthew 4:4); a fully developed civilization and economic well-being are not enough to satisfy all human desires. Even if all human sweat and toil were wiped from man's brow, the human heart is restless until it rests in the Lord and His love, as St. Augustine confesses.

Every man is imbued with the need for love. All of familial, professional and social life are the giving and taking away of some form of love. However, only God is the fullness of perfect love. The love of one's family, nation, state and profession are not enough for man;

becoming immersed in God is necessary for complete happiness.

Man's social aims flow from the fact that man is not only a person, but also a social being. Man must co-exist with others; this is his inevitable exigency. In order to achieve his natural and supernatural aims, man needs the cooperation of familial, national, state, professional and even religious communities.

Each of these communities corresponds to man's rational nature. Hence the conclusion that none of them can be destroyed; man cannot be deprived of co-existence with them.

Man must strive for heaven along with other people, as part of a religious community. According to Christ's will, man is dependent on the Church, which possesses supernatural graces, in his attitude towards God. Man's religious aspirations are, above all, public veneration of God, or common prayer.

These are man's aims that result from his nature. No one has the right to act against these aims, nor to separate man from them. All other aims of human life must be attuned with these basic and essential aims.

Every system that violates these aims would be contrary to man's nature; it would be unjust. Thus, liberalism, communism and totalitarianism all to varying degrees violate man's personal, social nature; they are a violation of human nature.

This is how man enters social, economic and political life. It must be ordered in a way that fully corresponds to the needs of human nature.

II. The Social Order

The social order must correspond to man's nature.

Man's personal-social nature is a model for the construction of all communities and systems. The social order must serve man, but man must not serve that order. Thus, we must first look at man, become intimately familiar with him, and only later devise political programs. Every social order must be constructed according to the properties of human nature. In the social order, man must feel as if in clothing tailored for him or as a tree in its bark; he must sense that the social order is something like the extension of his person. The order must be built specifically for man, who is to live and perfect himself within it. Thus, there must be place for both the individual and social aspirations of the individual in it.

We can find a perfect image of the human community in the human body. In it, we see their different, distinct and diverse functions that are so crucial to the human body that it cannot easily deny them. All the members cooperate with one another; all also suffer and experience joy together.

The social order is built according to the model of the human body. There must also be a multiplicity of members in the social order, for one body appears thanks to it. All are useful and necessary, and all are needed, hence their majesty and harmony.

Every community is a multiplicity of members. The wealthier and more developed a community, the more it needs new forms of co-existence that are increasingly intimate and better correspond to man's social nature.

The following emerge from co-existence between people: familial, tribal, national, state and other communities. Every human community that freely develops aims for the creation and preservation of these natural social groups, as it is only through them that their needs can be satisfied.

The destruction of these forms of social life would be an activity against the natural need of the human community. We see how devastating the destruction of the family was to social life in many states; how all the world's economic life was harmed by the destruction of professional associations; how tragic the lack of a religious society is for man. The family, profession, nation, state and Church fulfill social functions that are indispensable to the development of common life and for the good of the whole.

The same goes for individual segments of society. Each man and each social layer implement specific tasks. Hence the duty to recognize their role and importance. Failing to appreciate the role of the agrarian or working-class segments of society, their social impairment, and depriving them of co-existence lead not only to the sickness of one member, but to the suffering of the entire community. A state that is not concerned that all may feast at one table are paving the way for social anxiety and disorder.

Hence the conclusion that each person should be allotted his appropriate place, embraced with the care and respect of those on whom we are dependent, and those who work for us just as we work for them.

Just as in the human body, the social body must be coherent; otherwise, the suffering of the disenfranchised segments of society will impact the health of the entire social body.

III. Social Mechanisms

In the healthy system, social mechanisms should correspond to man's nature.

All these institutions and systems — the family, the profession, and the organization of production or labor — must be constructed according to the same overarching principle, because all are to serve man and help him achieve his aims. They cannot be contrary to human nature.

Let us look at several examples.

The Family

Just like the individual man, the family has a two-fold duty: personal and social. It should have powers that correspond to their tasks, with respect to both the individual and social life. Marriage should remedy man's own needs. However, it does not exist solely for individual purposes; it also has social purposes.

Thus, we cannot look at the institution of the family solely through the prism of utility and personal expediency. Therefore, the Church does not recognize divorces, which correspond to the whims and preferences of individuals, for the family, which is the basis of social life, serves not only individual aims but social ones as well.

The conclusion that the family must count on social privileges results from the fact that it bears witness to the nation and state and assists the development of economic life. Particular concern for the family is the duty of all those who draw their lifeblood from it. The separation of social benefits must take place according to the primacy of the family; hence the enfranchisement of the family and its living space; hence the entitlement to a family allowance and making use of public goods; hence the priority of the father of a family in employment.

345

The Labor System

Labor likewise has a twofold nature: personal and social. The mere duty to work comes not from the state, but from the Creator, who obliged man to do this in paradise, before original sin. Labor is the duty of the rational human being. Man should work even when all his needs are met. The useless wasting of time is one of the deadly sins.

The aim of labor is the development of the human person; it cannot be seen solely from the material perspective, as a sad necessity which is necessary to fill one's stomach. We cannot strive for the complete replacement of human labor with machinery. The efforts of labor are necessary for the full development of the person.

Through his labor, man should not only become useful for his community; he should cooperate with the common good. Man works in order to gain the resources to do good, be ready to serve his brothers, and show them some love in exchange for the help he has received.

This should be the organizing principle for the entire labor system, which considering such assumptions is not only the matter of the entrepreneur and the laborer but is also a social problem. Society should not be indifferent to how human labor is organized and how it progresses.

Property

Property serves to meet the needs of both its owners and their families, and the common good as well. It should serve the good of not only the individual, but of society as well. While possession is private, making use of property is communal.

Once again, this thought that brings man towards both himself and his surroundings frees him from selfishness and sloth that are justified by the statement that fewer goods are necessary for his own needs. The owner of property has the obligation to ensure that his goods meet the needs of society.

The entire system of property should develop both man's personality and his social disposition.

* * *

God has deposited perennial desires and aspirations in the human soul. One of them is the aspiration to become a child of God, who in the school of his Father, the God of love, has learned love.

Like God, man begins this love with himself. Encountering God's love, the love with which He first loved us, within oneself, man cannot disregard His image within himself. However, man cannot limit himself to love of himself; instead, like God, he must aim for love of his surroundings.

Man becomes united with society through this love. By co-existing with society, man perfects himself and learns social love. This love creates the proper attitude of man to the world created by God and to the laws that rule the world. "For the love of Christ controls us" (2 Corinthians 5:14). Thanks to it, a new social and natural — and, therefore, Divine — order is constructed.

10

The Christian Community: "One Body, One Spirit"

"For by one Spirit we were all baptized into one body" (1 Corinthians 12:13).

H AVING ENCOMPASSED ALL OF CREATION with His providential eye, the first and wisest organizer of the world, the Eternal Father, said: "It is not good that the man should be alone; I will make him a helper fit for him" (Genesis 2:18). As the Creator of human nature, He knew perfectly well what He was saying. His words are not only a constitution for co-existence in the family; they are a starting point for social life. This is the first chapter of written Catholic sociology, which is rooted in man's social nature. Drawing on this social nature, man has received "a helper fit for him" from God, which will be the model for all forms of social co-existence.

The greatest Catholic social activist, St. Paul, the Apostle to the Gentiles, referred to these same laws of human nature, which are enclosed in man, and introduced the entire system of Catholic sociology, using the example of the human body, in the famous twelfth chapter of the First Epistle to the Corinthians. The resulting conclusions are of fundamental significance to all social structures, both in the natural and supernatural order.

Let us scrutinize St. Paul's example and focus our attention on human nature to derive the most basic constitutional guidelines for human co-existence.

Every society must consist of many members.

Explaining the structure of the supernatural community, St. Paul says: "For just as the body is one and has many members, and all the members of the body, though many, are one body, so it is with Christ. For by one Spirit we were all baptized into one body" (1 Corinthians 12:12–13). If this is the truth with respect to the Church, and thus in reference to the supernatural community, this is all the more true in the natural order.

348

"For the body does not consist of one member but of many [. . .]. If all were a single organ, where would the body be?" (1 Corinthians 12:14, 19).

Every well-constructed society becomes one because of one well-constructed multitude. Just as there are arms and legs, a head and eyes in the human body, there must likewise be natural differences and a separation into diverse groups, professions, vocations and activities in society; the richer and more elevated the life of a community, the more diverse and complicated are its forms of human co-existence and cooperation.

In this division into members, we clearly see God's plan, or the role of the Creator who "arranged the organs in the body, each one of them, as He chose" (1 Corinthians 12:18). There are no whims in God's activity; everything is rational and intentional. His will, which molds vessels in accordance with their destiny, is expressed in His mind, just as it is expressed in the fingers of a potter. God renders the head and legs in the body of a human; He also implies that there must be a head, but also legs and arms, in every social construction. Naturally, the head is something greater than the legs because creation can live without legs, but life without a head is impossible. However, the body will not achieve all its life's aims when it is deprived of arms and legs or if it were to consist of only a head.

The same goes for human co-existence. Although there are social differences in relation to one's own life's tasks, this division is not a separation but a rational preparation for the fulfillment of the entirety of the tasks of social life.

Various reformist currents that strive for either the separation or the complete destruction of various social groups frequently oppose these very simple rules, especially today. In professional organizations, various classes hurl hostile and unfriendly slogans at one another.

The leading segments of society failed to appreciate the right of the persecuted segments to exist, stretching out all too comfortably in their common home, as if the social body existed only thanks to them. Meanwhile, the working segments of society sought revenge for their social debasement and were inclined to believe that the so-called intelligentsia were parasites and sluggards living off the work of others who brought no benefit to society. It was believed that only those who work with their hands, with "hammer and sickle," or the proletariat, are the creators of all riches and thus have the right to all of society's wealth. Meanwhile, the intelligentsia has not always appreciated the fact that its work is possible only when the physical labor of others creates for them the conditions that are needed for intellectual work.

The aversion to both "filthy hands" and the slogan *daloy gramotnyje*[1] must disappear. White hands must embrace those that are hardened from physical labor in an embrace of mutual love and the conviction that "there are many parts, yet one body" (1 Corinthians 12:20). This will be facilitated by the disappearance of a class mentality on behalf of the aristocracy, intelligentsia and proletariat; it will be facilitated by the disappearance of materialism in the evaluation of man, which has been ingrained not only through socialism, but also, in earlier times, through the owning classes that evaluated man's worth through the value of the estate one owned; finally, it will be facilitated by the return of Christian, universal love of one's neighbor, rather than basing love for one's neighbor on class, social stratum, or noble birth.

All the members of society perform the duties that are appropriate to them for the sake of the whole.

Having foreseen various disputes and disorder in social life, St. Paul asks: "If the foot should say, 'Because I am not a hand, I do not belong to the body,' that would not make it any less a part of the body. And if the ear should say, 'Because I am not an eye, I do not belong to the body,' that would not make it any less a part of the body. If the whole body were an eye, where would be the hearing? If the whole body were an ear, where would be the sense of smell?" (1 Corinthians 12:15–17). Just as every member of the human body has its tasks that led towards the good of the whole, the same occurs in the social body. In the appropriate range of abilities given to man, no one can replace him. How imperfect is the most refined sense of touch in the blind with respect to the usefulness of sight.

With regards to the scope of its functioning, every member of the human body is irreplaceable. This irreplaceability is the source of all its majesty and dignity, even if it received no praise from anyone else. Thus, man does not willingly dispose of even the most crippled members of his own body.

---

1 Russian: "Out with the educated!"

The same goes for social life. Both the head—the leaders of society—and the social "legs and arms," all these various segments and "states and professions," all the degrees of service to one another cannot be permanently replaced by other segments of society, and cannot allow themselves to be removed without causing injury to the whole.

Naturally, the head must always remain the head. Woe to the leaders of society, for if they were to forget about their social dignity, they would renounce it and humble themselves to a level that is inappropriate to their destiny and vocation. A body cannot live without a head! When the leaders of society fail in their duties, the instinct of self-preservation forces the lower segments to look for a competent new head in the empty place where it had been. Social revolutions and upheavals bring an end to the government of the elites, which is a salt that has lost its taste; it is incapable of bringing flavor to the earth, an extinguished candle without a flicker of light.

The responsibility of various members in social life with respect to the whole results from their own destinies and aims. God gives everyone gifts depending on the aim which they serve. The brain is in neither the arm nor in the leg; as a leading member, the head must be the brain for everyone else. In practice, we see that only those endowed with all sorts of goods have the conditions that are necessary to shape social, national and political culture. Although we want the broadest possible segments of people—both agricultural laborers and industrial workers—to make full use of this abundance through education and a high level of moral and social life, we know that the hardship of life and labor will make this very difficult. Perhaps social progress and a more just organization of labor will allow all access to those goods but will not succeed in completely obliterating the natural differences resulting from the division of social tasks. Thus, the burden of responsibility for providing broad segments of society with healthy spiritual nourishment primarily rests on the leaders of society.

We also demand of the "head" that, having been elevated to this dominant position in the structure of the body by the Creator, it will maintain its friendly benevolence and complaisance, mindful of the fact that it owes its elevation to God and that all its members are subordinate to His will. In the physical body, legs carry the head, although the human mind directs their functions. However, we will not be far from truth when we say that in the social body society's "arms and legs" lead to the elevation of the leading classes, not only in the democratic system.

Although it does not constitute the entire body, the head's activity depends on its cooperation with other components of the social body; it should recognize the importance and compatibility of all its members. Then the spirit of reluctance will disappear, while distrust and arrogance, which so often characterize the attitudes of the leadership classes to those subordinated to them, will disappear. All hostility to manual labor and unhealthy shame of it will disappear, for we will remember well that all such labor is blessed and holy, and it is necessary for the preservation and development of human life.

"On the contrary, the parts of the body which seem to be weaker are indispensable" (1 Corinthians 12:22). God admonishes proud ages and proud civilizations, showing them how fragile are the feet of clay that support them if they were to lack arduous, every day, hard and humble human labor; the majestic palaces they have built would crumble, while their arable gardens would become filled with weeds and the arrogant would die of hunger in their offices and laboratories, which are so hermetically isolated from the world.

All members of the social body need one another.

"The eye cannot say to the hand, 'I have no need of you,' nor again the head to the feet, 'I have no need of you.' On the contrary, the parts of the body which seem to be weaker are indispensable" (1 Corinthians 12:21–22). St. Paul has encompassed the conclusion from the previous reflections on these words.

We know from the experience of great revolutions how the "eyes and head," those leading segments that are used to constantly making use of the services of others, are inept, as someday the social order will be disrupted, while they will be left to their own resourcefulness. They will then come to understand how little they appreciated the tremendous labor performed by thousands of people thanks to which they could live comfortably.

The working and agricultural classes also know how great material and spiritual poverty they suffer when no one is concerned about them; when no one organizes education, social welfare, well-organized and successful places of work for them; when they lack a good book or newspaper, benevolent and wise counsel, and moral or religious assistance.

Social life develops like a cell that does not only feed but must also nourish others. In this life, one cannot only take and make use of what is available. That which one has taken is obliging!

Social justice demands that when we take something from others, we should give something to them in return as well. If we take so much good, assistance, and so many fruits of solid human labor; when we make use of the great love that is expressed in the effects of this labor, we cannot pay for this bread with the stone of anger. We must pay with charity, the entire richness of one's own soul, a salt that has not lost its taste, and light before the world "that they may see your good works and give glory to your Father" (see Matthew 5:16).

The source of life-giving water flows from here. In order to reliably pay for the gifts we have received, we must multiply goods; we must be ready for constant moral and religious progress and solid spiritual efforts, so that the birds of heaven that will rest in the shadow of our soul find nourishment without betrayal in its mustard branches.

The new social system must be based not only on the exchange of material and economic values, but also on the exchange of spiritual values. To be moral and valuable is as much a social duty as to be a conscientious official, artisan, laborer, writer, or journalist. Only then is the service of the mutual exchange of goods possible in the social body.

All the members of society should anticipate one another in their mutual kindness and self-sacrifice.

In every physical body, there is a strange solidarity of experiencing joy and suffering along with every other member. The same goes for the human body. As St. Paul writes: "If one member suffers, all suffer together; if one member is honored, all rejoice together" (1 Corinthians 12:26). This is a strange mystery that seems to reveal the better element of man, who rejoices at the glory, honor and elevation of the sons of his nation but laments their downfall and suffering. At the same time, this is a great social truth. It attests to the existence of social bonds, a common nerve that binds people together; about the fact that man is a being that cannot be separated from his society.

353

The prosperity of one social group will not bring it peace if it is surrounded by the poverty of the proletarian reminder of society. Great wealth is never healthy when it is accumulated amidst unparalleled poverty. Greasy bread is not tasty when all its bites are counted by hungry eyes. The specter of upheavals, revolution and unrest in the street brings anxiety to those who have excessively confided in their own goods and have ceased to be concerned about their brethren.

St. Paul tells us of the more and less respected members of a society, describing their respect for one another in a strange way: "And those parts of the body which we think less honorable we invest with the greater honor, and our unpresentable parts are treated with greater modesty, which our more presentable parts do not require" (1 Corinthians 12:23–24).

Like the head, eyes, mouth and arms in the human body, those "presentable" members, need nothing. They receive praise on account of who they are. They do not require separate protection from society. They are protected by their social status, title, surname and estate. Meanwhile, the "unpresentable" members require greater respect, protection and defense. Leo XIII speaks of them in his encyclical *Rerum novarum:* "When there is question of defending the rights of individuals, the poor and badly off have a claim to especial consideration. The richer class have many ways of shielding themselves and stand less in need of help from the State; whereas the mass of the poor have no resources of their own to fall back upon, and must chiefly depend upon the assistance of the State" (RN, 37).

The theme of the apostle, who explains the concern the "presentable" should have for the "unpresentable," is worthy of attention: "But God has so adjusted the body, giving the greater honor to the inferior part, that there may be no discord in the body, but that the members may have the same care for one another" (1 Corinthians 12:24–25).

Indeed, when we exercise all our duties with respect to the working class, when we surround it with the care it deserves, when we feel spiritual community and Christian fraternity with it, there is no place for division; the social body knows not hatred, class struggle, envy, upheaval or revolution. Nearly every upheaval is a mute protest against abuses that have often accumulated for decades; they are an accusation against the living generation, which did not want to or could not recognize a common social body and the stigma of fraternity in other members of the common social body. Responsibility for the violent unrest committed by the hands of the proletariat usually falls on the leadership classes, which have ceased to have a sense of community with the least of their brethren.

* * *

"Now you are the body of Christ and individually members of it" (1 Corinthians 12:27).

The Christian community should be built on the strong fundaments of the natural law, with which the Creator has imbued human nature. In its heart, this community will recognize the right to exist of all its members, fulfilling the aims of their life in accordance with God's plan. This community will respect all the activities of its members, which are performed by their own profession and vocation, in accordance with the natural aim of the community and the ultimate aims of people. A spirit of kindness, cooperation, sacrifice and Christian love will dominate in the heart of this community.

Such a conception of community will unite within itself its citizens as the children of one Father, who make a common effort in their earthly life to enter the gates of "Holy Jerusalem."

"One body, one spirit" is the "national anthem" of the Christian community. "For no man ever hates his own flesh, but nourishes and cherishes it, as Christ does the church, because we are members of His body" (Ephesians 5:29–30).

11

The State-Professional
System of the Future

*"A brother helped is like a strong
city" (Proverbs 18:19).*

*"The rich and the poor meet together; the Lord
is the maker of them all" (Proverbs 22:2).*

I N THE EPISTLE TO THE ROMANS, ST. PAUL
gives the community of believers guidelines on what their relationships with one another should be like: "Love one another with
brotherly affection; outdo one another in showing honor. [...] Contribute to the needs of the saints [...]. Live in harmony with one
another [...]. Repay no one evil for evil but take thought for what
is noble in the sight of all. If possible, so far as it depends upon you,
live peaceably with all" (Romans 12:10–18).

These principles once governed human co-existence not only before
God and in prayer books and churches, but before all people: in all
of public life, in the everyday relationships that bind together people
in labor, and in the pursuit of bread and clothing. Only when minds
were conquered by the pagan philosophy, which liberated economic
life from God's moral dictates and commandments, a system that
divided people into mutually hostile camps appeared in the name
of economic freedom. This system rejected all community between
the rich and poor; rejected concern for the common good of society;
and renounced not only love, but also all the imperatives of justice.
Peace was replaced with class struggle, which was constantly stoked
by the exploitation of defenseless laborers.

Although the razor of social evil has become significantly blunted
in recent years, the principles of the current system nonetheless bear
harmful fruits not only in the economic sphere, but even in the field
of social morality. Thus, the Church, which is the guardian of consciences, points out those serious deficiencies. Her social encyclicals
contain a calm yet powerful criticism of this system. The Holy See

considers a reform of the current system to be indispensable; in fact, Pius XI's encyclical *Quadragesimo anno* is subtitled: "On Reconstruction of the Social Order."

Of what should this reconstruction consist? In its most general aspirations, it wants to:

1. Imbue social and economic institutions with the Christian spirit;

2. End harmful class struggle and replace it with benevolent cooperation in the spirit of respect, justice and love; and

3. Overcome the opposition between laborers and entrepreneurs "until this opposition has been abolished and well-ordered members of the social body — Industries and Professions — are constituted in which men may have their place, not according to the position each has in the labor market but according to the respective social functions which each performs" (QA, 83).

Thus speaks the highest teaching authority in the Church. Although it is not the most solemn form of the Church's teaching and is not dogmatic in nature, it is greatly important and summons us to faithfully instruct others about the Holy Father's concerns.

In what direction is the state-professional system, also known as the corporate system, headed?

The Holy See reminds us above all about the general moral principles on which the new socio-economic life is to be built. The task of the Church is not the construction of this system, but instead the pointing out of unvarying truths that are tied to the nature of the world and are God's revealed will.

As a moral body, society is the natural basis for the future system.

St. Paul's instruction to the faithful of the Roman Church: "Live in harmony with one another" (Romans 12:16) is easy to implement, because here we are supported by the natural laws that God has granted to human nature and the nature of society. They must be recalled and implemented to have a systemic framework for peaceful co-existence.

The first truth proclaims that man is a person, a social being. Although he has his own life's aims that are greater than any social aims, and although having been redeemed by Christ's blood, he is the only immortal being among God's creatures, man is not a sovereign being; he is not a god that is independent in his activity. On the contrary, he is tied to society, without which he cannot achieve or fully develop his personality or all his life's aims, both temporal and eternal. Therefore, man's entry into social life is necessary for it. It is through this entry into social life that man become prone to various limitations related to the legal system, social mores, professional life, etc. However, the cost of these limitations brings hundred-fold profit thanks to the riches he receives from social life in exchange for his submission.

The second truth is that the society which man enters is not a collection of individuals, but it is a moral and physical unity although it consists of many members, just like the human body. St. Paul says: "All the members of the body, though many, are one body" (1 Corinthians 12:12).

Man is bound to society through numerous groups, "members" that bind people together through a community of problems and goods. The Christian spirit that unites people through their own life's aims and purposes in the common aim of society, the common good, is expressed in this co-existence of natural social groups. "Love one another with brotherly affection; outdo one another in showing honor. [. . .] Contribute to the needs of the saints [. . .]. Live in harmony with one another" (Romans 12:10–16).

The third truth is that man lives as a person in social community conceived in this way; all the forms of social co-existence assist the preservation and flourishing of his personality. Man maintains his life's personal and ultimate aims, preserving personal rights and exercising them within the limitations imposed by the common good. Man maintains the right to private property, the choice of his profession and life's vocation, and the freedom of labor and economic initiative that are subjected to limitations only within the framework of the good of the community.

The fourth truth recalls the basic principle of social philosophy: "Just as it is gravely wrong to take from individuals what they can accomplish by their own initiative and industry and give it to the community, so also it is an injustice and at the same time a grave evil and disturbance of right order to assign to a greater and higher association what lesser and subordinate organizations can do. For every social activity ought of its very nature to furnish help to the members of the body social, and never destroy and absorb them" (QA, 79).

According to this social truth of Christian philosophy, we must bring back the once-elaborated, natural forms of community that bind together man and the state to create the conditions for the renewal of social life in this way. Thus, the error of seeing the social initiative of the citizen as hostile to freedom must disappear, as must that which has enslaved the human person by the herd-like state, which transfers everything that man could do himself to state officials. When the state will entrust lower-level communities with the execution of less important tasks and duties, it will itself regain the liberty of elaborating general principles and will gain natural helpers in the healthy reconstruction of the state. It will ensure that its citizens will be capable of developing their personality on their own.

Further construction of the new order, modeled after the construction of Christ's community, will take place on this natural social bedrock: "The whole body, joined and knit together by every joint with which it is supplied, when each part is working properly, makes bodily growth and upbuilds itself in love" (Ephesians 4:16).

The construction of the new system should be based on professional status.

In his encyclical on the question of the worker, Leo XIII opposed the errors of Marx's teaching on the supposedly inherent hostility between the rich and poor: "The great mistake made in regard to the matter now under consideration is to take up with the notion that class is naturally hostile to class, and that the wealthy and the working men are intended by nature to live in mutual conflict. So irrational and so false is this view that the direct contrary is the truth. Just as the symmetry of the human frame is the result of the suitable arrangement of the different parts of the body, so in a State is it ordained by nature that these two classes should dwell in harmony and agreement, so as to maintain the balance of the body politic. Each needs the other: capital cannot do without labor, nor labor without capital" (RN, 19).

Revealed wisdom confirms these words: "The rich and the poor meet together; the Lord is the maker of them all" (Proverbs 22:2). The Creator of human nature wanted people to strive for one another;

He wanted them to encounter one another in work so that a knot of community and love would appear between them.

It is undeniable that there are differences resulting from the physical and spiritual properties of every person as well as the social, economic, climatic and other factors conditioning human life. However, it is also true that there are similarities, beginning with the community of nature, the purpose of life, human aspirations, and the community of exercised labor and permanent or temporary interests. All this creates the basis for people coming together. One of the most important of these commonalities is the similarity or identity of the labor that is performed, which brings people together in a professional community, which is the most natural after the family community.

Labor brings people together, creating among them a similar form of life, existence and mores. People share a common subject and aim of work; the necessity to coordinate their efforts to create new goods; a sense of interdependency; mutual need for one another; and the everyday evidence of the importance of their harmonious cooperation: the visible fruit of their labor.

Love is revealed in this labor; without it, labor will not bear fruit. Every form of working together is the result of some form of love. Thanks to this, a very strong social bond is forged, one that is stronger than that of class because it binds people together in the name of a certain community, related to the profession one exercises. The sense of this community leads, in a completely natural way, to the appearance of a professional organizational bond that illuminates the good of the profession, which once again is greater than the so-called class interest.

All those that exercise a specific form of labor, be they independent farm owners, entrepreneurs, or dependent laborers at all levels, concentrate around the good of the profession. In this way, there develops a natural community of people concentrated around what most brings and binds them together and around their professional work, rather than around what divides.

We will use this natural community as the fundament for the new state-professional system.

Because, in addition to the good of the profession there is also the good of all of society, the professional man exercises his social in addition to professional significance: that of cooperation for the well-being and satiation of the entire society.

From this flow the duties of each profession, which coordinate its aims with social aims and the professional good with the common good.

The first duty is the adjustment of professional work to the needs of the entire society and the subordination of the interests of individuals to those of the whole. "Repay no one evil for evil but take thought for what is noble in the sight of all" (Romans 12:17). This is an invitation to draw the social conclusions from God's love. "And this commandment we have from Him, that he who loves God should love his brother also" (1 John 4:21). In this way, we reveal the spirit of being children of God, a spirit we have received from God Himself, who is the beginning and the end of our aspirations.

The second duty requires that we cooperate with all who are interested in the results of professional labor. This cooperation must encompass above all the laborers and entrepreneurs. In this way, rampant class differences that divide people in their common labor will be overcome; the greatest obstacle to unity will be removed. Struggle will end, and it will be replaced by cooperation for the common good of the profession. According to Pius XI, the most important task of the new system must consist of the overcoming of class struggle and the grounding of the compatible cooperation of the "professional states."

"If possible, so far as it depends upon you, live peaceably with all" (Romans 12:18).

The third and final duty of a profession is cooperation with the state, which must be concerned about the good of not only one profession, but of that of the entire society. According to Pius XI "the interests common to the whole Industry or Profession should hold first place in these guilds. The most important among these interests is to promote the cooperation in the highest degree of each industry and profession for the sake of the common good of the country" (QA, 85).

It is more than obvious that great worth and dignity, not only of the individual but also of all who exercise the profession in the construction of the new system, flow from these duties. "The rich and the poor meet together; the Lord is the maker of them all" (Proverbs 22:2). "A brother helped is like a strong city" (Proverbs 18:19).

The road to the professional state leads through professional unions.

A supremely unifying, Christian social sense is expressed in the words of the Book of Ecclesiastes: "Two are better than one, because they have a good reward for their toil. For if they fall, one will lift up his fellow; but woe to him who is alone when he falls and has not another to lift him up [. . .]. And though a man might prevail against one who is alone, two will withstand him" (Ecclesiastes 4:9–12).

Man's aspiration towards social co-existence is a healthy and natural symptom. The Church always defended the social co-existence of people. Leo XII writes: "For, to enter into a 'society' of this kind is the natural right of man; and the State has for its office to protect natural rights, not to destroy them" (RN, 51). The Church has extended her loving concern to all forms of social co-existence. Throughout the ages, she bore witness to this, organizing the faithful in associations, guilds, religious fraternities, parishes, dioceses, ecclesiastical provinces, nations and states. She also always esteemed the organized society more than she did people living alone.

Catholic social teaching has demanded that socio-economic life be based on professional unions. Beginning with the centuries-old practice of the Middle Ages, when this economic balance supported guilds, up to the present day the Church recommends the constant association of laborers, entrepreneurs and the agreement between them with to the aid of unions.

The professional unions of laborers and entrepreneurs will be a significant phase in the creation of a new system. Unions have their own aims: defending the common good that is appropriate to a given social class. Thus, there can and should appear distinct labor unions for the protection of the moral-religious, social, economic and political goods of the laborers. There can also appear distinct labor unions for those professions. Thanks to these unions, the needs of individual social groups will be met more perfectly.

However, these unions do not limit their aims to themselves. They should aim to "set before themselves the task of preparing the way, in conformity with the mind of Christian social teaching, for those larger and more important guilds, Industries and Professions, which We mentioned before, and make every possible effort to bring them to realization" (QA, 87). Why? It corresponds to the Christian spirit of social wisdom, which preaches the need for universal unification; it brings together all who can and should be brought together to achieve the good of the entire community. Trade unions that serve these overriding aims should be "composed of delegates from the two syndicates (that is, of workers and employers), respectively, of the same industry or profession, and, as true and proper organs and institutions of the State, they direct the syndicates and coordinate their activities in matters of common interest toward one and the same end" (QA, 93).

Here in particular, in the bosom of corporations, there should appear a reconciliation of particular interests. According to "interests common to the whole Industry or Profession should hold first place in these guilds. The most important among these interests is to promote the cooperation in the highest degree of each industry and profession for the sake of the common good of the country" (QA, 85).

In this way, the Church wants to achieve something greater than justice and social peace. "But the Church, with Jesus Christ as her Master and Guide, aims higher still. She lays down precepts yet more perfect, and tries to bind class to class in friendliness and good feeling" (RN, 21). The social system must become like a unified body (*corpus*) with different members, each corresponding to its own predetermined purpose, but all those members harmoniously cooperate for one aim in the highest order, towards a common society.

In this way, the socio-economic system will recall the Pauline vision of the Church, that Mystical Body of Christ the Lord "from whom the whole body, joined and knit together by every joint with which it is supplied, when each part is working properly, makes bodily growth and upbuilds itself in love" (Ephesians 4:16).

* * *

Let us gather our thoughts. What will be the aim of a community organized in the state-professional system? It must overcome disorder in economic life and base it on healthy principles of Christian morality; furthermore, it should limit free competition, which cannot be the guiding principle of economic life (see QA, 88); finally, it must overcome class struggle by grounding the harmonious cooperation of the professional states. Class struggle will be replaced with social justice, which will be supported and complemented by love.

Thanks to this, there will first be peace in the heart of every profession and in every area of economic life, as the life of the profession will attain good customs and principles of professional morality, ordered labor relations and general conditions for prosperity and economic progress. The common good will also result from economic good, for the "strong bond" for all the states and professions is the "common good, to achieve which all Industries and Professions together ought, each to the best of its ability, to cooperate amicably" (QA, 84).

This is the "blessed vision of peace" (*beata pacis visio*) which the holy Church desires for humanity, which is exhausted by class struggle, envy and hatred. Hope will flourish under her wings: "Love one another with brotherly affection [...]. Contribute to the needs of the saints [...]. Repay no one evil for evil but take thought for what is noble in the sight of all. If possible, so far as it depends upon you, live peaceably with all" (Romans 12:10–18).

12

The Basis of the Christian
Workers' Movement

*"A brother helped is like a
strong city..." (Proverbs 18:19).*

N HIS ENCYCLICAL ON COMMUNISM, PIUS XI
laments that Catholic societies are distrustful of the workers' movement and labor unions, which the Holy See so ardently supports.
He writes: "What is to be thought [...] of those Catholic industrialists who even to this day have shown themselves hostile to a labor
movement that We Ourselves recommended?" (DR, 50).

Certainly, there are people in Catholic milieus who have devoted
their entire lives and even their estates to organize the workers' movement. However, the broad masses of society have not expressed significant interest and have not supported Christian laborers.

The truth is that the workers' movement often followed erroneous
paths. This did not happen because the demands regarding the rights
of workers were incorrect, but rather because they were improperly
expressed. Because of the lack of benevolent and rational people, the
workers' movement has fallen into the hands of career-oriented party
leaders. However, such errors do not discredit the right to association.

The right to association flows from man's natural properties.

Everyday experience instructs us that man's own efforts are insufficient; only cooperation with other people and accepting their assistance creates a "great man" who can overcome all obstacles.

Such wisdom confirmed by practice finds its basis in the words
of Divine Revelation: "Two are better than one, because they have a
good reward for their toil. For if they fall, one will lift up his fellow;
but woe to him who is alone when he falls and has not another to
lift him up [...]. And though a man might prevail against one who
is alone, two will withstand him" (Ecclesiastes 4:9–12).

This human social need is expressed in the natural tendency
received from God; the right to association flows from it. According

to Leo XIII, by indulging in this inherent tendency man becomes a member of the state community; however, apart from this he would be glad to be tied to his fellow citizens by the bonds of yet another community (see RN, 50). Various social institutions, systems and associations have resulted from man's social nature, from an aspiration driven by the needs of man's nature.

The cooperation of people in various associations creates a knot of mutual assistance and aid that are presented under various circumstances. This leads to the creation of various communities without which man would be incapable of meeting life's goals. They include: the family, Church, nation and profession. However, in his striving towards his fellow man, man does not limit himself to the necessary bonds; he creates other societies that, while not formally necessary, are very useful and helpful in everyday life. Hence the richness of the forms of social co-existence.

Although private unions are not necessary for the development of man's personhood, only for the better implementation of all his life's tasks, man's right to create them is based on this same natural law. Likewise, no one can deprive man of this right, not even the state community, because by suppressing the social life of individual units, the state would act contrary to nature and would saw off the branches on which it rests.

Leo XIII also correctly teaches that the laws of human nature allow man to create associations, while the state is established for the defense of the laws of nature and not for their annihilation. If the state prohibited citizens from joining associations, then it would contradict itself, for both private unions and the state result from the same singular cause, i.e., the inherent need for social life (see RN, 49).

The right of workers to their own associations flows from this same source. Leo XIII believes that, under natural law, workers should create their own associations. There may appear circumstances under which the creation of such associations is necessary, which the laborers should join to defend their economic interests, especially considering the existence of many anti-religious organizations. If, therefore, religion is prone to threats on the part of workers' organizations, Catholics should create their own associations and unite in this aim so that they can resist crushing and intolerable oppression (see RN, 54).

All those who bring together all sorts of craftsmen in various associations, supporting them with counsel and deed, thus providing them with honest and beneficial labor (see RN, 55) have the blessing of the Holy See.

Associations have the right to freedom in internal organizational life within the limits of the common good. Leo XIII goes on to say that the state should look after workers' associations based on the truth, but they should not infringe on their internal affairs, for life flows from internal sources and easily dies under the influence of outside sources. Thus, the internal freedom of associations should be secured, for it results from the same natural law from which it draws the aspiration towards social life in every person.

The aim of association is the harmonious cooperation of people for the common good.

The following instruction from the Book of Proverbs is the supreme wisdom of the association movement: "The rich and the poor meet together; the Lord is the maker of them all" (Proverbs 22:2). The Creator of human nature wanted people to seek out one another; He wanted them to encounter one another in work so that a knot of community and love would appear between them.

There are no internal contradictions between people, as if "the wealthy and the working men are intended by nature to live in mutual conflict." In fact, the complete opposite is true: "So irrational and so false is this view that the direct contrary is the truth. Just as the symmetry of the human frame is the result of the suitable arrangement of the different parts of the body, so in a State is it ordained by nature that these two classes should dwell in harmony and agreement, so as to maintain the balance of the body politic. Each needs the other: capital cannot do without labor, nor labor without capital" (RN, 19).

Thus, the aim of Catholic organizational efforts is not the division and juxtaposition of classes or their preparation for warfare, but rather unification in the common search for means of co-existence and cooperation in order to resolve the difficulties of social life. By joining professional associations, employers and laborers should bring the two worlds closer together and aid one another.

Having defended the right to association, the Church always opposed all social dispersion. Throughout her history, she provided an example of the social sense, unifying all the faithful in associations, religious fraternities, medieval guilds, religious provinces and nations. She also always esteemed the organized society more than she did people living alone. This same desire is evident in economic life, and the path to the new system passes across state-professional unions.

Leo XIII devoted a large part of his encyclical *Rerum novarum* to reflections on the aims of workers' association and gives them primacy in meeting all needs. "Such unions should be suited to the requirements of this our age — an age of wider education, of different habits, and of far more numerous requirements in daily life. It is gratifying to know that there are actually in existence not a few associations of this nature, consisting either of workmen alone, or of workmen and employers together, but it were greatly to be desired that they should become more numerous and more efficient" (RN, 49).

In his evaluation of the social legacy of the forty years that had passed since the publication of *Rerum novarum*, Pius XI expresses his joy that Leo XIII's teaching has succeeded in overcoming opposition and resolving doubts concerning labor unions; the pope is also satisfied that Christian workers have succeeded in creating professional organizations, thanks to which many people have not strayed from the path of Catholic law and morality (see QA, 33).

At the same time, the pope laments the fact that the associations of employers and the directors of economic life that Leo XIII had ardently recommended are few in number: "There is, however, strong hope that these obstacles also will be removed soon, and even now We greet with the deepest joy of Our soul, certain by no means insignificant attempts in this direction, the rich fruits of which promise a still richer harvest in the future" (QA, 38).

The aim is for the "rich and poor" to meet one another before the face of the Father, the Creator, in order to recognize within themselves the brotherhood of blood. Thus, the will to seek out one's neighbor should be perfected in this way.

The Church presents three aims to labor unions.

The first aim is religious and moral.

The present disorder in human co-existence is in part caused by moral factors. In order to oppose evil, religious-moral resources must be applied. Thus, labor unions will have in mind not only professional, but also religious-moral tasks. Leo XIII considers the growth of religiosity and good mores to be the most important tasks of these associations. This would therefore result from the fact that unions should be religious in nature, or they should at least be grounded in Christian ethics. "Otherwise they would lose wholly their special character, and end by becoming little better than those societies which take no account whatever of religion" (RN, 57).

Hence, Leo XIII's completely understandable guidelines: "Let our associations, then,

look first and before all things to God; let religious instruction have therein the foremost place, each one being carefully taught what is his duty to God, what he has to believe, what to hope for, and how he is to work out his salvation; and let all be warned and strengthened with special care against wrong principles and false teaching. Let the working man be urged and led to the worship of God, to the earnest practice of religion, and, among other things, to the keeping holy of Sundays and holy days. Let him learn to reverence and love holy Church, the common Mother of us all; and hence to obey the precepts of the Church, and to frequent the sacraments, since they are the means ordained by God for obtaining forgiveness of sin and fox leading a holy life" (*ibid.*).

People brought up in workers' organizations will embody Christian justice towards both God and their neighbors. "The foundations of the organization being thus laid in religion, We next proceed to make clear the relations of the members one to another, in order that they may live together in concord and go forward prosperously and with good results" (RN, 58).

Also momentous are the cultural and social tasks of workers' unions.

Through an organized social movement, the social and moral condition of those in the association can be achieved. Man becomes uplifted and filled with hope; this is the means for rescue! Hopelessness leads to passivity and the downfall of the spirit, to becoming subjected to the worst influences. People became influenced by revolutionaries not because they were evil, but because nobody ever thought about them honestly and never became concerned about their material well-being and the health of their spirit. The lack of Catholic workers' organizations caused people to join godless unions. The appearance of Catholic unions protects the religious life of workers from negative influences and at the same time allows them to fight for the rights they deserve.

Leo XIII's teachings "encouraged Christian workers to found mutual associations according to their various occupations [and] taught them how to do so" (QA, 31).

Workers' associations succeeded in gaining the right to exist, which "resolutely confirmed in the path of duty a goodly number of those whom socialist organizations strongly attracted by claiming to be the sole defenders and champions of the lowly and oppressed" (*ibid.*). This was a great victory. Its fruit was that "associations of this kind have molded truly Christian workers who, in combining harmoniously the diligent practice of their occupation with the salutary precepts of religion, protect effectively and resolutely their own temporal interests and rights, keeping a due respect for justice and a genuine desire to work together with other classes of society for the Christian renewal of all social life" (QA, 33).

Workers influenced by class-focused organizations formed in the spirit of war against society begin to lose their solely militant nature and become ready for cooperation, becoming capable of independently fulfilling some of the functions that had previously been exercised by public authorities.

This is a highly desirable change and corresponds to the expectations of the Holy See. Pius XI writes: "The supreme authority of the State ought, therefore, to let subordinate groups handle matters and concerns of lesser importance, which would otherwise dissipate its efforts greatly" (QA, 80).

The working classes, which are influenced by organizations, become a creative factor of civic life. They can be entrusted with social functions that require the spirit of community rather than that of class struggle; the spirit of service and not of power; and the spirit of love and not struggle.

Social change in this direction is necessary. Public authorities are increasingly inclined to hand over some functions to professional organizations, especially with regards to the agreement of employees and employers; they are willing to endow them with a public-legal character. Thanks to them, the meaning of these organizations will be elevated, which will gradually pave the way for a new system. Employers will return to their appropriate duties and their own role in society, which they had hitherto opposed.

Finally, there are the tasks of labor unions in the economic sphere.

They are numerous, and they are difficult. Here, the Christian exchange of services in the spirit of the guidelines of the Book of Proverbs should occur: "The rich and the poor meet together; the Lord is the maker of them all" (Proverbs 22:2).

Professional joint organizations should deal with the topics of social welfare and self-help as well as concern that the workers will never lack employment and that they may make use of the aid of associations during moments of economic crisis and stagnation, illness, misfortune and old age.

All differences of opinion in economic life should be adjudicated not only through political factors, but rather through social ones, through those who are concerned. Conflicts between workers and employers should be entrusted to join teams.

We must always have in mind the spirit of fraternal cooperation and collaboration. All the circumstances of everyday life should be utilized to hone this spirit.

* * *

These several reflections indicate that the spirit of the workers' movement is Christian, for the spirit of the Gospels is the spirit of community and unification. Christ the Lord has given us a model of unification in His Church, which is a living example for all forms of human co-existence.

In God's spirit, numerous earthly matters become one through fraternal love. Through Christ, "the whole body, joined and knit together by every joint with which it is supplied, when each part is working properly, makes bodily growth and upbuilds itself in love" (Ephesians 4:16).

Thus, the notion of uniting people in accordance with their natural needs is essentially Christian. The Church equally venerates the natural law and God's law; therefore, she wants human life to simultaneously follow both these laws. The Church cannot be indifferent to the human need for seeking associations.

Thus, that which is Christian in human social needs should be recognized, and we should extend a human hand to people so that they may rise to the level of social co-existence in the spirit of brotherhood and love.

13

The Word of God at the Threshold of a New Political System

"There are varieties of gifts, but the same Spirit; and there are varieties of service, but the same Lord; and there are varieties of working, but it is the same God who inspires them all in everyone" (1 Corinthians 12:4–6).

THE FEVERISH DESIRE FOR CHANGE HAS brought the world many painful experiences; we were witnesses to the appearance and downfall of bold programs, intentions and aspirations. Many of them are now dead and buried. How brief were their lives! The more zealous the desire for change, the more rapidly new programs appeared, and the faster they dissipated.

Was this not the cause of their failure, that the world and man were cleansed only externally, "the outside of the cup and of the dish" (Luke 11:39)? Meanwhile, a "new man" with an old heart was created inside. This old man has brought all the sins of his previous life to this new life: "For from within, out of the heart of man, come evil thoughts, fornication, theft, murder, adultery, coveting, wickedness, deceit, licentiousness, envy, slander, pride, foolishness. All these evil things come from within, and they defile a man" (Mark 7:21–23).

With this inherited burden, is there too little strength to demolish the most wondrous plans to level the construction of the future? Yet "the kingdom of God is in the midst of you" (Luke 17:21). The "fruit of the Spirit" is born in man's heart: "love, joy, peace, patience, kindness, goodness, faithfulness, gentleness, self-control; against such there is no law" (Galatians 5:22–23).

It is not difficult to write a program. But how difficult it is to prepare man for it! The closer this program is to the truth, the deeper this task reaches. It requires much time as well as the thorough and comprehensive efforts of the most diverse factors that shape human life.

The participation of the Church cannot be absent from such efforts. Although "My kingship is not of this world" (John 18:36), and the Church's aims are profoundly spiritual, the Gospels contain all the factors that are necessary to solve all contemporary social problems. The Church cannot lose sight of what is happening in socio-economic life.

The Church wants to fully express human life, and so she wants to direct all social mechanisms towards the glory of God to facilitate man's fulfillment of his destiny.

The Church does not believe that passing social orders are irreplaceable. The encyclical *Quadragesimo anno* speaks of the "reconstruction of the social order" in a state-professional spirit. Here, the Church sees its own task, which no one else can fulfill. Because the basic condition for effective change is the transformation of the human heart, the Church exercises a three-fold task by shaping the new man through her teaching, education and practical activity.

Through the entirety of her teachings, the Church fulfills the most perfect task. Catholic theology makes us believe in God the Omniscient Father, who is the Creator of not only the heavens, but also of earth. Just as the entirety of creation comes from the creative hands of the one God, likewise all the Catholic truths have come from His one mind; they encompass the entire man, whom they provide with the entirety of God. Christ has taken everything from the Father and given it to man. This is why the treasury of Church teachings contains no useless truths; to varying degrees, all of them grow like a mustard seed into a tree from which the birds in the heavens will gain strength and nourishment for the spirit and body. All Church teachings come together in a strange construction whose mortar is natural truths on whose fundament the lofty, radiant, luminous Revelation is based.

We see a beautiful model of harmony and unity between creation and its Creator in the fact that "from the greatness and beauty of created things comes a corresponding perception of their Creator" (Wisdom 13:5) and therefore "all men who were ignorant of God were foolish by nature; and they were unable from the good things that are seen to know Him who exists" (Wisdom 13:1). Thus, all truths bring us to those heights where man attains his complete unity with

God; all these dogmatic truths are of indispensable significance to moral life, which makes them useful to the most secular and worldly relationships of human life.

Church teachings contain numerous truths whose social usefulness is especially important; their social magnitude results from the fact that they are so strongly framed in God's truth. Here are several of them.

I. Catholic Teaching About Man

Why? Because in the future system of the world, man must be in second place after God. Unfortunately, the experience of recent decades demonstrates that man and his rights were only a slogan, while in practice man was subordinated to the complete slavery of objects. Have not objects, such as wealth, money, production, labor, race, the nation or the state, stood at the center of these socio-economic systems? And where is man? Man became a means to an end, a tool, a shapeless mass from which new pyramids of pride were built.

Almost all contemporary totalitarian systems strove for the rejection of man's personal rights. "Man? That sounds suspicious," they said. Man had no rights, aims or values; instead, he received everything from the grace of the state. Man's individuality was sacrificed for the sake of the collective.

These states have elevated old idols to the altars; with them, they have replaced God's place in man's life. Everything that had previously served man as a means to achieve his aim became the aim itself, requiring that things be venerated like gods and that people be sacrificed for them. We have seen how easily man, his life, and his most precious gifts have been sacrificed for those purposes. There are countless examples from the recent past attesting to this.

The contemporary world needs to be reminded of who man is. In his dignity and majesty, should he not be the subject of the greatest admiration? "O Lord, our Lord [. . .]. What is man? [. . .] Thou didst make him for a little while lower than the angels, thou hast crowned him with glory and honor, Thou hast given him dominion over the works of thy hands; thou hast put all things under his feet, all sheep and oxen, and also the beasts of the field, the birds of the air, and the fish of the sea" (Psalm 8:1–8).

Only man, slightly "lower than the angels," has been elevated to this great majesty by God. Apart from angels, only man is immortal, while the most powerful works of God's and man's hands are subject to death. Only man is created in the image and likeness of God. Only man has become the subject of redemption; God has loved only man; Jesus Christ has redeemed only man.

These truths cannot be forgotten while building a social system; every system that ignores it will contradict the deepest reasons for man's existence on earth. Important guidelines follow from these truths.

The certainty that man has his own aims to achieve results from this, as does the certainty that he is personally destined to be united with God in the perfect natural and supernatural order.

This aim must be considered the starting point for building any social system. The state cannot impose upon the individual an aim that contradicts man's own destiny, nor can it organize collective life in a way that would prevent man from achieving his own purpose. On the contrary, all earthly aims should be harmonized with this highest, ultimate aim. The entire social system must bear man in mind; it must care for his personality and provide him with the means that are necessary for this.

In this way, awareness of man's great dignity will be born, irrespective of the rights given to it by any community: "You were bought with a price. So glorify God in your body" (1 Corinthians 6:20).

II. Teaching on Social Bonds

By defending human dignity, the Church simultaneously gives man a lesson in humanity. However great the destiny of man may be, he would be incapable of achieving all his aims and of developing the fullness of his personality without the aid of the many communities in which he must live due to his social nature.

In His last prayer, Christ the Lord asked His Father for a great gift for people: "That they may all be one; even as thou, Father, art in Me, and I in Thee" (John 17:21).

God is the Creator of both the individual and of society; He has created man in such a way that he is a social being incapable of living apart from society, both in the natural order and in that of grace.

Christ the Lord has created Christian love to guard this unity: "A new commandment I give to you, that you love one another" (John 13:34). Christ's chosen apostle will elaborate on this commandment: "Love one another with brotherly affection; outdo one another in showing honor. [. . .] Live in harmony with one another" (Romans 12:10, 16).

The Church proposes love as the cornerstone for all social construction, social bonds, and unity; she teaches it through the one supernatural social bond that unites people into one supernatural body whose head she is.

This is the source of the social accomplishments of the Church: all relationships between people are built on the basis of supernatural ties. No bond is stronger than that which bonds those living in grace with the Church, neither that of external obligation nor that resulting from man's voluntary decision. This happens in the spirit of Christ's parable: "I am the vine, you are the branches" (John 15:5). A supernatural bond results from this relationship: "Now you are the body of Christ and individually members of it" (1 Corinthians 12:27).

The supernatural community in which man lives and is brought up by the Church is a model for any other community. St. Paul beautifully explains this, using the example of the unity of the human body: "For just as the body is one and has many members, and all the members of the body, though many, are one body, so it is with Christ. For by one Spirit we were all baptized into one body — Jews or Greeks, slaves or free — and all were made to drink of one Spirit" (1 Corinthians 12:12–13).

The Church of the believers creates one Mystical Body. Thus, it is unsurprising that it must be animated by mutual love: "For no man ever hates his own flesh, but nourishes and cherishes it, as Christ does the church, because we are members of His body" (Ephesians 5:29–30).

Where else can we better understand the commandment: "You shall love your neighbor as yourself" (Matthew 22:39) as in one's own soul filled with the one God, and one's own body, which is the dwelling of this Holy Spirit? What can bind man more closely to his fellow man, family, profession, fatherland or state if not the truth that "we are members of His body"?

Catholics brought up in the spirit of this truth are the best material for the construction of an earthly community. Thanks to the example of the supernatural community in which they live, they have learned the sociological truth that collective life necessitates a multiplicity of members, "for the body does not consist of one member but of many" (1 Corinthians 12:14).

This must also be so in the new social system, in the state-professional system whose internal strength is grounded in the loving mutual recognition of one another's laws, duties and spiritual usefulness: "The eye cannot say to the hand, 'I have no need of you,' nor again the head to the feet, 'I have no need of you'" (1 Corinthians 12:21).

No group that becomes a part of this social body can achieve its aims or demands without mutual assistance. These truths were rejected by liberalism, capitalism, socialism and communism, which are deaf to the conception of society as a moral organism. When this bore bitter fruits, there were attempts to replace the lack of internal coherence with a system of police coercion.

The mutual concern of social segments and groups for one another should result from this natural relationship: "That the members may have the same care for one another" (1 Corinthians 12:25). No state or profession can flourish without the aid of another. Recent experiences have taught us that we must say the same about nations and states about whose absolute sovereignty we cannot speak today. This is the rationale of the Christian community, which is the spirit of corporatism.

III. The Teaching on the Value of Goods

Capitalism has rejected the Gospel principle: "For what will it profit a man, if he gains the whole world and forfeits his life?" (Matthew 16:26). Instead, its slogan is Satan's temptation: "If you are the Son of God, command these stones to become loaves of bread" (Matthew 4:3). Capitalist morality has established new principles of evaluating people, depending on their material goods, skills and purely economic potential. Meanwhile, many who have cursed and struggled against capitalism have fallen to its errors.

The only principle of dividing people that socialism has found is the materialist principle; it has divided people into the bourgeoisie and proletariat according to the size of their material possessions. Communism, meanwhile, has evaluated man's worth using the measure of production capacities; the new communist "saint" is the Udarnik, the hero of labor.

This is a vicious circle in which both the exploiters and the exploited circulate to the rhythm of the same frenzied errors.

We must bring back Christ's law: "You cannot serve God and mammon. [. . .] Is not life more than food, and the body more than clothing?" (Matthew 6:24, 26). We must also bring back the belief that man's worth depends above all on his moral value, and all his rights in society must be measured by his morality, which must have primacy in the new system. Meanwhile, material goods must be subordinated to moral goods and must serve them. We must reject the principle of profit as the measure of people that is so common today; evaluating people by how much money they make, to what category their salary belongs, and what tax bracket they are in are the pagan measures of the new elite.[1]

* * *

"In the beginning was the Word [. . .]. All things were made through Him" (John 1:1, 3). God has acted in all His matters through the Word. He sent the Word to the earth so that it would become the Body and Wisdom of the world. Thus, the Word of God, sound teaching and thinking from which God's activity may be spurred, should be at the basis of every work.

Christ the Lord has taken the Word of God from His Father and given it to man: "I have given them the words which Thou gavest me, and they have received them" (John 17:8). All who accept the Word of God receive great strength so that they may "become children of God" (John 1:12).

Today, God's Word, strength and sons are necessary for the reconstruction of the world. May God's Word preached by the Church, then, aid His mystical body and life of the faithful.

---

1 At this point, the manuscript ends. The remaining blank space on the page allows us to infer that the author intended to elaborate his thoughts.

14

Catholic Education and the New Social Order

I N THE ETERNAL CONFLICT BETWEEN THE "new" and the "old," the Church is like "a householder who brings out of his treasure what is new and what is old" (Matthew 13:52). The Church has a strange talent: she never completely renounces that which has passed, nor does she close herself off from that which is approaching. The Church has a great gift for reconciling the old and the new; she is traditional in this way. How does she do this? By making the old new! She constantly renews the face of the earth. Through the mouths of thousands of priests, each day the Church brings prayers to the feet of the altars "to God my exceeding joy" (Psalm 43:4).

The Church gratefully recalls Christ the Lord's didactic advice: "And no one puts a piece of unshrunk cloth on an old garment, for the patch tears away from the garment, and a worse tear is made. Neither is new wine put into old wineskins; if it is, the skins burst, and the wine is spilled, and the skins are destroyed; but new wine is put into fresh wineskins, and so both are preserved" (Matthew 9:16–17).

The same goes for all the changes to the world. The entire world is filled with reformist aspirations. Some alter national borders, while others abolish old systems, introduce new constitutions and change legislation, but the old man remains.

Will the old man succeed in keeping within himself the blessings of the new system? A change of the system without a change of man will not bring the desired fruits. Thus, it is imperative to introduce a transformed man into the new system; to pour young wine into new wineskins.

The Church does not limit herself to preaching the Word of God. In fact, she implements it in the lives of people, preparing them for new tasks that each new generation is faced with. She becomes like the householder who "brings out of his treasure what is new and what is old" from the Gospels; she always knows how to properly bring man up. In the eternally living Church, new life and new citizens of God's state are born in the old world. In today's changes, the Church can play a significant role.

Moral transformation must be the basis of every reform of the social system.

Pius XI insisted on this in *Quadragesimo anno*: "Yet, if we look into the matter more carefully and more thoroughly, we shall clearly perceive that, preceding this ardently desired social restoration, there must be a renewal of the Christian spirit, from which so many immersed in economic life have, far and wide, unhappily fallen away, lest all our efforts be wasted and our house be built not on a rock but on shifting sand" (see Matthew 7:24) (QA, 127). The kingdom of God will come from the heart. The Christian state cannot be built without a Christian people.

There is a strict interdependency between the reform of mores, consciences and human hearts and economic orders. Leo XIII writes: "Christian morality, when adequately and completely practiced, leads of itself to temporal prosperity, for it merits the blessing of that God who is the source of all blessings; it powerfully restrains the greed of possession and the thirst for pleasure, twin plagues which too often make a man who is void of self-restraint miserable in the midst of abundance (see 1 Timothy 6:10); it makes men supply for the lack of means through economy, teaching them to be content with frugal living, and further, keeping them out of the reach of those vices which devour not small incomes merely, but large fortunes, and dissipate many a goodly inheritance" (RN, 28).

The following brief quotation from the Book of Proverbs is rich in great wisdom: "Better is a little with righteousness than great revenues with injustice" (Proverbs 16:8), for goods that are acquired in an honest way also lead to the acquisition of virtues; this is why fortunes that are dishonestly acquired collapse so quickly, because there is a lack of the moral virtues that are necessary to utilize them properly. A healthy economy must be irrevocably married to ethics. When brought into the new system, the immoral man thwarts the best laws and wisest systems and social institutions, as he will always follow his own inclinations in his new home.

The Church shapes a social disposition in the soul.

This is the second fundamental instruction, the second important task of education: "Let each of you look not only to his own interests, but also to the interests of others" (Philippians 2:4).

This is a logical consequence of the two-fold nature of man, which is simultaneously individual and social; this two-fold nature requires the need to perfect oneself and to broaden one's own soul.

As an individual, man has his own personal aims: he lives for the glory of God and the salvation of his soul. The angelic hymn of *Gloria in excelsis Deo* should always resound in that soul, while concern for God's glory must transcend that soul so that it may gain the praise of the world for God. We have heard the following command from God Himself: "You shall be holy; for I the Lord your God am holy" (Leviticus 19:2). This is a commandment to subordinate one's thinking to God in an act of faith; temper one's will and harmonize it with God's law; order one's emotions and passions; get rid of selfishness; and develop the virtue of love for one's neighbors and many others within one's soul.

As a social being, man receives God's instruction: "Bear one another's burdens, and so fulfill the law of Christ" (Galatians 6:2). This instruction contains the truth that man needs society for his personhood to fully flourish; only then will he possess the "fullness of God's law," as he will be supported by others and will support others in fulfilling his life's aims. Furthermore, as a being living in a social environment, man socializes with others and has a good or bad impact on them, sometimes even against his will. Thus, man is not merely a private being; his life, attributes, values, virtues, or addictions cannot separate him from his surroundings by an impenetrable wall. Everything will constitute not only his personal, but also his social property.

Numerous religious obligations that are profoundly social in nature result from this, especially the obligation of solidarity in the multiplication of good.

Man stands before his neighbor's eyes in a new light, as the second most important incentive for internal improvement, after God's love. The more spiritual values we have accumulated in our soul and the more virtues we have acquired, the better our influence on our surroundings will be. Here, the obligations towards "exchangeable justice" comes into place. Whenever our hearts experience kind deeds, we receive good examples and beautiful incentives to do good. All this is obliging; these are debts of gratitude that are constantly incurred.

Furthermore, we have received the social commandment to improve ourselves from Christ the Lord: "Let your light so shine before men, that they may see your good works and give glory to your Father who is in heaven" (Matthew 5:16). Here, the Lord Jesus has brought together two aims of our life: not only should we perform good deeds, but these personal deeds should have a social impact; they should be an example for the world and an incentive for imitation; they should multiply the glory of the good God, who gave the people the means so that they have the "power to become children of God" (John 1:12). This is the social resonance of good deeds, which debunks the myth that religion and personal morality are merely private affairs.

Man, who has been called to these tasks, must open himself to personal spiritual progress and the will to transform society by intensifying his personal values. This noble ambition to lift oneself up and elevate everyone and everything around oneself is at the very heart of Catholic action. Passive complaining about the rotten world will give way to a masculine attitude and a decisive willingness to destroy evil in its embryonic stage, at its source: in one's own heart. This will is even more masculine and social because it is essentially Christian. The second myth, that man must be like a wolf to his fellow man, will also be debunked when the world will see that the true Christian will sacrifice his soul for his brothers and sanctify his strongest attachments and affections to save people.

The most urgent task of education today is the social predisposition of man in the future system.

Indeed, the entire Christian moral order is opposed to this individualism, to the myth that morality is a private matter. Moral individualism kills the family; breaks down the indissolubility of marriage; ruins the socio-economic order; and slays professional morality, using man's supposed right to unlimited personal happiness and unhampered freedom to live as he wants.

This selfish, essentially anti-social attitude of contemporary man, "the man of the social age," infinitely multiplies sin, which opposes not only God, but also the social order He has grounded in the natural law. This is why sin is extreme individualism, for it is the cutting off all ties to God, people and the entire world, both living and dead; it is the violation of all laws that have been grounded by God, eternal laws that turn all of creation towards the Father and Creator of everything. It is unsurprising that the Lord Jesus considered the sinner to be a person who broke off all his ties to his community, just as the prodigal son broke ties with his father's household, and the lost sheep separated from its shepherd and herd. The pride of sin predisposes man to be hostile towards society: "I am not like other men" (Luke 18:11). Hence the divisions and constant wars. This disposition should be opposed by new social education.

The Church possesses moral truths whose educational value is exceptional.

The Church in particular supports education in the spirit of Catholic professional ethics, as this is the area of the greatest sins. The Christianization of man's soul has been too superficial; he is religious only in the church and only on holidays. Yet in the factory, workshop, store, chancellery or office, he continues to be a pagan who worships the principle of separating economics from ethics in his professional work.

Yet Christ cautions against this duality of conscience: "Beware of practicing your piety before men in order to be seen by them; for then you will have no reward from your Father who is in heaven" (Matthew 6:1). God must be in everything. "So, whether you eat or drink, or whatever you do, do all to the glory of God" (1 Corinthians 10:31). There is no honorable labor that would be free of God's anointing, moral duties and purposefulness.

Thus, profit, the idol of contemporary professional work, must disappear as the leading motivation and aim of economic activity. Such a motivation demoralizes human life, fills the heart with greed, overthrows the social order, and replaces honest work that feeds one's neighbors with the selfish chase after wealth.

To defeat this spirit of profit, the morality of professional life must be elevated; it must be permeated with the spirit of social service, enriched by Christian virtues, justice and love as well as the spirit of honesty and kindness, generosity, empathy and diligence, all virtues without which one cannot speak of an effective reconstruction of society.

The view of labor must be fundamentally changed. Labor can no longer be treated as an inevitable burden; it cannot be treated as equal to merchandise. Due to the factor of humanity, labor is an obligation. The working man manifests his social spirit when he is educated and edified through his labor, attaining personal perfection and seeing his value; he cooperates with Providence in the effort to feed humanity and cooperates with other people in the shaping of an internal spirit of solidarity. Labor conceived in such a way will appear to human eyes as the greatest human kindness, as the knot that binds people together with a spirit of practical love and the meek understanding of one another's interdependency. Here, the pride of rebellion against others ("I will not serve") disappears, because man begins to understand that we constantly make use of the aid of others.

The Church provides social education in the ecclesiastical community.

The Church's great merit is that she unites separated people through the material level of her existence. The complete unification of people solely through socio-economic bonds, even through shared professional work, is not completely possible, for this labor will focus on material goods; such is the nature of worldly and material goods that although they tend to divide people, the more we devote our hearts to them.

To unite people, stronger bonds are necessary; they must be united around the following Gospel truth, which is both spiritually and economically significant: "But seek first His kingdom and His righteousness, and all these things shall be yours as well" (Matthew 6:33). The common search for God's Kingdom, submitting oneself to Him and the service of spiritual goods unites people so closely that it binds together and ennobles them; thus, all other endeavors become more harmonious and fruitful, while people are united by not only love for God, but also love for man as well as by all hardships undertaken in the name of love.

Thanks to Christ, "the company of those who believed were of one heart and soul" (Acts 4:32). The same happens on the Sabbath day, which separates people from their workplaces and gathers them in the church of the heavenly Father we all share. As long as the Christian custom of the Lord's Day is preserved, despite being so frequently opposed today, the spiritual community of the faithful will be capable of quick renewal. The Church's treasury contains rich means for the unification of people who are otherwise divided and foreign to one another.

This is the Church's liturgy of the Mass. To this day, this bloodless sacrifice is offered up by the hands of the priest in the name of the entire Christian community; his hands raise up the entire community of believers in the Host. The Host is Christ's sacrifice, while the priest's hands, which are raised up, are held up by the intention of human hearts towards the Father, just as Moses' hands had once been elevated by Aaron's and Hur's arms (see Exodus 17:12). The Church is right in demanding that the faithful participate in the Mass more vigorously and actively, that they may be "in accord with Christ Jesus," so that "together [they] may with one voice glorify the God and Father of our Lord Jesus Christ" (Romans 15:5–6), that they may pray with the words with which the priest prays to God the Father in the name of the multitudes of believers. This community of human hearts and minds, forged through a shared sacrifice, becomes an even closer bond through our Lord Jesus Christ, who faithfully fulfills His joyous promise of "For where two or three are gathered in my name, there am I in the midst of them" (Matthew 18:20) in the sacrifice of the Mass. Here, we become one body; we are permeated and invigorated by one Spirit, while social prayer thwarts all forms of individualism, class hypertrophy and hostile divisions caused by matter; there is no longer a division into the bourgeoisie and proletariat or into employers and laborers, but we are all invigorated by one Spirit, "the same God who inspires them all in everyone" (1 Corinthians 12:6).

The culmination of this unification is the Eucharistic Feast, where Christ exercises a means of social equality that cannot be achieved anywhere else, containing the mystery of eternal life for all. "Because there is one bread, we who are many are one body, for we all partake of the one bread" (1 Corinthians 10:17).

Indeed, I say to all you who have been separated by life and its contradictory interests, which have separated factories and works and compartmentalized organizations and systems: "you are the body of Christ and individually members of it" (1 Corinthians 12:27).

That which has been initiated by the Church's sacramental life continues to be developed in her external organization, parish life, where people perform diverse forms of labor, while the people of different estates and professions become aware of the socio-religious bond that ties them together. The parish is God's municipality, a supernatural body whose strength results not from external coercion but from the completely free will to co-exist with our brothers in Christ.

We have come from the Father's hands, and we strive for the same God through His world. Can a world that is so well-organized divide us? On the contrary, the Catholicity of collective life is its only unity. The greatest ideal of the world's new social system is that "we are to grow up in every way into him who is the head, into Christ, from whom the whole body, joined and knit together by every joint with which it is supplied, when each part is working properly, makes bodily growth and upbuilds itself in love" (Ephesians 4:15–16).

15

The Christian State and Social Life

F ROM THE ENTIRETY OF THE SOCIAL
thought of the Church, we see that she gives the state a significant role in social life. Whenever this is discussed, it leads to
commotion among people who have suffered greatly at the hands of
the contemporary state and whose souls are hostile to everything that
is associated with any state.

Indisputably, the contemporary state has overstepped its powers
all too often, which its citizens have painfully experienced. Everyone
knows that there were many abuses of authority that often violated
the natural law itself. However, the mere abuse of power cannot
deprive the state of its essential powers.

It should be emphasized at the start that Catholic teaching understands state authority not as this or that form of government in this or
that nation, but in whatever form, as a divinely sanctioned necessity
under the natural law (see QA, 32).

Thus, we have before our eyes the Christian state. This does not
mean a confessional state, or a community whose entire life is governed by the principles of one denomination. Instead, we have in
mind a state community that is directed by the most general principles
of the natural law that result from its nature and true ends within the
limits of reason. A community striving for the common good with
the aid of the means with which it has been entrusted, respecting
the rights of its constitutive communities, is a state community that
is Christian in spirit.

What, therefore, is needed so that we may trust the state enough
to endow it with such extensive rights in the socio-economic sphere?

The Church teaches that the state is an indispensable community
in the worldly order as the Church is indispensable in the supernatural order. Both the Church and the state, each within their own scope,
are sovereign and free in their pursuit of their essential ends. However,

both these communities are indispensable to man, who can achieve all the aims of his own life only through co-existence within them.

In the Catholic conception, the state is an essential body, which means that one cannot speak of a Christian social system outside the state; it cannot be built without the state. However, the state is not the most important factor; under the natural law and God's law, it is dependent on the Church in a way that cannot be violated. The Church is the guardian of morality and God's law whenever that law is violated by the state.

The family and professional communities within the state community are the basis for the Christian social system; one cannot speak of such a system without them.

Classes, which are the walls of the social structure, also appear within these borders. They organize people around the interests that are most important to a given social group. However, they cannot lose sight of the good of other classes and should therefore enter into agreement with their representatives. For example, the working class should interact with the employer class and create a joint labor union as part of their cooperation.

Here, the aim of the state is to coordinate the interests of the family, profession, and class. Although these are distinct groups, they are not completely autonomous, but they should seek to achieve their good within the limits of the common good, the responsibility for which rests with the state.

These principles are the center of the unity and harmony of authority in the state community.

Nearly all of state life today deviates from these principles. It has its shadows, which obscure Christian social thought.

I. Contemporary Lights and Shadows

Almost all contemporary social reforms have resulted from extremely divergent assumptions.

The reforms of the previous century were not conducive to the social role of the state; they aimed for the liberation of the individual at the cost of one's neighbors and society. By contrast, the reforms of our century seek to expand the state's social authority, at times to the detriment of man. All these painful attempts and experiences should awaken a yearning for a proper Christian system.

In the upheavals of the previous century, the role of the state was seen as the least important. The ideal of these reforms and upheavals was freedom and independence at any cost. Church and state were separated in the name of this ideal, while the family was torn apart, labor organizations were destroyed, and all forms of social life were seen as limitations on freedom; in other words, the state was separated from its citizens. Especially fierce was the struggle for the family, during which there were efforts to isolate citizens from the Church (through civil marriages) and their social duties (through divorce). Human life, which had previously been bound together by numerous nodes of community, has been shattered into smaller spiritual-religious, economic, and political groups that are hostile to one another.

The application of the following principles was seen as the greatest wisdom: "A free Church in a free state" and "The individual must be free before the state." This led to the separation of religious, political, and economic life, while the entire previous century was filled with the struggle for primacy. Economic life is today becoming the highest measure of social life. All of human life must become subjected to economic life. As a result of this disruption of social balance, humanity has become prone to the temptation of the primacy of bread.

Social Christian thought wants to lead state life to structural community.

It wants to remind the state that it does not exist for the sake of individuals, as the revolutions of the previous century proclaimed. However, it also recalls that the individual does not exist for the state, either, as contemporary upheavals argue.

The Christian state is completely different.

In this state, man is at the forefront. He is the only real being in the state. Everything else is formed thanks to man and his social nature. Man is a person. The aim of the state is to serve, develop, and perfect the human person. This truth is professed by all of Christian philosophy, beginning with the Gospels and developing in the first centuries, the theories and practice of the Middle Ages, and ending with Pius XII's recent proclamations. Man and his nature, which God has created, is the starting point for the construction of any system. Therefore, man is the aim of social life.

However, this man is not separated from society. Although he is the most wonderful being, he acts in a group and is bound to it as its member who is dependent on the aims that a given group serves. There are intermediary groups such as the family and profession that exist between the state and individuals; they are the organs of the social body. Thanks to them, the state community is built; it embraces man and brings him into state life. Man's life cannot exist without the family, while every man naturally belongs to some professional group through the exercise of his professional tasks in society. Thus, citizens enter the state community within smaller communities that are related to one another through the common good for which these communities strive. This is the natural foundation for the construction of every state.

The autonomy of the family and profession are the basic requirement for the Christian system.

As the basic unit of all social life, the family is an important factor in the construction of the social system. It cannot be perceived as a regrettable necessity that is merely tolerated by the state; it possesses its own proper ends, which are antecedent to the rights of the state. Although it is a smaller community than the state, it is a real community, one that is older and comes first. Its natural laws come not from the authority of the state, but from God, the Creator of the family. Thus, the natural laws of the family are greater than any rights of the state, such that they cannot be infringed, are necessary to fulfill the proper ends of both. Christian social thought professes that the division of authority must be in accordance with the needs of the family.

Labor unions participate in the state; they are organs of the state and have not only private but also public tasks. We understand labor unions as social groups that are built not on the principle of conflict, but on that of professional community; they will bring together all the employers and employees of a given branch of economic life. As such, a union must fulfill its own aims, which are important to the entire state. It will represent the good of a given social group, expanding and, if necessary, defending it. It requires connection to other social groups in order to subordinate its particular good to the higher, common good. A labor union conceived in this way will be the center of socio-economic life. Being simultaneously public and private in nature, it relieves the state, while at the same time performing the important role of bringing up citizens.

Finally, there is the Church. She has the right to intervention in public life with regards to everything that concerns the family, education, and worship of God. This socio-religious bond is of great importance to the state community, for it becomes an additional force that binds people together.

These communities understood in such a way becomes the core of the Christian state system. One biological community (the family), one economic community (the nation), and one religious-moral community (the Church) are the bedrock on which further construction will take place.

We see here that Christian social thought is opposed to all forms of dispersion; it desires unification with the preservation of freedom that secures the aspiration for the common and universal good.

II. The Tasks of the Christian State in Social Life

The primary aim of the state is the coordination of the activity of individual social groups and classes.

Each community within the state pursues its own secondary good, which is inferior to the common good. The state that is concerned for the common good designates the conditions that are necessary to achieve the lesser goods; it coordinates the cooperation of groups, delineates the borders that cannot be crossed, and concentrates and binds together efforts that are isolated from one another. It is the builder that looks after the entirety of the construction.

Social classes should cooperate with one another. This cooperation is not class struggle, as the socialists claim, nor is it feverish competition, as the capitalists maintain. It is a common effort that is undertaken with respect for one another's rights. This cooperation is possible only with the aid of the intervention of the state; only it can designate the rights of individuals and social groups, providing them with the necessary protection and support.

The state is obliged to intervene when social groups themselves cannot coordinate their interests.

The social harmony which must be fostered by the state is the consequence of the cooperation and unification of economic, political, and religious authority.

The state is obliged to support and encourage the formation of professional groups in which the interests of classes and professions would be concentrated. The social encyclicals exhort the association of laborers and criticize those who resist this.

According to the Holy See, laborers have the natural right to create their own associations and cannot be disturbed in these efforts as long as they are within the boundaries of the common good.

Quadragesimo anno laments the fact that employers have not gone the path of association, which has hindered concordant cooperation with affiliated laborers. Catholic thought here is the same: to bring people together to pursue the common good.

Economic authority in the form of a public body of the organized society should emerge from these professional organizations. Economic life, which exists not only for the good of entrepreneurial individuals but for the needs of the entire society, is conducted under the oversight of the state.

Thus, the ideal of the Christian social system is not the omnipotence of the state, but rather an organized society that will develop its social efforts under the supervision of the state. This ideal does not venerate the state, but it does not reject its role, either. The state must become increasingly social and be based on a well-organized society; it must be the product of social life.

The state can cease to be the "land of Egypt and house of slavery" for its citizens only under such conditions. Only then will man create the conditions for the development of his personality. The citizen will cease to be a small child fed by the spoon of the state, always inept, expecting protection, submissive, suspicious, mistrustful, and mistrusted. He will finally feel that he is in his own home. He will take responsibility for his own life, which will have to be coordinated with the whole. His initiative and willingness to cooperate will be invigorated. The state will not be a competitor for its own citizens; as the social philosophy of the Church explains: "Just as it is gravely

393

wrong to take from individuals what they can accomplish by their own initiative and industry and give it to the community, so also it is an injustice and at the same time a grave evil and disturbance of right order to assign to a greater and higher association what lesser and subordinate organizations can do" (QA, 79).

In such a state, freedom, justice, and the peace of God will flourish. The state will be the sower of peace. That is why the blessings of the people and the Father in heaven will fall upon it.

VOLUME IV

The Labor System and Property

PART I

Economic Life

1
To the Gods of Production

"If any one does not provide for his
relatives, and especially for his own family,
he has disowned the faith and is worse
than an unbeliever" (1 Timothy 5:8).

"The land of a rich man brought forth plentifully;
and he thought to himself, 'What shall I do,
for I have nowhere to store my crops?' And
he said, 'I will do this: I will pull down my
barns and build larger ones; and there I will
store all my grain and my goods. And I will
say to my soul, Soul, you have ample goods
laid up for many years; take your ease, eat,
drink, be merry.' But God said to him, 'Fool!
This night your soul is required of you; and
the things you have prepared, whose will they
be?' So is he who lays up treasure for himself,
and is not rich toward God" (Luke 12:16–21)?

THE MADNESS REVILED IN THIS PARABLE continues to recur. Christ the Lord condemns not the abundance of goods itself, but rather the rich man's selfish attitude. He wanted to store his rich harvest to use them according to his own inclinations, ignoring others. "He who lays up treasure for himself" did not think about being "rich toward God." Apart from his own use and the satisfaction of his nutritive instinct, he did not recognize the world, neither people nor God.

Therein lies the topic that appears so often in today's global economy.

Where is contemporary economic life headed? It desires abundance and wants to multiply harvests at all costs. What is wrong with this? Naturally, the mere multiplication of goods can be beneficial and commendable. The error rests in the fact that goods produced in such a quantity are often stored in "new barns" and that no one is concerned about supplying them to the needy, the hungry, and the naked. Although the world is increasingly prosperous, the number of people living in poverty is not declining.

This is the madness of the world, which must encounter God's judgment: "This night your soul is required of you; and the things you have prepared, whose will they be?'" (Luke 12:20).

Production cannot in and of itself be the aim of human economic activity.

Influenced by the desire for profit and an excessive faith in the efficacy of labor, the principle of mass production, "production for production's sake" has triumphed in the economic world. Everything is drowned out by shouts of: Produce! Produce as much as you can! Create a new production record! Constant increases in production are noted. This is said with a certain pride and sense of superiority.

From where does this come? Certainly, there are many causes, above all an erroneous view of the aims of human labor.

In the contemporary pagan conception, labor has lost its internal purpose; it has become an aim in and of itself: labor for the sake of labor.

Because labor understood as such is not subordinated to any other value—personal, social, or supernatural—we can conclude that it is becoming an absolute value. Labor in its contemporary understanding has lost its aim outside of itself.

Such a concept must be straightened out. Labor must be directed towards a specified aim which it should achieve. This aim rests in the development of the human person and its value; in the exchange of social services; in the creation of means serving to satisfy needs; and, finally, in cooperation with God to fulfill His plan of feeding the world. Through his labor, man aims towards a higher good; labor becomes a means in the path towards goods of a higher value.

Meanwhile, the pagan conception of labor leads to its confinement within itself. This gives birth to the need to act for the sake of acting and the mysticism and exaltation of acting, which is expressed in the economic field in constantly increasing, dizzying production. Not the fruit of labor but the mere act of production, breaking records, and production techniques are loved, while the triumph of numbers and quantities is constantly proclaimed. Today, statistics are the mother of economic pride and selfishness.

It is telling that the lust for production to which the capitalist economy gives birth has also become apparent in the communist economy. The apple does not fall far from the tree. Can a sick tree give birth to good fruits?

Such a kind of activity knows no other possible progress than infinite multiplication. The labor of sport understood as a military strategy or the struggle against the opponent, competitor, or enemy of the state is created through labor and its fruits. Labor first becomes a weapon of battle and later a means of domination.

Furthermore, labor becomes something akin to gambling: production continues without end, and an artificial need is created. Clients for the produced merchandise are found through artificial propaganda. Contemporary man is constantly persuaded of something; he is persuaded that he should have such a need or another. Economic life no longer serves people, instead making use of all artificially stimulated human weaknesses, while man sacrifices himself to the idol of labor. Man ceases to be a man; he solely becomes a producer, consumer, or client.

This leads to the dislocation of the hierarchy of all values. In this way, economic life is dominated by the madness of production resulting from the heresy of labor to which both the capitalist and communist economies have submitted.

Depriving labor of its proper aim has led humanity astray. Thus, the proper purpose of labor must be restored. Only then will the illness of "production for production's sake" disappear. The agonizing question of: "The things you have prepared, whose will they be?" (Luke 12:20) will disappear.

Production must serve the satisfaction of man's needs.

Contemporary economic life has another concern: "What shall I do, for I have nowhere to store my crops?" (Luke 12:17). Having rejected the proper purpose of labor, it resolves its worries in a truly pagan way: "I will pull down my barns and build larger ones; and there I will store all my grain and my goods" (Luke 12:18). Everything is resolved in the spirit of this same feverish activity.

And what next? Take ease, eat drink, and be merry?

Economic life must recognize the truly hungry, truly homeless, and terribly naked man. Once it sees and approaches him, it will be revived, for it will have recovered its true aim.

If it does not notice him, it will begin to complain of . . . overproduction. This "overproduction" is an empty word of which one must be aware. It is seen when merchandise produced through the limitless exaltation of labor occupies warehouses outside of whose walls half-naked and eternally hungry people roam. To make note of overproduction, people, not stored merchandise, must be recognized. The economy of things must be replaced with the economy of man.

In reality, there is no overproduction of grain, as millions of people, including millions of children, are malnourished. There was talk of "overabundance" when entire counties and nations starved, while there was a mass export of grain in the communist state when millions died of starvation.

There is no overproduction of sugar, for children do not see it for months at a time. There is no overproduction of wool, cotton, or linen, for people walk without shirts, and at night they cover their freezing bodies with the rags in which they walked and worked during the day. The dearth of household supplies, spoons, and bowls were an everyday occurrence in Poland. Usually, there was one bed for three people.

Instead of "overabundance," we must speak of an erroneous distribution of goods, which is a major violation of economic balance and social duties that weigh on economic life as a result of which large masses of hardworking people lack access to the most basic goods.

This leads to the following instruction:

Limitless production must be replaced by production for the sake of one's neighbors.

Today, the principle of the production of goods for the unfamiliar, hypothetical, and oftentimes very distant consumer has come to dominate economic life. Labor is performed for the sake of needs that are sensed and predicted.

According to liberal economics, exchange must always increase and thus the means of production and transportation are constantly multiplied so that merchandise is sent to foreign, distant peoples, while one's own neighbor, who is nearby and needs goods that are sent over the hills and across the sea, is completely ignored.

The profit-focused man constantly benefits from such an exchange, while those who labor producing a given good do not have access to it.

Today, a struggle between the interests of the business owner and the good of humanity is waged in nearly every sphere of economic

402

life. Everywhere, the fast and easy profit of the individual dominates over the good of the human person.

It is forgotten that order is always created around the human person. All economic efforts must be focused on man.

In the Christian economy, our closest neighbor will be the center of the exchange of goods and services. This exchange must be based on justice and love. Meanwhile, justice and love must be first rendered to the neighbor closest to us, the neediest and most underprivileged.

There are duties to one's children and family, relatives, employees, and citizens as well as to one's city, province, nation, and, finally, the entire world. These duties are hierarchically arranged; they are gradated by the closeness with which one renders love to another.

The hierarchy of justice and love are also obliging in economic life. "If any one does not provide for his relatives, and especially for his own family, he has disowned the faith and is worse than an unbeliever" (1 Timothy 5:8).

Economic life must be above all motivated by the good of those closest to us: our families, co-workers, and compatriots. The satisfaction of their needs is a more imperative task than meeting the needs of people living overseas. Only what is left over can be given to strangers. This is organic thinking and acting. A society is a body in all areas, including in the economic sphere. A sense of community or social bonds does not allow one to cheat or to sell bread and sugar to strangers when one's one neighbors are hungry and thirsting, even if doing so is less expensive. The Christian state cannot engage in exports at the expense of its own hungry citizens.

The Christian economy is not free of duties in the exchange of goods. It must recognize the present situation and act for the benefit of that which lives and is sanctified through existence; that which lives has the right to life and to means necessary for the flourishing of that life. That which lives must be respected. We must strive for the sustenance of life in that which exists.

Therefore, the duty of economic life is above all acting for the benefit of one's neighbors. One must begin with his own household members, co-workers, and compatriots.

The aim of economic life must be the improvement of the quality of life rather than increasing the quantity of goods.

The purpose of the economy should not be an increase in the number of goods but rather the constant improvement of their quality. The contemporary struggle has occurred primarily through the prism of quantity. To create as much as possible as cheaply as possible; to flood the consumer market; to supplant less numerous but better merchandise: this is the aim of the economic efforts with which we are familiar.

The shift must occur with respect to the quality of produced goods. Only then will competition become fruitful. Then, man, who is the consumer, rather than advertising and propaganda, will have a voice.

Goods are produced for the consumer; he also has the right to evaluate them. The consumer and not he who emerges victorious through the massiveness of production usually seeks out better merchandise that corresponds to his needs. By choosing better merchandise, the consumer gives witness to value and truth. This is the moral prize for conscientious labor. Not quantity or advertising but the true value of things must be at the forefront.

By replacing quantitative exchange with qualitative exchange, professional morality is elevated because aiming for the perfection of merchandise is the basic and most necessary condition for the protection of public opinion and the professional conscience.

Today, the professional conscience is killed by the focus on quantity supported by advertising. As a result of the lack of a direct relationship between both the familiar and distant consumers and the producer, neglectful producers remain unpunished for all their abuses. Through qualitative competition, we arrive at a professional conscience.

The rejection of the myth of quantity will lead to the concentration of efforts around the constant improvement and elevation of the quality of produced goods, which will benefit both the producer and the whole of humanity. No limits should be imposed with respect towards the aspiration towards increasing perfection. Everything should aim for constant progress. Here, economics will become fused with asceticism. Subdue the earth better and better. The field of Christian progress is limitless. There is no danger here, although there is a place for healthy competition. "Let your light so shine before men, that they may see your good works and give glory to your Father who is in heaven" (Matthew 5:16).

May people honestly struggle for increasingly greater good, both in the worldly and spiritual spheres. May grace be the continuation of natural law here as well. May dead matter become infused with the incarnation of the spirit of God.

Considering this, may we strive for prosperity and wealth? We not only may, but in fact must do so! However, the aspiration towards prosperity must be guided by a moral aim: the desire to improve the culture of life. The aspiration towards prosperity and its sustenance will be justified by the improvement of the quality of life and not the materialistic focus on the quantity of goods.

When people are guided by this aim, they can seek wealth. The aim of wealth is not the motto: "Eat, drink, and be merry" (Luke 12:19), but the acquisition of increasingly greater material resources to enable oneself access to spiritual goods. The development of spiritual and religious life and culture and art; the improving quality of education and social welfare; the improving protection of man's spiritual and physical goods; and the development of all desires and honorable aspirations are all respectable aims. One can desire material goods so that an ever-greater number of people may be capable of obtaining them.

May the behavior of the Church, who receives great material goods from her faithful yet invests them in charitable works like hospitals, schools, and missions; decorates churches with gold; and surrounds the seat of the popes with the richness of the walls of the Vatican, thus collecting cultural treasures, serve as an example. The pope, a poor fisherman like Peter, lives among the greatest spiritual treasures of the earth.

How salvific is the exchange of gold into the treasures through which humanity becomes "rich toward God" (Luke 12:21)!

This is an honorable aim towards which one may infinitely aspire, for this worldly path slowly turns into service of God and neighbor.

The response is ready. "What shall I do, for I have nowhere to store my crops?" (Luke 12:17).

"And I tell you, make friends for yourselves by means of unrighteous mammon, so that when it fails, they may receive you into the eternal habitations" (Luke 16:9).

2

The Christian Aim of Managing People

"Fill the earth and subdue it" (Genesis 1:28).

I S IT NOT WORTH SPEAKING ABOUT THE AIM of economic efforts? Is it not obvious and clear enough? Certainly, every man who engages in economic activity strives for a good that he needs. From the perspective of the individual, the aim of labor is apparent. However, when we take into consideration the fact that man is a social being who is bound to society and dependent on it, his personal aspirations encounter his social aims. Man is obliged to serve not only his own good, but in every endeavor he should coordinate his own aspirations with the labor of other people. Man stands before the entire working mass and economic life as the organized effort of people striving for some aim.

What is and what should be the aim of the economic efforts of those who labor?

Does man engage in labor because hunger or the desire for profit force him to do so, or does he do this because there is an obligation to work for one's nation or state? What should be the proper aim of the collective effort of human labor. This problem is the subject of an implacable debate that has been going on for decades.

I. The Violation of the Proper Aim of Economic Life

The Christian Middle Ages did not know such a fierce conflict over the aims of economic life. Only during the age of the victory of the limitless economy and the nascent opposition to it did people begin to ask: what is our aim?

Some have sought to direct the entirety of economic life towards material goods and the wealth of the individual, sacrificing both man and society in that struggle, while others have rejected man, instead decreeing that society is the purpose of economic efforts. Finally, there are those who recall the most basic human rights.

Can wealth be the aim of economic life?

The history of economic life in recent decades provides a response to this. Economic doctrines that profess that wealth is the purpose of economic life have come to the fore. The slogan "Grow Wealthy" has become the credo of the new faith and the greatest morsel of wisdom. Many books that have justified it have been written, while economic and political currents whose purpose was the introduction of faith in the power of bread and gold appeared.

From that point, man has ceased to be the most important factor. In fact, man as such no longer exists; he is merely the producer and consumer of goods. Man is no longer a social being! His aim is not only the aspiration towards the common good but rather the struggle for his own income and capacity of multiplying his estate. Man is no longer a steward but a capitalist, while the worker becomes above all a mercenary and wage earner.

Because nothing binds the man who grows wealthy to others — in fact, because every man is merely a rival in the struggle for money, no one can be his neighbor; he can only be his competitor. Moral bonds between competitors have ceased to exist! One can grow wealthy at the cost of others, and all means of doing so are permitted: fraud, usury, cheating, deceit, violence, social revolution, and even war.

From that point, wealth has become the aim of human life rather than the means to achieve a goal, as in the past. Since then, it has completely overwhelmed man and made him its servant. The wealth of the individual has become his greatest glory, virtue, and social worth as well as the means of progress and an agent of exaltation and dignity. The more wealthy individuals there will be, it was proclaimed, the wealthier and more valuable society will be. Thus, people should be allowed to grow wealthy. They should not be disturbed in this. The state must maintain an attitude of conducive neutrality towards those who grow wealthy.

Economic life is free of ethical principles; it possesses its own laws that are not subjected to God's laws. The most powerful socio-economic currents of the previous era — capitalism, socialism, and communism — professed this independence of economic life.

"A bad tree cannot bear good fruit" (Matthew 7:18). Life itself has demonstrated how harmful the "temptation of bread" is to man. The principles of limitless economic freedom as well as the freedom from God's laws and social duties have led to a struggle between liberated capital and humiliated labor.

Economic life has ceased to be community and cooperation. It was forgotten that "no nation has ever risen out of want and poverty to a better and nobler condition save by the enormous and combined toil of all the people, both those who manage work and those who carry out directions" (QA, 53).

"The 'capitalist' economic regime has spread everywhere" (QA, 103), which has led to the separation of capital and labor, while it has been forgotten that "capital cannot do without labor, nor labor without capital" (RN, 15). This division has led to a struggle whose essential trait is the greedy extortion of produced goods and selfish pretenses.

Finally, the path of unbridled free competition has led to widespread economic slavery. "This concentration of power and might, the characteristic mark, as it were, of contemporary economic life, is the fruit that the unlimited freedom of struggle among competitors has of its own nature produced, and which lets only the strongest survive; and this is often the same as saying, those who fight the most violently, those who give least heed to their conscience" (QA, 107).

Both small industry and agriculture, including large properties, have become the slaves of finance, as has the proletariat. Finance has conquered, in turn: the economic life of the old society; state life, whose means and authority are utilized for its purposes; and, finally, international relations, in which wars are waged to consolidate the economic gains of finance.

"The ultimate consequences of the individualist spirit in economic life are those which you yourselves, Venerable Brethren and Beloved Children, see and deplore: Free competition has destroyed itself; economic dictatorship has supplanted the free market; unbridled ambition for power has likewise succeeded greed for gain; all economic life has become tragically hard, inexorable, and cruel" (QA, 109).

Indeed, "man shall not live by bread alone" (Deuteronomy 8:3). Today, the temptation of bread comes to Europe in yet another form. It must come to provide salvific experiences for the future.

In order to be rescued from the consequences of the service of things and the wealthy, a new aim of economic life was proposed.

408

People were summoned to work for the prosperity of the nation and sate. The nation would consume what it has produced together as one. Serving the proletarian state was replaced with serving one's own stomach. Man should sacrifice all his life's aims, tasks, and personal goods for the sake of the masses.

Does this resolve this problem? In the communist economic system, man is still a mere means, a tool for the multiplication of wealth. In the capitalist system, the businessman grew wealthy, while the state grows wealthy under communism.

II. The Aims of Human Life:

The Satisfaction of the General Needs of Humanity

In order to provide a rationale, we will above all indicate the basic assumptions of economic life conceived in a Catholic way and later its aspirations.

The Catholic Fundaments of the Economy

The Christian economy will indicate that God the Creator and His Providence will be the beginning and the end of all creation and therefore of human production, labor, and wealth. It is God Who gave to humanity the laws concerning use of the goods of the earth in accordance with their destiny to serve man.

The starting point for Christian management is God's commandment written down in the Book of Genesis in which God hands the earth over to man: "Fill the earth and subdue it" (Genesis 1:28). Not only the individual man, but also the community of people should subdue the earth. Thus, man can be subjected to any earthly measure, be it wealth or the service of wealth.

Each man — the entrepreneur, foreman, and laborer alike — becomes God's collaborator in the work of ruling the earth. God equips man with the necessary skills and makes him His collaborator; in fact, He makes him the lord of creation. Man is like a "priest of creation" from which his majesty in economic life results. Through his labor, man who cooperates with God elevates and offers up everything to God.

Hence, the order of economic life must begin with man, whose own aims and duties must be recognized, coordinated with those of society, and directed towards the service of the common good.

The order of economic life in the Christian economy will be arranged according to the following hierarchy: labor, nature, capital. Human labor is dominant; nature is increasingly tamed; and capital becomes increasingly proportional or divided more equally.

Labor strives for leadership. Its laws should be secured in an increasingly better way; the participation of laborers in the running of a business and in its profits should be greater; and the cooperation of people who labor together should be ever closer. Nature and capital are not factors that are human in their essence. This is why labor must be given primacy. God did so by subjecting nature to human labor. When conceived in such a way, as St. Antoninus of Florence teaches, production serves man rather than the reverse.

Nature must be increasingly tamed. This is the noblest factor in the human economy, for it has been received as a gift from God. Man's domination over the earth is the basic aim of the Christian economy; it is the implementation of God's commandment. The face of the earth must become worthy of man; it must be humanized in a way that man may live on earth without offending God. When conquering the earth, man cannot disappear under the weight of its wealth. That is what both capitalism and Bolshevik economic gigantism have done to man. Man is subjected to God's Providence, to which he must subject everything. God has renounced rule of the earth in favor of man. Man will conquer the earth only if he becomes subject to God. Otherwise, the earth will conquer man.

Man's right to the earth reflects God's right with respect to man. When man liberates himself from God's laws, the earth seeks revenge against man: the wealth of the earth increases, while the "king of the earth" becomes its slave. Today's millionaires are to an equal degree slaves of the earth as the proletariat. Both are *fabricae adscripti*.[1] An earth that is faithful to God seeks revenge on man for having betrayed God.

Meanwhile, capital must be in third place. Capital must be increasingly proportional; its division should be increasingly just so that the goods that have been accumulated may reach increasing strata of society.

All these factors should harmoniously work together in economic life, through the principles of a healthy morality and balance.

---

1   Latin: "Destined for the office."

2. The Proper Face of Economic Life

The ultimate aim of management rests in the full development of man's physical, spiritual, and moral strength. For this reason, the economy must be humanized, or liberated from the domination of things to give it a human face.

The economy is not a god before which man must bow, nor is it the most important part of human life. The Christian economy is based on the "economic man," and not on matter. Economic life and, therefore, its production, processes, aims, means of exchange, and distribution of social income as well as consumption itself must be organized and evaluated with respect to both individual and social human needs.

Man is more than the "economic man" or "human material" in the economic process. Economic life is not the entirety of human life, just as the economic sphere is not the entire life of the nation or even its most important part.

Man is something greater than a producer and consumer; his ultimate aims and tasks reach further and are more permanent than the most wondrous body of economic life.

The entirety of management must take into consideration not only man's economic good but also his personal character. It must respect and serve the supernatural aims of the human person.

We must also remember that economic life is merely a means to achieving man's ultimate aim. In the temporal order, it is the highest aim, for it achieves the fullness of its perfection there. Thus, economic life has its majesty and its momentous role as a factor in a certain essential order.

With respect to man's ultimate aim, economic life will be an indirect aim. Even though the common economic good is the ultimate aim in the temporal sphere, it is not the ultimate aim of human life.

The most learned economist and the most accomplished organizer and entrepreneur should remember that there is no permanent dwelling here and that the Father can come for your soul on any night.

The next task is the socialization of the economy.

Apart from personal goods, the aim of the Christian economy is striving for the common good. The common good is different from the good of individuals and the sum of private goods; it is greater than the interests of individuals as a part of society.

In the Middle Ages, the Christian economy was governed by the principle of the common good. Its activity was strictly subjected to moral principles and corporatist principles. The prohibition against usury and of the establishment of a fair price and a just wage originate from this time. This led to man's personal freedom, his economic independence, the spread of property, and social peace.

All management efforts must bear in mind the problem of coordinating the good of the person with that of society. The purpose of this requirement is that the goods created by God for all may be available to all according to the principles of justice and love (see RN, 11).

All selfishness and exclusiveness in the use of private goods as well as the search for one's own benefits is a blow to the social nature of economic life.

Now, the economy must become Christianized.

For this purpose, the concept of one's neighbor must return to economics. The good of every person should be coordinated with the equal good of one's neighbor, above all those who are closest to us.

The truth that pertains to private human life, the truth about the need to voluntarily renounce something and limit one's own needs, must also be obliging in economics.

Economic life should be developed within the context of service to our neighbors or our brothers, with whom we are one in God, our Father. To meet human needs—to feed the hungry, clothe the naked, and give drink to the thirsty—are not only the obligations of mercy but the most important obligations of economic life.

In all such efforts, "all things [must] be directed to God as the first and supreme end of all created activity, and that all created good under God be considered as mere instruments to be used only in so far as they conduce to the attainment of the supreme end. Nor is it to be thought that gainful occupations are thereby belittled or judged less consonant with human dignity; on the contrary, we are taught to recognize in them with reverence the manifest will of the Divine Creator Who placed man upon the earth to work it and use it in a multitude of ways for his needs" (QA, 136).

* * *

412

Subdue the earth, but do not become slaves to the earth, for the earth is not immortal like you, the friends and sons of God. Even though everything is ours, we never belong to ourselves but to Christ, Who in turn belongs to God (see 1 Corinthians 3:21–22).

3

The Church and the Directors of Economic Life

"Blessed is the rich man who is found blameless, and who does not go after gold. Who is he? And we will call him blessed, for he has done wonderful things among his people" (Sirach 31:8–9).

IN HIS EPISTLE TO THE BISHOP TIMOTHY, ST. Paul recalls the duties of the Church's teaching office with respect to the wealthy of this world: "As for the rich in this world, charge them not to be haughty, nor to set their hopes on uncertain riches but on God who richly furnishes us with everything to enjoy. They are to do good, to be rich in good deeds, liberal and generous, thus laying up for themselves a good foundation for the future, so that they may take hold of the life which is life indeed" (1 Timothy 6:17–19).

The Church is a kingdom not of this earth, and so she is not called to organize and manage economic life. To all her tempters, she responds with Christ's words: "Man, who made Me a judge or divider over you?" (Luke 12:14). The most important task of the Church is to teach all the nations to follow God's commandments. The Church will never abandon this role. However, she does not free anyone from the duty to listen to her teachings, either.

There is no sphere of human life and there is no profession or kind of labor that would be free of the commandments of God's laws; due to its moral nature, there is no human act that would not be subjected to the Church's judgment. Thus, the Church cannot consider economic life to be completely free of the laws of the Gospels. The Church is called to not only preach the Gospels to the poor, to slaves, paupers, proletarians, hired hands, and laborers, but also to the free, wealthy, the "bourgeoisie," factory owners, bankers, and capitalists. The Church proclaims the one and highest Truth of Christ, the Redeemer of the souls of both the rich and the poor, to

414

not only those whose eyes are red from bitter tears of poverty but also those whose glance is red from the glimmer of gold.

Thus, the Church has her own message to the "wealthy of this world"!

I. The Church's Primary Duty Towards the Wealthy

Set aside for a moment your balance sheets and budgets, your stock market quotations and market research; set aside all the registers of your bank accounts and payrolls and listen to the greatest contract for you: "You were bought with a price" (1 Corinthians 6:20).

We have been "bought"? But who has dared to sell us?! We are not merchandise but the producers of all wealth, of all merchandise! We pay this "price"! Who could be capable of buying us?

Who has sold you? He who was so easily tempted by all the kingdoms of the world and their glory: "All these I will give you, if you will fall down and worship me" (Matthew 4:9). You have sunk very low! Your fall is so great that you continue bowing servilely!

Who could succeed in buying you? Only He who can afford the great price, for it is the price of His own blood: "You know that you were ransomed [. . .] not with perishable things such as silver or gold, but with the precious blood of Christ" (1 Peter 1:18). "Do you not know that your bodies are members of Christ? [. . .] Do you not know that your body is a temple of the Holy Spirit within you, which you have from God?" (1 Corinthians 6:15, 19).

"Greater love has no man than this, that a man lay down his life for his friends" (John 15:13). It is Christ who has redeemed you for the price of His soul, not your factories, production halls, offices and agencies, banks and warehouses filled with merchandise, but your souls! Christ has laid down His soul for us, for His friends. You ask: do we have friends? It is true that do not have friends of your souls! You only have friends of your pockets and your purses. You know that all hate you. Strangely enough, you are hated by those to whom you provide labor and those whose wages—not only those of proletarians but also those of directors—you pay; by those to whom you sell your merchandise; by those from whom you receive raw materials; and those to whom you lend! There is no greater hatred than that which the world feels towards you. The world has been set aflame with revolution and class struggle, sabotage and strikes in the name of this hatred. "Communist manifestos" were written in the name of that hatred, while a proletarian state was built and you were crucified along with Christ, whom you had previously renounced! Take a stroll in the museums of atheism that are shown to your inquisitive, godless brothers from the internationale of gold: Christ and the capitalist are the most popular decorative motifs there.

Christ was once again hung on the Calvary of the twentieth century! Next to Him are two modern thieves: one clad in a shirt of gold and the other in a red one. What are their faults? One loved gold more than his soul, while the other sacrificed everything for hatred. Which of them will be in paradise today? Christ says to them both: "You are my friends if you do what I command you. No longer do I call you servants, for the servant does not know what his master is doing; but I have called you friends, for all that I have heard from my Father I have made known to you. You did not choose me, but I chose you and appointed you that you should go and bear fruit and that your fruit should abide [. . .]. This I command you, to love one another" (John 15:14–17).

He who will comprehend the words of life and will confess his sins and prayerfully express his contrition will enter paradise: "And we indeed justly; for we are receiving the due reward of our deeds [. . .]. Jesus, remember me when you come in your kingly power" (Luke 23:41–42).

Indeed, Christ never caused harm to anyone. Why, then, is He crucified in every century? "No one can serve two masters; for either he will hate the one and love the other, or he will be devoted to the one and despise the other. You cannot serve God and mammon" (Matthew 6:24). You have loved mammon, and this is why you hate Christ; you have renounced Him so that He does not stop you from "making money." You have given Him over to the commoner with a light conscience and have washed your hands like Pilate. Why are you surprised that in our age almost all the revolutions, from Annas to Caiaphas, trample on Christ, who is esteemed less than Barabbas, for He is crucified in His own Church again? "He who loves gold will not be justified" (Sirach 31:5). You are likewise not without fault!

"But woe to you that are rich, for you have received your consolation. Woe to you that are full now, for you shall hunger" (Luke 6:24–25). "They cast their silver into the streets, and their gold is like an unclean thing; their silver and gold are not able to deliver them in the day of the wrath of the Lord" (Ezekiel 7:19).

The Church says to the contemporary directors of economic life: "How could it benefit you if you possessed all the shares of great industrial businesses; if you created expansive corporations; if you seized the mining industry and dominated coal supply; if through the aid of money, you could influence elections and subject to yourselves parliaments and national governments; if you dominated all of public life? How could this help you if your soul suffered and you lost heaven, if even one soul died in this way?"[1]

Only the Church has the courage to stand amidst the crowded paths filled with people who have forgotten about the "One Almighty" in the pursuit of gold. "Do not lay up for yourselves treasures on earth, where moth and rust consume and where thieves break in and steal, but lay up for yourselves treasures in heaven, where neither moth nor rust consumes and where thieves do not break in and steal" (Matthew 6:19–20).

Only the Church has the authority to ask: "Is not life more than food, and the body more than clothing?" (Matthew 6:25).

The one Church, protected by Christ's gravity, says to all without exception: "But seek first his kingdom and his righteousness, and all these things shall be yours as well" (Matthew 6:33).

The Church by no means condemns this "everything" that shall be man's. Christ does not condemn honestly acquired goods; He only cautions to not attach our hearts to them too much. "For where your treasure is, there will your heart be also" (Matthew 6:21).

In accordance with the Book of Proverbs, the Church herself recommends restrained concern for the goods of this earth: "Remove far from me falsehood and lying; give me neither poverty nor riches, feed me with the food that is needful for me, lest I be full, and deny

---

1 *Katolicyzm, kapitalizm, socjalizm, List pasterski biskupów austriackich* ("Catholicism, Capitalism, and Socialism: A Pastoral Letter of the Austrian Bishops"); translated and annotated by Rev. Stefan Wyszyński, Lublin 1928 (second edition, Lublin 1935).

thee, and say, 'Who is the Lord?' or lest I be poor, and steal, and profane the name of my God" (Proverbs 30:8–9).

The Church cautions against giving one's entire heart over to wealth, which has a cursed impact and breeds economic domination and strength; wherever there is economic disorder, there are greater possibilities for moral abuses.

Excessive wealth blinds man's heart so greatly that people then forget about eternal goods and are overcome by a spirit of harshness, ruthlessness, severity, and terrible selfishness that softens even in the face of the greatest social failures and does not see that exploitation and human suffering inevitably invite the danger of revolution. The entire weight of the following curse befalls the people: "Let their feast become a snare and a trap, a pitfall and a retribution for them; let their eyes be darkened so that they cannot see and bend their backs forever" (Romans 11:9–10).

"Wakefulness over wealth wastes away one's flesh, and anxiety about it removes sleep" (Sirach 31:1). However, the illness of gold threatens not only the body. It is a thorn that drowns out the seed of the Word of God within the soul (see Matthew 13:7). This is why it is so difficult for the rich man to enter the Kingdom of Heaven (see Matthew 19:23).

God's Church constantly reminds the world how quickly everything that is worldly passes; she does not allow anyone to forget that even the greatest wealth "like the flower of the grass [...] will pass away. For the sun rises with its scorching heat and withers the grass; its flower falls, and its beauty perishes. So will the rich man fade away in the midst of his pursuits" (James 1:10–11). Immorally acquired wealth withers especially quickly: "Come now, you rich, weep and howl for the miseries that are coming upon you. Your riches have rotted, and your garments are moth-eaten. Your gold and silver have rusted, and their rust will be evidence against you and will eat your flesh like fire. You have laid up treasure for the last days. Behold, the wages of the laborers who mowed your fields, which you kept back by fraud, cry out; and the cries of the harvesters have reached the ears of the Lord of hosts" (James 5:1–4).

This is why the Church presents all rich men with Christ's instruction: "And I tell you, make friends for yourselves by means of unrighteous mammon, so that when it fails, they may receive you into the eternal habitations" (Luke 16:9). Blessed is he who will say to God: "Therefore I love Thy commandments above gold, above fine gold" (Psalm 119:127). Only then will the widespread hatred of the rich man turn into love. Your wealth will be in the service of God, and your life will be a blessing. The tears of the exploited will dried; the voices cursing you will resound with hymns of blessing; social relations will be transformed; and class struggle, the struggle of hearts and fists, will cease, while hatred and jealousy will disappear. And the estate that you will acquire after fulfilling your social duties, will it not be safer, closer to you, and more useful when it will not be burdened by sins of negligence, human injury, and jealousy? "Blessed is the man who walks not in the counsel of the wicked, nor stands in the way of sinners, nor sits in the seat of scoffers; but his delight is in the law of the Lord, and on His law, He meditates day and night. He is like a tree planted by streams of water, that yields its fruit in its season, and its leaf does not wither" (Psalm 1:1–3).

II. The Specific Duties of the Directors of Economic Life

The Church above all summons us to the Christian community and to the understanding of the different layers of society on the principles of justice and love.

The basis for this agreement will be Christian teaching that, as Leo XIII writes, has the strange but potent capacity to quell social conflict in its germinal stage. Thus, the sum of religious truths of which the Church is the translator and guardian is useful in bringing together and reconciling the rich and poor; namely, by appealing to both states that they fulfill their mutual obligations, especially those that result from justice (see RN, 19–20).

In the sphere of economic life, God intended to bind all people together through the community of labor. All, especially Catholic entrepreneurs and Catholic workers, should be concerned by this notion of binding together intended by God. In paradise, the Creator said to those who believe in God: "Fill the earth and subdue it" (see Genesis 1:28). He also counted on them the most, trusting that having confided in God, they will possess the land through their shared drudgery. We can refer Christ's words to Catholic workers bound together in sacrificial labor through the everyday knot of faith and love: "You are my friends if you do what I command you" (John 15:14).

Social peace and widespread prosperity can reign above all because of shared convictions, even if ongoing interests have at times divided people. To achieve this aim, they must comprehend that they are bound together by convictions more than they are separated by their respective interests. They share one God, one faith, one Church, the common good, the good of their profession, and the intentional community of the labor they perform. If they sometimes recognize this so-called "conflict of interests," it is obvious that they will comprehend their eternal destiny and the obligations resulting from the binding law of love and justice more, which will make this supposed conflict seem irrelevant and artificial. This conflict of interests will be replaced by the necessary and desirable cooperation of employers and workers in the Christian spirit of the community of labor.

Then, entrepreneurs will accept Christ's way of thinking, recognizing the worker as a man and Christian who deserves respect and veneration that he received from God's will to cooperate with Him in the effort to feed the world. The greater the dignity of the workers, the greater the honor of the workers called by Providence to be the directors of the social economy. They will also understand that the obligation to conscientiously cooperate with workers in the spirit of the words of Christ the Lord is not an affront but an honor: "And whoever would be first among you must be your slave" (Matthew 20:27). How easy it will be to achieve the recommended professional-estate system in which there is no longer a contradiction of interests, class struggle, or hatred in this way, as the common good and the cooperation of the classes based on social love are the leading ideals.

With respect to the cooperating workers, the Church demands that employers always be guided by the principles of love and social justice. They require that the worker is not treated like a slave; it is imperative "to respect in every man his dignity as a person ennobled by Christian character" (RN, 20). All forms of disrespecting human dignity are a treacherous stick with two ends that frequently falls on the head of those who have not respected the defenseless: "Whoever sheds the blood of man, by man shall his blood be shed; for God made man in his own image" (Genesis 9:6).

The Church harshly condemns the abuse of people as objects whose purpose is profit and their evaluation only according to the values presented by their muscles and strength and something shameful and inhuman (see RN, 20). In the encyclical *Quadragesimo anno*, Pius XI states that many employers say their workers as mere tools of labor but did not care about their souls or even thought about greater things (see QA, 135).

The Church prohibits employers against burdening their subordinates with excessive labor or that which does not befit their age or sex (see RN, 20). Seeing the magnitude of the abuses committed by employers, the encyclical *Quadragesimo anno* strongly condemns them: "Truly the mind shudders at the thought of the grave dangers to which the morals of workers (particularly younger workers) and the modesty of girls and women are exposed in modern factories" (QA, 135). Should we not lament the fact that while dead matter leaves the factories ennobled, people degenerate and are ruined there (see *ibid.*)? This is the fruit of neglected duties.

The Church considers the main duty of employers to give everyone what he justly deserves. She recalls that neither God's law nor human law allows for the exploitation of the needy and the poor and personally benefiting at the expense of another's poverty. Meanwhile, depriving anyone of the wage they have earned is a shameful crime (see RN, 20). "Behold, the wages of the laborers who mowed your fields, which you kept back by fraud, cry out; and the cries of the harvesters have reached the ears of the Lord of hosts" (James 5:4). "Woe to him who builds his house by unrighteousness, and his upper rooms by injustice; who makes his neighbor serve him for nothing and does not give him his wages" (Jeremiah 22:13).

The Church demands that the savings of the poor are respected. The rich should conscientiously avoid taking what the poor have saved from them by means of violence, deceit, or usury, especially since they are not sufficiently protected against injury and lawlessness. The more modest their estate, the more it should be respected (see RN, 20). Through God's intercession, improperly acquired goods will return to their rightful owners: "Though he heap up silver like dust and pile up clothing like clay; he may pile it up, but the just will wear it, and the innocent will divide the silver" (Job 27:16–17).

Employers should make sure that workers have the time that is necessary for their pious practices; they should not be prone to the temptations of seducers and incentives to sin (see RN, 20). How much justified concern there is in recalling this basic duty is evident in the accusation that Pius XI had to levy against employers, making note of numerous obstacles to the proper celebration of the holidays, "the universal weakening of that truly Christian sense through which even rude and unlettered men were wont to value higher things, and upon its substitution by the single preoccupation of getting in any way whatsoever one's daily bread" (see QA, 135).

How much effort, often in vain, must be undertaken to bring back the masses that have ceased to fulfill their duties towards God and their own souls through a defective economic system? Who will succeed in correcting this great evil? In the encyclical on godless communism, Catholics had to be correctly accused of having led, through their indifference and ruthlessness, to the spread of communism among the workers and to the erosion of their faith and trust in the Church.

III. Cooperation with God's Providence in the Work of Feeding Humanity

To achieve this purpose, the Church wants to oppose the spirit of selfishness and omnipotent profit, which should be replaced by the Christian desire for all economic activity to strive to meet the basic needs of the children of God.

The Church recognizes private property, which originates in the natural law, and emphatically proclaims that it is the source of not only income but also of duties. As Pius XI teaches in the encyclical *Quadragesimo anno*, property is not only individual but also social in nature; man possesses goods only in order that "individuals may be able to provide for themselves and their families but also that the goods which the Creator destined for the entire family of mankind may through this institution truly serve this purpose" (QA, 45).

By making use of private property, "men must consider in this matter not only their own advantage but also the common good" (QA, 49). All, especially the directors of economic life, are burdened with this duty.

Capitalism has erred, for "whatever was produced, whatever returns accrued, capital claimed for itself, hardly leaving to the worker enough to restore and renew his strength" (QA, 54). Such a system which "thinks it the right order of things for it to get everything and the worker nothing" (QA, 57) has been condemned in the Church's encyclicals.

The most important duties that direct economic life include making sure that "each, therefore, must be given his own share of goods, and the distribution of created goods, which, as every discerning person knows, is laboring today under the gravest evils due to the huge disparity between the few exceedingly rich and the unnumbered propertyless, must be effectively called back to and brought into conformity with the norms of the common good, that is, social justice" (QA, 58).

Bearing in mind this primary aim of human labor—the satisfaction of the basic needs of all members of society—Catholic teaching describes the obligations that befall superfluous income; that is, "income which [the person] does not need to sustain life fittingly and with dignity, is not left wholly to his own free determination" (QA, 50). Sacred Scripture, the Church Fathers, and Catholic social-moral teaching unanimously state that man does not have complete freedom in making use of them. On the contrary, the wealthy are obliged to practice alms, charity, and generosity.

Filled with God's spirit, wealthy Catholics have a beautiful history that has been written by the generous hand of charity and alms. How many charitable institutions that continue to wipe dry the tears of the poor and successfully struggle against human poverty have they founded.

However, the moral demands resulting from the Christian virtue of generosity, which has brought about so much good in the past, are strangely foreign to them today. The Holy Father Pius XI has recalled it by quoting St. Thomas (STh II–II, q. 9, a. 134), giving this virtue modern tasks that are so important during times of economic crisis. The pope writes in *Quadragesimo anno*: "Expending larger incomes so that opportunity for gainful work may be abundant, provided, however, that this work is applied to producing really useful goods, ought to be considered, as We deduce from the principles of the Angelic Doctor, an outstanding exemplification of the virtue of munificence and one particularly suited to the needs of the times" (QA, 51).

When we read these words, we see before our eyes the owner of the vineyard who, after having gone to the market many times during the day and seeing unemployed people there, asked them: "'Why do you stand here idle all day?' They said to him, 'Because no one has hired us.' He said to them, 'You go into the vineyard too'" (Matthew 20:6–7). This passage also reminds us that the long lines of the unemployed standing in front of labor offices whom "no one has hired" are the lifeless windows of factories, where labor dies and is so often killed by the cold breath of selfish calculation; they are the closed doors of factories from which hundreds of workers brought their daily bread to their families. They have been closed because the capital invested in the business brought too little profit to its owner or because it wanted to decrease production or increase the price of merchandise. Nobody asks about the "income" of society, which grows like a young forest, in the hundreds of places of employment. There is no such custom!

The Christian social sense, however, forces us to ask about it. It recalls that a good name is better than all wealth, while grace is better than silver and gold. "The rich and the poor meet together; the Lord is the maker of them all" (Proverbs 22:1–2). God has bound their hands together, while profit and money do not dare to separate. Here is an area where men should not "set their hopes on uncertain riches but on God who richly furnishes us with everything to enjoy. They are to do good, to be rich in good deeds, liberal and generous" (1 Timothy 6:17–18).

How many opportunities will Christian love find to multiply in this "chosen race, a royal priesthood, a holy nation, God's own people" (see 1 Peter 2:9). If it had become flesh, then the unfair legends about the social impotency of Catholicism and people brought up by it would have been debunked.

This virtue of generosity demands making use of wealth not only for one's own good but also for the good of others.

It can bring an end to soulless monetary speculation to create opportunities for work for those who look for it and to ensure means of earning money. Then, accumulated capital and superfluous income will not be used for speculation and stock market gambles; they will not be used for high, usurious interest rates or profits from currency exchanges but for the creation of workplaces and the providing of the sources of making money. Speculation on money, which is so detrimental to the peaceful development of economic life and the good of the entire nation, will give way to the Christian complaisance of money, which will bring the middle classes, farmers, and artisans the necessary resources for them to work independently. Will not the rich and the poor meet then, knowing that "the Lord is the maker of them all" (Proverbs 22:2)?

The Church recalls that superfluous incomes should be invested in a way that serves the production of truly beneficial goods.

Thus, it does not suffice to fulfill the duty of investing capital and paying workers employed in one's workplace. This duty must be performed socially; that is, superfluous income must be invested in enterprises that are useful to society; they must be used for the organization of workplaces, bearing in mind not only the exclusive interests of the entrepreneur but also the good of one's collaborators at all levels.

The Church speaks of the responsibility that befalls the owner for the use of his capital. It is not irrelevant if the money will be invested in a factory producing ammunition, poisonous gases, narcotics, or obscene merchandise or, on the contrary, in a factory that produces means that satisfy the most basic needs. Only a man governed by the capitalist mentality and the spirit of profit invests his superfluous income to increase his dividends. The Christian entrepreneur invests while taking into consideration his social usefulness and responsibility. Only when the invested money brings about good services, when it serves socially useful production is the entitlement to income from the services that are rendered justified. The reverse is also true: gaining profit from money invested in enterprises that produce useless or harmful products is injustice; it is making profit from poisoned wells.

This same consideration for the common good indicates to employers the need to limit their own needs to acquire the resources to help one's neighbor in this way.

Love of one's neighbor is a universal law that obliges not only monks and hermits, but perhaps especially entrepreneurs, employers, and the directors of economic life who live among people, who live off their labor.

Under exceptionally difficult circumstances, exceptional sacrifices are also required. If with respect to a just wage Catholic morality sometimes allows for an exemption from this proper principle for the sake of saving places of employment, not only the workers, but also the employers are obliged to make similar sacrifices. The pope recalls this duty in his encyclical on communism: "To be sure of eternal life, therefore, and to be able to help the poor effectively, it is imperative to return to a more moderate way of life, to renounce the joys, often sinful, which the world today holds out in such abundance; to forget self for love of the neighbor. There is a divine regenerating force in this "new precept" (as Christ called it) of Christian charity. Its faithful observance will pour into the heart an inner peace which the world knows not, and will finally cure the ills which oppress humanity" (DR, 48)

What is it like in practice? During times of great crisis, its burden completely befell the shoulders of workers. There were cases when the wages of factory owners amounted to 300,000 zlotys each year. In one enterprise, the wages of the twenty-nine directors of industrial plants exceeded the wages of 1,800 workers. According to estimates from the Great Depression, one worker engaged in public works would have had to work for one hundred years to earn the monthly salary of one company owner, which amounted to 100,000 zlotys.

The fact that in 1932 the President of Poland was forced to issue a decree on the limitation of excessive wages in enterprises attests to the economic relations in our poor country. According to one of the articles of this decree, the wage of the directors of companies had to amount to the sum of the wages of all employed in each enterprise. Tellingly, this decree did not concern wages amounting to 2,500 zlotys monthly and 30,000 annually.

It should be obvious that differences in taxation are justified because of the increasing duties of an economic group, the need for social benefits, and exceptional social usefulness. The social ideal is not to reduce these people to the proletarian level, as was prescribed in the Bolshevik state; on the contrary, all people must be raised up from proletarian existence. However, there must be sound reason and Christian righteousness along with prudence must dominate in these differences, which are loyally recognized by the world of workers.

Meanwhile, this is forgotten even in workplaces, which are falling into ruin. The wages of workers are lowered, or people are fired, which deprives workers of not only employment, but also the means to feed their families; oftentimes, places of work are allowed to disappear even though the incomes of managers do not decline. In Warsaw, there were banks that were several months behind in paying their workers so that their directors and owners could be paid to make up for their financial losses. Is it not evidence of a complete lack of morality when, after the bankruptcy of one factory in Lodz, where 6,500 workers had lost their jobs, the insolvency administrators were each paid 220,000 zlotys for two weeks of work?

This is a modest selection of examples that demonstrate how far removed our life is from Pius' salvific words and how selfishness and terrible harshness, ruthlessness, and indifference towards the sad fate of millions of fathers and their children have become rooted in this world. We leave too much gold to ourselves; thus, God is left with only frankincense and myrrh, while our neighbors are left with poverty.

And yet the strength of responsibility does not flag. The owners and directors of economic life are obliged to limit their egotistical use of riches for the sake of the common good. Persistence and renunciation result from the Christian commandments; they will wipe dry the tears of humanity. Only then will there be "the company of those who believed were of one heart and soul, and no one said that any of the things which he possessed was his own, but they had everything in common" (see Acts 4:32).

The spirit of Christian community obliges employers to be concerned not only about the worldly success of their enterprise, but also to ensure a just wage and, in difficult moments, to lower their own wages to at a rate equal to that of their workers. When there arrives the inevitable and ultimate necessity to close the enterprise, they must provide their workers with the means necessary for life, which have been lost because of the closure of their source income (see QA, 73). Indeed, economic supremacy and authority are above all service of society; this can never be forgotten.

When this spirit of Christian community will dominate your hearts and when it will become stronger in socio-economic life, you will become children of God who have the honorable role of cooperation with the Father, who feeds the world; you will become the beloved brothers in Christ of your collaborators, who in the spirit of kindness will lead to the multiplication of yours, ours, and the common prosperity, "not with eyeservice [. . .] but in singleness of heart" (Colossians 3:22).

* * *

Christ transformed the heart of a capitalist in the home of Zacchaeus, a tax collector who wanted to see Jesus from afar, from a "burning fig tree." Today, this would be the windows of a bank. However, such a distance does not suffice for Christ. The Lord looked into the depths of his heart and called: "Zacchaeus, make haste and come down; for I must stay at your house today" (Luke 19:5).

This one visit was enough for this opportunist to recognize the harmfulness of his greed, the deceptive triviality of his riches, and the incomparable value of good deeds. Perhaps the wisdom of Ecclesiastes, Son of David, flashed in his mind: "I also gathered for myself silver and gold and the treasure of kings and provinces [. . .]. So I became great and surpassed all who were before me in Jerusalem [. . .]. Then I considered all that my hands had done and the toil I had spent in doing it, and behold, all was vanity and a striving after wind, and there was nothing to be gained under the sun" (Ecclesiastes 2:8–11).

This is the salvific conclusion of the man who suddenly reconsidered: "Behold, Lord, the half of my goods I give to the poor; and if I have defrauded any one of anything, I restore it fourfold" (Luke 19:8).

Likewise today, Christ passes by your "flaming fig tree" in which you so confide; He passes by your factories, warehouses, and under the windows of your currency exchanges and banks. Today, it is no less urgent that salvation becomes your house. This is a very important time! Christ's calling is insistent: Quickly abandon those false hopes, that illusion of greatness that has been grown from the violation of God's laws. It is time for you to understand that "the kingdom of God does not mean food and drink;" it is not gold, silver, the stock market, a bank, or a commodity market, "but righteousness and peace and joy in the Holy Spirit" (Romans 14:17).

When you implement this justice, peace, and joy in your lives and your everyday labor, they will say of you: "Blessed is the rich man who is found blameless, and who does not go after gold! Who is he? And we will call him blessed, for he has done wonderful things among his people" (Sirach 31:8–9).

Blessed is the rich man "who does not put out his money at interest and does not take a bribe against the innocent. He who does these things shall never be moved" (Psalm 15:5).

The happy rich man? What do you say? What strange language! You, Christ's wretches, proclaim the happiness of wealth?

Yes, there is wealth that can be for the glory of man and that does not make him a wolf but rather the custodian of God's gifts. "One man pretends to be rich, yet has nothing; another pretends to be poor, yet has great wealth. The ransom of a man's life is his wealth" (Proverbs 13:7–8).

May you be rich in the Lord! And they will praise you for having done such things in your life, and your life "shall never be moved."

4

The State and Economic Life

EVER SINCE THE TIME WHEN LEO XIII reminded humanity of the principles that bring the world together through social love, a new spirit has entered human life. Selfishness, which has been flourished on the interests of the individual, is gradually disappearing, while the other extreme, which completely renounces man's activity on behalf of society, is likewise proving ineffective.

The sad experiences resulting from the destruction of the social body and the disappearance of the harmonious co-existence of people without respecting one another's rights forces us walk the paths indicated by the Church.

Although this is happening only slowly, it is becoming necessary to return to Christian social and economic community.

Under these circumstances, the attitude of the state to the citizen who is engaged in economic activity comes to the fore. Pius XI describes this topic as follows: "Just as it is gravely wrong to take from individuals what they can accomplish by their own initiative and industry and give it to the community, so also it is an injustice and at the same time a grave evil and disturbance of right order to assign to a greater and higher association what lesser and subordinate organizations can do" (QA, 79).

Thus, clear boundaries in which human activity should be ensured a certain freedom are being drawn. Such freedom should encompass the choice of one's economic activity, labor, freedom of exchange, and the freedom of adequate competition. These rights directly result from the freedom with which the human person is endowed as a free and independent being that is responsible for his own actions. The common good and the good of the other person will be the boundary of personal freedom. Within these boundaries, man has primacy over social initiative in the state.

Freedom conceived in such a way does not result from its conferral by state authority, but it directly results from the very nature of the human person. The state only recognizes it and applies it to the common good.

The activity of the state in the economic sphere must be resolved within this general framework. It will assist the entirety of economic life by creating the appropriate conditions; furthermore, it will aid individual social groups that have the right to it.

The state should create a system in which civic activity will flourish unhindered.

As a community, the state arises because of the natural needs of human co-existence. Its purpose is to meet the needs that citizens themselves cannot meet as they transcend their capacities and strength. From this flows the first task of the state. The state must strive to create such conditions and such a system in which economic life flourishes as advantageously as possible, which would give people the opportunity for a decent life and would allow them to fulfill all their personal and social duties.

Leo XIII recalls this very important principle: "The foremost duty, therefore, of the rulers of the State should be to make sure that the laws and institutions, the general character and administration of the commonwealth, shall be such as of themselves to realize public well-being and private prosperity. This is the proper scope of wise statesmanship and is the work of the rulers" (RN, 32).

Not every system facilitates the growth of the human person; not every state helps man in fulfilling his most essential duties. Hence the conclusion that the state cannot take on such political forms that would oppose the natural aspirations of man, a rational and free being destined for eternal life. In the selection of political systems, the state community is restricted by the natural law, which is expressed in human nature, in nature, and in the aims of the community itself. The state should choose a system in which man as a person may be provided with the best conditions for growth.

The fundaments of every state system should above all be: the purity of mores; order and justice; a restrained and righteous distribution of burdens and taxes; the growth of industry and trade; the flourishing of agriculture; and all other similar things (see *ibid.*). According to *Rerum novarum*, all to a large degree this leads to the prosperity of the state.

Here, Leo XIII recalls an infinitely wise Thomistic principle: "And the more that is done for the benefit of the working classes by the general laws of the country, the less need will there be to seek for special means to relieve them" (*ibid.*).

This is an extremely important principle for the construction of any permanent political system. When general institutions become healthier and come the closer to God and the natural law, the thousands of forms of state intervention become superfluous. Let us take family life as an example. When the family is based on sacred and indissoluble marriage, it will save the state the concern we see in the thousands of laws and decrees that have been implemented in France to save the family, encourage parents to fulfill their duty of creating new life, and so forth. All such legislative measures become pointless when they want to revive the branches of a tree whose trunk is dead. There are many such examples to which the countless pages of legislation, which seek to correct the effects of the widespread violation of the Ten Commandments, attest.

When the state protects the basic principles of a healthy system, it will have fewer problems with individual classes, groups, and segments of society.

The principle indicated above is at the same time the limit of the participation of the state in economic life.

The state should know how to limit its activity to the most important matters to which mere individuals cannot attend. If the government adopts economic statism and takes over the often-trivial aspects of everyday life, then, burdened with concerns, it becomes incapable of remedying its own more important and indispensable duties. A state that produces alcohol and matches and sells salt does not have the time to think about protecting its borders. May the state never debase its dignity; may it never stoop down to the level of merchants and peddles. The state should stand above them to effectively aid them; it should entrust to its citizens the problems of everyday life, stimulating and developing their mobility and entrepreneurship. May the state itself return to administering the common good; may it guide the national economy in the right direction in accordance with the needs of the common good; may it stand in defense of the national economy; may it administer unprofitable businesses that are necessary for the common good; finally, may it reserve itself the right to certain produced goods, those that would be harmful for social balance and the existence of the state itself if they remained in private hands.

The state has the duty to extend protection to all its citizens.

With respect to the citizens, the state should look out for all of them without exception. This is the guiding principle considering which the dignity of every person living within the borders of a given state grows. Leo XIII provides a rationale for this in his encyclical *Rerum novarum:* "As regards the State, the interests of all, whether high or low, are equal. The members of the working classes are citizens by nature and by the same right as the rich; they are real parts, living the life which makes up, through the family, the body of the commonwealth; and it need hardly be said that they are in every city very largely in the majority" (RN, 33).

There is a complex of personal rights with which all citizens must be equally endowed. Pius XII recalls them in his Christmas Eve address from December 24, 1942, by enumerating the basic rights of the human person that should be protected by the state:

1. The right to maintain and develop one's physical, intellectual, and moral life, especially the right to religious education and a religious upbringing.

2. The right to public and private veneration of God, including charitable religious activity.

3. The right to marry and to attain the natural purpose of marriage as well as the right to form a family community and one's own household.

4. The right to a job as an indispensable means of supporting one's family.

5. The right to freely choose one's state in life, which includes the priesthood and religious orders.

6. The right to use natural goods while respecting one's duties and the limitations of a social nature.

Therefore, the numerous and unfailingly difficult duties of the state include concern for the common good, especially within the above-described limits of the natural law. The state has the duty to provide equal protection to every social group, or to implement the kind of justice that is known as "distributive;" i.e., that which gives to all what they deserve and what should be given to them (see RN, 33).

In every state community, there are inevitable and desirable bedchambers. Will the duties of the state follow them?

There are different categories of citizens, which is a necessary fact because without these differences the social body could not exist. Within the borders of every state, there are people working for the public good and there are also those who work for themselves; there are workers, merchants, the poor... The state has numerous duties with respect to each of them.

Leo XIII describes the duties of those who directly work for the common good as follows: "Some there must be who devote themselves to the work of the commonwealth, who make the laws or administer justice, or whose advice and authority govern the nation in times of peace and defend it in war. Such men clearly occupy the foremost place in the State, and should be held in highest estimation, for their work concerns most nearly and effectively the general interests of the community" (RN, 34). The duties of the state are greater with respect to those who devote their entire lives to the public good.

With regards to citizens who directly work for their own good, they naturally "do not promote the general welfare in such measure as this, but they benefit the nation, if less directly, in a most important manner" (*ibid.*). The state also has certain obligations towards them; namely, to create the appropriate conditions for them to expand their activity which is directly useful for the whole of society.

Another category of people who deserve the protection of the state are the workers. Due to distributive justice, the state has its obligations towards them. Because it would be ludicrous if the state were concerned about only one part of its citizens while it ignored the other, public authority should take the appropriate steps to protect the working class and its interests (see *ibid.*).

This duty is bolstered by the great usefulness of the workers to society. Leo XIII writes that "the labor of the working class — the exercise of their skill, and the employment of their strength, in the cultivation of the land, and in the workshops of trade — is especially responsible and quite indispensable. Indeed, their co-operation is in this respect so important that it may be truly said that it is only by the labor of working men that States grow rich. Justice, therefore, demands that the interests of the working classes should be carefully watched over by the administration, so that they who contribute so largely to the advantage of the community may themselves share in the benefits which they create-that being housed, clothed, and bodily fit, they may find their life less hard and more endurable. It follows that whatever shall appear to prove conducive to the well-being of those who work should obtain favorable consideration. There is no fear that solicitude of this kind will be harmful to any interest; on the contrary, it will be to the advantage of all, for it cannot but be good for the commonwealth to shield from misery those on whom it so largely depends for the things that it needs" (*ibid.*).

The poor are another category of people that especially deserves protection from the state. The more helpless and abandoned a segment of society is, the greater the state's duties towards it. Why such a privilege? This is not privilege but justice. Leo XIII argues that the rich, whom prosperity protects like a levee, do not need as much protection of the authorities. By contrast, the poor, who are deprived of the protection of a large estate, are largely confined to the protection of the state. For this reason, the state should particularly care for the wage-earners, as many of them are not affluent (see RN, 34).

This aspiration towards social equilibrium expresses Christian nobility. The mandatory dependence of the poor cannot turn into their becoming slaves to the rich. In order to protect them from this humiliating dependency, the state is obliged to protect its citizens who lack property and to secure their personal freedom.

The state, which is entitled to protect all its citizens, must help them in their economic life through the aid of legislation, which will first meet the needs of the entire society and, later, will encompass all categories of citizens, each according to their social position and needs.

The state is obliged to protect the good of its citizens, which is undermined by the conditions of social life.

Although the state is concerned about the common good, according to Leo XIII the obligation of the rulers is to look after both the good of all and that of its various segments. It must look after the common good because according to the natural order protection of them is such an important duty of the central authority that the common good is not only the highest law but above all the cause and purpose of government as such (see RN, 33).

However, the state must look after the remaining parts of society as well. The state should bear in mind the interest not of the rulers but of their subjects; it must exercise its authority like God, whose fatherly protection is granted to both each individual and the entirety of society (see *ibid.*).

Thus, when the interests of the whole or the relations between each state are violated or even threatened, the intervention of public authority is indispensable (see *ibid.*).

This makes the legislative initiative of the state with respect to those workers who have experienced injury from an unjust economic system even more justified. Order and calm must be dominant everywhere for the sake of the common good and that of the individuals (see RN, 35). The state's duties include: the defense of the individual against injury; the struggle against usury, speculation, and the improper organization of labor; the proper solution of the problem of rent and wages; and the defense of the segments of society that are deprived of their own property.

The state's inspection of economic life will be necessary whenever law and justice are violated. This is both the cause and the limit of the state's authority.

The encyclical *Rerum novarum* enumerates a long list of spheres where the state should intervene. Let us cite some of them in the form of an example:

1. "There is the duty of safeguarding private property by legal enactment and protection" (RN, 38); private property must be the fundament of a healthy social system. It should be remembered that the state's protection extends to all private property, including wages for labor.

2. The state should study the causes of unemployment and work to prevent and eliminate them.

3. "The working man, too, has interests in which he should be protected by the State; and first of all, there are the interests of his soul" (RN, 40). The protection of the Church does not suffice here. Close cooperation between Church and state are necessary; different groups must work together for the common good, for this is the only

way to protect society from the injury caused by selfish individuals. This is more closely tied to the topic of the protection of holidays and "rest (combined with religious observances)" (RN, 41) in order to preclude the institutional destruction of man's moral and physical strength, which is caused by not only factory owners and the state, but also the workers themselves in their desire for a higher wage.

4. "If we turn not to things external and material, the first thing of all to secure is to save unfortunate working people from the cruelty of men of greed, who use human beings as mere instruments for money-making. It is neither just nor human so to grind men down with excessive labor as to stupefy their minds and wear out their bodies" (RN, 42).

5. "In regard to children, great care should be taken not to place them in workshops and factories until their bodies and minds are sufficiently developed. [. . .] Women, again, are not suited for certain occupations" (*ibid.*). Such labor is a sad necessity that should be eliminated through increasing the wages of the fathers of families and policies that are conducive towards family life.

6. The state should ensure that labor is rewarded with a just wage, which should suffice to meet the most important needs of the worker and his family.

* * *

By fulfilling these tasks, the state plays a paternal role with respect to all who live in a common home. Such a state will fully correspond to God's intentions: it will be just, Christian in spirit, a servant of God, and a servant of God's servants.

PART II

Labor

1
Labor as Man's Duty

"In toil you shall eat of it all the days of your life" (Genesis 3:17).

"You shall eat the fruit of the labor of your hands; you shall be happy, and it shall be well with you" (Psalm 128:2).

W E LIVE IN A TIME OF A RACE OF ORGA-nized work. We have countless evidence that the world is being transformed through labor. This image is so visible that man cannot resist its significance. Human labor is becoming increasingly purposeful, organized, and planned, while its scope gradually encompasses more and more people. Today, the question: "Why do you stand here idle all day?" (Matthew 20:6) sounds almost like a reproach.

Just as labor is in full swing and is bearing fruit, a fierce debate on the nature of labor is taking place. From where does this powerful law that has overwhelmed man and subjected him to its dictatorship originate?

Is labor a blessing? When we see the crowds of the unemployed shouting: "Give us work! Give us work!" we would be inclined to reply in the affirmative.

But maybe labor is a curse; a mania of humanity; some sort of Sisyphean toil? When we stand before the windows of factories and look at the exhausted, pale faces and the emaciated bodies of the workers rushing from their drudgery, this position also appears to be one we can accept.

When approached on its own, however, neither thought can succeed in convincing us. There is some unfathomable mystery here, some *mysterium laboris*.[1]

Why is it that "in toil you shall eat of it all the days of your life" (Genesis 3:17)?

Why is it that "man is born to trouble as the sparks fly upward" (Job 5:7)?

---

1 Latin: "The mystery of labor."

Can we ever expect an exhaustive answer to this question?

Is there not a speck of the mystery of faith here?

Labor has multifarious faces. It is simultaneously a sad necessity of life we perform avoid dying of starvation and a mystical service to love one's neighbor as well as mysterious, submissive cooperation that makes a servant a friend of God Himself.

Labor is not only physical exertion, but it is also an activity of the human person; it is an economic and social endeavor with a spiritual and even religious dimension.

I. Labor is Man's Personal Duty

When describing the arrangement of the world, the Psalmist has shown us how God has given every creature its proper place and time. Thus, darkness and the night are the kingdom of the beasts, all of which come out in its cover "seeking their food from God" (Psalm 103:21). When the sun comes up, they retreat to their dens and shelters to make room for man: "Man goes forth to his work and to his labor until the evening" (Psalm 104:23). The field has been opened to facilitate human labor! Why is there so much complaisance towards man's arduous labor? This is because Providence has designed nature to respect human labor.

Man's labor is his personal necessity.

It serves to keep man alive, meet his needs, and develop and hone his personality.

God has called man to labor. In paradise, man was obliged to labor in accordance with God's will: "The Lord God took the man and put him in the garden of Eden to till it and keep it" (Genesis 2:15). In exchange for work, Adam was given the right to receive nourishment from every tree in paradise except the tree of the knowledge of good and evil. When man violated God's commandment and was expelled from paradise, the obligation to labor remained, as man had "to till the ground from which he was taken" (Genesis 3:23). This everyday labor then became tied to redemptive toil: "In the sweat of your face you shall eat bread till you return to the ground, for out of it you were taken" (Genesis 3:18–19). Arduous labor thus became man's inseparable companion and the condition necessary for him to live: "In toil you

442

shall eat of it all the days of your life" (Genesis 3:17). From that point, it will always be that "a worker's appetite works for him; his mouth urges him on" (Proverbs 16:26). This necessity gives birth to two of life's basic laws: "Man is born to trouble as the sparks fly upward" (Job 5:7) and: "You shall eat the fruit of the labor of your hands" (Psalm 128:2).

The intention of our labor is not only the survival of human life, but it must above all satisfy all of man's needs.

Everything that man needs to preserve and maintain his own life is achieved through arduous labor; the fruits of the soil are gathered by the sweat of man's brow.

God has endowed man with a very valuable gift: reason. However, this honorable gift has the troublesome consequence that it must constantly be used. Thanks to reason, God can leave man to his own strength and hands. Only a rational being is capable of comprehending God's commandment: "In the sweat of your face you shall eat bread" (Genesis 3:18–19).

This concise instruction seemingly contains God's dialogue with man: I trust your reason, says the Lord. I will send you in the world naked; you will be cloaked in your own reason! I will send you forth without the means necessary for life; you will prepare the necessary nourishment from the gifts of nature! Although you are in a worse situation than the beasts, which have everything prepared for them, bear in mind how much higher than they you are! Your labor must satisfy your needs; it should therefore be rational and useful!

Labor cannot exist without understanding its usefulness. God designated a purpose for the labor of the first man: "to till and keep" the Garden of Eden (see Genesis 2:15). From that point, this purpose always accompanies human labor; it is a means to meet our needs with which we are so familiar.

We understand useful labor above all as adding a new value to the object or product that is the subject of our efforts. In the encyclical *Quadragesimo anno*, Pius XI speaks of the creation of truly useful goods in this sense. Meanwhile, Saint Paul instructs us that we "take no part in the unfruitful works of darkness, but instead expose them" (Ephesians 5:11). "I desire you to insist on these things, so that those who have believed in God may be careful to apply themselves to good deeds; these are excellent and profitable to men" (Titus 3:8).

Labor understood in this way is an important aim of man's efforts, but it is not the most important aim; to be fully useful, it must add importance not only to things, but also to man himself. It should shape and educate the worker. The influence of our will on matter does not suffice; our will also needs to influence those who work for their own will, reason, and feelings. Only then will labor reveal its full usefulness.

Labor leads to the full development and perfection of man.

Not only hunger, but also man's rational nature makes him labor. Labor is closely tied to the human person.

Labor is the effort of the entirety of man: his reason, will, feelings, strength, and physical endurance; all human faculties are tied to labor and participate in it. "You shall eat the fruit of the labor of your hands" (Psalm 128:2). Thus, human labor is above all personal in nature and the laborer above all should gain benefit from it: "It is the hard-working farmer who ought to have the first share of the crops" (2 Timothy 2:6).

For man, the most important fruit of labor is that it confronts us with our dignity. Indeed, our reason tells us of the need to secure nourishment for us, referring to our personhood and freedom and praiseworthily elevating us above the world of the beasts, which are governed by an impersonal instinct.

In his social encyclical, Leo XIII reminds us that man is his own steward and providence, for due to God's he should make use of his reason in satisfying the need to feed himself. Reason allows man to know holy things; reason has "prospered him in his labors and increased the fruit of his toil" (Wisdom 10:10). A breach between human labor and reason is impermissible.

This is the basis for our dutifulness, conscientiousness, and responsibility, as both duty and conscience are revealed in our labor. Thanks to them, we take on ever-greater human dignity as we use it to perform our labor better.

Labor must shape and develop man's value and gifts.

In every form of labor, twofold aims that are closely bound together concur and are simultaneously achieved: the perfection of the worker and the improvement of the fruit of labor itself.

In labor, man's physical, intellectual, and moral values and strength grow and become important. God's wisdom is a model for us: "The

Lord Himself created wisdom; He saw her and apportioned her; He poured her out upon all His works" (Sirach 1:9–10). God constantly acts in the radiance of His wisdom; because He is filled with love, He grants us His wisdom and expects its fruits in our labor.

Unfortunately, in the zeal of external labor man has frequently become so absorbed by his work and sacrificed himself so much for its good, perfection, and improvement that he became deaf to his own internal good. The only good that he recognizes is his salary, wage, bonuses for overtime, etc. Increasingly better factory products come from his hands, while he himself—as a man, a rational being—barely changes at all and does not improve.

There is something tragic about the fact that factory machinery is improving, technology is developing, and the value of products is increasing, while man himself falls further and further. Was Pius XI not right in complaining that "dead matter comes forth from the factory ennobled, while men there are corrupted and degraded" (QA, 135)? Through his labor, man has externally conquered matter, civilized the world, and made the face of the earth more beautiful but remained a slave in his soul.

Meanwhile, when engaging in external labor and improving and transforming matter, man cannot lose sight of the transformation of his mind, will, and heart. There cannot be a divorce between the perfection of man and the improvement of products, between perfection and labor, between the heart and the hand, and between morality and civilization because everything leads to the same, greatest aim: to God!

"Blessed is everyone who fears the Lord, who walks in His ways! "You shall eat the fruit of the labor of your hands; you shall be happy, and it shall be well with you" (Psalm 128:1–2). Man can be happy with his labor only when he makes his soul happier.

As a personal necessity, labor is a duty.

Our reflections make it clear that labor is indispensable; it is a necessary condition for attaining the full development of our rational nature and the making use of its gifts and authority. Furthermore, it is an obligation of the natural law, which demands preserving human life and adequately satisfying his personal and family needs.

Man is especially obliged to engage in labor for a wage when he lacks the adequate means to satisfy his needs. Leo XIII instructs us of this: "The preservation of life is the bounden duty of one and all, and to be wanting therein is a crime. It necessarily follows that each one has a natural right to procure what is required to live, and the poor can procure that in no other way than by what they can earn through their work" (RN, 44).

Paid labor is the personal duty of every person who lacks any other decent means of sustenance and is capable of working.

Under such circumstances, labor is an ordinary means of supporting oneself and all those we are required to provide with the means necessary for life as willed by Providence.

We find a beautiful example of this duty in the Book of Tobit, a once wealthy man who was driven to poverty due to the political conditions of his own people. "Now Anna his wife went daily to weaving work, and she brought home what she could get for their living by the labor of her hands" (Tobit 2:19).

St. Paul persistently encourages all Christians who can earn their bread through their own hands to not count on the help of their neighbors. He writes to the Thessalonians: "But we exhort you, brethren, to do so more and more, to aspire to live quietly, to mind your own affairs, and to work with your hands, as we charged you; so that you may command the respect of outsiders and be dependent on nobody" (1 Thessalonians 4:11–12).

The apostle, however, does not limit himself to only these recommendations. St. Paul has harsh words for those who have avoided work and idly wasted time although they could have gotten their daily bread themselves: "If anyone will not work, let him not eat" (2 Thessalonians 3:10).

By asking the faithful "to do their work in quietness and to earn their own living" (2 Thessalonians 3:12), they themselves have considered themselves to be an example of honorable paid labor. He writes: "For you yourselves know how you ought to imitate us; we were not idle when we were with you, we did not eat any one's bread without paying, but with toil and labor we worked night and day, that we might not burden any of you. It was not because we have not that right, but to give you in our conduct an example to imitate" (2 Thessalonians 3:7–9).

This servant of the Gospels, this laborer of Christ who was "worthy of double honor" wanted to give an example of love for labor and understanding its great worth with his life. At the same time, he taught that paid labor brings shame to no one.

Economic labor is the duty especially of those who have the appropriate skills.

Whomever God honors with the title of an owner should remember that his property should provide goods not only for his personal use but also for common consumption. This is why those who have skills must work.

Although the duty to work in one's own profession is not personal, as it can be performed better by well-qualified surrogates, the responsibility for the social usefulness of a given profession is personal. We can refer the words of Sacred Scripture to those who forget about this: "Extol not thyself in doing thy work and linger not in the time of distress: Better is he that laboureth, and aboundeth in all things, than he that boasteth himself and wanteth bread" (Sirach 10:29–30).

How often pride depletes itself in fruitless self-praise and satisfaction while idleness, sloth, ignorance, and stupidity are accusers that raise their voice against the owners of barren fig trees.

This leads to an obvious conclusion: paid labor and economic labor not only are not something that denigrates human dignity and are not a waste of one's life and strength, but they are a reason for worthiness; they are the source of exceptional dignity and opportunity to fully develop the talents one has received from God.

II. Labor Is Man's Social Duty

Christian philosophy teaches us than man cannot be isolated within himself; he is by nature a social being. To fully achieve his life's aims, which have been designated by Providence, man must co-exist with other people, make use of their cooperation and aid, and in turn provide them with works of justice and love.

The same goes with respect to human labor. Labor creates a social bond between people that not only brings people closer together but also teaches them social service to one another and bears witness to bilateral need and usefulness, thus teaching love of one's neighbor in practice. Labor creates all of history; binds together past and present epochs through its continuity; and creates a framework for those who have yet to come.

Thanks to labor, an organism of human solidarity, which results from the experience of man's own insufficiency and inadequacy, is formed. In labor, we recognize the necessity of dependence, subordination, cooperation, the exchange of goods and service, the division of labor, its coordination, and so forth. All these achievements are very important for co-existence in the spirit of Christian social love.

Labor should create the common good.

Labor is the service of not only oneself and one's own needs, but it is also service of one's neighbor. Man is a servant of God in all his activity; to serve, God has endowed him with various talents and, consequently, give him instructions.

One of them, "Be fruitful and multiply" (Genesis 1:28), fills the world with God's children. God has given socio-economic life its greatest contribution: that of a rational man without which we cannot speak of any progress or transformation of the earth.

Another instruction — "Fill the earth and subdue it" (see Genesis 1:28) — is a general mobilization by God once and forever. It is God's friendly summons to people, His collaborators, that they continue to develop God's creative work on earth.

The execution of these commands not only increases the glory of our Creator and Father; it not only perfects man, but it furthermore creates and expands the common good of society. This obedience to God's voice leads to the progress of civilization and prosperity.

Naturally, the degree to which we participate in creating the common good varies and depends on the kind of work one performs. One thing is certain: every kind of labor — executive and administrative; intellectual and physical; sophisticated and physically strenuous — indirectly leads to the multiplication of the common good, even if it primarily has one's own good in mind.

In this sense, our labor is service to our nation; as such, it should bear in mind not only one's own good but also the common good. Recalling this is especially important when we bear in mind that around the world, we, the Poles, have the reputation of good workers who toil on foreign acres. Let us demonstrate the will to work in our own backyard. Due to the foreign yoke and the decline of labor discipline, we are behind compared to the rest of the family of nations;

the productivity of our national economy is at one-third the level of other countries. Let us awaken within ourselves the will to bring up ourselves and our society.

Man's duty is to be socially useful.

This is the simple conclusion of our reflections so far. Each of us constantly receives services from others and thus must express gratitude for them. Everyone who lives in society and reaps any benefits from it must perform socially useful labor. This can be physical, intellectual, or cultural labor; it can also be the moral labor of sanctifying one's brethren. The basic law of Christian economics obliges us to work off our own useful labor and support those who cannot feed themselves. Ecclesiasticus admonishes us: "See ye that I have not labored for myself only, but for all that seek out the truth" (Sirach 24:47).

Labor provides us with the means that are necessary to help our neighbors.

By maintaining order in bearing witness to love, we should use the fruits of our labor for the use of those closest to us, especially our families, to all those who are incapable of working.

Man is obliged to work to support his family.

St. Paul instructs us: "If any one does not provide for his relatives, and especially for his own family, he has disowned the faith and is worse than an unbeliever" (1 Timothy 5:8). The Church derives the right to property from the duty to secure one's family's well-being. A just wage helps us to acquire a modest estate, while property creates the basis for securing the livelihood of one's family not only during the life of the father but after his death as well. Thus, whoever lacks other means of fulfilling his family duties must acquire the means necessary to do so through his own labor. The Apostle to the Gentiles says: "So then, as we have opportunity, let us do good to all men, and especially to those who are of the household of faith" (Galatians 8:10).

Our labor provides us with the means to perform acts of charity. To work means to produce useful goods; it means to want goods not only for oneself but also for others, for those who will make use of the fruits of our labor. Those who cannot work should make use of the toil of those who are capable and willing to work: children, the elderly, the sick and infirm, the poor and needy, the orphans and the abandoned, and all who are deprived of the care of their families. Labor conceived in this way is the exercise of natural love; it is the practical act of love of one's neighbor and is something greater than even the noblest words. The Apostle of Love admonishes us: "Little children, let us not love in word or speech but in deed and in truth" (1 John 3:18).

Labor opens for us the gates of Christian mercy and makes it possible for us to help to weak, the poor, and the powerless. The poor are God's family at God's feast. The Lord Almighty has made us stewards of the earth so that we may live and support those who expect our assistance by working on it. "The hapless commits himself to thee; thou hast been the helper of the fatherless" (Psalm 10:14).

Enumerating His acts of benevolence towards the Israelites, whom He led out of the land of Egypt and into the land of milk and honey, God calls us to through the work of our own hands share nourishment with "the Levite and the sojourner who is among you" (Deuteronomy 26:12). Today, the Church gives the faithful a similar admonition through the words of the Apostle, a weaver and laborer: "Let the thief no longer steal, but rather let him labor, doing honest work with his hands, so that he may be able to give to those in need" (Ephesians 4:28). In this way, the Church has transformed the fruits of human labor, the excessive wealth of the rich of this world, and even the generous penny of the worker into works of mercy, the wiping dry of tears, and the consolation of the proletariat; the history of Christian charity attests to this.

May we fulfill our vocation in light, in the spirit of complete subordination to the hard-working Father who voluntarily took upon Himself the duty to persistent and ever-fruitful labor.

Let us cooperate with God with willing hearts: "The point is this: he who sows sparingly will also reap sparingly, and he who sows bountifully will also reap bountifully. Each one must do as he has made up his mind, not reluctantly or under compulsion, for God loves a cheerful giver. And God is able to provide you with every blessing in abundance, so that you may always have enough of everything and may provide in abundance for every good work. As it is written, 'He scatters abroad, he gives to the poor; his righteousness endures forever.' He who supplies seed to the sower and bread for food will supply and multiply your resources and increase the harvest of your righteousness" (2 Corinthians 9:6–10).

2

The Christian Dignity
of Human Labor

*"Therefore, my beloved brethren, be steadfast,
immovable, always abounding in the work
of the Lord, knowing that in the Lord your
labor is not in vain" (1 Corinthians 15:58).*

THE LIGHT OF CHRIST'S TRUTH, WHICH illuminates all the people in the world, has also illuminated the darkness in which human labor had hitherto been hidden. When He led the world out of darkness, Christ the Lord exposed our works in the light of day so that they might be revealed to the world.

There was a time when the world did not yet know the laborious life of Nazareth; thus, it is unsurprising that human labor, especially manual labor, had been the subject of disdain before the coming of Christ the Lord. The greatest pagan thinkers and philosophers proclaimed that labor is an activity that degrades man and is unworthy of a rational and free being; they considered labor to be a sad material necessity. Much was said about the negative impact of physical labor on the human body and, it was believed, soul. It was believed that labor deprives man of freedom and his ability to exercise virtues and be engaged in civic life.

Only Christianity clearly rejected these views, instead pointing out the proper dignity of human labor. Labor has ceased to be a punishment, debasement, or form of slavery; instead, it is a human activity whose moral and religious value is great.

Christ the Lord said of the everyday labor of His Father and Himself: "My Father is working still, and I am working" (John 5:17); He called His Father a plowman, gardener, and homeowner with favor. Before beginning His apostolic work, Christ Himself was an artisan and was called "the carpenter's son" (see Matthew 13:55; Mark 6:3).

These were strange words, yet people must have desperately needed them since they were accepted so quickly and came to dominate the world, gradually transforming pagan views and customs. From that point, honest labor for one's own sustenance is a sign of true conversion and the basic duty of every person.

Now, labor serves not only to gain one's daily bread but also to make sacrifices in one's own life. Its significance is not only external, but it also demands internal life; it not only is not an obstacle to co-existence with God, but it is also major assistance in aspiring for heaven.

I. Economic Toil Is Cooperation with God

"Whatever your task, work heartily, as serving the Lord and not men, knowing that from the Lord you will receive the inheritance as your reward" (Colossians 3:23–24).

We will not have a deep understanding of the vocation, majesty, and greatness of human labor without invoking the teaching on the creation of the world and Divine Providence.

God is the first cause of all creation; everything that exists comes from God's hands, while everything that will exist in the future has a causative relationship with that which already exists. God is the beginning of everything that exists.

God governs all things and creatures. God rules the world through the laws that He has established Himself and to which He has subjected the existence and activity of all creatures. Meanwhile, God Himself respects them so much in governing that world that, apart from miracles, He does not violate or suspend them. In this way, God extends His Providence over the world through the physical laws of creation, the abundance of the chemical properties of created bodies, the fruitfulness of the earth, and the instincts given to the animals.

The Creator directs the world towards the aim He has designated.

The Book of Genesis presents to us the hard-working life of the Creator: "And on the seventh day God finished His work which He had done" (Genesis 2:2). The enormity of creation makes us admire God's limitless wisdom: "O Lord, how manifold are Thy works! "In wisdom hast Thou made them all; the earth is full of Thy creatures" (Psalm 104:24).

When we look at God's works more closely, we discern design and intention down to the smallest details: "Great are the works of the

Lord, studied by all who have pleasure in them" (Psalm 111:2). Each of God's works gives the most glorious testimony to its Creator; there is no shoddiness, feverish cursoriness, or impermanence here: "The Rock, His work is perfect; for all His ways are justice" (Deuteronomy 32:4). When seen up close, each creature, even the smallest and most mysterious, reveals its purpose; everyone justifies its own existence and is useful. The wise purposefulness of everything we look at overjoys us: "How great are Thy works, O Lord! Thy thoughts are very deep!" (Psalm 92:5)

The Creator, who is beautiful in all His essence, has poured all His beauty over all creation which has come from His hands. The subtlest Aesthete has provided a model for every labor so that it may bind together usefulness with its perfection and unique beauty. God has extended the most wondrous miracles over all who work the earth by a blue cloth of stars: "The heavens are telling the glory of God; and the firmament proclaims his handiwork" (Psalm 19:1).

Is this not the correct conclusion at which every person, every rational witness to God's creation can and should arrive? "All the earth worships Thee; they sing praises to Thee, sing praises to Thy name. Come and see what God has done" (Psalm 66:4–5).

"Come and see"—to whom is this invitation addressed? Only man, "the work of Thy hands" (see Job 10:3), is capable of comprehending it. Man is called to study the laborious God who continues to work and to love God in His works and acts.

Christ the Lord makes note of this: "My Father is working still, and I am working" (John 5:17). God did not stop at His first act of creation; instead, He constantly and actively sustains the world and fills the world with creation. God is a plowman, gardener, and owner of His vineyard, in which He constantly engages in the work of Providence. We see God in the world of creatures; we see how He exercises His authority and sustains and transforms life, even though He Himself never changes it: "Of old Thou didst lay the foundation of the earth, and the heavens are the work of Thy hands. They will perish, but Thou dost endure; they will all wear out like a garment. Thou changest them like raiment, and they pass away; but Thou art the same, and thy years have no end" (Psalm 102:25–27).

The Son of the most laborious Father has also filled His life with His activity and the fulfillment of the duty the Father has assigned to

Him (see John 17:4). He was so zealous that He wanted to accomplish everything during the day because "night comes, when no one can work" (John 9:4). In the world, Christ was "the light of the world" (John 9:5) and our model.

We stand admiring God's works. Should we limit ourselves to just admiration?

Man is called to cooperate with God.

The unemployed standing in the town square heard the vineyard owner ask them: "Why do you stand here idle all day?" (Matthew 20:6). God does not like passive viewers of His labor: "You go into the vineyard, too" (Matthew 20:7). We are called to cooperation, "for we are God's fellow workers" (1 Corinthians 3:9) both in the order of grace and in the natural order.

Man serves God in all His works; he has received all sorts of gifts, abilities, and talents for this purpose. We must be ready to respond to God's call: "Thou wouldest call, and I would answer Thee; Thou wouldest long for the work of Thy hands" (Job 14:15). God gives us His hand with the commandment: "Fill the earth and subdue it" (see Genesis 1:28).

Human labor is the continuation of God's creative work; it is God's extended arm and hand that multiplies in the billions of hands of working people. God calls us to work so that we may live. By endowing us with reason, He has commanded that we improve and finish the universe, making use of its goods and wealth.

The world that God has created is a perfect work, although it is not finished, unchangeable perfection. The world has not been created in a way that man may only make passive use of it, like the inhabitant of an enchanted castle. On the contrary, although the world has been designed for man it is so devoted to man that he can constantly add something to God's harmony.

Man should perfect the earth and subdue it to himself; he is called to humanize and ennoble it, to transform wild plains, woody jungles, impenetrable bogs, and roving sands into useful, arable, and fertile lands that are pleasing to the eye.

When we admire the enormity of the change that has happened to the earth through human labor, we see how obedient man was to God and what the resulting benefits were. To acknowledge this, it suffices to look at just one and the same landscape today with what it had looked like half a century before. When we stand before an old etching of our city and reflect on its historical details and the image of its present reality, we can perfectly discern the vocation of the working man.

Man must make the earth even more worthy of God. God's commandment, which was given in paradise, was full of concern for blind nature, which demands man's labor to maintain nature within the limits of God's designs. The earth needs man, for without his labor it would quickly turn into an impenetrable jungle.

Nature is meaningful when it serves man; it becomes important and useful only once it is conquered by man. For this reason, God not only wanted nature to be fertile for man, but He also that man may make it fertile. Bearing this in mind, God wanted man to be His collaborator, God's worker.

As God's collaborator, man's purpose is to constantly contribute to the perfection of God's work.

We ask: Does it suffice to contribute to it? We cannot we create? We cannot because human labor is only an addition to God's labor. Strictly speaking, human labor is not creative; it merely makes busy use of God's gifts and energies without which no one apart from God Himself can accomplish anything. "Do you know the ordinances of the heavens? Can you establish their rule on the earth?" (Job 38:33). "Who has put wisdom in the clouds?" (Job 38:36). "Do you give the horse his might?" (Job 39:19).

We are correctly reminded of this forgotten truth in the encyclical *Quadragesimo anno*: "But it is no less evident that, had not God the Creator of all things, in keeping with His goodness, first generously bestowed natural riches and resources — the wealth and forces of nature — such supreme efforts would have been idle and vain, indeed could never even have begun. For what else is work but to use or exercise the energies of mind and body on or through these very things?" (QA, 53).

Indeed! Man is only God's helper, not an independent creator of goods. God made a great contribution to the act of production. Is not too much said of capital and labor today? Is not too little said of the backbone that is at the fore of all production, of God? His nature is the gift that even the most strenuous human labor is incapable of creating. If God had not abundantly blessed us with His goods, we would have labored in vain like the fisherman in the Sea of Galilee. It was only through "the word of God" that the cast nets burst with the abundance of God's gifts.

Thus, man is only God's helper, not an independent creator of goods! At the same time, man's role as God's helper is an important one that is indispensable to his own good and the good of the cultivated land.

We cooperate with God by fulfilling the duties of our state and profession.

The greatest Owner of the earth demands that we fulfill our tasks and life's aims as best as possible in the spirit of conscientious cooperation with Him. Let us present ourselves "to God as one approved, a workman who has no need to be ashamed" (2 Timothy 2:15).

To be God's worker means to tie all our everyday labors to the aim and purpose that God wants to achieve: "Whatever your task, work heartily, as serving the Lord and not men, knowing that from the Lord you will receive the inheritance as your reward" (Colossians 3:23–24).

Meanwhile, God intends on bringing nourishment to all in the right time through the aid of our labor (see Psalm 145:15). For this reason, He has divided His numerous works among His people, burdening us with His concerns and the admonition: "But let each one test his own work, and then his reason to boast will be in himself alone and not in his neighbor. For each man will have to bear his own load" (Galatians 6:4–5).

The numerous burdens of human labor that are carried by man in his professional life take on true nobility, dignity, and beauty because of their relationship to God and His eternal creative efforts. Although they are far removed from the lofty efforts of scholars who study the paths of God's wisdom, they are close to that wisdom through God's reflection which is illuminated by our faith.

It is in the light of this faith that the farmer "sets his heart on plowing furrows" (Sirach 38:26) and the "craftsman and master workman [...] labors by night as well as by day [and] sets his heart on painting a lifelike image" (v. 27). Meanwhile, the "the smith sitting by the anvil [...] sets his heart on finishing his handiwork, and he is careful to complete its decoration" (v. 28) and the "potter [...] is always deeply concerned over his work, and all his output is by number" (v. 29). All of them sing God's glory, for "each is skillful in his own work" (v. 31), a molecule of God's wisdom without which "a city cannot be established" (v. 32).

God has placed a summons to zeal and persistence in the hearts of all: "And let us not grow weary in well-doing, for in due season we shall reap if we do not lose heart. So then, as we have opportunity, let us do good to all men, and especially to those who are of the household of faith" (Galatians 6:9–10).

In this way, all our lives, labors, and activities are fastened by our faith like a buckle; our deeds flow from faith, which is "active along with [...] works" and is "completed by works" (James 2:22). Having poured faith into our hearts, God has recommended that devote our lives to our labors, which are to attest to our faith, for "faith apart from works is dead" (James 2:26).

"You see that a man is justified by works and not by faith alone" (James 2:24). We become God's friends through our labors and hardship, which are performed under the sign of faith. The servant does not know what his master does, while through faith we have learned the entire meaning and significance of all of God's works as well as the meaning of human labors and deeds.

Jesus Christ, the Son of the Household Owner of Heaven, sees countless laborers burdened by the difficulty of arduous sacrificial labor carrying great weights and pulling their yoke in the field to help wearied beasts of burden in the difficult work of tilling and harvesting the earth's great abundance. These are all the collaborators of the beloved Father, His friends who do whatever is asked of them.

The Lord Jesus has addressed words of consolation to them: "Come to me, all who labor and are heavy laden, and I will give you rest" (Matthew 11:28).

II. Labor Is One of the Means of Our Sanctification

Ecclesiastes, a wise man from Jerusalem, looked at all human labor and difficulties and doubted their meaning: "What does man gain by all the toil at which he toils under the sun?" (Ecclesiastes 1:3). He worked much in his life but saw no fruit of his labor. "I have seen everything that is done under the sun; and behold, all is vanity and a striving after wind" (Ecclesiastes 2:14).

Is it true that nothing remains of our labors? What mystery is hidden here? A great one! It makes us grow silent in this din and in the maelstrom of hard work! It bashfully hides amidst its fruits, in the dizzying production records, amidst overflowing warehouses, thousands of tons of exports, and constantly increasing sales revenues.

However, when we looked at work-worn hands, at foreheads filled with beads of sweat and furrowed from exhaustion; when we hear a heart beating from hard work, all doubts abandon us!

Labor has given birth to goods that no statistic accounts for and that economists do not evaluate but that are the subject of "eternal economics." The worker is the first to receive nourishment from these goods, for "it is the hard-working farmer who ought to have the first share of the crops" (2 Timothy 2:6).

This fruit is the nourishment "of which you do not know" (John 4:32) or about which you forget: "He who reaps receives wages, and gathers fruit for eternal life, so that sower and reaper may rejoice together" (John 4:36).

We gather fruit for eternal life from this arduous work. Even if our factory wage were record-high and we received the greatest bonuses, they would be nothing compared to our abundant payment in heaven.

Labor is love for the Creator of all things.

St. Paul the Apostle instructs us: "Whatever your task, work heartily, as serving the Lord" (Colossians 3:23).

Man, who has been called to be God's helper, unites with God in his labor, becoming a "good and faithful servant" and God's friend: "No longer do I call you servants, for the servant does not know what his master is doing; but I have called you friends, for all that I have heard from my Father I have made known to you" (John 15:15). There are no secrets between God and us; we have learned His will and His labors, and we have learned the mysteries of nature and its purposes. We see God's paternal benevolence towards people scattered in nature's laws and treasures. Our love for God and His creation is born as we grow closer to God's works. In this way, our labor as service turns into a labor of love.

Wondrous is this educative path through which God elevates us in our labors. Our first vocation in which God called us to labor as His creation that we may live no longer suffices. As rational beings and Christians, God has called us to labor so that we may help Him to improve the universe and that we may perfect ourselves through making use of our talents; he calls us to increase God's glory through our filial submission to His will and, finally, to express our love for God through our work. Our dignity and the majesty of our labor have been revealed through this summons, as it not only accomplishes the salvation of nature, saves the world from the embrace of savagery, and ennobles matter, but it is above all man's salvation and redemption as well as his sanctification.

This strange power and love come not from nowhere but from the love that revives it. Labor for the sake of God's love is the apex of an active and laborious life, as it is not only participation in the work of creation but also in the work of redemption.

When we participate in the work of creation and cooperate with Providence, we experience the joy of labor; when we cooperate in redemption, we will experience its difficulty and burden. We praise God in both these works.

The work of the redemption of humanity took place once: on the Cross. From that point, all redemption flows from the Cross. Not even the most heroic labor can achieve our redemption. However, labor conceived of love for God helps us to achieve God and heaven.

Moreover, labor is prayer.

The fullness of activity is found in love. For this reason, labor performed from love for God cannot be separated from prayer. Labor resulting from love is prayer. To work means to pray. Labor is praise of God, who "is faithful in all His words and gracious in all His deeds" (Psalm 145:13). Prayerful labor is the sense of the honor of being called to cooperation with God in the work of feeding humanity and maintaining order on earth.

Labor as prayer is sacrificially giving oneself to God upon His summons: I do whatever You want me to, and I will give up to God everything that has come from Him: all my strength, abilities, talents, and gifts. "Take your share of suffering as a good soldier of Christ Jesus" (2 Timothy 2:3).

Finally, labor as prayer is the will to atone to God for all the ugliness of the devastation of sin: "Consider my affliction and my trouble and forgive all my sins" (Psalm 25:18).

Finally, labor is a place where Christian virtues are learned.

Labor resulting from love brings us closer to God: "For you alone are holy. You alone are the Lord. You alone, O Jesus Christ, are most high" (*Gloria*). It would be impossible for God to not impart on us His sanctity in such close cooperation.

God emanates all around, revealing His wisdom and benevolence in the work of His hands. When God creates beings and sustains their existence, God constantly gives Himself to man and to all of creation. We admire God's industriousness, limitless generosity, irrepressible creativity, and above all love and kindness.

Man working amidst these wonders cannot not be radiant. God gives us an example: "For I have given you an example, that you also should do as I have done to you" (John 13:15). This is the starting point of our diligence, our constantly increasing productivity, and our love and benevolence towards our neighbors who seek nourishment and provisions from our hands.

We are prompted to persistently overcome the recalcitrance of matter and the lack of human cooperation through the patience with which God nourishes the ungrateful and sinful world: "And let steadfastness have its full effect, that you may be perfect and complete, lacking in nothing" (James 1:4). Progress, civilization, and Christian culture, which make the earth subjected to man and, through him, God, receive their livelihood from this school of Christian patience.

Love for our labor, to which God has called us, will be something greater than just a civic virtue for us: it will be a ladder that will carry us higher, closer to heaven.

The more we love our labor, the more there is dignity and rectitude and the more pride we deserve; the false shame we feel for labor disappears, while our labor becomes transparent and is a solemn celebration on God's altar of creation. What is strange about this? Only he "who does evil hates the light, and does not come to the light, lest his deeds should be exposed. But he who does what is true comes to the light, that it may be clearly seen that his deeds have been wrought in God" (John 3:20–21).

We will see our worth in our labors. Our labor can reveal our hearts and be a test of who we are and our worth: "You will know them by their fruits" (Matthew 7:16). Therefore, our labor is a tribunal that can already tell us today what our Final Judgment will be like.

Depending on our deeds, our labor can be either our glory or our indictment. If our labor gives good fruits, God Himself ensures their glory before people "that they may see your good works and give glory to your Father who is in heaven" (Matthew 5:16).

This is the doubt that tormented the ancient wise man. What benefit does man have from his labor, "by all the toil at which he toils under the sun?" (Ecclesiastes 1:3)? May deeds themselves provide an answer! Not only land, agriculture, the factory, and the artisan's craft, and not only man's body but also his soul can be satiated and blessed by labor!

* * *

What, then, is labor? Is it a punishment for original sin? Or maybe it is a sad necessity so that we do not die of hunger? Or is it merchandise subjected to the harsh, irrational law of supply and demand?

Is labor tied to nature, or is it separated from it? The industrialization of the world and the machinism that takes on unheard-of dimensions is such that any attempt at stopping its march forward seems to be in vain. Man's domination over matter is consolidated and the earth becoming increasingly subordinated; this is the hitherto unknown greatness of labor!

Who is the working man? Maybe he is merely a working beast? In this triumph of labor, has man not become subjected to hitherto unknown servitude? Has the worker not become a mere tool in the capitalist system? Is he in essence not a slave and servant of the machine? Does he consider himself to be God's helper? Is his labor still love, prayer, and an experience that teaches virtue?

Such questions are numerous. The responses to them are often very sad. When labor was elevated, man was denigrated. Unprecedented labor became active, but it became sad, harsh, and hopeless. Although we are impressed by the achievements of labor, we are at the same time saddened by man's own losses.

In such a situation, we must earnestly recall the Christian elevation of human labor in which both internal and external labor are tied together: "And whatever you do, in word or deed, do everything in the name of the Lord Jesus, giving thanks to God the Father through Him" (Colossians 3:17).

The responsibility of our labor is as great as its dignity. By completely committing Himself to us in cooperation, God demands complete subordination on our behalf. There can be no talk of such subordination when man processes material without perfecting his own soul. The most laudable and economically productive labor remains mere chaff if we harm our souls while performing it.

We cannot deserve the accusation: "I have not found your works perfect in the sight of my God" (Revelation 3:2). There can be no sadder conclusion to a laborious life than hearing the sentence: "I tell you, I do not know where you come from; depart from me, all you workers of iniquity!" (Luke 13:27).

"Therefore, my beloved brethren, be steadfast, immovable, always abounding in the work of the Lord, knowing that in the Lord your labor is not in vain" (1 Corinthians 15:58).

3

The Toil of Factory Labor

*"Come to me, all who labor and are heavy
laden, and I will give you rest" (Matthew 11:28).*

ECCLESIASTICUS ADMONISHES: "DO NOT
hate toilsome labor" (Sirach 7:15). Can we speak of love for
factory labor? Should we free ourselves of aversion to it? Can
we expect that the warm rays of loves enter the drab, gray, and noisy
halls of factories without soiling love's white cloak? Life is too harsh
and too fast, while the clamor of hammers is too deafening for the
patient, gracious, and clement Lady to survive amidst this Dantean
hell. Inviting love into factory walls is madness! We respect and venerate it too much to degrade it in this way!

Is this not a silent acknowledgment of disbelief in the salvific power
of love?

After all, "love is strong as death [. . .]. Its flashes are flashes of
fire, a most vehement flame" (Song of Songs 8:6). To what will love
yield? What can it fear? Love is not always clad in white vestments;
it also knows the scarlet of blood and dark sweat stains. The love
that speaks most articulately to us is not the love in a myrtle wreath,
but the love from the stations of the cross; the love adorned with a
crown of thorns; the love that picks up sore feet off muddy streets;
the love that carries one's one cross with one's work-worn hands;
and every Simon of Cyrene we encounter in our everyday lives. Will
this love yield to "flashes of fire, a most vehement flame," or will it
fear immolation and the toil of factory labor? Will it be spooked by
the language of human suffering and matter?

No! Christ's voice must resound here: "Come to me, all who labor
and are heavy laden, and I will give you rest" (Matthew 11:28). Too
much misery has accumulated here for Christ to be absent. Human
efforts are too ineffectual for one's own strength to suffice. Only. . . "I
will give you rest"! Love will reign among you only in My name!

For love is stronger than machines, motors, cranes, turbines, and

463

everything that death sows; indeed, love is stronger than death itself. Thus, let us enter the factory gates with love in our hearts.

I. The Toil of Factory Labor on the Path to Love

Certainly, factory labor will never be mere pleasure, even with the best possible organization of the workplace and if man were granted the most perfect legal protection and the greatest possible human kindness. Every labor, and especially labor that is given a direction, should simultaneously bring us joy and difficulty. If labor were not subordinated to matter, executives, and the management of other people, it perhaps would be mere joy. Thus, in every organization of factory labor there will be drudgery, a particle of one's participation in salvation, one's own redemption. Today, this ordinary difficulty, which results from man's fallen nature, is supplemented by an additional difficulty that results from the flaws of the dominant socio-economic system. The conditions of labor, especially in the factory, often make it impossible to gain enjoyment from working.

The worker does not see the fruits of his labor. His labor is a good that is sold on a whimsical market according to the ordinary laws of supply and demand, which are valued more than the law of love. Thus, the product of labor no longer belongs to the worker.

Fundamentally, the exertion of human labor leads to the profit of the entrepreneur and only coincidentally leads to the satisfaction of human needs, which had once been the source of the greatest joy and social love.

Man becomes subordinated to machinery. His personal and professional needs are not taken into consideration; instead, the needs of machinery are. Thus, his moral and religious needs are even less important. This machine, which as a blind tool could always be man's servant, his most faithful helper, and even almost his friend in assisting him is pitted against the human person; in the way it is conceived today, the machine demands that man constantly renounces the most wondrous gifts of his nature. This fruit of human reason constantly struggles against its mother, reason, thus reducing man's participation in production, which ultimately leads to unemployment. Furthermore, to ensure that machinery constantly develops, unemployment is often seen as a necessary condition, which gives machinery the unusual task of the consumption of goods. Man deprived of labor through machinism is relegated to the ranks of irrational creatures.

This gives birth to this additional difficulty which has no causative relationship with original sin. This is the fruit of a flawed system that does not reduce the difficulty of labor, although it appears to move in that direction, but, on the contrary, exacerbates it.

Are there not human forces that would succeed in removing this source from which the greatest resistance to labor, the greatest hatred for it, flows? There certainly are! And they must be used!

II. The Spirit of Brotherhood and Friendship in Factory Labor

St. John the Apostle calls us to active love: "Let us not love in word or speech but in deed and in truth" (1 John 3:18). Where else do we have a space for active love if not in the maelstrom of labor, amidst one's workplace in which people gather to work together? The workplace seems to have been designed by nature to give birth to friendship and brotherhood.

Through labor, man transcends himself and notices other people working like himself around him. Labor leads to friendship between workers. The most intimate friendship is born amidst persistent and necessary labor.

A common object of labor is a factor that forges friendship, which is transmitted to persons and their souls. A sincere and open face appears in the sweat of one's brow; here, phoniness and the dishonest perversions of social life disappear.

Human friendship develops thanks to common labor. We see in it that we must make an effort to grow close to someone. Such is the case in all well-organized labor. Brotherhood is its natural result.

The responsibility of the organizers of workplaces is to ensure that everything is conducive to the spirit of brotherhood and friendship because of the organization itself. This is an indispensable condition for the fruitfulness of every labor.

In today's working conditions of factory labor, this spirit is nearly completely absent. The spirit of profit and subjection is an obstacle to friendship and brotherhood in the factory. The capitalist system has made labor a tool of hatred through the spirit of competition between workers and crises in which the labor of one deprives another of his bread.

Here, there is no room for loving one's neighbors in deed; everything is shackled to one's own selfish interest and subjected to profit, income, and wages.

Today, this is so marked that it is nearly impossible for man to experience joy from his labor and for a sense of brotherhood to be born through labor. Everything is done to make labor hate-filled for the worker.

We must correct this error that has been bred by capitalist civilization and reject the artificial aim of profit; the natural purposefulness of labor must be restored so that it may be useful to all, lead to brotherhood, and extinguish hatred.

The selfish concern for the acquisition of profit and income, which has been the leading factor, must disappear; money cannot be the aim of any kind of labor, including that in the factory. Universal usefulness and love of one's neighbor as oneself are the motivations that should illuminate the workplace.

Only then will friendship, love, and brotherhood be born, while silent struggle will disappear from the factory and workplace, which should be places where the Creator, who cooperates with people in the production of useful goods and in the path to heaven, is worshiped.

III. A Joyful Form of Labor

A man's work should correspond to his passions and talents. Labor cannot deafen and stupefy those who perform it; it cannot make a worker ignore and kill his great desires but instead should awaken them. Labor awakens within us our strength and our hidden gifts; through labor, we discover our vocation. It speaks to us in a comprehensible language to which we respond with love and filial tenderness, for in labor we give birth to a new work in our image and likeness. Can a woman forget her infant? Can we be indifferent to a work in which we have invested our own strength, thought, and heart, one which is the product of exhausting, sometimes bloody sacrifice?

Let us look at old workers who have devoted their entire lives to their profession; their labor is no longer tribulation, but instead it becomes a priestly sacrifice and toilsome joy. This is beautifully expressed in the poem "Iron Improvisation":

> The old locksmith's movements profess their credo faithfully,
> Like a child, he sheds tears of glee,
> Not knowing that the bell has rung, and it is time to leave,
> Thinking not of his supper, home, or bed,
> He hammers away, his weary face red.
> And praises the greatness of Omnipo-
> tence and the beautiful Design,
> His iron singing hymns to the heavens all the time.
>   (Wojciech Bąk, "The Heavenly Burden")

Here, we hear the steps of victorious creative joy over the arduous toil of labor. The love for toiling has entered the soul; this joy gives labor wings, make it easier and perfecting it. The worker is joyful "and like a strong man runs [his] course with joy" (Psalm 19:5).

In order to be joyous and enjoyable, labor cannot surpass man's strength and abilities. Because human strength is limited, man can perform only a strictly designated amount of labor. When the difficulty of labor exceeds this measure and violates proportions, labor can no longer be pleasant; it becomes burdensome and tedious, leading to sadness and depression. Works that are produced with such a disposition can never be useful. The difficulty of labor can be reduced while the joy resulting from it can be increased by prudently establishing how long it lasts and showing restraint in the use of human labor. Countless sins are committed against this natural law by both the private organizers of workshops and the systems and doctrines that are dominant today.

For labor to be accompanied by joy, it should be tied to a sense of hope. Above all, this should be the hope that the worker will receive a just and proper wage for his efforts, one that will allow him to satisfy all his needs and those of his family and to secure his existence through the acquisition of property.

This basic hope should be tied to the hope that zeal and conscientiousness will be recognized as the means of social advancement and distinction. If at every rung of the social ladder labor encounters recognition, merit, awards, and distinction, why should conscientious, sacrificial professional labor in the factory be deprived of this honor?

Finally, there is the greatest hope in the supernatural order in which God complements the insufficiency of the human dimension. When the human wage does not satiate, it cannot satisfy the human soul; when acquired hope does not give birth to God's joy, then waiting for God, a constant advent, and hope that only God can repay everything is born in labor.

We see how momentous this hope is wherever it has been destroyed. This is why factory labor has become so burdensome in the capitalist system; everything to which the worker had the right has ceased to be certain. He cannot be certain of anything. In the Bolshevik state, labor has become hopeless, for everything outside it has been negated. Love for labor superseded and opposed all other forms of love: for one's family, home, nation, and God Himself. Every aspiration of the heart had to be replaced by the love for labor and machinery. Labor and machinery can be the only holy thing, the only god. There is no hope for property, rest, or transformation. Can Bolshevik labor get rid of difficulty and suffering? On the contrary, its burden has achieved invincible dimensions. Neither the capitalist nor Bolshevik system can satisfy this hope: "Come to Me, all who labor and are heavy laden, and I will give you rest" (Matthew 11:28).

Only Christ has the power to transform.

* * *

Because human labor is not man's highest purpose, it cannot bring perfect joy. Even the joy resulting from labor cannot be fully satisfying.

Labor is not an absolute aim, but an indirect one: labor cannot be performed for labor's sake, but as a means of useful values both in the natural and supernatural order. Labor is not the meaning of human life.

After completing his work, man is happy for having completed his service. Then he has the sense that another joy, one that is a hundred times more perfect, is possible. The question of why we are forced to work continues to appear. Is it to make a profit, as the capitalists would like? Or is it to have a wage, as the communists claim? Both these aspirations agree with respect to the degradation of human efforts.

Christ gives us an answer: Only I will give you rest.

We will experience complete joy only when our working hands will be accompanied by the hymn of the youths from the fiery oven: "Bless the Lord, all works of the Lord, sing praise to Him, and highly exalt Him forever. [...] Bless the Lord, all powers [...]. Bless the Lord, fire and heat. [...] Bless the Lord, light and darkness [...]. Let the earth bless the Lord [...]. Bless the Lord, all things that grow on the earth [...]. Bless the Lord, you sons of men" (Daniel 3:35–60).

This Franciscan hymn of praise is extended; it resounds in human history with ever-new stanzas:

Bless the Lord, hands of plowmen and workers; bless Him, the efforts of the designs of workers, and the toil of artisans and miners.

Bless the Lord, fathers of families that work to get their own bread and that of Your children.

Bless the Lord, sweat of the brow and toil of redemptive hardship, in the grace of loving labor and salvation.

Sing the glory of the Lord, proud factory chimneys and beasts of terrible machines; and You, psalmody of production halls that sing to the Lord antiphons in the infinite paths of conveyor belts.

"Let everything that breathes praise the Lord!" (Psalm 150:6). All our strength, power, and movement are towards the Lord, towards God, towards the Father.

"Come to me, all who labor and are heavy laden, and I will give you rest" (Matthew 11:28).

4

Joyous Labor

*"So I saw that there is nothing better than
that a man should enjoy his work, for
that is his lot" (Ecclesiastes 3:22).*

*"Come to Me, all who labor and are heavy
laden, and I will give you rest" (Matthew 11:28).*

A S HE ADMIRED THE BEAUTY OF GOD'S works and the wondrousness of God's creation and dominion over the world, the Psalmist filled his heart with hope and joy: "It is good to give thanks to the Lord, to sing praises to Thy name, O Most High [. . .]. For Thou, O Lord, hast made me glad by Thy work; at the works of Thy hands, I sing for joy. How great are Thy works, O Lord! Thy thoughts are very deep! (Psalm 92:1, 4–5).

Our labor brings so much joy to the Creator that is difficult to express: the depths of adoration immerse us in the vastness of silence and adoration.

As the sons of humanity, God's helpers, and workers in His field, we are called to the same joy in our labors; we are called to participate in God's joy through our work. This was eloquently emphasized by Lemech, the son of Methuselah, in the name he gave to his son Noah after his birth: "Out of the ground which the Lord has cursed this one shall bring us relief from our work and from the toil of our hands" (Genesis 5:29).

God, creation, the entire world, and our neighbors all expect this consolation from the works and labors of our hands.

Can we speak of the joy of labor? Labor simultaneously attracts and repels. Is this not instead some intermingling of joy and suffering, freedom and compulsion, service and creativity? Indeed, labor is a necessity of nature. However, why is it also burdensome? Why are there efforts to free man of matter when he is subordinated to it?

Herein rests the mystery of labor. This contains some form of resistance which is found in man's grace-resistant nature. "I see in my members another law at war with the law of my mind" (Romans 7:23). Only the teaching of the holy faith can solve this mystery.

I. The Burden of Labor

Before original sin, labor was something unfamiliar and foreign to Adam. Although labor itself is not a fruit of the curse in paradise, since man knew labor in paradise, there it was something joyous, just like the labor of God Himself.

Starting with original sin, human labor became not only joyous but also burdensome, arduous, and exhausting: "Cursed is the ground because of you; in toil you shall eat of it all the days of your life; thorns and thistles it shall bring forth to you; and you shall eat the plants of the field" (Genesis 3:17–19).

Disobedience to God has contaminated human labor. Although the nobility of labor is the same as before sin and although man still needs it as a rational being, it has also become marked by indolence and resistance, which accompany the labors of the mind and the exercise of all virtues. The difficulty of labor results from man's sinful nature. Original sin first stupefied the human will, and so every human labor is sore from the wounds of sin. Since the appearance of original sin, resistance and obduracy accompany the exercise of acts of reason and virtue. Yet labor is a virtue and a rational activity.

Every effort is met with ordinary, normal difficulty because every effort encounters resistance.

The repetition and the resulting monotony in labor become tedious. Every working man knows the resistance of matter and how much thought, difficulty, and effort are needed to overcome it. This is some sort of painful mystery. Matter becomes subordinated to man only resistantly: "We know that the whole creation has been groaning in travail together until now; and not only the creation, but we ourselves, who have the first fruits of the Spirit, groan inwardly" (Romans 8:22). How much suffering is bound to the domination of matter and nature!

The ruins of fallen cities that had once been brimming with life but have sunken to the ground and are hidden from the human eye attest to the opposition of submissive human nature to labor; the hawthorn and thorn-covered ruins of the once-golden buildings of Aegean, Greek, or Roman civilization are so expressive of this. Meanwhile, are not the struggle against the hard boulder, rocky soil, rocky desert, or the threat of a raging flood the same rebellious words of matter with which man yelled at God: "I will not serve"?

This difficulty is supplemented with that of cooperation with people, which is also bitter. Original sin has caused man to wallow in selfishness and pride, which is a violation of man's social nature. Meanwhile, labor makes every man forget about himself; it makes him step outside of himself, become devoted to external works, and subject himself to their laws. This is repulsive to corrupted human nature, as it violates the conquests of original sin.

This magnifies the normal difficulty that accompanies human labor.

Yet the entire mystery of man's redemption is found in this suffering. The difficulty of labor is the healing of man's fallen nature; it is the struggle against the corruption that sin has sown. Burdensome labor that roughens one's hands and depletes one's strength is redemptive, salvific labor. Such labor seen through the lens of love for God leads to our redemption. Man repays his debts that have been accrued through original sin by the sweat of his brow.

Here we see that labor is not man's curse, while the difficulty tied to it is not demeaning misery; the sweat on our face and the toil of our hands is not humiliation. For every person, labor is a means of salvation, while the difficulty of labor is tied to the joy of victory over matter and over oneself.

The difficulty of labor resembles another hardship: that of giving birth. This is suffering that ennobles rather than debases. Both labor and giving birth to children are painful because they lead to the creation of something new. Yet the "joy that a child is born into the world" (John 16:21) flows from them.

Man can see his own resistance to God in the resistance that he encounters in his labors. Man's efforts in striving for the ennoblement of matter are similar to God's efforts with respect to our souls. God affects man in a way similar to how man affects matter. God constantly improves His work in man, in whom He wants His image to be reflected. Similarly, man, like God, wants to impress his face on matter.

Matter's submission to man should encourage man's submission to God. The fate of dead, useless, wild, and raw matter freeing itself from man's influence is the fate of man who has followed his own paths and abandoned God.

Is the toil of labor a punishment? Or is it not instead a lifeline given to man to help him to emerge out of the abyss of the flood of the rocky wave of sin?

II. The Joy of Labor

Arduous and burdensome human labor is permeated with joy. This fact was already reflected in ancient wisdom: "So I saw that there is nothing better than that a man should enjoy his work, for that is his lot" (Ecclesiastes 3:22).

From where does joy from human labor originate?

God wanted man to be the creator of his own prosperity. Although God in His goodness entrusted irrational beings with the tools of their labor, He entrusted man's total concern for them. God also endowed man with the most valuable gifts: his reason and his hands. Through them, He has allowed man to acquire what he has not received from nature.

Here is the source of all the joys of labor, both natural and supernatural. Thanks to our abilities, we are capable of constant self-improvement and changing our tools of labor, which leads to the sublimation of even the smallest human labor.

Not every labor is equally burdensome, arduous, and unpleasant; some labors are very pleasant, and there are very exalted periods in very exhausting labors. Even the most burdensome labor can be tied to some joy. Indeed, there is some natural joy of man triumphing in the work of creating things that respond to human needs. There are labors, especially those that are even more directly tied to nature, which give room for great joy. Let us reflect on the smile of the farmer who sees a plentiful harvest, abundant crops, and beautifully formed trees.

Do we not feel joy from the mere use of our energies, abilities, and physical and spiritual faculties? Look at those healthy, laughing, joyous, and tan faces; although they are sometimes filled with beads of sweat, these farmers understand the usefulness of their joyous labor. In this physical difficulty, man is happy "like a strong man [who] runs [his] course with joy" (Psalm 19:5).

We stand before an even deeper awareness of ourselves that results not only from the internal skillfulness in our labors but also from the sense of our personality, which is revealed in our works and is often extended in them. Man experiences nearly God-like joy as he reflects on the traces of his efforts in material works. Just as on the seventh day of creation, when God said that everything He created was very good, likewise man discerns his own likeness in his own works. How often we recognize a master by his works; an artist, scholar, or craftsman by the fruits of his labor. Such labor gives testimony to man; when we want to know a man, we ask what he does and what he has done.

In his labor, man constantly sees the improvement of his talents and qualities; the development of his personality; and his increasing physical and spiritual agility, to which the increasingly perfect works of his labor bear witness. Does this not make one joyful? In this joy, man completely forgets about his oppression and suffering. If he remembers the difficulty and the resistance he has overcome, should not this memory be the cause of new joy? After all, benevolent people express their admiration and recognition for us especially when we have gone through a forest of suffering and struggle.

When we achieve our aim; when our labor is crowned with a successful fruit; when the efforts of many years have led us to our aim, to the liberation of man because his desires have been fulfilled, we feel such great joy. It is most often in this joyous exaltation that the plans for new works most often appear, although they bring about sweat in the brow, "the burden of the day and the scorching heat" (Matthew 20:12), suffering, pain, and sleepless nights. This makes our joy even greater; an idle man will never experience such joy. Those who do not labor can never experience true rest. Even the total joy of play can be fully experienced only by the working man.

Finally, there is the joy that flows from the sense of having created a work that is useful for one's neighbors. Man is happy that he has given a rational form to matter; that he has created something in his image and likeness; that he and his work are useful to others through

474

this as well. When we reflect on the work itself and on its goodness, usefulness, and its admiration by others, we are filled with the joy of love for the works of our hands that is like God's love for the world.

Was not the wise man correct in saying: "So I saw that there is nothing better than that a man should enjoy his work, for that is his lot" (Ecclesiastes 3:22)?

Furthermore, God's supernatural joy is found in human labor.

Even if he has broken all records of production and the value of labor, the best worker can always recall St. Paul's words: "But earnestly desire the higher gifts" (1 Corinthians 12:31). Let us go further in this spirit: "And I will show you a still more excellent way" (*ibid.*).

In this way, our labor achieves a new source of joy because it will be love for God and for one's neighbor.

Labor is the response of the loving rational being to the summons of God's love through which God has invited us to cooperation with Him in His creative activity in the most honorable way. Man plays the role of the second cause in the rule of Providence over the world. Like Mary through her "fiat," man becomes "blessed among creation."

The great dignity of man who cooperates with God and the exceptional majesty of his labor flow from this: this is cooperation between man and God in both sadness and joy. This is the labor of prayer, praise, and love for God.

As such, it becomes a source of great joy for us: from its honorable vocation and exaltation; from the sense of cooperation with the Creator; from the grace of state that abundantly flows on human labor; and from useful grace as a good spirit to all our efforts, difficulties, and labors.

New joy flows from love for people. St. Paul zealously demonstrates how necessary it is in labor: "If I give away all I have, and if I deliver my body to be burned, but have not love, I gain nothing" (1 Corinthians 13:3). Many people burn themselves out from labor. There are those who look at labor through the lens of hatred, seeing it as a sad necessity, as they proclaim its exaltation. Such tragedies are widespread, given that labor is a universal phenomenon. Yet labor has its normal culmination in love for people and the world. Through labor, a bond is forged with other people that teaches us love. Man works to create and renew useful goods for his neighbors. Evidence of the fruit of our labor is friendship towards people. In this sense, labor brings us closer to love for our neighbors in God. This is why labor cannot be performed with a clenched fist and a shrunken heart. Both the hand and the heart must be open. Otherwise, there can be no truly fulfilled labor.

Only then, the toughest labor, like love, "bears all things, believes all things, hopes all things, endures all things" (1 Corinthians 13:7). Only then, free of class hatred, will it be capable of undertaking the greatest sacrifices and give birth to all the virtues without which there can be no fruitful labor: It is "is patient and kind; love is not jealous or boastful [. . .].

It does not rejoice at wrong but rejoices in the right" (1 Corinthians 13:4–7).

In the right. In the right is the truth that all creation is filled with blessings through open human hands, just like through God's open hands.

There is one more human joy that truly comes from God: the joy of man's redemption, which is performed through the joy of our loving labor. When we grow closer to God through labor and the act of love, this love revives us from our difficulties, and we wipe the sweat from our brow with that love.

When we engage in labor out of love of God, the merciful God will bring us to an exceptionally honorable and fruitful work: expiation. Thus, working by the sweat of one's brow is important for our expiation by God. Hence its salvific significance and its role that ennobles and purifies man.

* * *

"So I saw that there is nothing better than that a man should enjoy his work, for that is his lot" (Ecclesiastes 3:22). Looking into God's face gladdens us amidst difficulty and exhaustion. In God, our sorrows will turn into joy (see John 16:20).

5
God in the Factory

*"The works of all flesh are before Him, and
nothing can be hid from His eyes" (Sirach 39:19).*

*"Behold, I have created the smith who
blows the fire of coals and produces a
weapon for its purpose" (Isaiah 54:16).*

OD'S CHURCH HAS A STRANGE ABILITY
to bring together all the supposedly divergent areas of human
life. The one, holy, universal Church, who is the servant of
one God, brings about the harmony of the entirety of moral, religious,
social, economic, and even political life in God. In economic life, she
leads to the harmonious cooperation of nature, capital, and labor. In
the workplace, she expects the cooperation of owners, directors, and
engineers with workers without qualifications and without struggle.
For only the one Church believes in the ability to preserve this unity
because of its necessity to the common good.

God's peace must also reign in the factory, where the divergence
of aspirations has been exacerbated by class struggle and where many
efforts have been undertaken to drive a wedge between people to
replace mutual assistance with hatred; God's righteous peace must
also reign in the factory, which today is a hub of moral contradictions and sins.

For this peace to arrive in the factory, the Church recalls that the
word "worker" means "the working person" and so nowhere does he
cease to be a person, human, and child of God, not even in the factory.

The person who enters the factory cannot be treated as a machine
or tool; he cannot be expected to bow before the machine and serve
it. The machine is not man's god.

In the factory, the worker does not lose his God, the best Father:
"Behold, I have created the smith who blows the fire of coals and produces a weapon for its purpose" (Isaiah 54:16). Whoever works does so
for God, cooperating with Him and implementing His calling. That

is why God does not cease to protect him: "The works of all flesh are before Him, and nothing can be hid from His eyes" (Sirach 39:19).

Attempts at replacing God the Father with the idols of the factory are the cause of all conflict in the factory. All who have rejected service of the one God suffer because of this polytheism.

"God in the factory" is the call for social peace, man's moral good, and universal prosperity.

Does God reign in today's factories?

I. Will God Be Heard in the Factory?

The Book of Proverbs reveals to us one heart that must unite all people: "The rich and the poor meet together; the Lord is the maker of them all" (Proverbs 22:2). This truth has not ceased to be relevant in the factory. The spontaneous and compelling thought that arises in the soul of the honest manager is among the most elementary truths: "Did not He who made me in the womb make him? And did not One fashion us in the womb?" (Job 31:15). We are the children of one Father, which is a wonderful kinship that binds us together. Can there be forces that can divide people and pitting them against one another?

In light of these truths, the conflict between people at the workplace, which is where, according to God's plan, particularly fraternal love should be born, is particularly painful. Why, then, do the workplace and the factory, where human efforts are bound together through hands and thoughts, simultaneously tear hearts apart from one another?

Many specific causes come from one source. The source is where it has been forgotten that we are the children of one Father; that we are all called to cooperation with Divine Providence; that we do not cease to be God's children even in the factory; that God is the Lord of not only the stars and the sky, but also of... the factory.

The greatest evil is the disappearance of fraternal community between the employer and the worker.

When God's unifying love became absent from the factory, everything that remained was only matter that, having rejected God, could only divide. The direct, friendly relationship between the employer and his cooperators disappeared; they are separated by an ever-growing distance that makes the concept of the brother, neighbor, and even human alien. It is replaced by the notions of the employer, owner, director, employee, hired hand, and labor force. These terms almost imperceptibly turn into others that are popular today: the capitalist, exploiter, bourgeois, or proletarian.

The Christian attitude towards one's fellow brothers, humans, and persons has disappeared; all that is left are the ideas of the object, merchandise, money, and profit.

The manager no longer has a sense of duty to his elder brother; "Show yourself in all respects a model of good deeds" (Titus 2:7). We no longer care about St. Paul's guidelines: "Put on then, as God's chosen ones, holy and beloved, compassion, kindness, lowliness, meekness, and patience, forbearing one another and, if one has a complaint against another, forgiving each other; as the Lord has forgiven you, so you also must forgive" (Colossians 3:12–13). It has become difficult to listen to talk of justice. And what about love? Paternal and managerial virtues? This is a foreign and unclear language.

It is unsurprising that the dependence of the worker has become much more burdensome under such circumstances. Man has been separated from his strength and physical agility; he has ceased to be the focus of attention, while his physical strength has been subjected to the harsh laws of production to which he must constantly adapt. Bound by the lower part of human nature to the workplace and a slave to it in his higher, rational part, man painfully experiences his dependence, debasement, and spiritual impoverishment through labor. God created man as a rational and free being, while contemporary industry has a need only for human strength.

This is where all the harsh inequalities of social and human nature begin because God's law, the holy Church, Christian truths, and the entirety of religious life all elevate man, developing in him a sense of personal dignity and the equality of his ultimate aims. Meanwhile, the workplace in practice rejects these wonderful accomplishments of Christian culture despite God's designs.

All that is left is the complaint: "O Lord our God, other lords besides Thee have ruled over us, but Thy name alone we acknowledge" (Isaiah 26:13).

In the factory, the modern labor of technology has largely become inhuman.

Ecclesiasticus has expressively presented to us the burden of the debasement of human labor. This is the toil of the artisan and the carpenter "who labors by night as well as by day" (Sirach 38:27). Meanwhile, as the smith sits by his anvil "the breath of the fire melts his flesh, and he wastes away in the heat of the furnace" (v. 28) and the "potter sitting at his work and turning the wheel with his feet; he is always deeply concerned over his work, and all his output is by number" (v. 29).

The burden of human labor has become so much greater when compared with those distant times.

An additional difficulty resulting from the technology of organization itself supplements the ordinary difficulty that is common to all labor, especially in the factory: the new organization of labor strives to make use of the worker's time and energy as carefully as possible to increase his adeptness and efficiency. To achieve this, the entire production process is divided into a long series of simple and minor functions that are typically performed by the same people. All their movements, and even minor movements, are carefully calculated and subjected to the control of various clocks that unfailingly detect all shortcomings in the production process. This is so-called rationalization, the scientific organization of labor, whose aim, which is correct in principle, is the simplification of the performing of labor and the increase of its productivity.

In this complicated labor system, it is often forgotten that it is a living human who has his own laws of acting that differ from those of a machine that is under the control and pressure of all those chronometers, clocks, and calculations.

Because the achievements of machine technology have been applied too ruthlessly and too inhumanely, man's labor in the factory has become burdensome and devoid of any joy. Man is forced to perform the same mindless tasks for many years, which causes his intelligence, inventiveness, and resourcefulness to decline, thus stupefying and fatiguing him.

The productivity of human labor was artificially increased, having been calculated according to the achievements of the strongest people, which causes the greatest output to be expected of the weakest.

Look at how similar capitalism and Bolshevism are in practice with respect to this sphere of the exploitation of human energy. What the capitalist system has invented has been zealously adopted by the communists, who have promoted the heroes of labor, the udarniks, strong and healthy men who deplete all their energies within only a few years for the sake of a higher wage.

Having rejected the commandments of Christian morality, the new system of factory labor trusts the factory buzzer more than it does the conscience of the worker. He no longer trusts the noble virtues and human attributes of conscientiousness, zealousness, and rationality; his only measure is the chronometer. No one refers to humanity and conscientiousness any longer, which is a further cause of man's degradation.

The Church always teaches a different sort of conscientiousness: "Whatever your task, work heartily, as serving the Lord and not men, knowing that from the Lord you will receive the inheritance as your reward; you are serving the Lord Christ" (Colossians 3:22–24).

However, such morality is accorded no importance in the factory. A clock is hanging on the wall; it is your conscience, the eye and ear of your superior. You must know this, for otherwise your Saturday's wage will be small.

These are the fruits. A new burden is added to the ordinary toil of labor, that of Taylorization,[1] mechanization, and rationalization, which makes labor arduous, exhausting, stupefying, monotonous, and stripped of all joy and imagination. Human labor becomes impersonal, while reason begins to be an obstacle.

Man is handed over to the yoke of the machine. He no longer has control over the machine and production but instead becomes a supplement, much like every other sad necessity.

How accurately this human misfortune in today's factory is described by the poet:

> And you? Look at your sad dole:
> The idolater of the century, a nightmare of the soul!
> They have counted, calculated, and marked their spoils,
> And with an axe chopped you off the soil.
> In the hysterical sirens' wail,

---

1 In reference to the production methods of Frederick Taylor (1856–1915).

With a whip your heart they have flailed.
By the mad tempo of the machines,
A deaf and dull robot, barely walk you can.
You are no longer a man. Captured by the movement of the
cogs, the body becomes numb.
No longer a man, but a living or dead machine amidst clat-
ters and hums!

(Wojciech Bąk, "The Idolaters
of the Twentieth Century")

Today's technology of factory labor degrades man, stripping him of human dignity and God's joy.

Those who organize and perform labor must recall the admonition of St. Paul the Apostle: "You were bought with a price; do not become slaves of men" (1 Corinthians 7:23).

The one-sided excess of harsh physical labor causes injury to the worker's soul.

Catholic economics includes among its eternal principles the need to protect man's energies in labor so that he might make use of them as long as possible in order to serve both his own life's aims and society as creatively as possible. The rapid depletion of human energies, which suffice for barely a few years, in excessive labor are a sin against man's life's purpose and against a healthy national economy. The Lord's Wise Man teaches us a tested principle: "In all your work be industrious, and no sickness will overtake you" (Sirach 31:27).

Excessive and burdensome labor no longer shapes man or develops his personality. It fails to provide the necessary conditions for the activity of thoughts and feelings; it kills human thought and constricts one's interests, instead developing only the muscles. There comes a moment when every worker, who is stupefied by the monotony of his life, is no longer capable of understanding the essence of higher goods and no longer believes in his dignity and wonderful purpose because he cannot understand the discrepancy between the principles and practice of life, just like the Israelites who refused to obey Moses in Egypt "because of their broken spirit and their cruel bondage" (Exodus 6:9). Once man loses faith in his life's higher aims, he become embittered and filled with doubt: "Why did I come forth from the womb to see toil and sorrow, and spend my days in shame?"

(Jeremiah 20:18). All too often, such is the spiritual state of workers.

Man is no longer joyous in labor, which is accompanied by exhaustion and the awareness that his energies are unjustly used. Their spirit is similar to that of the oppressed Israelites from the time of the Egyptian yoke who "made their lives bitter with hard service, in mortar and brick, and in all kinds of work in the field" (Exodus 1:14).

What can prevent moral decline where personal dignity has been destroyed? In such a workplace, the mere organization of labor undermines morality; a second wave of demoralization that comes from the workers themselves must come. This is unsurprising "because [when] wickedness is multiplied, most men's love will grow cold" (Matthew 24:12).

When dishonest officials, supervisors, controllers, foremen, and so on make use of their advantage and the dependence of others on them, a chain of protection and exploitation in which one cannot survive at the price of his own honesty is created.

Pius XI writes: "Truly the mind shudders at the thought of the grave dangers to which the morals of workers (particularly younger workers) and the modesty of girls and women are exposed in modern factories" (QA, 135). Listen to the labor courts and read the reports of labor inspectors and you will see that these words are not thrown to the wind.

Acquaint yourselves with the factory dictionary in which not only the attitude of managers but also the workers themselves is expressed: that of foremen to their co-workers whose ranks they had recently left; that of professional workers to ordinary day laborers; that of older workers to younger ones; and that of men to women. How can others respect you if you have so little respect for yourselves? This absolves no one because, unfortunately, the example is often set at the top.

Constant haste and feverishness are unloaded in the lack of mutual respect, the mistreatment of people, anger, curses, and hatred. Can a work of cooperation with God the Father be created in such an environment and such a moral atmosphere? Can God's words: "Fill the earth and subdue it" (see Genesis 1:28) become our daily bread? Can man perfect himself through such labor?

Invigorated by the human spirit, the worker experiences terrible agony in such a factory environment, much like Lot in Sodom, who lived among corrupted people and "was vexed in his righteous soul day after day with their lawless deeds" (2 Peter 2:8).

Let us not be surprised at the pope's words that "bodily labor, which Divine Providence decreed to be performed, even after original sin, for the good at once of man's body and soul, is being everywhere changed into an instrument of perversion; for dead matter comes forth from the factory ennobled, while men there are corrupted and degraded" (QA, 135)

Could such a debasement of man be part of God's plans? This is neither God's will nor God's device, but the great sins of people who will someday stand before God for their unjust stewardship.

II. Let Us Bring God Into the Factory

Having gained dominion over his people, Solomon prayed to God, asking for the gift of wisdom in his rule: "Send her forth from the holy heavens, and from the throne of Thy glory send her, that she may be with me and toil, and that I may learn what is pleasing to Thee. For she knows and understands all things, and she will guide me wisely in my actions and guard me with her glory. Then my works will be acceptable, and I shall judge Thy people justly" (Wisdom 9:10–12).

If this ever-wise ruler sensed his inadequacy thousands of years ago and sought God's help in all his labors, today, in such an exceptionally convoluted world as today prayer should be the daily bread of all the organizers and directors of human life.

To organize the workplace in a way that it fulfills all its providential tasks and does not destroy man who instead flourishes and comes closer to both his worldly and ultimate aims through his labor, we need not only good will and professional skills but also wisdom that "reaches mightily from one end of the earth to the other, and [...] orders all things well" (Wisdom 8:1).

There are sacred truths that are obliging always and everywhere in human co-existence and in cooperation. They cannot be forgotten in the factory, where they must create an appropriate atmosphere to make labor truly fruitful.

St. Paul instructs us how to order the attitudes of people called to cooperate to one another. Being "individually members one of another" in Christ, we have received "gifts that differ according to the grace given to us;" some have received the gift to instruct and admonish, while others to serve "in our service" (see Romans 12:5–7). We should serve one another with these gifts, which have been given to ourselves and to our neighbors: "He who exhorts, (may he govern) in his exhortation" (Romans 12:8).

Cooperating in the spirit of mutual assistance, we will know how to improve the most difficult labor conditions and to ameliorate the harshest human labors and fill them with joy.

"Love one another with brotherly affection; outdo one another in showing honor. Never flag in zeal, be aglow with the Spirit, serve the Lord. [...] Contribute to the needs of the saints [...]. Live in harmony with one another [...]. Never be conceited [...]. Repay no one evil for evil but take thought for what is noble in the sight of all. If possible, so far as it depends upon you, live peaceably with all" (Romans 12:10–18).

This is the Christian "declaration of the rights of citizen and man" in the factory. Everything else will only be its application in practice and reference to specific circumstances created by life. This constitution requires that we protect all of man, all his faculties and aims so that he might fulfill his life's destiny by working in the factory.

In the factory, spiritual protection must extend to the working man.

In his encyclical *Rerum novarum*, Leo XIII argues that spiritual goods in the factory should be protected by the state. Meanwhile, in the encyclical *Quadragesimo anno* Pius XI condemns the abuses of the directors of economic life who have themselves departed from the path of righteousness and through their fall caused "to rush headlong also into the same chasm; and all the more so, because very many managements treated their workers like mere tools, with no concern at all for their souls, without indeed even the least thought of spiritual things" (QA, 135).

In the factory, there must be sensitivity to not only the good of the machine, tools, and technical devices, but above all the good of the human soul. Those who stand at the forefront of organized labor must lift themselves up and make their collaborators follow them through their example.

Why? Because economic life, production, and production are not the ultimate purpose of our existence. They are merely the means to exercise our worldly aims and to perfect our spiritual life by learning God's love and truth.

In the factory, protection of the good of the worker's body is not enough because our body is not the most important reason for our existence. Man has been given stewardship over creation not because of the advantages of his body but because of his rational soul in which God's image and likeness are inscribed.

God's commandment: "Be fruitful and multiply and fill the earth and subdue it" (Genesis 1:28) refers not only to the mighty or weak in body, to only the rich or poor, but to all, to every person. Considering this commandment, God has made all equal: "The same Lord is Lord of all and bestows His riches upon all who call upon Him" (Romans 10:12).

God Himself respects this declaration so much that He has not subjected it to revision or change throughout thousands of years. Thus, can a single workplace, factory, or mine be capable of destroying that which God Himself respects because of some economic laws or scientific organization of labor? Do the so-called laws of production have the power to overthrow the laws of the Ten Commandments?

The Holy Father rightly recalls that "no man may with impunity outrage that human dignity which God Himself treats with great reverence, nor stand in the way of that higher life which is the preparation of the eternal life of heaven" (RN, 40).

The conditions of labor in the factory, the very organization of the workplace, and the rules of factories can in no way transgress what God has established; they cannot degrade man's exaltation, nor can they pull his soul away from God, for they will not replace God with anything; they will neither bring him joy nor satiate his soul.

In the factory, man does not cease to be a child of God. Thus, his labor is something more than solely the labor of a rational being, for it is the labor of a man and a Christian and therefore is Christian labor. Our life is God's life in the members belonging to the Body of Christ. Our life's energies come from God's love. Thus, our activities are marked by great dignity and majesty. The sacred mark of the supernatural is impressed onto Christian labor.

Sacred labor cannot degrade man; for this reason, he must be treated in a Christian way. No one has the right to do otherwise; Leo XIII writes: "To consent to any treatment which is calculated to defeat the end and purpose of his being is beyond his right; he cannot give up his soul to servitude, for it is not man's own rights which are here in question, but the rights of God, the most sacred and inviolable of rights" (RN, 40).

The protection of man's bodily goods is no less an important duty of the management of a factory and of every employer.

In the encyclical *Rerum novarum*, Leo XIII writes: "If we turn not to things external and material, the first thing of all to secure is to save unfortunate working people from the cruelty of men of greed, who use human beings as mere instruments for money-making" (RN, 42). This is not only a duty that burdens the state; it is also the moral duty of every employer who cannot degrade any person for the sake of profit. If the spirit of profit dominates the workplace and if the energy, health, and even life of the worker is sacrificed for its sake, the employer incurs God's harsh threat in defense of His children: "For he who touches you touches the apple of his eye" (Zechariah 2:8).

The same applies to the organization techniques in the workplace. "It is neither just nor human so to grind men down with excessive labor as to stupefy their minds and wear out their bodies" (RN, 42). Not every technical system is good merely because it increases the factory's productivity. When organizing the workplace, one must remember that not only unfeeling machines but also living people will work in it. The physical well-being of the employers should be the framework for all technical plans and improvements. If production increases at the cost of the destruction of human energies, a scandalous injury takes place.

An organization of the workplace that rashly endangers the human body is also immoral and evil. It is difficult to exempt the factory owners who neglect the most basic preventative measures and thus expose people to work accidents, grave disability, and even the loss of life, which no compensation or insurance can restore, from moral responsibility before God. God's commandment "thou shalt not kill" demands that the entire technical legacy of labor safety laws and measures hone a delicate conscience and respect for the human body.

Bearing in mind not only the earthly good of the enterprise but also the permanent good of the individual and society, workers must be directed in such a way that their bodies and health are not harmed while working. The problem of the proper education of man is within the scope of the duties of the organizers of the workplace.

Another very important factor that belongs to this sphere is the level of the workers' wages. We should oppose the occasionally stoked covetousness of a greater wage at the cost of one's physical energies and detriment to one's health. After the capitalist experiences, the worst example is provided by Bolshevik Russia, which artificially bolsters the udarniks, leading to the premature depletion of man's physical strength. It cannot be allowed for the worker to have to take on more and more labor, motivated solely by the desire for earthly profit and to become burdened with excessive and harmful labor for the sake of profit.

Respecting man's spiritual and physical goods is of momentous economic importance.

God leaves nothing without reward. Respecting God's commandments is so abundantly rewarded by God's blessings that God will have such graces and gifts even for factory labor.

Respecting spiritual and physical goods elevates the spirit of employers, bolstering their bravery and joy in work; the healthier the mores in the factory, the fewer needs there are for complete submission to the obligation of labor. "The wage of the righteous leads to life, the gain of the wicked to sin" (Proverbs 10:16).

The violation of God's laws is not only an affront to the moral good of workers, but its effects impoverish economic life itself. "They conceive mischief and bring forth iniquity. [...] Their webs will not serve as clothing; men will not cover themselves with what they make. Their works are works of iniquity, and deeds of violence are in their hands" (Isaiah 59:4–6).

No economy can be healthier and more abundant in good than economic laws based on God's laws.

* * *

The factory is not a god, but its life and labor must serve God. The factory must praise God in the turbulence of work; it must ennoble and exalt man in his labor. It should accept man in a way as to not degrade him and not turn him into a slave of machinery. The factory should make the worker increasingly human so that he never loses sight of his own heart and soul.

The working people belong to the Lord, and God constantly struggles for the right to those people with the same strength as in the times of Egypt when "He smote all the first-born in Egypt, the first issue of their strength in the tents of Ham. Then He led forth his people like sheep and guided them in the wilderness like a flock" (Psalm 78:51–52).

Open the factory gates and let the King of glory enter.

Who is this King of glory? you ask. This is the One that will give everyone a wage according to his deeds. You will take the award or punishment for your stewardship from His right hand. "Then the righteous man will stand with great confidence in the presence of those who have afflicted Him and those who make light of His labors" (Wisdom 5:1).

Open the factory gates and let the King of glory enter.

Who is this King of glory? He is the common Father of the rich and the poor, of the factory owner and the worker.

6

The Catholic Organization
of the Workplace

I WILL BEGIN BY RECALLING TWO IMAGES.
The first is described by St. Paul: "Slaves, be obedient to those who are your earthly masters, with fear and trembling, in singleness of heart, as to Christ; not in the way of eye-service, as men-pleasers, but as servants of Christ, doing the will of God from the heart, rendering service with a good will as to the Lord and not to men, knowing that whatever good any one does, he will receive the same again from the Lord, whether he is a slave or free. Masters, do the same to them, and forbear threatening, knowing that He who is both their Master and yours is in heaven, and that there is no partiality with Him" (Ephesians 6:5–9).

The second is more concise: "A man's foes will be those of his own household" (Matthew 10:36); those who eat your bread and those whom you give work will be your foes. Why?

Why is there such a discrepancy in these two images? Why are we abandoning this most beautiful ideal for the reality of class warfare and hatred? This is the most important problem of our time and the most urgent one for Catholics. Indeed, it is an important problem. The matter in question is not one of dividing up goods but rather of sharing hearts. It is necessary to speak less of property, communism, or socialism and more of the Catholic attitude of the employer to the worker and the Catholic organization of labor.

Let us devote a few thoughts and comments to this most Catholic problem of social life. What is worth remembering? Above all, *in manual labor man first encounters his fellow man.*

In every labor, man first meets another man; one child of God meets another; a brother encounters his brother; and a Christian encounters a fellow Christian. This is the basic and essential relationship in which all community is forged. Only later does an employer encounter a worker or a supervisor his servant.

490

However, the first relationship is and always will be the most important: "The rich and the poor meet together; the Lord is the Maker of them all" (Proverbs 22:2).

The entire person, a whole rational and free person with all his temporal and supernatural aims and irrevocable human dignity that cannot be left outside the door of the workplace in the way one leaves his coat or knapsack, enters every factory and workplace.

The word "worker" still means above all "person." The human person and its dignity cannot be separated from man's physical energies, which serve the workplace.

The entirety of man must also be considered in the organization of the workplace and the relationships that are dominant there. The workplace should above all be a place of working people. Thus, all its arrangements must take into consideration not only the demands of production but also man's needs.

The relationship of the employer to the worker is above all that of one man to another; even if we have a manager above us or someone subordinate to us, in many ways they continue to be our equals.

In the organization of labor, no one can forget the physical good of the worker (the safety and integrity of his body); his spiritual good (the moral and religious good of the soul and its cultural needs); his social goods as a member of family, national, state, and professional communities; and, finally, his economic goods as a producer of new material goods who has the right to rest from the efforts of his labor.

The man who lives in the workplace should have the conditions to meet these numerous life's needs.

The relationship between the employer and the worker in the workplace must be Christian.

For this reason, it is imperative to:

1. Respect the dignity of the working person. The encyclical *Rerum novarum* teaches that employers cannot treat their workers like slaves; their human dignity, which is bolstered by the mark of the Christian, must be respected. There is a strict commandment: "No man may with impunity outrage that human dignity which God Himself treats with great reverence, nor stand in the way of that higher life which is the preparation of the eternal life of heaven" (RN, 40).

2. The workers' aspiration towards social progress should be maintained, developed, and honed. In its essence, this aspiration is honorable. Indeed, the entirety of Christian life consists of progress and self-improvement. The Church is marked by eternal transformation. If the worker demands respects for himself, this cannot be considered a communist element because it is in fact truly Christian. Instead, this aspiration should be maintained and reinforced. The contemporary aspirations towards progress among the working masses are mostly material and class oriented. The moral and social dimension of these aspirations must be noted, and so they should be put in their proper place.

3. Efforts to search for paths to a good solution to the social relationship should be sought. The distance between the intellectual and the manual laborer can and should be reduced not through demagogy and "lowering oneself to the people" but rather by elevating people to a higher level in the spirit of Christian love, brotherhood, and the resulting community. This will be facilitated by cooperation, respect, mutual assistance, improved social relations, and the rejection of the vulgar dictionary filled with insults and curses that absolutely dominates all workplaces today.

Calmly thinking people share a widespread conviction that the most difficult social question is the personal attitude of the employer towards the worker. According to Foerster, social problems "can be resolved only by changing the personal relationships between superiors and their subordinates and between the servants and the served; this can change only by making these relationships truly human and ethical. Ethics must be brought into the relationship with the railway porter, street sweeper, courier, waiter, tailor, nurse, cashier, doorman, and servant; there must be ethics with respect to all who serve."

The mere organization of labor in the workplace should improve rather than debase the person.

If this aim is not accomplished, then nothing will change with respect to social relations after the current terrible war.

The organization of every workplace must bear in mind not only the good of production but also the good of man in his entirety. One should ask if economic accomplishments are not paid for by too great a price and if they do not frustrate goods that are a hundred-fold more valuable than the benefit of increased production. The mere organization of labor should also help person, the entire person.

Indeed, the organization of the workplace should correspond to the aims of production, but it must also be remembered that the aim of production is not autonomous and is not the greatest purpose. Production is not a god. It takes place through the participation of people and is intended for people; thus, it cannot be above people.

Production technology is not a blind force that is immune to the laws of reason. Thus, human reason should take great effort to protect the person.

"It is neither just nor human so to grind men down with excessive labor as to stupefy their minds and wear out their bodies" (RN, 42).

Leo XIII writes that it is shameful and inhuman to exploit people as a tool for profit and judge them only according to the value presented by their muscles and physical energies.

The organization of the workplace should therefore remedy all the aims of human labor. Thus, it should develop man's mind, will, and moral values. To become sensitive to those values of workers that are underappreciated by both the organizers of the modern workplace and by the workers themselves requires great personal culture.

The workplace must ensure the maximal utility of human labor; thus, it should be ordered such that it does not prematurely deplete human energies, rejecting young old men after a dozen years of labor, as the Bolshevik udarnik movement has done. Man should work effectively for the greater part of his life. We attain the development of our skills only after working for an extended period. The energies of entire generations cannot be depleted; otherwise, this later becomes the burden of society.

Thus, the organization of labor must be concerned not only with earthly accomplishments but also the totality of man's duties. After his day's work, the worker should be capable of exercising his other duties: familial, professional, social, religious, civic, etc. A man who is so exhausted by labor that he is capable of only sleeping and eating after work ceases to be socially useful. In this area, he should be treated with the most caring concern.

In labor, the full development of man's personality must be facilitated.

In every workplace, the relationship of the employer to the worker should be didactic. People must be educated over the course of many years. This is why the view that labor is only a sad necessity must be opposed; instead, it should be professed that labor is a need of a rational being.

The employer should exhibit the virtues of not only a superior but also those of a father. Only then will he be able to educate the workers. This is of tremendous importance especially with regards to our relationships where there is a lack of respect for labor and there is so much false shame.

Finally, the spirit of serving one's working brothers is needed. Labor cannot be based on police controls or a system of punishments and compulsion. On the contrary, firmness should be tied to clemency and consequence. It should be ensured that the rationally given command is properly performed. When giving commands, however, one must bear in mind the admonition of the Gospels: "And whoever would be first among you must be your slave" (Matthew 20:27). The sense of mutual usefulness, dependence, value, and the spirit of service will alleviate this relationship and fill it with the Christian spirit.

The relationship in the factory can become a Christian relationship. When it reigns in the workplace, this spirit will facilitate the most important aim for which we strive in the Christian system.

A Christian environment of factory labor must be created.

We will attain this ideal through:

1. The principle of cooperation and the concurrence of employers and workers. Catholics should be the apostles of these principles. They should strive for the elimination of class struggle in which any fruits of labor are merely accidental. It should be surprising that economic life is possible in a dominant spirit of distrust, reluctance, and resistance. Attention should be given to the expansion of the scope of cooperation between people and establishing direct contact so that labor relations may become increasingly human.

2. Respect for Christian morality during work is another topic that has been completely forgotten. It should be undertaken to lead to the moral edification of the environment of human labor. The immorality of employers and carelessness of workers who have been given bad examples by their superiors change the workplace into a place where

God's laws are constantly violated. The divorce of economics from ethics and the acquisition of wealth at all costs must be opposed. We must strive to restore the conscience to the factory. Workers must be protected from the bad influences of immoral employers.

Pius XI explicitly demands the protection of the spiritual goods of factory workers, although this task is despised. However, employers must become sensitive to the spiritual goods of workers in order to oppose the dangers that threaten human souls. The employer cannot forget that the relationship outlined in the labor contract ends sooner or later but the soul, for which all who surround it bear responsibility, will remain.

There must be efforts to ensure that the workplace does not break up families, does not separate people from serving God and resting on the holy days, and that it does not denigrate and paganize souls, which have been redeemed through Christ's blood.

3. Finally, social legislation must be respected and defended. The Catholic employer should become the spiritual defender of labor legislation. The Catholic engineer must be a born labor inspector in the factory; he must be Christian in spirit, not because of his "office."

* * *

Are these utopias? Could this lead to the replacement of a sad image with a joyous one?

Let us ask what is more utopian, the current life, filled with struggle, disputes, and hatred, or the image of peaceful social service in mutual love?

A man's household members will cease to be his enemies only when both his superiors and workers will stand before the common God and Father. May they stand before one another not as servants but as beloved brothers (see Philemon 1:16).

7
The Workday and the Lord's Day

"Six days shall work be done, but the seventh day is a sabbath of solemn rest, holy to the Lord" (Exodus 31:15).

CONTEMPORARY MAN IS TORN APART BY contradictory aspirations. On the one hand, he has fallen prey to the myth of labor, feverish labor, and the idol of labor. He has come to believe that labor is the greatest virtue and that it is almost sacred, forgetting about the rest of the world in the process. There are people who anxiously fear rest as if it were some sort of phantom. The greatest productivity of labor and the increase of the labor force are the slogans of our day. The aim is to make as much money as quickly as possible irrespective of the cost. Millions of people are to be sacrificed to complete the work; these are not merely ambitions and dreams but reality as well. They are to complete the labor of the entire world, which has been spread out over all the generations and centuries. And what next? Will labor never run out?

On the other hand, there are efforts to arrange human life in such a way that man works as little as possible. He is to be replaced in his work by increasingly sophisticated machinery, working more and working faster without man's assistance; indeed, man is turned into a robot.

And what next? Can man be without labor? These are the contradictory contemporary aims. Labor is man's greatest virtue, ultimate purpose, and the meaning of his entire life. However, man cannot work in his life, for there is no work for him.

Do we still need to comprehend what the modern world wants?

In order to understand this, we must enter a different level, that of God's commandment: "Fill the earth and subdue it" (see Genesis 1:28), and remember another commandment: "Remember the sabbath day, to keep it holy" (see Exodus 20:8); "Six days shall work

496

be done, but the seventh day is a sabbath of solemn rest, holy to the Lord" (Exodus 31:15).

God's law has given man the duty to work, but it simultaneously instructed that this is not the only or ultimate duty. According to God's law, labor is a wonderful means of developing man's personhood, but it is not the only one. Thus, completely filling a man's life with labor is wrong, but the desire for its complete abolition is equally erroneous.

God's law presents us broad confines within which the rational person can enclose his life's aims.

Let us reflect on how to harmonize all these life's tasks with the everyday duty of labor so that we lose nothing of our eternal destiny. Let us encompass it within the framework of everyday work, weekly labor, and the labor of our entire lives.

I. The Burden of the Workday

The length of one's work is determined by the aim of the day's toil.

Our everyday work should take place in a time that best secures the productivity of the economy, which should above all justify the right to a proper wage; it should also lead to the normal development of man 's normal efficiency and man's personal faculties so that he does not exhaust all his human energies and can fulfill his life's other tasks.

A certain amount of time and a certain amount of both physical and spiritual energies are necessary to fulfill all these tasks.

The most joyous labor is tied to a certain inevitable difficulty that absorbs human energies. We sense this every day when we willingly go to work in the morning but return exhausted and weary. Bearing this in mind, Leo XIII recalls in his encyclical *Rerum novarum* that "daily labor, therefore, should be so regulated as not to be protracted over longer hours than strength admits" (RN, 42). The length of breaks from work should be determined when considering the various types of labor, the circumstances of their time and place, and, finally, the health of the workers. Catholic scholars have long opted for an eight-hour workday, even at times when the norm was to work more than a dozen hours a day.

To achieve all the demands of a day's labor, the workday can be neither too short nor too long.

It cannot be too short, for man requires a certain amount of time to develop his energies and make full use of them. However, it is a delusion to free man from labor in general, as is the ideal to reduce it to a minimum. It is also a delusion to replace all of human labor—the work of a rational and free being—with that of a machine or to limit it to the status of an insignificant addition. The machine unfailingly helps man by significantly reducing his time working. However, no one should want it to completely deprive us of labor or excessively facilitate it and free it of all effort and difficulty. This effort is a necessary condition for our progress and the development of our spiritual faculties and our humanity. This is why labor is necessary. And labor must be performed for the majority of a human's life. Our efforts should not seek to remove labor from life but instead to protect human dignity in labor so that we may remain human while working.

However, labor cannot last too longer. Human labor is efficient, useful, and joyous when it completely corresponds to man's preferences and does not overwhelm his energies and abilities. We know that our energies are limited and that they become depleted as the time spent working is extended: the intensity of labor flags, scrupulousness is reduced, and its efficiency and value decline. Excessively lengthy labor that transcends man's endurance becomes increasingly exhausting, burdensome, and even harmful and despised. The harmfulness of such labor is multifaceted: it harms the worker at the moral, psychological, and physical levels; it harms the very subject of labor, as the value of his production declines; and, finally, it harms society, which then consists of prematurely ruined and embittered laborers.

The length one spends in labor cannot be determined solely by economic benefits. We cannot fall prey to the temptation of excessively extending the day's toil at the cost of man and his remaining daily activities.

The time spent working should be such that man can fulfill his duty to cooperate with God in the work of feeding the world; to lead to the multiplication of economic labor and exercise of his moral duties through labor; to not prematurely deplete his physical and spiritual strength and become turned into a working machine; to have the ability to exercise his duties as the head or member of a family, nation, society, or profession; to be capable of making use of his religious life and participate in religious services to publicly and privately venerate God; and, finally, to have the desire to make use of cultural goods, education, books, self-improvement, or decent entertainment.

In order to fulfill all these duties, the worker should leave his workplace with such a disposition that excessive exhaustion does not deprive him of his desire and zeal to perform various works, so that man does not work the night away just like he does the day (see Sirach 38:28).

II. Man's Holy Workweek

The Book of Genesis, which describes the work of creation in six days, is an image of God's labor. It concludes with the following concise summary: "Thus the heavens and the earth were finished, and all the host of them. And on the seventh day God finished His work which He had done, and He rested on the seventh day from all His work which He had done. So, God blessed the seventh day and hallowed it, because on it God rested from all His work which He had done in creation" (Genesis 2:1–3).

The connection of "God blessed the seventh day and hallowed it" with "God rested from all His work," happy with what He had created, is significant.

From that time, the "seventh day" has a two-fold purpose in the history of God's world: to venerate God and to rest after having worked. Both the earthly and religious elements are bound together as closely as the bilateral sacrament of marriage and as the spiritual authority of the Church with the secular authority of the state in the political community. These are common things that are so important to man that they can be secured only through mutual efforts.

God blessed the seventh day and hallowed it.

Every labor is a knot that binds us to the created world, our neighbors, and God. Through this knot of friendship, our labor turns into prayer.

It is not enough for the human heart to devote the entire day —or six days of the week —to baling hale; to be completely happy, it must be capable of offering to God those bound bales at the end of a laborious week. Thus, six days of labor always prepare for God's seventh day.

Sundays and holidays are the voice of the working people calling out in the desert: "Prepare the way of the Lord, make His paths straight" (Matthew 3:2).

"These are the appointed feasts of the Lord, which you shall proclaim as times of holy convocation, for presenting to the Lord offerings" (Leviticus 23:37). The aims of this day are to give praise to God, the Father of all creation, life, and grace; to free oneself from matter and its overbearing influence; to become aware that creation does not have authority over man but that, on the contrary, man is the master of creation; and to recall the most wonderful and dignified service, the service of God, striving for it through one's own sanctification in order to resemble God more. This is a particularly important purpose of the holy day.

All these purposes should help make this day free of ordinary, everyday labor.

Religious life, the exercise of one's duties with respect to God, and the satisfaction of the needs of our heart and mind are the main aims of freedom from labor, a freedom that is beneficial to both body and soul. Holiday rest is not some fruitless idleness but, according to Leo XIII, "it should be rest from labor, hallowed by religion. Rest (combined with religious observances) disposes man to forget for a while the business of his everyday life, to turn his thoughts to things heavenly, and to the worship which he so strictly owes to the eternal Godhead" (RN, 41).

If the Church demands that the state protects all the interests of the worker, above all religious ones, this is not to promote sloth and idleness but to instead remind society and its members that there is another labor apart from that on this earth: in the vineyard of one's own soul. This exceptionally important truth must be constantly recalled today, amidst the dominant efforts to deprive the holy days of their religious nature.

Through the sanctification of the seventh day, man's right to rest is surrounded by a wall of inviolability.

When Nehemiah appeared in Jerusalem during a time of great religious decline, he saw the following image: "In those days I saw in Judah men treading wine presses on the sabbath and bringing in heaps of grain and loading them on asses; and also, wine, grapes, figs, and all kinds of burdens, which they brought into Jerusalem on the sabbath day" (Nehemiah 13:15). We see a similar image whenever God's commandment to keep holy the sabbath day is ignored, wherever a war is waged against religion to impose constant drudgery, from the cradle to the grave, on people more easily and without any scruples.

Those who violate the holy day and encourage others to renounce the Lord's days most effectively work for their own disadvantage. And what happens when the Lord's Day turns into sloth in the service of God and the destruction of human strength, health, and hard-earned money?

It must be remembered that disrespecting the holy day is usually (if not immediately, then in the near future) the means to the violation of the human right to adequate rest. The law of the holy day protects against the strong temptation to exploit human energies beyond their limits to which both capitalism and Bolshevism have fallen.

After all, the first violations of the human right to rest in general came from capitalism. Inspired by the fever of profit, it was eager to change the Catholic calendar and deprive it of all the Lord's holy days. "They said to themselves, 'We will utterly subdue them;' they burned all the meeting places of God in the land" (Psalm 74:8).

In his encyclical on communism, Pius XI complains that the capitalist exploitation of the time spent at work, as "even on Sundays and holy days, labor-shifts were given no time to attend to their essential religious duties. No one thought of building churches within convenient distance of factories, nor of facilitating the work of the priest. On the contrary, laicism was actively and persistently promoted, with the result that we are now reaping the fruits of the errors so often denounced by Our Predecessors and by Ourselves" (DR, 16).

The consequences of this violation of God's law with respect to those who work and the right of people to aspire for God have been reflected in the redoubled sense of the burden of labor, discouragement to work, the disappearance of all interests, indifference towards all other human duties, depression, a growing sense of the debasement of society, dissatisfaction, a spirit of opposition and rebellion, and, finally, all the bitter fruits of communism and the spirit of revolt. There is no time for God, prayer, and one's own children; there is only time for work, work, work. "Afflicted and close to death from my youth up, I suffer Thy terrors; I am helpless" (Psalm 88:15).

Is not the example of the tireless God giving way to rest not moving? We sense the true intentions of this act: "For I have given you an example, that you also should do as I have done to you" (John 13:15). God is the Lord of not only our soul but also of our body, which is why He defends the work of His hands, that it may not be prematurely destroyed.

Thus, like God Himself, man must rest from his labors to bring relief to his body and transformation to his soul. "For in six days the Lord made heaven and earth, the sea, and all that is in them, and rested the seventh day" (Exodus 20:11).

Amidst the drabness of the workday and the hopelessness of living amidst constant hardship without rest or a break, the Father of the heavens introduced a day of rest, relief, and joy.

Meanwhile, He instructed His Church to strive to implement God's commandment as a social right into human life and state legislation. How much effort the Church had to devote to this, to overcome human resistance so that the earth may recognize the right to rest as a social and cultural achievement!

Complete and fruitless rest after work is possible only in the atmosphere of a religious holy day.

We will understand and experience how important the holy day is to rest after work only later; then, we will also understand the momentous purpose of rest after working on the holy day.

It is telling that all the holidays and ceremonies that Moses introduced upon God's command bound together these two aims: the religious aim of praising God and the purely human one of rest. In Chapter 32 of Leviticus, this is frequently stated with emphasis. "And you shall make proclamation on the same day; you shall hold a holy convocation; you shall do no laborious work: it is a statute forever in all your dwellings throughout your generations" (Leviticus 23:21; see 23:8, 25, 28, 36).

The demand to pause one's work: "Six days you shall work, but on the seventh day you shall rest; in plowing time and in harvest you shall rest" (Exodus 34:21) is tied to the theme: "that your manservant and your maidservant may rest as well as you" (Deuteronomy 5:14).

Every labor is headed towards rest, to attain a moment when man has satisfied all his life's needs and realizes in the peace and calm of satisfaction that he does not live on bread alone.

Man stands before God's immense and holy energy when he is embraced by this respite and reflects on his completed work.

Here, when he encounters God and internally embraces him, man becomes filled with love, which will be abundantly poured out in further labor, in holy prudence. In this way, our labor rests in God and is ready for new efforts in Him. The God of our strength who constantly renews the youthfulness of our days is born in this restful silence.

According to God's plan, holiday rest must be shared and social.

Apart from its religious nature, rest from work requires several more conditions.

Above all, this rest must be universal.

God expressed this concern for the universality in His laws, which He established for the Jewish people. God proclaimed on Mount Sinai: "Six days you shall labor and do all your work; but the seventh day is a sabbath to the Lord your God; in it you shall not do any work, you, or your son, or your daughter, your manservant, or your maidservant, or your cattle, or the sojourner who is within your gates" (Exodus 20:9–10).

During universal, collective rest from work, when we partake in blissful respite and are surrounded by a feeling of relief and are sanctified by the beloved God's peace, we are exalted and calmed. The lord and servant grow closer to one another, for obliterated by the signs of harsh labor they have grown similar to another and have meet before the face of the common Father!

When the entirety of creation enjoys rest and all who can be encompassed by rest without causing damage to their most important tasks, a holiday atmosphere that elevates the value of physical rest itself is born. You know how great it is when this is tied to visiting a church together and man is forced to set aside his work clothes out of a sense of propriety.

Rest from work must above all be social.

The entire human community, all together at one time should praise God through collective prayer and ceasing to work. The Mosaic

503

Law persistently demanded that this social rest would be achieved through collective longer holidays upon the completion of the more important periods of human labor. Thus, for example: "You shall keep the feast of harvest, of the first fruits of your labor, of what you sow in the field. You shall keep the feast of ingathering at the end of the year when you gather in from the field the fruit of your labor. [...] The first of the first fruits of your ground you shall bring into the house of the Lord your God" (Exodus 23:16, 19).

This social nature of rest nullifies the excessive exceptions from labor legislation; thanks to it, a great number of people does not see a difference between the weekday and the holiday along with those who witness their labor. It should be remembered that such labor in an environment that celebrates is even more burdensome; all too often, it creates hubbub that unpleasantly disrupts the desired peace and quiet.

The experience of the Bolsheviks, who did away with Sundays free from work out of hatred for Christianity, confirms the great social injury caused by the struggle against God's wise laws. There, a sixth day free from work was introduced, but it was not for everyone in the entire state; thus, in practice there are no days free from work. In each family, it is celebrated on a different day, and so social life does not know joyous days.

III. The Burden of the Hardworking Life

The experience of the day teaches us that over the course of life human energies become completely and irreversibly depleted, which can in no way be prevented. The Psalmist of the Lord expressively places this before our eyes: "For all our days pass away under thy wrath, our years come to an end like a sigh. The years of our life are threescore and ten, or even by reason of strength fourscore; yet their span is but toil and trouble" (Psalm 90:9–10). Age, illnesses, misfortune, and sin all have their consequences. However, excessively arduous labor has a significant role in this process as well.

God has given man strength so that he may make skillful use of it, so that they suffice for him to fulfill the entirety of life's tasks. Only in certain cases and through God's grace, as the lives of the saints show, man attains the fullness of life in his youth. People in general need a certain longer period to achieve the perfection that is delineated by life's purpose. Hence,

Labor cannot make man's life shorter.

When working, man takes on certain abilities, experiences, and skills, all of which both shape man and increase the value of his labor. Much patience and time is needed for labor to fully develop man.

Thus, the production-related impatience, which does not allow the entire person to work and only unilaterally exhausts his physical energies in a brief time, is very harmful. Similarly, the udarnik labor system, which is so greatly praised in the Bolshevik system and depletes human energies in an accelerated tempo, does not allow for the use of all of one's life's experiences and the development of many virtues, which are shaped long and systematically.

The more ruthlessly human talents are used up for the sake of physical labor, the less time there is to fulfill life's remaining duties. By the time life ends, it has been used up unilaterally.

Are not Ecclesiastes' doubts concerning the life values of such labor justified here? "What has a man from all the toil and strain with which he toils beneath the sun? For all his days are full of pain, and his work is a vexation; even in the night his mind does not rest. This also is vanity" (Ecclesiastes 2:22–23).

Human strength must be secured for the entirety of man's life's duties.

For man to fulfill all his life's purposes, he must skillfully make use of the strength God has granted him.

Everyday work breaks or Sunday rest do not completely exhaust this topic. In the past, the Church regulated the time of labor, introducing customs that ensured regular breaks. The evening Angelus prayer meant the end of toil; on the eve of holidays, the first vespers were something like today's free Saturday, which is why they are attended by large numbers of guild members and artisans. We clearly see that in nearly every period of the Church's calendar there are several days' holidays that made it possible to rest and distract one's thoughts from the one-sidedness of human labor.

Today, when, because of human indolence, the number of holidays has been limited, we must make sure that the remaining holidays are carefully used in accordance with their appropriate purpose; further-more, one should look for additional means of protecting human strength so that it may fulfill life's aims.

These needs in part correspond to the social legislation concerning annual vacation for workers. They are truly the right of workers not only because they are based on legislation, but they are also a law that resides in the soul of the working person, in his personal nature, and in the complex purposefulness of his life.

Therefore, this right must be respected; it cannot be directly or indirectly violated, nor can it be considered an unjust burden because it concerns not only the workforce as an abstract entity, a wheel, or a screw that is inside a machine, but it is a topic pertaining to the entirety of the living person. The violation of man's right to vacation, which is secured by legislation, is a moral transgression and not the evasion of an unjust burden; it strikes not only at man's physical strength, but also his human, familial, social, and religious duties.

Free time is needed to fulfill these tasks.

Concern that one's time is used in accordance with its purpose is also a moral obligation before God and society.

Resulting from the natural law and God's law, a vacation break secured by state legislation should be honestly used for the physical and spiritual good of every worker.

We stand before our family, wife, and children who during the workdays cannot always come closer to their father, who is often outside the house, or in times of brief respite when we are too exhausted to completely give ourselves to our families.

We also stand before our own souls: how often have we ignored our daily prayer in our rush to work. Could we not have looked more closely at what is happening inside ourselves? We gain the possibility to devote some of that time to longer prayer, spiritual exercises, retreats, confession, and the deepening of our knowledge of God by reading.

How often have we forgotten of our civic, social, and professional duties! Are we freed of them because we work hard? This is also a time when we can reflect on our duties more, become acquainted with them, and become aware of our deficiencies and neglect and remedy them through the proper training, reading, and entering life.

These are not petty things because whether we are living and active members of our society depends on them. Leo XIII notes this by recalling that the workers' question must be resolved with the direct participation of the workers themselves. They must fulfill the duties that no one else will perform, as he will not reach for the plow.

We must make careful use of the time granted to us through God's and man's laws to exalt our lives above the level of everyday, drab human labor.

* * *

Before our eyes is the burden of the day, the burden of the week, and the burden of human life! This burden is mitigated by God's law, the teaching of the holy Church, and state legislation, which protect the worker's holiday rest after exhausting labor.

These laws are so important that, as Leo XIII teaches, that "in all agreements between masters and work people there is always the condition expressed or understood that there should be allowed proper rest for soul and body" (RN, 42).

"To agree in any other sense would be against what is right and just; for it can never be just or right to require on the one side, or to promise on the other, the giving up of those duties which a man owes to his God and to himself" (*ibid*).

Look at the harsh threats God uses to secure the holy day and rest after work: "You shall keep the sabbath, because it is holy for you; everyone who profanes it shall be put to death; whoever does any work on it, that soul shall be cut off from among his people. Six days shall work be done, but the seventh day is a sabbath of solemn rest, holy to the Lord; whoever does any work on the sabbath day shall be put to death. [. . .] It is a sign for ever between me and the people of Israel" (Exodus 31:14–17).

Today, nobody gives death sentences for those who violate the holy days, but we pronounce such sentences on ourselves. How many there are among us who are alive and have names yet are dead (see Revelation 3:1). Look at how often people prematurely wear themselves out and grow old and gray in the untamed tempo of labor. The tempo of work is faster and faster, while one's nerves become more and more depleted. Our soul perishes amongst the people (see Exodus 31:14).

Man becomes soulless, as do his laws and the whole world. "My soul cleaves to the dust" (Psalm 118:25).

Let us recall the soul of the world, God's law. "Look on my affliction and deliver me, for I do not forget Thy law" (Psalm 119:153). "Let my cry come before Thee, O Lord; give me understanding according to Thy word! Let my supplication come before Thee [...]. My lips will pour forth praise [...]. "Let me live, that I may praise Thee" (Psalm 169–171, 175).

8

Catholics and Labor Legislation

I N THE ENCYCLICAL *QUADRAGESIMO ANNO*, WE find the following words that are worthy of attention: "A new branch of law, wholly unknown to the earlier time, has arisen from this continuous and unwearied labor to protect vigorously the sacred rights of the workers that flow from their dignity as men and as Christians. These laws undertake the protection of life, health, strength, family, homes, workshops, wages and labor hazards, in fine, everything which pertains to the condition of wage workers, with special concern for women and children. Even though these laws do not conform exactly everywhere and in all respects to Leo's recommendations, still it is undeniable that much in them savors of the Encyclical, On the Condition of Workers, to which great credit must be given for whatever improvement has been achieved in the workers' condition" (QA, 28).

In these words, we find not only a statement of facts but also its praise. This new and great sphere of law deals with vast areas of human co-existence that the Church had once protected and supported but that today are deemed as indispensable and greatly useful by the state.

Tellingly, the concept of "labor law" today breeds opposition even among people of good will who are distrustful of all novelties.

"Labor law" was born in the harsh realities of social struggle, often coming from people who were negatively inclined towards Christian morality; thus, it can raise objections.

However, do we not see in contemporary labor legislation attempts at repairing all the sins of negligence and great sins against our brothers who are subjected to the difficulty of labor?

This is worth pondering!

I. What Is the Aim of Labor Legislation?

Its aim is the direct good of employees, primarily workers, and indirectly strives for the good of all society.

According to the encyclicals of the popes, we see that the scope of labor legislation is very broad and will probably be even broader as social morality deepens.

It must determine the mutual duties of workers and employers, their right to association, and the conditions of labor contracts; it must protect the laws of the working person, his health, strength, morality, and religiosity; it must protect wages and prevent unfortunate accidents at work in the spirit of God's commandment "thou shalt not kill;" this is the general framework of labor law.

Leo XIII frequently reminds the state that it has a particular duty to look after employees.

State legislation should aim to improve social conditions and the fate of the worker and secure his existence and rights. The state can refer to special legislation in the following cases: when the private property of the worker must be protected; to end disputes between business owners and their workers; the protection of workers from the exploitation of labor; the designation of the time spent at work during the day; breaks in daily work; the proper health conditions of labor; rest; etc. Furthermore, legislation must protect the spiritual good of the workers, the holidays, the possibility to fulfill one's religious duties and public veneration of God, the protection of women and children, etc.

In these examples, we see that what we find in today's labor legislation had long been recommended by the Holy See.

II. Are We Obliged to Respect Labor Law?

To respond to this question, one must above all recall several general principles of Catholic social teaching.

The duty of the state community is to respect the legal order and to defend civic rights.

In the workplace, there appears among people an exchange of rights and duties on the principle of justice. Because of various causes, including ill will, there can arise a danger that unquestionable rights may be violated. This danger is all the greater because of the immorality of economic life, human greed, the dominant principle of profit at all costs, class struggle, and so forth, labor relationships are also disrupted by political struggles.

One must avoid partiality in the evaluation and dimension of these laws; above all, the law must defend justice.

In the name of social and distributive justice, state authority is obliged to protect every state that lives within a society, as all — both the business owners and the workers — are part of it.

The less self-sufficient and more defenseless a segment of society is, the greater protection should be accorded to it by the state. In particular, workers living only hand to mouth and who are deprived of all property live under such conditions. Due to its legislative authority, the state has obligations with respect to those whose labor leads to an increase in the state's wealth but themselves live frugally among the goods they themselves have created.

Thus, is not the disrespect of labor law a sin?

The state and its laws are in their nature necessary for man, for the full development of his personality. As a part of society, man should strive for not only his own good but for the common good as well. The state has the right to demand its citizens' obedience with respect to everything that leads to the common good.

Thus, every rational state decree whose aim is the common good of society that is professed and proclaimed by the legitimate authority of that society is obliging and should be executed.

The transgression of any law established by God is a sin. The violation of a law established by legitimate state authority is a sin because the state's authority to make legislation comes from supernatural law, which is established by God. Thus, every direct violation of state law is an indirect violation of the natural law in which state society, which has been called to life through God's power, lives.

We arrive at the following conclusion: everything that directly or indirectly strikes at God's law, both the natural and revealed law, in Church or state law is sinful.

Thus, labor law obliges one's conscience as well.

The Church does not deprive the person of good will of legal protection; immoral people who care about neither God's law nor human law would benefit from this.

Thus, labor law is obliging in the conscience as part of state legislation, just like all rational legislation that is proclaimed by legitimate state authority.

If, then, human law is just (that is, if it strives for the common good, does not violate the authority of legitimate government, and correctly spreads out burdens), then it is obliging for the conscience.

The disappearance of morality from economic life has all too often led to the evasion of labor law and so-called "social burdens," which were considered to have been unfairly distributed. Mores must be improved so that they may lead to obedience "not only to avoid God's wrath but also for the sake of conscience" (Romans 13:5).

III. Catholics Have Particular Duties with Respect to Labor Law

Catholics should see in labor law a continuation of the legislation that God had once begun; they should see it as the spread of the Christian spirit of love of one's neighbor and the progress of the social morality and justice demanded by God.

Labor law has its beginning in the Ten Commandments.

The first labor legislation is God's commandments beginning with the Egyptian yoke and later developed on Mount Sinai, in the Gospels, the Apostolic Epistles, and the social encyclicals. One can say without exaggeration that God is the creator of labor legislation. It results from the Christian spirit!

The protection of the working person began when God sent Moses to Egypt; Moses saw "the affliction of [his] people who are in Egypt" and heard "their cry because of their taskmasters" (Exodus 3:7).

Legislation on holidays encompasses not only their religious aspect but also the right to rest from work. "Six days you shall do your work, but on the seventh day you shall rest; that your ox and your ass may have rest, and the son of your bondmaid, and the alien, may be refreshed" (Exodus 23:12). The worker was prohibited from working at night, which would incur God's wrath.

Wages for labor which are to be given to workers before sunset have been protected, "for he is poor and sets his heart upon it" (Deuteronomy 24:15). The prophet Jeremiah threatened those who did not pay their workers with a harsh "woe to you" (see Jeremiah 22:13). Job defended himself against accusations that he did not exploit laborers or torment plowmen (see (Job 31:40). We all know Christ's words that "the laborer deserves his wages" (Luke 10:7).

512

Meanwhile, the Apostle James admonishes those who do not pay due wages: "Behold, the wages of the laborers who mowed your fields, which you kept back by fraud, cry out; and the cries of the harvesters have reached the ears of the Lord of hosts" (James 5:4).

Thus, today's labor legislation has illustrious patrons. No one should forget this, especially not Catholics.

In labor law, we should see the spread of the Christian spirit of love for one's neighbor.

For the moment, let us set aside those who create laws and political parties. The same applies to matters that have come from a thoroughly Christian spirit and a conscience that has been honed by the influence of the Gospels. For us, this is the most important thing.

Labor law is a great chapter in Christian morality. It attests to the fact that the world is nonetheless becoming increasingly Christian, although this is occurring in diverse ways. We sometimes hear that the Church has lost her influence. No! It is true that the world has become secularized. However, the dose of Christian truths still works. It influences even the souls of the Church's enemies, such that they are beginning to demand the implementation of what the Church has long recommended.

On the contrary, Pius XII says: "the first effect of grace is the strengthening of our sincere efforts in exercising God's commandments every day, both as individuals and as members of society."

Thus, our world is moralized even more, although it is abandoning religious symbols for a secular society. This is secularization with the simultaneous spread of the Ten Commandments. How redemptive!

If you need examples, here are some. Many articles of the July 2, 1924, law concerning the labor of the young and women contain statues that are taken from the heart of Gospel morality.

Certainly, the Church prefers to see the mother of a family in the home rather than in the factory, which is why she demands a family wage for the father. However, under sad circumstances when labor becomes a woman's necessity, she wants the working mother to be surrounded by truly Christian protection.

Article 16 of this law demands protection of the pregnant woman. Whenever we speak of the family and the protection of children, we must remember that labor legislation assists the entire concern of the Church.

Meanwhile, we read in Article 4 of the law on the labor of youths and women: "The employment of youths and women is prohibited under conditions that are particularly dangerous or harmful for their health or in hard labor that is dangerous to their health, morality, and good customs." In this secular labor law, we hear an echo of all the commandments of God Himself that have emerged victorious in the twentieth century. The Ten Commandments are transferred to labor legislation. "The very stone which the builders rejected" (see Matthew 21:42) has again become the cornerstone. And it has fulfilled its duties designated by God. What does it matter who wrote and designed this legislation if it is essentially Christian and obliges the conscience?

There are many more such Divine voices. For example, Articles 6 and 7 of the law under discussion demand a physician's testimony so that a given job "does not exceed the worker's physical strength and harm his development;" this sounds like Moses' voice to the Egyptians.

And is not the demand that there be creches for infants in factories where more than one hundred women work in Article 15 not essentially Catholic?

Let us read the Law on the Time Spent Working from December 18, 1919. What good can the commandment: "Remember the sabbath day, to keep it holy" (see Exodus 20, 8) bring if state legislation has not protected its execution? What good is appealing to the faithful to attend Mass if people are bound to the cogs of factory machines from the early morning until the late night? How helpful is this law, which is violated today?

Let us turn to the Soviet state. There, public religious worship will be impossible even if religious freedom is restored without amendments to labor legislation.

Contemporary labor legislation can have a major impact on religious life.

The *Code of Conduct* demands that employees and their household members are guaranteed "the appropriate time for rest and religious practices" (Article 464). How helpful this is to us, and how it gives opportunities to refer to the employers' conscience. Are we allowed to lose sight of this law, which is like the John the Baptist of the question of God in the workplace?

Labor law facilitates a life worthy of man. In this way, it improves the moral social environment, which facilitates a life in accordance with God's laws.

In his speech on the fiftieth anniversary of *Rerum novarum*, Pius XII recalls that the aim of all Christian efforts is "to create social conditions that are only capable of facilitating everyone a life that is worthy of a human and Christian."

Finally, labor law is a form of executing the social duties that burden property.

Even if a wage were administered as justly as possible, there is still a great dissonance between the value of human labor and its renumeration.

Catholics should especially protect labor law.

Our models will be all whom Pius XI praises in the encyclical *Quadragesimo anno* and who assisted governments in implementing labor protection laws. Both priests and lay Catholics have major contributions with respect to creating and maintaining new labor law in nearly all countries.

Today, we have specific duties with respect to labor law:

1. We cannot oppose its assumptions but instead strive for its perfection and development. If there are deficiencies created by an environment, they should be improved rather than destroyed.

2. Catholics must strive for the increase of justice by separating labor legislation from political conflicts. It must be seized from the hands of politicians and elevated to the level of a higher social morality.

3. Respect for labor law should be promoted, while its violations must be condemned. In the past, Catholic society brought up by the Church fulfilled the duties inscribed in today's Labor Code even though it lacked rights. This has been done especially by religious fraternities, corporations, and professional associations. Today, Catholics must fulfill these tasks and be leaders in the sense of justice and social peace.

* * *

Social progress results from the spirit of Christian love. The more it encompasses the entirety of human life, the closer people will become to one another, while their co-existence will be filled with peace.

May love illuminate our hearts and allow us to understand everyone and respect their rights.

PART III

Using the Goods of the Earth

1
Property Between
God and Man

THE PSALMIST GIVES US A PERSUASIVE LES-
son in sobriety. The following strange words are heard amidst
the hubbub of clamorous struggles over the distribution of the
goods of this earth: "The earth is the Lord's and the fullness thereof,
the world and those who dwell therein" (Psalm 23:1).

These words are astonishing to so many people! Our rival for property? People are so familiar with the concepts of "mine" and "not
yours," so influenced by civil law, and so comforted by the security
of possessing and the desire of the proletariat that there can be no
talk of a new owner.

A new owner? Before God, is not everyone else a sleazy usurper
who extorts someone else's property?

The earth has forgotten God, its Creator. "For He has founded it
upon the seas and established it upon the rivers" (Psalm 23:2).

I. God Is the Highest Creator and the Only Owner

As Nehemiah was rebuilding the walls of the ruins of Jerusalem, he
called the people to a public confession of the sins that had led them to
slavery. Now, the time for a new life has arrived. We must stand before
God's face and recognize His authority. What should we start with?

We should start with the most basic truths and recognize that God
is the beginning and the end of all creation. "Thou art the Lord,
Thou alone; Thou hast made heaven, the heaven of heavens, with
all their host, the earth and all that is on it, the seas and all that is
in them; and Thou preservest all of them; and the host of heaven
worships Thee" (Nehemiah 9:6).

Every healthy reform of the world should begin with this inspiring
confession. Faith in "the Creator of heaven and earth" should be at
the fore. Order between heaven and earth and on earth itself results
from it.

God is the Creator of the world and its greatest owner!

The beginning of everything and all filiation in both heaven and on earth come from God.

The existence of everything that exists has its beginning in God's fatherhood. Nothing can come to exist on its own.

The one God is the highest Being: "I am who I am" (Exodus 3:14). The highest good is in Him. The highest good is complete good.

All existence comes from God's existence; all good comes from God's good. As the highest good, God is in His essence the greatest owner of everything. "The earth is the Lord's and the fullness thereof, the world and those who dwell therein" (Psalm 23:1).

God is greater than any being and any good existing outside Himself. The entire created world recognizes God's superiority to itself and grants to God the greatest existence, greatest authority, and greatest dominion and possession.

From where does this come? It comes from the fact that God did not conquer the world; instead, He created it. God rules over the world through creation and providence. God's absolute right to all things that exist comes from the fact that He has created the world.

God's ownership rests in everything, even that which has been processed by man. "The land is mine; for you are strangers and sojourners with me" (Leviticus 25:23).

Thus, the source of all property and any sort of possession comes from God.

II. All Human Property Comes from God's Property

With respect to man, the situation is different. Man possesses nothing because of his essence; instead, he receives everything. Man possesses only upon receiving. That which has been distant and foreign to him has grown closer to him.

However, man himself is not a possessed good. Man's existence is not identical to his goods; they can be distributed through exchange, loss, or death. There is an internal, necessary relationship between many and any good he possesses.

Whatever man possesses he has received from outside himself. Man cannot be identified with what he possesses, as is the case with God.

His possessions will always be outside himself and foreign to him, even though they are necessary from the cradle to the grave.

Here, there is also a huge difference between God and man. The conclusion that flows is that man does not have absolute authority over any object, as he himself does not create it; at most, he processes it. He takes what comes from God to add human properties to received things.

All possessed objects are acquired, distributed to us, and given for their use; however, they are never created by man. Man has not given essence to anything. Here rests the further difference between God's possessing and so-called human possession.

Considering these brief reflections, we see how simplistic it is to ascribe to man the absolute right to possession.

We can only repeat the proper conclusion by recalling the words of the Psalmist: "Make a joyful noise to the Lord, all the lands! Serve the Lord with gladness! [. . .] Know that the Lord is God! It is He that made us, and we are His" (Psalm 100:1–3).

From this, there are resulting guidelines on how we should act with respect to the goods we possess.

Above all, we should treat every good we have received as a gift. We cannot possess it in the way we possess what we owe to ourselves. We should above all be grateful to the Giver. Next, we should use what we have received according to the Giver's intentions and guidelines. However, we know that property, which is God's renumeration for man's cooperation in His creative activity is first intended for God's glory and, later, the good of the individual and society.

III. The Requirement of Social Love Comes from God's Gift of Ownership

Three laws are bound together in the institute of private property: the right of the giving God, the right of the gifted owner, and the right of one's neighbors.

"Nature, rather the Creator Himself, has given man the right of private ownership not only that individuals may be able to provide for themselves and their families but also that the goods which the Creator destined for the entire family of mankind may through this institution truly serve this purpose. All this can be achieved in no wise except through the maintenance of a certain and definite order" (QA, 45).

God has shaped the nature of every man by endowing him with the rational aspiration to permanently satisfying his own most immediate and future needs. Because of this property of human nature, private ownership has its origin in God. God confirms man's acquisition of ownership through the commandments: "You shall not steal" and "You shall not covet your neighbor's house" (see Exodus 20:15, 17).

All property has a twofold nature: it is personal, thanks to which man satisfies his needs and those of his family, and social, because of which he is obliged to rush to help his neighbor. We see here that although the ownership of property is private, its use is social.

Property is not only a source of income; it is also the source of responsibilities. The owner is not an absolute lord. He is obliged to use his goods not only for himself but also for the social good. He must exercise the social duties that weigh down on ownership. Thus, we must see property as a common good rather than as our own good.

Private property is simultaneously a right and service.

Wealthy people are the administrators of God's inheritance and of that of the poor.

With respect to God, the owners of property are the stewards of goods; they are the "officials of Divine Providence" who make sure that God's plan is fulfilled in their fragment of life so that all receive the necessary nourishment.

The owner is not the steward of society, for society itself does not own anything, either. However, he is God's steward and the administrator of God's goods.

As such, the owner does not have absolute authority over things; he cannot do whatever he fancies with it but must instead use it in accordance with God's will, its nature, and the needs of his needs and those of his neighbors.

Man's entire authority over goods results from the fact that they have been entrusted to him by God. As the administrator, he has the key to God's granary. Because "the laborer deserves his wages" (1 Timothy 5:18), he is the first to make use of the goods granted to him.

However, having satisfied his needs appropriately to the requirements of his state, God's administrator has the obligation to help others. The selfish use of goods is condemned by Christ in the parable of the rich man (see Luke 12:16–21).

The owner has the right to efficiently administer goods so that he may himself live, pay a just wage, bear good witness in public life, and lead to the satisfaction of the needs of the greatest number of people. A useless servant who buried the talent he has received in the ground has been thrown out "into the outer darkness; there men will weep and gnash their teeth" (see Matthew 25:30), while his talent has been given over to him who has multiplied goods for his Lord.

"But if anyone has the world's goods and sees his brother in need, yet closes his heart against him, how does God's love abide in him? Little children, let us not love in word or speech but in deed and in truth" (1 John 3:17–18).

The servant "whom his master will set over his household, to give them their portion of food at the proper time" (Luke 12:42). is called blessed. "Truly, I tell you, he will set him over all his possessions" (Luke 12:44).

IV. Reprisals for the Violation of God's Right to Property

Man is obliged to cooperate with God's management, to cooperate with God's creative activity. The owner does not have the right to reject cooperation in making the goods of the earth fruitful or their administration as a faithful steward of the goods that God has entrusted to him for the good of his neighbors.

This is the proper path to heaven for all owners. One goes to heaven through earthly goods; not through love of them, but through their proper administration. God demands the practical love of one's neighbor from owners; the poor live thanks to the love of neighbor.

However, sin obstructs man's path to achieving this ideal. He has brought disorder and chaos into the sphere of property. Under his influence, the desire for bread has expanded so greatly in man that it has drowned out love for one's neighbor. Thus, the exercise of the responsibilities bearing on property has become exceptionally difficult. The owner has found the tendency to completely reject or ignore them in his fallen nature.

However, the violation of God's laws gives birth to a particular retaliation on the part of nature, which wants to remain faithful to God. Ownership turned away from the service to all of God's aspirations through human nature burdens the soul with the "mammon of injustice" and the body with the "injustice of the steward."

The more prudent "sons of light" (Luke 18:8) noticed that they lost themselves and became slaves to property after having possessed everything.

Today, not only is man the owner of things, estates, money, and property; all these "possess" man, tie him down, and buy him. The owner of the earth is *glebae adscriptus*;[1] the owner of the "treasures of the world" fears rust, moths, and thieves. The owner of a comfortable home becomes the guardian of junk. The growing attachment to goods leads to man's enslavement to things. The desire for ownership deprives us of solitude, peace, and freedom. This is the retaliation of untamed desire from which one can be freed only through justice, alms, charity, and generosity.

This personal anxiety can easily transform into social anxiety, as the violated rights of one's neighbors grow into a great revolutionary force that threatens improperly acquired goods and arouses the fear of all who are guilty, at the same time sometimes causing injury to the innocent. This terrible, blind revolutionary fervor sometimes adds a new injury in the name of bringing justice to the oppressed, although in practice it harms almost everyone. The hurricane of social revolutions overturns both rotten and healthy trees. This is the lesson of history, an admonition to not violate the laws whose God will someday seek vengeance.

However, there is one law that is greater than property. It is the law of death, which befalls even the most affluent owner. It best demonstrates that man is not an absolute lord of the goods of this earth. "For we brought nothing into the world, and we cannot take anything out of the world" (1 Timothy 6:7); "As he came from his mother's womb he shall go again, naked as he came, and shall take nothing for his toil" (Ecclesiastes 5:14).

However much man can impress the traits of his personality on his property through his work, he will never become irrevocably tied to any material thing; material things will always be beyond man, even if

---

1 Latin: Attachment to the soil.

524

he has devoted his entire heart to them. We see this tragedy in death, when one's beloved property is handed over to someone else, when not only material goods but even cultural ones come to be of use of others. Only then man knows "vanity of vanities" (Ecclesiastes 1:2); then he laments that he neglected to "make friends for [himself] by means of unrighteous mammon" (see Luke 16:9), that he "is not rich toward God" (Luke 12:21). He will take nothing with him.

* * *

The only good that will not abandon man is the supernatural merits that have been achieved through faithfully serving God's grace. Through grace, man becomes one with Christ, the Word that becomes the participant of all values. "All are yours; and you are Christ's; and Christ is God's" (1 Corinthians 3:22).

"But seek first his kingdom and his righteousness, and all these things shall be yours as well" (Matthew 6:3).

2
Man, God's Steward

*"The private possession of goods [...] the Author
of nature in His most wise providence ordained
for the support of human life" (QA, 49).*

NOT ONLY GOD'S LAW BUT ALSO, BECAUSE
of His benevolence, the rights of the owner and one's neighbors are reflected in private property.

The right of the owner is related to his rational and free will and
his personhood. The human person is the fundament of all private
property. All social systems must correspond to man's nature and
serve it. They can serve man well as long as they reflect the properties
of human nature. Then, man's activity finds its natural extension
in the social system, which creates forms that best correspond to
human needs.

Man is simultaneously an individual and a social being. He is a
rational and free being with his life's own earthly and eternal purposes
that have been given to him by his Creator. The individual achieves
these aims through his connection to society: in his familial, professional, national, political, and Church communities.

The appropriate social system that would develop all of man's
aspirations must correspond to such a conception of human nature.
In this system, every social, economic, and political institution must
follow human nature.

Thus, the system of property should above all correspond to the
human person and his own, social, earthly, and ultimate aims. Thus,
property is personal and social in nature; it serves man's aims as an
individual and, through its owner, it serves society, to which it has
been consciously directed by him.

In his encyclical *Quadragesimo anno*, Pius XI writes: "Nature,
rather the Creator Himself, has given man the right of private ownership not only that individuals may be able to provide for themselves
and their families but also that the goods which the Creator destined

for the entire family of mankind may through this institution truly serve this purpose" (QA, 45).

Let us make note of the relationship of private property and the so-called right of nature to appropriately evaluate man's aspirations, which are particularly strong today, to secure his existence through the aid of any form of possession.

I. Private Property Is a Need of Human Nature

In the Church's teaching, it is a theological certainty that "private ownership [. . .] is the natural right of man" (RN, 22).

Leo XIII says this many times in the encyclical *Rerum novarum*.

He is echoed by Pius XI: "The private possession of goods [. . .] the Author of nature in His most wise providence ordained for the support of human life" (QA, 49).

Likewise, Pius XII said on the fiftieth anniversary of *Rerum novarum*: "As a living being endowed with reason, every man's nature gives him the right to make use of the material goods of the earth, although it is left to the human will and the legal forms of individual nations that regulate their practical application in greater detail. The natural order, which comes from God, demands private property and a free bilateral exchange of goods through a payment."

The question of the natural law requires explanation.

It flows from God's eternal law, according to which God established the order of everything, giving it a specific nature, character, properties, and aims. Natural law and revealed law flow from God's law like two streams and are the source of man's both state and ecclesiastical rights.

The natural law is superior to all human laws as it results from our nature with which our Creator has endowed us.

This law strives for the preservation and development of human life through activities that are in accordance with the needs of human nature. If people acted contrary to the needs of nature and if they constantly violated its rights, they would lead to the annihilation of the human race.

Human nature, which registers the effects of activity contrary to nature, instructs man on what is conducive and what is harmful to his nature. The former acts are called good, while the latter are evil.

Through his rational nature, man realizes that he must make use of good deeds, or those that are not contrary to nature, to achieve aims corresponding to his nature. Otherwise, he will not achieve his aim and realize his life's goals. Our reason cautions us and morally obliges us to make use of such means that aim for goods that are proper to human nature.

In this way, man comes to know the constant, unchanging norms of behavior that lead to the aim that is proper to his nature and is known as the natural law. He comes to know it even better in God's revealed teaching, which is developed and explained by the Church.

Man arrives at the direct conclusions of these basic principles on what best corresponds to his nature and is conducive to his full development through his own experiences.

Institutions that are supposed to help man to fully develop his personality are created in light of these conclusions, which shape human nature.

Such institutions include private property. This results from the conclusion that man, who is obliged to support his own life and that of those closest to him, must have the right to the means that are necessary for the development of human life. He can make use of these means as long as he has the full freedom to do so. Therefore, man must have the right to possess material goods as his property.

Private property corresponds to the needs of the human person.
We must recall two basic truths:

1. Man is a rational and free person. This means that he has his own aim, is aware of it, and is responsible for the course of his own life. Hence man's great dignity. This is also the source of his freedom with respect to society.

Man must have this freedom at least with respect to what is necessary to preserve his basic life's needs.

2. The denial of man's right to private property is equivalent to disrespecting his personal freedom and a denial of freedom. Man has rights and obligations with respect to his own life. The obligation to preserve his life is a personal obligation. Not the state but man himself has this duty. Therefore, the state cannot deprive man of access to resources that are necessary to fulfill this obligation.

Thus, there is a necessary knot around private property and man's personhood. Personality is the nature of rational and therefore free and responsible beings. Animals are not owners because they are not persons. People have a vocation to property because they are persons and therefore rational and free beings.

Leo XIII explains this elementary truth whose formulation would sound grotesque today if not the experiences of communism that were based around this practical denial of the difference that must be remembered when ruling over men and animals.

Thanks to his reason, man is "the steward of God's providence," as Leo XIII beautifully writes. God has distributed rule over the world in such a way that he placed some of the providential activities in the hands of man, a rational being, obliging him to cooperate with him in the work of feeding the world.

Property is inscribed in human nature and in the nature of things. It is the radiation of human personhood in things. Human personhood inclines one to property, just as the nature of animals inclines them to eating and drinking. The desire for ownership is as natural as physical hunger and thirst.

The desire for ownership is a desire of our highest nature. Every man has an owner's soul, even those who oppose the private property of others have maintained their own, directed by hatred towards the property of others perhaps only because it was greater than their own.

How close this relationship is also results from the fact that through labor man impresses his personality on property. "Now, when man thus turns the activity of his mind and the strength of his body toward procuring the fruits of nature, by such act he makes his own that portion of nature's field which he cultivates — that portion on which he leaves, as it were, the impress of his personality; and it cannot but be just that he should possess that portion as his very own, and have a right to hold it without any one being justified in violating that right" (RN, 9).

Through labor, man expresses himself in things; he reflects all the properties of his nature in them. Let us look at the farmer who tills his field. There are people who have put their entire souls into tilling the soil. To rupture man's relationship to a plowed field is to strike at the child of his thoughts, will, and heart. Let us enter the office of a scholar. Every book on his shelf speaks to him as a sort of community of thought that binds this man together with this possession; anyone who would want to work there would feel like a stranger. Let us stand before a painting by Matejko hanging in Zachęta.[1] No one needs to be convinced that this is Matejko's, and not Zachęta's, painting. The human soul is reflected in this hall, library, and work of art; it is the stamp of an artist.

This is how far-reaching this community of property and the human person is.

Man has always exercised the right of private property.

This statement results from man's nature. From the very beginning of his existence, he had to possess the means that were necessary to support himself. He could not have expected that a communist state that would endow him with the means necessary for life would appear. Man had to live from the beginning of his existence on earth. If man counted on the providence of the collective state, humanity would never see such a state, because its creators would be absent.

Thus, man is correct in having abandoned expectations that the state would provide him with property. "Man precedes the State, and possesses, prior to the formation of any State, the right of providing for the substance of his body" (RN, 7).

During the times of the omnipotence of the state, this simple truth seemed likely to generate conflict. It is forgotten that man had to have received the right to possession from another, higher source; that he took it from the dominion and inspiration of nature.

Not only the state, which is too inclined to replace the citizen by taking upon itself the duties that it sometimes cannot exercise, should be reminded of this truth; so should people who neglect to make use of their rational and prospective nature and all too easily expect that the state will take upon itself their helplessness, expecting not only general but also elaborate assistance from it.

---

1   Jan Matejko (1838–1893): Was a Krakow painter who depicted Poland's past at a time when the country was partitioned. His most famous works include *Astronomer Copernicus, or Conversations with God* (1873); *The Battle of Grunwald* (1878); and *John III Sobieski at Vienna* (1883), which was a gift of the Polish nation to Pope Leo XIII and is now on permanent display in the Vatican Museums. Founded in 1860, the Zachęta National Gallery of Art is a prestigious Warsaw art museum.

Thus, the basic truth for every social system is the statement that the arrangement of the life of the private person belongs to him and not to society.

A society that would like to replace man in every problem and exercise all of man's private duties with the aid of the social system would make people childlike, helpless, and prone to a quick death.

II. Private Property: The Need of the Working Class

In his evaluation of the communist program of the transformation of the social system — the replacement of private property with communal property — Leo XIII emphasizes three stipulations according to which this new system harms those it wants to help the most. Communal property deprives man of the aim to work; it deprives him of his savings, the fruits of his labor; and, finally, it makes social progress impossible.

The aim of human labor is to acquire the means that are necessary for life.

Leo XIII writes: "When a man engages in remunerative labor, the impelling reason and motive of his work is to obtain property, and thereafter to hold it as his very own. If one man hires out to another his strength or skill, he does so for the purpose of receiving in return what is necessary for the satisfaction of his needs; he therefore expressly intends to acquire a right full and real, not only to the remuneration, but also to the disposal of such remuneration, just as he pleases" (RN, 5).

How deeply human is the pope's reference to man's most basic aspirations, which result from man's rational nature!

Man has personal needs first and is obliged to satisfy them with the aid of his reason and his own will. These are basic needs, for their satisfaction makes existence possible, which is a necessary condition for all other activities and the exercise of one's social duties.

Meanwhile, socialist thinking is different. In the socialist system, man is obliged to first think about the state and work for its ideal; only its implementation can satisfy even the most basic human needs. Therefore, we must first act and only later exist and live!

How can one fail to see how artificial and unnatural this construction is?

Is it not obvious that the cause that inclines us towards labor is above all our personal good and the good of our immediate family that can be achieved through this activity that leads to the reasonable acquisition of property, which allow man to satisfy his needs and secure one's existence?

Is not every intense effort, doubling of energy, and zeal in labor not awakened or intensified by one's needs or an ardent desire for a better existence?

The aim of human labor is the acquisition of property by saving.

Through his reason, man becomes aware of not only his current, most immediate needs that are satisfied from day to day. Man senses that his needs will have to be constantly replenished, so he thinks about meeting them in the future. Thus, the prudent man is inclined to not consume all the goods he has achieved through labor but to save some of them for the future. This occurs with the assistance of savings, thanks to which man limits his expenditures and uses his saved resources to acquire permanent goods.

Man has the right not only to the property that satisfies his needs but also that that which has been saved because it is a different form of renumeration for his labor. Thus, man has the authority to manage his property, which is acquired through saved resources just like his wage. This is the essence of the right to property, "whether the property consist of land or chattels" (RN, 5).

Thus, if private property becomes communal, it causes great injury to people who have acquired a modest estate through hard work. This "would deprive him of the liberty of disposing of his wages, and thereby of all hope and possibility of increasing his resources and of bettering his condition in life" (*ibid.*).

Finally, the aim of human labor is social progress with the participation of property.

Property that has been acquired and increased with the aid of savings that secures the family's stable existence and development through the education of youths gives man the ability to attain a higher and more dignified level of social life. The greater the means at the disposal of the working class that are appropriate to its environment, the more normally can a society move upwards, thanks to which a society gains new strength. This is a healthy phenomenon that is conducive to development.

In a system without private property, this is almost impossible. The communist system condemns working-class children to an eternal proletarian existence without any hope for a better future.

III. Private property as a Necessary Pre-Condition for the Existence of the Family

There is a necessary relationship between the family and property that is so obvious that the supporters of communism, who did not want to reject the notion of communal property, have sacrificed the family for its sake.

All considerations that speak in favor of the defense of man's private property are further bolstered by the right to a family life. This right must correspond to the ability to possess the appropriate resources that are necessary to support the existence of the family.

The socio-economic system should respect this right of the individual especially since the exercise of family duties is immensely socially important. The family is the basic cell of social and state life. Society does not consist of individuals but rather of social cells, the most important of which is the family.

* * *

Our reflections make it obvious that the right to property is closely related to man's personal nature.

The right to property corresponds to man's nature in such a way that man must possess it in any form for his full development. Naturally, the form must respond to the essential need of human nature and cannot be subjected to changes that disqualify its tasks with respect to man.

The family's permanence and stability come from human nature. As long as the human species exists, the family

must be tied to human nature. With respect to its essential properties, human nature does not change.

A state system that would deprive its citizens of all forms of property would be incompatible with the natural law and God's law.

Meanwhile, the Creator leaves the organization of ownership to human prudence and human laws, which decide on the designation of boundaries and definition of private property.

By protecting man's basic right to property, competent state authority can change forms of possession with the common good in mind. This good is at the same time the limit of the scope of activity of the community that is entitled to this.

Above all, it is obliged to make sure that private property fulfills its social task.

Property is subjected to the personal responsibility of the owner; however, it is not unlimited. The common good is the limit of the initiative and freedom of the owner.

Only at the price of exercising all duties weighing down on property, which is the basis of the social system, will human life be facilitated as the ever-wise intentions of Divine Providence intend.

3

The Rights of One's Neighbors Weighing on Property

"Now the company of those who believed were of one heart and soul, and no one said that any of the things which he possessed was his own, but they had everything in common" (Acts 4:32).

T HE ACTS OF THE APOSTLES PRESENT US NOT only the beginnings of Christ's Church on earth but also the birth of new principles that from that point will regulate social life. Although there are no new laws, there is new life. Slavery had not yet disappeared, and the Church had not yet issued any decree condemning it, but in the everyday lives of Christians "there is neither slave nor free [. . .] for you are all one in Christ Jesus" (see Galatians 3:28). There were no decrees hindering the uninhabited use of private goods, yet the Christian spirit opened hearts, hands, and treasuries. The new life of the faithful preceded the Christian laws without any dictates or coercion.

In everyday life, the generous hearts of the Christians of the first centuries presented the best explanation of how to understand the possession of private property. They continue to be obliging today; the best evidence of this is the incident with Ananias and Sapphira who were punished not for having kept part of the property they had sold but because they had lied to the Holy Spirit. "While it remained unsold, did it not remain your own? And after it was sold, was it not at your disposal?" (Acts 5:4).

The Church did not abolish private property; instead, she imbued human hearts with a readiness to share their goods with their neighbors. "Give of your bread to the hungry, and of your clothing to the naked" (Tobit 4:17). Since then, an important chapter on the social duties weighing on private property has been added to the Church's teaching.

I. The Dual Nature of Property

The purpose of private property is "not only that individuals may be able to provide for themselves and their families but also that the goods which the Creator destined for the entire family of mankind" (see QA, 45).

This dual nature of property cannot be separated without injury to the owner, society, or the institution of property itself. Every violation of it turns property into plunder and the earth into a land of tears and exploitation.

"Nature, rather the Creator Himself, has given man the right of private ownership not only that individuals may be able to provide for themselves and their families but also that the goods which the Creator destined for the entire family of mankind may through this institution truly serve this purpose" (QA, 45).

The private nature of property is indisputable. This is expressed in the fact that property serves the good of the individual and that property exists so that "individuals may be able to provide for themselves and their families" (*ibid.*).

The belief, so common today, that property is merely a social function exercised by the owner upon the authority of his fellow brothers, nation, and state is erroneous. The owner is not an official of society.

Commutative justice defends the right to private property (see QA, 47). It demands the repayment of debts, the paying of wages for labor, trade obligations, and the avoidance of fraud and theft in the sale and protection of goods.

This right gives the owner the freedom to dispose of his property without the participation of third actors within the limits of the natural law, morality, and the common good.

However, private property is not the rejection of the rights of others to possessed goods, nor is it the sealing off of things from one's neighbors.

Hence the social nature of property. This is expressed, first, in the fact that property respects the common good (see QA, 45) of all people. Second, the material goods "may through this institution truly serve this purpose" of the common good (*ibid.*). Next, the private good must be consistent with the needs of the public good both in

536

its system and its use, which does not hinder but instead helps the private good. Finally, "men must consider in this matter not only their own advantage but also the common good" (QA, 49).

II. The Social Bases of the Duties of Property

The obligation to share property with one's neighbors is indisputable. Sacred Scripture frequently reminds us of this duty. The Mosaic Law is beautiful in its deeply human intention.

"When you reap the harvest of your land, you shall not reap your field to its very border, neither shall you gather the gleanings after your harvest. And you shall not strip your vineyard bare, neither shall you gather the fallen grapes of your vineyard; you shall leave them for the poor and for the sojourner" (Leviticus 19:9–10).

"When you go into your neighbor's vineyard, you may eat your fill of grapes, as many as you wish, but you shall not put any in your vessel. When you go into your neighbor's standing grain, you may pluck the ears with your hand, but you shall not put a sickle to your neighbor's standing grain" (Deuteronomy 23:24–25).

Christ's predecessor says: "He who has two coats, let him share with him who has none; and he who has food, let him do likewise" (Luke 3:11).

According to the apostolic constitutions of the first centuries of Christianity: "Share your estate with your neighbors and do not call your property unlimited, for everything is a gift from God, Whom all people should serve."

St. John Chrysostom demands that the rich man and the owner consider themselves to be zealous and good stewards of the goods entrusted to them by God and act accordingly (Homily on Matthew 24).

By what authority are these laws binding?

Pius XI teaches that "the duty of owners to use their property only in a right way does not come under [commutative] justice, but under other virtues, obligations of which "cannot be enforced by legal action" (QA, 47).

These words require an explanation.

Human co-existence is governed especially by two virtues: justice and love. They both complement one another. In the sphere of the possession and use of goods, they harmoniously work together.

537

The arms of justice are very long. Moralists see in it two aspects: general and particular justice.

General justice, also known as legal or social justice, is also the resolute and persistent will to return to the community its rights.

In his nature, man is a social being; he must live in the human community and thus has duties towards it.

Social justice inclines man to fulfill these duties. All of man's acts and talents should be directed towards the common good. The soldier is obliged to fight for his fatherland; the citizen must pay taxes and respect established laws; everyone has a duty to cooperate with that which is necessary for the maintenance of the common good.

We see here how important the virtue of justice is; a lack of it disrupts social peace and causes great injury to one's fellow citizens.

Pius XI has applied this virtue to the entire sphere of socio-economic life.

Particular justice is the resolute and persistent will to give the rights to people that they physically or morally deserve. With respect to private persons, it appears as commutative justice and defends all contracts and bilateral documents. As distributive justice, in public relationships it makes use of the leader of a community in order to distribute public burdens, awards, honors, and punishments according to proper and proportional measures.

The duties that incline one to make honest use of property are governed by "other virtues, obligations of which 'cannot be enforced by legal action'" (QA, 47).

The basis of these virtues, which regulate the use of property, is love and the following resulting virtues: alms, charity, and generosity.

Although these are not legal obligations, in certain exceptional circumstances, such as natural disasters or public hazards, they can become legally binding. However, they are real duties; their violation burdens the human conscience.

"The Sacred Scriptures and the Fathers of the Church constantly declare in the most explicit language that the rich are bound by a very grave precept to practice almsgiving, beneficence, and munificence" (QA, 50).

Giving alms makes us directly turn towards our neighbors and morally obliges us to bring succor to the poor who are suffering.

Charity obliges us to support works of mercy, remedying human penury and reducing the effects of poverty.

Meanwhile, generosity, as a virtue that mitigates the evil love of money, will incline one for their generous use to create great, socially useful works. The role of generosity is very important. It obliges the souls of wealthy people who can share great monetary resources. Years ago, during a time of vibrant faith, a surplus of goods was used to build churches, abbeys, and foundations that multiplied the glory of God. Today, the Holy See wants to increase the scope of this virtue to create new opportunities for human labor.

The exercise of these virtues is dictated by the imperative of social justice, as a result of which each man is obliged to cooperate with the common good and maintain social order and well-being.

III. The Fulfillment of Social Obligations Weighing on Property

Naturally, the starting point is the disposition of the heart. We should follow the example of the first Christians: "Now the company of those who believed were of one heart and soul, and no one said that any of the things which he possessed was his own, but they had everything in common" (Acts 4:32).

To achieve the social good, it is not enough to distribute and divide land, factories, and capital. If the human heart is not divided, everything will return to new, selfish hands. The example of Bolshevism attests to this. The division of material is not of major importance to the maintenance of social justice.

According to St. Thomas, external things must be considered common rather than individual. Man should be ready to share his goods, even necessary ones, although there is no obligation to do so. Property owned only for oneself is avarice and moral perversion.

Such an internal disposition will open our eyes to all our brothers, which is beautifully expressed in the prayer said when blessing one's table: "The eyes of all look to Thee, and Thou givest them their food in due season. Thou openest Thy hand, Thou satisfiest the desire of every living thing" (Psalm 145:15–16).

Human thoughts and actions will flow from this spirit.

Man will first understand what the private possession, but common use of goods means.

This is the basic principle for the entirety of the Church's teaching on property. She distinguishes between the right to possess property, which is private, and its use, which should be common. While strongly defending possession as tied to the natural law and the needs of the human person, the Church simultaneously emphasizes that the demand of social justice is helping others through the aid of one's own goods, to "give for alms those things which are within," as Christ the Lord has taught (see Luke 11:41), thus pointing towards one of the means of fulfilling the social duties that weigh on property.

Leo XIII writes: "Whoever has received from the Divine bounty a large share of temporal blessings, whether they be external and material, or gifts of the mind, has received them for the purpose of using them for the perfecting of his own nature, and, at the same time, that he may employ them, as the steward of God's providence, for the benefit of others" (RN, 22).

The goods of this earth achieve their proper destiny through human hands so that "the right of private ownership [exists] not only that individuals may be able to provide for themselves and their families but also that the goods which the Creator destined for the entire family of mankind may through this institution truly serve this purpose" (QA, 45). By giving goods to people, God simultaneously puts pressure on the conscience that an abundance of goods many be achieved through good organization and, thanks to good will, reach the needy with the aid of the virtue of love.

Thus, we see that we are speaking here not of some form of management or organization of property but rather of the very destiny of property. The purpose of goods is such that they should serve all and fulfill the needs of the whole of society.

The use of common goods therefore comes from the natural law, just like possession itself. This is the most important aspect of the Catholic teaching on property. Not only the private right to possess but also the right to common use is based on God's law. The entirety of the teaching on alms attests to this.

In every piece of property to which I have "my right" there is also something of "the rights of others." Property is not only divided into what is mine and yours; there is also something that is ours between what is mine and what is yours.

"A person's superfluous income [. . .] is not left wholly to his own free determination" (QA, 50).

This is the second principle of the Catholic teaching on property; it is a conclusion of the first.

Pius XI explains what "superfluous income" is; it is "income which [man] does not need to sustain life fittingly and with dignity" (*ibid.*).

Disposable goods are no longer tied to their owner through his personal needs; thus, they are subjected to the general destiny of goods and should be distributed.

There are two reasons why this duty is exercised: first, there is the danger of a life that engenders the needy; second, there is the mere fact of possessing disposable goods.

Even if there were no people threatened by death from starvation, the second reason remains. Naturally, the existence of paupers is a decisive factor, for the poor are the natural consumers of disposable goods.

He who has disposable goods is no longer their owner. St. Thomas called those who do not respect this commandment the violators of the rights of others. St. Basil of Caesarea expresses this very clearly: "Are you, who considers what you have received only to give to others to be yours, not a plunderer? Bread that is stored for later is the bread of those who hunger; clothing held under lock and key is the clothing of the naked; the shoes you allow to rot are the property of the barefoot; stored money is the property of the poor."

The possession of disposable goods is like the management of goods for others.

This obligation applies to such income that remains after the satisfaction of one's personal and family needs and after the exercise of one's own duties within boundaries that are designated by one's social environment and position. Naturally, this does not pertain to property that brings income.

Rather, this applies to disposable goods, whereas necessary goods are subject to inviolable personal rights.

Naturally, so-called necessary goods can differ, depending on the conditions of existence, one's social environment, quality of life, and decent mores. This obligation is not constant and the same for all, but it instead is subject to fluctuations depending on both ordinary and exceptional circumstances. Such a conception allows for a greater possibility to act, one that is free and without coercion. However, this conception cannot be expanded; all misdeeds, abuses, social requirements, morbid fashions, luxury, and human vanity cannot be applied to it. On the contrary, this is where the social obligation to a frugal life that greater means to help others may be acquired begins. A balance between one's own quality of life and the needs of one's surroundings is a social obligation.

This is where the duty of love and social justice begins. St. Augustine teaches: "The disposable goods of the wealthy are the necessary goods of the poor. You seize the property of others when you have a surplus of goods" (Homily on Psalm 142).

The social obligation weighing on property can be exercised through alms, generosity, and charity.

With respect to people who are incapable of working, such as the elderly, sick, invalids, and orphans, private property is bound to the obligation of alms, charity, and mercy. "The hapless commits himself to thee; Thou hast been the helper of the fatherless" (Psalm 10:14). Giving alms is the simplest form of exercising the duties weighing on property. This is a religious, moral, and social obligation.

"Therefore I command you, you shall open wide your hand to your brother, to the needy and to the poor, in the land" (Deuteronomy 15:11).

"Share your bread with the hungry and bring the homeless poor into your house; when you see the naked, to cover him" (Isaiah 58:7).

"Give, and it will be given to you; good measure, pressed down, shaken together, running over, will be put into your lap. For the measure you give will be the measure you get back" (Luke 6:38).

There is communion between the poor and Christ and, through Christ, between the poor and us. We are one body in Christ. Alms is serving Christ through our neighbors. Thus, during the Final Judgment our deeds towards the poor will be judged as acts of negligence or merit with respect to Christ Himself (see Matthew 25:40).

Hence the commandment given to those who possess: "As for the rich in this world, charge them not to be haughty, nor to set their hopes on uncertain riches but on God who richly furnishes us with everything to enjoy. They are to do good, to be rich in good deeds, liberal and generous" (1 Timothy 6:17–18).

However, alms are not the last word with respect to the social duties weighing on property. Alms are not a sufficient means of life for the poor, while they are not the entire social duty of the rich. Charity will not solve the social problem.

The rich cannot ignore their duty to look after the unfortunate; only then can they fully attest to love.

The rich cannot limit themselves to charity, convinced that they are implementing social justice.

In order to renew society, there must be a bond between love and social justice.

Another obligation weighing on private property is the creation of sources of income.

This obligation should be fulfilled with respect to those who can and want to work. Here, alms can only be a form of temporary assistance; in the long term, this problem must be resolved in a different way.

We must recall the virtue of generosity. Pius XI writes: "Expending larger incomes so that opportunity for gainful work may be abundant, provided, however, that this work is applied to producing really useful goods, ought to be considered, as We deduce from the principles of the Angelic Doctor, an outstanding exemplification of the virtue of munificence and one particularly suited to the needs of the times" (QA, 51).

To use one's goods for the benefit of one's neighbors when they are in need means to provide them with work and the opportunity to make a wage to support themselves. In this case, the owner of produced goods has an essential, responsible role to fulfill. He is obliged to best direct the subject of property and make use of all the production capabilities of his workplace. The exercise of this moral obligation determines if private property will achieve its purpose.

Naturally, such efforts are also for one's own benefit, for the work of the owner gives him the right to a reward. However, this activity also benefits employees and the good of society.

Such activity is not a demand of commutative justice, but it is not ordinary love. The discipline of economics instructs us that capital should work; it turns out that not only man, but also material objects cannot remain idle.

The laws of the revealed books are consistent with the laws of economics. According to Ecclesiastes: "There is a grievous evil which I have seen under the sun: riches were kept by their owner to his hurt, and those riches were lost in a bad venture" (Ecclesiastes 5:13–14).

This is the continuation of Christian love, which is initiated through alms. The owner is obliged to use his wealth for the good of all. To a large degree, he owes it not only to his own work and ingenuity but also to the living conditions, social order, and cooperation of his neighbors who make an increase in prosperity possible. Thus, surplus income should not lay fallow; instead, it should be used for the service of society.

In his radio address of June 1, 1941, Pius XII said that not the accumulation of goods but the participation of the maximum number of people in those goods attests to the true wealth of the nation. "Work so that this kind of just division is truly accomplished in a permanent way and you will see that even nations who have at their disposal smaller goods will become economically healthy."

This social well-being is attained through the exercise of the social duties that weigh on property.

* * *

God's Wise Man once prayed using words that sound strange to the ears of today's man: "Give me neither poverty nor riches, feed me with the food that is needful for me, lest I be full, and deny Thee, and say, 'Who is the Lord?' or lest I be poor, and steal, and profane the name of my God" (Proverbs 30:8–9).

These words contain an unusual moderation with respect to wealth and socio-economic realism. This is balanced possession. This is achieved not through the justice of measure and weight, but through one heart and soul. This is possible only before the face of God. "The rich and the poor meet together; the Lord is the Maker of them all" (Proverbs 22:2).

The mathematical equality of possession between people is neither possible nor necessary. However, the reduction of income disparities is both possible and desirable. This will take place through the aid of private possession, as one's own social obligations will be executed in a Christian way.

We will achieve the desired balance. Arguments and struggles will end, as will jealousy and jaundice; meanwhile, love, the mother of justice and peace, will blossom.

4

The State and Property

NABOTH'S VINEYARD HAS BECOME A HIStorical symbol of the relationship between state authority and private property. This distant, perhaps forgotten event repeats itself so often today in various forms. This is the story of the eternal conflict between the rights of man and his community, between the citizen and the authorities, and between Naboth and Ahab.

Naboth's vineyard borders on royal gardens, just as in everyday life the border between the right of private property and state authority is thin. Ahab is allowed to have his plans, while Naboth is allowed to defend his rights.

Ahab says: "Give me your vineyard, that I may have it for a vegetable garden, because it is near my house; and I will give you a better vineyard for it; or, if it seems good to you, I will give you its value in money." Naboth replies: "The Lord forbid that I should give you the inheritance of my fathers" (1 Kings 21:2–3).

The king has the right to ask, but the citizen can likewise reject such a request. Such a rejection may anger the ruler, but he cannot listen to Jezebel's suggestions.

The ordinary course of the dispute begins to be tragic. The king's wounded pride is worked up with irony. "Do you now govern Israel?" (1 Kings 21:7). Indeed! Is the king incapable of dealing with a modest subject? He allows wicked people to act. Naboth dies because of the queen, which opens the way to another's property. Who can resist the wish, will, and authority of the king?

Yet it turns out that the road to Naboth's vineyard is obstructed; it is closed off even for the king, who goes to see it. Elijah the Tishbite, God's messenger, had the following communication for Ahab: "Thus says the Lord, 'Have you killed, and also taken possession?'" (1 Kings 21:19). God's punishments will befall the king, queen, and the entire royal household. "You have sold yourself to do what is evil in the sight of the Lord" (1 Kings 21:20).

This harsh sentence on the royal family is a warning to those who exercise state authority, that they not abuse their dominance in order to destroy inviolable human rights and so that they do not place their own good over that of the common good and not sacrifice natural rights for their own benefit.

I. What Can We Not Forget in the Management of Goods?

We cannot forget that the state has man before itself. Every man is a person, a rational and free yet simultaneously social being.

All social institutions should correspond to man's two-fold nature. If there is a discrepancy here, social life will be filled with constant dissonance and upheaval. A system and legislation that determine the destiny of property should correspond to human nature.

The right of the state to direct the activity of man and social groups towards the common good results from the necessity of social co-existence.

Man himself is obliged to coordinate his own good with the common good and cooperate to achieve the common good. Only then will man be capable of achieving the fullness of his personal development, when his relationship to the common good will be arranged within the limits of God's law and the natural law.

From this also results the right and duty of the state concerning the arrangement of social life and, within its framework, the designation of the right to property.

When we speak of the rights and obligations of the state, we emphasize that: "By the State we here understand, not the particular form of government prevailing in this or that nation, but the State as rightly apprehended" (RN, 32). Thus, we mean a public community based on the natural law that respects God's positive law; in other words, we must strive for a Christian state, not in the sense that it is a confessional state but that its fundaments are Christian in nature.

A state conceived in this way is obliged to concern for the common good, which is greater than the good of any individual and at the same time higher than the total of the good of all individuals.

In the sphere of property, a requirement of this common good is the right of all to life. According to the teaching of St. Thomas, the authority of the state extends to ensuring that things within the domain of private property are used together.

The state's task is to bind the private property of the individual to society. This aspiration must be bilateral: the community must sacrifice itself and always defend the citizen's right to possession, while citizens must serve society with their social goods.

Thanks to this aspiration, a social bond strengthened in the sphere of earthly goods will be forged.

Because private property has a two-fold purpose (simultaneously individual and social), the role of the state is also two-fold: with respect to the common good and the individual destiny of property as well as with respect to the social good and the social purposes of property.

Let us reflect on each aspect of this.

II. The Role of the State and the Individual Purposes of Property

The state must above all recognize private property as the basis of the social system.

Private property is the result of human nature and the need for social co-existence. It must always serve man. It should protect human needs and assist in the development of personhood. The state is obliged to respect the institution of property and must consider it a necessity resulting from the nature of the human person.

Man must be concerned about the development of the person and the means that are necessary to achieve this. The duty to satisfy one's needs is the most personal and earliest duty. Pius XII has made note of this fact in his speech on the fiftieth anniversary of *Rerum novarum*: "Indeed, man has a completely personal duty to protect and perfect his material and spiritual life in order to achieve the religious and moral aim that God has given to all people and that He has given as the highest norm, obliging before all other duties always and in every case."

The state must recognize the laws of God and nature, which are older than its own. Pius XII says: "The protection of the inviolable scope of the rights of the human person and their fulfillment must be an essential task of all public authority. Is this not the true meaning of the common good to whose support the state is called?"

The state cannot destroy private property and deprive citizens of the right to possess.

In the above-mentioned speech, Pius XII denies the state the right to such broad authority over the members of society that it may renounce or question the efficacy of the natural right to material goods out of concern for the public good.

The state can do this neither directly nor indirectly, nor through taxation. Pius XI teaches that "it is grossly unjust for a State to exhaust private wealth through the weight of imposts and taxes" (QA, 49).

Why? We find an answer in *Rerum novarum*: "The natural right itself both of owning goods privately and of passing them on by inheritance ought always to remain intact and inviolate, since this indeed is a right that the State cannot take away" (RN, 49).

The state is obliged to protect private property.

Rerum novarum brings the following principle to the fore: "First of all, there is the duty of safeguarding private property by legal enactment and protection" by the state (RN, 38).

The duties of the state are supreme, as with respect to property they cannot be at the same level as the citizen. However, they are not absolute, as they are limited by the natural law. The state is not an owner, but a mediator between owners; the ordinary role of the state in the field of property is to adjudicate disputes between owners and to protect, direct, and promote private initiative.

Whenever the state becomes a competitor in the sphere of property, it usually degrades its dignity, becoming a merchant, broker, or entrepreneur, often cheating its citizens whereas it should be the defender of both man and the public good. If it plays the role of an owner, the state is often prone to all the flaws and sins of its citizens; it often evades the laws it has established, in the process destroying rather than protecting the legal order. As an employer, the state can be no less exploitative of laborers than the private owners of workplaces.

The state cannot reduce property to a social function because property is not a function. The owner is not a state or collective official who can be removed when he improperly runs his workplace.

The state has the right to protect the common good, but it cannot forget that property above all serves to meet the needs of the owner and only later can serve society. The concept of property consists of private possession and common use; thus, man cannot be deprived of his right to possess, as the use of property does not completely correspond to society's needs.

The protection of the property of labor by the state means its protection against the selfishness of those who possess as well as against the designs of social authority.

The state should seek to promote private property.

A system in which the attainment of property would be possible for every willing, hardworking, and far-sighted person should be created.

The promotion of property must protect people from the slavery to which they would be bound if they were handed over to the only owner and provider of bread, the state. Slavery to the state becomes even more burdensome than the capitalist yoke. In the capitalist economy, the worker can always change his place of employment and improve his conditions of existence; however, the state, being the only owner, is capable of starving man, for even his most basic needs are then dependent solely on it.

Private property should protect man's freedom not only from the private entrepreneur but also from the state.

Christian social thought strives for the social balance of possession. This happens especially through the aid of a just wage.

The state has the duty to respond to man's will to possess, which is his natural need, and to develop that need. According to Leo XIII: "The law, therefore, should favor ownership, and its policy should be to induce as many as possible of the people to become owners" (RN, 46). The disappearance of the will to possess is a negative social symptom.

According to Pius XII, the aim of the "national economy" is not the mere accumulation of goods by the state but their just distribution to the largest possible segments of the nation.

III. The Role of the State and the Individual Purposes of Property

Private property is not freed of the duty to respect moral laws and commandments as well as the demands of the conscience; it gives no one the right to use property while violating God's law and human laws. The protection of these laws will be the first and best form of exercising the social duties weighing on property.

In this field, the state has its unique duties.

Concern for the common good of citizens rests on the state.

The state appears as a factor of social balance. It is concerned for the common good and for this reason it is interested in property.

Because private property corresponds to the needs of human nature, it is a constant institution; the state cannot seek its abolition.

However, the forms of property are volatile, for they depend on development, technology, and the conditions and needs of human life. "For God has granted the earth to mankind in general, not in the sense that all without distinction can deal with it as they like, but rather that no part of it was assigned to any one in particular, and that the limits of private possession have been left to be fixed by man's own industry, and by the laws of individual races" (RN, 8).

Indeed, people who cultivate and develop economic life have a major impact on the development of the system of property. Man can dispose of his property.

However, he cannot limit himself to this self-determined role in ordering private property. Man's mere nature does not determine which object should belong to this man or another, just as it does not determine the means of acquiring and distributing property.

However, the determination of these rights is indispensable to social peace. Here, there is room for the activity of the state community. The state's duties include more precisely determining everything that is not determined by the natural law and what is indispensable to maintaining the social order.

The state determines the necessary conditions to recognize something as the property of an individual. "Public authority, under the guiding light always of the natural and Divine law, can determine more accurately upon consideration of the true requirements of the common good, what is permitted and what is not permitted to owners in the use of their property" (QA, 49).

The necessity to ensure that the system of property corresponds to the common good and to justice is also a real right and important duty of the public authorities.

According to Pius XII: "The natural order, which comes from God, demands private property and the free, bilateral exchange of good through trade and contributions as well as public authorities regulating these activities with respect to both these functions" (radio address, June 1, 1941).

Public authorities could not remedy the public good if they did not have the right to implement certain changes in the management of property within the limits of the natural law.

To achieve this aim, public authorities along with citizens must look for increasingly better forms of the organization of private property so that they may fully correspond to their destiny.

Naturally, the main purpose of the public authorities is the creation of an appropriate framework for economic activity.

To maintain social balance and justice, it is necessary to remove major income inequalities. For this purpose, "the State has the right to control its use in the interests of the public good alone, but by no means to absorb it altogether" (RN, 47).

Constantly bearing in mind the assumption of the common good wherever the free initiative of those who manage goods is unsuccessful, the public authorities should support small and medium places of employment and farms. They should seek to promote property and oppose proletarianism. In this way, it will strive for accordance between the system of private property and the needs of the common good.

Pius XI writes: "Yet when the State brings private ownership into harmony with the needs of the common good, it does not commit a hostile act against private owners but rather does them a friendly service; for it thereby effectively prevents the private possession of goods, which the Author of nature in His most wise providence ordained for the support of human life, from causing intolerable evils and thus rushing to its own destruction; it does not destroy private possessions, but safeguards them; and it does not weaken private property rights, but strengthens them" (QA, 49).

Wherever great social inequalities exist, and masses of paupers live alongside the very wealthy, their property cannot be safe.

Citizens must be brought up in the spirit of serving society through their own property.

The state is not an owner; it cannot be a competitor in debates on property. However, it has authority over owners.

The state always should bear in mind the fact that property does not give the right to make absolute use of one's estate, as one is burdened by duties with respect to God and neighbor.

Naturally, the exercise of these duties above all belongs to the owners themselves. However, experience shows that owners frequently do not exercise them. In that case, the public authorities must use legal coercion, especially with respect to people of ill will.

Furthermore, according to St. Thomas the state should not only seek legal coercion with respect to people of ill will, but it can even distribute the disposable goods of the negligent and the slothful to the needy.

The state has this right to preserve the general good in the name of justice, which is violated by a wicked owner; this does not refer to particular justice, which is with respect to a specific individual, but to general justice.

However, it does not give the state the right to the expropriation of those who make improper use of property or make it useless.

The state may transfer property in the name of the public good.

The state's duties include looking after the common good; with respect to the individual, the state has, under various conditions, the same duties. Thus, the state cannot achieve the transfer of private property from one person to another, solely referring to its good.

The common good may incline the state to transfer property; however, certain conditions must be met.

Factors that justify expropriation by the state include:

1. There is an excessive number of agricultural proletarians who lack employment and are condemned to emigration;

2. The lack of food, which afflicts the general population and leads to malnourishment, starvation, or the necessity to transport means of nourishment at excessive prices;

3. The necessity for good cultivation of the soil in order to achieve a surplus of products or to repay foreign debts;

4. Public safety and the peace of certain spheres of the state, such as its borders or places of employment.

Under such circumstances, when there is no other, less radical solution, the distribution of land is justified, for the common good demands that a large number of people does not live in poverty and hunger, to restore social calm, and to secure the existence and security of the state.

A condition for decent expropriation for public purposes is prior just compensation for the owner. We must remember that this is not the only and most effective means.

* * *

Naboth's vineyard must be taken back from the hands of king Ahab. The authority of the state sovereign over private property is limited by God's law, the rights of the owner, and the rights of society.